The story of the vanishing automobile is a fairy tale told by certain architects, urban planners, and environmental groups. It is about *smart growth*, their very real plan to rebuild American cities to higher densities, construct expensive rail transit lines, and encourage people to live in high-density transit-oriented developments rather than low-density suburbs.

The fairy tale is that smart growth will reduce congestion, clean the air, provide affordable housing, and protect urban open space. Don't believe it! *The Vanishing Automobile and Other Urban Myths* shows that smart growth increases traffic congestion, air pollution, and housing costs, and reduces urban open spaces available for families to enjoy. The automobile is not going to vanish.

This book reveals the truth about smart growth:
- How the real goal of smart growth is to increase urban congestion;
- Who makes up congestion coalition promoting smart growth;
- The facts behind scores of smart-growth myths.

This book also presents a comprehensive alternative that will protect the American dream of mobility, affordable housing, and a clean environment with accessible open spaces. If you are one of the 200 million Americans who lives in a city or suburb, then you need to read *The Vanishing Automobile* to understand the plans being prepared for your region and neighborhood.

Randal O'Toole is senior economist with the Thoreau Institute and the author of *Reforming the Forest Service*.

The Vanishing Automobile

How Smart Growth Will Harm American Cities

and Other Urban Myths

Randal O'Toole
The Thoreau Institute
Bandon, Oregon

"In wildness is the preservation of the world." "That government is best which governs least." *Henry David Thoreau*

Cover photo: The joke is on the taxpayer as one of Portland's expensive light-rail cars chuckles its way into downtown.

Title Page Photos

1. A house in Sunnyside Village, a neighborhood planned by Peter Calthorpe, with tiny lots, minimal spaces between homes, narrow streets, and garages slightly recessed behind the fronts of the houses (p. 78).
2. Center Commons, a subsidized transit-oriented development being built on land formerly occupied by the Oregon Department of Motor Vehicles. Despite subsidies to the developer, individual condominiums will cost nearly $200,000—a high price even by Portland housing standards.
3. This 35-unit-per-acre apartment next to the Gresham light-rail line received $327,000 in subsidies to build to higher densities than the developer thought were marketable (p. 105).
4. The four-story Russellville apartments tower over the one- and two-story homes in the nearby area. A banner offering free rent to anyone signing a lease testifies to double-digit vacancy rates due to planner-driven overproduction of apartments (p. 121). *Photo by Myles Cunneen.*
5. Beaverton Round was supposed to be a housing, retail, and office development surrounding a light-rail station, but after receiving close to $10 million in tax breaks and other subsidies the developer went bankrupt. The building now stands unfinished and the region is trying to see how much more it will have to pay to convince a developer to complete it (p. 106).
6. Portland streetcar. The city is spending $40 million building a downtown streetcar line as one of many subsidies designed to attract high-density residential developments (p. 104). *All photos by the author unless otherwise noted.*

O'Toole, Randal, 1952–
The Vanishing Automobile and Other Urban Myths :
      How Smart Growth Will Harm American Cities / Randal O'Toole
        p. cm.
      Includes bibliographical references and index.
      ISBN 0-9706439-0-X

This book is dedicated to the freedom fighters of Oak Grove and other parts of the Portland area who are working for freedom of choice, mobility, and local control; especially:

Liz Callison
Craig Flynn
Jerry Foy
Thelma Haggenmiller
Jeanne Johnson
Milt Johnson
Richard Jones
David King
Susan King
John Liljegren
Sharon Phillips
Eugene Schoenheit
Bob Tiernan

This book is also dedicated to my father, Robert O'Toole, who taught me how to use numbers, and my mother, Vivian O'Toole, who taught me how to use words.

Contents

Chapters

Smart-Growth Myths

THE PORTLAND CASE STUDY

OTHER CASE STUDIES

Facts and Statistics

Web Tools

More web tools can be found on the Thoreau Institute's web site at www.ti.org.

Appendices and Index

Acknowledgments

This book is the product of many minds and assistance from many people. John Charles, Bob Behnke, Liz Callison, Myles Cunneen, Craig Flynn, Richard Jones, Gerard Mildner, and Mel Zucker provided useful information and clues about Portland regional problems and politics. Bruce Gaardner, Daniel Hunt, Fritz Knaak, Phil Krinkie, Lisa Lee, John Periard, Bob Shipman, and Craig Stone sent me a steady stream of information about the Twin Cities. Peter Gordon, James Moore, Daniel Simmons, and Sam Staley provided advice and information about other urban areas. Special thanks are due to Wendell Cox and Peter Samuel, whose tremendous and often uncompensated research on transit and highways deserves the gratitude of all mobility supporters.

I want to extend my great appreciation to Don & Dorothy McCluskey, the Charles G. Koch Charitable Foundation, and the Sarah Scaife Foundation for funding three productive semesters at Yale and Berkeley where I was able to study urban, forest, and other environmental problems as well as bounce my ideas off of many sharp minds. I also appreciate the support and assistance of Jerry Taylor and Ed Hudgins at the Cato Institute; Robert Poole, Lynn Scarlett, Virginia Postrel, Nick Gillespie, and other staff members at the Reason Foundation; Joe Bast of the Heartland Institute; and Tony Obadal of Obadal & MacLeod. I corresponded with many other people while researching this book and I wish to thank everyone and apologize for not being able to list all your names here.

Special thanks to Sally Fairfax for mentoring me at the University of California and elsewhere. I also want to thank Benn Coifman for many productive discussions about congestion, as well as for many of the graphics that made this book more fun to design and, I hope, a little more fun to read. Finally, without my partner, Vickie Crowley, and our dogs, Chip and Buffy, this book would not have been possible. While these and many other people deserve credit for whatever is worthwhile about this book, I alone am responsible for any and all mistakes and errors.

Smart-growth planners call a house with a garage in front a "snout house" (top). The city of Portland has recently outlawed the construction of such homes on the theory that prominent garages encourage people to drive more (p. 65).

A high-density, smart-growth development looms over a conventional neighborhood shopping center in east Portland (bottom). Regional plans for the Portland area call for more such high-density developments and discourage auto-oriented shopping centers (pp. 63, 71).

The Myth of the Vanishing Automobile

Once upon a time there was a great and wealthy city. But the people in the city were beset by a race of terrible, fire-breathing dragons known as *automobiles*. When the dragons first arrived, they seemed to be helpful: carrying people to work, to markets, and even to visit grandma in the next city. But the dragons multiplied and soon there were so many that there was hardly room for people. The dragons demanded more and more of the city for their own use. Sometimes they would get into terrible fights with one another, often killing innocent people. What's more, their flaming breath was noxious and poisoned the air.

One day the people met in a great council to decide what to do. There was long debate but few could agree, for the dragons were fierce. Besides, many people liked being carried around by the dragons and it was a status symbol to have a big one sitting in your yard.

During a lull in the debate, a stranger stood up. "I can rid your city of the dragons," he said. "What is more, I promise that you will be happier when they are gone."

"And what will it cost us to gain this tremendous service?" asked the mayor.

"All you have to do is give me the power to redesign your city," replied the stranger.

So the stranger went to work. First, he moved people's homes closer together. That way the dragons couldn't squeeze between them or lie around in the front yards. He also made the streets smaller, so no more than one dragon could pass through at a time. He built sharp peaks on all of the roofs so that the dragons couldn't land on top.

As the stranger worked, the people of the city found that, since all of their houses and shops were closer together, they didn't need the dragons after all. They could now walk to work or market and arrive as fast as when they rode the dragons. Those who had to go further could ride a new creature the stranger brought to the city that he called a *light rail*. Unlike the dragons, the light rail didn't breathe fire and never got into fights or hurt anyone.

The dragons were angry but they were helpless to stop the stranger. "You've made this city unlivable for us," said Suburban, the largest and fiercest of the dragons. And they all vanished.

The people cheered and thanked the stranger, for he had kept his promise and they were happier than ever before.

"I have more cities to save," said the stranger as he started to leave. But before he could go, a little boy ran up to him.

"Wait a minute," shouted the boy. "Who are you? Are you a dragon killer?"

"No," answered the stranger. "I am a smart-growth planner."

Urban planners tell this pleasant fairy tale to urban and suburban residents in community meetings all over the nation. Like most fairy tales, this one has a clear sense of good and evil, villains, a hero, and a happy ending. If this fairy tale were made into a movie, however, it would have to be a *film noire*, with the hero turning out to be the villain; the villains turning into semi-heroes; and a messy, and probably unhappy, ending. Reality is far more complicated than fairy tales and it is not always easy to tell good from evil.

Our cities are far from perfect. Highways are congested and skies are dirty from exhaust fumes. Strip developments along the roads are eyesores and remain inaccessible to anyone who can't drive. Many architects and planners say that they can fix these problems—*if* we give them the power to redesign our cities. They want to stop building freeways and build more light rail and other transit facilities. They want to halt suburban growth and move people into higher density developments. Some of them want to control the shape of our houses, our front porches, even the pitch of our rooftops. They say that all of these things, which they call *smart growth*, will reduce our dependence on the automobile and make our cities better places to live.

Nearly all cities employ urban planners, but few have granted them this kind of power. One that has is Portland, Oregon, where a single regional planning agency has the ultimate authority for land-use and transportation planning over three counties and twenty-four cities. The Portland area has begun to implement a smart-growth plan, including high-density housing, design codes, light-rail transit, and disincentives to drive autos.

As a result, city officials and civic leaders from across the United States consider Portland the model for urban growth management. Attend an urban planning conference and you will hear Portland touted as a prime example of excellent planning. Advocates of mass transit will tell you that Portland's light rail is one of the most successful in the nation. The American Planning Association has given Portland and Oregon numerous awards for their growth and transportation planning activities.

Yet as growing numbers of Portlanders learn what it means to be a part of this great experiment, many are not so sure they like it. Some of them are quite positive that they hate it. Portland's growth management techniques will require major changes in neighborhoods and lifestyles—changes few residents want to make. And Portland's acclaimed light rail is looking more and more like a multi-billion dollar boondoggle.

New lifestyles and heavy taxes for mass transit might be acceptable if they produced the benefits that planners claim for them. It is more likely that these programs will make congestion, pollution, and other urban problems worse than ever. In fact, even as regional planners publicly state that their goal is to keep Portland from becoming like Los Angeles, internal agency documents reveal that in several important ways their real aim is to make Portland more like Los Angeles than any other metropolitan area in the country. Having lived most of my life in Portland, I've written this book to provide people in other urban areas with an answer when someone asks, "Why don't we do here what they are doing in Portland?"

The title of this book is a paraphrase of *The Vanishing Hitchhiker*, the popular book of urban folklore by Jan Brunvand.[1] Folklore can be a fascinating topic to study. But as the basis of coercive government policy, it is extremely dangerous. The Myth of the Vanishing Automobile is just one of the many pieces of smart-growth folklore that this book will examine. "Myths tacitly provide an alluring simplification," says urban expert Jonathan Richmond. "Telling simple but powerful stories, they point to specific cures." Such cures depend "on the often invisible assumptions inherent in the myth. But those assumptions can steer the way to bad planning decisions which fail to provide the hoped-for benefits.[2] This book will examine these myths by looking at the effects of smart growth on Portland and other cities that have tried it.

When I first worked on urban issues in 1972, I was a starry-eyed believer in mass transit, a bicyclist who wouldn't even get a drivers license for several more years, and an idealist who suspected that sinister forces were keeping my dreams of urban utopias from coming true. But my work over the next twenty years on a variety of environmental issues taught me to be skeptical about government planning and to rely on hard data rather than attractive but unproven myths and fantasies.

In 1995, I was living in the Portland suburb of Oak Grove, when one of my neighbors asked me to a attend a meeting on "growth management and transportation planning." I soon learned that Portland's entire establishment—the mayor, the city council, most other elected officials, newspaper editorial writers, and nearly every major civic group—had turned into naïve, starry-eyed idealists like I had been in 1972, and with none of my skepticism. The Portland area was growing at 2 percent per year, and they all had an inordinate faith that the area's growing pains could be solved with light rail and urban planning.

But the new urban planning ideas accepted by the establishment were far more draconian than anything I had considered in the 1970s. Their vision for Portland included promoting transit by making highways intolerably congested; spending most of the region's transportation budget on a rail transit system that less than 2 percent of Portlanders would use; fining employers if too many of their employees drove to work; and forcing people to live in much higher densities than they would choose on their own. Today, these ideas, under the name of smart growth, are spreading across the country.

This book can be read from cover to cover, but it was written to be more of a reference book. Browse through it, or skip around and read the parts that are most pertinent to your urban area. Each section is designed to be as self-contained as possible, including complete endnotes, while minimizing repetition.

The book divides into nine roughly equal parts which fall into three unequal groups: Parts one through three present an introduction to smart growth, the history of the movement, and the people who support it. Parts four through eight provide a detailed discussion of each major smart-growth prescription: density, rail transit, anti-auto policies, land-use planning, and regional governments. Part nine describes an alternative to smart growth that can help solve many urban problems without smart-growth's negative consequences.

Each part is broken into chapters, myths, case studies, facts, and web tools:

- Numbered *chapters* provide a brief introduction to the issues;
- The *myths* respond to smart-growth claims such as that suburbs cause congestion or light rail promotes neighborhood redevelopment;
- *Case studies*, the longest of which is about Portland, describe the effects of smart growth and other policies in various urban areas;
- *Facts* present a few important statistics about each major issue;
- *Web tools* give you access to more information and data.

If you want to get involved in these issues, you can find further sources of information in the appendices. You will also find tools on the Thoreau Institute's web site (www.ti.org/urban.html) that will help you analyze issues in your own region and organize support for mobility and freedom of choice. A book like this can never be finished and I will update it with new data and information as it becomes available. If you are interested in receiving these updates, send a blank email to mobility@ti.org. If you have any questions, feel free to email me at rot@ti.org.

Notes

1. Jan Harold Brunvand, *The Vanishing Hitchhiker: American Urban Legends and Their Meanings* (New York, NY: Norton, 1981), 208 pp.
2. Jonathan E. D. Richmond, "The Mythical Conception of Rail Transit in Los Angeles," http://the-tech.mit.edu/~richmond/professional/myth.pdf.

Part One

The Dark Side of Smart Growth

Residents of this tree-lined street in Oak Grove (top) are considered "auto-dependent" because of low densities and lack of sidewalks. Yet the area has so little traffic that there is minimal interference between autos and pedestrians (see p. 9). When planners proposed to rezone Oak Grove to as much as four times the current densities so that people could "walk and bicycle more," residents asked what existing neighborhood looked like planners' vision for the area. They were told to look at Portland's Northwest 23rd (bottom), where "people are learning to walk more." It turns out that people in that area are walking more mainly because they can't find parking near their destinations (p. 72).

1. Introduction to Smart Growth

On January 11, 1999, Vice President Al Gore announced the "Clinton-Gore Livability Agenda," which the media immediately dubbed the *war on sprawl*.[1] "Too frequently, a gallon of gas is used up just purchasing a gallon of milk," claimed Gore. "Too often, if a parent wants to read a child a bedtime story, they call on a cell phone while they're stuck in a traffic jam, and try to explain why they can't be home in time for the child to go to sleep."[2]

As in so many wars, the first casualty was the truth. Few suburbanites live so far from a grocery store that they must consume a gallon of gasoline to buy milk. Contrary to popular belief, average commuting times have remained remarkably constant for many years and are fairly similar among cities large and small.

Vice President Gore might be excused a little hyperbole if the war on sprawl were challenging truly important problems. But it is not. Russians say that "Americans don't have any serious problems, so they have to invent them."[3] Sprawl is one of those invented problems. Low-density suburbanization—which is what people usually mean by *sprawl*—not only is *not* responsible for most of the problems that its critics charge, it is the *solution* to many of the problems that sprawl opponents claim they want to solve.

The war on sprawl is really a war on American lifestyles. It combines a war on the suburbs that house half of all Americans with a war on the automobiles that carry Americans four out of every five miles they travel. Yet the suburbs provide an ideal medium between rural open spaces and crowded cities while occupying just 2 percent of the nation's land. Meanwhile, for most urban-length trips, the automobile is the fastest, most convenient, and most economical form of personal transportation ever devised.

Americans live a wide range of lifestyles. A fourth of all U.S. residents live in rural areas outside any cities or towns. Another 10 percent live in small towns outside major urban areas. While 65 percent of Americans live in urban areas of 50,000 people or more, just a third of those live in the central cities such as New York, Seattle, or Dallas. Urban lifestyles range from low-density suburbs through medium-density edge cities to high-density city centers. All of these are valid lifestyle choices and they work for the people who live there.

But smart growth does not consider most of these lifestyles valid. If smart-growth planners had their way, almost everyone except a few rural workers and their families would be confined to high-density, mixed-use urban neighborhoods.

- Oregon land-use regulators are trying to prevent anyone from building in rural areas except actual farmers. They deride exurbanites who want to live in rural areas as "hobby farmers" trying to get around state land-use laws.[4]
- Smart-growth guru Andres Duany would outlaw the further construction of low-density suburbs that are currently the choice of half of all Americans.[5] He and other smart-growth planners want to redevelop existing suburbs to much higher densities, more like the inner cities that suburban residents left.
- Planners consider the edge cities that are the major source of job growth in this country to be "chaotic," a "threat to central cities,"[6] and in desperate need of planning.[7]

This book will show that, when smart-growth planners say they want to give people choices, they mean they want to take choices away. When they say they want to relieve congestion, they mean they want to increase congestion so that people will be forced to ride transit. When they say they want affordable housing, they mean they want to make single-family housing unaffordable so that all but the wealthiest people will live in high-density housing. When they say they want to preserve open space for people, they mean they want to preserve it *from* people.

Smart growth is a convoluted web of policies and ideas, many of which only make sense in the context of the supporters who expect to benefit from them. Part 3 will discuss those supporters and show why most of them want more congestion and the other problems smart growth brings. But first we will examine some of the basic issues that led to the smart-growth debate in the first place.

Notes

1. Judith Havemann, "Gore Proposal Aims to Tame Urban Sprawl," *Washington Post*, 11 January 1999, p. A2.
2. Remarks by Vice President Gore on Announcement of Livability Agenda, Washington, DC, January 11, 1999.
3. Russell Working, "Pardon me if I'm rusty on what protests mean," *The Oregonian* 5 December 1999, pp. G1–G2.
4. Robin Franzen, "Preserving farms or abetting hobbyists?" *The Oregonian*, December 14, 1998, http://www.oregonlive.com/todaysnews/9812/st121401.html.
5. Andres Duany, Elizabeth Plater-Zyberk, and Jeff Speck, *Suburban Nation: The Rise of Sprawl and the Decline of the American Dream* (New York, NY: North Point Press, 2000), p. 146.
6. Oliver Byrum, "Edge Cities: A Pragmatic View," *Journal of the American Planning Association*, 58:395–396.
7. Charles Lockwood, "Edge Cities on the Brink," *Wall Street Journal*, December 21, 1994.

The Battle of
Oak Grove

My first personal experience with smart growth was in the spring of 1995, when a neighbor I hardly knew named Jeanne Johnson sent me a note asking me to come to a meeting of the "Oak Grove Growth Management and Transportation Planning Committee." I almost ignored it, but the note had a slightly desperate tone to it that made me wonder what was going on.

Oak Grove is what planners call an *inner ring* suburb. Never incorporated, the community is about eight miles south of downtown Portland on the east side of the Willamette River. It was platted in 1892, when the nation's first electric interurban rail line was being built between Portland and Oregon City. Wealthy Portlanders soon realized that they could "get away from it all" by building homes along the rail line and commuting. By 1930, the part of Oak Grove along the rail line was a streetcar suburb, with modest homes centered on a small business area. But much of the community had large houses on parcels of an acre or more, interspersed with farms and dairies. Over succeeding generations, the large parcels and farms were broken up and sold off. Today, the community has a wide variety of lot sizes and home styles.

The block I lived on, for example, covers more than twenty-five acres. This itself is unusual—blocks in most cities are a tenth that size—but it is by no means the largest in Oak Grove. Individual lots on our block range from 7,000 square feet to 50,000 square feet or more (an acre is 43,560 square feet). At least one vacant lot is well over an acre in size. My own home was on a 15,000-square-foot lot, just over a third of an acre. The oldest homes on the block were built around the turn of the century; the newest less than a decade ago. Since the houses were built one by one over a one-hundred-year period, each is unique, with some made of native rock by a pioneer family of Italian stonemasons—rare in the timber-rich Northwest.

The community has less than 70 percent of the population density of other Portland-area residential areas. The neighborhood has few sidewalks, but that doesn't matter because such a low density means there is little auto traffic. My dog and I walked about four miles a day through the neighborhood, meeting many of our neighbors who were also out walking. Many people take advantage of their large yards to grow flowers and vegetables, and a few own small livestock such as poultry, goats, sheep, horses, and even a donkey.

Oak Grove's glory days as a wealthy community are long past: Today, except for those living on the river, most residents are blue-collar workers. The decline in wealth is probably due to the community's age and the many subdivisions of formerly large estates, neither of which are attractive to yuppies. This is fortunate for moderate-income people like me who otherwise couldn't afford to live in such a low-density area.

At the meeting, I learned that county planners had been working for six months with local residents on a "transportation and growth management plan." The purpose of the plan, planners claimed, was to give people more opportunities to walk and ride their bicycles. This seemed peculiar since no one I know has ever felt hesitant to walk or bicycle around the neighborhood.

Then they showed us a map of the plan. The block I lived on and several nearby were to be rezoned for 5,000-square-foot minimum lot sizes. Homeowners in this zone would also be allowed to build "granny flats," or small apartments, into their homes—effectively turning many of them into duplexes. The block across the street from my home plus many others would be rezoned for multifamily dwellings with 24 units per acre (about 1,800 square feet of land per unit).

To give people a place to walk to, a significant chunk of our neighborhood would be "mixed use," with stores and other businesses located a few steps from residences. In particular, planners hoped that many of the multifamily dwellings would be three stories high—two stories is the current limit—with businesses occupying the street floor.

The goal was to quadruple population densities in downtown Oak Grove and double them elsewhere. We were assured that this "densification," as the planners called it, was for our own good and that it would encourage walking and discourage cars. We were also told that we had little choice in the matter, because the *2040 Plan* being prepared by Metro, Portland's regional planning agency, would require planners to densify Oak Grove whether we liked it or not.

Neotraditionalism

When my neighbors and I began criticizing the county plan for Oak Grove, we were immediately asked why we hadn't been to earlier meetings of the planning group, which had been going on for several months. It turned out that a notice of the first meeting had been sent to most Oak Grove residents as a part of a newsletter put out by the local sewer, water, and fire districts. But the meeting notice said nothing about densification, mixed uses, or multifamily zoning. Instead, it concentrated on "making the Oak Grove community more pedestrian-oriented, with walking trails and bicycle paths." It also talked about "revitalizing the downtown area," but not about design codes, granny flats, or any other controversial idea.

At the beginning of the planning process, the county also conducted a "scientific survey" of local residents. As it happens, I was one of the people surveyed. Like the meeting notices, the survey concentrated exclusively on transportation, asking if I would like more bike trails or lanes, and so forth. There was nothing in the survey to hint that the county was thinking of rezoning the neighborhood for higher densities.

The emphasis on transportation wasn't simply a cover for something more sinister. Planners today believe that transportation and land use are inextricably related—not just that transportation facilities influence land use, which makes sense, but that land-use patterns influence whether people drive, walk, or take mass transit. This was an important part of *neotraditionalism*, which one of the county planners described to me as "the latest planning fad." In 1995, the term *smart growth* had not yet been coined. When my neighbors and I asked about the reasoning behind neotraditional design, planners responded with totally circuitous logic. Why did planners want to densify our community? "Because densification is part of the neotraditional concept." What is neotraditionalism? "Neotraditionalism is a planning concept that calls for densification."

Clackamas County planners had already zoned a parcel of distant farmland to become a high-density, neotraditional development. But Portland planners knew it was not enough to build new neotraditional suburbs. To dramatically increase density and reduce auto use, they would also have to redesign existing suburbs along neotraditional lines. No one knew if that was possible. To find out, the Oregon Department of Transportation offered federal grant moneys to local jurisdictions that would volunteer to impose neotraditional designs on existing neighborhoods. Clackamas County decided to volunteer Oak Grove and received a $34,000 grant from the state.

How did the county happen to pick Oak Grove? Because, planners said, Metro had designated Oak Grove a *town center* in its draft 2040 plan. A town center, as Metro describes it, has "compact development and transit service" with "local shopping and employment." Its population density would be more than 30 people per acre—about four times Oak Grove's current average density.

At the time, I knew little about Metro except that it had something to do with garbage collection and recycling. It turned out that Metro is a regional government whose jurisdiction extends over 24 cities and three counties. "Metro is predicting that 500,000 people are going to move to Portland in the next twenty years, and we have to find room for them," we were told. "Metro is writing a plan to densify the entire Portland metropolitan area, and we have to do our part."

Part of the Oak Grove plan called for giving people more "access." This meant that planners wanted to build more streets to break Oak Grove's large blocks into smaller ones. After all, it is hard to subdivide properties into 50-by-100-foot lots when the blocks are 600 feet or more on a side. But nearly everyone in the neighborhood agreed that they didn't want new streets.

Planners then said they wanted to build bikeways and pedestrian paths across some of the larger blocks. That sounded all right with most people, and they drew lines on maps to show where they might go. Then someone asked, "Are these pedestrian ways going to be barricaded so people can't drive their cars down them?"

"Oh, no," said a planner. "We can't deny anyone access to their property." Why would people need access to their backyards—unless the "pedestrian ways" were really just another way of encouraging people to subdivide their large lots on Oak Grove's large blocks? Sensing this, residents unanimously vetoed the bike path idea.

Another part of the plan called for "revitalizing" Oak Grove's "downtown," which includes a number of shops and a machine works located near the former streetcar line. In 1933, the state built a "superhighway"—Oregon's first four-lane road—paralleling the interurban line but about a half-mile east of downtown Oak Grove. The downtown area declined as most businesses moved out to or were replaced by ones on the highway. Remaining downtown shops include, among others, two convenience stores, a karate studio, a tavern, and a beauty parlor.

A neotraditional redevelopment of Oak Grove would replace most of the buildings downtown with three- or four-story mixed-use apartments that had shops and businesses on the ground level. But planners didn't dwell on this, emphasizing instead sidewalk configurations, planting trees, and other features of street design—most of which would have to be paid for by local businesses.

Curiously, planners maps defined downtown as not just the four blocks of businesses but also a half-mile-long stretch of residential between the businesses and the highway. The homes on this street included one of the largest and most beautiful solid stone houses in the Portland area. So I was stunned when the planner from the revitalization committee announced that, "To preserve the historic character of downtown Oak Grove, we propose to allow zero-foot setbacks of buildings." A setback is the minimum or maximum distance allowed between a property line and a building. A zero-foot setback would allow homeowners to add false fronts on their houses that reached the sidewalk. How do false fronts on historic houses "preserve" their historic character?

I wondered if I had misheard this statement. But at a later meeting planners distributed the proposed zoning codes for "town centers" and "town center residential." The town center code allowed no setbacks. The town center residential code changed traditional minimum setbacks of thirty feet from the street into maximum setbacks of eighteen feet, while setbacks between properties were changed from a traditional minimum of five feet to zero.

In other words, the codes encouraged owners of the historic homes on Oak Grove Boulevard to tear down their homes and build row houses or apartments. Someone who owned a home on a one-acre lot would not be allowed to subdivide

and build one or two new homes. If they subdivided at all, they would be required
to build apartments, row houses, or other suitably dense developments. No one
would be forced to subdivide, but when one or more did, others who preferred to
live in a less dense neighborhood would probably sell out, leading to more subdivisions.

The codes also included numerous neotraditional design frills. Roofs must be
hipped or gambreled, not flat; shops had to have at least 19 feet of window space
for every 25 feet of street frontage; "consistent design elements shall be used
throughout the district to ensure that the entire area is visually and functionally
unified." Unity and cute design would replace individualism and history.

Several Oak Grove residents who attended their first meeting with me were less
upset about the design code or setbacks than the huge increase in density. I wondered how the plan got as far as it did with no protests from local residents. But
looking around the room, I realized that most of the people who had regularly
attended planning meetings were not residents. Some were business owners, others were employees of the local sewer, water, or fire districts who lived elsewhere.

Some of the residents invited the planners to walk through the neighborhood
so they could explain why they were uncomfortable with densification. After walking around the area on a sunny spring day, the planner exclaimed, "What a lovely
neighborhood. The only other time I've ever walked around Oak Grove, it was
raining, the edges of the streets were muddy, and I couldn't figure out why anyone
would want to live here." But after people, some of whom had grown up in Oak
Grove, told her that they didn't want higher density zoning, she replied, "People
come and go, but the land remains. I plan for the land." What we thought didn't
count because we were only people. When I suggested that problems such as
congestion, pollution, and open space could be solved with incentives rather than
coercive zoning, the planner answered that my ideas "aren't part of our business-
as-usual" and "would take major paradigm shifts to accomplish." As if quadrupling densities wasn't a "paradigm shift"!

The Oak Grove Plan

After several meetings, planners presented the task force with a three-quarter-inch
thick document called the Oak Grove Plan. The plan contained little or no data
about the area—when we asked for data, we were told "we haven't got our geographic information system working yet." Nor did it contain any alternatives.
Instead, it simply called for a massive increase in density.

Planners scheduled a public meeting at the local school gymnasium so that
they could present their plan to the community. To let people know about the
meeting, planners distributed another innocuous flyer that talked about bikeways,
"public space," and "common sense zoning," whatever that is. In response, Oak
Grove residents wrote their own flyer that emphasized high density, multifamily

dwellings, mixed use, and prescriptive zoning and passed out the flyer to nearly two thousand homes.

Obviously expecting a small turnout, planners had set out around 100 chairs in the gym. In fact, nearly 200 angry residents showed up. But planners were ready, spending an hour-and-a-half on boring presentations about bike paths and pedestrian ways before saying anything about zoning. The presentations were made by citizen members of the planning committee, thus deferring people's anger from the planners to these people.

At the end of the presentations, planners refused to accept any public comment and allowed only 15 minutes for questions and answers. But it was clear the people opposed the plan, and the meeting was punctuated by frequent outbursts such as "go home" and "who asked you, anyway?" An informal poll showed that fewer than 20 people attended in response to the planners' leaflet, while at least half came as a result of the local residents' leaflet. Earlier in the planning process, one of the planners had lamented that "It is too bad that Oak Grove doesn't have a community identity because it isn't incorporated." At the end of this meeting, she announced, "Well, if nothing else, at least we've helped you get a community identity."

After the meeting, planners decided that they "made a mistake in not allowing more people to talk, and in not letting people make more comments." So they held another meeting three weeks later. Oak Grove residents leafleted again and more than 150 people attended. Two hours of questions and acrimonious debate made it clear that the community was unanimously opposed to the plan.

The meetings completely transformed the situation. The original committee members distanced themselves from the plan, saying they were duped. A poll of committee members who actually lived in the neighborhood revealed them to be 100 percent opposed to the plan that they had previously acquiesced to. In fact, it was almost impossible to find anyone who actually admitted to being on the land-use committee—everybody claimed to have been "someplace else."

Planners could see they weren't getting anywhere, and said they would drop the plan if that is what the community wanted. "But if you don't let us pass this plan now," warned one, "then Metro will make us impose even more densification on you next year."

Why Oak Grove?

Since planners were threatening Oak Grove residents with the bogeyman of Metro, people began to wonder why Metro had picked Oak Grove to be a town center in the first place. Metro's September, 1994, draft plan did not include Oak Grove among the town centers, but a later draft in December did. County planners said that the town center designation came "at the request of North Clackamas business leaders." But Oak Grove business people anxiously assured residents that they had nothing to do with it.

It turned out that the requests came from the sewer, water, and fire districts. The heads of these districts told residents that they believed town center designation would make them eligible for more federal funds. "Funds and resources would be channeled into these centers," the fire chief told his district board of directors. Town centers "will be focal points for development and funds" said the water board. The boards for all three districts petitioned Metro to add Oak Grove to the list of town centers.

I reviewed Metro documents and interviewed Metro staff, but could find no evidence that town centers would be special recipients of any funds. "There might be some transportation funds to make the areas more pedestrian friendly," Metro staffer Mark Turpel told me, "but that's all."

Curiously, the fire chief opposed neotraditional designs. "My fire trucks sometimes have to get into people's backyards," he told me. "That's why we need at least five feet of setbacks along property lines" (which would mean at least ten feet between buildings). When I told him that the town center zoning codes would forbid such setbacks, he was surprised but didn't think such buildings would ever be constructed.

A memo I found written by the fire chief revealed something else. "Metro planning staff, specifically John Fregonese [at that time Metro's growth management director], agrees" that Oak Grove should be a town center. "He stated that it was designated but the county planning staff removed it." Later, county planners told me that they had opposed town center designation because they remembered that in previous planning efforts Oak Grove residents had fought long and hard against any zoning denser than four units per acre.

"We Aren't Even Going to Read this Plan"

A few weeks after the public hearing, the planning committee met with two of Clackamas County's three county commissioners. The meeting had a large turn-out. After listening to comments from many more people—some of whom said they had felt misled by planners—the chair of the county commission held up the 120-page Oak Grove plan and said that "the commission will probably not approve this plan." "Does that mean that you might approve this plan?" someone asked. "We probably aren't even going to read this plan," she said, and slammed it down on the table.

On July 24, 1996, Clackamas County Commission Chair Judie Hammerstad sent a letter requesting that Metro remove the town center designation from Oak Grove. "There is no community support for a 'town center,' " she wrote. Planners held a final meeting with residents a few days later. The planning team leader somewhat wistfully recalled that "Metro staff told me that a public hearing would get people upset. They said I should just hold open houses, like they do." But, she said, she didn't believe that open houses gave the public a fair chance to comment on a plan.

A few months later, Metro sent out a newsletter including the latest map of its 2040 plan. Oak Grove was not listed as a town center. Except for the corridor around the superhighway, Oak Grove is classified as an *inner neighborhood*. This means that Metro expects no more density increases than might happen through ordinary infill. Local residents are still working to protect the highway corridor from further densification.

In 1998, when Yale University offered me a fellowship, I moved out of Oak Grove and now live in Bandon, Oregon, a small town of about 2,800 people. As small as it is, Bandon is under pressure from the state to densify, so we are witnessing further battles over smart growth—as neotraditionalism is now popularly known.

While Oak Grove won its battle, other Portland-area neighborhoods have not been as successful, and debates over density are springing up all over the metropolitan area. In a small way, Oak Grove's successful effort to avoid densification may impose a little more densification on other Clackamas County neighborhoods.

Meanwhile, smart growth is sweeping the nation. State after state has passed or is considering smart-growth legislation, often modeled after Oregon's 1973 land-use planning laws. City after city is considering creating a regional government and giving it sweeping planning powers, modeled after Portland's Metro. More than sixty cities want to build light-rail lines and they all point to Portland as a light-rail success, even though residents of Oak Grove and the nearby suburb of Milwaukie helped kill a light-rail line planned in their area. Oak Grove has shown that people can protect their neighborhoods from smart growth.

 Web Tools: Tour of Oak Grove

For a tour of Oak Grove, see www.ti.org/og.html.

The Sprawl Myth

Myth: Congestion, pollution, high taxes, and other problems in rapidly growing areas are due to urban sprawl.

Reality: Growth can be painful but the problems of high-density growth are the same or worse as those of low-density growth.

The rapid growth of many urban areas, particularly those in the West and South, means that their residents are experiencing serious growing pains. A region growing faster than 2 percent per year will double its population in less than thirty-five years. At this rate, development takes place so rapidly that people can almost see it from day to day. Traffic increases faster than new roads can be built, vacant lots fill up, and sleepy towns around the urban fringes quickly become urban subcenters as new homes, offices, and shopping malls spread across the countryside. Residents of such fast-growing places worry about increasing congestion, air pollution, the loss of open space, affordable housing, and whether their taxes are somehow subsidizing the fancy homes being built by newcomers.

Smart-growth advocates are quick to exploit these fears. They blame congestion, pollution, disappearing open space, unaffordable housing, and high taxes on "sprawl," by which they mean low-density suburbs served by automotive transport. Yet, as will be shown in myths examining each specific issue, all of these problems tend to be worse in the high-density areas that smart growth favors.

University of California planning professor Elizabeth Deakin points to surveys showing "resident satisfaction to be higher in communities that were growing moderately than in either fast-growth or slow-growth jurisdictions."[1] An area with very slow or no growth feels stagnant; people worry that their children won't find jobs or that if they lose theirs they won't be able to find another. This problem is common to many Northeast and Midwest urban areas.

Despite slow or no growth, many of these regions are still changing. People are moving out of dense city centers and into low-density suburbs. The result is an overall decline in density and increase in land use despite little or no increase in population. Smart-growth advocates oppose this form of sprawl as well as the fast-growing form.

Janet Rothenberg Pack, a professor of public policy at the Wharton School, notes that large differences in the development of various urban areas "suggest the need for flexible urban policy rather than for one-size-fits-all metropolitanism."[2] Yet the smart-growth prescriptions for urban areas in the Northeast and Midwest is the same as for cities in the West and South: increased densities, rail transit, auto-hostile design, all overseen by regional planning authorities.

Rapid change, as experienced by growing cities in the West and South, can be painful. Lack of change, as experienced by the stagnating cities of the Northeast and Midwest, can also be painful. But either of these pains is only peripherally related to low-density suburbanization. Smart growth will do nothing to relieve the pains and may even make them worse.

Notes

1. Elizabeth Deakin, "Growth Controls and Growth Management: A Summary and Review of Empirical Research" *in* David Brower, David Godschalk, and Douglas Porter, eds., *Understanding Growth Management: Critical Issues and a Research Agenda* (Washington, DC: Urban Land Institute, 1989), pp. 3–21.
2. Janet Rothenberg Pack, "Metropolitan Areas: Regional Differences," *Brookings Review*, Fall, 1998, p. 27; http://www.brook.edu/press/review/fa98/pack.pdf.

Urban Growth Facts

The United States is experiencing a major shift in population from the climatically inhospitable and densely populated Northeast and Midwest for the sunny South and the thinly populated West. Census estimates indicate that since 1990:

• The twenty fastest-growing states include every western state except Wyoming and every southern coastal state except Mississippi and Alabama, but only two states in the Northeast or Midwest.
• The forty fastest growing metropolitan areas are all in the West or South.
• All but one of the nation's twenty slowest-growing states are in the Northeast and Midwest.
• All but five of the thirty-five urban areas that lost population were in the Northeast or Midwest.
• The cities of Boston, Cleveland, Minneapolis, Detroit, Cincinnati, Milwaukee, Philadelphia, and St. Louis all lost population, but their metropolitan areas grew.

The Ten Fastest-Growing States, 1990–1999

State	Annual Growth
Nevada	4.7%
Arizona	3.0%
Idaho	2.4%
Utah	2.4%
Colorado	2.3%
Georgia	2.1%
Washington	1.9%
Texas	1.9%
Florida	1.7%
Oregon	1.7%

The Ten Slowest-Growing States, 1990–1999

State	Annual Growth
Louisiana	0.4%
Iowa	0.4%
Massachusetts	0.3%
Maine	0.2%
New York	0.1%
Pennsylvania	0.1%
West Virginia	0.1%
Connecticut	0.0%
North Dakota	-0.1%
Rhode Island	-0.1%

The Ten Fastest-Growing Urban Areas, 1990–1999

State	Annual Growth
Las Vegas, NV	5.5%
Laredo, TX	4.2%
McAllen, TX	3.8%
Boise City, ID	3.6%
Naples, FL	3.5%
Austin, TX	3.4%
Fayetteville, AR	3.4%
Phoenix, AZ	3.4%
Provo, UT	3.1%
Atlanta, GA	3.0%

The Ten Slowest-Growing Urban Areas, 1990–1999

State	Annual Growth
Buffalo, NY	-0.4%
Scranton, PA	-0.5%
Lawton, OK	-0.5%
Jacksonville, NC	-0.6%
Pittsfield, MA	-0.6%
Pine Bluff, AR	-0.6%
Binghamton, NY	-0.7%
Steubenville, OH	-0.7%
Utica, NY	-0.9%
Grand Forks, ND	-0.9%

Source: Census Bureau, www.census.gov.

2. What Is Sprawl?

ebates about sprawl are not helped by the fact that there is little agreement about what the term means. When it first became widely used in the 1950s, *sprawl* generally referred to *leapfrog* development, that is, developments well beyond the edge of existing urban areas. Eventually, the spaces between old and new developments were filled in, but in the meantime leapfrog development supposedly imposed high urban-service costs and required wasteful commuting.

The term *sprawl* is used as a pejorative, as when Charles Abrams defined sprawl as "the awkward spreading out of the limbs of either a man or a community. The first is a product of bad manners, the second a product of bad planning."[1] People can debate the merits of high- vs. low-density housing, highways vs. transit, or WalMart vs. downtown stores. But there is no debating the merits of sprawl: Like bad manners, anything called sprawl is simply *bad*. The vagueness of the definition works in favor of its opponents. To some, sprawl means congestion; to others, air pollution; to others, urban poverty; and to others, high taxes, or the decline of downtowns. Anyone who says "I oppose sprawl" wins to their side people who worry about any of these problems.

Professional sprawl warriors do have something in mind when they say sprawl, though it may not be quite the same as what others think. Abrams' 1971 definition added that "Sprawl is a by-product of the highway and automobile, which enabled the spread of development in all directions. As builders scramble for lots to build on, the journey to work is lengthened and green spaces are consumed by gas stations and clutter."[2] Thus, as early as 1971, the term *sprawl* linked suburbs with the automobile. This linkage remains the key defining feature today.

In 1998, the Sierra Club defined sprawl as "low-density development beyond the edge of service and employment, which separates where people live from where they shop, work, recreate, and educate—thus requiring cars to move between zones." James Kunstler, author of *The Geography of Nowhere*, says sprawl's "chief characteristics are the strict separation of human activities, mandatory driving to get from one activity to another, and huge supplies of free parking."[3] Such *auto dependency* is severely criticized by people worried about *sustainable transportation*, which apparently means transportation that doesn't rely on automobiles.

21

Smart-growth advocates love to cite European cities as examples that Americans should emulate. Australian planners Jeffrey Kenworthy and Felix Laube claim that European cities are better than those in Australia and the U.S. because they are less auto dependent. Their 1999 *International Sourcebook on Automobile Dependency* presents data from more than forty-six cities around the world.[4] They conclude that Europeans drive less because their cities are denser, inhospitable to cars, and have excellent mass transit. As the European case study will show, Europeans drive less than Americans because their incomes are lower, not because their cities are designed differently. As their incomes rise, the miles Europeans drive is growing faster than in the U.S. despite their dense cities and transit systems.

Sprawl opponents are not always consistent in describing sprawl. The Sierra Club calls Atlanta and St. Louis the two "most sprawl-threatened large cities" in the U.S. because their population densities are declining. Yet it calls Los Angeles "the granddaddy of sprawl" even though, between 1980 and 1990, its density increased by 12 percent. The Club also lists Las Vegas as one of the cities most threatened by sprawl, yet Las Vegas' density increased by nearly a third from 1990 to 1996, the years the Sierra Club used to measure sprawl.

The Club rates Washington, DC, as the nation's third most sprawl-threatened major urban area while it lauds Portland, Oregon, as "one of the nation's most livable cities."[5] Yet Portland's transit system carries a much smaller share of travelers than Washington's; Portland's population density is 15 percent less than Washington's; and between 1980 and 1990 Portland's density increased less (i.e., it "sprawled" more) than Washington's.

The Sierra Club also rates McAllen, Texas, as the most sprawl-threatened medium-sized urban area. McAllen's population density declined by 17 percent between 1990 and 1996 while its transit system carries 4 percent of all commuters. By comparison, Eugene, Oregon, experienced a 29 percent decline in density during those years and its transit service carries only 2.5 percent of commuters. Yet the Sierra Club does not consider Eugene to be threatened by sprawl.

Portland and Eugene escape the Sierra Club's attention because they are leading the nation in applying smart-growth prescriptions to their areas. Apparently, to smart-growth supporters, it doesn't matter if their prescriptions are working, it only matters that they are being used.

Notes

1. Charles Abrams, *The Language of Cities* (New York, NY: Viking, 1971), pp. 293–294.
2. Ibid.
3. James Howard Kunstler, "Home from Nowhere," *Atlantic Monthly* September 1996, pp. 43–66.
4. Jeffrey R. Kenworthy and Felix B. Laube, *An International Sourcebook of Automobile Dependence in Cities 1960–1990* (Boulder, CO: University of Colorado, 1999), 704 pp.
5. Sierra Club, *The Dark Side of the American Dream* (San Francisco, CA: Sierra Club, 1998), p. 27.

The Myth of Community

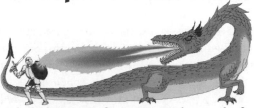

Myth: The suburbs lack a sense of community that can be found in traditional, high-density neighborhoods.

Reality: Communities are based on human networks, not geography, and modern transportation and communications allow people to be a part of many communities well beyond their residential neighborhoods.

"People living in sprawling developments," says the Department of Housing and Urban Development, "gather less often in public places and feel less responsible to one another and to shared surroundings than residents of more dense communities." The department offers not a shred of evidence for this other than that "some observers" say so. This "decline in sense of community" is supposed to be due to "leapfrog development patterns, lack of a central community focal point, and reliance on automobiles."[1]

The "observers" who worry about the loss of community include Richard Sexton, who writes that "automobile suburbia" has allowed America to focus "on the generous freedom granted the individual, while the collective concept of community languishes in apathy."[2] James Kunstler claims that the "extreme individualism of property ownership. . . has been the source of many of the problems" he sees in the suburbs, and in particular the loss of "the public realm."[3] Milwaukee Mayor John Norquist sees dense urban neighborhoods as the solution. "People are seeking more from life," says Norquist. "They are looking for a sense of belonging and community, and much of what they are looking for can be found in real cities and their neighborhoods," as opposed to the "faceless" suburbs.[4]

One of the most important communitarians is Robert Putnam, whose book *Bowling Alone* argues that something he calls *social capital* is rapidly declining in America. Although the book is filled with statistics and charts, he makes a completely subjective guess that suburbanization is responsible for "perhaps 10 percent" of the loss of social capital.[5] Without any analysis, he adds that it is "plausible that design innovations like mixed-use zoning, pedestrian-friendly street grids, and more space for public use should enhance social capital."[6] Curiously, Putnam's data don't support his supposition that the suburbs reduce social capital. To the extent that his data mean anything at all, they show that suburbs have more social capital than central cities and small towns have more than big cities.[7] Since central cities are denser than suburbs and big cities tend to be denser than small ones, Putnam's data suggest that social capital is fostered more in lower density areas. If so, then Putnam's support for smart growth is completely mistaken.

Today's claim that the suburbs lack a sense of community is ironic, for in the 1950s suburban critics maintained just the opposite: that suburbs were draining Americans of their individualism and turning them into "organization men" who believed a "social ethic" that stressed "the group as the source of creativity."[8] Whether they lack community or lack individuality, the conclusion is that suburbanites lead shallow and unhappy lives compared with what they would have in more compact inner-city neighborhoods. As will be shown in the Unhappy Suburbs Myth (p. 59), polls of suburban residents repeatedly find otherwise.

Architecture critic Philip Langdon says suburbanites are not even aware of the problem because they aren't "as knowledgeable about the implications of community design as professional planners are."[9] So they buy houses that "squelch neighborhood and public life."[10] To fix this, "houses must be designed in ways that encourage people to spend time in public."[11] As architect Andres Duany details, this means replacing private backyards with public parks, private automobiles with public transit, and large private homes with public community centers.[12]

These architects and planners have failed to understand both the detail and the grand scale of modern American society. They blame the disappearance of the front porch, for example, on a declining sense of community. In fact, in most parts of the country, shady front porches where the place people went to escape the indoor summer heat. The invention of air conditioning, not a declining sense of community, doomed the front porch.

Despite the lack of front porches in Levittown, New Jersey, sociologist Herbert Gans found many examples of community spirit, including participation in religious and social organizations, zoning and planning, and other community activities. "Architects and planners insist that every community must have a single physical and symbolic center," wrote Gans, but he doubted that such a center "would have created a major impact on people's lives" because few events required the entire community to "come together as a group." "In most cities," added Gans, "demand for and use of centers is generated by tourists," not by residents.[13]

Before living in Levittown, Gans spent two years in Boston's West End, a traditional, high-density urban neighborhood. He found West Enders had strong feelings about their ethnic or social group, but not about their neighborhood. "Life for the West Ender was defined in terms of his relationship to the [peer or ethnic] group," not the neighborhood.[14] Levittown "may displease the professional city planner," concluded Gans, "but perhaps more than any other type of community, Levittown permits most of its residents to be what they want to be—to center their lives around the home and the family, to be among neighbors whom they can trust, to find friends to share the leisure hours, and to participate in organizations that provide sociability and the opportunity to be of service to others."[14]

More fundamentally, suburban critics confuse *community* with *geography*. Since automobiles are evil, smart growth would limit people to choosing their friends from among their neighbors within immediate walking distance. This is absurd. As *Washington Post* writer Joel Garreau notes, "the main idea behind community now is voluntary association, not geography."[16] In today's jet-speed, internet economy, people have a far greater sense of community than ever before. Only their communities are not geographic, they are based on personal interests. Communities can be related to work, family, recreation, or hobbies. Soccer moms, pet owners, ethnic groups, skiers, and collectors all have their own communities.

Most people belong to many different communities. With so many different ones to choose from, no one wants to limit themselves to just the communities that can be found within walking distance from their homes. The automobile has become an essential part of community spirit and efforts to restrict driving will impede, not improve, that spirit.

Notes

1. HUD, *State of the Cities Report, 1999* (Washington, DC: HUD, 1999), finding #2.
2. Richard Sexton, *Parallel Utopias: The Quest for Community* (San Francisco, CA: Chronicle Books, 1995), p. 15.
3. James Howard Kunstler, *The Geography of Nowhere: The Rise and Decline of America's Man-Made Landscape* (New York, NY: Simon & Schuster, 1993), pp. 26–27.
4. John Norquist, "Free Market: Key to Public Choice," *Commonground*, 2 (1, Winter, 1999): p. 32.
5. Robert Putnam, *Bowling Alone: The Collapse and Revival of American Community* (New York, NY: Simon & Schuster, 2000), p. 283.
6. Ibid, p. 408.
7. Ibid, pp. 206–207.
8. William H. Whyte, Jr., *The Organization Man* (New York, NY: Simon & Schuster, 1956), pp. 4–8, 330–331.
9. Philip Langdon, *A Better Place to Live: Reshaping the American Suburb* (New York, NY: Harper Perennial, 1994), p. 79.
10. Ibid, p. xiii.
11. Ibid, p. 148.
12. Andres Duany, Elizabeth Plater-Zyberk, and Jeff Speck, *Suburban Nation: The Rise of Sprawl and the Decline of the American Dream* (New York, NY: North Point Press, 2000), pp. 59–60.
13. Herbert J. Gans, *The Levittowners: Ways of Life and Politics in a New Suburban Community* (New York, NY: Pantheon, 1967), pp. 282–283.
14. Herbert J. Gans, *The Urban Villagers: Group and Class in the Life of Italian Americans* updated edition (New York, NY: Free Press, 1982), p. 172.
15. Gans, *The Levittowners*, pp. 412–413.
16. Joel Garreau, *Edge City: Life on the New Frontier* (New York, NY: Doubleday, 1991), p. 275.

3. What Is Smart Growth?

Years before the term *smart growth* had been coined, *Washington Post* writer Joel Garreau asked an urban planner how he would change a low-density urban area. "I would increase dramatically the real residential population," he replied. "Give me 100,000 people. . . not living within a mile or two miles. I want them living right here. I'd raise the gasoline tax by 300 percent. I'd raise the price of automobiles enormously. I mean I would just limit movement. . . and there would be a massive rush to live near your work, your social or commercial activity. And then I would put enormous costs on parking. I think just take transportation alone, you could change these places dramatically"

"Given vast powers," comments Garreau, what this planner would do "is force Americans to live in a world that few now seem to value."[1] Today, we recognize the planner's prescription as smart growth: Use transportation policy to immobilize people so that, like nineteenth-century urbanites, they will be happy living in high densities.

For more than a century, rising incomes and new technologies have given American urbanites greater choices about where to live and how to travel, and most of them have decided to live in lower density areas and to travel by auto. Now smart-growth planners want to turn back the clock by rebuilding cities to nineteenth-century densities and forcing people to use nineteenth-century transportation technologies. If *sprawl* is defined by auto usage, then the sprawl opponents' idea of a *livable city* is a city with fewer automobiles. "A livable city is one in which you can buy your morning orange juice without driving a car," says Portland's Mayor Vera Katz. "Livable cities occur when all one's needs can be met within walking distance, public transport distances, or short drives," agrees Portland planning advocate Robert Bremmer.[2]

Sometime around 1996, sprawl warriors coined the term *smart growth* to describe their alternative to low-density suburbs. Unlike the terms they previously used, such as *compact cities*, *neotraditionalism*, and *new urbanism*, smart growth has attracted national attention. After all, people will argue about whether they want compact cities or traditional neighborhoods, but who will argue in favor of dumb growth or sprawl when a smart-growth alternative is available?

As planners describe it, smart growth is an attractive vision of people living and working in pedestrian-friendly communities, walking to the store, taking light rail on longer trips, and using the automobile only as a last resort. As a result, smart growth supposedly allows urban areas to grow without increasing congestion, pollution, taxes, or the loss of open space.

The reality of smart growth is far from the vision:

- Smart growth not only causes congestion, many smart-growth advocates believe that increased congestion is needed to make it work;
- Yet even with increased congestion, smart growth does not lead significant numbers of people to trade in their cars for transit, walking, or cycling;
- Smart growth's effects on air pollution are ambiguous, since the effects of increased congestion on auto emissions are likely to offset the minor reductions in auto driving;
- Similarly, smart growth not only causes single-family home prices to rise, but some smart-growth advocates may believe that such price increases are needed to convince people to live in high-density, transit-oriented developments;
- As a result, rates of home ownership can be expected to decline and low-income people will have a harder time paying for decent housing;
- Far from keeping its promise of reducing urban-service costs, smart growth imposes extra burdens on taxpayers to cover the costs of subsidized rail transit and subsidized high-density housing;
- Smart growth is likely to lead to increased costs for consumer goods due to a reduction in retail competition and an emphasis on small, noncompetitive stores;
- Urban open spaces will rapidly disappear to infill;
- Nor does smart growth guarantee protection of rural open spaces—instead, it may lead to accelerated exurbanization of rural areas;
- finally, smart growth causes a tremendous loss of both freedom and mobility.

Despite these problems, the smart-growth vision is widely shared among the nation's political and urban leaders, led by Vice President Al Gore. Smart-growth supporters include the governors of Oregon, Maryland, Minnesota, and Georgia, among others; the mayors of Albuquerque, Atlanta, Minneapolis, Nashville, Portland, Sacramento, San Diego, Seattle, and many other big cities; editorial writers for such major newspapers as the *Los Angeles Times*, *Minneapolis Star-Tribune*, the Portland *Oregonian*; and numerous interest groups ranging from the Sierra Club to the National Trust for Historic Preservation, plus of course rail transit builders and other businesses that expect to profit from smart growth.

One place where the vision is *not* supported is in the data produced by the government agencies promoting smart growth. This book will show that the background data for almost every proposal for higher densities, light rail, transit-oriented development, and other smart-growth proposals show that these plans will lead to increased congestion and declining urban open space. Many of the plans admit that air pollution will get worse and they inevitably lead to higher housing prices and require higher subsidies and therefore higher taxes.

Smart growth is *not* no growth. Debates over growth vs. no growth that characterized the 1970s were largely won by the growth side. A significant no-growth or slow-growth minority remains, represented by Eban Fodor's recent book, *Better Not Bigger*. Fodor argues that smart growth "fails to address the amount of growth that is desirable." He believes that "we may be able to identify an optimal size for each community, or at least a 'maximum size' beyond which the quality and livability will decline." Although he never says how this optimal size is to be calculated, once it is calculated he argues that smart growth and no growth are "completely compatible and even complementary."[3]

If smart growth really meant no growth, most of smart growth's supporters would abandon the movement. The war on sprawl is fought by a coalition of pro-growth forces in the cities combined with anti-auto, anti-suburb forces among planners and environmentalists. While some sprawl opponents may not like growth, most recognize that accepting growth is necessary to maintain this coalition: The no-growth minority is expected to support smart growth as the lesser of evils.

People on both sides of the smart-growth issue sometimes portray their opponents as no-growth advocates. But most interest groups on both sides accept that growth is not the issue; the question is how we grow. The twin goals of the war on sprawl are to:

- "Grow up, not out"—that is, grow by increasing densities rather than by spreading across the land.
- "Reduce auto dependency" by emphasizing transit and walkable neighborhoods rather than roads and autos.

Smart-growth advocates have a precise idea of what they want American cities to look like in the future. As detailed in parts four through eight, smart growth consists of five major prescriptions:

1. Significantly increase urban and suburban population densities (part four);
2. Spend scarce transportation dollars on rail transit that few people will ride instead of taking steps that can genuinely relieve traffic congestion (part five);
3. Discourage auto driving by, among other things, mandating so-called pedestrian-friendly, but really automobile-hostile, design codes (part six);
4. Redevelop existing neighborhoods into high-density, mixed-use, transit-oriented developments (part seven);
5. Create regional governments that can impose these policies on reluctant suburbs and neighborhoods with little or no democratic consent (part eight).

Taken together, smart-growth policies amount to the immobilization of America. Contrary to its proponents' claims, smart growth does not reduce congestion; it increases it. Privately—and sometimes publicly—smart-growth supporters admit that they consider increased congestion to be a benefit.

The surprising part is that anyone supports smart growth. Yet smart growth's chief supporters—urban planners and urban environmentalists—have built a powerful coalition with a wide range of other interest groups by portraying smart growth as all things to all people. Are you worried about congestion? Smart growth will get cars off the road. Annoyed by high taxes? Smart growth will save money. Concerned about the future of the inner city? Smart growth will save it. Air pollution, poverty, historic buildings? Smart growth, it is claimed, will fix or save them all. In fact, the opposite is more likely to happen.

Ultimately, smart growth is about power:

- Who gets to decide how you travel and where you live, work, and shop: you, or a government planner who thinks cars are immoral and that you should walk to the grocery store and take mass transit to work?
- Who gets to collect taxes and make land-use decisions in your neighborhood: decentralized local governments or a centralized metropolitan government?
- Who decides how your gasoline taxes and other highway user fees are spent: people interested in promoting mobility, or a government agency that frets and moralizes over people's travel preferences?
- Who will set the agenda for your city's future: local residents or Washington bureaucrats in the Environmental Protection Agency?

Smart growth is about the centralization of power over American lifestyles in an age when nearly every other country in the world has given up on central planning. Smart-growth advocates seek to give regional governments the exclusive power over land-use and transportation planning in urban areas. Under the thumb of the Environmental Protection Agency, which will favor urban areas that follow smart-growth prescriptions with federal funds, these regional governments will force cities to rezone neighborhoods to higher densities and divert highway user fees to transit.

As part nine will detail, opponents of smart growth favor instead the decentralization of power and responsibility to local municipalities rather than regional governments; to neighborhoods rather than cities; and to individuals rather than any government authority. Some government services can better be provided by the private sector. Where government is needed, it should respond to public needs and desires, not attempt to manipulate people into changing their behavior to suit bureaucratic whims or misconceptions.

Notes

1. Joel Garreau, *Edge City: Life on the New Frontier* (New York, NY: Doubleday, 1991), p. 239.
2. Robert Bremmer, "Portland's livability doomed without Metro," *The Oregonian*, August 28, 1997, letters to the editor page.
3. Eben Fodor, *Better Not Bigger: How to Take Control of Urban Growth and Improve Your Community* (Stony Creek, CT: New Society, 1999), pp 27–28.

The Choice Myth

Myth: Smart growth gives people more housing and transportation choices.

Reality: Smart growth isn't about giving people more choice; it is about taking away choices.

One of the most pernicious criticisms of modern urban and suburban areas is that they have taken away people's choices of housing and transportation. Low-density suburban zoning, the story goes, prevents developers from building and people from choosing to live in walkable or transit-oriented neighborhoods. The popularity of the automobile led transit companies to dismantle most streetcar lines and has reduced urban transit choices.

"People want choices," says Milwaukee Mayor John Norquist. "The key is to allow the free market to produce a broad spectrum of choices consumers want."[1] But Norquist thinks that, in a free market, people will choose to abandon the suburbs and move to the cities where they will abandon their autos in favor of transit. In fact, it is clear that most people prefer mobility and low densities to transit and crowding.

Many U.S. cities have both traditional high-density neighborhoods and rail transit. Yet people are not exactly swarming to move to these areas. Most cities with both rail transit and traditional high-density centers—cities such as Boston, Baltimore, and Philadelphia—are losing population, while their suburbs are growing. The few fast-growing rail-transit cities, such as San Jose and San Diego, do not have dense, nineteenth-century cores, and even they are growing more slowly than their suburbs.

Of course, many cities without rail transit are losing population, and those losing the fastest tend to be the dense, older cities. Suburbs are growing faster than central cities in virtually all urban areas. No central city is turning people away and most are eager to grow as fast as their suburbs. Yet people continue to move away from congested areas. Similarly, many cities have built new rail transit lines in the past three decades, yet few of them have attracted significant numbers of auto drivers out of their cars.

Smart growth's overt solution, of course, is to give people choices by building new rail transit lines and rezoning rail corridors for transit-oriented developments. Rail transit is so expensive, however, that this is like giving house guests a choice of ordinary California wine or a $500-per-bottle Bordeaux. Similarly, far from being affordable, housing in high-density areas tends to be more expensive, due to higher land values, than housing in low-density areas.

As noted in chapter 7 (p. 130), the architects who developed many smart-growth ideas originally tried to convince developers to build them and sell them to people who wanted to live in higher densities. These architects expected that people would jump at the chance to walk or ride transit instead of driving cars. But the few such developments that were built tended to sell slowly. So smart-growth supporters soon turned to government coercion to promote their ideas. "All development," not just the developments that the market will support, "should be in the form of compact, walkable neighborhoods," says the Congress for the New Urbanism.[2]

All or nearly all transportation construction dollars, argues the Surface Transportation Policy Project, should go to rail transit, not new highways, despite the fact that the trains carry few people while the highways are jammed. Yet many cities that build rail transit end up cutting back on bus services in the transit corridors. Nonstop buses that once took 20 to 25 minutes between two points are replaced with a rail line that requires 30 to 40 minutes, including several stops, to cover the same distance. Neighborhoods that once had direct bus connections to downtown find that they now have a feeder bus to the rail station where they must transfer and wait for the train—often at an additional cost.

Transit agencies that beat the drum to build expensive rail systems and then devote the enormous resources required to oversee construction end up neglecting other, more useful transit services. Meanwhile, auto drivers face increasing congestion because funds that should have gone into reducing highway bottle-necks that delay hundreds of thousands of travelers each day are spent instead on rail transit that is used by only a few tens of thousands of travelers.

If all smart growth proposed to do was give developers the option of building higher density housing and give people the option of transit that was economically competitive with autos, then hardly anyone would object. But smart growth isn't about giving people more choices; it is about taking away choices by making low-density housing unaffordable for most people and making highways intolerably congested.

Notes

1. John Norquist, "Free Market: Key to Public Choice," *Commonground*, 2 (1, Winter, 1999): 30, 32.
2. Congress for the New Urbanism, "New Urbanism Basics," http://www.cnu.org/newurbanism.html.

The Myth of Voter Support

Myth: Voters support the war on sprawl.
Reality: Voters tend to support actions that keep population densities low and tend to oppose actions that increase density.

With architects and planners providing a patina of expertise and endorsements from environmental and other interest groups, many elected officials have concluded that smart growth is the route to political popularity. This conclusion is apparently affirmed by a Brookings Institution study that is said to have identified 240 local smart-growth ballot measures in the November, 1998 election, more than 72 percent of which passed.[1] Al Gore specifically cited this study in announcing the administration's war on sprawl, and it may have helped convince him to make sprawl a centerpiece of his presidential campaign.

However, a close examination of the 240 measures cited in the Brookings study reveals that none of them were truly smart-growth measures. Almost all of them were simply tax levies for purchasing parks and open space. Voters see parks and urban open space as ways of *reducing* density and congestion, not increasing it.

A few of the ballot measures in California involved urban-growth boundaries or some other form of growth control. But, unlike those in Oregon, California growth boundaries limit density and growth, not increase density. California cities have been adopting boundaries and other growth-control measures since the 1970s, and such boundaries are widely viewed as a way of maintaining low densities. In 1988 alone, voters in various California cities passed 147 growth-control measures. Some of these limited commercial and industrial development, but most restricted residential densities, placed caps on population, rezoned as open space lands that had been available for development, or required voter approval or council supermajorities for any increases in residential density.[2]

While ballot measures limiting density are usually successful, few measures have ever asked voters if they want to significantly increase densities within their neighborhoods or communities, and most if not all have been soundly defeated. In 1997, the city council of one Portland suburb asked voters whether they wanted to accept the higher densities Portland's regional planners wanted to impose upon them. The residents voted four-to-one against higher densities.

The November, 2000, election saw the resounding defeat of two smart-growth measures in Arizona and Colorado. Arizona's proposition 202 would have required urban-growth boundaries with strong limits on development outside the boundaries.[3] Colorado's amendment 24 would have forbidden development outside of existing urban areas without voter approval.[4] Both measures lost by more than a two-to-one margin. As in previous elections, several San Francisco-area counties and cities passed growth-control measures that limited density rather than increased it.[5] Several places passed open-space measures, but again these are seen by voters as limiting density, not increasing it.

As noted in the Neighborhood-Redevelopment Myth (p. 334), rail transit construction is closely connected with neighborhood densification. This makes rail an important if not crucial part of the smart-growth platform. Yet the Brookings study did not consider any of the six rail ballot measures voted on in November, 1998, five of which were decisively voted down. In fact, more than two out of three rail ballot measures voted on between 1995 and 2000 were defeated.[6] In the November, 2000, election, Florida and Seattle passed vague rail ballot measures that allocated little, if any, money for rail projects,[7] while Austin turned down an expensive light-rail plan.[8]

Politicians who endorse smart growth on the strength of the Brookings study are likely to be very surprised. Voters can be persuaded to support transit if they think transit subsidies will reduce congestion. They will support open space purchases if they think such open spaces will reduce densities. But they will oppose plans that call for increasing the densities of the neighborhoods in which they live and would certainly oppose plans that proposed to increase urban congestion.

Notes

1. Phyllis Myers, *Livability at the Ballot Box: State and Local Referenda on Parks, Conservation, and Smarter Growth, Election Day, 1998* (Washington, DC: Brookings, 1999), 17 pp., http://www.brook.edu/es/urban/myers.pdf.
2. Glickfeld, M., and N. Levine, *The New Land Use Regulation "Revolution": Why California's Local Jurisdictions Enact Growth Control and Management Measures* (Los Angeles, CA: UCLA Extension Public Policy Program, 1991).
3. Tony Davis and Macario Juarez, "Growth control fails overwhelmingly," *Arizona Daily Star*, November 8, 2000, http://www.azstarnet.com/vote2000/eday-propositions.shtml.
4. Michele Ames and Todd Hartman, "Growth-control amendment fails," *Rocky Mountain News*, November 8, 2000, http://www.rockymountainnews.com/election/1108am24a.shtml.
5. Ken McNeill, "Growth-control plans gain favor with voters," *Tri-Valley Herald*, November 8, 2000, http://www.herald-ang.com/default.ASP?puid=258&spuid=258&Indx=522938&Article=ON.
6. Wendell Cox, "U.S. Urban Rail Referendum Results Through May 2000," http://www.publicpurpose.com/ut-railv.htm.

7. Tyler Bridges, "Florida bullet train heads towards approval," *Miami Herald*, November 8, 2000; Jim Brunner, "City voters push monorail expansion one step closer to reality," *Seattle Times*, November 8, 2000, http://archives.seattletimes.nwsource.com/cgi-bin/texis/web/vortex/display?slug=mono08&date=20001108.

8. Kelly Danie, "Light rail dies," *American-Statesman*, November 8, 2000, http://austin360.com/news/features/local/8railvote.html.

Part Two

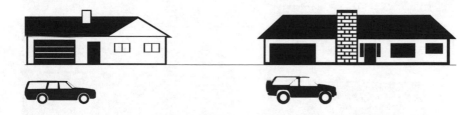

The War on the
American Dream

Large yards are being infilled with apartments in this former single-family Gresham neighborhood since planners rezoned it for high-density multi-family dwellings (top). If someone's house burns down, zoning requires them to replace it with an apartment (p. 62).
Accessory apartments are a way of increasing density in single-family neighborhoods (bottom). Residents of single-family neighborhoods strongly protested whenever Portland-area planners proposed to allow such units, which can effectively turn some homes into duplexes. So Metro simply required that all single-family zoning ordinances be rewritten to allow accessory units, thus assuring that local residents will have no say in the matter (p. 61).

4. The War on the Suburbs

*M*ost people unconsciously divide the world between Us and THEM. US includes the people we know and love, who are smart, witty, and creative, and who lead exciting, influential lives. THEM includes the faceless crowd of millions or billions who lead sad, banal lives that are mostly wasted. Exactly who THEY are depends on who you are. If you are a Manhattan writer, a Berkeley architect, or a professor of urban planning at one of our great universities, then THEY probably include the unfortunates who live in placeless, ugly, and chaotic suburbs.

"As anyone who reads the fiction in *The New Yorker* knows," says *Newsweek*, "Americans mostly live in banal places with the souls of shopping malls, affording nowhere to mingle except traffic jams, nowhere to walk except the health club."[1] It doesn't seem to have occurred to *Newsweek* that few Americans regard the fiction in *The New Yorker* as the last word on how they should live. After all, it is only fiction. More recently, the *Economist* concluded that suburban "alienation is inevitable in places that lack both natural centres and public spaces." As evidence, the magazine cited two eminent authorities: *The Simpsons* (which isn't even about the suburbs) and *King of the Hill* cartoon shows.[2]

Intellectuals have insisted that suburbs are boring, sterile, and culturally oppressive ever since the 1920s, when Henry Ford's affordable cars made suburbs accessible to ordinary people. Indeed, it appears that what disturbed intellectuals was not the suburbs themselves but the fact that they were occupied by ordinary—and therefore, to the intellectuals, boring—people.

Suburbanization began long before the 1920s, and originally it was met with approval by intellectuals, architects, and designers. For as long as humans have lived in great cities, the wealthiest in those cities had their rural estates to which they removed, particularly in the summers, to avoid the disease, crime, and pestilence of the crowded cities. But true suburbs—places outside the city where urban workers lived and commuted from and to each day—did not appear so long as transportation was limited to foot or horsepower.

Harvard landscape historian John Stilgoe traces the earliest American suburbs to the 1820s and 1830s, when the nation's first railroads were built.[3]

Suburbanization received a boost, he notes, in the 1850s, when the steam-pow-
ered intercity railway was supplemented within cities by the horse-powered rail-
car. An even bigger boost occurred in the 1880s and 1890s, when first cable cars
and then electric streetcars replaced the horse cars. Each innovation reduced the
cost of transportation and made the suburbs accessible to more people. But as late
as 1910, suburbs remained the preserve of the upper classes.

To the urban planners and intellectuals of late nineteenth century, suburbs
were not a problem but a solution—*the* solution to what was regarded as the chief
urban problem of industrial America: overcrowded cities. Between 1850 and 1890,
three-quarters of the population of New York and other major cities lived in tenements, with several families often jammed into single apartments.[4] Intellectual
and social leaders considered the high-density tenements of that time to be unsanitary and unsafe, and planners and reformers spent their time trying to find
ways to reduce densities.

"Many turn-of-the-century observers viewed the inner city. . . as a social men-
ace from which the masses should make every effort to escape," writes transportation historian Mark Foster.[5] Planning historian Peter Hall adds that, "Twentieth-
century city planning, as an intellectual and professional movement, essentially
represents a reaction to the evils of the nineteenth-century city."[6]

Planners came up with all sorts of utopian solutions for helping the downtrod-
den masses. But, says Hall, the "central irony" turned out to be that "even as the
first tentative experiments were made in creating a new planned social order, so
the market began to dissolve the worst evils of the slum city through the process
of mass suburbanization."[7]

To say that "the market" solved the problems of urban slums, while true enough,
is an oversimplification. It is just as accurate to credit Henry Ford, recently named
Businessman of the Century by *Fortune* magazine, with the solution.[8] In 1909,
when Ford introduced the Model T, he sold it for as little as $825. By 1915, he
dropped the price below $400, and in 1925 you could buy a new Model T for just
$260.[9] Ford also implemented the mass production system and doubled workers
pay. As this system spread from industry to industry, it became possible for most
workers to earn enough money that they could afford to buy not only cars but
their own homes. Low prices and high pay liberated average working people from
the crowded cities; by the mid 1920s, more than half of all American families
owned a car.

Suburbs were attractive because they contributed to the mobility made possible by the automobile. "The resident in a city found it more difficult and expensive to own a family car than the rural or suburban resident," wrote Joseph Barnett,
the federal official in charge of urban roads, in 1950. "Garaging in cities was more
expensive, insurance rates were higher, ability to reach a destination more difficult
than in rural areas, and upon arrival at a destination a garage or car park could
easily be added to a suburban home and little delay was experienced in reaching

an arterial route."[10]

If the suburbs made it easier to own an automobile, autos made it easier to enjoy the benefits of the suburbs. "Garden-type housing projects on large tracts are better places in which to live than individual apartment houses or even separate homes in some real estate developments designed for quick profits," noted Barnett in 1950. "The 'park and shop' is becoming common and the retail sales buildings of the mail order companies are assuming huge proportions."[11]

"The suburban car and automobile have rendered confinement within the City unnecessary for large numbers of people," noted Ford himself in 1922. "And one of the most hopeful facts is that, whereas only the well-to-do once found it possible to get away from the city, now the workingman finds it not only possible but advantageous to live in the country."

The roaring 1920s were accompanied by rapid suburbanization as American incomes soared. Prescient observers could see that cities no longer needed dense urban centers. "In the days of electrical transmission, the automobile and the telephone," said Frank Lloyd Wright in 1922, urban concentration "becomes needless congestion—it is a curse."[12] He added later that "The traffic problem, if tied up with the skyscraper"—by which he meant dense inner cities—"is insoluble by any busy big city in the United States or elsewhere."[13]

"Cities are doomed," agreed Ford. "There is no city now existing that would be rebuilt as it is, if it were destroyed; which fact is in itself a confession of our real estimate of our cities."[14] Ford was right, observes Joel Garreau in his 1991 book, *Edge City*. A huge percentage of jobs in the New York urban area are in Manhattan. But cities largely built in the twentieth century, such as Los Angeles, Phoenix, and Las Vegas, lack major downtown employment centers. "We have not built a single old-style downtown from raw dirt in seventy-five years," notes Garreau.[15]

Most American metropolitan areas can be classified as either *nineteenth-century* or *twentieth-century* urban areas. The nineteenth-century cities developed before the automobile and so have dense urban cores. Manhattan, which is twelve times as dense as the New York urbanized area as a whole, is the classic example. The twentieth-century cities developed with the automobile, and so do not have particularly dense cores. In one of the most recent, San Jose, the city is hardly denser than its urbanized area.

Too many planners and writers act as though only the nineteenth-century urban area qualifies as a "true city." San Francisco is "a great and true city," says one writer, while Dallas and Salt Lake City are merely "ugly, dysfunctional, anti-human blight."[16] Yet the nineteenth century city "is only one way to think of a city," responds Garreau. Crowded, industrial cities such as New York, Chicago, and San Francisco "are the aberrations. We built cities that way for less than a century. . . , from perhaps 1840 to 1920."[17] Pre-industrial cities did not look like that, and neither do post-industrial cities. Yet it is those industrial cities—the ones that late-nineteenth-century planners were so eager to be rid of—that most planners today have in mind when they talk about compact cities, downtown revitalization, light-rail transit, and smart growth.

Henry Ford could see that cities "may continue to exist" as work places, "but people will live outside them."[18] "We shall solve the city problem by leaving the city."[19] But as the masses began leaving the fire-trap tenements and disease-ridden slums for the fresh air and wide-open spaces of the suburbs, intellectual Americans began to have second thoughts about the suburbs.

"Not until the 1920s did those suburbs substantially unnerve American intellectuals," says historian Stilgoe. "Indeed until that time most intellectuals favored their creation." But when they discovered that those living in the suburbs were "slow to accept the European avant garde," then "urban writers, especially in New York, turn[ed] on the suburbs as the home of narrow-mindedness."

> Architects entranced with the flat-roofed, cement apartment houses of 1930s Berlin reeled from steadfast suburban love of single-family, pitched roof houses; interior decorators announcing the wonders of tube-steel furniture found a burgeoning interest in American wooden antiques; city planners championing great boulevards and public parks learned of gardeners anxious to shape their own private spaces; and social critics and historians struggling to interpret the great forces guiding the passage of the Republic found families making separate peace with urbanization, corporate employment, and high-paced political and social change.[20]

Nor was this unique to America. Peter Hall notes that British suburbs of the 1920s and 1930s were "universally derided and condemned," and that "the prosecutors were all upper-middle class and the offenders were mostly lower-middle class." The people moving to the suburbs, says Hall, "were enjoying a quantum leap in their quality of life." Yet, as in America, architects led the opposition to the suburbs. "The suburbs' chief fault seems to have been that they conspicuously diverged from either of the then main standards of good taste: the neo-Georgian. . . or the uncompromisingly modern," remarks Hall. "Whether it was sour grapes or not, the architects were angry; they wanted revenge."[21]

In both Britain and America, the architects were joined by nature lovers who worried that the countryside would soon be overrun with suburbs. Hall describes this as the "terror" of "the democratization of the countryside: the lower-middle-class and working-class invasion of an area that had hitherto been the preserve of an aristocratic and upper-middle-class elite." Hall cites a 1938 anti-suburb essay by C. E. M. Joad that "revealingly" referred to the "hordes of hikers cackling insanely in the woods. . . . People, wherever there is water, upon seashores or upon river banks, lying in every attitude of undress and inelegant squalor, grilling themselves, for all the world as if they were steaks, in the sun." The solution, Joad believed, was "the extension of the towns must be stopped, building must be restricted to sharply defined areas, and such re-housing of the population as may be necessary must be carried on within these areas." Such housing, another anti-suburbs writer suggested, would be in "great new blocks of flats which will house a considerable part of the population."[22] This sounds a lot like smart growth, and the case study on European cities will show that this is exactly what most European nations did after World War II.

In the United States, however, freedom of choice in housing prevailed after World War II, and the choice of many was to move to the suburbs. The construction of Levittowns on Long Island and suburban Philadelphia were social, business, and economic triumphs in many ways. They were the largest private housing projects in history, with one of them housing 82,000 people.[23] William Levitt applied Henry Ford's mass-production techniques to home construction, going so far as to have one crew dedicated to white paint and another dedicated to red.[24] This process, imitated by builders across the nation, did for housing what the Model T did for transportation: It made home ownership accessible to the masses.

The Levittowns also so riled up the intellectuals that today the name *Levittown* is synonymous with all that is supposed to be bad about the suburbs. "Sterility is designed into them!" exclaimed *Newsweek*. John Keats' 1956 book, *The Crack in the Picture Window*, called the suburbs "conceived in error, nurtured by greed, corroding everything they touch."[25] "Little Boxes," a 1960s song by Berkeley writer Malvina Reynolds and popularized by Pete Seeger, labeled the suburbs "ticky-tacky."

These elitist views fail to explain why the suburbs are so popular. Suburban residents were a tiny minority of the U.S. population in 1915. Within fifty years they outnumbered central city dwellers and today they make up half the U.S. population. This is very annoying to those who believe that everyone would be happier if they just lived in higher densities. As an Oregon smart-growth advocate is fond of saying, "I grew up on a 50-by-100-foot lot, and what was good enough for me should be good enough for anyone."[26] The arrogant notion that a small elite can and should make important lifestyle choices for everyone else is at the heart of the war on the suburbs.

Notes

1. Jerry Adler, "Bye-Bye, Suburban Dream," *Newsweek*, May 15, 1995 pp. 40–53.
2. Lexington, "When life is more interesting than art," *The Economist*, March 31, 2000, p. 36.
3. John R. Stilgoe, *Borderland: Origins of the American Suburb, 1820–1939* (New Haven, CT: Yale University Press, 1988), 353 pp.
4. Benson Bobrick, *Labyrinths of Iron: Subways in History, Myth, Art, Technology, and War* (New York: Henry Holt & Co., 1981; Owl Book edition, 1994), p. 210.
5. Mark S. Foster, *From Streetcar to Superhighway: American City Planners and Urban Transportation, 1900–1940* (Philadelphia, PA: Temple University Press, 1981), p. 7.
6. Peter Geoffrey Hall, *Cities of Tomorrow: An Intellectual History of Urban Planning and Design in the Twentieth Century* (Cambridge, MA: Blackwell, 1988; updated to 1996), p. 7.

7. Ibid, pp. 7–8.
8. *Fortune*, "The Businessman of the Century," November 22, 1999 (v. 140, no. 10), p. 108, http://library.northernlight.com/PN19991109040000085.html?cb=13&sc=0.
9. The Model T Ford Club International, "Original Model T Ford Prices by Model and Year," http://www.modelt.org/tprices.html.
10. Joseph Barnett, "The Highway in Urban and Suburban Areas," in Jean Labatut and Wheaton J. Land (ed.), *Highways in Our National Life: A Symposium* (Princeton, NJ: Princeton University Press, 1950), p. 146.
11. Ibid, p. 150.
12. Quoted in Robert fishman, "The Post-War American Suburb: A New Form, A New City," in Daniel Schaffer (ed.), *Two Centuries of American Planning* (Baltimore, MD: Johns Hopkins, 1988), p. 266.
13. Frank Lloyd Wright, *The Living City* (New York, NY: Horizon Press, 1958), p. 81.
14. Henry Ford, *Ford Ideals: Being a Selection from 'Mr. Ford's Page' in The Dearborn Independent* (Dearborn, MI: Dearborn Independent, 1922), pp. 426–427.
15. Joel Garreau, *Edge City: Life on the New Frontier* (New York, NY: Doubleday, 1991), p. 25
16. Carolyn Lochhead, "Strip Malls and Sprawl: Is There Any Escape?" *San Francisco Chronicle*, March 28, 1999.
17. Joel Garreau, *Edge City*, p. 25.
18. Ibid, p. 428.
19. Ibid, p. 156–157.
20. John R. Stilgoe, *Borderland: Origins of the American Suburb, 1820–1939* (New Haven, CT: Yale University Press, 1988), p. 4.
21. Hall, *Cities of Tomorrow*, p. 79–80.
22. Ibid, p. 82–83.
23. Kenneth T. Jackson, *Crabgrass Frontier: The Suburbanization of the United States* (New York, NY: Oxford University Press, 1985), p. 235.
24. Ibid, p. 234.
25. John Keats, *The Crack in the Picture Window* (Boston, MA: Houghton Mifflin, 1956), p. 7.
26. Robert Liberty, director of 1000 Friends of Oregon, interview with Randal O'Toole, April, 1996.

Smart Growth's
Potemkin Village

From all over the world, people visit my hometown of Portland, Oregon, to learn the wonders of smart-growth planning. Urban mayors ooh and ah over Portland's light rail, planners thrill to the region's urban-growth boundary and transit-oriented development, and reporters write glowingly about the city's vitality and walkability.

Typical is *New York Times* reporter Timothy Egan, who finds that "Portland is arguably the most European-feeling city in the West, a place where the pedestrian is king." According to Egan, Portland is so "dense and compact" that a "curious pedestrian can wander for days and never miss the inside of a car."[1] Minneapolis *Star-Tribune* writer Steve Berg found himself "dumbfounded at the beauty and vitality of the streets" of Portland. "Every spare inch seems planted in flowers."[2] Travel writer Robert Kaplan calls Portland "perhaps the most architecturally pleasing and meticulously planned downtown of any major city in the United States."[3]

Portland-area residents may wonder if these people saw some different city entirely, for these descriptions don't come close to reality. Far from being a pedestrian paradise, more than 92 percent of all travel in the Portland area is by auto, with walking and bicycling together totaling only 5 percent.[4] Portland-area auto traffic increased by more than 50 percent between 1990 and 1998,[5] while transit lost market share, now carrying well under 3 percent of travel. The light-rail lines that other city officials envy carry only about a quarter of transit riders.

As a result, Portlanders are experiencing rapidly increasing congestion.[6] They also suffer some of the least affordable housing in the nation,[7] shrinking parks and open spaces, and an increasing tax burden to pay for both the light-rail lines that hardly anyone uses and subsidized high-density developments that many people live in only because the lower-density housing they would prefer is artificially priced out of reach. No wonder transportation consultant Wendell Cox calls Portland "smart growth's Potemkin Village."[8]

Most reporters and official visitors to Portland appear to have spent their time exclusively in the downtown area, where less than 2 percent of Portland-area residents live, or along the light-rail line that serves only a small segment of the Portland area.[9] Timothy Egan gives this away when he writes that Portland "city blocks are small—an American urban anomaly at just 200 feet square." This is true only in downtown: Nearly all other parts of Portland have city blocks at least twice that large, and in the suburbs that occupy two-thirds of the Portland area they are often much larger than that. Even downtown the reporters seem more dazzled by the vision than the reality. Egan writes about a parking lot "at the heart of the city's retail district" that was removed and replaced with a brick-covered park. "No one misses the parking lot," enthuses Egan. For good reason: When the city removed the parking lot, it built two multilevel parking garages just two to three blocks away. Downtown may be vibrant, but Portlanders haven't given up their cars.

Thanks more to local entrepreneurs than to light rail, downtown has become an interesting place to shop. As a center of employment, however, downtown Portland continues to decline. Most new jobs in the Portland area are in the edge cities of Beaverton, Hillsboro, and Tigard, several miles west of downtown. For more than a decade, the only new downtown office buildings have been built either by government agencies or with government subsidies. Downtown employment would be even lower were it not for executive orders from President Clinton and Oregon's governor directing federal and state agencies with offices in the Portland area to stay or relocate downtown.[10] The Bureau of Land Management was forced to move its state office from an east Portland office park to downtown despite higher rents and less convenience to its employees. The State Highway Division was forced to abandon its beautiful craftsman-style offices at the edge of the city and add to downtown congestion.

Even as a retail and entertainment center, downtown Portland serves mainly people who live close to downtown. Many Portland-area suburbanites rarely go downtown because it is too congested with cars and transit is too slow and inconvenient. Portland's downtown is just one of many entertainment, shopping, and office centers in Portland, albeit a little larger than most. But to understand Portland, you have to understand more than just downtown, which, after all, occupies less than a half a percent of the region's area.[11]

One person who learned this was Andres Duany, the architect who developed neotraditional planning. On four public speaking engagements in Portland, Duany says, "I was 'handled' by my hosts and shown the many wonderful places that make it a great, livable city." But on his fifth visit, he "escaped" his hosts and left the downtown area. To his "surprise," he found that as soon as he left the inner city "the sectors all the way to the urban boundary were chock full of the usual sprawl that one finds in any American city." He concluded that Portland's famous urban-growth boundary had done little "other than to neutralize the environmentalist opposition [to low-density suburbs] and to build the Portland myth."[12] Duany dislikes low-density suburbs. But he is right about one thing: Portland's planning reputation is largely a sham, due more to a great public relations effort than to any real differences between Portland and other American cities.

Portland's reputation for planning excellence dates back to 1973, when the Oregon legislature passed what remains the strongest statewide land-use planning law in the nation. Among other things, this law required Portland and other Oregon cities to establish urban-growth boundaries outside of which development is heavily restricted. In 1979, Portland further enhanced its reputation when it halted construction of a freeway and elected to use its federal highway dollars to build a light-rail line instead. That line was completed in 1986.

In 1992, Portland-area voters were promised that they could save Portland from becoming like Los Angeles by creating Metro, a regional authority with dictatorial planning authority over twenty-four cities and three counties. Metro has jurisdiction over parks, solid waste, Portland's Zoo, and various convention facilities. Most important, brag planners, Metro has "regional planning with teeth"[13]—the strongest transportation and land-use planning powers of any metropolitan government in the nation.

In December, 1997, Portland's seven-member Metro council approved its *2040 Plan*, the strongest, most comprehensive smart-growth plan ever written for a U.S. urban area. Metro planners predicted that the region's population would increase by nearly 80 percent between 1990 and 2040. To accommodate these people, the plan called for:

- Increasing population densities by 70 percent;
- Building and operating a total of 93 miles of light-rail lines and 33 miles of commuter rail;
- Adding only 14 percent new lane miles of roads, mainly to serve industrial areas, while reducing road capacities in many other parts of the region;
- Redeveloping dozens of neighborhoods into high-density, mixed-use areas;
- Requiring city and county planners to rezone neighborhoods at higher densities to meet specific population targets so that new residents could be accommodated with minimal expansion of the urban-growth boundary.

Many of the hundreds of newspaper and magazine articles written about Portland's plan take planners at their word when they say that the 2040 plan is turning the region into a pedestrian- and transit-oriented community. Few mention the tremendous costs that the plan imposes on Portland-area residents:

- Thanks to the urban-growth boundary, Portland went from being one of the nation's most affordable single-family housing markets in the late 1980s to one of the least affordable in the late 1990s.
- Thanks to Metro's spending most of the region's transportation dollars on light rail instead of roads, Portland has suffered a rapid increase in congestion—and Metro planners predict it will get much worse.
- Thanks to demands that an expected 500,000 new residents be housed without greatly expanding the urban-growth boundary, thousands of acres of open space inside the growth boundary, including farms, golf courses, and even

city parks, are being rezoned for development.

Even fewer articles in the popular press note that Metro planners predict that nearly 90 percent of travel in the Portland area will continue to be by auto, while the billions invested in light-rail transit will carry less than 3 percent of all travel. These predictions are probably optimistic: Portland-area driving has already exceeded Metro's expectations.

Despite these problems, civic leaders in fast-growing cities throughout the nation eye Metro's planning authority with envy. Georgia, Maryland, Minnesota, Washington, and Wisconsin are among the states that have recently passed land-use or growth-management planning laws. More than sixty cities are seeking federal funds to build light-rail or other rail transit lines. Regional planning agencies in more than three hundred U.S. metropolitan areas wish they had the authority that Portland has granted to Metro. Urban-growth boundaries, light rail, and regional planning agencies have become textbook solutions to almost any urban problem. A hard look at Portland will show that the textbook is wrong.

Notes

1. Tim Egan, "Portland On Foot: The best way to see Oregon's Rose City is not in a car," *Delta Sky Magazine*, August 1999, p. 54.
2. Steve Berg, "Portland offers up its recipe for making a better city," Minneapolis *Star-Tribune*, May 16, 1999, http://www.startribune.com/stOnLine/folder.
3. Robert Kaplan, *An Empire Wilderness: Travels into America's Future* (New York, NY: Random House, 1998), p. 330.
4. Metro, *Region 2040 Recommended Alternative Technical Appendix* (Portland, OR: Metro, 9-15-94).
5. Federal Highway Administration, *Highway Statistics 1990* and *Highway Statistics 1998* (Washington, DC: FHwA, 1991 and 1999), table HM-72.
6. Texas Transportation Institute, *Urban Roadway Congestion Annual Report 1998* (College Station, TX: Texas A&M, 1998), table 3.
7. National Association of Home Builders, *Housing Opportunity Index, first Quarter 1999*, http://www.nahb.com/mandl.html.
8. Wendell Cox, "Portland: Planning Potemkin Village," 1995, http://www.publicpurpose.com/.
9. Metro, *Region 2040 Recommended Alternative Technical Appendix* (Portland, OR: Metro, 1994), table 5.
10. William Clinton, Executive Orders 12988 and 13006 on Locating Federal Facilities (Washington, DC: White House, 1996); Barbara Roberts, Executive Order No. 94-07, "Siting State Offices in Oregon's Community Centers," 7 June 1994.
11. Metro, *Region 2040 Recommended Alternative Technical Appendix* (Portland, OR: Metro, 1994), table 5.
12. Andres Duany, "Punching holes in Portland," *The Oregonian*, December 19, 1999, p. E1.
13. G. B. Arrington, *Beyond the field of Dreams* (Portland, OR: Tri-Met, 1996), http://www.tri-met.org/reports/dreams.htm.

Population Facts

The federal government defines a *metropolitan area* as an area of 50,000 people or more. The U.S. has nearly 400 such metropolitan areas. Some of these, such as Los Angeles and Riverside-San Bernardino, are contiguous with one another. When these are combined, there are about 276 noncontiguous metropolitan areas. The most important city in each metropolitan area is called the *central city*. Some metropolitan areas, such as Minneapolis-St. Paul and Dallas-Ft. Worth, have more than one central city.

The Census Bureau tracks data for both *metropolitan statistical areas* (MSAs) and *urbanized areas*. The former include entire counties, the latter just the portions of the counties with more than 1,000 people per square mile (about one house every two acres). MSAs should not be used when measuring density: The Riverside-San Bernardino MSA, for example, includes the Mojave Desert and extends all the way to Nevada.

Smaller towns not a part of metropolitan areas are considered *urban*. Surprisingly, one out of four Americans live in *rural* areas, that is, outside of any town or metropolitan area. Nearly two out of three Americans live in metropolitan areas, leaving 10 percent in small towns.

Population of U.S. in 1990: 248.7 million
    Urban: 187.1 million (75 percent)
    Rural: 61.7 million (25 percent)
    276 major urbanized areas: 158.3 million (64 percent)
    281 central cities: 60.7 million (24 percent)

Population of U.S. in 1998: 270.3 million
    276 major urbanized areas: 176.1 million (65 percent)
    281 central cities: 62.8 million (23 percent)

 Web Tools: Population Data

For population data for your city or suburb, see www.census.gov.

Portland Geography

At about 1.5 million people, the Portland-Vancouver metropolitan area is the twenty-fifth largest urban area in the nation. The Columbia River separates the Oregon and Washington portions of the area. Known as the Rose City, Portland itself has about a third of the total population and is divided by the Willamette River into distinctive east and west sides, with downtown Portland located on the west side. On the east side is a major shopping mall and office complex known as Lloyd Center. Where downtown employment has remained stagnant for decades, Lloyd Center jobs have grown tremendously and the area now rivals downtown as an employment center. Portland-area planners sometimes combine Lloyds and downtown and call it the *central city*.

The city of Portland's 125 square miles are almost entirely in Multnomah County, which also includes the Portland's largest suburb, Gresham, and a few smaller suburbs including Fairview. A light-rail line completed in 1986 connects Gresham with Portland. The Oregon portion of the Portland urban area also includes parts of two other counties: Clackamas County is south of Portland while Washington County is west of Portland. Clackamas includes the suburbs of Lake Oswego, West Linn, Oregon City, Milwaukie, and Oak Grove. Washington includes Beaverton, Hillsboro, Tigard, and Tualatin. Since 1998, a light-rail line passing through Beaverton connects Portland with Hillsboro.

Table One: The Portland-Vancouver Urbanized Area

	1950	1990	1998
Population (thousands)	558	1,172	1,471
Land area square miles	124	388	468
Density	4,509	3,021	3,143

Source: Census Bureau for 1950 and 1990, FHwA, Highway Statistics 1998 for
1998. FHwA data are not exactly comparable with Census Bureau data since they
use slightly different criteria for determining urbanized area boundaries.

A comparison of tables one and two show that the Portland urban area of 1950 included about the same number of square miles as the city of Portland contains

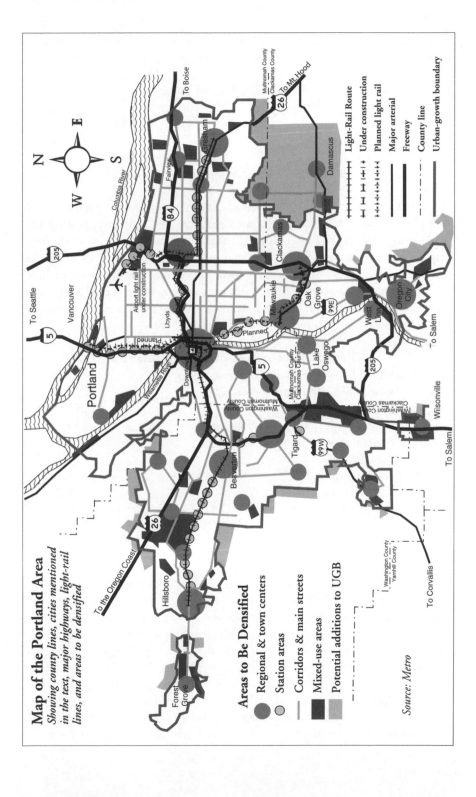

Map of the Portland Area

Showing county lines, cities mentioned in the text, major highways, light-rail lines, and areas to be densified

Areas to Be Densified

● Regional & town centers
○ Station areas
— Corridors & main streets
▓ Mixed-use areas
░ Potential additions to UGB

Light-Rail Route
Under construction
Planned light rail
Major arterial
Freeway
County line
Urban-growth boundary

Source: Metro

today. Yet the 1950 urban area population was 10 percent greater than Portland's population today, reflecting a significant reduction in population density.

Table Two: The City of Portland

	1950	1990	1998
Population (thousands)	374	437	504
Land area square miles	64	125	125
Density	5,828	3,508	4,000

Source: Census Bureau. Land area and density for 1998 are estimated.

Table three shows that Portland-area residents traveled an average of 12,320 miles by auto in 1998. At just 235 passenger miles per capita, transit accounted for less than 2 percent of all motorized travel in the region. The table also indicates that transit carried about 5.6 percent of all commuters in 1990. This percentage appears to have declined since then. Vancouver, Washington, is included in most of these urban-area statistics. But because Vancouver is outside the jurisdiction of Metro, Portland's regional planning agency, it will rarely be mentioned in this case study.

Table Three: Portland-Area Transportation

Miles of freeway per million people	93
Annual miles driven per capita	7,702
Passenger miles per capita	12,320
Annual transit miles per capita	235
Annual transit trips per capita	59
Auto commuters	89.4%
Transit commuters	5.6%
Walk/cycle commuters	5.0%

Source: FHwA, Highway Statistics 1998, FTA, Transit Profiles 1998, 1990 Census. All data are from 1998 except commuting data, which are from 1990. Passenger miles per capita are 1.6 times miles driven per capita.

In 1969, Oregon required all cities and counties to have comprehensive land-use plans and zoning. A 1973 law required those plans to comply with standards set by a state commission. The 1973 law also required all cities to draw an urban-growth boundary, outside of which development was severely limited. Portland's urban-growth boundary, which embraces all of the suburbs mentioned above, was drawn in 1979 to include about 362 square miles of land. The boundary was not significantly altered until 1998, when about six square miles were added.

Past planning and zoning have left the three Portland-area counties with severe land imbalances. In particular, Clackamas County is short of industrial lands, while Washington County has a surplus. As a result, Washington County has been the state's main beneficiary of the high-tech boom. The county grew by nearly 100,000 people in the first nine years of the 1990s, compared to only 60,000 in Clackamas and 50,000 in Multnomah counties. Though jobs continue to grow in Washington County, the county has nearly run out of vacant land suitable for residential use inside the urban-growth boundary.

This problem could be solved by expanding the growth boundary in Washington County. But Washington County lands west of the boundary are considered prime farm lands, while Clackamas County lands east of the boundary are not. Oregon has over a million acres of prime farm lands that aren't even used for growing crops— they are mostly pasture or woodlands—but Oregon's land-use planning system protects prime farm land no matter what the cost. So recent expansions of the boundary have mostly been in Clackamas County, and regional planners hope to place 100,000 residents on that land. Since Clackamas County has no good east-west highway routes, any of these residents who work in Washington County will face a circuitous commute of at least thirty miles each way. Thus, many of the headaches facing today's regional planners were caused by past generations of planners.

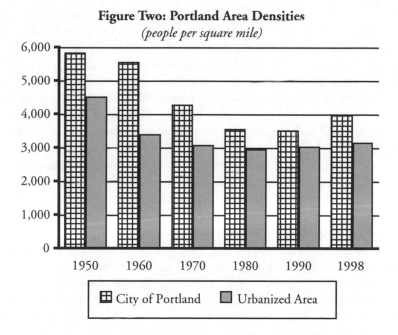

Figure Two: Portland Area Densities
(people per square mile)

Portland-area densities declined dramatically between 1950 and 1980, and have increased slightly since then. Source: Census Burea for 1950 through 1990, FHwA for 1998.

The Sterile-Suburbs Myth

Myth: Suburbs are sterile, cultureless places that can only be saved through better planning.

Reality: Though few suburbs are popular tourist attractions, they serve their residents well.

Do mass-produced, ticky-tacky suburbs lead to mass-produced, ticky-tacky people? William Whyte suggested this in *The Organization Man*, which was based on his studies of the postwar Chicago suburb of Park Forest. Whyte believed that the suburbs were a part of a process leading to a decline of individualism and an increase in conformity.[1] This led to what sociologist Herbert Gans called the "myth of suburbia": that the suburbs were breeding Americans "as mass produced as the houses they lived in," and that suburbanites were "bored and lonely, alienated, atomized, and depersonalized." "In unison," wrote Gans, the mythmakers "chanted that individualism was dying, suburbanites were miserable, and the fault lay with the homogeneous suburban landscape and its population."[2]

Having helped with Whyte's initial studies of Park Forest, Gans says that he "watched the growth of this mythology with misgivings." Gans himself had found that suburbanites "were happy in their new homes and communities, much happier than they had been in the city."[3] When Gans realized "that city planners also swallowed the suburban myth and were altering their professional recommendations accordingly," he decided to do a new study of the suburbs.[4] So he bought a house in Levittown, New Jersey, when that community was under construction, and lived there for nearly two years. "Hair raising stories about the homogeneity of people and conformity of life in the first two Levittowns made it clear that if any of the evils ascribed by the critics of suburbia actually existed, they would be found in a Levittown," he reflected.[5]

The myths, he found, were all wrong. Levittowners "are not apathetic conformists ripe for takeover by a totalitarian elite or corporate merchandiser; they are not conspicuous consumers and slaves to sudden whims of cultural and political fashion; they are not even organization men."[6] In fact, he found Levittown culture to be strikingly similar to that which "DeToqueville reported in his travels through small-town middle class America a century ago. . . . The equality of men and women, the power of the child over his parents, the importance of voluntary association, the social functions of the church, and the rejection of high culture seem to be holdovers from his time, and so is the adherence to the traditional values: individual honesty, thrift, religiously inspired morality, Franklinesque individualism, and Victorian prudery."[7]

Suburban critics, Gans decided, view "the lower middle and working class people with whom I lived in Levittown as an uneducated, gullible, petty 'mass' which rejects the culture that would make it fully human, the 'good government' that would create the better community, and the proper planning that would do away with the landscape-despoiling little 'boxes' in which they live." Gans called criticism of the suburbs "upper-middle class ethnocentrism."[8]

Ironically, the claim that the suburbs were breeding mass conformity has been turned on its head today, when people such as architectural critic Philip Langdon charge that the suburbs are *too* individualistic[9]—probably because suburbanites refuse to go along with their compact utopias. The conformity claim and the individualistic claim may both mask the real problem the critics have: The suburbs tend to be more conservative than the critics. "Republicans generally are more in tune with the Suburban Agenda than the Democrats," says G. Scott Thomas, author of *The United States of Suburbia*.[10] Could Al Gore think that forcing suburbanites to live in higher densities will turn them into Democrats?

Despite Gans' work, the myth of evil suburbia remains alive and well and is deeply imbedded in smart growth. James Kunstler, author of *The Geography of Nowhere*, describes the suburbs as "a trashy and preposterous human habitat with no future"[11] and "the mindless twitchings of a brain-dead culture."[12] With no supporting evidence, Langdon blames the suburbs for everything from insecurity at work to teenage suicides to "a barrage of distressing news and information from near and far." "A well-designed community might enable us to fight" these "contaminants," he claims.[13]

Many of the people who criticize the suburbs have never lived in the suburbs. Most of what they know about the suburbs they learned from other writers, most of whom never lived in the suburbs themselves. Philip Langdon, for example, admits that he has lived his entire life in small towns, where he could walk to a corner grocery store, or inner cities such as New Haven, where he can still walk to a corner grocery store.[14] Indeed, he seems to hate the suburbs mainly because, when he visits them, he can't walk to a corner grocery store. His only other real evidence against the suburbs comes from anecdotes told to him by alienated suburbanites who never seem to have last names, making readers wonder if their stories were taken out of context.

In contrast, Gans found few suburbanites bothered by the fact that they had to drive to the supermarket. Indeed, when a planner proposed to allow businesses in their residential areas, so that they could walk to a store, the Levittowners fiercely opposed the idea. They wanted to keep residential areas separate from shopping and other commercial areas, and this remains the desire of many suburbanites today.

Critics of suburbs "look at suburbia as outsiders, who approach the community with a 'tourist' perspective," said Gans, "The tourist wants visual interest, cultural diversity, entertainment, esthetic pleasure, variety (preferably exotic), and emotional stimulation. The resident, on the other hand, wants a comfortable, convenient, and socially satisfying place to live—esthetically pleasing, to be sure, but first and foremost functional for his daily needs. Much of the critique of suburbia as community reflects the critics' disappointment that the new suburbs do not satisfy their particular tourist requirements; that they are not places for wandering, that they lack the charm of a medieval village, the excitement of a metropolis, or the architectural variety of an upper-income suburb."[15]

Notes

1. William H. Whyte, Jr., *The Organization Man* (New York, NY: Simon & Schuster, 1956), pp. 4–8, 330–331.
2. Herbert J. Gans, *The Levittowners: Ways of Life and Politics in a New Suburban Community* (New York, NY: Pantheon, 1967), pp. xv–xvi.
3. Ibid, p. xvi.
4. Ibid, p. xvii.
5. Ibid.
6. Ibid, p. 417.
7. Ibid, p. 419.
8. Ibid, p. vi.
9. Philip Langdon, *A Better Place to Live: Reshaping the American Suburb* (New York, NY: Harper Perennial, 1994), p. 19.
10. G. Scott Thomas, *The United States of Suburbia: How the Suburbs Took Control of America and What They Plan to Do With It* (New York, NY: Prometheus, 1998), 290 pp.
11. James Howard Kunstler, *The Geography of Nowhere: The Rise and Decline of America's Manmade Landscape* (New York, NY: Simon & Schuster, 1993), p. 105.
12. Ibid, p. 112.
13. Langdon, *A Better Place to Live*, pp. 2–3.
14. Ibid, pp. x–xi.
15. Gans, *The Levittowners*, p. 186.

Stack 'Em & Pack 'Em

Despite Timothy Egan's claim that Portland is "dense and compact," Portland-area densities are quite conventional, and well below the densities of such "sprawling" urban areas as Los Angeles, San Jose, or Seattle. When Portland's urban-growth boundary was drawn in 1979, its 362 square miles was about three times the size of Portland itself. It included just three-eighths of one percent of the state of Oregon, yet about a third of the state's population, or some 900,000 people, lived and worked on about 220 square miles inside the boundary. Most of the remaining land was considered "vacant" and most of this was suitable for development. Of course, most "vacant" lands had working farms, forests, or other rural activities.

Planners estimated that the boundary contained enough vacant land to satisfy Portland-area population growth until the year 2000, provided that half of all new housing was multifamily and much of the rest was on smaller lots. But there was no regional planning authority to enforce this target, so new developments were mostly conventional, low-density suburbs. As a result, by 1990, most of the major pieces of land available for development had been developed. More than 13,000 acres of farm land remained inside the growth boundary, but most of these farmers, encouraged by significant tax breaks on Oregon agricultural lands, wanted to keep farming. After 1990, land prices started rising rapidly, and the cost of a vacant acre of land increased by 600 percent in six years. Where Portland was ranked as one of the fifty most affordable housing markets in the nation in 1989, by 1996 it was one of the five least affordable.[1]

Homebuilders pressed to expand the boundary. But what was once a planning tool had for some people become a sacred line that should never be moved. A few political leaders and planners formed a "zero-option committee" that opposed any expansion at all.[2] They were supported by people living near the boundary who wanted to protect their views and by 1000 Friends of Oregon, whose goal was to protect farmlands outside the boundary at all costs.

Farms inside the boundary, however, were considered ripe for development. "Metro planners say the farm tax [break] is counterproductive to good planning,"[3] says the *Oregonian*. A typical farmer pays less than $10 per acre in property taxes on land that, if it were available for development, might be taxed at $3,000 per acre or more. A farmer who decides to stop farming and develop the property must pay five years of back taxes at the higher rate, adding to the disincentive to develop. Eliminating the tax break would force farmers to quickly sell to developers. But when Metro proposed to do so, farmers strongly protested and the proposal was killed.

Metro estimated that the region's population will grow by 425,000 people in the next twenty years. But it added less than 6 square miles to the boundary, increasing the amount of land within the boundary by 1.6 percent. Instead of a larger expansion, Metro gave population targets to the twenty-four cities and three counties in the area. These cities and counties were required to rezone neighborhoods to high enough densities to house and employ the added population. Many city officials and planners enthusiastically accepted their targets, hoping that they would translate into a larger tax base and perhaps federal funds for neighborhood redevelopment. Portland State University's Institute for Urban Studies noted that "This unusual competition among planners for growth tends to overestimate the amount of densification" that can take place, because "local residents are unlikely to have the same preferences for high density" as planners.[4]

Some suburban elected officials seemed to be more aware of this. Portland, the slowest growing city in the region, lobbied for a target that was much higher than Metro wanted to give it. Lake Oswego, however, bitterly complained when Metro gave it a target of 4,900 home sites—city officials there didn't think they could find more than about 1,500 to 2,000. One local official referred to Metro's plans as "stack 'em and pack 'em."

The only member of the Metro council who supported a major boundary expansion was Don Morissette, a home builder who was regularly demonized by the *Oregonian* for having a "conflict of interest" (as if anyone in the Portland area did not). In 1996, for example, the paper erroneously accused Morissette of owning land outside the urban-growth boundary which he hoped to profit from by expanding the boundary.[5] The paper also raised "questions about his motives" when Morissette spent his own money on an independent study of the growth boundary.[6]

When Metro finally decided to expand the boundary, the location of the expansion was highly politicized. Two areas considered for expansion were Stafford, a wealthy community south of Portland, and Damascus, a working class community east of Portland. Many people in both areas opposed expansion, but "the political influence of the upper-middle class residents" of Stafford prevailed, and most of the land in the final expansion plan was near Damascus.[7]

The shortage of developable land led to a huge difference in values of land inside and outside of the boundary. Vacant land inside the boundary might be worth $100,000 an acre or more, while identical land outside the boundary is generally worth less than $1,000 an acre. A religious order called the Sisters of St.

Mary owns 463 acres of land just outside the urban-growth boundary in Washington County. Currently, the land is nearly worthless. Inside the boundary, it might be worth $200,000 per acre to a developer. Otherwise identical lands just over the boundary are rapidly being developed. But 1,000 Friends of Oregon and other groups strongly oppose including the Sisters land in the boundary because it is farmland. The Sisters lose, but it is hard to say who gains.[8]

Effectively, the boundary has confiscated, without compensation, most of the value of people's land outside the boundary even as it forces home buyers to pay hundreds of millions more for their housing inside the boundary. After destroying people's land values, a state commission has proposed to tax the "windfall profits" that would be gained by any landowner whose land is included in a boundary expansion.[9] Oregon City planner Richard Carson suggested an "annexation charge" of 33 percent of the value of the land once it is inside the boundary.[10] What the government taketh away, it taxes when it giveth back.

In order to fit hundreds of thousands of expected newcomers without making significant further expansions of the boundary, Metro's 2040 plan requires that most areas of undeveloped land inside the boundary be zoned for high-density development. About three dozen existing neighborhoods are defined as regional or town centers, and must be rezoned to about double their existing densities. Dozens of corridors between these centers, as well as any neighborhood within a half-mile of a light-rail station, are also to be rezoned to higher densities, preferably for mixed-use, transit-oriented developments. All remaining neighborhoods are expected to gain significant population through infill. As shown in the map on page 49, almost everyone in the region lives a short distance from an area that is to be densified. To meet Metro's population targets, Portland and other cities have rezoned many of the neighborhoods shown in white on the map to higher densities as well.

No final decisions have been made about expanding the boundary over the next forty years. But all planning projections for the 2040 plan are based on the assumption that the land within the boundary will grow by no more than 15,000 acres, a 6-percent increase, while the number of people living within the boundary will grow by 830,000, an 80-percent increase from 1990. The 2040 population density will thus exceed 4,800 people per square mile, a 70-percent increase. Only the Los Angeles, New York, Miami, and Davis, California, urbanized areas were denser than this in 1990.

After adding just under 6 square miles to the boundary in 1998, Metro said it would add more in the following year or two. But in October, 2000, Metro decided to include no more acres within the boundary.[11] Metro's dogged insistence on maintaining, or only slightly expanding, the current boundary may prove self-destructive in the long run. People who don't want to accept high-density lifestyles are likely to leapfrog the boundary by moving to satellite towns outside of Metro's jurisdiction, living on large lots of rural land, or becoming exurbanites. If enough people move to Newberg or Woodburn, Oregon or Battleground, Washington, then employers are likely to follow, thus creating new, and even more distant, edge cities.

In line with Peter Drucker's prediction that "any government activity almost at once becomes 'moral,'"[12] the urban-growth boundary that was originally viewed as flexible and growing as needed has now become a religious icon for planning advocates. Thus, the boundary has actually become a hindrance to rational planning, because any plan or analysis that suggests that the boundary should be changed is immediately considered tainted.

Notes

1. National Association of Home Builders, *Housing Opportunity Index 4th Quarter 1989* and *4th Quarter 1995* (Washington, DC: NAHB, 1990 and 1996).
2. R. Gregory Nokes, "Support multiplies for 'zero' growth option," *The Oregonian*, November 11, 1995, p. A1; R. Gregory Nokes, "Backers pitch zero option to Metro," *The Oregonian*, November 30, 1995, p. C2.
3. R. Gregory Nokes, "Taking a stand," *The Oregonian*, March 16, 1995, p. C1.
4. Gerard C.S. Mildner, Kenneth J. Dueker, and Anthony M. Rufolo, *Impact of the Urban Growth Boundary on Metropolitan Housing Markets* (Portland, OR: PSU Center for Urban Studies, 1996), 70 pages.
5. Editorial, "Metro and Ethics," *The Oregonian*, June 26, 1996, p. D6. The paper corrected its error on June 28. See also R. Gregory Nokes, "Morissette study says boundary must expand," *The Oregonian*, May 1, 1996, p. B4; R. Gregory Nokes, "Don Morissette: Land Lord," *The Oregonian*, July 1, 1996, p. A1, both of which refer to Morissette's alleged conflict of interest.
6. R. Gregory Nokes, "Morissette challenges boundary projections," *The Oregonian*, March 6, 1996, p. B1.
7. R. Gregory Nokes, "State board rejects Metro Council's Stafford expansion," *The Oregonian*, June 21, 2000, http://www.oregonlive.com/news/oregonian/index.ssf?/news/oregonian/00/06/lc_42luba21.frame.
8. Steve Mayes, "Developer Steps Across Line," *The Oregonian*, March 20, 1996, p. C1.
9. Task Force on Growth in Oregon, *Growth and Its Impacts in Oregon* (Salem, OR: Governor's Office, 1999), p. 6-6, http://www.governor.state.or.us/governor/download/taskrpt.pdf.
10. Richard Carson, *Paying for Our Growth in Oregon* (Oregon City, OR: New Oregon Meridian Press, 1998), p. 80, http://members.aol.com/odumonarch/Pogo-rpt.pdf.
11. R. Gregory Nokes, "Metro won't expand urban growth boundary," *The Oregonian*, October 27, 2000, http://www.oregonlive.com/news/oregonian/index.ssf?/news/oregonian/00/10/lc_62metro27.frame.
12. Peter Drucker, *The New Realities* (New York, NY: Harper & Row, 1989), p. 64.

The Unhappy-Suburbs Myth

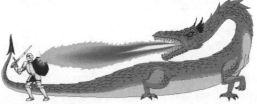

Myth: Suburbanites are unhappy.
Reality: Numerous polls show that suburbanites love their homes and neighborhoods.

Despite have never lived in a suburb, Philip Langdon is convinced that suburbanites are unhappy. "The United States has become a predominantly suburban nation, but not a very happy one," he says. "There is more distress in the suburbs than people like to admit."[1] While he feels the inner-city neighborhood where he lives is a true community, he thinks the nearby suburbs are "only a collection of unconnected individuals."

The suburbs aren't for everybody, and neither are the dense inner cities. As it turns out, given a choice most Americans prefer to live in low-density suburbs, where there is less congestion, pollution, and crime; where schools are better and their children can play in a large yard or in the streets without worrying about being run over by a car; where they could have privacy, freedom from noise, and the greater freedom to make noise yourself without bothering your neighbors; where they could grow a garden and let their pets run around the yard.

Herbert Gans's two years living in Levittown, New Jersey, convinced him that suburbanites did not suffer from "depression, boredom, loneliness, and ultimately mental illness" as charged by the critics. Instead, he found "that suburban life has produced more family cohesion and a significant boost in morale through the reduction of boredom and loneliness."[2]

A recent *Los Angeles Times* poll found that most L.A. suburbanites "generally love their lives." Not only do they not regret living away from the city, "the farther they get from Los Angeles, the more they love" their lives.[3] Interviews with 2,400 residents of several different suburban communities found only 29 percent who think they would be happier somewhere else. But most weren't unhappy because they were in the suburbs: Instead, they feared that their suburb was being "swallowed up by the big city."

Another poll by the *Albuquerque Tribune* found that 70 percent of suburban residents of Albuquerque didn't want "more retail stores and services within walking distance of their homes."[4] Similar results were found in a Milwaukee, Wisconsin, poll by the *Milwaukee Journal-Sentinel*.[5] This preference for low density means that many central cities are losing population even as their suburbs are growing. The thinning out of central city populations actually makes them less congested and more livable, so many parts of most cities are gentrifying as people move back in to take advantage of the lower densities.

Nor are suburbanites eager to accept smart-growth prescriptions for high-density, mixed-use neighborhoods where they can walk to the stores and take transit to work. Garreau interviewed a community activist who was so agitated by such attitudes that she eventually ran for and won a seat on the Phoenix city council. Linda Nadolski rehearsed for Garreau her responses to those who want to densify her neighborhood.

"If I wanted to live in New York, I wouldn't have left," she says. "How dare you take this away from me. Again. And P.S., you can take your light-rail system and shove it." "Increasingly," concludes Garreau, suburban values are "not parading in lock step with the city's elders and betters and the planners and the development interests. Instead, [they are] questioning density and height and mass transit."

Suburbs are "not utopia," says Mark Weber, editor of the Twin Cities' suburban newspaper, *Eden Prairie News*. "We travel pretty much everywhere by car, and architecturally you could mistake Eden Prairie for almost any suburb that boomed in the 1980s and '90s. But all the political wonks now touting Smart Growth as 'people-friendly development' need to know this: The suburbs offer most of what nearly every young family wants. Good luck reprogramming us."[6]

Notes

1. Philip Langdon, *A Better Place to Live: Reshaping the American Suburb* (New York, NY: Harper Perennial, 1994), p. 1, p. 19.
2. Gans, *The Levittowners: Ways of Life and Politics in a New Suburban Community* (New York, NY: Pantheon, 1967), p. 220.
3. Daryl Kelley, "As Suburbs Change, They Still Satisfy," *Los Angeles Times*, October 19, 1999, http://www.latimes.com/news/reports/suburbs.
4. Leanne Potts, "Poll Shows City Residents Won't Get Out of Cars to fight Sprawl," *Albuquerque Tribune*, October 31, 1999, http://www.abqtrib.com/archives/business/110199_leecol.shtml.
5. Tom Vanden Brook, "Residents want best of both worlds, poll shows: They support efforts to curb sprawl, but many wish to live in rural area," *Milwaukee Journal-Sentinel*, January 30, 2000, p. 1.
6. Mark A. Weber, "Don't you feel guilty about Eden Prairie's 'Dumb Growth?'" *Eden Prairie News*, October 21, 1999.

Suburbs Are Passé

In May, 2000, the Portland area's largest home builder, West Hills Development, stunned the region by announcing that it was cutting its operations in half. The Portland area population continues to grow at 2 percent per year, but the company's owner says that the region is "running out of land and we don't see a bright future in this area."[1]

Portland-area home builders and home buyers face a major dilemma. Since 1997, Metro expanded the urban-growth boundary by just 6 square miles, less than a 2-percent increase. Nearly all of this land was in Clackamas County, one of the three counties in the Metro area. Due to past planning errors, Clackamas County has become the region's "bedroom county" because it has a severe shortage of industrial land.[2] Meanwhile, Washington County has a surplus of industrial and a shortage of residential land. Any Washington County worker who settles in Clackamas County's Damascus urban-growth expansion area faces a circuitous, thirty-mile or longer commute to work. In fact, it takes less time to commute to Intel's plant in Hillsboro from Seaside, on the Oregon Coast, than from Damascus. As result, West Hills Development and other home builders have been slow to build in Damascus when the real market for housing is in Washington County.

Metro's solution to the land shortage is to encourage or require cities to rezone land to higher densities, including more multifamily housing, mixed-use developments, and single-family homes on tiny lots. As a result, all over the Portland area, vacant lots are being filled by row houses, old homes are torn down and replaced with apartments, and former one- and two-story storefronts are being turned into massive, four- and five-story mixed-use developments. Metro's plan demands a 17-percent increase in the share of people living in multifamily housing[3] and a 23-percent decrease in the average lot size of new homes.[4]

Metro requires minimum-density zoning in all areas. Its rules say that, retroactive to 1990, developments must have at least 80 percent of the maximum density allowed in each zone. If developments between 1990 and the present failed to meet that target, new developments must achieve higher densities to compensate. In single-family zones, no restrictions are allowed on *accessory apartments* (also known as *granny flats*) within homes.[5] This will effectively turn many smaller single-family homes into duplexes. This last requirement was a response to major protests from residents whenever Portland or other cities had proposed to allow accessory units in single-family neighborhoods. In one case, over 200 people packed Portland's city hall to protest such a zoning change, which they felt would add to congestion and reduce property values. Metro simply overruled the public's desires by requiring that all single-family zoning codes be rewritten to allow accessory units.

Metro planners are particularly proud of Orenco Station, a huge, high-density development on the west end of the light-rail line. Just a few years ago, Orenco was prime farm land—the name stands for OREgon Nursery COmpany.[6] Since it was inside of the urban-growth boundary, regional planners deliberately routed a light-rail line near it so they could zone it for high-density development.

Much of Orenco now consists of massive three- and four-story apartment buildings. Four city blocks have been built to resemble a Brooklyn or San Francisco neighborhood, with bay windows, ground floor restaurants and other businesses, and apartments or condominiums upstairs. Orenco also has single-family homes, many of them large enough to please up-and-coming software executives. But lot sizes average 3,500 square feet, so their front yards are tiny and their backyards nonexistent: Their rear doors open on an alley. Houses are built on the property lines, so that homeowners have a ten-foot-wide patch of yard on one side and no yard on the other. Given Washington County's acute housing shortage, homes in Orenco sell reasonably quickly. Yet a representative of the developer calls Orenco his company's "nonprofit wing" and says they have no plans to build another development like it.[7]

Fairview Village, a subdivision in Multnomah County, has received many accolades for its neotraditional home styles, front porches, and mixture of single-family homes with row houses and town homes. Being far from Washington County jobs, it has sold poorly, and some of the original home builders dropped out of the project.[8] Although the development includes only 600 units of housing, many of the units remain unbuilt and unsold after seven years.[9] In 1997, the region helped rescue the development with a $368,000 federal grant.[10]

Subsidies for Orenco were limited to waivers of impact fees. But Metro and local governments have had a difficult time promoting the redevelopment of existing neighborhoods to higher densities without considerably greater subsidies (see the Field-of-Dreams Myth, p. 103).

Gresham, a city on the east end of the light-rail line, tried to promote transit-oriented development by rezoning a neighborhood of single-family homes near the light-rail station to high-density, multifamily housing. The new zone did not allow single-family homes, even to replace one destroyed by a fire or other accident. Neighborhood residents who did not want to live near high-density apartments found that they could not sell their homes. When potential buyers asked banks for loans on the properties, the banks discovered that zoning rules would not allow the owner to rebuild anything less than an apartment if the house burned down. The banks said that meant there was no collateral and refused to make the loans.[11] The neighborhood is slowly changing, but existing home owners have lost tens of thousands of dollars in their property values.

The latest fad in Portland is the four- to five-story mixed-use development. The Multnomah County Commission is pressuring county librarians to use funds approved by voters for library expansions to build four- or five-story apartment buildings with the libraries on the ground floor. Library Director Ginnie Cooper says she is "quite concerned" about "the potential added cost, the time delays, and the major change in scope" of the libraries. "Would I do it if it were up to me?" she asks. "No. At some point, we have to ask ourselves, 'How do we make sure we don't lose sight of the fact that this is a library?'" Yet county commissioners insist upon combining such mixed-use developments with libraries.[12]

Outside of the greater downtown area, nearly all buildings in the Portland area are just one- or two-stories tall. In fact, four- and five-story mid-rise buildings are uncommon anywhere in the country except New York City. The four- and five-story buildings that have been built to date in Portland loom over their neighbors like fat, ugly dinosaurs. "It's not really something that fits into the character of the neighborhood," says a resident commenting on one of the new library proposals. Yet the region's leaders say such buildings are a part of the "vision" for Portland. "If you cannot live with these values," says Portland's Mayor Vera Katz, who grew up in New York City, "then don't come and live here."[13]

Yet many of the people who already live in the Portland area don't share Katz' desire to see forty- and fifty-unit per acre apartments spring up in their neighborhoods. This could be seen as early as 1995, when—in response to Metro's density targets—Portland and suburban planners initiated rezoning plans for selected neighborhoods. Though few neighborhoods were as successful as Oak Grove in halting densification, many heated battles were fought.

Of Oregon's forty cities with more than 10,000 people, Portland ranked thirty-seventh in rate of population growth between 1990 and 1998.[14] So it eagerly accepted a target of 70,000 new housing units. To meet that target, it has been rezoning numerous neighborhoods to much higher densities over the strong objections of local residents and officially recognized neighborhood associations. In 1995, Portland drafted a plan to double and triple housing densities in much of the outer southeast area. Local residents protested, and they say that planners agreed to scale back their proposals. When the plan was approved, residents were shocked to find that it was just as dense as when first proposed. They claim city planners betrayed them; planners say the residents just misunderstood.[15] Now residents are protesting each new development as row houses go up in the area.[16]

In 1996, more than 400 residents of Portland's Multnomah neighborhood jammed a high school cafeteria protesting a proposal to allow row houses on 2,500-

square-foot lots in much of their neighborhood, which is now mostly 7,000-square-foot lots. Spontaneous remarks such as "down with the Planning Bureau" rang out through the three-hour meeting to the applause of those attending.[17] The plan for that neighborhood, which is wealthier and more politically savvy than the outer southeast area, is still in contention, but the city has backed off on its most extreme proposals.

In November, 1997, the Milwaukie city council approved a Calthorpe-designed, high-density, mixed-use zoning plan that was bitterly opposed by local residents.[18] The council also strongly supported Metro's proposed light-rail line through Milwaukie even though most Milwaukie voters had opposed it in a 1996 election. Outraged residents used Oregon's recall process, gathering signatures and convincing a majority of Milwaukie voters to remove the mayor and two councilors from office in December, 1997. "People were not voting against [Mayor] Craig [Lomnicki] and company," said Tualatin Mayor Lou Ogden, "but voting against growth and congestion."[19]

The West Linn city council put a measure on the 1997 ballot asking residents if they approved of the targets Metro gave their community. The voters rejected them by four to one—but it was only an advisory vote as neither the voters nor the West Linn city council have the power to overrule Metro.

In Oregon City, Kathy Hogan has earned the title "Mrs. R-10" because of her advocacy for maintaining residential densities at 10,000-square-foot lots. "She wants a rural lifestyle," said Oregon City planner Richard Carson (who has since taken a job with Clark County, Washington). "If you buy property within the urban growth boundary, you probably should know it will develop someday."[20] Yet a 10,000-square-foot lot is not a rural lifestyle; it is a suburban lifestyle.

John Jackley, who is on the West Linn city council, says that "a serious and unforeseen flaw" in Oregon's land-use planning system is that it recognizes only two lifestyles: "urban and rural." Suburbs are not considered legitimate. "Metro planners moan about the suburbs as if they were a disease and do their best to plan us out of existence with their 'urban village' concepts, functional plans and density dictates," says Jackley. "The suburbs are not a problem," he argues. "They are a legitimate demographic choice as equal as urban and rural."[21]

Metro executive director Mike Burton disagrees. "Suburbs are passé," he sniffs.[22] "A lot of the trash around the edge of Portland is as trashy as the trash around any other city," concurs Portland City Councilor Charles Hales. "It's godawful subdivisions right up to the line."[23] Hales obviously has little sympathy for Jackley's argument that suburbs are a legitimate choice.

Debates spread to nearly every part of the region in 2000 as planners struggled to meet a December deadline to rezone according to Metro's plan.

• In March, 2000, residents of Portland's Hollywood district argued late into the night about the city's proposal to raise height limits adjacent to their homes to 65 feet. The city council finally agreed to a 45-foot height limit next to single-family zones, but left the 65-foot limit in commercial areas.[24]

- In April, "density appears to be the plan's hot-button word" as West Linn planners presented their proposal for adding 10,000 residents, half in multi-family housing, to the south-of-Portland suburb just three years after the town's residents voted four-to-one against any density increases.[25]
- In May, Cedar Hills residents began fighting high-density plans and subdivisions in their low-density, Washington County neighborhood.[26]
- Also in May, Milwaukie residents protested a revised plan for densifying their community. Though not as dense as the earlier plan which led the town to recall its mayor and most of its city council in 1997, the plan still left residents and business owners angry that their land was zoned for mixed uses.[27]

These and many other debates over neighborhood densification led Richard Carson to observe that Portland "is no longer the Mecca of good planning and is on its way to becoming the new Beirut."[28] "As the city promotes the idea of infill development, there have been more disputes," agrees the *Oregonian*.[29]

Ironically, after pushing for row houses during much of the 1990s, planners now say that row houses aren't dense enough. "If row houses had not been allowed, we would have seen condos of a higher density and better design," says a member of the Portland Planning Commission. Part of the problem is that row houses "are very ugly" because they have garages in front.[30]

Indeed, Portland-area planners are not content to mandate higher densities. They also want to control building design. They particularly object to housing with garages in front, which they derisively refer to as "snout houses." In 1999, Portland adopted a neotraditional design code that requires all new housing in the city to have garages recessed behind the front of the home and that "at least 15 percent of the area of each façade that faces a street lot line must be windows or main entrance doors."[31] Despite worries that the new rules would boost housing costs in a market whose prices are already above the heads of most residents, the council unanimously approved the code. West Linn and other Portland suburbs are considering similar codes.

"They tell us it's for our own good," says proud snout-house owner Naomi Kaufman Price, "that we will be happier in their garage-less infill bungalows and multifamily bunkers. . . on itty-bitty lots with neighbors a loud cough away." Price, an assistant editor for the *Oregonian*, thinks that the snout-house ban is part of a class war. "We of the ordinary classes can't be trusted to choose our own homes. We are expected to make economic sacrifices so someone else can select for us."[32]

Opinion polls consistently show that Portland-area residents support the urban-growth boundary. Their support weakens slightly when told that the boundary means increased densities inside. It fades considerably when told that it means higher densities in their own neighborhood. Proposed densification of his neighborhood "has taxed my support greatly for the boundary," says Hillsdale Neighborhood Association President Wesley Risher.[33] Just as people support light rail because they hope others will ride it and reduce highway congestion, people support density as long as it is somewhere else. "I'm all for high-density housing," says one resident of a low-density neighborhood where row houses are being debated, "but this is too close for comfort."[34]

Ultimately, what makes it possible for Portland and its suburbs to impose higher densities on existing neighborhoods is Metro. When the regional planning agency approved its comprehensive plan in 1997, few Portland-area residents knew what was going on. It was not until planners marched into their neighborhoods with density targets in hand that people began to understand. By that time, it was too late: The decision to densify the region had already been made, and only the most politically savvy and aggressive neighborhoods will escape transformation.

Notes

1. R. Gregory Nokes, "Area's Largest Builder Will Cut Back," *The Oregonian*, May 19, 2000, p. A1.
2. Joseph Rose, "Clackamas study locates industrial land," *The Oregonian*, April 27, 2000, http://www.oregonlive.com/news/oregonian/index.ssf?/news/oregonian/00/04/lc_52land27.frame.
3. Metro, *Regional Framework Plan Discussion Draft* (Portland, OR: Metro, May, 1997), p. 28.
4. Metro, *Region 2040 Recommended Alternative Technical Appendix* (Portland, OR: Metro, September, 1994), table 11.
5. Metro, *Urban Growth Management Functional Plan* (Portland, OR: Metro, November, 1996), title 1, section 2(C).
6. Lewis A. McArthur, *Oregon Geographic Names*, Fifth Edition (Portland, OR: Oregon Historical Society, 1982), p. 564.
7. Randy Gragg, "The New Urbanism: Laboratory Portland," *The Oregonian*, June 11, 2000, p. E10.
8. Connie Potter, "Fairview Village: New east Multnomah County subdivision recaptures look, feel of small-town America," *The Oregonian*, 2 May 1999, pp. H-1–H-2.
9. Randy Gragg, "The New Urbanism: Laboratory Portland," *The Oregonian*, June 11, 2000, p. E10.
10. U.S. Department of Transportation, *CMAQ Annual Reports (FY 1997)* (Washington, DC: US DOT, 1998), p. 14.
11. Dionne Peeples-Salah, "Rezoning for Transit Traps Downtown Homeowners," *The Oregonian*, January 18, 1996, p. A1.
12. David Austin, "Library system checks out mixed-use branches," *The Oregonian*, February 2, 2000, http://www.oregonlive.com/news/00/02/st020217.html.
13. Vera Katz, "State of the City," speech before the Portland City Club, January 28, 2000, p. C3, http://www.ci.portland.or.us/mayor/press4/soc2000spc.htm.
14. Census Bureau, "Population Estimates for Cities with Populations of 10,000 and Greater, 1990 and 1998," http://www.census.gov/population/estimates/metro-city/SC10K98-T3-DR.txt.
15. Brent Hunsberger, "Centennial: Misled or misunderstood?" *The Oregonian*, December 15, 1998, p. A10; interview with Bruce Cody, Centennial Neighborhood Association

president, April, 1998.

16. Wade Nkrumah, "Proposed infill development in Lents snags, and its a sign of a growing problem in Portland," *The Oregonian*, May 30, 2000, p. D2.

17. Janet Christ, "SW neighborhood residents furious over zoning plan," *The Oregonian*, October 17, 1996, p. C4.

18. Calthorpe Associates, *South–North Corridor Study: Milwaukie, Oregon* (Portland, OR: Metro, 1994), 24 pp.

19. R. Gregory Nokes, "Milwaukie recall wake-up call for region's planners," The Oregonian, December 22, 1997, pp. A14.

20. Dennis McCarthy, "Taking on City Hall," *The Oregonian*, January 2, 1997, p. MS7.

21. John Jackley, "Endangered Species: Suburbs slowly realize that land-use plans may be end of them," *The Oregonian*, November 24, 1996, op-ed page.

22. Peter Fish, "2040: A Portland odyssey," *Sunset*, November, 1996, p. 16.

23. Alan Ehrenhalt, "The Great Wall of Portland," *Governing*, May 1997, p. 21.

24. Fred Leeson, "City oks plan for Sandy and Hollywood," *The Oregonian*, April 6, 2000, p. B2.

25. Aimee Green, "Plan revisions for West Linn go to public tonight," *The Oregonian*, April 24, 2000, p. E2.

26. Richard Colby, "Housing density looms over spacious Cedar Hills," *The Oregonian*, May 25, 2000, p. A1.

27. Dennis McCarthy, "Milwaukie rezoning plan plays to mixed reviews," *The Oregonian*, May 31, 2000, p. B2.

28. Richard Carson, "Why would someone want planning job?" *The Oregonian*, November 29, 1999, http://www.oregonlive.com/oped/index.ssf?/oped/99/11/ed112951.frame.

29. Wade Nkrumah, "Proposed infill development in Lents snags, and its a sign of a growing problem in Portland," *The Oregonian*, May 30, 2000, p. D2.

30. Gordon Oliver, "Once a solution, row houses fall out of city favor," *The Oregonian*, August 11, 1999, http://www.oregonlive.com/news/99/08/st081115.html.

31. City of Portland ordinance number 173593, effective 9/3/99, §33.110.232, "Street-Facing Facades in R10 through R2.5 Zones."

32. Naomi Kaufman Price, "Cultural snoot-ism is what this is about: We of the ordinary class can't be trusted to choose a home," *The Oregonian*, July 26, 1999.

33. Brent Hunsberger, "Portland's desire for density stirs up residents' worries," *The Oregonian*, December 15, 1998, p. A1.

34. Brent Hunsberger, "Beaumont-Wilshire: Roadblocks along busy street," *The Oregonian*, December 15, 1998, p. A11.

The Ugly-Suburbs Myth

Myth: "Real" cities are beautiful and orderly; suburbs are ugly and chaotic.

Reality: The true test of an urban area is not its attractiveness to tourists but how well it functions for its residents.

Dallas and Salt Lake City are "ugly, dysfunctional, antihuman blight," says a *San Francisco Chronicle* columnist. Unlike San Francisco, which is "a great and true city," Dallas and Salt Lake "aren't cities."[1] Salt Lake City "consists of mile upon mile of franchise stores and six-lane streets." Dallas's downtown skyscrapers "do little more than mimic a living city." Apparently, a true city needs streetcars, unaffordable high-density housing, and extremely congested roads. The writer may not have noticed that San Francisco's 750,000 people are surrounded by nearly five million more people in the San Francisco-Oakland-San Jose urban regions who all live in areas very similar to Salt Lake and Dallas.

A large part of the criticism of the suburbs is simply an aesthetic judgment: suburbs are ugly, older cities are beautiful. This judgment is based on a nineteenth-century idea of what a city should be. Since modern urban areas don't match fantasies of what cities should look like, they are therefore ugly.

"Traditional-downtown urbanites recoil because a place blown out to automobile scale is not what they think of as 'city,'" says Joel Garreau. "They find the swirl of functions intimidating, confusing, maddening. Why are these tall office buildings so far apart? Why are they juxtaposed, apparently higgledy-piggledy, among the malls and strip shopping centers and fast-food joints and self-service gas stations?"[2] But, he adds, people felt the same way about London, Paris, and Venice when they were young, fast-growing cities as well.

When James Kunstler, the author of *The Geography of Nowhere*, visited Portland, he was totally repelled by the Beaverton-Hillsboro area, west of downtown Portland. He decried "the abysmal quality of the stuff that is being built right now. . . out in Washington County: Route 26, Beaverton, and all that bullshit. Building any more of it is going to carry an extremely high price."[3] Kunstler's solution? More planning and government regulation. "You need to bring the same level of excellence to the suburbs that you brought to the city of Portland. You can mandate that any new growth must adhere to higher standards of [design and building]."

By "level of excellence," Kunstler probably refers to downtown Portland, with its bus mall, light rail, and waterfront park. But Beaverton and Hillsboro are producing 30 percent more jobs and far more economic value than downtown Portland will ever see. Beaverton-Hillsboro, the fastest growing urbanized area in Oregon, is one of Garreau's edge cities. Kunstler's prescription would bring order to Washington County by stifling economic growth.

Joel Garreau observes that the adjective people most often apply to fast-growing edge cities is "chaotic." Garreau's own first response when he discovered an edge city is instructive:

> It seemed insane to me. It was a challenge to everything I had been taught: that what this world needed was More Planning; that cars were inherently Evil and our attachment to them Inexplicable; that suburbia was morally wrong; and that if Americans perversely continued to live the way they have for generation after generation, it couldn't be because they liked it; it must be because They Had No Choice.

As a good reporter, Garreau researched and wrote *Edge City* to "get to the bottom of this." What he learned, Garreau says, can be "summed up in the wisdom of Pogo. I have met the enemy. And he is us."

The desire for "order" instead of "chaos" particularly motivates aesthetic judgments of the suburbs. "Stockholm has very little rural-urban fringe: the use of land is either rural or urban, not a mixture of the two," says compact city advocate David Popenoe. "Visually, this yields a strong sense of order, and signals a clear ideological separation of town and country as two very distinct worlds." By comparison, he says, in American cities "the visual appearance is one of ambiguity" because "one is never quite sure at what point the rural countryside ends and the physical metropolis. . . actually begins."[4] Popenoe considers the fact that Americans have more lifestyle choices than Swedes to somehow be a disadvantage.

Garreau notes that, through a process of trial and error, developers have identified a number of "rules of thumb about human behavior" which they hope will increase the likelihood that their projects will succeed. These include such rules as:

- To succeed, a large mall must have a quarter of a million people within a fifteen-minute drive;
- Offices need about 250 square feet per worker plus four hundred square feet of parking for each worker's car;
- Ten million square feet of office and retail space produces forty thousand vehicle trips per day.
- For developers to profit, new homes must sell for four times the cost of the land. In other words, an expensive house won't sell on cheap land because a wealthy buyer won't want to live there, while a cheap house won't sell on expensive land because a poor buyer won't be able to afford the land.

These rules of thumb, says Garreau, "reveal an underlying order in what appears to the uninitiated to be chaos."[5] Planners and architects often miss this underlying order because their notions of what a city should look like are based on the nineteenth-century city, not on what makes sense today.

Something else may lie even deeper beneath the demand for order. In his perceptive book, *Seeing Like a State*, James Scott notes that government officials "strive to shape a people and landscape that will fit their techniques of observation." The "chaotic, disorderly, constantly changing social reality" of the suburbs is hard to model; difficult to predict; difficult to tax; impossible to manage. Just as foresters plant trees in neat rows so they may be more easily counted and controlled, suggests Scott, government officials want to impose "uniformity and order" on cities and suburbs so that the masses may be more easily controlled.[6]

In the end, beauty is in the eye of the beholder. There is nothing wrong with living in a beautiful, unique area if it does not mean forgoing other things that may be more important to the people who live there. But government planners should not try to force a few architects' ideas of beauty on everyone else.

Notes

1. Carolyn Lochhead, "Strip Malls and Sprawl: Is There Any Escape?" *San Francisco Chronicle*, March 28, 1999.
2. Joel Garreau, *Edge City: Life on the New Frontier* (New York, NY: Doubleday, 1991), p. 9.
3. Bob Young, "The World According to Kunstler," *Willamette Week*, July 4, 1995, p. 24.
4. David Popenoe, *Private Pleasure, Public Plight: American Metropolitan Community Life in Comparative Perspective* (New Brunswick, NJ: Transaction, 1985), pp. 42–43.
5. Joel Garreau, *Edge City*, p. 463.
6. James C. Scott, *Seeing Like a State: How Certain Schemes to Improve the Human Condition Have Failed* (New Haven, CT: Yale University Press, 1998), p. 82.

Boutiques Yes,
Shopping Malls No

Like Americans everywhere, Portlanders today do much of their shopping at major supermarkets and shopping malls. Metro and the state's goal is to change people's shopping habits so that they will do most of their shopping in "neighborhood shopping centers within convenient walking and cycling distance of residential areas."[1]

Metro's plan forbids the construction of any retail areas larger than 60,000 square feet in "employment and industrial areas."[2] Despite the name, "employment areas" include most of the remaining large blocks of vacant or relatively undeveloped land inside the urban-growth boundary, and Metro hopes that they will be developed into mixed-use areas with a combination of high housing and high commercial densities. A 60,000-square-foot store is about the size of a supermarket built in the 1950s. Metro's rules effectively forbid any more WalMarts, Costcos, K-Marts, or medium- to large-sized shopping malls in the Portland area.

Metro is attempting to turn back the clock to the era of mom-and-pop grocery stores within walking distance of people's homes. Yet this era was remarkably brief and in fact was only a transition from late nineteenth-century public markets and mid-twentieth century supermarkets.

Since Metro has effectively forbidden any new large shopping areas, it intends that future new retail construction will be pedestrian-friendly and transit-oriented. On "main streets," says Metro, "buildings move right up to the sidewalk and may gain a second or third story."[3] Parking will be on the street or behind the stores. Stores will be allowed no more than 6.2 parking spaces per thousand square feet of leasable space, and if the store is served by frequent transit service this is reduced to 5.1 spaces.

These restrictions will put new stores at a severe competitive disadvantage with the existing Fred Meyer and other large stores in the region. On-street parking is totally inadequate for most businesses, but many shoppers don't feel safe parking in an area not visible from the street, particularly at night. These parking limits can put stores at a severe disadvantage. "Retailers can lose 2 percent of their sales just by having a door that is hard to open," one developer told me. "What happens if people won't shop at night because they don't feel safe in the parking lots?"

71

Architecture critic Craig Whitaker notes that, if cars are moved to the back, "front doors would start following the cars."[4] Small shops may only have enough personnel to monitor one entrance to the store, and that will usually turn out to be the entrance to the parking lot. Portland writer Bob Elliot has already observed a store in Southeast Portland where the door fronting the street "is barricaded with merchandise on the inside" and "a sign directs you to the back entrance off the automobile parking lot."[5]

New retailers will respond to Metro's enforced competitive disadvantages by becoming "heavily concentrated toward specialty retail," says Hobson Johnson, a Portland-area real estate consultant. As can be seen in existing Portland neighborhoods that have developed pedestrian-friendly retail design, such as the Northwest 23rd area and the Hawthorne district, stores have found niche markets. This means that people from all over the region travel to these stores, creating major traffic and parking problems for the neighborhoods. Meanwhile, says Hobson Johnson, neighborhood residents continue to make "the bulk of retail transactions for groceries, clothing, home improvements, furnishings, electronics, and automobiles" in conventional shopping areas, meaning that they have to drive out of their neighborhoods. Hobson Johnson predicts that, under the 2040 plan, "residents may have to travel farther to get the goods and services that they want, or have to pay more for these goods and services, or a combination of both."

In 1992, Metro asked Peter Calthorpe to redesign Clackamas Town Center, the region's largest shopping mall, "to show how surface parking lots can be a redevelopment resource."[6] According to *The Oregonian*, the plan was based on Calthorpe's belief that "large regional shopping malls such as the Town Center, built to attract motorists throughout the region, would soon be a thing of the past as more communities turn to mass transit."[7] Calthorpe suggested using "the downtown [Portland] 200-foot block pattern laid onto the parking lots and infilled with multistory mixed-use buildings."[8] "The future of regional retail centers is in question," argued Calthorpe. "With the rise of telecommunications and frustration with our overreliance on automobiles, it is quite possible that retailers will have to return to basics by serving neighborhoods well."[9] Calthorpe recommended building 1,800 to 2,900 units of multifamily housing plus office space for 3,900 to 4,600 workers on the parking area.[10]

The 2040 plan designates the shopping mall and the area around it as a regional center, which requires the highest densities of development outside of downtown Portland. The plan calls for 95 jobs *and* 25.9 housing units per acre. Outside of downtowns, a typical high-density development might provide up to 80 jobs *or* 24 apartments per acre. Metro's goals for the Clackamas regional center "are unlikely to be realized" in Portland's market, says real estate consultant Hobson Johnson. A development exceeding both these densities on the same acre "is unprecedented outside of the Portland" downtown area. Of course, the only way to add housing and office spaces to an existing shopping mall will be to greatly increase available parking. As Calthorpe's plan recognizes, this means building parking garages.[11] Such garages cost two-and-one-half times as much per space as a parking lot,[12] and it is unlikely that any developer will build them without public subsidies.

The shopping mall's huge parking lots represent land that is "not very well utilized," claims Metro Executive Mike Burton. Burton points out that Lloyd Center, which uses parking garages, has more parking spaces and more retail space in 35 acres than Clackamas Town Center has in 100 acres.[13] But Lloyd Center is directly across the Willamette River from downtown Portland, and land values are much higher than at the edge of the metropolitan area where Clackamas Town Center is located.

Located next to Interstate 205, Clackamas Town Center is the most congested area in Clackamas County, mainly because of poorly designed intersections near the freeway. The owners of the shopping mall have little interest becoming apartment landlords. They are willing to turn parking lots into offices or more retail spaces only if land values become high enough to justify the construction of parking garages or the garages are subsidized.[14] But they discreetly withheld comment on Calthorpe's plan because they want Metro to approve roadway improvements that will reduce local congestion.

To meet Metro's population targets, Clackamas County rezoned the Clackamas Town Center area to exceed Metro's density goals. The minimum density for multifamily housing is 30 units per acre. Land zoned for offices and commercial uses also allows up to 30 housing units per acre on the same site.[15] Much of the land around the mall has been rezoned to mixed uses, with up to 30 units of apartments per acre plus office and retail space.

Using their zoning authority, Portland-area local governments will be able to prevent the construction of any new large stores, as Metro intends. The mixed-use developments and neighborhood shopping areas they want to create are not likely to reduce Portland-area driving. Instead, they will simply reduce consumer options and increase consumer costs.

Notes

1. LCDC, Transportation Planning Rule, OAR 660-012-0035(2)(c).
2. Metro, *Urban Growth Management Functional Plan* (Portland, OR: Metro, November, 1996), title 4, p. 17.
3. Metro, *Main Street Handbook: A User's Guide to Main Streets* (Portland, OR: Metro, 1996), p. 19.
4. Craig Whitaker, *Architetcure and the American Dream* (New York, NY: Potter, 1996), p. 72.
5. Bob Elliot, "Building Orientation Means—How Do I Get Into This Place?" *SE Chronicles*, March 15, 1996, http://www.teleport.com/~relliott/MAR96/gallery.html.
6. Calthorpe & Associates, *Region 2040* (Portland, OR: Metro, 1994), p. 4.
7. Dennis McCarthy, "Town Center design gets a 'Portland' look," *The Oregonian*, May 11,

1994, p. E2.

8. Calthorpe, *Region 2040*, p. 4.
9. Ibid, p. 19.
10. Ibid, p. 22.
11. Ibid, pp. 25–26.
12. Joel Garreau, *Edge City: Life on the New Frontier* (New York, NY: Doubleday, 1991), p. 119.
13. Robert Goldfield, "Clackamas Town Center studies growth options," *The Business Journal*, July 1, 1996, http://www.bizjournals.com/portland/stories/1996/07/01/story6.html.
14. Ibid.
15. Clackamas County, "Summary of Special Zoning Districts," http://www.co.clackamas.or.us/dtd/zoning/htmls/sum_spe.html.

Portland's Downtown Myth

Myth: Light rail and sound planning have revitalized Portland's downtown.
Reality: Downtown's growth as a shopping and entertainment district is largely
due to local entrepreneurs. To improve their downtown statistics, planners
expanded the definition of downtown.

Thirty years ago, downtown Portland was nearly dead after 6 PM and on
weekends. Today, the area is so lively that congestion and parking problems are nearly as bad on evenings and weekends as they are during weekdays. Naturally, planners are quick to take credit for this, but the real story is
much more complicated.

Importers Bill and Sam Naito owned several old buildings north of the current
downtown. In the 1970s, they began restoring the ground floors of those buildings and leasing them to restaurants and shops. The area soon became known as
Old Town. Many Oregon craftspeople began using an empty parking lot near
Old Town to sell their wares on Saturdays. The Saturday Market quickly became
a popular institution and reaffirmed Old Town's status as a trendy area. Later, the
Naitos purchased a derilict department store and turned it into the Galleria, a
mall with numerous shops and eateries. A few blocks away, Michael Powell bought
a former car dealership and turned it into one of the world's largest independent
bookstores, offering over a million different new and used titles.

All these businesses were thriving well before Portland's light-rail line was completed in 1986. Downtown businesses were promoted more by the construction
by the city of two multi-storied parking garages, one across the street from the
Galleria. Another action taken by the city that helped downtown was to replace a
street fronting on the Willamette River with a large park. Traffic on the street was
rerouted to an expanded freeway system. The park is now used for festivals almost
every weekend in the spring and summer.

Entrepreneurial efforts combined with better parking and freeway access made
downtown Portland into a lively shopping and entertainment district. But as an
employment district, downtown is still dying. Metro claims that "about 20 percent of all employment in the region is in downtown Portland."[1] But Metro is

confusing "downtown" with an area it calls the "central city," which includes the Lloyd Center and other areas outside of Portland's traditional downtown. The downtown area itself only has a little more than half the jobs of the central city.

Over the past decade, downtown employment has failed to grow enough to maintain its share of regional jobs. In fact, while jobs in the Lloyd district and the suburbs have grown rapidly, downtown jobs have not grown at all. Almost all new construction downtown has been government or government-subsidized buildings. Almost all new jobs downtown have been relocations of government offices in response to presidential and gubernatorial executive orders that federal and state offices be downtown. But these have been balanced by the departure of private business to other areas.

Metro's 2040 plan promises to maintain central city employment at 20 percent of regional employment. This will require adding nearly 122,000 jobs to an area already congested with 146,000 jobs.[2] Metro simultaneously wants to increase the central city's residential population by more than 150 percent. Given the amount of subsidies that the city of Portland is giving developers to build central city housing, including property tax waivers, infrastructure subsidies, and below-market land sales, this goal may be achievable. But a 150-percent increase in residential population will simply add to the district's congestion, making it even less attractive for businesses.

As in most cities, Portland's downtown is the most congested part of the metropolitan area. Downtown's small, two-hundred-square-foot blocks actually mean that the district has a greater percentage of its land area in streets than any other part of the region. Yet its job density is ten times greater than the regional average. Even though a high percentage of downtown workers use transit, congestion is daunting to most area residents. With congestion comes pollution. Since carbon monoxide (CO) dissipates rapidly, CO pollution violations only happen when motor vehicles are concentrated. All of Portland's historic violations of CO air standards have been downtown. If the 2040 plan manages to keep downtown at 20 percent of regional employment, more violations are almost certain.

Allowing downtown's share of employment to shrink should not be equated with letting downtown die. Despite its historic loss of employment share, Portland's downtown is a lively entertainment center, with concerts, theater, festivals, and conventions throughout the year. The area has a wide variety of shops, including Powell's landmark bookstore. These aspects of downtown can survive without wedding Portland to an expensive, pointless, and counterproductive effort to maintain downtown's job share.

Notes

1. Metro, *Metro 2040 Growth Concept* (Portland, OR: Metro, 1994), p. 7.
2. Metro, *Region 2040 Recommended Alternative Technical Appendix* (Portland, OR: Metro, 1994), table 8.

The Placeless-Suburbs Myth

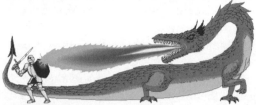

Myth: All suburbs look alike.
Reality: If you know how to look, suburbs have as much variety as any inner city neighborhood.

Built between 1949 and 1951, Levittown, Long Island, housed 82,000 people in 17,447 homes. While the houses had different interior floor plans, all of the early homes were built in an outwardly identical Cape Cod style, while later homes were all an outwardly identical ranch style. These cookie-cutter homes led to jokes and cartoons about people not being able to find their home and commuters entering the wrong house. Eventually, the myth grew up that not only the homes but all suburbs were the same: identical houses on identical *cul de sacs* a few blocks away from identical strip malls. James Kunstler, Peter Calthorpe, Jane Holtz Kay, and other sprawl opponents endlessly repeat the word *placeless* or some variation.[1] "There is a growing sense of frustration and placelessness in our suburban landscape," writes Calthorpe, "with chain-store architecture, scaleless office parks, and monotonous subdivisions."[2]

In fact, new suburban homes are no more monotonous than new inner city developments. While multifamily dwellings tend to retain their exterior uniformity, suburban single-family homes began to change almost from the day people move in. "Uniform and monotonous as they might seem from the outside," says Peter Hall of early suburbs, "for their new occupants each house embodied tiny variations, built in or bought in, which gave it individuality: a stained-glass window, a porch, a kitchen fitting, even a garden gnome."[3]

"The old Levittowns are now interesting to look at," says Joel Garreau. "People have made additions to their houses and planted their grounds with variety and imagination."[4] "The roofs [in Levittown] have developed so many dormers it seems like they've grown dormers on dormers," noted a writer for *Esquire* in 1988. "Fronts have sprouted pergolas and porches, roof lines have been raised, pitched, expanded, corniced, and cupolaed."[5]

Just as the individual homes in Levittown are now different, so do suburbs differ from one another. Suburbs of Phoenix look quite different from suburbs of the Twin Cities. The Portland suburb of Lake Oswego looks very different from Oak Grove, right across the river.

Calthorpe, Kunstler, and Kay consider the suburbs "placeless" because they don't offer unique tourist attractions such as the Empire State Building or San Francisco cable cars. But as Herbert Gans points out, people are mostly residents, not tourists.[6] Suburban residents want privacy, so they buy large lots and land-scape their yards. They want easy access to groceries and other consumer goods, so they drive to the commercial strips that offer them a wide variety of competi-tive stores. When they want aesthetic variety, they go to a movie or take a vacation in a national park. Aesthetic variety in their neighborhood or local supermarket wouldn't mean much to them as residents; only a tourist would even notice it.

Outside of Portland is Sunnyside Village, built by several developers who fol-lowed a detailed design code mandated by county planners. The development's cookie-cutter homes on tiny lots are painted in identical off-whites. A walking path connects the homes to a conventional strip mall with a supermarket and a few other stores. "The development is considered a failure by new urbanism stan-dards," says *The Oregonian*. "Homes don't possess the turn-back-the-clock archi-tecture [and] residents face the same commuter headaches as any other suburb-to-city schlepper."[7] One of the residents' biggest complaints is that the narrow streets don't provide enough parking space. The neighborhood's design codes were written by an architect hired by Clackamas County. His name? Peter Calthorpe.

"Houses are for people, not critics," said William Levitt, the builder of Levittowns. He added that his houses looked similar when new because they were mass produced—just like the clothes we wear and the cars we drive. "This isn't something to grieve over. It's something to glory in" because such mass produc-tion brought unprecedented material goods to people of nearly all incomes. Levitt added that we need to "keep in mind the difference between material values and those of the mind and spirit."[8] Just because the houses look similar doesn't mean that the people inside are the same.

Notes

1. See, for example, Kay, *Asphalt Nation*, p. 4; Kunstler, *Geography of Nowhere*, p. 131.
2. Peter Calthorpe, *The Next American Metropolis: Ecology, Community, and the American Dream* (New York, NY: Princeton Architectural Press, 1993), p.18.
3. Peter Geoffrey Hall, *Cities of Tomorrow: An Intellectual History of Urban Planning and Design in the Twentieth Century* (Cambridge, MA: Blackwell, 1996), p. 79.
4. Joel Garreau, *Edge City: Life on the New Frontier* (New York, NY: Doubleday, 1991), p. 271.
5. Ron Rosenbaum, "The House That Levitt Built," *Esquire*, December, 1988, p. 388.
6. Herbert J. Gans, *The Levittowners: Ways of Life and Politics in a New Suburban Commu-nity* (New York, NY: Pantheon, 1967), p. 186.
7. Harry Esteve and Joseph Rose, "Urban by design," *The Oregonian*, February 13, 2000, http://www.oregonlive.com/news/00/02/st021304.html.
8. William Levitt, "What! Live in Levittown?" *Good Housekeeping*, July 1958, 176.

Open Space Yes, Accessible Open Space No

Metro has two programs aimed at protecting Oregon farms, forests, and open spaces. First, of course, is its high-density development plans, which call for most new housing to be on tiny lots or in multifamily dwellings. Second is a program of purchasing green spaces so that future Portland-area residents will always have plenty of open space.

Despite Metro's draconian high-density program, a continued spread of Portland's low-density suburbs would have a negligible effect on Oregon's farm and forest base. All of the developed land in Oregon—including both urban and rural developments—amounts to less than 2 percent of the land area of the state. The land inside the Portland's urban-growth boundary—only some of which is developed—amounts to less than three-eighths of a percent of the state and just 12 percent of the three counties that contain the Portland area.

Only 17 percent of those three counties are farms, so there is plenty of room for urban growth without even consuming farmlands. In 1997, more than a million acres of Oregon land suitable for growing crops was instead in pasture or idle.[1] That's 29 percent of Oregon's croplands and well over four times the land in the current urban-growth boundary.

Nor is there any danger of running out of open space. Half of all the land in the three Portland-area counties is publicly owned—most in national forests—so it is not likely to ever be developed.

Part of the misperception regarding sprawl is that most people think that the vast majority of an urban area is residential. Forcing people to live on smaller lots is presumed to have a significant impact on the amount of urbanized land. Yet in 1990, residential neighborhoods made up only about 25 percent of the land inside Portland's urban-growth boundary.[2] If every Portland-area household—including one- and two-person households—moved onto an 8,000-square-foot lot, those lots would still consume under half the land inside the boundary. If the boundary were expanded to provide 8,000-square-foot lots for every new household that Metro expects to arrive by the year 2040, as well as schools and other services needed by those households, the boundary would still contain just one-half percent of the state.

Meanwhile, Metro has promised Portland-area residents access to a constant number of acres of open space per capita.[3] Thus, as the region's population increases, the amount of open space must increase as well. Metro expects to accomplish this apparent feat of magic by using a definition of open space that is at once cribbed and expansive: cribbed because Metro limits its definition of open space to mainly include lands in public parks; expansive because most of the land that Metro is preserving as open space is outside of the urban-growth boundary and inaccessible to most Portland-area residents.

Metro certainly does not consider people's large back yards to be open space. Vacant lots, woodlands, and the more than 10,000 acres of prime farm land that happen to be within the urban-growth boundary are also excluded from Metro's calculations of open space. All of these, including many of the back yards, are considered "vacant" lands suitable for infill. Yet when they are developed, the amount of land that is truly open space will significantly decline.

Metro's plan calls for developing nearly 29,000 acres of land inside the original urban-growth boundary plus about 6,500 acres that have been or will be added to the boundary since 1997.[4] Most of these acres are now "vacant," meaning they are farms, forests, or other open spaces. To meet their population targets, local governments have promoted the development of many areas that local residents thought were open spaces even by Metro's definitions.

Residents of north Portland were outraged when the city sold 14 acres of Johnswood Park, at well below market value, for high-density residential development.[5] "Until now we have regarded public parks as part of the unbuildable stock of land, valuable amenities held aloft from the development frenzy," former 1000 Friends of Oregon staff member Anthony Boutard told the Portland city council. "Taking any park in the name of holding the urban-growth boundary would erode people's confidence in the city of Portland, Metro, and the growth boundary."[6] Yet the city sold and rezoned the park because it was "in keeping with the overall 2040 concept of increasing housing density inside urban growth boundaries."[7]

To meet Metro's population targets, Clackamas County rezoned most of the 92-acre Top o' Scott Golf Course for offices and housing.[8] Only 30 acres will remain as open space. Nearby residents are angry that land they believed would be permanently green will be intensively developed. Metro insists that it has nothing to do with these decisions, since they were made by local governments. But Clackamas County felt pressured to develop Top o' Scott to meet its density targets because Oak Grove, the largest unincorporated urban part of the county, had rejected plans for denser development. Of course, what's appropriate for one neighborhood shouldn't depend on what happens in another neighborhood ten miles away. But under Metro's planning, it does.

On top of this, planners are still talking about eliminating the tax breaks that allow people inside the urban-growth boundary to farm. Some planners hint that the tax breaks are merely protecting "hobby farmers" and "encourage sprawl" by allowing people to live on large pieces of land.[9]

Meanwhile, Metro convinced voters to approve a $136 million "open spaces, parks, and streams" bond measure in 1995. Most of the money was to be used to purchase about 6,000 acres of parks and open spaces. Nearly 85 percent of these acres are in greenbelts *outside* the urban-growth boundary. Since they are outside the growth boundary, they were protected from intensive development by state rules even before their purchase by Metro. Metro plans to keep most of these acres in a wild state, so they will not be easily accessible to even residents who live near them.

"The land outside the UGB provides a different type of benefits from that provided by neighborhood parks," says Randall Pozdena, an economist with the consulting firm ECONorthwest. Metro "implicitly argues that households are indifferent between an acre of nearby park or woods and one that is at the periphery of the region," which Pozdena finds dubious.[10] He could have added that Metro also implicitly argues that local residents are indifferent between a developed playground and an undeveloped wildlife sanctuary.

One reason why Metro has purchased so much land outside the urban-growth boundary is that land there costs less. The average price Metro has paid for land outside the boundary is $8,621 per acre; while the average inside the boundary is $49,543, or nearly six times as much per acre.[11] This puts Metro in the ethically dubious position of having destroyed more than 80 percent of people's property values by excluding their land from the boundary, then buying that land at the much reduced rates so that it can claim it has maintained urban open space. But another reason for Metro's greenbelt strategy is suggested by architect Andres Duany, who argues that such greenbelts work better than simple growth boundaries because they are "not as susceptible to the development pressure" as private lands outside the boundary.[12]

While claiming to preserve open space, Metro's policies are in fact destroying many open spaces that are commonly used by urban residents. The greenbelt that Metro is preserving is inaccessible to residents who do not like to tramp through forests or swamps that lack trails or other facilities. Moreover, residents who don't like living in Metro's high-density neighborhoods are likely to go outside the Portland urban-growth boundary entirely, whether to satellite cities or as exurbanites living in rural areas.

Notes

1. Natural Resources Conservation Service, *Natural Resources Inventory 1997* (Washington, DC: USDA, 1999), table 3.
2. Metro, *Region 2040 Recommended Alternative Technical Appendix* (Portland, OR: Metro, 1994), table 8.
3. Metro, *Regional Framework Plan* (Portland, OR: Metro, December, 1997), p. 169.

4. Metro, *Region 2040 Recommended Alternative Technical Appendix* (Portland, OR: Metro, 1994), table 8.

5. Scott Learn, "City oks Johnswood land deal," *The Oregonian*, June 24, 1999, p. D3.

6. Anthony Boutard, quoted from testimony in personal communication to the author, 29 May 1997.

7. Portland City Council, "Johnswood Park Supplemental Findings," January, 1997.

8. Brian Miller, "Clackamas County," *Business Journal*, January 18, 1999, http://www.bizjournals.com/portland/stories/1999/01/18/newscolumn4.html.

9. Robin Franzen, "Tax breaks turn out to have some unwanted side effects," *The Oregonian*, December 14, 1998, p. A11.

10. Randall Pozdena, "Review of Metro's Urban Growth Report, September 1999 Update," ECONorthwest, October, 1999.

11. Metro, *Four Years and 4,400 Acres: Metro's Open Spaces Land Acquisition, Report to Citizens* (Portland, OR: Metro, 1999), pp. 14–15.

12. Andres Duany, Elizabeth Plater-Zyberk, and Jeff Speck, *Suburban Nation: The Rise of Sprawl and the Decline of the American Dream* (New York, NY: North Point Press, 2000), p. 144.

The Paved-Over-Suburbs Myth

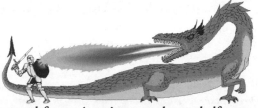

Myth: Urban sprawl forces Americans to devote half to two-thirds of urban land to roads, streets, parking lots, and other automobile purposes.
Reality: Low-density suburbs devote less land to pavement than high-density cities.

"The amount of pavement" in suburban areas "is extremely high," says Andres Duany, "especially when compared to the efficiency of a section of an older city."[1] In fact, in most urban areas, the exact opposite is true: Because suburbs tend to have larger blocks, they devote a smaller portion of their areas to pavement.

Ray Brindle, an Australian transportation researcher, asked how much land in Melbourne was devoted to streets. He found that close to a third of the land in older parts of the city—parts built before the automobile became dominant—was used for streets. But modern suburbs of Melbourne used well under a quarter of their land for streets. He concluded that "urban areas designed for car use in fact devoted less land to roads and streets" than areas designed before the car.[2]

This pattern can be found in U.S. cities as well. With 200-foot-square blocks and 66-foot-wide streets, 43 percent of Portland's downtown is covered by streets. Portland neighborhoods typically have 200-foot by 400-foot blocks with 66-foot streets, meaning 35 percent of the land area is streets. These patterns were established by 1900, well before there were more than a handful of automobiles in Portland. Street patterns in Portland suburbs vary widely, but blocks tend to be about twice as large as in Portland. If blocks are 400-feet by 400-feet and streets are still 66 feet wide, then only 26 percent of the suburbs is devoted to streets.

A related myth is that the auto "consumes" half or more of all urban land. A recent book claims that "In the urban United States, the automobile consumes close to half of the land area of cities; in Los Angeles the figure approaches two thirds."[3] UCLA planning Professor Donald Shoup was intrigued by this number and decided to trace it to its source. The book cited an article in the *Journal of the American Planning Association*. The article cited a 1988 study by the World Watch Institute. The World Watch report cited a 1980 book by Kirkpatrick Sale. Sale gave no source and would not return Shoup's phone calls.[4]

Shoup points out that land used for streets is not the same as land "consumed by automobiles" if that land would have been used for streets before the auto. Although more land is used for parking lots today than before the auto, this is partly if not entirely balanced out by the reduction in street area in auto-oriented suburbs. In any case, far less than half of urban land is devoted to streets, and most of those streets would be there with or without autos.

Notes

1. Andres Duany, Elizabeth Plater-Zyberk, and Jeff Speck, *Suburban Nation: The Rise of Sprawl and the Decline of the American Dream* (New York, NY: North Point Press, 2000), p. 7.
2. Ray Brindle, ARRB Transport Research Ltd, email to Stephen Marshall, available at http://socrates.berkeley.edu/~uctc.
3. Michael Southworth and Eran Ben-Joseph, *Streets and the Shaping of Towns and Cities* (New York: McGraw-Hill, 1997), pp. 4-5.
4. Donald Shoup, "Pedigree of a Statistic," *Access* 11 (Fall, 1997): p. 41.

5. The War on the Automobile

More than anything else—more than electricity, more than the telephone, perhaps even more than computers—the automobile has transformed American society.

- Workers no longer have to live within walking distance of dirty factories.
- Employers have a greater choice of workers and employees have a greater choice of jobs, allowing people to be better suited, happier, and more productive in their work.
- Supermarkets provide year-round access to fresh produce and a huge variety of other foods previously available, if at all, only to the very rich.
- Shopping malls provide many goods and services that were unavailable to most Americans just a few decades ago.
- Consumers enjoy lower prices because retailers know that, if they charge too much, people can drive down the road to a lower-priced store.
- Recreationists can spend a weekend up in the mountains or down at the shore without using up all of their time in travel.
- Medical care is minutes away from almost every American.
- Farm families once isolated from the rest of the world for most of the year can now journey to town in minutes.[1]

"Americans are individualists," says Joel Garreau. "The automobile is the finest expression of transportation-individualism ever devised." But the automobile is more than just individual transportation. It has changed our whole way of life in ways that we barely comprehend. The auto industry and all of the industries related to it—oil, steel, and so forth—not only brought wealth to the Fords and the Rockefellers but are largely responsible for the wealth of America's huge middle class. Without these industries, America would be much more of a dual-class society—rich and poor—than it is today.

In addition, most of the urban amenities that we take for granted today are only possible because of the auto. Take, for example, supermarkets, which didn't exist before cars. What do you buy at the supermarket: anchovies? sun-dried tomatoes? masa harina? plantains? Such foods were unavailable, or available only to the very few, before supermarkets. Trucks made it possible to deliver large quantities of a wide variety of goods to supermarkets and other stores. But such stores could not have succeeded if they did not serve large numbers of people who could buy and take away relatively large quantities of groceries or other products. The largest supermarkets, which offer the greatest variety and tend to have the lowest prices, draw customers from a market area of many square miles.[2] Such stores could not exist without autos to bring them customers.

The automobile, which city planning Professor Melvin Webber describes as "the most effective surface-transportation system yet devised,"[3] has brought Americans unheard-of mobility. Unlike mass transit, the auto allows people to go where they want to go when they want to go there. Unlike walking, cars make it easy to carry the groceries or other goods for long distances. And cars are far cleaner than the main form of nonhuman powered individual transit before 1900—imagine the effects of 8 million horses in New York City today.

Table One: American Travel in 1900 and 1996
(Annual miles traveled per capita)

	1900	1996
Cars and light trucks	10	14,000
Air	0	1,700
Heavy trucks	0	700
Intercity bus	0	530
Urban transit	400	160
Motorcycles	0	40
Intercity rail	200	20
Walking/cycling	1,000	350
TOTAL	1,610	17,500

Sources: Motorized in 1996: Bureau of Transportation Statistics, National Transportation Statistics 1998 *(Washington, DC: U.S. DOT, 1999), table 1-10.*
Intercity rail in 1900: Census Bureau, Historical Statistics of the United States: Colonial Times to 1970 *(Washington, DC: Census Bureau, 1975), series Q307. The figure for 1900 is 211 miles, but an unknown part of this is commuter rail which overlaps with urban transit.*
Urban transit in 1900: Extrapolated from American Public Transportation Association, Transit Factbook *(Washington, DC: APTA, 1998). APTA only has data for total passengers back to 1907 and passenger miles back to 1975. During the 1970s, transit trips averaged 4 miles. Assuming 4 miles per trip, per capita transit mileage was 484 in 1910 and 589 in 1920. Extrapolating, 400 miles per capita is a reasonable figure for 1900.*
Walking/cycling are estimated, see text.

The average American travels 14,000 miles per year by auto, which makes up more than 80 percent of all motorized travel (table one). While exact numbers for walking and bicycling are not known, less than 5 percent of all commuters walk or cycle to work and the distances they go are much shorter than the distances motorized commuters travel. Walking and cycling probably account for less than 2 percent of passenger miles, or about 350 miles per person per year.

In contrast, in 1900 the average American traveled around 200 miles per year on intercity trains and around 400 miles per year on streetcars and other urban transit. These averages disguise huge disparities: Except for the wealthy and businessmen in selected fields, most Americans did not regularly ride intercity trains or even streetcars and rarely went more than 10 miles from home. The amounts of non-motorized travel are more difficult to estimate. But most urban Americans did not own horses or bicycles: In 1899, American factories produced less than one horse-drawn carriage or buggy for every thirty urban Americans[4] and one bicycle for every seventy Americans.[5] By comparison, in 1990, one auto was sold in the U.S. for every nineteen Americans.[6] This suggests that walking was the main mode of transportation for most urban Americans in 1900. In total, the average American probably traveled less than 2,000 miles per year in 1900, most of it on foot.

Auto opponents have a nostalgic view of a past in which transit systems and intercity rail networks were dense enough to carry everyone where they wanted to go. They like to think that we would be better off today if we hadn't discarded those systems in favor of autos. Yet the average American urbanite travels more than 12,000 passenger miles per year by auto within the city, and another 2,000 passenger miles between cities. By comparison, at their peak in 1920, urban transit carried American urban residents only about 1,400 passenger miles per year[7] and intercity rail carried the average American only 440 miles per year.[8] Considering the near quadrupling of urban populations since 1920, transit systems would have to carry people thirty-two times as many passenger miles, and intercity rail seventeen times as many passenger miles, as they did in 1920 to equal auto transportation today. Such systems would be far more costly to build and operate than the autos and highways we have today.

Thanks mainly to the automobile, Americans are roughly ten times as mobile today as they were a century ago. Moreover, this mobility is much more evenly spread throughout society. In sharp distinction with the transportation disparities in nineteenth-century travel, the automobile is a great equalizer. A Mercedes may cost more than a Geo, but their drivers deal on equal terms for space on the highway, parking at the shopping mall, and fuel in their tanks. Anyone who owns a car today has enormous freedom and opportunities not available to people a few generations ago. And almost every American family *does* own a car: In 1995, better than nine out of every ten households owned at least one car[9] and America had more cars than people old enough to drive them.[10]

What critics often call our love affair with the automobile has actually been a marriage of convenience. In 1908, before Mr. Ford began selling inexpensive cars, Americans owned only one auto for every one hundred households. Within twenty years, over half of all households owned a car. Growth in auto ownership was slowed by the Depression and World War II, but even in 1938 Americans drove more than 2,000 miles per capita. Per capita driving doubled by about 1960 and by the early 1990s Americans owned an average of more than two cars per household.

Table Two: U.S. Vehicles Per Household and Auto Travel

	Vehicles per Household	Miles Driven (billions)	Miles Per Capita
1908	.01		
1918	.26		
1928	.85		
1938	.87	271	2,086
1948	.98	398	2,709
1958	1.34	665	3,846
1968	1.66	1,016	5,123
1978	1.92	1,545	6,963
1988	2.03	2,026	8,294
1998	2.23	2,625	9,711

Source: Federal Highway Administration, Highway Statistics Summary to 1995, tables MV-201, VM-201; FHwA, Highway Statistics 1998, tables MV-1, VM-2. Driving per capita differs from table one because table one is in passenger miles while this table is in vehicle miles.

Growth rates in auto ownership and driving continued throughout the twentieth century and are likely to continue in the twenty-first. But growth has slowed in the last couple of decades. Until the late 1970s, per capita driving increased by about 3 percent per year. Since then, growth has been less than 2 percent per year. This slowdown is not because urban congestion is discouraging driving: Growth in rural driving is slowing even faster than growth in urban driving. It is also not because of increased fuel costs; while fuel costs do influence auto travel, in real dollars today's gasoline prices are about the same as ever. The slowdown in the growth of driving appears to be simply due to market saturation: With more than one auto for every person of driving age, most Americans are driving just about as much as they want.

Auto Opponents

Cars are not an unmitigated blessing. They pollute the air, consume energy, congest the roads, lead to injurious and sometimes fatal accidents. But critics of the auto have been far too quick to complain about the problems while they ignore the benefits. Criticism of the car began in the 1960s and often came from the same elites who disliked the suburbs. Since then, auto opponents have put out a torrent of books about the evils of the auto.

- A. Q. Mowbry's 1968 book, *Road to Ruin*, warned that "highway advocates are already laying plans for an accelerated effort to blanket the nation with asphalt."[11]
- John Jerome's 1970 book, *The Death of the Automobile*, claimed that the mobility offered by the automobile is a "dubious benefit that is wrapped in the most tragic self-delusion."[12]
- *Autokind vs. Mankind*, written in 1971 by Kenneth Schneider, argued that the "brutal grip" of "auto tyranny" is causing "physical deprivation, injury, and death."[13]
- In 1972, Richard Hébert's *Highways to Nowhere* claimed that autos were "the most inefficient mode of transportation ever devised by man."[14]
- In addition to criticizing the suburbs, James Kunstler 1993 book, *The Geography of Nowhere*, describes the auto-centered world as "the evil empire." Kunstler believes we need to redesign our cities to live without autos because rising gas prices will soon mean that "only the rich will be able to own cars."[15]
- Stephen Goddard's 1994 book, *Getting There*, claimed that auto subsidies totaled $293 billion per year, but including traffic congestion, auto insurance, and other costs paid for exclusively by auto users.[16]
- "The nation is in 'lifeclock' to the automobile," says Jane Holtz Kay in her 1997 book, *Asphalt Nation*. "It is in its grip so securely that we can barely perceive how both the quality of mobility and the quality of life have diminished."[17]

Newspaper and magazine writers commonly say we are "addicted" to the auto. The strong implication is that our use of automobiles is irrational. In fact, it is the opposition that is irrational.

Jane Holtz Kay, for example, describes her meeting with Sandra Rosenbloom, a University of Arizona researcher who studies the importance of autos to women. Unlike men who tend to drive straight home from work, women use cars to do errands such as shopping and picking up the kids. "Working mothers are much more dependent on driving alone than comparable male parents," she says. Efforts to discourage auto driving, she says, penalize women much more than men.[18]

"Isn't that depressing?" asks Kay, who thinks that it is "grim" that women have to suffer "vehicular bondage." But Rosenbloom answers, "You wouldn't believe how owning their first car frees women." Kay's response? "How like a man"![19]

As with the suburbs, opposition to the auto is highly emotional. "The adversaries of the auto seemed to feel toward it a kind of Old Testament moral and esthetic aversion," observes James Dunn in his book, *Driving Forces*.[20] Auto opponents, he goes on, do "not want to solve specific problems caused by the automobile. They define the automobile as a problem in and of itself."

There is no doubt that autos do cause problems, but to make their case auto opponents greatly exaggerate those problems. According to them, autos are heavily subsidized, they poison the air, they waste people's time in congestion, and they caused the decline of our cities. These myths will be discussed later in this book.

In 1939, American cities came about as close as they ever will to smart-growth ideals. Suburbs were growing but the vast majority of urbanites still lived in cities. Many of the suburbs that did exist were fairly dense because they were built around streetcar or interurban rail lines. Four-lane roads were rare and, except for a few intercity toll roads such as the Pennsylvania Turnpike, limited-access highways were almost unheard of.

Despite this apparent paradise, the most popular attraction at the 1939 New York World's Fair was the General Motors Futurama, a huge diorama showing the highways of the future: limited-access freeways linking cities, towns, and rural areas; six- and eight-lane roads with hundreds of tiny moving cars zipping over bridges and through tunnels, across cities and into downtowns. Five million people stood in lines that often stretched more than a mile long to take a sixteen-minute tour of this exhibit. Norman Bel Geddes, Futurama's designer, predicted that, as these future highways were built, "cities [will] tend to become centers for working, the country districts centers for living."[21] This was widely agreed to be a good thing, because (according to a sociologist quoted by Bel Geddes), "The extreme concentration of population at centers has deplorable effects upon the health, intelligence and morals of people."[22]

Today, we have gone from the smart-growth paradise of the early twentieth century to the Futurama paradise of the twenty-first. Despite their critics, American highways perform yeoman service for the nation, carrying nearly a trillion ton-miles of freight and four trillion passenger-miles of travel. And most of this service is performed by the highways that most resemble those that awed Futurama observers: the interstates and other freeways that today's auto opponents hate the most.

Interstate freeways make up just 1.2 percent of the nation's road miles, yet they carry 24 percent of the passenger traffic (figure one). Other freeways and multilane roads make up another 4.1 percent of road miles, yet carry 30 percent of the traffic. Between them, the 5.3 percent of the nation's roads that auto opponents hate the most are responsible for well over half the traffic. These percentages are approximately the same in both urban and rural areas.

Even when adjusting for the fact that interstates and other freeways have more lanes than smaller roads and streets, they are still very productive. In 1998, interstates in the nation's 392 urbanized areas made up 10 percent of lane miles but carried 25 percent of the traffic. They also did so more safely than non-interstates: Transportation expert Wendell Cox estimates that interstate highways have saved 187,000 lives and prevented 12 million injuries.[23]

For decades, the number of automobiles and the number of miles driven in the U.S. have grown faster than the nation's population. Transportation experts have long predicted that these trends would level off. While the trends have slowed,

Figure One: Miles of Urban Road and Urban Miles Driven by Road Type

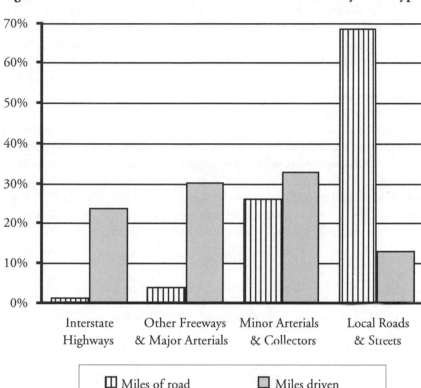

Freeways and major arterials carry most traffic even though they make up only a small share of road mileage. Source: FHwA, Highway Statistics 1998, *tables HM-50 and VM-2.*

they haven't leveled off: both the number of autos and the number of miles driven continue to grow faster than the population.[24]

Will these trends continue? As baby boomers retire, transportation experts predict that the growth in peak-hour travel may decline. But many baby boomers may end up retiring later than their parents, thus reducing the effect on peak-hour travel. Overall travel by footloose baby boomers is likely to be as much or more in retirement as when they are working. Even today, the growth in travel for people over age 65 is greater than for any other age group.[25]

Still, some have doubts about the future of auto driving. "Anyone who thinks we're going to be using cars twenty-five years from now the way we've been accustomed to using them in the recent past ought to have their head examined," proclaims James Kunstler. "That phase of our national history is over."[26] Believing this, Kunstler has no hesitation in urging that we spend billions of dollars "remaking" our cities as if cars did not exist.

Joel Garreau disagrees. "In an affluent America," says the author of *Edge City*, "the dominant mode of transportation for generations is likely to be something with four tires and a steering wheel."[27] Urban designs that ignore this likelihood will be as disastrous as the urban renewal and public housing disasters of the past.

"While many scholars have vilified the automobile as the destroyer of the city," says urban historian Peter Muller, a "more balanced assessment" would find that automobiles and highways are "the long-hoped-for attainment of private mass transportation that offered users almost total freedom to travel whenever and wherever they chose."[28] Such freedom, pouts James Kunstler, "is the freedom of a fourteen-year-old child."[29] The freedom that auto-haters Knustler and Jane Holtz Kay disdain is much more than just freedom to move around. "The most important aspect of the automobile," says Garreau, "is that it shifted the balance of power from centralized modes of organization toward the individual."[30] As part three will show, the smart-growth movement is partly driven by those who wish to increase central authority at the expense of individual freedom.

Notes

1. Michael Berger, *The Devil Wagon in God's Country: The Automobile and Social Change in Rural America, 1893–1929* (Hamden, CT: Archon Books, 1979), pp. 55–74.
2. Michael Rothschild, *Bionomics: Economy as Ecosystem* (New York, NY: MacRae, 1990), p. 372.
3. Melvin Webber, "The Marriage of Autos and Transit: How to Make Transit Popular Again," *Access* 5:26–31.
4. Census Bureau, *Historical Statistics of the United States, Colonial Times to 1970* (Washington, DC: Census Bureau, 1975), series P296.
5. Ibid, series P298.
6. Census Bureau, *Statistical Abstract of the United States 1994* (Washington, DC: Census Bureau, 1994), table 1007. Includes passenger vehicles and light trucks.
7. American Public Transportation Association, *Transit Factbook* (Washington, DC: APTA, 1998), table 39.
8. Census Bureau, *Historical Statistics of the United States,* series Q307.
9. Patricia Hu and Jennifer Young, *Draft Summary of Travel Trends: 1995 Nationwide Personal Transportation Survey* (Oak Ridge, TN: US DOE, 1999), table 16, http://www-cta.ornl.gov/npts/1995/Doc/trends_reportl8.pdf.
10. FHwA, *Highway Statistics 1998*, table MV-1; Census Bureau, "Population Estimates by Age and Sex," http://www.census.gov/population/estimates/nation/intfile2-1.txt.
11. A. Q. Mowbry, *Road to Ruin* (Philadelphia, PA: J. B. Lippincott, 1969), 240 pp.
12. John Jerome, *The Death of the Automobile: The Fatal Effect of the Golden Era, 1955–1970* (New York, NY: W. W. Norton, 1972), 288 pp.
13. Kenneth R. Schneider, *Autokind vs. Mankind: An Analysis of Tyranny, A Proposal for Rebellion, A Plan for Reconstruction* (New York, NY: W. W. Norton, 1971), p. 6.
14. Richard Hébert, *Highways to Nowhere: The Politics of City Transportation* (Indianapolis, IN: Bobbs-Merrill, 1972), p. 188.
15. James Howard Kunstler, *The Geography of Nowhere: The Rise and Decline of America's Man-Made Landscape* (New York, NY: Simon & Schuster, 1993), p. 124.

16. Stephen B. Goddard, *Getting There: The Epic Struggle between Road and Rail in the American Century* (New York, NY: BasicBooks, 1994), 351 pp. As a railfan, I find one of Goddard's claims particularly amusing. Extolling the virtues of passenger trains, he writes, "Passengers on [the Chesapeake & Ohio Railroad's] 'Chessies' streaked from Cincinatti to Washington while dancing to live music and enjoying movies, aquariums, and children's playrooms." In fact, the railroad purchased equipment for the Chessie, but cancelled the train before it ever ran and sold the equipment to other railroads.

17. Jane Holtz Kay, *Asphalt Nation: How the Automobile Took over America and How We Can Take It Back* (New York, NY: Crown, 1997), p. 19.

18. Sandra Rosenbloom and Elizabeth Burns, "Do Environmental Measures and Travel Reduction Programs Hurt Working Women?" Drachman Institute for Land and Regional Development Studies, University of Arizona, October, 1993.

19. Kay, *Asphalt Nation*, pp. 22–23.

20. James A. Dunn, Jr., *Driving Forces: The Automobile, Its Enemies, and the Politics of Mobility* (Washington, DC: Brookings Institution, 1998), p. 6.

21. Norman Bel Geddes, *Magic Motorways* (New York, NY: Random House, 1940), p. 288.

22. Ibid, p. 293.

23. Wendell Cox & Jean Love, *40 Years of the US Interstate Highway System: An Analysis* (Washington, DC: American Highway Users Alliance, 1996), http://www.publicpurpose.com.

24. FHwA, *Highway Statistics Summary to 1995*, tables MV-200, DL201, and VM-201.

25. Patricia Hu and Jennifer Young, *Draft Summary of Travel Trends*, p. 22, http://www-cta.ornl.gov/npts/1995/Doc/trends_reportl8.pdf.

26. James Howard Kunstler, *Home from Nowhere: Remaking Our Everyday World for the Twenty-First Century* (New York, NY: Simon & Schuster, 1996), p. 58.

27. Joel Garreau, *Edge City: Life on the New Frontier* (New York, NY: Doubleday, 1991), pp. 126–127.

28. Peter O. Muller, "Transportation and Urban Form: Stages in the Spatial Evolution of the American Metropolis," *in* Susan Hanson (ed.), *The Geography of Urban Transportation* (New York, NY: Guilford Press, 1986), p. 45.

29. Kunstler, *Home from Nowhere*, p. 61.

30. Garreau, *Edge City*, p. 108.

Auto & Highway Facts

Miles of urban road per million urban residents: 3,845
  Miles of urban freeway per million urban residents: 110

Urban freeway miles as percent of all urban road miles: 2.9%
  Urban freeway miles driven as percent of all urban miles driven: 36.0%

Urban miles driven each day per capita: 22.4
  Urban miles driven each year per capita: 8,180

Urban passenger miles each day per capita: 35.8
  Urban passenger miles each year per capita: 13,100
  Source: FHwA, Highway Statistics 1998.

Average number of people per automobile: 1.6
  Average number of people per commuter auto: 1.1
  Source: FHwA, Nationwide Personal Transportation Survey.

Percent of morning rush hour traffic that is *not* commuter traffic: 40
  Percent of afternoon rush hour traffic that is *not* commuter traffic: 60
  Source: Alan Pisarski, Commuting in America.

Web Tools: Highways and Traffic

Download information about highways and traffic in your urban area at http://www.fhwa.dot.gov/ohim/hs98/roads.htm. Get tables HM-71 and HM-72 in either PDF format or Lotus format. Similar tables for years back to 1993 (and possibly, by the time you read this, 1999) are available at http://www.fhwa.dot.gov/ohim/ohimstat.htm.

Forward Into the Past

During the 1970s, Portland's transit agency, Tri-Met, made many low-cost improvements to its bus services, including:

- Doubling frequencies on popular routes;
- Creating park-and-ride stations; and
- Eliminating fares downtown.

As a result, transit ridership grew by an incredible 12 percent per year, three times as fast as auto driving. This made Portland one of the few regions in the nation where transit increased market share over the automobile. That trend abruptly ended in 1980, when Portland began building light rail. To pay for it, Tri-Met raised fares and reduced bus service, leading to steady decline in ridership. By 1986, when the light rail first opened for operation, Tri-Met had lost 15 percent of its riders. After 1986, transit ridership began to grow again, but much more slowly than the growth of auto travel. As a result, transit continues to lose market share.

Yet Metro is spending as many federal and local dollars as it can on light rail. Metro and Tri-Met proudly insist that Portland's two light-rail lines were built "on time and under budget and achieved projected ridership levels." The truth is quite a bit different. The first line was projected to cost $188 million and take four years to build. It actually required $240 million and five years.[1] The second line was originally supposed to cost $240 million and be built in four years. Its final cost was $944 million and it too required an extra year. This high cost led Portland State University urban studies professor Kenneth Dueker to describe Portland's light rail as "gold plated."[2] It is certainly far removed from the original conception of a low-cost alternative to buses.

In January, 1999, Vice President Gore claimed that Portland's light rail is "beloved by its users."[3] In fact, between 1990 and 1998, support for light rail declined from 75 percent to 48 percent of the region's voters. Although supporters consistently outspent opponents by ten-to-one, each successive election saw declining support as more people realized what a boondoggle it is. Suburbanites who live near existing or proposed light-rail lines, and therefore have the most incentive to study the proposals, provided the greatest opposition. In the last election, nearly all precincts in all the suburbs on existing and proposed lines voted against it, along with many east Portland precincts on the existing line.[4]

The light rail "has never developed the momentum its fans envisioned," says Portland's liberal *Willamette Week* newspaper. "It's expensive; it asks people to make themselves less mobile; and it's been sold as an anti-car religion instead of a low-stress option for car owners."[5] Worse, it is deadly: In just a few months after Gore's statement, Portland's new westside light rail had run over and killed five people, and severely injured a sixth. This made it one of the most dangerous stretches of rail line in the nation. Ironically, most of the victims were light-rail riders on their way to or from a station.[6]

Fortunately, there aren't very many riders for light rail to kill. Though Portland planners rarely admit it, ridership was as much below estimates as costs were above them. The first line was supposed to carry 42,500 riders per day within five years of opening and 57,000 after ten years. Actual ridership proved to be less than half those projections. The second line is only two years old, and ridership so far is only half of what was originally projected for five years after opening. Most of the people who are riding light rail were previously bus riders, while some former bus riders have switched to driving because light rail is so slow. As a result, traffic on the highways paralleling the two lines continues to grow as fast or faster than before the lines were built.[7]

Light-rail's slow speeds shocked many transit riders who were used to taking express buses from Gresham, Gateway, Hollywood, Beaverton, and Hillsboro to downtown Portland. After briefly circulating through the local neighborhood, these buses got on the nearest freeway and zipped downtown at 50 to 60 miles per hour. These express bus routes were cancelled when the light rail lines opened, which nearly doubled trip times for many transit riders. The current light-rail schedules take one hour and thirty-seven minutes to go 33 miles from Gresham to Hillsboro, or just over 20 miles per hour. This makes the notion that many Intel employees will live in Gresham and commute by light rail pretty unrealistic.

More important than moving people, a major motivation behind Metro's light-rail planning is neighborhood densification. One reason why the second light-rail line cost four times as much as first estimated is that it was originally planned to terminate in Beaverton, six miles west of downtown Portland. Metro decided to build it another five miles to Hillsboro, even though its analyses showed that doing so would add only 430 riders per day, or about 1 percent, when compared with low-cost bus service improvements. Why was it worth spending $250 million on so few riders? Because the route passed through Orenco, a huge patch of prime farm land ripe for transit-oriented development.

Metro also planned a third light-rail line to Clackamas Town Center, the region's largest shopping mall. Metro's initial analysis indicated that the last five miles of the line would generate only 600 riders per day.[8] But Metro wanted to turn the shopping mall's huge parking area into apartments, offices, and other transit-oriented developments, and even hired Peter Calthorpe to write a plan for doing so.[9]

Another motivation behind Metro's light-rail obsession is the desire to get federal transportation dollars. Having decided to build few new freeways, Metro needs to get its federal transportation dollars for transit or lose out. Between 1992 and 1997, Oregon received more dollars from the federal mass transit trust fund, relative to what Oregon auto and truck drivers paid into the fund, than any other state except New York.[10] In 1996, Metro's executive director, Mike Burton, warned in a letter to other officials in the region that "the region must take action to bring Oregon's fair share of federal transportation dollars back home or they will be lost to other regions of the country."[11] The action he wanted them to take was to endorse the construction of more light-rail lines.

Portland first faced this problem in 1973 when Mayor Neil Goldschmidt wanted to cancel construction of the Mt. Hood Freeway, which was planned from downtown Portland to Gresham. Congress would allow Portland to spend the freeway dollars on transit. Light rail was only one of the options being considered. "It's easy to forget how much resistance there was to light rail," says Alan Webber, then an aide to Goldschmidt. "It sounded like something from another planet, and it sounded too fancy for Portland."[12] A 1973 study by the state of Oregon estimated that Portland light-rail service could begin on four routes totalling 46 miles for less than $84 million, or about $2 million per mile.[13] But when Tri-Met planned to build an entirely new light-rail line, the costs jumped to nearly $8 million per mile.

One alternative to rail was an exclusive busway between Gresham and Portland. The busway had several advantages over rail. It cost less to build. Once off the busway, buses could vary their routes into many different neighborhoods, so the busway would attract more passengers than rail. But a busway would cost more to operate, partly because it was serving more neighborhoods and carrying more riders. The deciding factor in favor of light rail may have been the federal government's funding patterns: Congress was free with capital funds but stingy with operating funds. This biased the analysis towards a system that cost a lot to build but less to operate—even if it carried fewer passengers. So Tri-Met decided to build light rail. The final cost turned out to be $14 million per mile, nearly double the original estimate.

By the time Portland was ready to consider a second light-rail line, the canceled-freeway law had been replaced with a new law offering federal matching funds on a one-to-one basis. This meant that local taxpayers would have to come up with 50 percent of the funds. But Oregon's senior senator, Mark Hatfield, was the ranking Republican on the Senate Appropriations Committee. With his help, the federal government paid 75 percent of the cost of the second line, which cost an average of more than $50 million per mile.

Metro then wanted to build a third light-rail line, known as the "south-north route," to Vancouver, Washington, at a cost of well over $100 million per mile.

Since Hatfield had retired, the federal government would pay only half, so Metro expected the state of Oregon and Vancouver to each pay a sixth, leaving just a sixth of the cost to Portlanders. In separate elections, Vancouver and Oregon voters each rejected the idea. Portland-area voters then turned down Metro's fallback proposal that they pay half the costs. Not to be defeated, Metro is planning to build the north part of the line anyway with 70 percent federal funding, an idea endorsed by the Clinton administration but not yet approved by Congress.

The south-north light-rail proposal turned into such a boondoggle that the Association of Oregon Rail and Transit Advocates, a group that had strongly promoted the idea of light rail, actively campaigned against it. While insisting that light-rail made sense in concept, the group argued that the south-north line's "costs [are] too high" and projected "ridership too low" to make it worthwhile.[14]

Meanwhile, a light-rail branch off of the Gresham line to Portland's airport is under construction as a part of a sweetheart deal with the Bechtel Corporation. Under the deal, Bechtel is building the five-mile light-rail line and is supposed to pay about a fifth of the cost.[15] In exchange, Bechtel will get a 99-year no-cost lease on 120 acres of commercial and industrial land near the airport. Metro estimates that the lease is worth $20 to $30 million.[16] Without competitive bidding on the contract, no one knows how much Bechtel is really paying, but taxpayers are paying more than $130 million for the line plus the light-rail vehicles to run on it. Yet many Portland-area officials, including Portland Mayor Vera Katz, claim that the airport line is being built without tax dollars.[17] "What is unusual about the airport MAX proposal," says Portland State University urban studies professor Gerard Mildner, "isn't the lack of taxes, but the slick way in which they are hidden."[18]

Both the airport and the north light-rail lines will significantly increase congestion in the Portland area. The Bechtel industrial park will generate far more traffic than the airport rail line is expected to carry. No airport light-rail line in the country carries as many as 6 percent of air travelers, and most of those travelers would otherwise have taken taxis, buses, or airport limos.[19] The north light-rail line is going to replace two lanes of a busy four-lane arterial. As a result, Metro expects a significant increase in traffic congestion over the "no-build" alternative.[20]

When light rail was first being considered, Goldschmidt's top aid and transportation expert was Ron Buel, whose book, *Dead End: The Automobile in Mass Transportation*, recommended numerous transit alternatives to automobiles. Today, he—along with many other Portland transit advocates—is skeptical about light rail's high cost, low ridership, and the fact that it unrealistically asks people to make themselves less mobile. "If I could have $1 billion to spend on non-light-rail transit," he says, referring to the cost of Portland's second light-rail line, "I could get an enormous amount done."[21]

Buel was able to learn from the experience of the first light-rail line because he retired from politics and is now an outside observer. What Buel and others did not realize in the 1970s was that, once the decision to build light rail was made, it would create a huge constituency for building more light-rail lines no matter what the cost and no matter how unsuccessful the first line.

Metro's desire for light rail makes sense if the goal is to capture federal dollars or to have an excuse to densify reluctant neighborhoods. But it does not help most of the region's residents, even those who ride transit. Metro admits that building more light rail imposes such high operating costs on Tri-Met that it "limits future bus expansion."[22] In particular, with more light rail, Tri-Met will only have enough operating funds to expand bus service at about 1 percent per year—little more than half the rate of population growth. If no more rail is built, Tri-Met will have enough operating funds to expand bus service at 3.8 percent per year—about twice the rate of population growth.[23]

For example, says Metro, just $66 million could begin a new bus service on twelve major routes that Tri-Met calls *FastLink*—faster, frequent, more comfortable service that Tri-Met describes as "the bus equivalent of light rail." This suggests that, for less than a fifth of the cost of the south-north line, Tri-Met could run light-rail-like schedules and service on *all* of its 85 major bus routes. Although Tri-Met first proposed FastLink services in 1993, none have yet been started because the agency is preoccupied with light rail.[24] The agency has also had to reduce bus service on some of its most popular routes.[25]

Despite the limits it places on bus service, Metro's *Regional Transportation Plan* still calls for building the south light-rail line to Milwaukie and Clackamas, a branch line to Oregon City, and extending the north line into Vancouver.[26] Metro is also seeking $75 million in federal funding to start commuter rail service from Beaverton to Wilsonville.[27]

Over the next two decades, Metro would like to spend at least 56 percent of the region's transportation budget on transit. Roughly a third of that is to go for capital improvements, mainly light rail construction.[28] Of the other 44 percent, as will be discussed below, roughly half will be spent either reducing roadway capacities or adding bikeways and pedestrian facilities to roads. Only a tiny share will be spent on capacity increases, and that will mainly be for freight routes.

Notes

1. Don Pickrell, *Urban Rail Transit Projects: Forecast vs. Actual Ridership and Costs* (Cambridge, MA: US DOT, 1989), p. 33.
2. Ken Dueker, "Portland's Love Affair with Light Rail: Assessing the Risk Factors," Portland State Univeristy Center for Urban Studies Discussion Paper 95-6, 1995.
3. Remarks by Vice President Gore on Announcement of Livability Agenda, Washington, DC, January 11, 1999.
4. Gordon Oliver and Brent Hunsberger, "Holding the line on light rail," *The Oregonian*, December 9, 1996, p. B1. Map accompanying article shows precinct-by-precinct results

    of 1996 vote on south/north light-rail line.

5. Bob Young, "1986 Train in Vain," *Willamette Week 25 Years*, November 10, 1999, p. 50.

6. Nancy Keates, "Light-Rail Addition Comes to Portland At a Heavy Price: MAX Moves Lots of People—And Runs Some Down," *Wall Street Journal*, December 2, 1999, p. A1.

7. Melvin Zucker, "Did Westside Light Rail Really Reduce Traffic Volumes?"(Portland, OR: Oregon Transportation Institute, 1999), http://www.hevanet.com/oti/may99westsidecorridor.htm.

8. Gordon Oliver, "Returning to Light Rail: Clackamas Town Center," *The Oregonian*, February 12, 1998, p. A20.

9. Calthorpe Associates, *Region 2040* (Portland, OR: Metro, 1994), pp. 19–28.

10. Federal Transit Administration, "Comparison of Projected Federal Highway Trust Fund Receipts for the Mass Transit Account to Federal Apportionments and Allocations for Transit, FY 1992 - 1997" (Washington, DC: FTA, 1997), 1 p.

11. Memo from Mike Burton to JPACT re: South/North LRT Proposal, 11 December 1996, Portland, Oregon.

12. Young, "1986 Train in Vain," p. 50.

13. Railroad Division, Public Utilities Commission of Oregon, *Light Rail Transit: Portland Area Rail Corridor Study* (Salem, OR: PUC, 1973).

14. Association of Oregon Rail and Transit Advocates, "Argument in Opposition to Measure No. 32," *Voter's Pamphlet, General Election, November 5, 1996* (Salem, OR: Secretary of State, 1996), p. 63.

15. Tri-Met, *Draft Finance Proposal: Airport MAX Extension* (Portland, OR: Tri-Met, 1998), p. 5.

16. Amy Carlson Kohnstamm, Tri-Met, personal communication to Craig Flynn, July, 1998.

17. Statement of Portland Mayor Vera Katz on *Talk of the Nation*, National Public Radio, July 27, 2000.

18. Gerard Mildner, "Rethinking the Airport MAX," *The Oregonian*, October 5, 1998, p. B9.

19. Myles Cunneen, "Summary of Forecasts, Air Passenger Use of Rail Transit," unpublished paper, 1998, p. 1.

20. Metro, *North Corridor Interstate MAX Light Rail Project Final Environmental Impact Statement* (Portland, OR: Metro, 1999), table 3.3-3.

21. Young, "1986 Train in Vain," p. 50.

22. Metro, *Interim Federal Regional Transportation Plan* (Portland, OR: Metro, 1995), p. 7-8.

23. Metro, *Interim Federal Regional Transportation Plan*, p. 5-21 and p. 7-18.

24. Tri-Met, *Strategic Plan FastLink Sloping Report* (Portland, OR: Tri-Met, 1993), 24 pp.

25. Bob Young, "Save the 14!: Cutting service on one of the city's most popular routes reveals bigger problems at Tri-Met," *Willamette Week*, 23(26, April 4, 1997), p. 1.

26. Metro, *1999 Regional Transportation Plan* (Portland, OR: Metro, 1999), p. 4-3.

27. Joseph Rose, "Clackamas County stalls in race for transit funds," *The Oregonian*, February 14, 2000, http://www.oregonlive.com/news/00/02/st021403.html.

28. Metro, *1999 Regional Transportation Plan*, pp. 4-7–4-8.

Portland's Light-Rail Myth

Myth: Portland's light rail is highly successful.
Reality: Portland's light rail has had virtually no effect on congestion.

When compared with some light-rail lines in the country, Portland's light rail *is* moderately successful. In 1998, Portland's rail line carried 20 percent more passenger miles, per route mile, as the average light-rail line. By this measure—which is the best measure of congestion relief that transit can provide—Portland ranked sixth out of seventeen major U.S. light-rail systems. But when considered as an investment in urban transportation, Portland's light rail is an unmitigated failure.

When originally proposed, planners projected that Portland's first light-rail line would carry more than 42,000 passengers a day five years after it opened, an in another five years it would carry 57,000 passengers a day. Actual ridership proved to be less than half of this amount. In 1987, the line's first full year of operation, it carried just 19,500 riders per weekday. Overall, the region's transit system gained about 4,700 riders per weekday, so three out of four light-rail riders must have been former bus riders.

Ten years later, rail ridership had increased by less than 10,000 riders per weekday.[1] This compares very poorly with the growth of travel in Interstate 84, which parallels the rail line over much of its route. Far from reducing congestion, the opening of the light rail led to an acceleration of freeway traffic growth. By 1997, the highway was serving 55,000 vehicles carrying 88,000 passengers per weekday more than in 1986.[2] The growth in freeway passenger movement was eight times faster than light-rail growth.

Ridership results were more positive when Portland's second light-rail line opened in late 1998. In the year following the line's opening, weekday rail ridership increased by 23,200 while weekday transit ridership increased by 19,500 trips. This suggests that close to 10,000 people may now be taking round trips on transit who previously were using another form of transportation or not traveling. Of course, more people may simply be transferring from buses to rail cars, and transit ridership would have grown without the new rail line simply due to population growth.)

Yet the impacts of the new line on congestion have been imperceptible. As before, traffic growth on the highway paralleling the light-rail line, U.S. 26, has accelerated. In the first year after the line opened, highway traffic grew more than twice as fast as in the previous two years.[3] The highway serves 153,000 vehicles a weekday, or roughly 245,000 weekday passengers, so new transit riders amount to less than 8 percent of the corridor's traffic.

Light rail has an insignificant impact on congestion over the entire Portland area. In 1999, Portland-area residents and visitors rode about 222 million passenger miles on public transit buses and 101 million miles on light rail. Meanwhile, they traveled about 1.8 billion passenger miles by auto.[4] This means that about 1.5 percent of all motorized travel was by transit, and only a third of that, or 0.5 percent of the total, was by light rail. Tripling light-rail route miles, as Metro wants to do, might triple that percentage, but it won't significantly reduce the total share of travel by auto.

In short, Portland's light-rail lines:

- Carry less than half the people originally projected by planners;
- Carry less than 10 percent of the people in their corridors;
- Did not prevent accelerated growth of highway traffic in their corridors;
- Carries just 0.3 percent of all traffic in Portland.

Considering the $1.2 billion spent on these two light-rail lines, such tiny ridership is of little comfort to auto drivers stuck in traffic. Nor did light rail benefit transit riders. Those in the light-rail corridors suffered slower transit service than the express buses the light-rail lines replaced, while transit riders outside the rail corridors end up with less frequent and lower-quality service because, says Metro, light-rail's huge costs "limit bus expansion" in the Portland area.[5]

Notes

1. Ridership data on file at Tri-Met offices, Portland, Oregon.
2. Oregon Department of Transportation, "I-84 Vehicle Counts," Salem, Oregon. Weekday traffic is about 5.5 percent greater than daily traffic (including weekends); cars carry an average of 1.6 people per car.
3. Oregon Transportation Institute, "Did Westside Light Rail Really Reduce Traffic Volumes?" 1999, http://www.hevanet.com/oti/may99westsidecorridor.htm.
4. Federal Highway Administration, *Highway Statistics 1998* (Washington, DC: Federal Highway Administration, 1999), table HM-72.
5. Metro, *Interim Federal Regional Transportation Plan* (Portland, OR: Metro, 1995), p. 7-8.

The Field-of-Dreams Myth

Myth: Portland-area light-rail transit led to a significant amount of urban redevelopment.

Reality: The vast majority of development along Portland's light-rail line is government-built, government-subsidized, or unrelated to the light-rail line.

Light rail "is not worth the cost if you're just looking at transit," says Portland smart-growth planner John Fregonese. "It's a way to develop your community at higher densities."[1] But Portland's heavily subsidized light-rail line didn't even do that until developers were given even more subsidies.

Portland's transit agency, Tri-Met, claims that more than a billion dollars worth of investments made in the eastside light-rail corridor since that rail line opened in 1986.[2] This has led journalists to report that "the light-rail system has boosted the downtown and spawned $1.2 billion in new development."[3] In fact, the vast majority of the construction on Tri-Met's list has little to do with the light rail. Moreover, many of those that meet smart-growth criteria for "transit-oriented development" were heavily subsidized.

Tri-Met's list includes, among other things:

- A new, $262 million basketball arena adjacent to the existing basketball arena. The older arena was built a quarter of a century before the light rail, and no one seriously considered a different location for the new arena.
- The $220 million remodeling of the Lloyd Center shopping mall, which was demanded by merchants to keep up with more modern malls elsewhere in the region.
- An $85 million convention center built by Metro, Portland's regional planning authority. Metro may have decided to build the center near the light rail, but Metro would have built it if Portland had no light rail.
- Several government office buildings costing around $110 million. By executive order of the governor and the president, most state and federal offices in Portland must be located in the greater downtown area. Since light rail happens to serve that area, the buildings are located near light rail.
- At least $72 million of routine remodeling of various commercial properties, including office buildings and retail stores outside of Lloyd Center. For ex-

ample, Tri-Met credited the $27 million remodeling of the Gateway Fred
Meyer store to light rail. In fact, in the decade after the line was built the Fred
Meyer chain remodeled 86 percent of its dozens of stores, all but two of them
well away from any light-rail line.[4]

- More than $14 million spent on two government-built parking garages, one
a little-used light-rail park-and-ride station and the other located downtown.
If light rail works so well, why is a new parking garage needed downtown and
how can the light rail be said to have stimulated its construction?

The above properties account for two-thirds of Tri-Met's list, yet none are the
mixed-use, transit-oriented developments that smart-growth advocates want to
see. In 1996, ten years after the Portland-to-Gresham light-rail line opened for
business, city planner Mike Saba sadly reported to the Portland city council that
"we have not seen any of the kind of development—of a mid-rise, higher-density,
mixed-use, mixed-income type—that we would've liked to have seen" along the
light-rail line. City Councilor Charles Hales noted that "we are in the hottest real
estate market in the country," yet city planning maps revealed that "most of those
sites [along the light-rail line] are still vacant."[5] To correct this, Hales convinced
the council to offer developers ten years of property tax waivers for any high-
density housing built near light-rail stations.

A 1997 analysis by Portland State University's Center for Urban Studies agreed
with Saba and Hales about light rail's lack of effects on land use. The study found
that "light rail alone has not been sufficient to have an appreciable impact on
development patterns, residential density, auto ownership, and transit modal behavior."[6] Most, if not all, of the true transit-oriented developments built along
Portland's light rail required government subsidies such as tax waivers, infrastructure subsidies, below-market land sales, and in some cases direct grants to the
developers.

In 1998, Metro received a $3 million grant from the Federal Transit Adminis-
tration to buy land near light-rail stations and then resell it at a loss to developers
on the condition they will build transit-oriented developments.[7] The Oregon
Department of Transportation has provided land at bargain rates to developers
who will build such developments near existing or proposed light-rail lines.

Portland has been particularly aggressive in subsidizing high-density housing
near the downtown area. The city is providing at least $80 million in various
subsidies for some 3,000 units of high-density housing in the River District, just
north of downtown.[8] People who move there can expect increased congestion,
since among the subsidies are the removal of traffic lanes and local access to one of
the city's Willamette River bridges.

The city also increased downtown parking fees in order to help raise $42 mil-
lion to build a streetcar line for short-wheelbase trolley cars to run from downtown to Northwest Portland. Jim Howell, a leader of Citizens for Better Transit
and former planner with Portland's transit agency, thinks that the streetcar "is a

waste of money." He notes that the route it will follow is used by so few people that it "doesn't even have a bus line." While buying buses to serve the route would cost only about $300,000 per bus, each streetcar will cost $2 million and the tracks and wires another $30 million.

"What gripes me is we spend a lot of money because people who don't ride transit think its neat," responds Howell. "At the same time, we don't spend money on what's needed," which, in his opinion, includes better bus service on most routes and rail service only when it can be built at a low cost and serve a lot of people.[9]

Howell admits that the real goal of the streetcar is to promote high-density housing. "When did anyone ever build transit-oriented development around bus service?" asks City Commissioner Charles Hales. The answer, it turns it, is "when it was subsidized." Tax waivers and other incentives have often proved sufficient to convince developers to build high-density housing with or without light rail. Such transit-oriented developments have been built on Belmont Street, Martin Luther King Avenue, and in parts of downtown Portland that are well away from the light-rail line. But just building a light-rail line without also providing subsidies has not led to neighborhood redevelopment in the Portland area.

The city of Gresham, at the east end of the light-rail line that opened in 1986, discovered this in the early 1990s. Gresham hoped the line would produce an economic boom, but little materialized. A developer told the city that the market for high density was so poor that he would need more than $300,000 in subsidies to build. So in 1995 Gresham waived $137,000 in property taxes and development fees and provided a $200,000 grant from federal funds. The result was a 33-unit-per-acre apartment and one of the region's first high-density (but not mixed-use) transit-oriented developments.[10]

Gresham also wanted a 130-acre mixed-use development, which it called Gresham Civic Neighborhood, built on prime farm land. The landowners wanted to build a conventional shopping mall, but the city refused to allow it. Although the city's plan won an award from the American Planning Association, no developers were interested even after Gresham offered $11 million worth of subsidies to encourage development.[11] To promote the plan the city spent $1.8 million building a four-lane road through the middle of the area which critics quickly dubbed "the road to nowhere."[12] It also spent $2.1 building a light-rail station in case anyone should ever develop the property. After years of planning and promotions, some developers are building in the area, but progress is slow.

"To get higher density in suburbia, you have to support it with public money," said Gresham Mayor Gussie McRobert in 1995.[13] "The public subsidy for many other such projects ranges from 25 percent all the way up to 50 percent," notes the *Oregonian*.[14]

Sometimes even light rail and subsidies together aren't enough. When Portland's second light-rail line opened in the suburb of Beaverton, the city council there planned a grandiose development called Beaverton Round—because it would almost completely surround the light-rail station. The Round was supposed to include three to five stories of apartments, shops, and offices. To support it, the city provided $10 million worth of land, infrastructure, and property tax breaks. Yet the developer went bankrupt before it was completed, contractors complained that they were owed nearly $5 million, and the project stands empty and hollow.[15]

Beaverton Round was to be a classic example of the mid-rise, mixed-use, transit-oriented developments that are springing up in many other parts of Portland, mostly with the help of tax waivers and other subsidies. Portland's experience shows that the field of dreams is a myth if it means "build light rail, and they will come." It only becomes a reality if it means "subsidize it enough and they will come." Light rail is not important to the subsidies; instead, the key subsidies are tax waivers, below-market property sales, and direct grants to developers. So why bother with building light rail?

Notes

1. Dee J. Hall, "The Choice: High Density or Urban Sprawl," *Wisconsin State Journal*, July 23, 1995.
2. G. B. Arrington, "Beyond the Field of Dreams," Tri-Met, 1996, http://www.tri-met.org/reports/dreams.htm.
3. Dee J. Hall, "The Choice."
4. Fred Meyer Inc., "The transition years: 1990 through 1996," http://www.fredmeyer.com/fms/fmshist/hist90s.shtml.
5. Quotes from the October 23, 1996, city council meeting were transcribed from a videotape of that meeting made by the city of Portland.
6. Kenneth Dueker and Martha Bianco, *Effects of Light Rail Transit in Portland: Implications for Transit-Oriented Developement Design Concepts* (Portland, OR: Center for Urban Studies, 1998), p. 2, http://www.upa.pdx.edu/CUS/PUBS/PDFs/DP97-7.pdf.
7. Linda McDonnell, "Metro looks for help to put developments on track," *Daily Journal of Commerce*, April 9, 1998, p. 3.
8. Robin Franzen and Brent Hunsberger, "Oregon's land-use rules have city folks feeling too tightly packed," *The Oregonian*, December 13, 1998, p. A1.
9. Bob Young, "Runaway Train," *Willamette Week*, January 28, 1998, pp. 14–15.
10. Kara Briggs, "Council Approves Tax Break for Apartments," *The Oregonian*, October 25, 1995, p. C2.
11. Kara Briggs, "Gresham Pushes Auxiliary Downtown Project," *The Oregonian*, September 23, 1997, p. C2.
12. Harry Esteve, "Gresham decides to take new path on central project," *The Oregonian*, August 7, 1999, p. C1.
13. Kara Briggs, "Gresham Nudges Apartments Plan Up the Scale," *The Oregonian*, June 27, 1995, B2.
14. *The Oregonian*, "The Round: White elephant or diamond in the rough?" *The Oregonian*, May 1, 1999.
15. Aaron Fentress, "Beaverton pays to save Round," *The Oregonian*, July 23, 1999.

The Auto-Dependency Myth

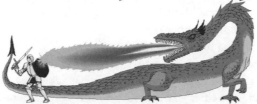

Myth: Poorly designed neighborhoods force people to be dependent on expensive, polluting automobiles.

Reality: Modern suburbs reflect people's preferences for the increased mobility provided by the automobile.

The automobile enabled people to leave the crowded, polluted city, but it exacted a price: Suburbanites are now forced to drive to anywhere they want to go. This means that the suburbs are unlivable for those who cannot drive, such as children and many seniors, and expensive for those who can. As Jane Holtz Kay says, the freedom promised by autos "is reduced by the servitude of a car-bound society that denies movement any other way."[1]

"In most American cities," claims Andres Duany, "the worst traffic is to be found not downtown but in the surrounding suburbs."[2] Duany cites no evidence for this and it is probably not true. But Anthony Downs suggests that "the dominant vision" of urban America "generates excessive travel." "A pattern of single-family housing and low-density workplaces spreads homes and jobs widely. People have to travel long distances from where they live to where they work, shop, or play."[3] Because of this, Downs continues, there is "more traffic congestion, expense, time spent driving, and air pollution." So Downs thinks "it is reasonable to conclude that people are traveling much more than they would prefer."[4]

This "reasonable conclusion" is based on several assumptions:
1. People get no pleasure from driving (see the Accessibility Myth, p. 109);
2. Driving is very expensive (see the Cost-of-Driving Myth, p. 117);
3. People would drive less if they lived in more compact, mixed-use cities;
4. So low-density suburbs are responsible for congestion and air pollution.

If low-density suburbs make people auto dependent, then it must follow that people drive significantly less in higher-density parts of the same urban areas. If not, then the whole idea that increasing densities will reduce auto dependency is wrong. This is the main argument of this book, and different chapters and myths will examine it from many different angles. The simple answer is: Yes, people who live in higher density areas do drive a little less, but *not* because they live in higher

densities. Instead, they want to drive less and so they choose to live in neighborhoods where they can minimize driving.

MIT planner Paul Schimek studied this question and found that "greater neighborhood residential density is associated with lower household vehicle travel," but
that this was mostly explained by "income and household size."[5] For example,
one-and two-person households were more likely to locate in higher density areas
than families with children. Other factors may account for much of the remaining reductions in driving found in higher densities.

The 1990 census asked one out of six households how the workers in those
households went to work. The Census Bureau has tabulated their answers for
each of 23,435 different cities, towns, villages, and unincorporated places in the
U.S. A comparison of densities with the share of people who drove to work reveals
that doubling the density of the average place reduces auto commuting by less
than 0.03 percent. The correlation between the two sets of numbers is no better
than random (statistically, r-squared is 0.004).

The Department of Housing and Urban Development notes that "the average
suburban household drives approximately 30 percent more annually than its central city counterpart."[6] The department calls this a "cost of sprawl." But maybe it
is a benefit of suburbanization; maybe they are going somewhere they like. Maybe
the city residents would like to go places too, but can't because there is too much
congestion. Or maybe the people who live in the cities don't like to drive, but the
people who live in the suburbs do. In any case, the simple fact that some people
drive more than others does not mean that they are suffering.

In nearly every urban area in America, people have a choice between low-
density suburbs and moderate- to high-density central cities. For those who want
to drive less, there are plenty of homes in inner-city neighborhoods that are well
served by mass transit. If these densities were really popular and convenient, home
builders would fall all over themselves to replicate them elsewhere. But in most
places, the demand for higher densities is satisfied by the densities that already
exist in the cities.

Notes

1. Jane Holtz Kay, *Asphalt Nation: How the Automobile Took over America and How We Can
   Take It Back* (New York, NY: Crown, 1997), p. 26.
2. Andres Duany, Elizabeth Plater-Zyberk, and Jeff Speck, *Suburban Nation: The Rise of
   Sprawl and the Decline of the American Dream* (New York, NY: North Point Press, 2000),
   p. 22.
3. Anthony Downs, *New Visions for Metropolitan America* (Washington, DC: Brookings
   Institution, 1994), p. 7.
4. Ibid, p. 8.
5. Paul Schimek, *Household Motor Vehicle Ownership and Use: How Much Does Residential
   Density Matter?* (Washington, DC: Transportation Research Board, 1996).
6. HUD, *State of the Cities 1999* (Washington, DC: HUD, 1999), p. iv.

The Accessibility Myth

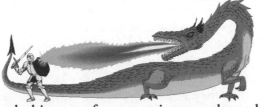

Myth: People only drive to get from one point to another and would be glad to avoid driving if neighborhoods were better designed.

Reality: Many people enjoy the journey and prefer to live some distance away from work, shopping, and other urban areas.

"Why go anywhere?" asks University of California planning Professor Robert Cervero. "Millions of people could be liberated from their vehicles" if neighborhoods were redesigned to make things accessible without requiring mobility.[1] Cervero says it is "axiomatic" that "the physical act of traveling is a derived behavior." In other words, "people travel to engage in activities at other places—work, recreation, shopping, worship, health care, and so on—not because they wish to ride a car or bus."[2] The transportation planner's goal, Cervero argues, should be to increase accessibility, not mobility. This means locating things that people need—jobs, stores, parks, schools—close to home.

Smart-growth advocates distinguish between *mobility* and *accessibility*. The first is the ability to move around; the second the ability to reach desired destinations. Smart-growth planners say that data showing that Americans drive more each year only show that urban areas are increasingly dysfunctional: People shouldn't have to travel around so much to do the things they want to do.

This seems so sensible, especially to young college students used to living in an apartment above a grocery store a few blocks from campus in high-density Berkeley. But can we really put everything people want—restaurants, supermarkets, variety stores, specialty shops, doctors' offices, hospitals, libraries, daycare centers, schools, parks, swimming pools, hiking areas, offices, factories, government buildings, friends, family, community centers, and everything else—all within walking distance or at most a convenient rail transit trip away from residential areas? The answer is almost certainly "No."

Just as questionable is Cervero's fundamental premise. Is travel merely a "derived behavior"? Do people move around only because they have to, not because they enjoy the wind in their hair and the comfort of their private auto, as the ads for BMW, Acura, Jeep, and so many other auto makers would have us believe?

Sociologist Herbert Gans found that suburbanites do "not share the critics' and the planners' distaste for commuting." In fact, he found the most dissatisfaction among people who used transit. Gans also found that "longer hours on the job" were more significant than commute length in keeping employees from spending time with their families.[3]

More recently, University of California engineering Professor Patricia Mohktarian and Hebrew University geography Professor Ilam Salomon point out that "recreational travel has been an outgrowth of virtually every means of transportation ever known. . . consider horseback riding or sailing."[4] Why not the automobile or transit? Transportation analysts have long known about "joyriding"—driving solely for the pleasure of going somewhere. Census data and other information show that U.S. commute times average about 22 minutes.[5] Mohktarian and Salomon surveyed 1,900 households in the San Francisco Bay Area and found that people preferred an average commute time of 16 minutes—only a little less than average. Three out of four commuters said that they often drove out of their way to explore new places or just for the fun of it.[6]

"Some people just love to go, even when they're going nowhere in particular," conclude Mohktarian and Salomon. Nor is the "thirst for mobility. . . peculiar to Americans or Californians," as Mohktarian and Salomon point out that studies in Australia, Israel, and elsewhere reached similar conclusions.[7]

"The view that a path to an explicit goal is worthy of architectural concern, whereas a path without an apparent goal is not, has led to an unrealistic nostalgia among some architects and critics for a preindustrial pedestrian-dominated world," says architecture critic Craig Whitaker. Most people agree that travel is more than just a nuisance, something to be avoided whenever possible. "Americans already believe the climax of the trip has no special meaning," continues Whitaker. "Inasmuch as life is an unending journey, the end, as it were, is simply a place to turn around and start back in the opposite direction."[8]

Notes

1. Robert Cervero, "Why Go Anywhere?" in *Fifty Years of City and Regional Planning at UC Berkeley: A Celebratory Anthology of Faculty Essays* (Berkeley, CA: Department of City and Regional Planning, 1998).
2. Robert Cervero, "Tracking Accessibility," *Access* 11 (Fall, 1997): p. 27.
3. Herbert J. Gans, *The Levittowners: Ways of Life and Politics in a New Suburban Community* (New York, NY: Pantheon, 1967), p. 222.
4. Patricia Mokhtarian and Ilam Salomon, "Travel for the Fun of It," *Access*, 15 (Fall 1999): p. 27.
5. Alan Pisarski, *Commuting in America II* (Washington, DC: Eno, 1996) , p. 85.
6. Mohktarian and Salomon, "Travel for the Fun of It," p. 29.
7. Ibid, p. 31.
8. Craig Whitaker, *Architecture and the American Dream* (New York, NY: Potter, 1996), p. 188, p. 244.

Congestion Signals Positive Urban Development

Between 1990 and 1998, the population of the greater Portland area grew by 25 percent, but the miles driven in the region grew by 52 percent.[1] According to a report issued by the Oregon Department of Transportation, "suburban development and highway construction contributed to" this increase in driving, "but were not the primary causes." Instead, the main causes were "population, employment, and income increases." Because huge increases in driving were accompanied by only a tiny increase in new road capacity, says the report, the region experienced a 140 percent increase in travel delay due to congestion between 1982 and 1994.[2] The report concludes that "Large increases in highway capacity will be needed to avoid growing congestion unless Oregonians agree to substantially reduce their personal mobility."[3]

Yet a substantial reduction in mobility appears to be Metro's goal. Metro anticipates a 70-percent increase in population within the urban-growth boundary, but proposes to build only 14 percent new lane miles of roads. In fact, the agency's *Regional Transportation Plan* will probably result in a net decrease in road capacities because it proposes to turn many major arterials and collectors into "boulevards"—meaning existing lanes will be removed and various barriers placed in the roads to slow traffic.

Traditional transportation planning places a high priority on congestion reduction, second only to maintaining safety. But Metro says that "the 2040 Growth Concept requires a departure from past transportation planning practice." The agency wants to minimize congestion around "industrial areas and intermodal facilities" because the region's "continued economic vitality. . . largely depends on preserving or improving access to these areas and maintaining reasonable levels of mobility on the region's throughways." Elsewhere, however, the 2040 plan's concentrations of housing and jobs will "produce levels of congestion that signal positive urban development for these areas."[4]

Highway engineers give letter grades A through F to traffic conditions or *levels of service*: A is about 30 percent of a road's capacity, B is 50 percent, C is 75 percent, D is 90 percent, E is 100 percent, and F is near gridlock. Levels of service

A through C allow normal speeds, but to achieve the higher flows of D and E cars must drive closer together and so drivers slow down. Because E is at capacity, traffic flows are unstable and any small disruption can quickly lead to stop-and-go traffic, or level of service F. Traditional traffic engineers generally aim for level of service C or at worst D and base construction priorities on meeting these goals.

Metro's own mobility standards consider level of service F to be acceptable on many of Portland's major freeways as well as the central city, in the centers, main streets, and light-rail station areas. Metro states that "this level of congestion is acceptable in these 2040 Design Types because the opportunity to use alternative modes of travel is greatest in these areas."[5] In fact, it adds, "transportation solutions aimed solely at relieving congestion are inappropriate" in these areas.[6] Service level E, which traffic engineers previously considered unacceptable during peak hours, is actually considered acceptable during midday periods in these same areas as well as at peak hours everywhere else.

Table Two: Metro's Mobility Standards
(Acceptable Level of Service)

Location	Midday Peak	AM/PM Peak Hour
Concept areas[1]	E	F
Major freeways[2]	E	F
Other Principal Arterials	D	E
Other areas[3]	D	E

1. Central Portland, regional and town centers, light-rail station areas, and main streets.
2. Interstate 5 north of downtown, Interstate 84, Interstate 405, U.S. 26, & 99E from downtown to highway 224.
3. Including corridors, industrial areas, and neighborhoods.
   Source: Metro, Regional Transportation Plan (Portland, OR: Metro, November, 1999), p. 1-29.

When asked why planners designated some freeways F and others (such as Interstate 5 south of downtown) E, Metro transportation planning director Andy Cotugno said that the F freeways are paralleled by existing or proposed light-rail lines, while the E freeways were not. Increasing highway capacities on the F freeways, he stated, "would eliminate transit ridership."[7] He also warned that adding new freeway capacity would be expensive, but neglected to mention that it would be less expensive than building Metro's proposed light-rail lines.

Beyond minimizing the need to reduce congestion on major freeways, the new mobility standards actually allow Metro and the state to reduce roadway capacities in many places. Metro's plan calls for turning numerous arterial and collector roads into *boulevards*.[8] This means reducing the number of lanes of travel, using curb extensions to block former right-turn lanes, replacing left-turn lanes with median barriers, widening sidewalks, and adding bike lanes.[9] The state has already budgeted such changes for several state highways in the Portland area. Numerous streets that Metro's *Regional Transportation Plan* designates as "major arterials for motor vehicles" are slated for such downgrading, including Beaverton-Hillsdale Highway, Canyon, Farmington, Interstate, King, Macadam, and Sandy, to name a few.[10] These changes will greatly increase congestion and force auto traffic to use other routes—but Metro's standards allow service level F on the major highways paralleling these arterials.

The city of Portland spends $2 million per year on traffic calming. When such projects began in the 1980s, they were limited to neighborhood streets where residents requested help to reduce speeding and accidents. But in the 1990s Portland expanded them to many busy streets, often reducing the number of lanes of traffic, reducing parking spaces, adding extensions to curbs to limit right turns, and building concrete median strips to limit left turns and other options.[11] Major routes that have already been traffic-calmed include Northeast Martin Luther King, Northeast Broadway, and parts of Sandy.

Sometimes road capacity reductions are made in conjunction with increases in residential density. Portland is spending $13 million removing one of the two ramps leading off the west end of the Broadway Bridge across the Willamette River. This will make room to build hundreds of units of high-density housing in the area. But residents of that housing will face traffic jams if they want to cross the river because half of the bridge's road capacity will be gone.[12]

The boulevards and other traffic calming measures are supposed to promote walking and cycling. Chapter 23 will show that bike paths, bike lanes, pedestrian-friendly design, and traffic calming techniques often make roads and streets more dangerous for bicyclists and pedestrians. Cycling on bike paths which mix pedestrian and bicycle traffic is considerably more dangerous than cycling in streets. Cycling on streets that have been "calmed" with traffic circles, curb extensions, and other barriers greatly increases the hazard of bicycle-auto accidents. Changing one-way streets to two-way streets increases hazards to pedestrians. Despite the rhetoric, the primary motivation for these practices is not to promote cycling and walking but to increase congestion and discourage driving.

In 1998, over the objections of local residents, the state of Oregon applied several traffic calming measures, including curb extensions and median barriers, to selected intersections on McLoughlin Avenue, state highway 99, in Oak Grove. In January 2000, a woman and her granddaughter tried to cross McLoughlin at one of these intersections. They made it to the median island. A car in the left-hand lane of the four-lane road waved them to cross, which they did. They were struck by a car in the right-hand lane which could not see them because of the car in the left lane. The woman was killed and her granddaughter injured.[13] Many local residents believe that the pedestrian refuges gave the woman a false sense of security.[14]

Metro's *1999 Regional Transportation Plan* calls for dividing the next two decades worth of the region's capital funds for transportation—an estimated $7.3

billion—as follows:
- 27 percent on light-rail and commuter-rail construction;
- 14 percent on new buses and bus facilities;
- 6 percent on bikeways, pedestrian ways, traffic calming, and subsidies for transit-oriented developments;
- 1 percent on marine or rail freight facilities;
- Leaving 52 percent for highways and roads.[15]

At least 5 of the 52 percent for roads is going for "preservation" (meaning major maintenance projects), mainly of Portland's many bridges. Another 19 percent is going for local roads, including some road widenings but also some traffic calming, bike paths, sidewalks, and freight routes. The remaining 29 percent is to be spent on "regional roads," mainly interstates and other freeways. Some of this will be spent reconstructing existing roads, but some will be spent on genuine capacity expansions.

In short, Metro plans to spend perhaps a third of the region's capital transportation budget increasing road capacities. Significantly more, roughly half, will be spent on rail, bus, bikeways, and pedestrian facilities, part of which will be spent reducing the capacities of many arterials and collectors to carry traffic. The vast majority of this money comes from highway taxes, and most of the remainder comes from taxes paid by people who frequently drive and rarely use transit. On top of this, the region's workers, 90 percent of whom drive to work, will pay well over $2 billion in payroll taxes to operate transit in the next two decades.[16]

Given this spending, Metro anticipates that average auto speeds will decline from 25 miles per hour today to 21 miles per hour in 2020. The number of hours of traffic delay due to congestion is expected to increase by more than five times.[17] In 1994 driving was faster than either bus or light-rail transit.[18] But Metro expects that by 2020 some light-rail journeys will beat auto drive times and that the time penalty for taking buses will shrink.

Table Three: Driving Indicators

	Average speed mph	Travel delay, hours	Trucking speed mph
1994	25	7,509	37.2
2020 transportation plan	21	37,690	32.6

Source: Metro, 1999 Regional Transportation Plan, tables 2.7, 2.9, 5.9, and 5.11. Speeds are during peak hours.

To further discourage auto driving, Metro has adopted strict parking limits for new developments and redeveloped areas. The agency has different limits for nineteen types of land uses, ranging from tennis courts to warehouses. The limits also vary depending on whether or not the site is in a "transit-accessible area," meaning near a transit stop with peak-hour service at least every twenty minutes. In transit-accessible areas, churches may have no more than 0.6 parking spaces per seat; movie theaters no more than 0.4 spaces per seat; and colleges and universities no more than 0.3 spaces per student or staff. Limits are only slightly higher in the rest of the region.[19]

The ultimate goal of all of these auto restrictions is to reduce auto driving and increase the number of people in those cars that remain on the road. Portland's Mayor Vera Katz says "we are losing to the traffic congestion and gridlock that too often strangles cities" because "71 percent of commuters drive alone to and from work."[20] Metro's director, Mike Burton, says more pithily that the region's transportation problems can't be solved "until people stop traveling SOV in their SUV's, which decreases the LOS and makes us SOL" (*SOV* is single-occupant vehicle, *LOS* is level of service).[21]

The state land-use goal is to reduce Portland-area per capita auto driving by 15 percent. The state's highway plan specifically sets a goal of reducing the number of commuters driving alone to 62 percent.[22] Metro's goals are even more ambitious: It wants to reduce single-occupancy driving to less than 40 percent of trips to and within central Portland and less than 55 percent to and within centers, station areas, main streets, and corridors. That covers just about all travel in the Portland area. The single-occupancy goal for travel to and within industrial areas and residential neighborhoods is only 60 percent, but very little driving stays strictly within these areas. To help achieve these goals, Metro has ambitious plans for Portland-area transit.

"Congestion is bad and getting worse," worries Burton. "It's a nightmare for commuters" that has increased travel delay by "37 percent in 5 years."[23] Yet rather than admit that his agency's policies are responsible for this, he prefers to lecture Portlanders on why they should stop driving.

Notes

1. Federal Highway Administration, *Highway Statistics 1990* and *Highway Statistics 1998* (Washington, DC: FHwA, 1991 and 1999), table HM-72.
2. Brian Gregor, *Statewide Congestion Overview for Oregon* (Salem, OR: ODOT, 1998), p. 2.
3. Ibid, p. 3.
4. Metro, *Regional Transportation Plan Update* (Portland, OR: Metro, 1996), p. 1-20.
5. Metro, *Regional Framework Plan* (Portland, OR: Metro, December, 1997), p. 74.
6. Metro, *1999 Regional Transportation Plan* (Portland, OR: Metro, November, 1999), p. 6-38.
7. Metro, "Minutes of the Metro Council Transportation Planning Committee Meeting," July 18, 2000, p. 7.
8. Metro, *1999 Regional Transportation Plan*, p. 1-17.
9. Ibid, p. 1-21.
10. Metro, *1999 Regional Transportation Plan*, p. 1-27 and figures 5-11 through 5-16.
11. City of Portland, "Traffic Calming Home Page," http://www.trans.ci.portland.or.us/Traffic_Management/trafficcalming/default.htm.

12. Bill Stewart, "Lovejoy Ramp will soon be a memory," *The Oregonian*, June 10, 1999.

13. *The Oregonian*, "Van hurts girl, kills woman crossing street," January 18, 2000.

14. Richard Jones, personal communication, January 19, 2000.

15. Metro, "RTP Project Lists," January 28, 2000.

16. Federal Transit Administration, *Transit Profiles, Agencies in Urbanized Areas Exceeding 200,000 Population: 1997 Report Year* (Washington, DC: FTA, 1998), p. 200. Payroll taxes covered $106 million of Tri-Met operation costs in 1997; over two decades this will add up to well over $2 billion.

17. Metro, *1999 Regional Transportation Plan*, p. 5-5.

18. Ibid, p. 2-17.

19. Metro, *Urban Growth Management Functional Plan* (Portland, OR: Metro, November, 1996), p. 43.

20. Vera Katz, "2000 State of the City Address," January 28, 2000, http://www.ci.portland.or.us/mayor/press4/soc2000spc.htm.

21. Mike Burton, "State of the Region Address," January 7, 2000, http://www.multnomah.lib.or.us/metro/glance/exec/cityclub00.html

22. ODOT, *1999 Oregon Highway Plan*, http://www.odot.state.or.us/tdb/planning/highway/vision.doc.

23. Mike Burton, "State of the Region Address."

The Cost-of-Driving Myth

Myth: Automobiles are a costly burden forced on Americans by poor urban design and sprawl.
Reality: Over most urban distances, the automobile is the most efficient and convenient transport mode ever devised.

Auto opponents frequently decry the costs of automobiles without acknowledging that they provide any compensating benefits. One favored technique is to point to the per mile cost of auto ownership calculated by the U.S. Department of Transportation or some other authority. For example, in 1996, a subcompact car was estimated to cost 32 cents per mile, while a full-sized sports-utility vehicle was estimated to cost 45 cents per mile.[1] This cost assumes that someone borrows money to buy a brand-new car, repays the loan over five years, and drives the car less than 12,000 miles per year.

In fact, many of these costs are fixed costs, including depreciation, finance charges, and insurance. People who drive more miles per year, own the car longer than five years, buy a used car, or pay off the car in less than five years will substantially reduce these fixed costs per mile. Partly because of increased competition between auto manufacturers, higher-quality autos have allowed Americans to reduce costs by keeping cars longer or buying older used cars.[2] The average age of a car in the U.S. increased from 5.6 years in 1970 to 8.6 years in 1996.[3] This trend has also brought auto ownership within reach of lower income families.

Actual operating costs, including fuel, maintenance, and repairs, average only about 12 cents per mile; used cars cost slightly more per mile to operate than new ones.[4] When counting cost per passenger mile, autos are even less expensive: about 7.5 cents per mile for the average trip, which carries about 1.6 people. This is far lower than typical transit fares, which average about 20 cents per mile.

Of course, car owners must ultimately pay both the fixed and variable costs of driving. But after they make a decision to purchase a car, whether it is primarily for commuting, driving the kids to school, or intercity driving, then they naturally consider only the variable cost for any additional driving they do. People who buy their first cars after years of riding transit often find that transit rarely makes much sense anymore.

This is because autos are not only inexpensive, they are fast and flexible. For most people, automobiles excel for carrying passengers and up to several hundred pounds of goods over any distance from less than half a mile to several hundred miles.

- Bicycling makes sense only for short distances and walking for even shorter distances. Neither are good at carrying any but the smallest packages.
- Transit is slow and only goes to certain locations. Autos are not only faster than transit, the difference between the two is increasing. In 1983, auto commuters averaged 30.2 miles per hour, 69 percent faster than transit. By 1995, auto commuters averaged 35.4 miles per hour, or 83 percent faster than transit.[5]
- Airplanes are expensive and door-to-door time is not much faster than autos for trips under 200 or so miles.

Automobiles have other advantages over transit. University of California (Davis) sociology Professor J. F. Scott notes that autos are "status enhancing" while transit is "degrading." The role of autos as status symbols may make them more expensive than necessary if people buy new cars before the old ones are worn out. But that is not a cost of driving; it is a cost of the status symbol. Meanwhile, the demand of most transit systems for such things as exact change "is itself a form of status insult," says Scott.[6] Imagine car dealers or gasoline stations that would only sell their products to people who had exact change!

The higher speeds and extraordinarily low operating cost of autos frustrates auto opponents; they feel it is somehow unfair and that automobile owners should be penalized for enjoying such low transportation costs. Yet it is a fact of life: For most urban and shorter interurban trips, automobiles provide greater benefits and cost less to operate than any other mode of transportation.

Notes

1. Federal Highway Administration, *Our Nation's Highways: Selected Facts and Figures* (Washington, DC: FHwA, 1998), p. 14.
2. Don Pickrell and Paul Schimek, *Trends in Personal Motor Vehicle Ownership and Use: Evidence from the Nationwide Personal Transportation Survey* (Cambridge, MA: USDOT, 1998), p. 21.
3. Ibid, p. 13.
4. Anonymous, "New Car Driving Costs Increase Slightly for Southern Californians," http://www.theautochannel.com/news/press/date/19990729/press027453.html.
5. Patricia Hu and Jennifer Young, *Draft Summary of Travel Trends: 1995 Nationwide Personal Transportation Survey* (Oak Ridge, TN: US DOE, 1999), table 25, http://www-cta.ornl.gov/npts/1995/Doc/trends_reportl8.pdf.
6. J. F. Scott, email "Re: Transit vs Freeway Capacity," to transport-policy group, 25 January 2000.

The Costs of Smart Growth

Metro has apparently succeeded at slowing highway expansion, building light-rail lines, shrinking house lot sizes, and building more multi-family dwellings. But these are only means to an end, and the end is supposed to be a more livable Portland. By objective standards of livability—including congestion, pollution, the cost of living, and accessible open space—Metro's plan is a spectacular failure.

Travel habits: Metro itself predicts that its plan will fail to attract significant numbers of people out of their automobiles. Using a state-of-the-art transportation computer model, Metro planners predicted in 1995 that the effects of density, rail transit, traffic calming, and transit-oriented development on driving habits would be minimal: a 5-percent decline in per capita driving (table four).

Table Four: Trip Shares in 1990 and 2040
(percent of trips inside the urban-growth boundary)

	1990	2040	Percent Change
Auto	92.1	87.8	−4.6
Transit	2.8	6.4	129.5
Walk/bike	5.2	5.8	12.8

Source: Metro, Region 2040 Technical Appendix, *Transportation tables.*

Metro's *1999 Regional Transportation Plan* provides more recent estimates of the effects of Metro's plans on travel by the year 2020. They are not much different: Assuming Metro gets as much funding as it would like for transit, transit's market share doubles, walking/cycling increases by 30 percent, driving decreases by 6 percent.[1] Given the smaller amount of transit funds actually available, transit's share increases by only 15 percent, so driving loses just 2.7 percent market share.[2] In either case, Metro predicts that per capita miles driven will increase by 2 to 4 percent, which is extremeley optimistic considering that the *annual* increase in per capita miles driven has not been much less than 2 percent per year.

In short, Metro predicts that huge changes in land use and major investments in transit result in insignificant changes in travel habits. Even this prediction may be optimistic. Metro's model assumes that travel habits depend on such factors as age, household size, income, education, housing density, and pedestrian-friendly design. The model would predict that a family of four of particular income and education living in a low-density suburban neighborhood would, if moved to a high-density transit-oriented development, start to behave the same as families of four with similar incomes and educations who already live in high-density areas. While this is better than simply basing predictions on density, the fact remains that personal preference does not enter into the model. Ultimately, the model assumes that, for any given family, density has a greater influence on travel habits than preference. If it turns out that people of a given age and family size who prefer to drive less have chosen to live in high-density areas so they can live without driving, the model will overestimate the reduction in driving when other people are forced to live in such housing.

This error is suggested by the fact that the actual increase in Portland-area driving since planners began putting the plan into effect have been greater than Metro predicted. The 1995 predictions started from a 1990 baseline, while the 1999 transportation plan starts from a 1994 base. According to the Federal Highway Administration (using data provided by state departments of transportation), between 1990 and 1998 Portland-area auto owners increased per capita miles driven by 21 percent. The increase from 1994 to 1998 was 4 percent—the amount Metro predicted would take place by 2020. If there are any further increases at all, then Metro's predictions of congestion will be underestimated.

Congestion: If Metro succeeds in reducing per capita driving by 5 percent, it will not do much to reduce congestion considering that Metro also expects a 70-percent increase in population. Since Metro plans only a 14-percent increase in lane miles of roads, planners predict a tripling of congestion by 2040.[3] As noted in table three, above, the 1999 transportation plan says that congestion in 2020 will reduce average auto speeds from 25 to 21 miles per hour and quintuple the number of hours that auto drivers spend in congestion.[4]

The Texas Transportation Institute estimates that the number of hours the average Portland-area driver sat in congestion nearly doubled between 1990 and 1997. The total dollar cost of congestion, calculates the institute, nearly tripled during this time period.[5] If the institute is correct, Portland-area congestion in seven years already went a considerable way to the tripling predicted by Metro in fifty years.

Air pollution: With congestion comes increased air pollution. While Metro uses a state-of-the-art transportation model, its air pollution model is less credible. It does not accurately account the extra pollution generated at the slow speeds experienced in stop-and-go traffic.[6] Its pollution predictions are therefore based mostly on the number of miles driven, not the traffic conditions in which driving takes place. Even so, the model predicts a 10-percent increase in nitrogen oxides, a component of smog.[7] Other pollutants are expected to decline, but the model probably underestimates pollution that will be produced by congestion.

Housing costs: A third area in which Metro's plan imposes clear costs on Port-land-area residents is housing. Since 1990, the price of an acre of land available for housing developments has grown from $20,000 to upwards of $200,000. By 1996, the land shortage was so acute that *The Oregonian* reported that every major home builder in the region was "now aware of every single buildable parcel of 10 acres and up inside the Portland area's urban growth boundary," including who owned it and whether they might want to sell it. As a result, housing prices more than doubled and in some parts of the region they tripled.

The National Association of Home Builders publishes a quarterly index rating the affordability of nearly 200 U.S. housing markets. The index is based on the percentage of families in an urban area that can afford a median-priced home. The group also compares the median home price with the median income in each housing market. In 1989, all four Oregon housing markets on the list—Portland, Salem, Eugene, and Medford—were among the nation's fifty most affordable housing markets. By 1996, Portland was the second least affordable housing market—after San Francisco—and the other three were among the twenty least affordable. Oregon cities have been among the twenty least affordable markets ever since.

Defenders of Metro and the urban-growth boundary say that the increase in housing prices is due solely to growth and has nothing to do with the land supply. But many urban areas which are growing much faster than Portland have much more affordable housing. From 1990 to 1998, the nation's fastest growing urban area was Las Vegas, which grew more than twice as fast as Portland. Yet the home builders estimate that 67 percent of Las Vegas families can afford a median priced home, compared with just 33 percent in Portland. Phoenix and Atlanta each grew considerably faster than Portland, yet the percentage of families in those cities that can afford to buy a home is even greater than Las Vegas.[8]

Metro expects the region to add about 360,000 new households by the year 2040.[9] Assuming half of these buy single-family homes, and assuming that the land premium due to the urban-growth boundary averages $20,000 per home—both assumptions are very conservative—then the urban-growth boundary is adding $3.6 billion to the cost of housing. Of course, this cost is realized by landowners and developers in the form of windfall profits, but it still represents a huge and unnecessary transfer of wealth which will probably be, on average, from poorer to richer people.

Intentionally or not, unaffordable housing actually helps Metro achieve its density goals. With land prices artificially inflated, home buyers are more willing to consider living on smaller lots. With house prices artificially inflated, new residents are more willing to consider living in multifamily housing.

In sharp contrast to the cost of home ownership, Portland apartment rentals have barely kept up with inflation. At the end of 1999, the apartment market was considered "saturated," and vacancy rates were high. Spurred by high-density zoning and subsidies, developers built 31,000 new multifamily units between 1995 and 1999. By early 1999, vacancy rates were at 7 percent, their highest in the decade, and reached 11 percent for apartments built in the 1990s. To attract tenants, apartment owners were offering a free month's rent on a year's lease, amenities such as computer labs and community kitchens, free cable, and high-speed internet hookups. Where house prices had doubled in the 1990s, apartment rents grew by a measly 31 percent.[10] After deducting inflation, they were actually declining.[11]

Some of the people who suffer the most from Portland's distorted housing market are low-income people and potential first-time home buyers. One of the quirks of the market is that housing prices have risen the fastest in low-income neighborhoods as people with higher incomes buy the only homes they can afford. A study by the Coalition for a Livable Future found that, between 1990 and 1996, home prices in some parts of Portland tripled, while they at least doubled in much of the rest of the city.[12] Increases in poverty rates in other parts of the city led the group to speculate that home prices forced many low-income people, particularly renters, to move out of their homes and neighborhoods to other, lower-priced parts of the region. Many also probably moved to smaller homes or apartments. The coalition, of course, refuses to blame the urban-growth boundary for this problem and recommends that it be solved by forcing developers to build low-income housing.[13]

Portland's response is to require builders of more than sixteen housing units to include a certain percentage of low-income housing in the development. This is known as *inclusionary zoning*. This assuages liberal consciences, but at the existing rate of construction it will take hundreds of years for all low-income families to benefit. In the meantime, everyone else's housing costs—including the vast majority of low-income people not fortunate enough to find a mandated low-income housing unit—go up as they have to subsidize the low-income homes.

Other consumer costs: So far it is too early to tell, but it is likely that Metro's restrictions on retailing will drive up the cost of groceries and other consumer goods. Large stores tend to offer lower prices, greater selection, and have a higher turnover, which means that they sell fresher produce and other perishables. Yet under Metro's plan, no new large stores can be built in Portland. Instead, pedestrian- and transit-bound residents of high-density and mixed-use neighborhoods are expected to shop and smaller grocery stores and other shops.

Stunting growth: Regional leaders credit the livability created by Portland-area planners for the region's rapid growth. Yet the fact is that Portland and Oregon have been growing slower than many other western communities and states that have little or no regional planning or smart-growth policies. Between 1990 and 1999, Las Vegas, Reno, Phoenix, Denver, Boise, Colorado Springs, and Olympia urban areas all grew faster than any urban area in Oregon. During the same time period, the relatively unregulated Washington portion of the Portland-Vancouver metropolitan area grew faster than even the fastest-growing county in the Oregon portion (table two). Meanwhile, Washington, Idaho, Utah, Colorado, and Arizona all grew faster than Oregon.[14] No-growth advocates may cheer at Portland's slower growth, but when that slower growth is combined with faster-growing congestion and unaffordable housing, there is little to cheer about.

Table Two: Growth of Portland-Area Counties, 1990–1999

County	Percent Growth
Clark County, Washington	41.3
Clackamas County, Oregon	21.3
Multnomah County, Oregon	8.4
Washington County, Oregon	31.4

Source: Census Bureau.

Taxes: Although density advocates claim that high-density cities have lower urban service costs than low-density areas, Metro and local governments are imposing huge costs on local taxpayers to pay for transit and subsidize high-density housing. Portland-area transit operations are paid for out of a payroll tax that gives Portland transit riders some of the highest subsidies in the nation. The local share of Portland's west-side light-rail line was paid for out of a property tax approved by voters in 1990.

When voters turned down a similar property tax to pay for the north light-rail line, Portland created a tax-increment finance district to pay for it instead. This means that all future increases in tax revenues from land and improvements in a broad area around the light-rail line will be used to repay the costs of building the line. Those increases otherwise would have gone to pay for local schools, police, fire, and other services—services that now must be reduced or paid for by taxpayers elsewhere in the region.

Similar schemes, including tax waivers, developer impact fees, and sales of public land to private developers at below-market rates, have been used to entice developers to build high-density transit-oriented developments. The costs, of course, are passed on to other taxpayers in the area. Finally, property taxes are repaying $135 million worth of bonds used to purchase open space—most of which is outside of the urban area and will not be accessible to most local residents.

Given all of these problems, it is hard to see why anyone would support Metro's smart-growth plan. In fact, the plan creates new enemies every time one of the cities or counties in the Portland area rezones a new neighborhood. Portland-area residents are beginning to understand that Metro's real goal is to create congestion, not reduce it. Despite strong opposition from land-use planning supporters, a citizens' group called Oregonians in Action, convinced Oregon voters to pass a measure requiring compensation whenever the state or local government passes a rule, such as a zoning ordinance, that reduces the value of someone's property.[15] The same group has petitioned to place a measure on the March, 2001, ballot that would strip Metro of its authority to dictate densities and other planning goals to local jurisdictions. Metro is enough worried about this measure that it is spending hundreds of thousands of dollars on a public relations campaign.[16]

Around the world, nations that have turned their economies over to central planners ended up with surpluses of things that no one wanted and shortages of goods and services that people did want. What makes Metro's plan special is that the shortages of road capacity, single-family housing, and urban open spaces and surpluses of rail transit, apartments, and rural open spaces are all deliberately contrived and ideologically based. Time will tell whether Metro survives voter challenges and if local residents truly come to see the area as more livable. But residents are keenly aware of the increasing congestion, unaffordable housing, and disappearing urban open space even if many do not yet understand that Metro's planning is responsible.

Notes

1. Metro, *1999 Regional Transportation Plan*, table 5.10, http://www.multnomah.lib.or.us/metro/transpo/highcap/rtp/rtp.html.
2. Ibid, table 2.8.
3. Metro, *Region 2040 Technical Appendix*, Transportation tables.
4. Metro, *1999 Regional Transportation Plan*, tables 2.7, 2.9, 5.9, and 5.11. Speeds are during peak hours.
5. Texas Transportation Institute, Mobility spreadsheet for Portland, 1999, http://mobility.tamu.edu/study/XLSs/portland.xls.
6. Jean Sumida, *Link Based Emission Calculation Methodology* (Portland, OR: Metro, 1995), p. 5.
7. Metro, *Metro 2040 Growth Concept* (Portland, OR: Metro, 1994), exhibit C, page 19.
8. National Association of Home Builders, *Housing Opportunity Index: First Quarter 2000* (Washington, DC: NAHB, 2000), http://www.nahb.com/facts/hoi/2000_1Q/complete_ranking.htm.
9. Metro, *Region 2040 Technical Appendix*, table 7.
10. Gordon Oliver, "Apartment hunters move in on deals," *The Oregonian*, December 6, 1999.
11. Alan Pulaski, "Freebies await westside renters," *The Oregonian*, April 18, 1998, p. A1, A10.
12. Coalition for a Livable Future, *Displacement: The Dismantling of a Community* (Portland, OR: CLF, 1999), "What Does the Data Show?" http://www.clfuture.org/displacement/data.html.
13. Ibid, "We Can Fight Displacement," http://www.clfuture.org/displacement/resources.html.
14. Census Bureau, "Population Estimates," http://www.census.gov/population/www/estimates/popest.html.
15. Charles Beggs, "Property compensation measure passes," *The Oregonian*, November 8, 2000, http://www.oregonlive.com/electionsflash/index.ssf?/cgi-free/getstory_ssf.cgi?o0057_BC_OR-ELN--PropertyCompe&&news&vote2000-loc.
16. R. Gregory Nokes, "Campaign in Works to Polish Metro's Image," *The Oregonian*, October 7, 1999.

Part Three

U.S. DEPARTMENT OF HOUSING AND URBAN DEVELOPMENT

DEPARTMENT OF TRANSPORTATION · UNITED STATES OF AMERICA

UNITED STATES ENVIRONMENTAL PROTECTION AGENCY

The Congestion Coalition

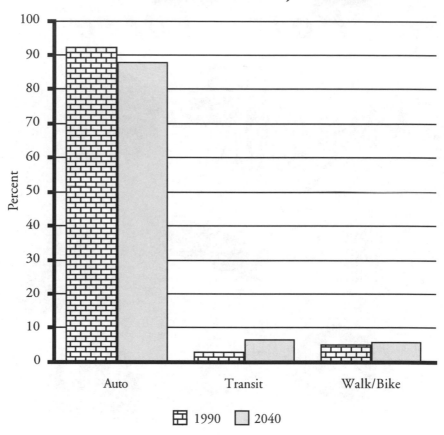

Portland-Area Travel in 1990 and Projected for 2040

Percent

| | Auto | Transit | Walk/Bike |

⊞ 1990   ▢ 2040

After increasing the density within Portland's urban-growth boundary by 70 percent, building and operating a total of 120 miles of rail lines, promoting the construction of scores of transit-oriented developments, and traffic calming dozens of travel corridors, Metro planners project that transit usage will double and walking and bicycling will increase slightly. But the auto's share of regional travel will fall by only about 5 percent. With 80 percent more people, this means there will be 70 percent more miles driven each day. Metro projects that the number of miles of congested roads will triple and the time Portlanders spend waiting in traffic will more than quintuple. Source: Metro, Region 2040 Plan technical appendix.

6. A Grassroots Movement?

The war on sprawl is "a real, grass-roots effort," says the *Christian Science Monitor*. "Because their favorite ribbon of remote highway has become a line of cookie-cutter housing tracts or strip malls, Americans in every state are saying, 'enough is enough.'"[1] The newspaper cited, among other evidence, the Brookings Institution study that claimed that voters passed hundreds of anti-sprawl ballot measures in the November, 1998, election, plus the fact that "a record 1,000 state land-use reform bills have been introduced in legislatures across the country."

In fact, smart growth is not a grassroots movement. A true grassroots movement is supported, funded, and motivated by large numbers of people in a wide variety of regions, locales, and walks of life. The smart-growth movement is a coalition of elites, heavily funded by a few foundations and several government bureaucracies. These interests often have hidden agendas which are very different from the goals they claim for smart growth. In political campaigns, for example, a major source of support comes from corporations that stand to profit from urban rail construction and other smart-growth projects.

This is not to say that the smart-growth movement is monolithic. Instead, it is a loose coalition of professionals, bureaucrats, elected officials, nonprofit organizations, and business interests. Each has its own agenda, but they have learned to share one another's rhetoric. For example, the Sierra Club will fret that "sprawl erodes the city's tax base"[2] when it really cares much more about preserving rural open space, while former Albuquerque Mayor David Rusk will pay lip service to the effects of low-density development on open space when his real goal is adding suburban tax bases to central city budgets.[3]

Many smart-growth advocates have the best of intentions and truly want to create livable cities and neighborhoods. Many others have hidden agendas. Some are idealists and moralists who dislike autos and low-density lifestyles. Others are businesses that hope to make money from rail construction, neighborhood redevelopment, or other aspects of the smart-growth agenda. Still others are government officials seeking to expand their jurisdictions or budgets. The core smart-growth agenda—density, rail transit, anti-auto measures, land-use planning, and

regional government—has evolved to meet the goals and needs of all these supporters.

Despite the claims of smart-growth advocates, increased densities combined
with anti-auto measures such as narrow streets and parking restrictions will be
certain to increase urban congestion. Though it seems hard to believe that anyone
would want more congestion, it turns out that most members of the smart-growth
coalition will benefit from such congestion. Indeed, it is just as accurate to call it
the *congestion coalition* as the smart-growth coalition.

Few will admit to supporting congestion and some may not even realize that
the policies they advocate will increase congestion. But the twin goals of smart
growth—increased urban densities and decreased auto driving—will inevitably
increase congestion, partly because congestion is one of the tools smart growth
uses to reduce auto driving. Many smart-growth advocates hope there will be a
feedback relationship: increased congestion will lead people to drive less as well as
to live closer together so they won't need to drive as much. Like so much of smart
growth, this turns out to be wishful thinking.

The vast majority of Americans live in low densities and do most of their travel
by automobile. While smart-growth propaganda might persuade some voters that
light rail will get other people off the roads or that high-density development will
reduce crowding in the suburbs, few will willingly shift to transit or move into
apartments simply because they are available. Once people realize that the goal of
smart growth is to make driving as difficult as possible and low-density housing as
expensive as possible, they quickly come to oppose it. This means that the smart-
growth coalition must disguise its true goals. Though it wants to increase urban
congestion, it gets support by blaming congestion on sprawl. Though it wants to
put single-family housing out of reach for most new households, it blames
unaffordable housing on the suburbs.

The smart-growth coalition has developed what it hopes will be a winning
strategy to achieve its goals:
- Raise public alarm over congestion, loss of open space, air pollution, inner-
  city decline, and taxes. This is particularly effective in fast-growing cities where
  people see rapid change and where they can provoke suspicion that existing
  residents are subsidizing urban services for newcomers.
- Build a coalition of a wide range of interest groups by somehow linking each
  group's goals to urban sprawl and convincing group leaders that smart growth
  will benefit the group.
- Publicly focus on a few potentially popular and highly-visible remedies for
  urban problems, including rail transit, purchases of open space, and developer impact fees.
- Quietly tie in less visible (and potentially less popular) parts of the smart-
  growth package, including neighborhood densification, density floors for new
  development, subsidies for transit-oriented development, urban-growth

boundaries, traffic calming, parking limits, and limits on low-density retail and commercial development.

This strategy will succeed in city after city so long as people believe smart growth's rhetoric and remain unaware of smart growth's true goals.

Notes

1. Daniel B. Wood, "Backlash Against Urban Sprawl Broadens," *Christian Science Monitor*, December 16, 1999.
2. Sierra Club, *The Dark Side of the American Dream* (San Francisco, CA: Sierra Club, 1998), p. 2.
3. David Rusk, *Cities Without Suburbs* (Washington, DC: Woodrow Wilson Center Press, 1993), 146 pp.

7. The Architects

Though not politically powerful, architects provide a patina of intellectual authority and an apparently scientific rationale for smart-growth policies. In the 1920s and 1930s, two internationally famous architects developed urban designs that profoundly influenced American cities. Le Corbusier was a Swiss designer who proposed high-density cities featuring high-rise apartments surrounded by green spaces. He called his plans *Radiant City* and they were the inspiration for many public housing projects. Le Corbusier's vision, says urban historian Peter Hall, was "that the evil of the modern city was its density of development and that the remedy, perversely, was to increase that density."[1]

At the opposite extreme from Le Corbusier was Frank Lloyd Wright, who sought a complete decentralization, with an acre of land per family in his *Broadacre City*. An occasional office building might be a high rise, but most buildings were only one or two levels. His 1930 designs turned out to roughly predict the modern American suburb: His *usonian house* became the ranch house; his scattered high-rise offices and manufacturing plants became today's edge cities.

Architects and planners today consider the Radiant City inhumane and lifeless. Peter Hall calls Le Corbusier "an authoritarian centralist" and "the Rasputin" of urban planning.[2] His "urban vision was authoritarian, inflexible and simplistic," says Wharton Professor Witold Rybczynski. "Wherever it was tried, it failed. Standardization proved inhuman and disorienting. The open spaces were inhospitable; the bureaucratically imposed plan, socially destructive."[3] Yet planners also revile Broadacre City as sprawl. The American Planning Association's *Planning* magazine notes the "head-on collision between the current professional fashion for centralization and Wright's wholehearted embrace of the opposite."[4]

Smart growth prefers Le Corbusier's density and authoritarian centralism over Wright's decentralization. Urban architectural planning and design has changed Radiant City mainly in the details, preferring postmodern mid-rise buildings to Le Corbusier's severely modern high rises. Smart growth takes its most recent inspiration from three major architects: the husband-and-wife team of Andres Duany and Elizabeth Plater-Zyberk on the East Coast and Peter Calthorpe on the West Coast.

Duany and Plater-Zyberk

"Suburban sprawl is cancerous growth rather than healthy growth, and it is destroying our civic life," write Duany and Plater-Zyberk. They believe that the suburbs fail to provide residents with a "sense of community."[5] Americans, they continue, "are happy with the private realm they have won for themselves, but desperately anxious about the public realm around them." Duany and Plater-Zyberk believe that well-planned higher-density housing would promote such a sense of community. In fact, Duany says, if people had a sense of community, they would welcome higher density housing since "every new house would enhance" the community.[6]

To promote that sense of community, Duany and Plater-Zyberk include public buildings and other "communal spaces" in the communities they design, including parks, daycare facilities, libraries, and community buildings. They advocate transit not because it is cleaner or more energy efficient than cars but as a way of getting people into more communal spaces and out of the automobile, which they call a "private space as well as a potentially sociopathic device."[7]

Duany and Plater-Zyberk model their plans after *traditional neighborhoods*, which they loosely and somewhat inaccurately describe as any neighborhood built before World War II.[8] Traditional neighborhoods, they claim, were mixed use and pedestrian friendly. Their ideal neighborhoods were those built around the streetcar in the 1920s. "Urban planning reached a level of competence in the 1920s that was absolutely mind-boggling," claims Duany.[9] In fact, the private developers who built the streetcar suburbs were no more competent than developers today, they just based their designs on the transportation technology that then existed as opposed to the technology that exists today.

Since most people in the 1910s, if not the 1920s, walked, bicycled, or rode streetcars rather than drove autos, Duany and Plater-Zyberk presume that replicating the neighborhoods of that time period will reduce driving. They therefore propose multifamily dwellings or houses on small lots with tiny front years and garages in back, as well as the mixing of housing with grocery stores and other shops. Because of their emphasis on the term *traditional neighborhood*, their style of planning has come to be dubbed *neotraditional*.

More than just higher densities, traditional neighborhoods typically had garages recessed behind the homes or facing back alleys while the fronts of the homes had large porches where people can sit and meet their neighbors. "In the suburbs you have backyard decks; in towns you have porches on the street," he says. Naturally, he believes that towns offered a better sense of community.

Ironically, Duany blames previous generations of planners for the suburbs' supposed lack of community and other problems. "It is the professionals of recent decades that have ruined our cities." Most importantly, he objects to the separation of housing from other uses that is characteristic of most zoning codes.[10] Those separations came about, of course, because the urban planners of the 1920s didn't think that their cities were anywhere near as wonderful as Duany proclaims. In fact, they thought those cities were awful, and to fix them they wrote the zoning codes Duany objects to today. From the first zoning code, written for New York City in 1916, nearly all zoning codes have had two major features in common:

- Separation of uses, so that factories and stores wouldn't be next to residential areas; and
- Protection of high-value residential areas from apartments and other high-density residential through the use of minimum lot sizes.

In short, high-density, mixed uses were considered the bane of American cities in the 1920s, while low-density, separated uses were the salvation. Beyond that, Plater-Zyberk observes, "most zoning codes are *pro*scriptive—they just try to prevent things from happening without offering a vision of how things should be." In contrast, says Plater-Zyberk, neotraditional zoning is "*pre*scriptive. We want the streets to feel and act a certain way."[11]

- Where current zoning calls for maximum densities (or minimum lot sizes), neotraditional codes call for *minimum* densities (or maximum lot sizes);
- Where current zoning may say that houses must be set back at least 30 feet from the street (but set no upper limit), neotraditional codes may say that houses can be *no more* than 20 feet from the street.
- Where existing zoning codes may require at least 20 feet between homes, neotraditional codes may requires that homes be *no more* than 10 feet apart.
- Where existing zoning codes may say little or nothing about home design, neotraditional codes prescribe recessed garages, large front porches, and other traditional designs.
- Where existing zoning codes may say little or nothing about street design, neotraditional codes prescribe narrow streets on gridded patterns instead of broad, winding streets with cul de sacs.

Neotraditional prescriptions can get amazingly detailed. Based on the traditional communities they have studied, Duany and Plater-Zyberk say they "have derived a good operational rule for creating sense of space:. . . the street width as measured from building front should not exceed six times the height of the buildings." Unfortunately, Americans today "like their houses low and their front yards deep." Since this is "a formula for exceeding the ratio," Duany and Plater-Zyberk want design codes that enforce the standards they consider "timeless" rather than the designs that ignorant Americans might choose on their own.[12]

One of their most famous designs is the resort community of Seaside, Florida, which was used to film much of Jim Carrey's movie, *The Truman Show*. The town has narrow streets; houses share public walkways separate from the streets; most of the houses look like they were built in the Victorian era; and businesses are all within walking distance. The community was planned to have 300 houses, 30 row houses, up to 200 hotel rooms and apartments, and various retail spaces on just eighty acres.[13] Duany and Plater-Zyberk did not design the individual buildings, just the town's layout and design code.

Seaside is not perfect. Some of the houses face the backs of stores, giving them unsightly views of trash bins, loading docks, and air conditioning units.[14] More important, Seaside is not even a true community, being mainly a resort town with second homes and rooms for short-term visitors. It is difficult to say why Seaside's plans should be adopted by any suburb. It is one thing to provide sandy walking paths for barefoot children heading to a Florida beach. It is another thing to design a pedestrian community for Minnesota winters or Arizona summers. Seaside's artificial design and controlling qualities is what attracted it to the makers of *The Truman Show*. "*The Truman Show* poses the uneasy question, 'At what price New Urbanism?'" commented *Architecture* magazine.[15] To which Duany defensively responded, "Believing that Seaside is actually as depicted in the film, you join the audience of chumps that *The Truman Show* satirizes."[16]

Another Duany/Plater-Zyberk development is Kentlands, in Gaithersberg, Maryland. Kentlands has houses on small lots, row houses, and low-rise apartments mixed with retail and commercial uses. It has successfully mixed various uses as well as people with various income levels together, and Duany claims it has attracted many professionals who are nostalgic for the older towns that Duany regards as traditional. However, it is not particularly transit oriented and its residents drive as much as other suburbanites.

Peter Calthorpe

On the other side of the continent, Peter Calthorpe is far more interested in transportation issues than in questions of community. Calthorpe believes the automobile is not sustainable, so he promotes communities that are oriented around transit and walking. He combines high density, mixed use, and easy access to mass transit to create *pedestrian pockets*, small neighborhoods of people who (Calthorpe hopes) work and shop near their homes. Transit stations at the center of every neighborhood would take people to other parts of the city. Stores, cafés, and civic and social centers mixed among the housing and especially near the transit station allow people to walk instead of drive to buy a loaf of bread, purchase a cup of coffee, or enjoy an evening with their neighbors.[17]

"The old suburban dream is increasingly out of sync with today's culture," says Calthorpe, who likes to refer to suburbs as "placeless."[18] Despite his lack of respect for suburban quality of life, he decries the growth of suburban office parks as an invasion that has "seriously eroded the quality of life in formerly quiet suburban towns."[19] In any case, he claims that his transit-oriented developments would be "more affordable for working families, environmentally responsible, and cost-effective for business and government."[20]

Calthorpe put his ideas into practice in his plan for Laguna West, a suburb outside of Sacramento. The plan called for a transit center surrounded by low-rise apartments, and that surrounded by single-family homes on relatively small lots. Scattered throughout the area would be a variety of stores and businesses that would be within walking distance of the residents.

Calthorpe convinced a developer to start Laguna West, but the developer couldn't sell the high-density condominiums at the center and went bankrupt. A new developer turned the condos into a senior center and decided to put in ordinary suburban homes instead of more high density. Since Calthorpe doesn't believe in cars, he didn't plan any parking at the transit center, so people who used transit often parked in front of other people's homes. Annoyed, the residents near the transit center convinced the transit agency to move the transit stop away from the development.

Meanwhile, residents do all of their shopping at an ordinary strip mall. The only businesses in the development itself are gas stations and a quick lube, suggesting that people haven't exactly given up on their cars. In keeping with Calthorpe's original vision, the current developer plans to eventually build some high-density housing in the area, but has been unable to attract investors.[21]

Even auto-hater Jane Holtz Kay is unhappy with Duany/Plater-Zyberk and Calthorpe. "For all the idea of community," she says, their plans "failed to ease dependency on the automobile." Both Kentlands and Laguna West "still lacked the mass transit or the neighborhood mix to allow freedom from the automobile."[22]

Despite the apparent failure of Laguna West, Calthorpe's transit-oriented developments are wildly popular among planners. Calthorpe now gets much of his business in contracts from city planning agencies who want similar designs in their areas. Sunnyside Village, a Calthorpe-designed suburb of Portland, Oregon, consists of low-rise apartments and houses on tiny lots near a rather ordinary supermarket mini-mall. Houses in the area did not sell well until all of the alternatives—homes on larger lots—were pretty much gone.

Recently, the local fire department decreed that Sunnyside Village residents would lose half their street parking because emergency vehicles could not fit in the narrow streets when cars were parked on both sides. At a public meeting, one angry resident declared that the planners should all be required to live in Sunnyside Village for two years before they inflict such a design on another area.[23]

Notes

1. Peter Geoffrey Hall, *Cities of Tomorrow: An Intellectual History of Urban Planning and Design in the Twentieth Century* (Cambridge, MA: Blackwell, 1988; updated to 1996), p. 9.
2. Ibid, p. 3, p. 5.
3. Witold Rybczynski, "The Architect: Le Corbusier," *Time*, June 8, 1998, p. 92.
4. Harold Henderson, "Planners Library," *Planning*, May, 1996, p. 29.

5. Andres Duany and Elizabeth Plater-Zyberk, "The Second Coming of the American Small Town," *Wilson's Quarterly*, Winter, 1992, pp. 19–48.
6. Andres Duany, "New Urbanism Quotations," http://www.periferia.org/publications/Quotes.html.
7. Andres Duany, Elizabeth Plater-Zyberk, and Jeff Speck, *Suburban Nation: The Rise of Sprawl and the Decline of the American Dream* (New York, NY: North Point Press, 2000), p. 60.
8. Ibid, p. 3.
9. Quoted in James Kunstler, *The Geography of Nowhere: The Rise and Decline of America's Man-Made Landscape* (New York: NY: Simon & Schuster, 1993), p. 255.
10. Duany, et al., *Suburban Nation*, p. 5.
11. Quoted in James Kunstler, *The Geography of Nowhere*, p. 259.
12. Duany and Plater-Zyberk, "The Second Coming of the American Small Town," pp. 19–48.
13. Richard Sexton, *Parallel Utopias: The Quest for Community* (San Francisco, CA: Chronicle Books, 1995), p. 112.
14. Craig Whitaker, *Architecture and the American Dream* (New York, NY: Potter, 1996), p. 63.
15. Reed Kroloff, "Suspending Disbelief," *Architecture*, August, 1998, p. 11.
16. Andres Duany, "Closing the Circle" (letter to editor of *Architecture*), August, 1998, http://www.dpz.com/Writings-FilesInserted/B-02-P01-architec.htm.
17. Peter Calthorpe, *The Next American Metropolis: Ecology, Community, and the American Dream* (New York, NY: Princeton Architectural Press, 1993), p. 17.
18. Ibid, p. 15.
19. Ibid, p. 18.
20. Ibid, p. 17.
21. Mel Zucker, personal communication, 20 April 1999.
22. Jane Holtz Kay, *Asphalt Nation: How the Automobile Took over America and How We Can Take It Back* (New York, NY: Crown, 1997), p. 274.
23. Richard Jones, personal communication, January 1999.

The Design Myth

Myth: Architects are professionally qualified to design cities.

Reality: Architects are not always the best designers of ordinary buildings; cities are far beyond their capabilities.

Architects throughout history have believed that, since they could design buildings, they were also the best suited professionals to design cities. "Architecture and urbanism are in fact one problem only and are not separate questions," Le Corbusier grandly proclaimed. "They demand one solution only and this is the work of one profession only"—architecture. This view is somewhat like a doctor presuming that, because he can reconstruct a shattered hip or install an artificial heart, he can also build a human being from scratch—something which is so far beyond their abilities.

"There is this strange conceit among architects," says Peter Gordon, "that people ought to live in what they design."[1] Some people wonder whether architects are even qualified to design decent buildings, much less cities. At almost any major university with an architecture school, that school is easy to find because it is in the ugliest, most inhumane-looking building on campus. Since many university urban planning departments are located in the architecture schools, it is useful to remember that this is the building that is inspiring graduates who think they can plan better cities and suburbs.

Joel Garreau points out that "Doctors and lawyers enjoy near monopolies in their professions; architects control a mere 30 percent of their market—the market for the design and execution of buildings." According to this market evidence, he concludes, "Contractors and engineers are viewed as far more sane."[2]

Whole Earth Catalog founder Stewart Brand thinks that architecture's flaws outweigh its benefits and says there is a good reason why architects design so few buildings: Most architects are lousy at what they do. Architects build their businesses, says Brand, by winning design awards. These awards are judged solely on the outside appearance of the building, usually as seen in a photo. So architects get good at designing buildings that are pretty to look at—without worrying about whether the buildings serve the user.[3]

In fact, many architect-designed buildings are highly dysfunctional. Hated by their occupants, expensive to maintain, the buildings are often inflexible and un-suited to expansion or adaptation to new uses. Few architects ever bother to find out how owners like their buildings. One study of fifty-eight buildings found that "in only one case in ten did the architect ever return to the building—and then with no interest in evaluation," says Brand. "The facilities managers interviewed for the study had universally acid views about the architects."

Brand asked one architect what he learned from his earlier buildings. "Oh, you never go back!" the architect exclaimed. "It's too discouraging." A few architects do go back and do "post-occupancy evaluations," but architectural reputations remain based on outer design, not inner solutions to users' problems. Brand's criticism of the architecture profession is neatly summed up in two sentences: "All buildings are predictions" and "All predictions are wrong." Given that this is true, Brand thinks buildings should "be designed and used so it doesn't matter when they're wrong"—in other words, so that they can be readily modified and adapted to new uses. Buildings built by non-architects often meet this goal; buildings designed by architects usually fail.[4]

As an example, Brand points to the classic Cape Cod house—a box with a roof slanted at 35 to 45 degrees—as a popular and flexible traditional building. Con-struction and maintenance costs are low, and as the owners' needs change they can add dormers, extend the building, build a new wing, expand or enclose the porch, or easily make all sorts of other changes. In contrast, Brand points to the postmodern homes popular among architects today. With all sorts of right angles in the floor plan and changes in the roof line, a postmodern house "attempts to look as if it has been added on to for generations." Yet this "fussy complexity greatly increases the construction and maintenance costs" and makes it much more difficult to make real modifications later on.[5]

Architecture's mistakes are greatly magnified at the urban level. Urban archi-tects, like building architects, focus on aesthetics over function; fail to find out how users really feel about plans; and tend to make inflexible plans that cannot be adapted to new needs and uses. Yet the architects of individual buildings have the virtue of imposing their mistakes mainly on the people who hired them. Urban planners impose their mistakes on millions of people who may not even be aware that the planners existed.

Notes

1. Jerry Adler, "Bye-Bye, Suburban Dream," *Newsweek*, May 15, 1995 pp. 40–53.
2. Joel Garreau, *Edge City: Life on the New Frontier* (New York, NY: Doubleday, 1991), p. 241.
3. Stewart Brand, *How Buildings Learn: What Happens After They're Built* (New York, NY: Viking, 1994), pp. 54–55.
4. Ibid, p. 178.
5. Ibid, p. 201.

8. The Planners

Calthorpe and Duany/Plater-Zyberk argue that many zoning codes do not permit the high-density, mixed-use developments they advocate. Originally they were content to urge developers and planners to try their ideas and tell potential home buyers that they might prefer more compact or traditional neighborhoods. In 1991, in a conference at Yosemite Park's Ahwahnee Hotel with a group of other architects and urban planners interested in their ideas, they decided to go a more authoritarian route.[1]

One of the purposes of the conference was to reconcile differences between the Calthorpe and the Duany models. While Duany stressed community, Calthorpe stressed transportation. More important, while Duany stressed neotraditional design features such as front porches, Calthorpe stressed planning features such as mixing housing with retailing and placing both near transit stations. While the group agreed to keep the rhetoric of community, they dropped many of the neotraditional design features from their agenda and focused instead on transportation issues.

As a result, the conference adopted a set of design concepts known as the *Ahwahnee Principles*.[2] "Existing patterns of urban and suburban development seriously impair our quality of life," said the principles. Those impairments include "congestion and air pollution resulting from our increased dependence on automobiles, the loss of precious open space, the need for costly improvements to roads and public services, the inequitable distribution of economic resources, and the loss of a sense of community."

The principles include many ideas that later became known as smart growth:
- Communities in which "housing, jobs, daily needs and other activities are within easy walking distance of each other";
- Narrow streets to "encourage pedestrian and bike use";
- A "transportation network built around transit rather than freeways";
- The idea that "rather than allowing developer-initiated, piecemeal development," "governments shall take charge of the planning process";
- A "regional land-use planning structure" should be the focus of such planning. As Duany says, "Think globally, act locally, but plan regionally."[3]

Planners had been thinking about density and transit issues long before Duany and Calthorpe published their ideas. One of the first smart-growth-like proposals can be found in the 1973 book, *Compact City: A Plan for a Livable Urban Environment*, written by urban planners George Dantzig and Thomas Saaty.[4] They advocated "total-system planning" to insure that housing would be dense and people would be able to get around on foot or by transit rather than by driving. Their compact city was openly "based on Radiant City lines—it would have a central work core ringed by residences and there would be a general separation of functions."[5] But the authors admitted that an alternative could combine Radiant City with Jane Jacob's "lively neighborhoods," which planners now call "transit-oriented developments." After this book was published, many planners advocated urban-growth boundaries and other means to densify cities.

Not all planners support smart growth, but the exceptions are a definite minority. Many are centered around the University of Southern California, including Peter Gordon, Harry Richardson, Genevieve Giuliano, and James Moore. Richardson and Gordon, for example, argue that planners should not try to regulate cities and interfere with free markets but instead to make sure that markets are working properly. "We are not against planning," they say, "but we are against inefficient and inequitable interventions" in the market. Instead, they support "innovations in the employment of price incentives in land use planning."[6] Other planners skeptical of smart growth can be found at the University of California and no doubt other universities as well, but except at USC they tend to be in the minority.

Planners today are represented chiefly by the American Planning Association and its state chapters. In addition, an organization named the Congress for the New Urbanism consists mainly of planners who support smart growth.

American Planning Association

The American Planning Association (APA) is "dedicated to advancing the art, science, and profession of urban, rural and regional planning."[7] Under the guise of providing social benefits, the association lobbies for legislation that will keep planners employed. The association's predecessor group, the American Institute of Planners, was formed in 1917. Today, it has 30,000 members, most of whom are planners and planning officials.[8]

In 1994, the association started a project it called "Growing Smart" (a term it actually trademarked). The project "aimed at helping states modernize statutes affecting planning." Most state planning laws, the APA notes, are based on model legislation written in 1928, the Standard City Planning Enabling Act. This model law was written by the Department of Commerce under the supervision of then-Secretary of Commerce Herbert Hoover.[9] Of course, this model planning legislation was strongly endorsed and promoted by the APA for many decades. But because it led to the sprawl they so dislike, planners today consider it to be as much a problem as a solution. The Growing Smart project aims to replace the older laws with smart-growth statutes.

State chapters of the association are lobbying legislatures for smart-growth laws in each state. When the *Christian Science Monitor* says that state legislatures are considering a thousand land-use planning bills, most of those bills have been drafted by the American Planning Association or its state affiliates. Chapters have been particularly effective in Arizona, Colorado, Georgia, Illinois, Massachusetts, Minnesota, New York, North Carolina, Pennsylvania, and Washington.[10] They have also had an influence in California, Iowa, Kentucky, New Hampshire, Virginia, Wisconsin, and many other states.

The American Planning Association presents itself as a benevolent organization that merely has the best interests of urban and rural residents at heart. It is merely a coincidence that the legislation it proposes will give its members more power and many more jobs.

Congress for the New Urbanism

After the Ahwahnee Principles were written, the style-conscious term *neotraditionalism* was slowly replaced by the planning-oriented term *new urbanism*. In 1993, planners and architects formed the Congress for the New Urbanism (CNU). The group exists solely to promote new urban policies by holding annual conferences and workshops.

The organization is uncompromising in its goals: "All development should be in the form of compact, walkable neighborhoods,"[11] it says, while it supports "the reconfiguration of sprawling suburbs into communities of real neighborhoods."[12] Of course, to new urbanists a "real neighborhood" is a compact neighborhood. So the Congress for the New Urbanism appears to not only oppose the construction of new low-density suburbs, it apparently stands for increasing the densities of all existing suburbs.

In 1996, the group produced a *Charter of the New Urbanism* which in many ways is an update of the Ahwahnee Principles:
- "Neighborhoods should be compact, pedestrian-friendly, and mixed-use";
- The region's edges should not be "blurred" by unplanned development, which implies an urban-growth boundary of some sort;
- Transit corridors should "organize metropolitan structure and revitalize city centers";
- "In contrast, highway corridors should not displace investment from existing centers," which would seem to proscribe any new roads;
- Development should focus on "transit, pedestrian, and bicycle systems. . . while reducing dependence upon the automobile."
- Blocks should "encourage walking and enable neighbors to know each other."

- Since the "metropolitan region is a fundamental economic unit," all planning should be done at this level.[13]

Notes

1. Judith Corbett and Joe Velasquez, "The Ahwahnee Principles: Toward More Livable Communities," http://www.lgc.org/clc/ahwnprin.html
2. Ahwahnee Principles, http://www.lgc.org/clc/ahwahnee/principles.html.
3. Andres Duany, Elizabeth Plater-Zyberk, and Jeff Speck, *Suburban Nation: The Rise of Sprawl and the Decline of the American Dream* (New York, NY: North Point Press, 2000), p. 225.
4. George Dantzig and Thomas Saaty, *Compact City: A Plan for a Liveable Urban Environment* (San Francisco, CA: Freeman, 1973), 244 pp.
5. Ibid, p. 26.
6. Harry W. Richardson and Peter Gordon, "Market Planning: Oxymoron or Common Sense?" *Journal of the American Planning Association* 59(3) [Summer, 1993]: pp. 347–352.
7. American Planning Association, *Planning Communities for the 21st Century* (Washington, DC: APA, 1999), p. i, http://www.planning.org/plnginfo/GROWSMAR/images/APA_complete1.pdf.
8. American Planning Association, "*American Planning Association*," http://www.planning.org/abtapa/factsht.htm.
9. Rodney Cobb, "Toward Modern Statutes: A Survey of State Laws on Local Land-Use Planning," *in* APA, *Planning Communities for the 21st Century*, pp. 7–8, http://www.planning.org/plnginfo/GROWSMAR/images/APA_complete1.pdf.
10. Stuart Meck, "Executive Summary: Status of State Planning Reform," *in* APA, *Planning Communities for the 21st Century*, p. 2, http://www.planning.org/plnginfo/GROWSMAR/images/APA_complete1.pdf.
11. Congress for the New Urbanism, "About New Urbanism," San Francisco, CA: CNU, 1998), http://www.cnu.org.
12. Congress for the New Urbanism, "Charter of the New Urbanism," (San Francisco, CA: CNU, 1996), http://www.cnu.org/charter.html.
13. Ibid.

The Planning Myth

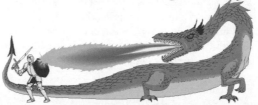

Myth: Planning—and *only* planning—can solve urban problems.
Reality: Urban planning has more often than not led to disaster.

"Long-term planning is central to achieving better land use and growth management," says a book titled *Land Use in America*. "Land use planning. . . is not radical doctrine. It is rational decision making. It is time the country gives up its fear of planning and embraces its benefits."[1]

Rational decision making. Community goals. Growth management. Better land use. The benefits of planning. These phrases sound so warm and appealing. Similar if not identical phrases have been used to promote planning for more than a century. But when we go back to see the results of urban planning, we repeatedly find the same thing: disaster. Past urban plans nearly all have three things in common:

- They cost far more to implement than projected by planners;
- They produce far fewer benefits than claimed by planners;
- They have serious negative unintended consequences.

While architects have sometimes designed unsatisfactory buildings, one wonders why the planning profession exists at all. The chief lesson of the cold war, if not the entire twentieth century, has been that centralized, government planning succeeds mainly at creating shortages of things that people want, surpluses of things they don't want, and in general keeping people poor. Perhaps this makes it appropriate that planners should lead the smart-growth movement, since smart growth's chief goals are to create shortages of highways and low-density housing and surpluses of rail transit and high-density housing. Such shortages and surpluses often merely lead to more calls for urban planning to solve the problems.

Everyone plans, and planning is essential to everyday life. We plan what we are going to do each day, what we are going to have for dinner, where we are going to spend the weekend. We might plan someone's birthday party a few weeks ahead of time. If we know we are going to travel somewhere or move to a new home or new job, we will plan ahead for those changes.

Yet few people plan their lives more than a few weeks in advance. The reason is simple: There are just too many uncertainties. There might be a family crisis, a new work opportunity, an invitation to some exciting adventure. Planning too far ahead means we either waste time preparing for things that never happen or get locked in to less desirable activities because we can't predict new opportunities. People do make some long-term plans, such as setting aside money for their children's education or their own retirements. But other than saving money, such plans remain vague: Few thirty-year-olds fix in advance which university their toddlers are going to attend or in which resort town they are going to spend their retirements.

Corporations sometimes have to plan many years in advance. When timber companies cut their trees, they plan for the next crop by planting a new forest even though that crop might not mature for forty or more years. The construction of a fifty-story office building may not pay off for decades. The companies that make such investments are basing them on expectations that people will continue to want to buy wood and work in offices instead of at home. Smart companies attempt to balance their risks by investing in a variety of products. Even then, expectations may prove wrong, in which case the company loses money or even goes out of business. One advantage of the corporate structure is that investment in the company, and therefore in the risk, is entirely voluntary.

Government planners—the people this book refers to when simply using the word *planners*—also try to make plans for years or decades in advance. The problems they face are much more complex than those faced by individuals or corporations. For a corporation, long-term planning usually boils down to a few investment choices within the expertise of the company. A timber company, for example, may have to decide whether to invest in fertilization, herbicides, or other activities designed to make the trees grow faster. To make such decisions, they need to know how fast the trees will grow with and without the treatments, how much the treatments cost, and how much the trees will be worth when they are cut.

As law professor Bernard Siegan points out, urban planning "is enormously more complex." Planners must consider "questions of compatibility, economic feasibility, property values, existing uses, adjoining and nearby uses, traffic, topography, utilities, schools, future growth, conservation, and environment" for each parcel of land. Just to determine the feasibility of one use for one site at one time "would require a market survey costing possibly thousands of dollars."[2] Yet planners claim to be able to determine the optimal uses for most or all sites in a city for many years into the future.

Urban planners need far more information to make long-term land-use and transportation decisions. They need to know how fast a region will grow in the future, what kind of work its people will do, where they will live, where they will shop, where else they will want to travel, how much land will be needed for industry, retail, commercial, multifamily residential, single-family residential, parks, natural areas, farms, and many other uses. As the planners who wrote the book, *Compact City*, say, urban planning requires "*total-system planning*. . . evaluating the effects of a proposed design on as many aspects of the urban system as possible" (emphasis in original).[3] It is not too much to say that urban planning requires perfect omniscience about the future. Unlike individual or corporate planning, urban planning also requires omniscience about the needs and desires of all of the current and future residents of the urban area.

Urban planners have no better crystal ball for predicting the future than individuals or corporations. Nor do they have special insights into the hearts of all current, much less future, residents. Planning an individual city or suburb is an impossible job.

The problems planners face increase exponentially at a regional level. Andres Duany and his partners unhesitatingly urge regional planners to write "detailed physical plans for the development and redevelopment of neighborhoods." "Merely zoning for higher density in these locations is not enough," they add. Instead, plans should be "drawn with such precision that only the architectural detail is left to future designers."[4] This places an incredible burden on regional planners, who barely know how much land in their region is available for development, much less exactly how every block and building lot should be used right up to, but not including, the architectural detail.

Urban planning has one advantage over individual or corporate planning: For the government agencies and planners, it is nearly risk free. The cost of a bad plan is not paid by the planner. Nor is it shared among a few investors who are voluntarily accepting the risk. Instead it is imposed, often without their consent, on the taxpayers and residents of the urban area. The risk-free nature of planning means that there is no shortage of people willing to impose the costs of their mistakes on urban areas.

Since it is impossible to know the future or to understand in any significant detail the needs and desires of urban residents, urban planning relies instead on fads. Zoning, urban renewal, public housing, central city interstates, rail transit, and transit-oriented developments are all fads that allow planners to substitute a one-size-fits-all prescription and their own personal preferences for accurate knowledge about the future and the preferences of urban residents.

Fads can only become popular if there is one or more powerful constituencies behind them. Some things that planners might like to do never happen because no powerful interest group wants them. Other things that planners might not like become planning fads anyway because downtown interests, developers, or some other group thinks they will benefit. Planners may idealistically go along with such compromises hoping that their involvement will "make a difference," or they may feel that such compromises are merely a part of the democratic process and that the end result of such a process must be good because it was democratic.

Many of the urban planning fads of the past half century have turned into disasters. Urban renewal programs destroyed lively neighborhoods and replaced them with sterile monuments. Public housing projects inspired by Le Corbusier's Radiant City turned into crime-infested nightmares and had to be torn down. Inner-city freeways that planners thought would revitalize downtowns helped to kill them. Most recently, heavy- and light-rail projects have consumed billions of dollars yet attract few people out of their cars.

Smart-growth advocates such as Andres Duany admit that many if not most urban problems have been caused by past planning disasters. "It is the professionals of recent decades that have ruined our cities and our landscapes," says Duany.[5] Zoning, urban interstates, and federal housing policies are responsible for the problems of sprawl. Duany has a simple prescription for those problems: Give planners more power and authority than ever. That is exactly what cities are doing when they adopt smart-growth policies.

Smart growth is the perfect fad for urban planners because it eliminates the need to know anything about the present or future of the urban area or about the desires of its residents.

- How will people want to travel in the future? It doesn't matter because smart growth says cities should spend most of their transportation budgets on transit, sidewalks, and bike paths.
- What kind of housing will people want to live in? It doesn't matter because smart growth says people should live in multifamily housing or at best in single-family housing on small lots.
- Where will people want to shop? It doesn't matter because smart growth says people should all shop at corner stores just downstairs or down the street from where they live.

Thus, planning has moved from helping people live the way they want to live to telling them to live the way planners think they should live. This is an inevitable consequence of giving anyone the power to plan anyone else's life.

Notes

1. Henry Diamond and Patrick Noonan, *Land Use in America: The Report of the Sustainable Use of Land Project* (Washington, DC: Island Press, 1996), p. 7.
2. Bernard Siegan, *Land Use Without Zoning* (Lexington, MA: Lexington Books, 1972), p. 6.
3. George Dantzig and Thomas Saaty, *Compact City: A Plan for a Livable Urban Environment* (San Francisco, CA: Freeman, 1973), p. 9.
4. Andres Duany, Elizabeth Plater-Zyberk, and Jeff Speck, *Suburban Nation: The Rise of Sprawl and the Decline of the American Dream* (New York, NY: North Point Press, 2000), p. 228.
5. Andres Duany, "New Urbanism Quotations," http://www.periferia.org/publications/Quotes.html.

Oregon's Land-Use Planning

PORTLAND CASE STUDY

I n February, 2000, a state land-use official shocked Portland-area religious leaders by telling the Sunnyside United Methodist Church in southeast Portland that it could allow no more than 70 people at one time into its 400-seat sanctuary for Sunday services.[1] A local uproar soon led this decision to be rescinded, but numerous other restrictions on the church's activities remain.

When the First Presbyterian Church in the southern Oregon town of Jacksonville had outgrown its building, it applied for a routine permit to build a larger church. The city said it would permit the new church only if no more than 40 cars used the church parking lot on weekdays; there were no services on Sunday evenings; the church would be closed on Saturdays; and the church would hold no more than five weddings and/or funerals per year.[2] When the church refused to accept these conditions, the city simply denied the permit, saying that it would lead to too much congestion. The church is appealing the decision.[3]

This sort of micromanagement by government officials has become common in Oregon, and it is led by the Land Conservation and Development Commission (LCDC), which oversee's Oregon's land-use laws. LCDC is a seven-member body appointed by the governor which writes standards for and reviews county and city planning. The 1973 land-use law required every city and county to submit its land-use plans for commission approval, and the law provided an appeal process for anyone who objected to any planning or zoning decision anywhere in the state.

The law was strongly supported by Oregon's popular governor at the time, Tom McCall. Though McCall is famous for saying "Please visit Oregon, but don't move here," during his term of office Oregon began to grow rapidly. To support that growth, McCall encouraged "clean industry," such as silicon wafer manufacturers, to move to Oregon, while telling polluters to stay away. There is a persistent myth that McCall had Oregon post signs at the borders asking people not to move to the state and that a later governor removed those signs.[4] In fact, all the sign said was, "Welcome to Oregon — We Hope You Enjoy Your Visit."[5]

Initially, few people understood what the land-use planning law would really do. Would it be a "growth-control" law, one that attempted to stifle immigration and population growth (as many accused McCall of trying to do)? Or would it be a "growth-management" law, which accepted growth but merely tried to channel it into acceptable locations? The answer came when the Land Conservation and Development Commission approved its first goals.

The goals required that all cities identify an urban-growth boundary that contained enough, but no more, vacant land to accommodate projected "long-range urban population growth."[6] A housing goal required all cities to provide for "adequate numbers of needed housing units at price ranges and rent levels which are commensurate with the financial capabilities of Oregon households."[7] No city or town could zone itself exclusively for large-lot, single-family housing affordable only to upper-income residents. Outside of the urban-growth boundaries, most farms, forests, and other open spaces were to be protected from development on parcels smaller than 80 to 160 acres. Smaller lots could be used only if the county could show that such sizes would "maintain the existing commercial agricultural enterprise within the area."[8]

Under the Oregon plan, then, growth would be *controlled* outside the urban-growth boundaries through the combination of tax incentives and zoning at very large—80 to 160 or more acres—minimum lot sizes. But growth would be *managed* inside the urban-growth boundaries using zoning and other systems to insure that there would always be sufficient affordable housing for everyone.

As the law was implemented for nearly two decades, nearly all of the burden fell upon landowners outside of the urban-growth boundaries who were unable to use their land as they liked. There were some controversies inside the growth boundaries when cities or counties proposed to rezone to higher densities. But generally, the growth boundaries were drawn large enough to allow development at low densities for many years. When rural opponents of the planning rules attempted to overturn them at the ballot box, the much larger number of urban residents who benefitted from enforced rural open space without paying any costs voted in favor of retaining the law.

Inside the urban areas, the law was supported by a coalition of environmentalists and developers. Since state rules prohibited any community from limiting growth inside its growth boundary, realtors, home builders, and other developers had no objections to the law.

Until 1990, no one talked about compact development, neighborhood densification, or "growing up, not out." With a few exceptions such as the Portland suburb of Happy Valley, most Oregon communities already had a mix of high- and low-density housing and so had no problem meeting the state housing goal. The initial urban-growth boundaries were drawn to include huge areas of vacant land—enough, it was hoped, for twenty years' worth of growth. When the land-use goals were first being written, I asked Steve Schell, one of the original members of the Land Conservation and Development Commission, what would happen when the vacant land inside the boundaries was filled up. "Then we breach the boundary," he said.

In other words, the original intention of the growth boundaries was not to contain cities within those boundaries for all time but simply "To provide for an orderly and efficient transition from rural to urban land use"[9]—in other words, to prevent leapfrog development. Such leapfrog development was assumed to be inefficient for both urban residents and farmers. Urban residents would have to pay more taxes to deliver urban services to suburbs that had leapfrogged the urban area. Farmers whose land was isolated by leapfrog development would have to pay more to farm their land. Though never proven these assumptions were widely accepted.

Despite this original intention, once the growth boundaries were put into place they immediately created a constituency. Anyone who lived on or near a boundary had an interest in keeping the boundary intact so that they could maintain their views of rural open space outside the boundary. They were joined by people who bought homes and "hobby farms" outside the boundary who wanted their neighborhoods to remain rural. Intended to be a flexible planning tool, the boundaries soon became, in many people's minds, sacred lines that should never be changed.

Table One: Change in Selected Urban Area Population Densities

Urban Area	1990 Population (thousands)	1990 Density (people/sq. mi.)	% Density Change from 1980
Denver	1,518	3,309	7
Eugene	189	2,888	-2
Las Vegas	697	3,018	29
Los Angeles	11,403	5,801	12
Minneapolis-St. Paul	2,080	1,956	7
Phoenix	2,006	2,707	23
Portland	1,005	3,133	2
Vancouver	167	2,489	11
Sacramento	1,097	3,285	15
Salem	157	2,760	6
Salt Lake City	789	3,107	40
Seattle	1,744	2,967	3

Source: Census Bureau

Oregon's land-use laws may have discouraged leapfrog development, but they did not discourage low-density sprawl. Between 1980 and 1990, the population density of the Portland urbanized area increased by just 2 percent, while the Eugene urbanized area density actually fell by 2 percent. Meanwhile the densities of many other cities of similar size, but without similar land-use laws, increased by far more (table one). Las Vegas, which the Sierra Club says is one of the nation's most sprawl-threatened cities, increased its density by 29 percent, while Phoenix, which received a "dishonorable mention" from the Sierra Club, increased its density by 23 percent. Salt Lake, another city accused of sprawling, increased its density by 40 percent, and even Los Angeles, the Sierra Club's "granddaddy of sprawl," increased its density by 12 percent.

Despite its sprawl, Oregon was not exactly running short of farms, forests, or open space. In 1986, when all cities and counties had completed LCDC-approved land-use plans, they had zoned 49 percent of the state for agricultural uses, 44 percent for forest uses, and 5 percent for other rural uses such as parks and rural residential. Only 1.24 percent of the state was inside of an urban-growth boundary, and much of that remained undeveloped. Rural residential was the only rural zone allowing developments on lots as small as five acres, and it occupied just 1.03 percent of the state.[10]

Over the next decade, minor adjustments brought a few thousand more acres inside urban boundaries, but still left 98.74 percent of the state in rural zones.[11] Much of the land within the urban-growth boundaries also remains undeveloped. According to the 1990 census, all developed "places," including unincorporated areas with as few as 8 residents, occupied just 1.02 percent of the state.[12]

Despite these numbers, the Land Conservation and Development Commission imposed increasingly draconian rules to prevent rural developments it did not think appropriate. Some of the rules are inscrutable. For example, the commission allows "regulation" golf courses—courses with "a par of 64 to 73 strokes" for eighteen holes—on agricultural land. But it does not allow "par 3" golf courses, that is, courses with a par of just 54 for eighteen holes.[13]

To protect the countryside, the commission also regulates the things farmers can sell in roadside stands: At least 75 percent of sales must be "farm crops and livestock grown on farms in the local agricultural area."[14] One farm family, whose land is located just 1,000 feet outside of Salem's urban-growth boundary, sold fresh blueberries at a roadside stand. This was so successful that they expanded to selling blueberry muffins and pies. Eventually the fruit stand evolved into the popular Blueberry Cafe, selling such things as blueberry pancakes, Norwegian potato lefse, and coffee. The cafe was a boon for local farmers, consuming three tons of blueberries as well as many other farm products each year. But in January, 2000, after three years of operation, planning officials ordered that it be shut down because the share of locally-grown products had fallen below 75 percent.[15] The owners reluctantly converted it back to a fruit stand.[16]

More important, the commission has tried to discourage housing in rural areas. The commission's original rules required counties to zone most farm and forest lands to at least 40-acre, and preferably 160-acre, minimum lot sizes. This was based on an unproved assumption that smaller farms are not economically viable. The fact that the average farm size in many European countries is less than 5 acres, and most Asian farms are smaller than that, was ignored. For many, the real goal is not to maintain viable farms but to preserve land outside of urban-growth boundaries as open space.

Oregon's land-use commission soon decided that 40- and even 160-acre minimum lot sizes were not enough: In Oregon's growing economy, increasing numbers of people were wealthy enough to buy this much farm land and build "starter castles"—the anti-sprawl movement's derisive term for large exurbanite homes. So the commission passed a new rule: Landowners must actually farm their land for three years before they are allowed to build on it. Some landowners met this requirement by planting blueberries, a low-cost crop that required little tending and whose first harvest would not even be ready until after the three years were up.

The commission responded by passing an even more stringent rule: Owners of "high-value" farmland (class I and II farmlands as defined by the U.S.D.A.) must earn at least $80,000 per year from farming for two years (or three of the last five years) before they can build a home on their land.[17] Owners of low-value farm land (located mostly in eastern Oregon) need earn only $40,000 per year. Only one out of six Oregon farmers actually earns $80,000 per year farming, so if they did not already have houses on their land this rule would prevent most Oregon farmers from living on their own land. This rule will also have an unintended consequence: The lands that are most valuable for farming will be the ones that are developed first because they will most easily produce the minimum revenues.

"This farm income test is an essential safeguard for the state's economy," says the director of the Department of Land Conservation and Development. "Before we started using this test, lawyers, doctors, and others not really farming were building houses in farm zones," which threatened "years of progressive farmland protection policy."[18] The department brags that, in the first three years after adopting this rule, only 322 new homes were approved on farm lands.[19] During that same time period, the state's population grew by 140,000 people, nearly all of whom were forced by LCDC rules to crowd into urban areas.

Having greatly restricted development of nearly 98 percent of the state, the commission has most recently placed further restrictions on the use of the 1.03 percent classified rural residential. While most rural residential zones allow lots as small as five acres, a new rule passed by the commission heavily restricts further subdivisions of any lands in this zone and encourages counties to zone such land in 10-acre minimum lot sizes. To prevent urbanization of rural residential land that is close to urban-growth boundaries, land on urban fringes must be zoned in lots as large as 20 acres.[20] This will help contain Oregon's growing urban population inside the growth boundaries.

Notes

1. Wade Nkrumah, "Portland church at center of gathering storm," *The Oregonian*, February 11, 2000.

2. Associated Press, "Jacksonville Church," *The Oregonian*, March 2, 2000, p. D9.
3. Associated Press, "Vote puts kibosh on Jacksonville church expansion," *The Oregonian*, March 9, 2000, http://www.oregonlive.com/news/00/03/st030924.htm.
4. Edwin Mills, "No Growth/Slow Growth Presentation January 19, 1994," *in* ECO Northwest, *Evaluation of No-Growth and Slow-Growth Policies for the Portland Region* (Portland, OR: Metro, 1994), p. D-2.
5. Brent Walth, *Fire at Eden's Gate: Tom McCall & the Oregon Story* (Portland, OR: Oregon Historical Society, 1994), p. 3.
6. LCDC Goal 14, http://darkwing.uoregon.edu/~pppm/landuse/GOALS/Goal_14.html.
7. LCDC Goal 10, http://darkwing.uoregon.edu/~pppm/landuse/GOALS/Goal_10.html.
8. LCDC Goal 3, http://darkwing.uoregon.edu/~pppm/landuse/GOALS/Goal_3.html.
9. LCDC Goal 14.
10. LCDC, "Zoning Acres by County - 1986," http://www.lcd.state.or.us/backinfo/zontot.htm.
11. LCDC, "County Acres Replanned and/or Rezoned from One Rural Zone to Another Rural Zone by Type of Zone and Year," http://www.lcd.state.or.us/backinfo/pamapsum.htm.
12. Census Bureau, http://www.census.gov/population/www/censusdata/places.html.
13. Oregon Administrative Rule 660-033-0130(20).
14. OAR 660-033-0130(23).
15. Associated Press, "Blueberry Cafe finds itself in a jam," January 18, 2000, http://www.oregonlive.com/news/00/01/st011815.html.
16. Cheryl Martinis, "Blueberry Cafe will close March 1," *The Oregonian*, February 20, 2000, http://www.oregonlive.com/news/00/02/st022009.html.
17. OAR 660-033-0130(24)(b)(B).
18. LCDC, *Using Income Criteria to Protect Commercial Farmland in the State of Oregon* (Salem, OR: LCDC, 1998), p. 2, http://www.lcd.state.or.us/issues/rural/dlcdfly.pdf.
19. Ibid.
20. Oregon Administrative Rule Chapter 660, Division 4, amended June 9, 2000, http://www.lcd.state.or.us./rural/rrrule.htm.

9. Environmental Groups

Polls show that the vast majority of Americans are worried about the environment and consider themselves environmentalists. Yet many if not most Americans are also suspicious that the solutions proposed by major environmental groups are too extreme. Environmental groups have learned to raise alarm over problems of broad public concern without getting too specific about the details of their solutions. Although most Americans prefer to live in uncongested, low-density areas, environmental groups who want to force people to live in congested, high-density cities have made sprawl a major political issue.

What has long been called "the environmental movement" is in reality two different movements: one focused on human health problems due to pollution and toxics; the other focused on preserving the natural environment. Though these movements rarely overlap, the war on sprawl has brought them together. Those concerned with pollution have declared war on the automobile. Those concerned with nature have declared war on low-density development. Since autos and low densities go together, the two sides support one another.

The Surface Transportation Policy Project

The anti-auto part of the movement is chiefly represented by the Surface Transportation Policy Project (STPP), a group formed in 1990 to lobby Congress on transportation legislation. With the help of the American Planning Association, American Public Transit Association, and other environmental, planning, and interest groups, the group achieved spectacular success in 1991 when Congress passed the Intermodal Surface Transportation Efficiency Act (ISTEA). Transportation analyst Peter Samuel notes that STPP represents "a new breed of transportation policy experts [who] aim to replace fact-and-figures transportation technocrats." While the "old breed" was dominated by "engineers from blue-collar, small-town backgrounds," STPP consists of "ideologues who are more committed to 'taming' highways than to building them."[1]

STPP claims that "250 organizations from most states around the country belong to STPP's grassroots network."[2] In reality, it has no formal members. Foundations and government grants provide nearly all of the funding needed to maintain its dozen or so staff members. Its self-selecting board of directors includes a variety of transportation lobbyists, foundation officials, and legal experts. Its director, Hank Dittmar, was previously the chief lobbyist for the San Francisco Bay Area Metropolitan Transportation Commission. The group is extremely prolific, producing publications with titles like *At Roads End*, *Crying Wolf: The False "Crisis" of America's Crumbling Roads and Bridges*, *Reclaiming Our Cities and Towns*, and *Car Trouble*. STPP monitors federal spending on transportation and lobbies both Congress and the administration to spend more on transit and less on roads.

The Sierra Club

The Sierra Club represents the nature-lover branch of the environmental movement. While the Sierra Club objects to new roads, its chief concern is that "suburban sprawl destroys habitats and wild areas, threatens endangered species and moves natural areas farther away from where most people live." "We are running out of greener pastures," says the club, adding that sprawl is "the fastest-growing threat" to local quality of life. "Instead of massive suburbs where it is impossible to get around without a car," says the club, "we envision urban neighborhoods where jobs, shopping, services, and recreation are all nearby." In particular, the group supports urban-growth boundaries, infill development, revitalization of downtown areas, and purchase of open space around city edges.[3]

The Sierra Club sometimes appears confused about its goals. It applauds Oregon's urban-growth boundaries, which aim to increase densities. But it also applauds the very different urban-growth boundaries in California and Boulder, Colorado, which aim to preserve existing low-densities. The San Francisco Chapter of the Sierra Club supported 1999 ballot measures in several Bay Area cities that would have required a vote of the people for any increases in density.[4] As planning professor Bernard Frieden noted in 1979, the Sierra Club seems to oppose any new development in the Bay Area, often for contradictory reasons.[5] The result is that the San Francisco-Oakland regional housing market is the least affordable in the nation.

One conclusion may be that Sierra Club members support high density as long as it is somewhere else. Unlike the Surface Transportation Policy Project, the club is truly a membership organization. Local policies on sprawl and other issues are decided by local chapter members. The result is a group whose national goal is to favor high density but whose local chapters often favor low densities.

The Environmental Defense Fund

The Environmental Defense Fund (EDF) is an unusual environmental group in many ways. Although nominally an environmental law firm, it also employs many

economists and scientists. Unlike many other environmental groups, it often advocates free-market solutions to environmental problems. Though it is a national
group, its staff is highly decentralized and individual offices set their own policies.
Though it has members, it gets most of its funding from foundations.

EDF's Berkeley office has studied congestion pricing of roads. But the
organization's Washington office has focused mainly on smart-growth regulatory
programs. Michael Replogle, who works in the Washington office, works almost
exclusively on alternatives to autos. For nearly a decade, he directed transportation planning in Montgomery County, Maryland, which in many ways is the
home of smart growth. Now with EDF, he writes reports and gives frequent speeches
lauding urban-growth boundaries, light rail, and transit-oriented developments.

1000 Friends

Supplementing the national environmental groups such as STPP, EDF, and Sierra
Club are numerous statewide environmental groups that focus on land-use and
transportation planning. The model for such groups is 1000 Friends of Oregon,
which was founded in 1975 to monitor and enforce Oregon's land-use planning
laws. Initially, the group's focus was on halting or limiting development of farms,
forests, and open spaces outside of urban areas. But since around 1990, the group
has strongly promoted density, light rail, and other smart-growth ideas inside of
the state's urban areas while it opposes development in the 98 percent of the state
which is rural.

Henry Richmond, the founder of 1000 Friends of Oregon, later founded the
National Growth Management Leadership Project, whose main role was to inspire the creation of more 1000 friends groups in other states. Such 1000 friends
organizations have been formed in at least twenty different states, including Florida,
Hawaii, Maryland, Pennsylvania, and Washington. They are joined by a number
of similar organizations with slightly more creative names such as Grow Smart
Rhode Island and Coalition for Utah's Future.

1. Peter Samuel, "The Transportation Lobby: The Politics of Highway and Transit,"
   Organization Trends, February, 1996, http://www.capitalresearch.org/trends/ot-
   0296.html.
2. Surface Transportation Policy Project, "The Surface Transportation Policy Project: Who
   We Are," 1997, 1 p.
3. Sierra Club, *The Dark Side of the American Dream* (San Francisco, CA: Sierra Club,
   1998), http://www.sierraclub.org/transportation/sprawl/sprawl_report/.
4. *Contra Costa News*, "CAPP Initiative," various dates, http://www.hotcoco.com/elec-
   tion99/capp.htm.
5. Bernard J. Frieden, *The Environmental Protection Hustle* (Cambridge, MA: MIT, 1979),
   p. 9.

The Open-Space Myth

Myth: Urban growth is threatening prime agricultural lands, forests, and open space.

Reality: More than 95 percent of America is rural open space. Urban areas occupy less than 2 percent of the nation's land and all cities, towns, and villages of ten or more people occupy less than 3 percent of the nation's land.

As everyone who travels on interstate freeways knows, urbanization is filling every corner of the land. "Too much of our precious open space is being gobbled up by sprawl," claims Vice President Gore.[1] "We are running out of greener pastures," says the Sierra Club, adding that unchecked sprawl "destroys the agricultural heritage of this country."[2] Only urban-growth boundaries and more dense, compact cities, it seems, will save prime farm lands, wilderness, and open space from destruction.

The problem is that interstate freeways present a highly distorted view of the United States. Since those freeways are so convenient to trucking, they are a prime attraction to business and industry. Most freeways also follow rail lines that were the main source of freight transportation for more than a century, and hence were often developed before the interstates were built. The fact is, once you get off the freeway and outside of major urban areas, vast portions of the country remain undeveloped.

"Space is one of America's plentiful resources," says Brookings Institution urban analyst Pietro Nivola. It makes no sense "to expect that space should be utilized as parsimoniously here as in countries with precious little of it."[3] "There is an immense amount of vacant land even within that alleged belt of city running from Boston to Norfolk," says Herbert Gans. "The destruction of raw land," he adds "seems a small price to pay for extending the benefits of suburban life to more people."[4]

The total land area of the United States is about 3.6 million square miles. According to the 1990 census, major urbanized areas housed 64 percent of all Americans, yet occupied just 61,000 square miles of land. This is 1.7 percent of the nation as a whole. Census takers measured the amount of land in all of the

390 urban areas with a population greater than 50,000 people. All of the land inside the central city plus all adjacent land that had more than 1,000 people per square mile (roughly one house every two acres) was counted as part of the urbanized area.

According to the Federal Highway Administration, by 1998 these metropolitan areas expanded to cover 82,500 square miles of land. This is a 35 percent increase even though the population of these areas grew by only 10 percent. While this is possible, the Federal Highway Administration is not as meticulous in identifying urbanized areas as the Census Bureau. In fact, it relies on state highway agencies to collect the data, and some agencies may expand their urbanized areas in the hope that it may make them eligible for more federal funding. Still, 82,500 square miles represents just 2.3 percent of the nation's land.

The 1990 census also found that all cities, towns, and villages, no matter how small, covered just 126,000 square miles, or less than 3.5 percent of the entire U.S.[5] This includes all incorporated towns, even those with zero population, and unincorporated villages of as few as 2 people. Many of these places include vast areas of open space within their borders. The Census Bureau included 2,600 square miles in Juneau, Alaska, and 2,300 in Sitka, yet the actual developed portions of these cities are much smaller. Bay Lake, Florida, has no residents yet occupies 18.6 square miles, while Circle Hot Springs, Arkansas, has 29 residents yet covers 53.3 miles of land. With so few residents it is unlikely that all of these square miles are developed. So 126,000 square miles greatly overstates the amount of urbanized land in the U.S. If urbanized areas are generously defined as having a density of at least 500 people per square mile (about one house every four acres), then no more than 91,000 square miles, or 2.5 percent of the nation, were urbanized in 1990.

Another source of data about the development of open space is the Natural Resources Inventory conducted every five years by the Natural Resources Conservation Service (formerly known as the Soils Conservation Service). The 1992 inventory found that just 4.0 percent of the land area of the U.S. has been developed. This includes both urban developments as well as rural roads and railroads.

In December, 1999, Vice President Al Gore claimed that the 1997 Natural Resources Inventory proved that sprawl was accelerating and action was needed immediately to protect open space. The numbers Gore released indicated that 165,000 square miles, or about 5.4 percent of the nation's land, were developed, including both urban and rural developments. Gore claimed that this represented a rate of development between 1992 and 1997 that was twice as fast as the rate between 1987 and 1992.

In fact, it turns out that the 1997 inventory data were severely flawed and may have been manipulated to support Gore's position. There are several indications that the data were flawed. First, the numbers that Gore claims for the 1987 and 1992 inventories differed from the actual numbers in those inventories. Gore's numbers for 1987 indicated 7,350 square miles more developed land than found by the 1987 inventory, while Gore's numbers for 1992 found 4,700 fewer square miles of developed land than in the 1992 inventory.[6] Where Gore's numbers show an accelerating pace of urban development, the actual numbers show no change in pace.

The second problem is that Gore's numbers for individual states make no sense when compared with other data for those states. The numbers for Pennsylvania showed a huge increase in developed lands between 1992 and 1997. Yet Pennsylvanians actually built fewer homes between 1992 and 1997 than between 1987 and 1992. For Gore's numbers to be correct, the average home lot would have had to increase from less than one-half acre to more than 5 acres.[7] Gore's numbers also conflicted with the USDA Census of Agriculture for Pennsylvania. Where Gore's numbers found a 900,000 acre loss in farmlands, the Census for Agriculture found only a 21,600 acre decline.[8]

While the Census of Agriculture is based on an actual count of every acre used to grow agricultural products, the Natural Resources Inventory which Gore used is based on a statistical sample. This sample includes 800,000 "points" which are evaluated to see if they are urban, crops, pasture, forest, or whatever. These 800,000 points are assumed to accurately represent the nearly 1.6 billion acres of non-federal land outside of Alaska. As it turns out, they weren't so accurate. In March, 2000, the Department of Agriculture warned that it had found a "problem" with the Natural Resources Inventory data that Gore had used and was withdrawing the data pending revision.[9]

Was the problem an accident or were the data manipulated to lend credence to the war on sprawl? One indication comes from a preliminary Natural Resources Inventory report that had been published a year before Gore's announcement. This preliminary report conflicted with Gore's claims in two major ways:

- Where Gore claimed that the U.S. lost 1.9 percent of its croplands between 1992 and 1997, the preliminary report indicated less than a 0.5 percent decline in croplands.
- Where Gore claimed that pasture lands and range lands both also declined, and forest lands increased only slightly, the preliminary report found that increases in pasture, range, and forest lands accounted for most of the decline in crop lands.

One reason why crop lands are declining is that improved farming techniques are producing greater yields from fewer acres. One hundred years ago, the average Iowa farmer produced about 20 bushels of corn to the acre. Today the average is 150 bushels and in 1999 one Iowa farmer managed to get 394 bushels per acre. As a result of these yields, says the *Wall Street Journal*, "the world is awash in corn" and corn prices are "deeply depressed."[10]

Nor is there any danger of running out of farm lands. Although farmers only cultivated crops on a little over 500,000 square miles in 1997, the U.S. has nearly

1 million more square miles of agricultural lands. These lands are being used for conservation reserves, pastures, range, and other non-crop purposes. "Preconceptions about the 'assault' of urban development on farmland may be even more misplaced," says Nivola. "The United States is one of the world's most productive agricultural producers, with ample capacity to spare."[11]

The above figures do not even count the more than 620,000 square miles of forest lands, many of which were used for agriculture until rising farm production led farmers to turn them back into woodlands. Because of the regrowth of forests on former farms, the U.S. has more forest lands today than it did a century ago. Moreover, timber is growing faster than forest landowners are cutting it, and this has been true for at least eighty years. In 1996, American forests grew nearly 24 million cubic feet of wood, but landowners cut only 16 million cubic feet.[12] According to projections by the Forest Service, this is likely to remain true for the next fifty years, which is as far ahead as the agency tries to see into the future.

Even if Gore's data were correct, they show that, outside of Alaska:

- The federal government owns more than 400 million acres of land;
- Non-federal agricultural lands cover 930 million acres;
- Non-federal forest lands cover 400 million acres;
- For a total of 1,730 million acres of open space.
- By comparison, Gore's data show that less than 81 million acres are urbanized, which means we have more than 21 acres of open space for every urbanized acre.

If Gore's 1997 numbers are believed, on a state-by-state basis, urbanization covers:

- 100 percent of DC;
- About a third of New Jersey;
- About a quarter Connecticut, Massachusetts, and Rhode Island;
- 10 to 15 percent of Maryland, Delaware, Florida, Ohio, Pennsylvania, and North Carolina;
- 5 to 10 percent of New York, Michigan, Georgia, South Carolina, Tennessee, Virginia, Indiana, Illinois, Alabama, and Kentucky; and
- Less than 5 percent of all remaining states.

Roughly a third of the nation, and more than half of the West, is in federal or state forests, parks, or range reserves. These lands will probably never be urbanized and in the future their primary goal will be to provide outdoor recreation for urban residents. Their capacity for handling that goal is far ahead of their current usage; although a few areas of a few national parks are crowded—notably Yosemite Valley, the South Rim of the Grand Canyon, and parts of two or three other parks—99 percent of these lands are hardly used for recreation today.

Notes

1. Office of the Vice President, "Vice President Al Gore Releases New Figures Showing Accelerated Loss of Farmland to Development," December 6, 1999, p. 1.
2. Sierra Club, *The Dark Side of The American Dream*, http://www.sierraclub.org/transportation/sprawl/sprawl_report/.
3. Pietro S. Nivola, *Laws of the Landscape: How Policies Shape Cities in Europe and America* (Washington, DC: Brookings, 1999), p. 5.
4. Herbert J. Gans, *The Levittowners: Ways of Life and Politics in a New Suburban Community* (New York, NY: Pantheon, 1967), p. 422–423.
5. Census Bureau, "Places," http://www.census.gov/population/www/censusdata/places.html.
6. USDA, *Summary Report, 1987 Natural Resources Inventory* (Washington, DC: USDA, 1989), table one; USDA, *1992 Natural Resources Inventory* (Washington, DC: USDA, 1994), table one; USDA, *Summary Report, 1997 Natural Resources Inventory* (Washington, DC: USDA, 1999), table one.
7. Diana Mastrull, "U.S. Study on Land Development Was Wrong," *The Philadelphia Inquirer*, April 28, 2000.
8. USDA, *Census of Agriculture* (Washington, DC: USDA, 1999).
9. U.S. Department of Agriculture, "Announcement," March 27, 2000, http://www.nhq.nrcs.usda.gov/NRI/1997/summary_report/original/contents.html.
10. Scott Kilman, "King of Corn Has Tips for Farmers, But More Isn't What They Need," *Wall Street Journal*, February 28, 2000, p. A1.
11. Pietro S. Nivola, *Laws of the Landscape: How Policies Shape Cities in Europe and America* (Washington, DC: Brookings, 1999), p. 39.
12. W. Brad Smith, *1997 RPA Assessment of the Nation's Forests* (Washington, DC: Forest Service, 1999), review draft, table 13.

1000 Friends of Oregon

The Land Conservation and Development Commission would not be able to do all that it does without the support of the nonprofit group known as 1000 Friends of Oregon, which files appeals and lawsuits to enforce the Commission's rules. The group was started in 1975 by Henry Richmond, who had been staff attorney for the Oregon Student Public Interest Research Group (OSPIRG). Governor McCall enthusiastically chaired the group's original board of advisors. The group is named after Richmond's initial fundraising strategy: He hoped to convince one thousand people to each donate $100 per year. While he never reached that target, he raised enough funds to hire Robert Stacey and Richard Benner, two recent University of Oregon law graduates and former OSPIRG interns, to work for the organization. Robert Liberty, another recent law school graduate, was hired a few years later.

Today, 1000 Friends may be the most powerful nonprofit group in the state of Oregon. Urban analysts at Portland State University note that, "although 1000 Friends bills its membership as including 'wine producers and woodlot owners, office builders and orchardists, farmers, environmentalists, ranchers, teachers, computer software engineers,' this group's most important members are perhaps its attorneys." This is because the group gains its power from "a powerful weapon: the threat of lawsuits against any entity, be it private or public, that violates the sanctity of the land use laws." The analysts add that "it is clear that the [Land Conservation and Development Commission] relies on the support of 1000 Friends in the implementation of its policy."[1]

Though many viewed it as an environmental group, 1000 Friends of Oregon was really a coalition of environmental and developer interests. On one hand, 1000 Friends successfully challenged city and county plans that drew overly large urban-growth boundaries or that failed to zone lands outside of urban-growth boundaries to sufficiently large lot sizes. On the other hand, 1000 Friends also challenged towns that proposed to limit or place a moratorium on building permits or to zone their entire communities for very large lot sizes, actions violating the state's housing goal. The coalition was based on an understanding that the environmentalists would gain protection of rural open space while the developers would be allowed to accommodate growth by building homes inside the urban-growth boundaries.

By 1986, all city and county land-use plans had been completed, approved by LCDC, and (in many cases) rewritten in response to appeals by 1000 Friends. More than 98 percent of the state was zoned for large-lot development, mostly in lot sizes so large that it prohibited subdivisions. For a time, 1000 Friends appeared to be a group in search of something to do.

Then the Oregon Department of Transportation proposed to build a new freeway from Tualatin to Hillsboro, Washington County communities which were beginning a high-tech boom. Though both cities are inside the Portland urban-growth boundary, the direct route from one to the other went outside the boundary. Highway opponents charged that the highway was a "boundary buster" that would encourage expansion of the boundary and development on prime farm lands.

In response, 1000 Friends raised money from a number of foundations to do a major study of alternatives to the road. The study, called Land Use, Transportation, Air Quality (LUTRAQ), purported to show that transit improvements and compact, transit-oriented development would reduce traffic demands enough that there would be no need to build the highway (see the LUTRAQ Myth, p. 165).

In 1990, 1000 Friends was fifteen years old and highly influential in Oregon politics. But most of that influence had been used to protect rural farms, forests, and open space; the group made almost no effort to alter the lifestyles of urban and suburban residents. But now the group used LUTRAQ to build a network of seemingly independent groups that lobby for transit, compact development, and zero expansion of the urban-growth boundary. Led by Robert Liberty, who took over as 1000 Friends' director when Henry Richmond left the organization, its staff and board serve on the boards of many other non-profits while its former staff have taken major government posts influencing Oregon's land-use planning system.

As a part of the LUTRAQ project, 1000 Friends helped start Sensible Transportation Options for People, later renamed Citizens for Sensible Transportation.[2] The group lobbies in favor of light rail, providing a counterweight to the fact that other Portland transit advocates, including the Association of Oregon Railway and Transit Advocates and Citizens for Better Transit, oppose Portland's light-rail plans. The latter groups want better transit, while Citizens for Sensible Transit sees rail transit as a part of the 1000 Friends land-use agenda.

When the debate over expansion of the urban-growth boundary heated up, 1000 Friends helped form the Zero Option Committee, a group of local officials and activists who opposed any expansion of the boundary.[3]

As Metro started developing its 2040 plan, 1000 Friends started the Coalition for a Livable Future, bringing together more than fifty other groups, including the League of Women Voters, environmental groups such as the Sierra Club, antipoverty groups such as the Oregon Food Bank, planning groups such as the Portland chapter of the American Planning Association, and several churches to lobby for compact development and transit. Until recently, the group used 1000 Friends' server and web address for its web site; the web site directed that orders for the group's publications must be accompanied by checks made out to "1000 Friends."[4] Ironically, one of the members of the Coalition for a Livable Future is the Sunnyside United Methodist Church, the church that was ordered to limit its services to seventy people (see p. 146). Perhaps the church's leaders now realize that a government that tells farmers, suburbanites, auto drivers, and retailers how to live their lives and run their businesses is bound to get around to telling churches what they can and cannot do as well.

Oregon's governor started the Willamette Valley Livability Forum to consider the future of farms, forests, and urban areas in the Willamette River Valley, where most Oregonians live, and appointed Liberty to the group's steering committee. Liberty in turn organized the Willamette Valley Alternative Futures Project, whose goal is to provide technical support for and influence the Livability Forum.[5] The organization's web site is located on the server of ECONorthwest, a for-profit consulting firm that does most of the economic consulting to state and local governments in Oregon.

Like many tax exempt political groups, 1000 Friends has a lobbying arm, the 1000 Friends Action Fund. The group lobbies in the state legislature, participates in ballot measure campaigns, and rates legislators for their support or opposition to 1000 Friends policies.[6] The organization's offices and staff are the same as 1000 Friends, but having a separate group on paper enables 1000 Friends to obtain foundation grants that would not be available to a lobbying group.

The 1000 Friends network is supported by former 1000 Friends employees who have moved into government positions. Former staff attorney Richard Benner is now director of the Department of Land Conservation and Development, the state agency that oversees the land-use planning and zoning done by every city and county in Oregon. Under his leadership, the Land Conservation and Development Commission passed the rule requiring that rural land owners earn $80,000 per year farming before being allowed to build a home on their land.

Robert Stacey, 1000 Friends' other early staff attorney, went on to be director of planning for Portland, Oregon for several years and now is the head planner for Tri-Met, Portland's transit agency. He also chairs a nonprofit organization called Livable Oregon, which is funded by Oregon's Department of Transportation to "help" communities all over the state write smart-growth plans.[7]

Various board and staff members of 1000 Friends also serve on the boards of other Oregon non-profits or on various government commissions. For example, Gail Achterman chaired the 1000 Friends board at the same time as she served on the Governor's Task Force on Growth. Staff member Evan Manvel is on the board of the Bicycle Transportation Alliance, which lobbies for funding for bikeways and against "our out-of-balance reliance on the automobile."[8] Robert Liberty was a member of Portland's Future Visions Commission which developed the vision on which Metro's 2040 plan was based.

Meanwhile, Henry Richmond started the National Growth Management Leadership Project, which helps create 1000 friends organizations in other states, including Colorado, Florida, Hawaii, Iowa, Maryland, Minnesota, New Mexico, Ohio, Pennsylvania, Utah, Washington, and Wisconsin. Many of these groups are gaining the same sort of influence in their states as 1000 Friends has in Oregon. The group is chaired by Robert Liberty.

The list of groups influenced by 1000 Friends would not be complete without mentioning Portland Audubon Society, whose staff naturalist, Mike Houck, is Robert Liberty's close friend and neighbor. Houck helped start the Coalition for a Livable Future and was instrumental in creating Portland's Greenspaces program, the region's large-scale land acquisition effort for parks and wildlife.[9]

Liberty lives in inner-city Northwest Portland, within walking distance of stores and walking or cycling distance of 1000 Friends' offices. He once told me that "I grew up on a 50-by-100 lot, and what's good enough for me should be good enough for anyone." While he seems willing to impose his lifestyle choice on hundreds of thousands of other Portlanders, even he has his limits. When someone proposed to allow coffee shops and other commercial uses on the ground floors of multifamily housing in his neighborhood, he strongly objected to "commercial creeping up the side streets." Said Liberty, "I love cappuccino as well as anyone, but I don't want the whole neighborhood to be a regional boutique."[10]

In addition to interlocking boards and other ties with each other and 1000 Friends, many of these groups share the same funding base. The Energy Foundation, the Ford Foundation, the James C. Penney Foundation, the Nathan Cummings Foundation, the Northwest Area Foundation, the Surdna Foundation, and the Environmental Protection Agency have all given money to more than one, and in many cases several, of the above groups.

Not all Oregon environmentalists support the 1000 Friends agenda. Some, led by former Oregon Natural Resources Council director Andy Kerr, have started Alternatives to Growth Oregon (AGO), a nonprofit group dedicated to slow- or no-growth policies. In contrast, the 1000 Friends agenda has always accepted growth and the group built its coalition of developers and environmentalists on that premise. Alternatives to Growth Oregon has developed enough of a following to lead Governor Kitzhaber to create his Task Force on Growth to examine slow-growth and no-growth policies. But with Gail Achterman as chair and two other 1000 Friends board members on the task force, the group's conclusions were foreordained.[11] Although the task force proposed new and increased taxes to pay for growth, it did not propose to try to limit growth in urban areas.[12]

A different view is provided by John Charles, who for seventeen years was director of the Oregon Environmental Council. Charles supports incentive-based policies, such as pollution fees and congestion pricing of highways, rather than regulatory policies aimed at discouraging driving and low-density housing. But Charles's freedom to promote these policies was hampered by the fact that Robert Stacey or other 1000 Friends staff members were almost always on his board of directors. At one point, the board censored twelve out of sixteen pages of comments Charles wrote on Metro's plans. Charles eventually left the organization and now works for Oregon's libertarian think tank, the Cascade Policy Institute. Stacey made certain that Charles's replacement supports the 1000 Friends' agenda.

Both Kerr's and Charles's dissenting views probably represent a substantial number of Oregonians. But as yet neither has come anywhere close to the success of 1000 Friends in promoting their policies. While still vulnerable to challenge, the 1000 Friends agenda has become the firm policy of Oregon, Portland's regional government, most major city governments, and many county governments. Many people fear that land-use planning is controlled by developers, but in Oregon the real power is in the hands of 1000 Friends of Oregon.

Notes

1. Martha J. Bianco and Sy Adler, *The Politics of Implementation: Oregon's Statewide Transportation Planning Rule—What's Been Accomplished and How* (Portland, OR: PSU Center for Urban Studies, 1998), pp. 20–21, http://www.upa.pdx.edu/CUS/PUBS/PDFs/DP98-8.pdf.
2. Citizens for Sensible Transportation, "Citizens for Sensible Transportation," http://www.cfst.org/ and http://www.cfst.org/history.html.
3. R. Gregory Nokes, "Support multiplies for 'zero' growth option," *The Oregonian*, November 11, 1995, p. A1.
4. Coalition for a Livable Future, "Mission," www.clfuture.org/aboutclf.html; "Members," www.clfuture.org/members.html, "A Brief History of the Coalition," www.clfuture.org/history.html. Until March, 2000, the group's web address was www.friends.org/clr/index.html.
5. Willamette Valley Alternative Futures Project, "About this Project," http://www.econw.com/wvaf/about.html and "Researchers and Advisors," http://www.econw.com/wvaf/research.html.
6. 1000 Friends Action Fund, "Mission," http://www.1000friendsaction.org/about.html.
7. Livable Oregon, "About Livable Oregon," http://www.livable.org/about.html.
8. Bicycle Transportation Alliance, "History of the BTA," http://www.teleport.com/~bta4bike/info/about.html.
9. Audubon Society of Portland, "Board Officers and Staff," http://www.audubonportland.org/come_see/brdstaff.htm#staff.
10. Lee Perlman, "Residents air thoughts on Northwest infill plan," *The Oregonian*, November 23, 1992, p. B2.
11. Richard Carson, "They may have 1000 Friends, but none are builders," *The Business Journal*, May 4, 1998, http://www.amcity.com/portland/stories/1998/05/04/editorial3.html.
12. Task Force on Growth in Oregon, *Growth and Its Impacts in Oregon* (Salem, OR: Governor's Office, 1999), pp. 6-5–6-6, http://www.governor.state.or.us/governor/download/taskrpt.pdf.

The LUTRAQ Myth

Myth: The Land Use-Transportation-Air Quality (LUTRAQ) study proves that higher densities and transit-oriented development will reduce congestion.

Reality: LUTRAQ overestimated the effects of density and transit-oriented development on travel habits, but even with those overestimates it predicts that these policies will increase congestion.

With the financial support of numerous foundations, the Land Use, Transportation, Air Quality (LUTRAQ) study was commissioned by 1000 Friends of Oregon with the aim of stopping a new highway. In numbers of people, Washington County was the fastest growing part of Oregon, and state transportation officials had proposed a highway connecting Tualatin to Hillsboro to reduce the county's rapidly growing congestion.

LUTRAQ proposed a combination of high-density, mixed-use developments in the centers of Hillsboro, Tualatin, and other Washington County cities; a light-rail line connecting these centers; and numerous transit-oriented developments located within a mile of light rail or express bus routes. The high-density developments would accommodate increased numbers of people without expanding the urban-growth boundary while the rail and bus service would allow those people to move around without congesting the roads.[1]

The groups hired several professional consulting firms to predict the effects of its alternative. They estimated that people living in transit-oriented developments would be far less likely to own an automobile and far more likely to walk, cycle, or ride transit than people living in a standard suburban development.[2] Based on this, they estimated that, compared with building the Western Bypass, the LUTRAQ alternative would:

- Reduce auto commuting from 89 to 78 percent;
- Increase the share of auto commuters riding in carpools from 15 to 26 percent;
- Increase the share of commuters using transit from 9 to 18 percent;
- Increase the share of commuters walking or cycling from 2.5 to 3.5 percent; and

• Reduce total vehicle-miles traveled by 8 percent.[3]

Many of these estimates were based on highly speculative assumptions about the effects of density and design on people's travel behavior. For example, the model assumed that people would drive less if stores and offices fronted on sidewalks instead of being separated from the street and sidewalk by a parking lot. In particular, a 63-percent increase in commercial buildings fronting on the sidewalk was supposed to reduce driving by 10 percent.

To support assumptions like these, 1000 Friends hired experts such as the Parsons Brinkerhoff engineering consulting firm and Peter Calthorpe's architectural firm. While ostensibly objective, Parsons Brinkerhoff is making tens of millions of dollars helping cities design and build light-rail systems. Calthorpe, of course, is a strong proponent of smart growth policies.

Many outsiders, however, doubted whether LUTRAQ's assumptions were valid. Wayne Kittleson, a Portland transportation consultant, reviewed the Parsons Brinkerhoff studies that supposedly supported the claim that building design would change travel behavior. He found that the methods and data in the reports were "too weak to support the conclusions that have been reached." In particular, the statistical analyses in the reports themselves showed that "the actual relationship [between building design and travel] is questionable." In fact, he concluded, "the LUTRAQ data actually help to demonstrate that building orientation [whether buildings front on the sidewalk] is not likely to materially affect these mode choice decisions."[4]

Table One: Commuting Choices under LUTRAQ Alternatives
(percent share and percent change from bypass alternative)

All travel	Bypass	LUTRAQ	% Change	LUTRAQ+	% Change
Walk	2.5	3.5	40.0	3.5	40.0
Transit	8.8	10.0	13.6	12.8	45.5
Drive alone	75.1	72.7	-3.2	63.9	-14.9
Carpool	13.6	13.8	1.5	19.7	44.9
Total auto	88.7	86.5	-2.5	83.6	-5.7

LUTRAQ predicted that, if the Bypass were built, 75 percent of commuters would drive alone. Land-use changes would reduce this by just 3 percent; TDM reduces it by nearly 12 percent more. Source: Genevieve Giuliano, "The Weakening Transportation-Land Use Connection," Access 6 (Spring, 1995): p. 8.

Even if all of the assumptions in LUTRAQ were valid, LUTRAQ's results show that rail transit and transit-oriented development have little effect on people's behavior. University of Southern California planning Professor Genevieve Giuliano points out that LUTRAQ compared several different alternatives. One assumed that the Western Bypass was built. A second assumed that light rail would be built instead of the bypass and land use would emphasize transit-oriented developments. A third alternative was the same as the second, but also assumed that all workers would get free transit passes but have to pay for parking if they drove to work. This was called the *transportation demand management* or TDM alternative.

Table one indicates that the TDM alternative reduces drive-alone commuting by nearly 15 percent. But land-use policies and rail transit alone reduce drive-alone commuting by only 3 percent. Clearly, the assumed parking fees and free transit are much more important than land-use and design codes. Despite the huge change in land-use patterns, comments Giuliano, "without TDM, travel impacts of the LUTRAQ alternative are minor."[5]

LUTRAQ predicts significant effects on transit *if* parking fees and free transit are included. But 1000 Friends and other LUTRAQ supporters go beyond even these results to falsely claim that LUTRAQ predicts that smart growth would reduce congestion. In fact, even with free transit and costly parking, LUTRAQ numbers show auto commuting (including carpooling) is reduced by less than 6 percent while total auto travel, including non-commuter travel, is reduced by just 2.2 percent. Commuters make up only about half of all rush-hour travel, so LUTRAQ-plus-TDM reduces the auto's share of rush-hour travel by only about 4 percent. Since LUTRAQ's increases in density are much greater than 4 percent, total traffic is increased at all hours of the day.

Despite these problems, LUTRAQ became one of the most influential smart-growth studies ever done, and certainly the most influential study done by a non-government organization. Although LUTRAQ only studied the Washington County portion of the Portland area, Metro ended up applying its recommendations to the entire Portland area. In 1998, Oregon Senator Ron Wyden convinced Congress to spend $20 million per year on LUTRAQ-like studies in other cities. The money goes to local governments but may be shared with "nontraditional" organizations, meaning nonprofit groups such as 1000 Friends. In 2000, for example, the program gave $205,000 to Envision Utah, which is promoting smart growth in the Salt Lake City area.

Notes

1. 1000 Friends of Oregon, *Making the Connections: A Summary of the LUTRAQ Project* (Portland, Oregon: 1000 Friends, 1997), pp. 8–10.
2. Ibid, p. 9.
3. Ibid, p. 15.
4. Wayne Kittleson, Letter to Keith Bartholomew, 1000 Friends of Oregon, June 24, 1994, 3 pp.
5. Genevieve Giuliano, "The Weakening Transportation-Land Use Connection," *Access* 6 (Spring, 1995): p. 8.

Transportation Planning in Oregon

Inspired by efforts to link transportation and land-use planning, in 1991 the state Land Conservation and Development Commission issued a new transportation planning rule requiring Oregon's major cities to halt and reverse the historic trend towards more per capita driving. In particular, cities were to:

• Prevent any increase in miles per capita in the next ten years;
• Reduce miles per capita by at least 10 percent in the next twenty years;
• Reduce miles per capita by at least 20 percent in the next thirty years; and
• Reduce per capita nonresidential parking by at least 10 percent in the next twenty years.[1]

The rule directed Metro and its counterparts in Salem, Eugene, and Medford to increase population and job densities; place "neighborhood shopping centers" within walking distance of residential areas; reduce the number of nonresidential parking spaces per capita by 10 percent; require transit stops at all major industrial, retail, and office centers; and build bikeways and sidewalks along all arterials and major collector roads, among other things. The original rule contained many other requirements, such as that many businesses should front on sidewalks instead of providing parking in front.

"I find it difficult to believe" that the state would even consider such a rule, says Alan Pisarski, author of *Commuting in America*.[2] No wonder: Americans have increased their use of motor vehicles (including cars, trucks, and buses) by 2 to 3 percent per year since 1930. Even during the oil-shocked 1970s, the trend averaged 2.1 percent per year. Increases in driving aren't frivolous, nor are they related to poor urban design. Pisarski points out that they are due to such things as more women entering the work force and demographic trends as baby boomers get older.

As it turns out, the state land-use commission partly recognized the hopelessness of this rule in 1998, when it eliminated the ten-year requirement and reduced the twenty- and thirty-year requirements. In addition, in 1995 the commission relaxed the regulations on building orientation, limiting them to businesses near major transit stops. But the commission still expects Portland-area residents to reduce their driving by 15 percent within thirty years. The commission claims that its rule will "make it more convenient for people to walk, bicycle and use transit."[3] In fact, all it really will do is make it less convenient to drive. There is little evidence that it will actually change people's travel behavior.

In 1997, the Coalition for a Livable Future and 1000 Friends of Oregon convinced Governor John Kitzhaber to issue an executive order directing all other state agencies to "promote compact development" and "encourage mixed-use development designed to encourage walking, biking, and transit use."[4] The governor-appointed Oregon Transportation Commission complied with enthusiasm. The state's highway plan predicts that auto driving will increase by 40 percent in the next two decades. "If nothing is done to improve currently high volume highway segments," says the plan, "highway mobility will decrease, travel times will increase, and user costs will increase for each user."[5] But rather than try to maintain mobility in urban areas, the plan's goal is to "foster compact development patterns in communities."

Towards that end, the state Department of Transportation has funded Livable Oregon, a nonprofit group chaired by former 1000 Friends attorney Robert Stacey, to run a "smart development" program. This program, says the department, "provides public information on alternative development patterns and designs."[6] Livable Oregon goes further, saying that they help community leaders "advocate" for "main street revitalization."[7]

According to the Department of Transportation's *Smart Development Primer*, the "ideal community" is one in which people can "walk to the store, the library, the post office, or the bank."[8] The primer presents all of the usual arguments about the costs of sprawl and the need "for more transportation options." It says that compact development "reduces traffic" and claims that "gasoline taxes and user fees cover only 60 percent of the costs of building and maintaining roads, leaving a $21 billion shortfall annually to be paid from general taxation." As will be shown in the Subsidized-Highway Myth (p. 380), this claim is false.

The transportation department also gives local planning agencies grants for transportation and growth management planning. Typical grants include:
- $44,600 to Clackamas County for "traffic calming and skinny streets standards";
- $52,000 to Beaverton for "property redevelopment alternatives for Beaverton's automobile-dependent downtown";
- $40,000 to Salem to plan mixed-use developments;
- $40,000 to Eugene to plan "infill and redevelopment areas";
- $30,000 to Ashland for a "neotraditional subdivision ordinance."

The grants are not confined to urban areas. Morrow County has a population of 10,000 and its largest city has a population of just 1,700. Yet it has received more than $150,000 in grants for urban growth and transportation planning. Dayville, Long Creek, and Monument (combined populations: under 500) received $55,000 for transportation plans; Talent (population: 4,300) received

$15,000 for a "transit-oriented downtown plan" plus another $30,000 for a "transportation system plan"; and Hermiston (population: 11,500) received $50,000 for an "infill and redevelopment strategies plan."

In total, the transportation department gives out about $2.5 million per year for such planning, about half of which goes into the Portland metropolitan area. On a statewide scale, grants in the tens of thousands of dollars do not seem like much, but they can represent a lot of money for small town and thinly-populated county governments. As Oregon City planner Richard Carson says, the grants provide incentives "to local governments to pursue this alternative-transportation philosophy in every planning effort."[9]

Another thing that the state has done is to significantly reduce the mobility standards for Oregon's urban roads. In a major departure from past practice, Oregon's 1999 highway plan calls for significantly lower mobility standards in urban areas than in small towns and rural areas (table one). Even lower standards apply to *special transportation areas*, which are "designated compact district[s] located on a state highway within an urban growth boundary." In other words, they include the main streets and business districts in any incorporated town. Within these areas, mobility standards will be so low that "traffic congestion will be allowed to reach levels where peak hour traffic flow is highly unstable and traffic queues will form on a regular basis." In such areas, the state will emphasize transit, bicycle, and pedestrian facilities over auto capacities.

Table One: Oregon Mobility Standards
(Highway volume-to-capacity ratios)

Location	Range of 1999 Standards	Comparable LOS
Rural areas	0.70–0.75	C
Unincorporated communities	0.70–0.80	C
Inside small-town UGBs	0.70–0.85	C
Eugene, Medford, Salem UGB	0.80–0.90	C–D
Special transportation areas	0.85–0.95	D
Portland non-concept areas	0.90–0.95	D–E
Portland freeways	0.9	D
Portland concept areas	0.95–1.00	E

Source: ODOT, Oregon Highway Plan, tables 6 and 7. Concept areas include central Portland, regional and town centers, light-rail station areas, and main streets. Generally the higher standards (lower number) in a range are for major roads and freight routes, while the lower standards are for regional, local, or non-freight routes.

The very lowest mobility standards are in the Portland area. Central Portland and areas that Metro has designated regional or town centers, main streets, and areas around light-rail stations all have a volume-to-capacity standard of 1.0. This effectively means that even when these areas are gridlocked the state will not feel any need to increase road capacities. Only freight routes in these areas get any break, with a standard of 0.95. Outside of these areas, Portland standards are 0.9 to 0.95, which still means they have to reach near-gridlock conditions before planners will consider increasing road capacities.

"Current state planning policy," says Carson, "is being driven by a desire on the part of environmentalists and sympathetic planning officials to change the American automobile culture." LCDC's and ODOT's plans aim to "radically change our lifestyles, get us out of the car and have us walk, ride a bike or use transit" so that we save fuel and pollute less. Yet Carson notes that the justification for such social engineering is weak, since high-mileage, low-emission cars are technically feasible. Recently, for example, Honda began selling a seventy-mile-per-gallon car. The state, he concludes, should end its "denial about the automobile" and stop "gambling the taxpayers' money on an outdated conviction that government can convince us to do something we don't want to do."[10]

The commission's policies represent a radical turnaround from historic practice. A recent report by one state transportation analyst warns that "large increases in highway capacity will be needed to avoid growing congestion unless Oregonians agree to substantially reduce their personal mobility."[11] But the chair of Oregon's State Transportation Commission has told the legislature that "I don't believe we can build our way out of congestion."[12] Worse than doing nothing about congestion, the state is actually increasing congestion by helping Metro reduce the capacities of many Portland-area state highways (see "Congestion Signals Positive Urban Development," p. 111).

Notes

1. LCDC, *Transportation Planning Rule*, OAR Chapter 660-12-035(4), adopted 1993.
2. Gordon Oliver, "Transit expert sees continual desire for sprawl, autos," *The Oregonian*, December 6, 1994.
3. LCDC, *Transportation Planning Rule*, "Purpose."
4. John Kitzhaber, "1997 Executive Order creating Oregon's Quality Development Objectives," executive order number EO 97-22, 16 December 1997.
5. ODOT, *1999 Oregon Highway Plan* (Portland, OR: ODOT, 1999), "State Highway Needs Analysis," http://www.odot.state.or.us/tdb/planning/highway/vision.doc.
6. ODOT, "Smart Development," http://www.lcd.state.or.us/issues/tgmweb/smart/smart.htm.
7. Livable Oregon, "About Livable Oregon," http://www.livable.org/about.html.
8. ODOT, "Smart Development Primer," http://www.lcd.state.or.us/issues/tgmweb/smart/primer.htm.
9. Richard Carson, "Rethinking the Car," *The Oregonian*, October 16, 1997, (op-ed page).
10. Ibid.
11. Brian Gregor, *Statewide Congestion Overview for Oregon* (Salem, OR: ODOT, 1998), p. 3.
12. Henry Hewitt, testimony before Interim Committee on Natural Resources, April 1, 1998.

10. Central City Boosters

A huge portion of the smart-growth debate results from a single historical fact: the political division between central cities and suburbs. The central cities are generally the most powerful political entity in any urban area, yet most if not all of the population and employment growth is taking place in the suburbs. Central city officials maintain the nineteenth-century view that a city should consist of a job-dense downtown surrounded by dense residential areas. They often express aesthetic revulsion against the suburbs, but their real gripe is that they have no control over the property taxes and other taxes paid by suburbanites.

City Officials

To central city officials, suburbanites are parasites, enjoying the advantages of an urban area without paying their fair share of the costs. Annexations and city-county consolidations were attempts to include the suburbs in the central city tax base. The suburbs fought back by voting against annexation, when they had that option, or incorporating towns of their own, making them immune to hostile takeovers—or so they thought. Smart growth's push for regional governments is an attempt to overcome that immunity.

Portland, Oregon, has a nineteenth-century downtown, but two-thirds of its residents live (and most work) in the suburbs. Charles Hales, Portland city commissioner and leading smart-growth proponent, calls low-density suburbs around Portland "trash."[1] But he is probably most upset that most suburbanites voted against increasing their property taxes to pay for more light-rail construction.

Before becoming a U.S. representative, Earl Blumenauer also held a seat on Portland's city council. Today, he is promoting smart growth in Congress. Sometimes, he says, we need "the federal government to make the rules, to help us do what we know we need to do."[2] Such rules would insure that every city adopts smart-growth policies even if their suburbs or other residents do not want to.

Albuquerque is largely a twentieth-century city, with only a tiny downtown. Yet its former mayor, David Rusk, never understood that this was the inevitable result of urban growth in a automotive society. "As mayor," he says, "I often spoke of Albuquerque as 'a giant suburb in search of a city.'" His goal is "reunifying city and suburbs, creating, in effect, 'cities without suburbs.'"[3] One tool toward that goal is regional government, and Rusk urges central cities to form "regional growth management compacts" to gain control over reluctant suburbs.[4]

Milwaukee Mayor John Norquist believes that federal highway, housing, and other subsidies favored suburban growth and "undermined the natural advantages of cities." He believes that a free market, with no federal interference, would lead to more central city growth and less suburban sprawl. Right or wrong, his argument that "urban superhighways should be relegated to the scrap heap of history" is inconsistent with his strong support for federal funding of a light-rail transit system in Milwaukee.[5]

Whether they are Republicans or Democrats, free marketeers or big-government planners, most central city officials agree that suburban growth is bad and that urban policies should aim to force suburbanites to return to the cities. Their efforts toward that end are supported by two organizations of local government officials, the Local Government Commission and the International Council for Local Environmental Initiatives.

The Local Government Commission is a nonprofit organization that "is composed of forward-thinking elected officials, city and county staff, and other interested individuals." Its goal is to provide "information to mayors, city council members and county supervisors and others regarding innovative, creative programs and policies and assists their implementation through technical assistance, networking and peer support, workshops, policy development, and publications."[6]

One of the commission's major projects is the "Center for Livable Communities," which promotes smart growth policies, including the Ahwahnee Principles, transit-oriented development, and alternatives to automobiles. The organization works mainly in California.

The International Council for Local Environmental Initiatives also has its U.S. headquarters in California, but it works in cities throughout the country as well as in other nations. The organization was formed "in 1990 as the international environmental agency for local governments under the sponsorship of the United Nations Environment Programme."[7] It distributes information about smart growth and "sustainable communities" to any local government official or agency.

The tension between central cities and their suburbs over federal funding plays into the hands of anti-auto interests. The central cities have well-established transportation networks and their populations are growing slowly, if at all. The suburbs are growing rapidly and have much greater needs for new transportation facilities. If the federal government is going to spend money on transportation, it makes sense that it would be spent in the suburbs. Yet the Surface Transportation Policy Project is critical of the fact that federal transportation spending has "favored new development at the fringes of metropolitan areas to the detriment of existing communities."[8] Since central city neighborhoods generally oppose new highways, while suburban neighborhoods support them, spending more money in the cities means spending it on transit to the detriment of suburban highways, which is the Policy Project's real goal.

Downtown Businesses

Major downtown businesses consider downtowns to be the indispensable hearts and souls of their regions. Built to high densities in the nineteenth century, downtowns are generally the most congested portions of urban areas. In many areas, most of the measured air pollution violations are downtown. To escape congestion, pollution, and other problems associated with density, residents and businesses have moved to the suburbs as fast as they are able. Naturally, downtown property owners and merchants resent the erosion of their former prominence.

Typically, city halls and regional governments are also located downtown, as are the editorial offices of the main newspapers in an urban area. This gives downtown businesses the closest access to political and opinion leaders in each urban region. Over the years, this has led to huge federal, state, and local subsidies and programs aimed at propping up downtown densities which no longer make sense in modern urban areas. These subsidies and programs have included:

- Urban interstates, which were built to, through, and around downtown areas in the hope of reducing congestion and making those areas attractive to people and businesses that might otherwise move to the suburbs;
- Urban renewal, often clearing low-income housing and replacing it with urban monuments, civic centers, or high-income housing; and
- Most recently, rail transit projects aimed at supporting downtown commuters and reviving downtown areas.

President Clinton has issued executive orders aimed at "revitalizing downtowns" by directing federal agencies to locate their offices in downtown and historic districts "wherever operationally appropriate and economically prudent."[9] The governor of Oregon and, no doubt, other states issued a similar order for state agencies.[10] Regional planning agencies often write into their plans the assumption or expectation that downtown jobs will increase to keep pace with regional employment. Many cities use "tax increment financing" and other creative accounting to subsidize downtown development. Despite these subsidies and programs, downtowns continue to lose jobs outright or at least as a share of regional jobs.

USC planners Peter Gordon and Harry Richardson observe that the "main effect" of many of these subsidies "has been a fiscal drain, further weakening the central cities they are supposed to save." As urban improvements, they say, many downtown projects "might qualify as 'planning disasters,'" though they benefited some special interests at everyone else's expense.[11]

Ironically, many downtown areas have thrived in recent years, though not in the ways planned or anticipated by the officials generating these subsidies. Instead of remaining manufacturing, retail, and other employment centers, they have become entertainment districts. To some degree this is due to subsidies, such as public support for museums and theaters. But mostly it is because downtown businesses have carved out this niche for themselves based largely on their historic character, while other parts of urban areas serve other niches. Yet the idea of downtown being only one of several specialized districts, instead of being the main business and retail district in an area, infuriates downtown leaders.[12] One recent book, *Fantasy City*, by John Hannigan, even claims that downtowns' success as entertainment areas will merely "further accelerate the fragmentation and loss of community which have been the hallmarks of recent urban history."[13]

Smart growth represents a perverse solution for downtown areas. Though past solutions such as freeways and urban renewal aimed to make downtowns attractive, they still could not compete with suburban shopping malls and office parks. Smart growth promises to make the suburban areas as congested as downtown, thus eliminating their attraction to shoppers and employers.

Notes

1. Alan Ehrenhalt, "The Great Wall of Portland," *Governing*, May 1997, p. 21.
2. Earl Blumenauer, "Livable Communities," http://www.house.gov/blumenauer/livable.html.
3. David Rusk, *Cities Without Suburbs* (Washington, DC: Woodrow Wilson Center Press, 1993), p. xiv.
4. David Rusk, "The Exploding Metropolis: Why Growth Management Makes Sense," *Brookings Review*, Fall, 1998, p. 14.
5. John Norquist, "Free Market: Key to Public Choice," *Commonground*, 2 (1, Winter, 1999): 30.
6. Local Government Commission, "About the Local Government Commission," http://www.lgc.org/lgc/lgc.html.
7. International Council for Local Environmental Initiatives, "Welcome," http://www.iclei.org.
8. Surface Transportation Policy Project, *Getting a Fair Share: An Analysis of Federal Transportation Spending* (Washington, DC: STPP, 1997), http://www.transact.org/Reports/Money/GETTING.HTM.
9. William Clinton, Executive Orders 12988 and 13006 on Locating Federal Facilities (Washington, DC: White House, 1996).
10. Barbara Roberts, Executive Order No. 94-07, "Siting State Offices in Oregon's Community Centers," 7 June 1994.
11. Peter Gordon and Harry Richardson, "Are Compact Cities a Desirable Planning Goal?" *Journal of the American Planning Association* 61(1), http://www.smartgrowth.org/library/apa_pointcounterpoint/apa_sprawl.html.
12. Joel Garreau, *Edge City: Life on the New Frontier* (New York, NY: Doubleday, 1991), pp. 243–244.
13. John Hannigan, *Fantasy City: Pleasure and Profit in the Postmodern Metropolis* (New York, NY: Routledge, 1998), p. 197.

The Central-City Myth

Myth: Central cities must maintain their populations and densities at all costs.
Reality: Letting central city populations decline may be the best way to improve their livability.

Central city officials resent the fact that suburbanites don't pay taxes to the cities. The fact that most central cities are stagnant or declining in population while their suburbs are rapidly growing convinces many officials that suburbs are parasites that should be forced to pay for central city revitalization.

The recent economic boom has halted the decline in central city populations and jobs. A recent Brookings Institution report found that jobs grew in three out four central cities between 1993 and 1996. Yet in most cases, suburban jobs increased faster. Rather than consider the growth in city jobs good news, the report concluded that "cities are losing ground even in good times" and warned that "further employment expansion could [further] erode their competitive position vis a vis their suburbs."[1] This tendency to see bad news in good has become ingrained in many urban officials and scholars.

Pre-automobile cities were much denser than most cities today and the chief urban problem at the turn of the twentieth century was how to reduce this density. But as the automobile enabled more and more people to leave the crowded cities, urban property owners saw their property values decline. In many cases, this was not because the people who were left behind were poor. Instead, it was because transportation improvements had reduced the value of being within walking distance of other businesses.

To prevent this loss in their property values, central city businesses convinced urban leaders to change the goal of urban planning from reducing density to maintaining or increasing density. Urban renewal of the 1950s, urban interstates of the 1960s, rail transit of the 1980s, and smart growth today are all variations on this theme. The urban planning profession ended up following the money and redesigning itself to meet the demands of powerful special interests.

Huge subsidies are needed to increase or even maintain central city densities. One of the motives for annexation and regional governments is to increase the tax base for subsidizing density. One reason suburbanites resist annexation and regional governments is that they do not want to see their taxes go for sports stadiums, convention centers, rail transit systems, and other frivolities that benefit only a few people. They know it is much more difficult to stop such projects in a larger government than in a smaller one. Central city tax rates tend to be higher than those of the suburbs, and these taxes are more likely to go to subsidize big business than to help the poor.

Short of being able to tax the suburbs directly, the cities have treated the Department of Housing and Urban Development as a source of transfer payments from suburban taxpayers to the cities. As previously noted, as much as 90 percent of the agency's $33 billion budget represents subsidies to the cities. One argument for such subsidies is that it would be wasteful to abandon central city buildings and infrastructure. "However admirable the sentiment behind such pleas for urban husbandry," says Brookings scholar Pietro Nivola, "they beg a fundamental query: are national living standards always enhanced by saving existing communities instead of starting new ones?" He answers that "a political obligation to indiscriminately salvage 'communities' at any cost is irrational and untenable."[2]

What would American cities be like if they had tightly constricted urban expansion? Nivola suggests that housing for the poor would be more cramped and substandard, and yet more expensive; that more people would be exposed to crime, congestion, and environmental hazards; and that the restraints "would have pinched the national economy," making most Americans less prosperous. Such afflictions, Nivola finds, have "sapped the economies of several European countries and Japan" because those nations have tried to restrain urban expansion. Suburbanization, Nivola concludes, "has been largely a natural process, accommodating a vibrant, technologically dazzling economy and a growing population in a land with vast territories and resources."[3]

Blaming the "decline" of cities on suburbanization is killing the messenger. The message is: density and congestion are costly and people avoid them. Cities should allow their densities to decline to levels that will make them attractive to a wide variety of income groups without subsidies. Cities will remain higher in density than suburbs, partly because some people like higher densities and partly because at some point the cost of further reducing densities will exceed the benefits. But trying to impose density on the suburbs makes no more sense than taxing the suburbs to support inefficiently high densities in the cities.

Notes

1. John Brennan and Edward Hill, *Where Are the Jobs? Cities, Suburbs, and the Competition for Employment* (Washington, DC: Brookings, 1999), p. 8.
2. Pietro S. Nivola, *Laws of the Landscape: How Policies Shape Cities in Europe and America* (Washington, DC: Brookings, 1999), p. 38.
3. Ibid, pp. 88–89.

The Downtown Myth

Myth: We need to save downtown areas.
Reality: The idea of downtowns as the single center of urban areas is obsolete.

Downtowns are seen by many planners as the key to a healthy urban area, so they devote an inordinate amount of time to downtown planning. New transportation facilities are designed to serve downtown, subsidies are provided to build new housing downtown, and retailers and offices are encouraged to stay downtown. "Downtown renewal" has been a major feature of urban planning for at least five decades. "Many urban visionaries. . . have nobly devoted their entire lives to reviving the old downtown," says Joel Garreau. Yet, Garreau continues, downtowns "are relics of a time past."[1]

An old-fashioned downtown—sporting tall concrete-and steel buildings with walls that touch each other, laid out on a rectangular grid, accented by sidewalks, surrounded by political boundaries, and lorded over by a mayor—is only one way to think of a city. In fact, it is only the nineteenth-century version. . . . We built cities that way for less than a century.[2]

High rises were technologically infeasible before about 1840. After about 1920, the automobile and the telephone made downtowns unnecessary. Today, Garreau's edge cities spread out over large spaces. They may include some high rises, but they are not necessarily bumping up against one another.

Dense downtowns were originally built because nineteenth-century transportation made it difficult for people to live and work far apart. They survived into the late twentieth century partly because some businesses, particularly financial firms, found it convenient to remain close to one another. At the dawn of the twenty-first century, urban analysts debate whether this advantage, which economists call agglomerative economies, outweighs the cost of congestion and infrastructure required to maintain high-density areas.[3]

What is not debatable is that no areas as dense as the old downtowns are being built. Garreau estimates that "traffic jams become a major political issue" in edge cities when they become a fifth as dense as "a typical old downtown" and that the densest edge cities never become more than 30 percent as dense as downtowns.[4]

Downtown Portland produces less than 20 percent of the economic activity of the Portland urban area. Downtown Los Angeles produces less than 5 percent of the Los Angeles urban area's activities. In today's decentralized cities, it makes no sense to focus resources on a tiny segment of the urban area.

Yet planners continually ignore the economic insignificance of downtowns. Jack Linville, a former official with the American Planning Association and now a designer in Houston, explained the problem to *Edge City* author Joel Garreau:

> What the architects and the planners, the trained professionals, all believe is that Edge City is wrong. It all goes back to the Costs of Sprawl report. The whole concept is—the suburbs growing is the wrong way to develop. That what you really want to do is protect the vitality of downtown. So everything you do is aimed at bringing people back to the CBD [central business district].[5]

Yet planners have been unable to restore downtowns to the economic significance they once had. As USC planners Peter Gordon and Harry Richardson note, "downtown renewal efforts have failed." Despite huge government investments in downtown areas during the 1980s, downtown "job growth was slow, negligible, or negative. Together, the top ten cities' CBDs [central business districts] grew at just over one percent per year in the period 1980–86."[6]

This doesn't mean that downtowns are dead. Thanks in part to those investments, most U.S. large-city downtowns have become major entertainment centers, drawing people in to shops, theaters, parks, festivals, and other activities. But just as they are only one possible entertainment destination people can go to, so are they only one of many centers for retailing, office space, manufacturing, and warehousing in our cities.

"I can make a case for a downtown as essentially a tourist, entertainment, and business center," says historian David Dillon. But when he suggests to planners "the notion of a downtown as one of five or six specialized districts," he says, "it's oh, no, the worst possible thing. It's kind of a blindness."[7]

Other than utopian visions, planners have had at least two reasons to concentrate on downtowns. First, at least until recently, most urban planners worked for central cities, not the suburbs. With city halls located downtown, elected officials and planners must get an inflated sense of the importance of downtowns.

If that isn't enough, downtown interests lobby hard to get moneys, especially federal dollars, flowing into their districts. "Declining sectors turn to politics for remedies," say Gordon and Richardson, who note that "Los Angeles' downtown-focused rail transit projects account for more lobbying activity than does the entire California state government!"

Unfortunately, Gordon and Richardson continue, attempts to prop up declining sectors of the economy sets up "a vicious cycle. . . that further weakens the viability of traditional city centers." Taxes to pay for downtown improvements "drive more and more economic activities out from central cities" even as they strengthen the bureaucracies, effectively rewarding them for their misguided policies.[8]

MIT planner Bernard Frieden notes that planners often fund downtown programs using creative finance efforts that "shield their own ventures from budget reviews and voter approval." Tax-increment financing, for example, consists of dedicating future increases in property taxes from a given part of a city to urban renewal or other local projects. Existing recipients of property taxes do not object because they get no less than they got before. It has become "one of the leading downtown strategies," says Frieden, because "cities can commit to one project after another without ever having to make a choice among competing plans." Such programs, he says, "are troublesome to people who value accountability based on the informed consent of the governed."[9]

Politics have insured that planners who focused on saving downtown were rewarded for doing so. Planners who thought about ways to enhance the suburbs or Garreau's edge cities received no positive feedback. After several decades of this pattern, it is no wonder that planners remain focused on downtown and, as Garreau notes, view economic prosperity outside of downtown "as nothing but a threat."[10]

Notes

1. Joel Garreau, *Edge City: Life on the New Frontier* (New York, NY: Doubleday, 1991), p. 59.
2. Ibid, p. 25.
3. Richard Voith, "The Downtown Parking Syndrome: Does Curing the Illness Kill the Patient?" *Business Review*, January-February, 1998, p. 11.
4. Garreau, *Edge City*, p. 470.
5. Ibid, p. 232.
6. Peter Gordon and Harry Richardson, "Are Compact Cities a Desirable Planning Goal?" *Journal of the American Planning Association* 61(1), http://www.smartgrowth.org/library/apa_pointcounterpoint/apa_sprawl.html.
7. Garreau, *Edge City*, pp. 243–244.
8. Gordon and Richardson, "Are Compact Cities a Desirable Planning Goal?"
9. Bernard Frieden, *Downtown Inc: How America Rebuilds Cities* (Cambridge, MA: MIT Press, 1989), p. 251.
10. Garreau, *Edge City*, p. 59.

Business Support for Metro

In September, 1996, Portland light-rail proponents held a luncheon in a downtown hotel to raise campaign funds for a member of Congress. The member was not anyone from Oregon, but Pennsylvania Representative Bud Shuster. Shuster chairs the House Transportation Committee, which in 1997 would consider the largest transportation spending bill in U.S. history—and the largest source of pork barrel in the 105th Congress. Some idea of Shuster's importance can be gauged by the fact that so many members of the House of Representatives clamored to be on the Transportation Committee that it ended up being the largest committee in the House's history.

Shuster is actually a highway proponent and is somewhat skeptical of rail transit. But, according to his campaign treasurer, he agreed to come to Portland to look at a proposed light-rail line once local officials met his "fund-raising criteria." Officials of Tri-Met, Portland's transit agency, donated $1,500. Portland city Commissioner Charles Hales donated another $500. Other people, mostly from companies that help plan or build light-rail lines, donated $6,000 more.[1] While the trip did not prove particularly lucrative for Shuster, it revealed some of the sources of support for light rail and other aspects of Metro's plans.

Home builders and realtors had long supported 1000 Friends' land-use planning efforts. But many of them lost their enthusiasm for land-use planning when the scarcity of land within the urban-growth boundary limited the possibilities for large-scale home developments. Still, those who specialize in infill, transit-oriented developments, or other high-density programs are strongly supportive of Metro's 2040 plan. In many cases, the housing these developers build is heavily subsidized with tax waivers, infrastructure subsidies, and other supports. Many of these developers contributed to the recent reelection campaign of Portland City Councillor and smart-growth advocate Charles Hales.[2] One developer of many of Portland's transit-oriented developments, Walsh Construction, is co-owned by Tom Walsh, who also served for several years as general manager of Tri-Met, Portland's transit agency.

In recent light-rail ballot measures, supporters of light rail tended to outspend opponents by about ten to one, and most of the financial support came from businesses that expect to profit from rail construction. In the 1996 campaign, major contributors included:

- Electric companies that will not only sell electricity to the rail line but would have major upgrades to their facilities done at taxpayers' expense: $100,000;
- Banks likely to make huge fees selling and handling the bonds needed for billion-dollar light-rail projects: $60,000;
- Engineering consulting firms and construction companies that could build the line: $42,000;
- Labor unions whose members will build the line: $25,000;
- Rail car manufacturers: $20,000;
- The advertising company that uses light-rail vehicles as rolling billboards: $10,000;
- Realtors: $22,500; and
- Downtown businesses not including those listed above: $58,500.

In addition, the city's leading builder of transit-oriented developments, Walsh Construction, donated $1,000, while Tom Walsh, the general manager of Tri-Met and part owner of Walsh Construction, donated $2,000. Walsh has since retired from Tri-Met but Walsh Construction is still building transit-oriented developments. Out of more than $400,000 in contributions to the campaign, less than $2,000 came in donations of under $100 and less than $5,000 came in donations of under $500.[3]

Some Portland-area retailers welcome Metro's restrictions on future retailers since those restrictions limit the competition that existing stores will face for the 700,000 new residents expected to move to the region in the next few years. Fred Meyer, Portland's hometown store, operates more than two dozen grocery and variety stores in the Portland area, all but one of which are well over Metro's 60,000-square-foot size limit. Although very few people travel to a Fred Meyer store on light rail, the company donated $50,000 to the light-rail campaign in 1996. It also donated funds to Metro for a pro-smart-growth publicity campaign and allowed Metro to distribute its materials at Fred Meyer stores. At the same time, the company refused to allow Metro's opponents to distribute anti-Metro or anti-light rail materials near their stores because they are "political."

Downtown business interests are another strong backer of Metro. In the past decade, the Portland area has gained some 200,000 new jobs—virtually none of which located downtown. This has outraged downtown businesses, led by the Association for Portland Progress (which itself donated $1,000 to the light-rail campaign). "Our city and the region's quality of life depend on employment in the core," says Gregg Kantor, who chairs the association's Business Development Committee. If downtown doesn't "capture its share of [job] growth, suburban communities will face even more serious traffic, housing and taxation problems," Kantor claims.[4]

Downtown interests back light rail because it maintains the preeminence of the downtown area. Many of the downtown businesses that contributed to light-rail campaigns are building and land owners who no doubt hope that more light-rail lines will add to the values of their properties. Surprisingly, City Center Parking, which operates city-owned parking garages, two of which are on the light-rail line, contributed $10,000 to the light-rail campaign—which may not be so surprising if the company thinks that such donations will help it keep its lucrative concessions.

Even more ironically, downtown businesses want light rail downtown—but only if it keeps its distance. When Tri-Met built its downtown bus mall in the 1970s, most of the businesses on the mall suffered during the construction period and many never recovered. When the city began talking about building a north-south-oriented light-rail line, downtown interests insisted that it go downtown even though that meant adding an expensive river crossing. But those same interests also insisted that it not go on their streets downtown. Hotels and restaurants opposed routings by them. Other major businesses, including Powell's Book Store and the Blitz-Weinhardt Brewery, threatened to leave downtown if light rail was built on their streets. So the city decided to build it on the bus mall, where there were few businesses left to protest. The decision wasn't swayed when Tri-Met analysts showed that the bus mall did not have room to handle buses and streetcars, especially if transit ridership grew. If it got too crowded, the buses would have to go somewhere else.

Downtown interests appreciate other parts of Portland's smart-growth plans. Huge housing subsidies are bringing thousands of new residents to the downtown area. Plans to increase congestion and reduce parking in the suburbs will take away the advantages that suburban shopping malls and office parks have over downtown. Most important, the plans call for locating thousands of new jobs downtown. The Association for Portland Progress, which represents scores of downtown businesses, hopes that these plans will maintain "the central city as the dynamic heart of the city and region."[5]

Ruth Scott, the president of the Association for Portland Progress just happens to be married to Brian Scott, the president of Livable Oregon, which is chaired by former 1000 Friends attorney Robert Stacey. Both work hard to promote downtown interests. "He goes down to Salem, jumps up and down, and screams and cries that we need the money or downtowns will suffer," says a downtown business leader about Brian Scott. "He's very good at it. He gets the money."[6]

President Clinton's executive order that federal agencies should locate their urban offices in downtown areas led the Bureau of Land Management to move from an east Portland office park. In 1994, the Coalition for a Livable Future and 1000 Friends convinced then-Governor Barbara Roberts to issue a similar executive order requiring state agencies to locate their offices in downtowns in order to "reduce reliance on the single-occupant automobile."[7] This led the Oregon Department of Transportation to abandon its Craftsman-style offices on the edge of

Portland and move downtown. Employees of these government agencies now must suffer downtown congestion and the inconvenience of being located farther from the resources they are supposed to manage. Despite all of this, the growth in government jobs downtown has barely kept pace with the loss of private jobs.

Another major backer of Metro's policies is Intel, whose manufacturing facilities in Hillsboro employs more than 10,000 people. In 1993, Intel convinced the state legislature to allow counties to give tax breaks to companies building huge silicon chip factories. Since then, a dozen companies have decided to build more than $10 billion worth of facilities in the Portland area. More than half of those companies applied for and received tax breaks totaling well over $200 million.

Such tax breaks were probably not needed to convince most of the companies to build in Oregon. Several of the companies did not even bother applying for the breaks. One that applied for the break and didn't get decided to build in Oregon anyway (but later changed its mind for other reasons). Another got the tax break but then made it clear it would have built a plant even without such a break.

Intel was a major contributor to light-rail ballot measures. It has also purchased transit passes for all of its employees, although only a few of them actually ride transit to work. Intel may believe it needs to take such actions to gain the political support it needs to operate and expand its Hillsboro operations. In 1999, not without controversy, it obtained another huge tax break for a new facility that it is building in Hillsboro.[8]

Notes

1. Brent Walsh and Gordon Oliver, "Light-rail fans play D.C. cash game," *The Oregonian*, November 29, 1996, p. A1, A27.
2. Scott Learn, "Hales reaches new heights for city election fund raising," *The Oregonian*, April 18, 2000, p. B2.
3. Oregonians for Roads and Rail, "November 1996 General Election: First Pre-Election Report," on file with the Secretary of State, Salem, Oregon.
4. Gregg Kantor, "Central city jobs key to region's health," *The Oregonian*, February 4, 1998, (op-ed page).
5. Association for Portland Progress, "Welcome to the Association for Portland Progress Website," http://www.portlandprogress.org/.
6. Sarah Thomas, "Ruth & Brian Scott Downtown Dynamos," *The Oregonian*, January 17, 1995, p. C1.
7. Barbara Roberts, "1994 Executive Order giving downtowns priority for locating state offices," executive order number EO 94-07, 7 June 1994.
8. Steve Duin, "Stampeded by the advancing high-tech horde," *The Oregonian*, July 13, 2000, http://www.oregonlive.com/news/oregonian/index.ssf?/columnists/00/07/lc_51duin13.frame.

11. Transit Agencies & Builders

*T*ransit agencies have much to gain from smart growth policies. Even if smart growth fails to convince many automobilists to ride transit, smart growth policies would transfer increased shares of highway user fees to mass transit.

More than 500 transit agencies are members of the American Public Transportation Association (APTA), which grandiosely changed its name from the American Public Transit Association in 1999. Private companies that manufacture transit equipment and sell services to transit agencies are also members of APTA. This gives APTA a larger budget than the Surface Transportation Policy Project, Sierra Club, and Environmental Defense Fund combined, and it has a staff of more than seventy employees to help lobby for more transit funding.[1] APTA publishes a weekly newspaper, produces numerous position papers and publicity brochures, and maintains a grassroots program to organize telephone and letter-writing campaigns.

The vast majority of federal transit funds go to a few major cities, including New York, Chicago, Boston, and San Francisco. The distribution of these funds is far less fair, proportional to population, than the distribution of highway funds. Yet every transit agency gets at least a little money, and on a per passenger basis the smaller agencies tend to get the most, so there is little complaint about fairness.

Transportation builders and engineering consulting firms are divided over smart-growth issues. Many of these firms thrived when the Interstate Highway System and other major roads were built, but only some are able to transfer their expertise to the construction of rail lines. A number of engineering consulting firms, notably Parsons Brinkerhof, and major contractors, notably Bechtel, have profited immensely from rail projects. Companies that lay asphalt have done less well.

Housing developers are also split over smart growth. Building in the suburbs costs less and is less risky than in the cities, partly because land prices are lower and partly because it costs less to build fifty houses on one vacant parcel than to infill two houses here, three houses there, and a set of row houses over there. A few home builders have specialized in such infill projects and therefore support smart growth. Others are not so sure.

Nevertheless, the companies that do benefit from smart growth are quick to make contributions to political campaigns for light rail or for candidates that support smart growth. As noted on page 182, donors to light-rail campaigns typically include:

- Electric companies that will sell the electricity and may enjoy major improvements to their infrastructure at taxpayers' expense;
- Banks that expect to finance the bonds that will be sold to build the rail system;
- The engineering and consulting firms that will plan the rail line;
- Construction companies that will build it;
- Real estate developers who expect to take advantage of high-density rezoning planned around station areas; and
- The companies that manufacture light-rail vehicles.[2]

"The rail lobby typically includes the entrenched transit bureaucracy, powerful architect-engineering firms, wealthy contractors, labor unions, the downtown business community, and assorted civic boosters," says Ken Orski, the editor of *Innovation Briefs*, a newsletter covering urban mobility issues. "The forces lobbying in favor of rail projects are far more powerful than the so-called 'highway lobby.'"[3]

Notes

1. Peter Samuel, "The Transportation Lobby: The Politics of Highway and Transit," *Organization Trends*, February, 1996, http://www.capitalresearch.org/trends/ot-0296.html.
2. Oregonians for Roads and Rail, "Statement of Contributions and Expenditures, November, 1996, General Election," on file at the Oregon Secretary of State's office, election division, Salem, Oregon.
3. Ken Orski, "Atlanta Debates Its Transportation Future," *Innovation Briefs*, Vol. 11, No. 5, Sep/Oct 2000, p. 2.

Metro

Metro is the result of decades of effort by Portlanders who wanted a strong regional government against suburbanites who valued their independence. Previous attempts to create a Portland-area regional government failed largely because of voter resistance in the suburbs:

- In 1924, a proposal to consolidate Portland with Multnomah County, which includes four other incorporated cities, was rejected by voters;
- During the 1960s, Portland's attempts to annex suburbs led suburbanites to incorporate at least a half a dozen cities to stave off annexation;
- In 1966, voters rejected a plan to include the entire Portland urban area in one supercity.

In the 1960s, local governments responded to federal mandates for a metropolitan planning organization by creating the Columbia Region Association of Governments (CRAG). This was purely a coordinating body that had no power to tax or regulate anyone. In 1970, the Oregon state legislature created the Metropolitan Service District (MSD) to make some sense out of all of the hundreds of sewer, water, parks, garbage, and other special service districts in the Portland area. The agency quickly learned that most of the service districts valued their local prerogatives and did not want help from a regional agency. Portland, for example, jealously made certain that MSD had no authority over its water supply or port district. The agency had little to do other than deal with solid waste problems, and it did not deal with those very well.

In 1976, a federally funded committee of local citizens proposed to create a true regional government, with an elected commission and broad planning powers over the entire urban area. CRAG and MSD would merge and become an agency that planned land use, provided services such as waste disposal, managed the zoo and other parks and entertainment centers, and did anything else "of metropolitan concern." In May, 1978, voters approved this proposal by a small margin. Metro historians admit that "the wording of the ballot measure—'Reorganize MSD, Abolish CRAG'—was confusing. Voters may have backed the measure expecting to rid the area of a metropolitan planning agency rather than create a more powerful one." As a result, "the result is hard to interpret as a mandate for regional government."[1] Most voters in Clackamas County sided against it, but the county couldn't convince the courts to let it stay out of the new agency, which retained the name Metropolitan Service District.

The agency soon expanded its parks and entertainment business. It convinced voters to pay for the construction of a large convention center. It began managing several parks and wetlands in the Portland area. It also took over management of an exposition center, a basketball/hockey arena, and a football/baseball stadium. After various proposals to build solid waste incinerators went nowhere, the district dealt with Portland's garbage by trucking it to a private landfill hundreds of miles away in eastern Oregon.

These activities were highly visible. Less well known to most of the public was the agency's planning activities. In 1979, in response to Oregon's 1973 planning laws, the district defined the urban-growth boundary around Portland. It also slowly took over transportation and other planning activities for the region. The agency paid for its growing planning staff out of surcharges on garbage collection.

In 1991, the Metropolitan Service District got ambitious and started dreaming again of city-county consolidation. Staff members drew up a proposal to replace all city and county governments in the tri-county area with a single agency. This idea didn't go over too well with other government officials. Instead, a committee of city and county elected officials proposed to revise the district's charter to give the agency almost the same powers that a city would have to tax and annex adjacent lands. It could take over almost any special district or government activity if it felt that the work of that district or activity was a "matter of metropolitan concern." The new charter would also change the name to Metro and replace its thirteen-member council with an elected council of seven.

It is doubtful whether most of the voters knew what they were voting on, since the ballot title was "limits regional government." "If this measure passes, most voters will think they have struck a blow to limit regional government, which is exactly the opposite of what it does," said MSD staff member Ken Gervais before the election. "In nearly all respects, the charter expands Metro's powers over current state law."[2] Indeed, the charter gave Metro dictatorial planning powers over the twenty-four cities and three counties in the Portland area.

The charter made planning Metro's top priority.[3] Metro would write a "future vision" for the region and a fifty-year land-use and transportation plan. By 2000, all local governments in the region would have to revise their zoning laws to comply with Metro's plan. The most important expansion of power was Metro's ability to force three county and twenty-four city governments to adopt zoning patterns that complied with Metro's comprehensive plan. Admitting that this idea was "radical," Portland city Commissioner Charles Hales, who helped write the charter, says "I'm still amazed we got away with that."[4]

At about the time the charter was on the ballot, Metro's growing planning staff needed new office space. The agency proved its skills at dealing with taxpayers' dollars by moving into a new building. Rather than build a brand-new building, Metro decided to demonstrate the value of recycling by converting an old Sears department store to an office building. Metro spent $30 million on the effort and ended up with a building worth only $15 million. It could have leveled the store and built a new building for just half of what it spent. When it left its old office, Metro still had two-and-one-half years remaining on its lease. Its planners proved their forecasting skills by estimating that the agency could sublease most of the old building within four months. This didn't happen, and taxpayers ended up paying hundreds of thousands of dollars for vacant office space.[5]

Several years after Metro moved into its new building, someone discovered untreated human sewage leaking into the Willamette River. They traced it to toilets in the old Sears building that had never been hooked up to city sewer lines. As the agency chartered to reduce regional pollution, Metro was embarrassed to admit that it was a polluter—pollution that could have been avoided if it had saved taxpayers $15 million by simply building a new office.[6]

During the five years Metro was preparing its 2040 plan, its director of growth management planning was John Fregonese. In this position, Fregonese supervised all of Metro's contracts with Peter Calthorpe, including Calthorpe's plans for Clackamas Town Center, Gresham, Orenco, and many other areas. Fregonese is a strong supporter of compact development, though he himself lives in a very low-density neighborhood in southwest Portland.

In November, 1997, just a few weeks before the Metro council approved the 2040 plan, Fregonese left Metro to take a job with Calthorpe Associates.[7] Fregonese opened a new Calthorpe office in Portland (sometimes identified as Fregonese, Calthorpe Associates), from which he spreads the gospel of new urbanism and Portland to other cities across the nation. He helped run the Envision Utah process that is seeking to bring smart growth to the greater Salt Lake region. No one at Metro ever publicly suggested that there might be something unethical about Fregonese going to work for Calthorpe.

Notes

1. Carl Abbott and Margery Post Abbot, *Historical Development of the Metropolitan Service District* (Portland, OR: MSD, 1991), p. 24.
2. James Mayer, "Metro Charter a Puzzle Even for Those in Know," *The Oregonian*, October 20, 1992, p. B4.
3. Metro charter, section 5(3).
4. James Mayer, "Home rule plan to be on ballot," *The Oregonian*, August 1, 1992, p. D1.
5. Gordon Oliver, "Old Metro offices drain its budget," *The Oregonian*, December 15, 1993, p. F1.
6. R. Gregory Nokes, "Metro pollution could invite potty shots," *The Oregonian*, March 6, 1998.
7. R. Gregory Nokes, "Metro's chief planner will move to a new job," *The Oregonian*, November 18, 1997, p. E3.

Public Involvement

Through the 1980s, Oregon's land-use planning system was popular with urban residents because it cost them little yet guaranteed them a huge area of permanent open space. But in the early 1990s, 1000 Friends' LUTRAQ study and the state transportation planning rules revealed to anyone who was watching that planning advocates wanted to impose huge changes in urban and suburban living and travel habits. But very few were watching.

Although many Portland-area residents would strongly oppose the densities and congestion in Metro's plans, Metro had two advantages that allowed it to build these policies into its 2040 plan. First, regional planning is boring. The 2040 process took five years to complete, and few people other than paid professionals are willing to plow through the endless documents and attend the interminable public meetings required for a planning effort of this scope. Other than home builders and retailers, both of whom were divided on the issue, most of the paid professionals were from 1000 Friends and their spin-off groups.

Second, Metro used an intricate public involvement process that made it appear as if the plan sprang forth from the minds of local residents, and was not simply derived from the transportation planning rule. The process included numerous mailings to residents, solicitations for comments, hearings, and other public meetings. Yet Metro made no real effort to get an accurate cross section of public opinion or even to really listen to members of the public.

For example, as required by Metro's new charter, Metro appointed a Future Vision Commission to write a vision statement on which the final plan was to be based. The commission included Robert Liberty and was dominated by people who supported increased densities and rail transit rather than low-density suburbanization. The commission met many times but held no public hearings. While members of the public were allowed to attend the meetings, those who wanted to speak were given just two minutes.

Although the commission's final report lists eighteen "commentors on the future vision,"[1] these were people who were invited to submit comments—but not all of them did. Economist Ed Whitelaw wrote that "the document I reviewed is a good preface to a Ray Atkeson book" (i.e., coffee-table books of Oregon scenery), but "I don't think I can be of much help" unless the vision "talks about policy prescriptions."[2] Historian E. Kimbark MacColl simply wrote that "I really have nothing to add" to the Ray Atkeson-like vision.[3] This hardly suggests that the vision statement was the result of a grassroots involvement process.

Metro brags that it sent questionnaires "to more than 500,000 households, asking residents about real choices" such as whether they wanted higher-density development or an expansion of the urban-growth boundary.[4] The reality is far different. Only one publication went to every household in the region, and it did include a questionaire. But nine of the ten questions were strictly process questions, such as "would you rather write letters or testify at a hearing?"

The one substantive question asked, "do you agree or disagree with the values outlined in the draft vision statement?" An 1,800-word summary of the vision statement was printed elsewhere in the brochure. If anyone read the statement, the questionnaire offered just a few square inches in which to make any comments. But it did not matter what people wrote since the mailing was sent to people *after* the Future Vision Commission was finished.[5] Anyone who took the time to respond would have no effect on the vision.

The future vision statement is just one example of the disdain Metro had for public opinion. Other mailings went to no more than 10 percent of the region's households, mostly to light-rail supporters, transit activists, various allies of 1000 Friends, and other people who had expressed an interest in the 2040 planning process. Most people who might be upset to learn that Metro was going to increase Portland-area congestion or densify their neighborhoods did not receive copies of most Metro mailings, and in any case the brochures did not say anything about these plans.

Metro's public meetings were mostly "open houses" where Calthorpe-type architectural renderings were displayed alongside of multicolored maps of the region. Planners answered questions but made no formal presentations and accepted no public testimony so there was little opportunity for real debate over Metro's plans or even to find out what those plans were. Metro held about three dozen such open houses on the 2040 plan, and fewer than a hundred people wandered in and out during the average open house.

Metro also held eighteen public hearings on the 2040 plan. Since many were during business hours, they were mainly attended by professional advocates. Many of these "hearings" were simply ordinary Metro council business meetings with a short period open for public comment. A typical such hearing took testimony from just a half-dozen people, five of whom identified themselves as representatives of a lobby or interest group. Testimony was normally limited to three minutes, which barely gave witnesses time to introduce themselves.

Metro did not tolerate dissenters at its hearings. While it passed out its own publications and brochures to anyone who attended, it tried to forbid anyone else from passing out flyers questioning Metro's plans. When light-rail opponents tried to pass out copies of their testimony at a hearing on light rail, Metro ordered them to leave. When they persisted, Metro called three sheriff's deputies and threatened to arrest the leafletters. Metro backed down only when light-rail opponents alerted the press that they expected to get arrested at the next hearing.

People who wanted to do more than write a letter or fill out a survey form encountered formidable barriers. Other than its newsletters and a few other documents prepared for public consumption, Metro charges "user fees" for its publications. A 70-page population forecast, for example, costs $20. Most such documents are unavailable at local libraries, partly because until recently Metro even charged the libraries for copies of most publications. Metro also charges more than $50 per hour to transfer data, which is enough to discourage many people from critiquing Metro's computer models.

Even many public officials had a hard time getting involved in 2040 planning. The mayor of Tigard, Jim Nicoli, worried that Metro has been "pushing too hard, too fast."[6] A September, 1995, letter from the Tigard city council to Metro complained that "Metro did not seem to value significant involvement by other governmental bodies. . . A speedy conclusion to the plan appeared to have higher priority than did careful analysis." "We never got the time to get comfortable with 2040," says Hillsboro's head planner, Winslow Brooks. "The process moved so fast, it really didn't allow us time to become a reasonable part of the discussion and analysis." When he was a Metro councilor, Don Morissette complained that even he had a hard time getting data from Metro's staff.

Metro claims that it received more than 20,000 comments on the 2040 plan and that they strongly supported "growing up, not out."[7] But it does not say how many unique individuals made comments. Since it sent several slightly different questionnaires to its self-selected list of interested people, it is possible that several thousand people submitted more than one of the 20,000 comments. So it is not likely that this represented an accurate cross-section of people in the Portland area. Nor did Metro ever ask people such hard questions as, "would you want your neighborhood of single-family homes invaded by high-density, mixed-use developments?" or "do you favor a tripling of congestion on Portland-area roads?"

However, several surveys commissioned by Metro found that support for compact development and other smart-growth ideas was weak. A 1992 survey asked people what they disliked the most about living in their part of the Portland area. The most frequent response was "too much traffic/congestion" (22.6 percent), followed by "lack of parking" (17.6 percent). "Urban sprawl" was mentioned by only 3.1 percent.[8] Metro must have paid little attention to this, because they plan they adopted increases congestion and reduces parking.

A 1993 Metro poll specifically warned that the people responding to Metro's public involvement processes "hold views that are not necessarily reflective of the community as a whole."[9] A 1996 poll found that most people agreed that "No amount of planning and design can make higher density development near where

I live acceptable to me." People were willing to go along with one more house on their block, but "a few more houses and some apartments over garages" was considered undesirable. While most Portland residents said they would like to live within walking distance of shopping, most suburban residents said they would not. "The overall awareness of Metro's 2040 planning process is still very low," said the pollster just a few months before the plan was finished. "Those people with an awareness of Metro's 2040 planning process hold views that are not necessarily reflective of the community as a whole." In other words, the opinions of those who actually commented on the plan are probably skewed.[10]

A 1997 survey found that the biggest concern people had about growth was traffic congestion.[11] Since Metro's plan calls for letting congestion increase to stop-and-go traffic in many parts of the city, it clearly does not reflect most resident's desires. Another 1997 poll found that, if you ask people whether they support the urban-growth boundary, only 15 percent said no. But if you ask whether they support the boundary if it means increases in population densities, opposition jumps to 41 percent.[12]

Polls also show that most people who support light rail never plan to ride it; they only support it because they hope it will reduce the congestion on the highways where they plan to drive. Similarly, Portland polls show that most people support the urban-growth boundary, but they themselves want to live in low-density areas. When the choice between higher densities in your neighborhood versus expanding the urban-growth boundary is made absolutely clear, support for Metro's plan disintegrates.

If Metro were sincerely interested in getting an accurate cross-section of community opinion, it would not get it through public involvement. Planners know that most members of the public get involved in land-use issues only when plans threaten peoples "back yards." When planners came to his home neighborhood with an infill proposal, Robert Liberty noted that "there are more people here tonight to talk about future development in one neighborhood than Metro had in its workshops last month to talk about the future of the whole region."[13]

Almost no one other than a few invited speakers commented on the Future Vision statement for the Portland region. Twenty-two people testified when the Metro Council approved the final 2040 framework plan. But when it came time to rezone a Southwest Portland neighborhood to high densities, at least four hundred people jammed a high school cafeteria in protest.[14]

The success of a regional government such as Metro depended on this principle. The public remains unconcerned or unaware as Metro writes a plan that mandates higher urban densities and increases congestion. City and county planners have to take the heat when neighborhoods rise up in opposition to high densities, but fall back on the fact that the decision is already made: Metro is making them do it. When motorists complain about traffic congestion, Metro says it doesn't have enough money to build roads, so people should walk or ride the billion-dollar light rail which Metro somehow found the money to build.

The fact that Metro was created by a vote of the people and is theoretically run by an elected council is supposed to insure that the 2040 plan is democratic. In fact, many voters had no idea what they were voting on and many have no idea still that Metro even exists, except possibly as a garbage-collection district. A 1997 poll done for Metro found that three out of four Portland-area residents knew and had opinions about their mayor and city council. But only 56 percent of residents knew and had opinions about the Metro council.[15] Voters weary of monitoring their federal, state, county, and city officials are reluctant to spend much time watching a fifth layer of government.

Advocates of civic life may find such reluctance deplorable, but people in fact have two good reasons not to bother to learn about government agencies such as Metro. First, they know that their own votes or actions are extremely unlikely to change the outcome of an election or decision. Second, they know that even if they make a mistake with their vote—or if they don't vote and other voters vote wrong—that the cost of the their mistake will be shared with many other taxpayers. So overall, people have little incentive to learn about something like the 2040 plan. But when a local government proposes to radically change neighborhood zoning, the cost of the plan is shared among only a few residents while the likelihood that opposition will succeed is higher. A true, representative democracy does not mean more representatives—such as thirteen rather than seven elected positions on the Metro council—but smaller political jurisdictions.

In short, a good way to prepare a potentially controversial plan without public awareness is through a large regional planning agency that covers so much ground that public involvement will be extremely low. That may not have been the intention of the people who created Metro. But, if their goal was truly democratic public involvement, they should have pushed planning to a more local level, not a regional level.

Between the Land Conservation and Development Commission and Metro, Oregon land-use planners are inching closer to Andres Duany's goal of planning every parcel in the state "with such precision that only the architectural detail is left to future designers."[16] "The growing intrusion of planners into Americans' everyday lives is not the result of democratic endorsement, but rather reflects a spirit of abdication," say USC planners Gordon and Richardson. They add that when political participation "is uniformly low," as it is today, "the hidden costs [of planning] are unlikely to be seriously challenged. Instead, these [growth management] policies will probably flourish."[17]

"We need to have a Portland so that we can see how new urbanism works," says Joel Garreau, "just like we need to have a Houston so we can see how land use without zoning works.[18] It is easy for Garreau to remain detached: He doesn't have to live in Portland. Even if Portland is a worthwhile experiment, says Portland State University's Ken Dueker, "Portland area residents have not knowingly consented to be willing research subjects in a radical experiment."[19] Unlike planners, economists, medical doctors, and most other professionals consider it unethical to experiment on human populations without their consent.

Metro's 2040 plan had the strong backing of powerful interests, including 1000 Friends and other non-profits along with selected businesses. Many political leaders also supported the plan, including Portland officials eager to gain control over the suburbs and suburban officials eager to get federal dollars that Metro promised to parcel out. But Metro could only adopt such a plan because most of the people of the Portland area had no idea what Metro was doing.

Notes

1. Future Vision Commission, *Future Vision Report* (Portland, OR: Metro, 1995), appendices A, B, and D.
2. Letter from Ed Whitelaw to the Future Vision Commission, February 24, 1994, available in Metro files.
3. Letter from E. K. MacColl to the Future Vision Commission, January 31, 1994, available in Metro files.
4. Neal Pierce, "Portland Revered Up as Model for Combatting Sprawl," *The Oregonian*, April 3, 1995, p. B9. (This article was syndicated by the *Washington Post*.)
5. Metro, *2040 Framework Update*, Spring/Summer 1995, p. 15.
6. Harry Bodine, "Metro's growth plan: too much, too fast?" *The Oregonian*, March 25, 1996, p. B3.
7. Pierce, "Portland Revered."
8. Decision Sciences, Inc., *Telephone Survey for the Region 2040 Project: A Quantitative Research Report*, April, 1992, p. 3.
9. Western Attitudes, "A Community Attitude Survey for Metro" (Lake Oswego, OR: Western Attitudes, 1993), p. 4.
10. Metro Means Business Committee, Public Opinion Survey (Portland, OR: Metro, 1996).
11. Davis & Hibbits, *1997 Growth Management Survey Summary* (Portland, OR: Metro, 1997), http://www.multnomah.lib.or.us/metro/growth/surveysum/sld005.htm.
12. R. Gregory Nokes, "Portlanders want some elbow room," *The Oregonian*, April 27, 1997.
13. Lee Perlman, "Residents air thoughts on Northwest infill plan," *The Oregonian*, November 23, 1992, p. B2.
14. Janet Christ, "SW neighborhood residents furious over zoning plan," *The Oregonian*, October 17, 1996, p. C4.
15. Davis & Hibbitts, *1997 Growth Management Survey Summary* (Portland, OR: Metro, 1997), p. 20.
16. Andres Duany, Elizabeth Plater-Zyberk, and Jeff Speck, *Suburban Nation: The Rise of Sprawl and the Decline of the American Dream* (New York, NY: North Point Press, 2000), p. 228.
17. Harry W. Richardson and Peter Gordon, "Market Planning: Oxymoron or Common Sense?" *Journal of the American Planning Association* 59(3) [Summer, 1993]: pp. 347–352.
18. Joel Garreau, interview with the author, November 13, 1998.
19. Ken Dueker, "Portland's Love Affair with Light Rail: Assessing the Risk Factors," Portland State University Center for Urban Studies Discussion Paper 95-6, 1995.

12. The Environmental Protection Agency

Less than a month after Gore declared war on sprawl, the administrator of EPA's Northeast Region, John DeVillars, announced that the agency will "use the full force of federal environmental law to oppose or seek modification of those projects which by their very nature contribute to sprawl."[1] Using a carrot-and-stick approach, he promised millions of dollars in grants to cities that adopted smart-growth policies, while threatening to use its authority under various laws to oppose anything it regarded as sprawl. Noting that the EPA has already restricted some highway spending in New Hampshire, DeVillars promised "to intensify these efforts."[2]

The EPA traces its authority over urban planning primarily to the Clean Air Act Amendments of 1990, which require that state and metropolitan transportation plans be designed to bring polluted areas into compliance with federal air pollution standards.[3] The EPA has oversight over those plans and can impose sanctions on urban areas that it classifies as polluted and that have failed to implement plans to clean up that pollution.

In the 1970s, the agency tried to use this authority under the original Clean Air Act of 1970 to pressure cities to impose "disincentives for the automobile" such as high parking charges and limits on access to certain areas. This resulted in a storm of protest by local officials to members of Congress. Congress responded by directing the EPA to focus on technological improvements to autos rather than on attempting to suppress auto driving.[4]

The 1990 amendments to the law, with their emphasis on planning, did not lead to such protests, nor did the 1991 transportation bill, the Intermodal Surface Transportation Efficiency Act (ISTEA). This law specifically tied federal transportation dollars—nearly all of which are generated by gasoline taxes and other highway user fees—to clean air. Under the law, the EPA must deny federal highway funds to polluted cities unless those cities have written approved plans for cleaning their air. A recent court case brought by the Sierra Club against Atlanta, Georgia, affirmed that cities may not spend highway dollars, even for preapproved projects, unless they have an EPA-approved plan.

More than 113 million people live in *nonattainment areas*, that is, cities that the EPA classifies as having air pollution problems. This includes nineteen of the nation's twenty largest urban areas (the Twin Cities is the exception), but it also includes such smaller cities as Baton Rouge, Louisiana; Nashville, Tennessee; and Boise, Idaho. New ozone standards recently issued by the EPA could significantly increase this number.

In 1998, Congress passed the Transportation Efficiency Act for the 21st Century (TEA-21). The act authorized a large increase in federal highway funding, which has highway officials and contractors excited about the possibility of using these increased funds to expand highways and reduce congestion. But cities in EPA nonattainment areas will get those funds only if they adopt pollution-control plans approved by the EPA. EPA wants to use this power not to clean up the air but to reduce people's driving.

The EPA is now strongly pushing cities to adopt "smart-growth" plans to curb urban sprawl and reduce urban driving. Some sense of EPA's goals can be obtained from an internal "EPA TEA-21 Workgroup Report" that was approved by the agency's Office of Policy in September, 1998. The report, titled "New Approaches to Integrate Environmental and Transportation Policy through TEA-21 Implementation," describes the EPA's current role in local transportation decisions as "marginal" and proposes new interventions to give pro-environment officials, environmental activists, and regulators—many of whom are EPA partners—more power in transportation planning at the local and regional levels. The "new approach" will be to kill projects that increase highway capacity early on rather than bring them to the point where their benefits and costs can be compared with EPA-favored approaches.

The report states that "Current strategies are leading to very rapid increases in driving and sprawl with escalating environmental damage."[5] In fact, the growth in driving has declined from nearly 5 percent per year in the 1930s through 1960s to only about 3 percent per year since the 1970s.[6] Meanwhile, EPA's own data show that the environmental damage caused by this driving is steadily declining as cleaner cars and fuels replace older ones. While the EPA report erroneously claims that "vehicle-caused pollution doubles periodically in most metropolitan areas," in fact it is declining almost everywhere.

Based on these false premises, the report calls for EPA's "involvement in the early stages of transportation plan development." Within each EPA region, says the memo, the EPA will "work with MPOs [metropolitan planning organizations] and other stakeholders to promote demand management [i.e., reduced auto use] and other innovative alternatives" to highways. The document also calls for EPA to aggressively oppose "auto dependency and urban sprawl."

TEA-21 provisions to streamline environmental clearance, intended by the Congress to reduce the power of environmental regulators to block road projects, are seen by EPA as "an opportunity to change the transportation planning process by building on our involvement in plan development to ensure that demand management strategies with broad multimedia benefits are addressed at key points in the planning process." ("Multimedia" is EPA jargon referring to air, water, and land.) In other words, a "streamlined process" will have the EPA and its allies killing highway projects before anyone knows they are being considered, thus "reducing the need for stakeholder involvement at later stages."

The report applauds a number of local plans that meet EPA's approval:
- In northwest Indiana, several highway projects were eliminated "before project selection," meaning before they could be fairly compared with EPA preferred alternatives;
- In Philadelphia, environmental indicators were established that bias the analysis against roads;
- In San Francisco, a Regional Alliance for Transit has produced a "significant increase in public [i.e., activist] involvement in the regional planning process."

The EPA's Region III (mid-Atlantic) has also been getting involved in transportation planning "before key political decisions are made." The report notes that this prevents the formation of a political constituency for highway projects: "Currently most environmental reviews occur after projects have a political constituency behind them, making change very difficult."

One important fund created by ISTEA and continued in TEA-21 is the Congestion Mitigation/Air Quality (CMAQ) fund. This is about a billion dollars per year, but the administration has proposed to increase it to $1.6 billion. The EPA report calls for spending the money on "air quality" (i.e., reducing auto use) and not "congestion mitigation." For example, improved traffic signals can reduce congestion, but the paper suggests that such improvements should be ineligible for CMAQ funds because the reduced congestion can "induce more overall travel." To carry out these schemes, the report concludes by recommending that an additional 31.5 full-time equivalent staff, and $3.15 million in support funds, be allocated to EPA's TEA-21 campaign.

Federal Grants to Sprawl Warriors

One of the Environmental Protection Agency's most important roles in the war on sprawl has been to give more than $9 million in federal funds in the last five years to anti-auto and smart-growth groups. Those groups then lobby for smart-growth policies at the national, state, and local level, including lobbying to give more power and funding to the Environmental Protection Agency. EPA grants to anti-auto, anti-suburbs groups fall into two major categories:
- The agency's Transportation Partners program has given millions of dollars to nine major organizations whose goal is to reduce vehicle travel.

- The EPA's Smart Growth Network gives large grants to a number of national and state organizations to promote smart growth.

Transportation Partners

According to the EPA, "the mission of the Transportation Partners program is to reduce the growth in Vehicle Miles Traveled (VMT) throughout the U.S."[7] Note that, although EPA's goal is supposed to be to reduce pollution, the emphasis here was to "reduce travel." The EPA traces the program's history to Vice President Gore's Climate Change Action Plan.[8] This plan calls for reducing U.S. "greenhouse gas emissions to 1990 levels by the year 2000." The Transportation Partners program was supposed to bring about nearly half of the transportation portion of that reduction.[9] This means reducing people's driving by 20 billion miles per year, or slightly less than one percent of the total.

Since early 1996, the EPA has given more than $6 million to the following "principal transportation partners":[10]

- the International Council for Local Environmental Initiatives ($2,034,216);
- the Surface Transportation Policy Project ($855,000);
- the Center for Clean Air Policy ($678,939);
- the Environmental Defense Fund ($650,000);
- the Local Government Commission ($500,000);
- the Bicycle Federation of America ($465,000);
- the Association for Commuter Transportation ($315,000);
- Renew America ($215,000); and
- Public Technology Incorporated ($154,765).

The above amounts are only for transportation programs. Many of these groups get additional EPA funding for a variety of other issues. These numbers, which are taken from an EPA web site, may be low.[11] For example, documents obtained from the EPA by *Tollroads* newsletter editor Peter Samuel indicate that EPA gave the Surface Transportation Policy Project $775,000 through 1998. But the web site shows grants totaling only $625,000 through 1998. Adding a 1999 grant of $230,000 produces a total of either $855,000 or $1,050,000.

A few of these grants went for what might be considered legitimate work to solve congestion and air pollution problems. The Association for Commuter Transportation promotes alternatives to commuting in single-occupancy vehicles. The organization focuses on "transportation demand management," meaning that it works with large employers to promote employee vanpooling and transit ridership.[12] The grant to the Environmental Defense Fund was aimed at market-based transportation reforms in California and New York. The organization also employs Michael Replogle, who popularized the term "smart growth" when he worked for the state of Maryland. Replogle supports market tools such as congestion pricing of roads, but also endorses smart-growth plans such as those being adopted in

Maryland and Oregon.

Despite these exceptions, most of the EPA grants went to organizations whose sole purpose is to lobby federal, state, or local governments, or to provide assistance to other groups doing such lobbying. Four of these groups claim to be associations of state or local governments or government officials:

- The Center for Clean Air Policy is an association formed by state governors to promote innovative approaches to pollution. EPA funding is supporting the organization's "Collaborative to Improve Transportation, Land Use, and Air Quality," meaning smart growth.
- The International Council for Local Government Initiatives describes itself as "an association of local governments dedicated to the prevention and solution of local, regional, and global environmental problems through local action."[13] EPA funding is directed to its "Cities for Climate Protection" program which encourages cities to adopt smart growth policies and plans.
- The Local Government Commission is a nonprofit association of "forward-thinking public officials."[14] EPA funding goes to the council's "livable communities" program to promote smart growth in local transportation planning.
- Despite its name, Public Technology, Inc., is a nonprofit group affiliated with the National League of Cities and National Association of Counties.[15] EPA funding is used to promote smart-growth planning at the local level.

Three other recipients are strictly nonprofit lobby groups:

- The Bicycle Federation of America (now known as the National Center for Bicycling and Walking) helps cyclists work with local transportation planning to promote bicycle and pedestrian facilities.[16] Often this means reducing road capacities even though many roads are already at capacity and bicycling and walking typically make up a tiny percentage of all commuting.
- Renew America's main purpose is to present awards to groups for their sustainability projects.[17] EPA funding supports about eight awards per year to groups working on sustainable transportation—meaning non-automotive transportation. One 1998 award, for example, lauded Metro, the regional planning agency for Portland, Oregon, for "developing innovative street design policies intended to reduce auto usage."
- The Surface Transportation Policy Project was created in 1990 to promote diversions of federal highway user fees to non-highway transportation. According to an EPA memo supporting this grant, "STPP has nurtured a network of local transportation activists, its 'grassroots Network', and provided Network members and the public at large with the TransAct electronic information service."[18] The group also sponsors a "Transportation Action Network" web site that strongly promotes smart growth and that was originally paid for, at least in part, by the EPA.[19]

Although not the largest recipient of grants, the Surface Transportation Policy

Project was in many ways the most important Transportation Partner. Transcripts of EPA's monthly telephone conference calls with transportation partners are at least 50 percent conversations with Surface Transportation Policy Project staff.

In 1997, the EPA claimed that its Transportation Partners program led Americans to drive 1.25 billion fewer miles in 1997 than they might have driven without it.[20] This claim is difficult to believe, especially since few of the projects funded by the program did anything other than lobby and propagandize against automobiles. Americans drove 76 billion miles more in 1997 than in 1996, the largest increase in driving in nearly a decade.[21] Driving continued to grow by nearly as much in 1998. This suggests that U.S. drivers were not much influenced by the Transportation Partners program.

In May, 1999, hearings before the Senate Appropriations Committee, Senator Robert Byrd asked EPA Administrator Carol Browner critical questions about the Transportation Partners program. In response, Browner sent a June, 1999, letter to Byrd promising "changes that will substantially improve the program's accountability and balance."[22] Among other things, Browner promised to replace its noncompetitive grant process with a competitive one "open to all transportation and environmental organizations." But in December, 1999, the EPA quietly announced that it would simply discontinue the Transportation Partners program.

In the meantime, EPA continued to make grants to its former Transportation Partners, including Renew America, the Environmental Defense Fund, and the Local Government Commission. The only change is that the grants are now for smart growth instead of transportation partners.

Smart Growth Network

Although the Transportation Partners program has been formally discontinued, the EPA continues to give grants to a Smart Growth Network that heavily overlaps the Transportation Partners. A smart growth web site, www.smartgrowth.org, lists twenty-one partners, including the Congress for New Urbanism and the Surface Transportation Policy Project. Two-thirds of these partners are headquartered in Washington, DC. According to the web site, the Smart Growth Network Partners program consists of "outreach programs, technical assistance, research, publications, and other collaborative projects."

Normally a web site with a dot-org address would be run by a nonprofit, while a government web address would end dot-gov. The smartgrowth.org web site claims it is run by one of the partners, the Sustainable Communities Network. In reality, it designed by the EPA to be a front for its activities. On one page, the site stated, "For more information, please contact the UEDD at (202) 260-2750, or see our Web site: http://www.smartgrowth.org." UEDD is the Urban and Economic Development Division of the EPA.

The site also invites email inquiries to info@smartgrowth.org. In early 1999

Tollroads newsletter editor Peter Samuel sent an email asking, "who controls the content of this web site?" The response came from Branagan.Michael@ epamail.epa.gov, meaning an EPA employee. The email confirmed that the Smart Growth Network "is an EPA initiative" and that the smartgrowth.org "web page is written and funded by EPA." Branagan admitted that the information was not placed on EPA's web site (www.epa.gov) because "the association with EPA may have discouraged/alienated potential users from even entertaining any ideas, articles, etc. that were posted on the site from the start."

Table One: Smart Growth Network Partners

American Farmland Trust
American Planning Association
Center for Neighborhood Technology
Congress for the New Urbanism
The Conservation Fund
International City/County Management Association
Joint Center for Sustainable Communities
Local Government Commission
National Association of Counties
National Association of Local Government Environmental Professionals
National Growth Management Leadership Project
National Neighborhood Coalition
Natural Resources Defense Council
National Trust for Historic Preservation
The Northeast-Midwest Institute
Scenic America
State of Maryland
Surface Transportation Policy Project
Sustainable Communities Network
Trust for Public Land
Urban Land Institute
Source: http://www.smartgrowth.org/

Branagan states that "the idea was to neutrally encourage dialog in the ideas on the site," but the site is far from neutral. A large portion is devoted to pushing the "Clinton-Gore Livability Agenda," and the site includes many speeches by Al Gore and EPA officials. In late 1999, the site was formally transferred to the Sustainable Communities Network, but its content remains largely unchanged.

A typical quote from the site states that "Advertisers have been saying for years that automobiles signify freedom and social acceptability. Many Americans are discovering that automobiles also mean pollution, congestion, increased commuting time, frustration and road rage." In other words, people only drive because they have been manipulated by advertisers. The director of EPA's Urban and Economic Development Division, Harriett Tregoning, carries this theme further in an article posted on the web site. People live in low-density suburbs, she says, because the federal government has subsidized highways—ignoring the fact that these "subsidies" have come entirely from gas taxes and other highway user fees.

If the smart growth web site is managed by the Sustainable Communities Network, other partners take on other responsibilities:

- The American Planning Association publishes a legislative guidebook on smart growth;
- The Congress for the New Urbanism provides (with EPA funding) "technical assistance to local governments";
- The International City/County Management Association runs (with EPA funding) the Smart Growth Network and publishes a smart-growth newsletter;
- The National Association of Counties "publishes a primer on sprawl";
- The National Association of Local Government Environmental Professionals is finding ways to use "existing and potential federal regulatory incentives to encourage smart growth";
- The National Trust for Historic Preservation promotes "main streets" as alternatives to conventional shopping malls as well as infill development;
- The Urban Land Institute holds (with EPA funding) a national Partners for Smart Growth conference.

As noted, many of these programs are partly or entirely funded by the EPA. EPA smart growth grants include:

- $700,000 to the Growth Management Institute for "workshops, focus group meetings, and other activities" aimed to be an "antidote to sprawl";
- $505,000 in two grants to the Coalition for Utah's Future to support Envision Utah's community workshops and promote similar initiatives in "communities across the country";
- $363,395 to the International City/County Management Association to create a smart-growth network.
- $237,250 to Grow Smart Rhode Island to promote "sustainable development" in the Ocean State;
- $175,000 to 1000 Friends of Oregon to create a National Growth Management Leadership Project (a Smart Growth Network partner) that would promote smart growth in other parts of the country.
- $165,000 to the Congress for the New Urbanism for workshops and conferences on smart growth;
- $155,000 to the Urban Land Institute for a national conference on smart growth
- $50,000 to the National Governors Association to "help states develop smart growth strategies";

- $35,000 to the Center for Watershed Protection to develop smart growth zoning codes;
- $20,000 to the Local Government Commission for a conference on smart growth;
- $10,000 more to the Urban Land Institute to promote smart growth in a portion of Washington, DC.

In the year 2000 alone, EPA has given nearly $1 million in "smart growth" or "transportation choice" grants, many to state organizations. As with the transportation partners grants, some of these grants may be larger than indicated here. For example, the EPA's grants web site reports a $512,000 grant to the Growth Management Institute, while that organization's web site says that the grant was $700,000.[23] There may also be additional grants not found in the database. For example, the EPA gave the National Association of Counties $429,312 for the Joint Center for Sustainable Development. This organization is a part of the smart growth network, but the term "smart growth" does not appear in the grant description. Other grants to smart-growth groups may lack this or similar terms so were not found by searches of the web site.

EPA's combination of funding and support to state governments, local governments, and non-profits has had a powerful effect in many places. For example, Envision Utah is a smart-growth program promoted by Utah's governor—no doubt influenced by the EPA smart-growth grant to the National Governor's Association. The EPA grant to the Coalition for Utah's Future will help spread this program to other states.

EPA's transportation and smart-growth funding is only a small share of all EPA grants to nonprofit organizations. According to *Phony Philanthropy*, a report by Citizens Against Government Waste, in 1995 and 1996 the EPA gave $236 million in 839 grants to non-profits. As the report dryly comments, "Many of these organizations are promoting agendas that many Americans might not agree with."[24]

"When an organization receives government funding, it frees up funding obtained through membership or other nongovernment sources to be used for more controversial activities, such as lobbying or promoting a particular philosophy," notes the report. "Some organizations even use government money directly to promote their political and lobbying activities." While this is illegal, the report found several instances of EPA funds being spent directly on lobbying.

The approximately $8 million identified here as grants to transportation and smart growth is a tiny share of EPA's total budget. But the individual grants represent a significant share of the budgets of the non-profits receiving them and also gives those non-profits a major boost over opponents to smart growth, most of whom are poorly funded and have no support network like the EPA's Transportation Partners or Smart Growth Network.

This severely distorts the supposedly local planning process that Congress created in ISTEA and TEA-21. Bicyclists, for example, make up just 0.4 percent of all commuters in America, yet EPA's $465,000 grant to the Bicycle Federation of America makes sure that transportation planners in cities across the country pay close attention to the demands of cyclists. Close to 90 percent of all commuters drive autos to work, but EPA gave no grant to any automobile groups and the views of auto drivers are often unheard in local transportation planning.

Congress based this planning process on the philosophy that state and local governments should make final transportation decisions after considering public input and a full range of alternatives. Yet EPA grants are designed to subvert local public input by allowing outside or minority views to dominate. As previously noted, the EPA is also trying to prevent local planning agencies from considering a full range of alternatives if those alternatives involve highway building.

The EPA grants have other disturbing qualities. Naturally, the groups receiving EPA funding will be at the witness stand at budget time to endorse increases in EPA's budgets. EPA funding also creates the appearance of a grassroots movement against sprawl when in fact much of the "movement" is supported by a federal agency seeking increased funding and power over local governments.

Al Gore was able to confidently propose a war on the lifestyle of most Americans because he knew he would be supported by numerous citizens' groups that have been getting funding and support from the EPA. After Gore's January 11 announcement, the January 12 edition of the Land Letter, a newsletter for natural resource professionals, ran a lead article headlined, "Amidst great applause, Gore announces plan to curb urban sprawl."[25] The groups cited as "applauding" the plan, including the Surface Transportation Policy Project and the Environmental Defense Fund, were nearly all EPA transportation or smart-growth partners.

From a legal standpoint, the EPA grants and its other support for smart growth may go beyond its authority, which is to clean the air of pollutants such as hydrocarbons, nitrogen oxides, and carbon monoxide. Reducing people's mobility by creating traffic jams and forcing them to live in congested cities may slightly reduce total vehicle-miles driven. But it is likely to increase the production of those pollutants that EPA is supposed to control.

Notes

1. This section is partly based on Peter Samuel and Randal O'Toole, *Smart Growth at the Federal Trough* (Washington, DC: Cato Institute, 1999). My thanks to Peter Samuel for helping to develop much of the information.
2. John DeVillars, "Opening Remarks, Smart Growth Strategies for New England Conference," February 2, 1999, http://www.epa.gov/region01/ra/sprawl/speech.html.
3. Clean Air Act Amendments of 1990, §101(f), Conformity Requirements.
4. Arnold M. Howitt, Joshua P. Anderson, and Alan A. Altshuler, *The New Politics of Clean Air and Transportation* (Washington, DC: US DOT, 1997), p. 37.
5. Environmental Protection Agency, "New Approaches to Integrate Environmental and Transportation Policy through TEA21 Implementation," memo dated 26 August 1998 and adopted by the EPA Office of Policy on 14 September 1998.

6. Federal Highway Administration, *Highway Statistics Summary to 1995* (Washington, DC: FHwA, 1996), table VM-201.
7. EPA, *Transportation Partners 1997 Annual Report* (Washington, DC: EPA, 1998), Executive Summary, p. 1.
8. Ibid, p. 1-1.
9. Ibid.
10. Financial information on these grants comes from the EPA's Grants Information and Control System database, http://www.epa.gov/envirofw/html/gics/gics_query.html.
11. Environmental Protection Agency, "Grants Information Query Form," http:// www.epa.gov/envirofw/html/gics/gics_query.html.
12. Association for Commuter Transportation, "Association for Commuter Transportation," http://tmi.cob.fsu.edu/act/act.htm.
13. International Council for Local Environmental Initiatives, "Home Page," http:// www.iclei.org.
14. Center for Livable Communities, "Welcome to the Center for Livable Communities," http://www.lgc.org/clc.
15. Public Technology, Inc., "Public Technology, Inc.," http://www.pti.nw.dc.us.
16. National Center for Bicycling and Walking, "bikefed.org," http://www.bikefed.org.
17. Renew America, "Renew America," http://solstice.crest.org/sustainable/renew_america.
18. Memo titled "Decision memorandum - Supplemental Incremental Funding for the Surface Transportation Policy Project under Cooperative Agreement CX-825013-01-0" from Michael Shelby, Energy and Transportation Sectors Division, to Mildred Lee, Grants Operations Branch, EPA, 4 pp.
19. Surface Transportation Policy Project, "The Transportation Act," http:// www.transact.org.
20. EPA, *Transportation Partners 1997 Annual Report*, p. 4-1.
21. FHwA, *Highway Statistics 1997* (Washington, DC: FHwA, 1998), table VM-1; FHwA, *Highway Statistics 1996*, table VM-1; and FHwA, *Highway Statistics Summary to 1995*, table VM-201.
22. Carol Browner, letter to Honorable Robert Byrd, 16 June 1999.
23. Growth Management Institute, "GMI Projects," http://www.gmionline.org/projects.htm.
24. Citizens Against Government Waste, *Phony Philanthropy: How Government Grants are Subverting the Missions of Nonprofit Organizations* (Washington, DC: CAGW, 1998), available at
25. Colleen Schu, "Amidst great applause, Gore announces plan to curb urban sprawl," *Land Letter* 18(1): 1–3.

 Web Tools: EPA Grantees

To see recent EPA grants to non-profit groups for smart growth, go to http://www.epa.gov/envirofw/html/gics/gics_query.html. Because of abbreviations, looking up under the name of the organization doesn't always work and looking at all non-profit grants produces too many results. To narrow down your search, limit your search to "Surveys Studies Investigations (66.606)" and try various search terms under "Text Search," such as "smart," "growth," and "transportation."

13. Other Federal Agencies

Al Gore announced the administration's war on sprawl in January, 1999. Yet the Clinton-Gore administration had already been promoting smart-growth policies in many different arenas. As noted in chapter 12, such support originated in the Environmental Protection Agency. More recently, the Department of Transportation and the Department of Housing and Urban Development also jumped on the smart-growth bandwagon.

Department of Transportation

Under the Clinton administration, the Department of Transportation has become a strong proponent of smart growth. Among other things, the department is strongly promoting rail transit, increased urban densities, and regional planning. Support for these policies comes in the form of funding to various states and metropolitan areas; numerous publications promoting smart-growth ideas; and support for conferences and other public relations activities.

The Federal Transit Administration has taken the lead in the department's smart-growth efforts. The agency has issued many publications promoting density, transit-oriented developments, and of course transit improvements.[1] Federal transit officials also encourage local planners to build more rail transit and other highway alternatives into their regional transportation plans.

Ever since the Department of Transportation was created in 1966, the major agencies it has overseen have represented different modes of travel: air, rail, waterways, highways, and urban transit.[2] Given that each mode has its own constituencies that want to monitor federal actions that affect them, this structure was inevitable. Also inevitable was the consequent battles between agencies. The Federal Highway Administration and Federal Transit Administration, for example, compete for funds from the same pot of money and are not likely to be objective about the true benefits and costs of what they do.

Historically, the federal highway budget has been much larger than its transit budget. But the Clinton administration has given priority to transit and consistently slanted its programs against auto travel. One place that this is visible is in the department's strategic plan, written to comply with the 1993 Government Performance and Results Act. This law requires every federal agency to define its mission, goals, and objectives in terms of the outcomes it wants to produce so that agencies can be held "accountable for achieving program results."[3]

The Department of Transportation's strategic plan identifies safety and mobility as its major goals. The mobility goal is described as "Shape America's future by ensuring a transportation system that is accessible, integrated, efficient, and offers flexibility of choices." One obvious measure to use for mobility is passenger miles of travel since that represents the outcome or results of agency actions. The problem is that this measure would reveal public transit to be very inefficient, since transit subsidies per passenger mile are about one hundred times greater than highway subsidies per passenger mile. American transit systems are so poorly managed that "efficiency" conflicts with "flexibility of choices."

To avoid measuring mobility by the passenger mile, the department uses four other measures:

- The percent of national highway miles with poor ride quality;
- The percent of national highway bridges that are deficient;
- The average age of bus and rail fleets;
- The number of people living within 0.5 miles of transit stops.[4]

Contrary to the requirements of the law, none of these are truly outcome-related. Instead, they are all based on inputs: how much is spent on pavement, bridges, transit hardware, and transit operations. In particular, none of these measures will reveal that transit carries less than 2 percent of all urban trips. The department will deem itself successful if it floods cities with transit vehicles even if they all run empty.

The department also administers the Congestion Mitigation and Air Quality (CMAQ) fund, a billion-dollar per year fund created in 1991. Cities may apply to use these funds but can only spend them on activities which the secretary of transportation has found will effectively reduce congestion and air pollution. Many cities have used the funds to improve traffic flows, such as by synchronizing traffic signals. Since cars pollute more in stop-and-go traffic, this is clearly an effective use of CMAQ funds. For example:

- At a cost of $450,000, traffic signal improvements in Fresno, California, are estimated to reduce carbon monoxide emissions by almost 1600 kilograms per day and nitrogen oxide emissions by nearly 300 kilograms per day.
- At a cost of $320,000, traffic signal improvements in Syracuse, New York, are expected to reduce carbon monoxide emissions by more than 200 kilograms per day;
- At a cost of $9.8 million, computerization of New York City traffic signals is expected to reduce hydrocarbon emissions by 220 kilograms per day and nitrogen oxide emissions by 60 kilograms per day.[5]

But many other cities have used CMAQ funds for highly questionable activi-

ties, including:
- New Jersey spent $9 million building a new train station, which it says will reduce air pollution (hydrocarbons) by just 4 kilograms per day;
- Fairview, Oregon, spent $368,000 subsidizing a high-density, transit-oriented development that will probably increase air pollution by increasing congestion in the development's vicinity. The town made no estimate of pollution effects;
- Santa Clara County (San Jose), California, spent $15 million in CMAQ funds to build a light-rail line. It made no claims about air quality improvements and there probably will be none;
- Portland, Oregon, spent $373,000 on a light-rail park-and-ride station, which it claims will reduce carbon monoxide emissions by a paltry 4 kilograms per day and nitrogen oxide emissions by just 1 kilogram per day.[6]

Not all traffic signalization projects perform so well as the ones listed above and not all of the transit projects perform so poorly; nor should the estimates always be considered reliable. But when millions of dollars are spent on activities that aren't even claimed to produce significant pollution benefits, the Department of Transportation is clearly failing in its duty to insure that these funds are spent effectively. In particular, it should deny funds to transit-oriented developments and other projects that will increase congestion and air pollution. But it will not do so as long as the smart-growth ideology dominates the department.

The transportation bill of 1998 created another new fund, the Transportation and Community and System Preservation Pilot Program. Introduced by Oregon Senator Ron Wyden and inspired by a Surface Transportation Policy Project proposal, the fund is being used to promote smart-growth in communities throughout the nation. A provision in the laws states that funds can be given to "nontraditional partners," meaning nonprofit organizations instead of just government agencies.[7] After the law was passed, a newsletter of the Surface Transportation Policy Project urged local groups to take advantage of this provision to fund their campaigns to "redirect highway funds" to transit and transit-oriented development.[8]

In its first year, the fund was used for thirty-five different smart-growth projects, including:
- Promoting transit-oriented developments in Kansas City, Missouri, Cleveland, Ohio, and Philadelphia, Pennsylvania;
- Creating a "sprawl index" in Lansing, Michigan;
- Educational workshops aimed at making New Jersey towns more "transit friendly";
- Subsidizing a manufacturing business park in downtown Dayton, Ohio;
- Rewriting land-use rules to promote neotraditional neighborhoods in Johnson City, Tennessee.

Some of these funds were used to support ostensibly objective public-involvement processes, including the Envision Utah program and similar programs in Anchorage, Alaska, central Kentucky, and Saginaw, Michigan. But, as the Public-Involvement Myth (p. 469) describes, these so-called public involvement processes are usually a sham with smart-growth prescriptions being the foregone conclusion no matter what members of the public say they really want.

Department of Housing and Urban Development

Although the Department of Housing and Urban Development (HUD) did not formally endorse smart growth until 1999, it more than any other federal department would welcome a war on the suburbs. Since its creation in 1965, the department's stated mission has been to secure a "decent, safe, and sanitary home and suitable living environment for every American." But to judge by its behavior, its real mission is to use federal tax dollars collected from the suburbs to prop up declining central cities.

Recent department annual reports on the state of the cities are one long whine about how the suburbs are growing faster than the cities and so therefore the cities deserve more federal subsidies. This is particularly incongruous in the late 1990s, when most central cities are doing very well: incomes and homeownership rates are up, unemployment and crime are down. Yet to HUD, the glass is always half empty: The fact that jobs in central cities are growing is less important than the fact that jobs in the suburbs are growing faster.

"A new digital divide in high tech jobs is emerging between cities and suburbs," announced the *State of the Cities 2000* report with alarm. Although high-tech jobs are rapidly growing in the cities, they are growing even faster in the suburbs. "Despite the positive gains in high-tech job growth in central cities, suburbs continue to outpace central cities," warns the report.[9] More good news: "Homeownership has reached all-time highs in both central cities and suburbs."[10] But the bad news is that suburban homeownership rates are higher, so the cities need more housing subsidies.

The 1998 *State of the Cities* report blames the differences between cities and suburbs on "middle-class flight that began two decades ago."[11] In fact, this "flight" began well over a century ago, long before any federal urban programs or housing subsidies, and represented peoples' desires to live in lower densities and outside the jurisdictions of the often-corrupt central city governments. With a few notable exceptions, central cities are less corrupt today. But their tax rates are often significantly higher than in the suburbs, and much of these taxes go not to help poor people but to subsidize big businesses, including such things as football stadiums and convention centers.

Frustrated by suburban resistance to annexation, the cities have come to rely on HUD as a source of transfer payments from suburban taxpayers to the cities. About $23 billion of HUD's $33 billion budget is for public housing, nearly all of which is spent in the cities. Another $7.6 billion is for community development, which is also mostly spent in the cities. Of the remainder, about $2.3 billion goes to the Federal Housing Administration, mostly for mortgage insurance which benefits both cities and suburbs, and almost all the rest is overhead. Thus, as much as 90 percent of HUD's budget is aimed at propping up the central cities.

The 1998 *State of the Cities* report called for conventional solutions to urban problems, namely more federal spending and housing and other programs. But the 1999 and 2000 reports have lengthy sections about "promoting smarter growth and livable communities." The reports repeat a familiar litany against "sprawl," including claims that sprawl increases urban-service costs, threatens open space, and concentrates poverty.

The 1999 report calls for developing "Smart-Growth strategies across jurisdictional lines." The report lauds Georgia for creating the Georgia Regional Transportation Authority and giving it "the authority to stop construction of highways or shopping malls that don't promote smart growth" in the Atlanta area.[12] HUD is spending $50 million in 2000 to promote such "regional connections" in other metropolitan areas.[13] In other words, suburbs are to lose their independence to various regional or metropolitan councils promoted by federal policy.

The 2000 *State of the Cities* admits that internet technology, "coupled with rising incomes, population growth, and infrastructure spending patterns," continue to promote "decentralization," and warns that this "threatens to undermine the quality of life in both cities and suburbs." One of the "dangers" of such decentralization, the report claims, is that "There is evidence that the high-tech economy reinforces the need for strong central cities." The report doesn't cite any evidence other than to say that what economists call "agglomerative economies"—the value of locating businesses near other businesses—"are also valuable in the New Economy."[14] So all of those high-tech firms must be making a mistake when they locate in the suburbs—a mistake that can be corrected by smart growth and government planning.

HUD's endorsement of smart growth puts its stated goals in conflict with many of its on-the-ground proposals:

- The *State of the Cities* reports all applaud increasing rates of urban home ownership. But smart growth and the 1999 report call for more construction of apartments and other multifamily dwellings.
- The 1998 report lauds a "bridges to work" program that helps poor people get to work by—among other things—increasing rates of auto ownership. But the 1999 and 2000 reports support smart-growth programs that increase urban congestion, which will make it harder for poor people to get to work.
- The 1999 report claims to support "local and bottom-up strategies." But a major new initiative calls for funding metropolitan planning organizations in urban areas whose suburbs concede power to the regional planners.
- In the biggest conflict of all, smart growth's proven track record of creating

the nation's least affordable housing markets is completely contrary to HUD's traditional mission of providing affordable housing.

It appears that HUD's old mission of helping to house the poor has been superseded by a more recent one of helping cities grab political power over the suburbs. The Department of Housing and Urban Development clearly sees itself as an advocate for the cities against the evil suburbs—and there is no Department of Suburban Development to advocate for the suburbs.

Other Federal Agencies

Many other federal agencies have been recruited in the administration's war on sprawl. For example,

- The National Park Service has a program aimed at "revitalizing urban America" with "urban greening efforts" in, among other cities, Chicago and Milwaukee.[15]
- NASA is providing satellite data that supposedly shows the problems with sprawl.[16]
- The Forest Service is promoting conservation easements on private lands to protect "traditional uses against rapid urban expansion."[17]
- The Department of Commerce is emphasizing "sustainable development" in its economic development grants to cities.[18]
- On the Pacific Coast, the National Marine Fisheries Service is promoting transit ridership and compact development in order to help save salmon—even though it admits that it has no idea whether driving and low-density development have anything to do with salmon declines.[19]

In addition, to help "revitalize downtowns," President Clinton issued executive orders 12988 and 13006, which direct federal agencies to locate their offices in downtown and historic districts "wherever operationally appropriate and economically prudent."[20] In short, it is clear that the entire Clinton administration is pushing hard for smart growth using every agency of the federal government that is even remotely related to domestic affairs.

This book is going to press after the November, 2000, election but before it is known whether the next president will be Al Gore or George Bush. As president, Al Gore would clearly continue to push federal agencies to support smart growth. George Bush is not likely to push for federal smart-growth programs, but there is no indication that he would try to halt such programs in the Environmental Protection Agency or other agencies. With a weak election mandate, Bush will probably not be able to replace smart-growth proponents in the EPA and other federal agencies. Once bureaucratic programs get going, it is very difficult to stop them. With its Congressional mandate, the Department of Transportation in particular is likely to continue to give grants to smart-growth proponents and projects no matter who is president. Nor will the presidential election slow the momentum for smart growth in Georgia, Maryland, the Twin Cities, and the many other states and cities whose governors, mayors, and other elected officials strongly support such policies.

One little-noted aspect of the 2000 election is the growing split between central city and suburban voting patterns, noted in 1998 in Scott Thomas's book, *The United States of Suburbia*.[21] In most states, the central cities voted heavily for Gore while their suburbs voted heavily for Bush. It may be that Gore's war on sprawl exacerbated this split.

Notes

1. See, for example, Federal Transit Administration, *Transit and Urban Form* (Washington, DC: US DOT, 1996), 94 pp.
2. John L. Hazard, *Managing National Transportation Policy* (Washington, DC: Eno, 1988), p. 130.
3. Government Performance and Results Act of 1993, §2(b)(1).
4. U.S. Department of Transportation, *Strategic Plan for Fiscal Years 1997–2002* (Washington, DC: DOT, 1997), http://www.dot.gov/hot/dotplan.pdf.
5. US DOT, *CMAQ Annual Report 1997* (Washington, DC: DOT, 1998), http://www.fhwa.dot.gov/environment/cmaq97st.pdf.
6. Ibid. The Fairview, Oregon, example came from the 1996 annual report, available at http://www.fhwa.dot.gov/environment/cm1fy96.pdf.
7. Transportation Equity Act of 1998, public law 105-178, section 1221.
8. Surface Transportation Policy Project, "A New Shot at the Land Use & Transportation Question," *Progress*, June, 1998, pp. 9–11.
9. Department of Housing and Urban Development, *The State of the Cities 2000* (Washington, DC: HUD, 2000), p. v, http://www.huduser.org/publications/pdf/socrpt.pdf.
10. Ibid, p. vii.
11. Department of Housing and Urban Development, *The State of the Cities 1998* (Washington, DC: HUD, 1998), p. vii, http://www.huduser.org/publications/pdf/soc98.pdf.
12. Ibid, p. 21.
13. Ibid, p. 49.
14. HUD, *State of the Cities 2000*, p. 61.
15. EPA, "Revitalizing Downtowns," http://www.epa.gov/region5/sprawl/downtowns.htm.
16. EPA, "Regional Planning," http://www.epa.gov/region5/sprawl/regional.htm.
17. EPA, "Infill Development," http://www.epa.gov/region5/sprawl/farmland.htm.
18. EPA, "Farmland Preservation and Rural Communities," http://www.epa.gov/region5/sprawl/infill.htm.
19. National Oceanic and Atmospheric Administration, "Salmon and Steelhead; Final Rules," *Federal Register*, July 10, 2000.
20. William Clinton, Executive Orders 12988 and 13006 on Locating Federal Facilities (Washington, DC: White House, 1996).
21. G. Scott Thomas, *The United States of Suburbia: How the Suburbs Took Control of America and What They Plan to Do With It* (New York, NY: Prometheus, 1998), 290 pp.

The Myth of Urban Decline

Myth: Sprawl contributes to poverty and urban decline.
Reality: Low-density suburbanization has little to do with poverty or urban decline.

"Poverty in cities is higher than in the suburbs," says HUD's 1998 *State of the Cities* report, which adds that poverty is "highly concentrated in certain neighborhoods."[1] According to some, this is at least partly due to urban sprawl. Ned Farquhar, the director of 1000 Friends of New Mexico, says that "lower-income people would have more opportunity to find rewarding work and build lifetime equity if we didn't let sprawling growth undermine our economic performance."

Sprawl, claims Farquhar, forces poor people to live in expensive housing in the cities because they can't afford the cars they would need to live in more affordable housing in the suburbs. Moreover, as jobs relocate to the suburbs, they move out of the reach of the urban poor.[2] In 1998, Anthony Downs summed up the problem by saying that "suburban sprawl concentrates poor households, especially poor minority households, in certain high-poverty neighborhoods."[3]

This argument has been elaborated by former Albuquerque Mayor David Rusk. Rusk believes that cities that have been able to annex most of their suburbs are "fairer" than urban areas with separate cities and suburbs because the former have a more even income distribution and slightly more integrated neighborhoods. Rusk urges central cities to form "regional growth management compacts" to gain control over reluctant suburbs and help reduce poverty.[4]

In reviewing Rusk's book, *Cities without Suburbs*, Columbia law professor Edward Zelinsky noted that Rusk's comparisons of individual cities were not statistically valid.[5] Rusk would pick two cities, such as Houston and Detroit, and credit any advantages Houston had over Detroit to Houston's ability to annex suburbs without a popular vote. Zelinsky pointed out that Detroit was an early twentieth-century manufacturing city with a dense urban core, while Houston grew up in the late twentieth century and never had a dense core. Thus, historical differences were more important than sprawl or regional government in explaining differences in poverty concentrations.

In 1999, none other than Anthony Downs did the statistical analysis Zelinsky demanded. Downs compared various measures of sprawl, such as overall urban area density and the ratio of central city to suburban density, with measures of urban decline, including poverty, crime, and population changes in the central city. "I came to the conclusion that there is no meaningful and significant statistical relationship between any of the specific traits of sprawl, or a sprawl index, and either measure of urban decline," says Downs. "This was very surprising to me and went against my belief that sprawl contributed to concentrated poverty and therefore to urban decline." He now believes that poverty would be concentrated in certain areas "even if sprawl did not exist. . . . Even compact growth would produce the same problems."[6]

In fact, policies aimed at stopping sprawl could actually increase the concentrations of poverty in certain neighborhoods. Urban-growth boundaries or the purchase of land for open space will increase the price of inner-city housing. This could "compel many low-income households now living there (and future poor immigrants) to live elsewhere," says Downs. In response, they might "start overcrowding existing units in older areas or older suburbs and generate large-scale slums."[7]

USC planners Peter Gordon and Harry Richardson examined the question of whether the dispersal of jobs was hurting poor minorities who could not afford cars. They compared travel times to work for whites and blacks in five cities, and found "no disadvantages for blacks." In fact, blacks had significantly shorter journeys than whites in three of the five cities, while only slightly longer ones in the other two cities.[8]

At the same time, there is plenty of research suggesting that the best way to help poor people is to give them access to automobiles. Katherine O'Regan, an economist at Yale, and John Quigley, an economist at UC Berkeley, have found that poor people who own cars are more likely to find better-paying jobs than ones who do not. Ironically, until recently welfare policies prevented poor people from owning cars, lest they lose their welfare benefits. To reduce poverty, they conclude, we should "promote the mass transit system that works so well for the nonpoor—the private auto."[9]

Poor people make up a larger percentage of central city residents than suburban residents. But, says Pietro Nivola, this doesn't mean that changing this pattern "for a different pattern would be unquestionably better."[10] Nivola believes efforts to curb sprawl will only make housing less affordable for the urban poor.

In his book, *Crabgrass Frontier*, suburban analyst Kenneth Jackson points out that concentrations of poverty in the cities are largely due to historic federal policies. The Department of Housing and Urban Development and its predecessor agencies placed most low-income housing projects in central cities that were eager for federal subsidies. Meanwhile, its mortgage loan programs "red lined" poor and minority neighborhoods, so that middle-class whites were often able to buy homes only if they purchased in the suburbs or wealthier parts of the cities. The Federal Housing Administration actively discriminated against blacks and other minorities at least through 1948[11] and passively allowed discrimination for much longer.[12]

Most such federal policies were changed many years ago. Today, as soon as inner city poor can afford cars and a down payment on homes, they often move to the suburbs. "During the 1980s and 1990s," says Edwin Mills, "African Americans and Latinos have been moving to the suburbs in record numbers."[13]

There is no evidence that suburbanization contributes to or causes poverty or concentrations of poverty. Autos and suburbanization have helped tens of millions of Americans escape poverty and improve their lives. While some people remain poor, and some of these have been "left behind" as others moved to the suburbs, it doesn't make sense to punish everyone else by forcing them to live in costly, congested cities. What is clear is that smart growth harms poor people by making housing and transportation more expensive.

Notes

1. Department of Housing and Urban Development, *1998 State of the Cities Report* (Washington, DC: HUD, 1998), http://www.huduser.org/publications/polleg/tsoc98/tsoc_98.html.
2. Ned Farquhar, "Sprawl and Poverty," *Albuquerque Tribune*, January 6, 2000, p. C1.
3. Anthony Downs, "How America's Cities Are Growing: The Big Picture," *Brookings Review*, Fall, 1998, p. 9, http://www.brookings.org/press/REVIEW/fa98/downs.pdf.
4. David Rusk, "The Exploding Metropolis: Why Growth Management Makes Sense," *Brookings Review*, Fall, 1998, p. 14.
5. Edward A. Zelinsky, "Metropolitanism, Progressivism, and Race: Cities Without Suburbs by David Rusk," *Columbia Law Review* 98:665.
6. Anthony Downs, "Some Realities about Sprawl and Urban Decline," *Housing Policy Debate* 10 (4): p. 961, http://www.fanniemaefoundation.org/research/policy/pdf/HPD104/HPD104/downs.pdf.
7. Ibid, p. 972.
8. Peter Gordon and Harry Richardson, "Congestion Trends in Metropolitan Areas," *in* National Research Council, *Curbing Gridlock: Peak-Period Fees to Relieve Traffic Congestion* (Washington, DC: National Acadamy Press, 1994), volume 2:1–31.
9. Katherine O'Regan and John Quigley, "Cars for the Poor," *Access*, 12 (Spring, 1998): pp. 20-24.
10. Pietro S. Nivola, *Laws of the Landscape: How Policies Shape Cities in Europe and America* (Washington, DC: Brookings, 1999), pp. 45–46.
11. Kenneth T. Jackson, *Crabgrass Frontier: The Suburbanization of the United States* (New York, NY: Oxford University Press, 1985), pp. 208–216.
12. Gwendolyn Wright, *Building the Dream: A Social History of Housing in America* (Boston, MA: MIT Press, 1983), pp. 247–248.
13. Edwin S. Mills, "Truly Smart 'Smart Growth,'" *Illinois Real Estate Letter*, Summer, 1999, p. 3.

14. Funding the War on Sprawl

ar from being a grassroots movement enjoying monetary support from a broad range of people, the war on sprawl is predominantly funded by major foundations and government agencies. In addition to grants from the Environmental Protection Agency, U.S. Department of Transportation, and other federal agencies, the nonprofit groups that are leading this war are often supported by special interests, such as the American Public Transportation Association, or by foundation and state and local grants. Some apparently grassroots organizations, such as 1000 Friends of New Mexico and the Growth Management Institute, get more than three-quarters of their funding from government grants and less than 4 percent from individual contributions.[1]

Foundation Support

In January, 1999, representatives of close to thirty major foundations held an inaugural meeting of the Funders Network on Sprawl, Smart Growth and Livable Communities. Participants included the Ford, the John D. and Catherine T. MacArthur, Charles Stewart Mott, David & Lucile Packard, and Turner foundations.[2] Most of these foundations had already been funding anti-auto and anti-suburb activities for more than a decade.

In 1989, the Joyce Foundation supported a national conference on surface transportation which led to the creation of the Surface Transportation Policy Project in 1990. Since then, most of that organization's funding has come from Joyce, Surdna, Nathan Cummings, and the James C. Penney foundations.

Oregon's 1000 Friends was another early pioneer in fundraising for smart growth, starting in 1988 with the Land Use-Transportation Air Quality (LUTRAQ) project, which claimed to prove that density and transit-oriented development could reduce congestion and air pollution. Over the next several years, LUTRAQ received millions of dollars in funding from the Energy, Nathan Cummings, Surdna, ARCO, and Joyce foundations.

In 1991, the Pew Charitable Trusts, the John D. and Catherine T. MacArthur Foundation, and the Rockefeller Foundation jointly began the Energy Foundation, seeding it with tens of millions of dollars. This foundation typically gives nearly $10 million per year to a variety of environmental groups. The Surface Transportation Policy Project, for example, recently received $250,000 for a two-year project to "support national policy advocacy and the Transportation and Quality of Life Campaign." Other pro-rail and/or anti-auto grants went to 1000 Friends of Oregon, the Bicycle Federation of America, the Coalition for Utah's Future, the Colorado Public Interest Research Foundation, Friends of the Earth, the Environmental Law and Policy Center of the Midwest, the Georgia Conservancy and Georgians for Transportation Alternatives, the Oregon Environmental Council, Rails to Trails Conservancy, Sensible Transportation Options for People, and the Tri-State Transportation Campaign.[3]

The Surdna Foundation is another big giver to anti-sprawl groups. In its 1998–1999 funding cycle, it gave nearly $4 million to anti-auto and anti-suburbs groups. Recipients included 1000 Friends of New Mexico, the Colorado Public Interest Research Foundation, the Congress for the New Urbanism, the Hoosier Environmental Council, the National Smart Growth Coalition, and the Surface Transportation Policy Project.[4]

From 1990 to 1999 the Nathan Cummings Foundation has given at least $3.5 million to smart-growth projects. This includes $900,000 to the Surface Transportation Policy Project, plus grants to the Sierra Club, Environmental Defense Foundation, 1000 Friends of Oregon, and many other national and state anti-auto and anti-auto groups.

There is nothing wrong with these foundations giving money to the causes they choose. However, foundations that think their money is going to make cities more livable by reducing congestion and improving air quality have been deceived. At the same time, groups that are largely funded by such foundations should not pose as grassroots organizations. "The growing campaign against suburbanization is at root elitist in that it would deny people what they want," writes Capital Research Center researcher Daniel Oliver after reviewing foundation funding of smart-growth groups. "This elitism is the smart growth campaign's Achilles' heel."[5]

State Funding of Smart Growth

Several states, including Oregon, and Utah, have funded nonprofit groups that advocate for smart growth to conduct supposedly objective public involvement processes aimed at changing land-use and transportation.

Livable Oregon is a nonprofit organization that "promotes shaping urban growth with less dependence on automobiles." With funding from the state Department of Transportation, the organization holds workshops and meetings in various communities to develop "a collective vision" for the community's future. The organization claims to be committed to letting "all community members. . . participate in planning and decision-making about their community's future." Yet the organization's "collective vision" is already predetermined: "Main Street revitalization," "community development centered on mixed-use downtowns," and houses on "narrow and small lots."[6]

When Livable Oregon held a workshop in the town of Hood River, it stated in advance that Hood River's "undirected sprawl is sobering with its ever-expanding asphalt-covered landscapes." The group wanted Hood River to "take charge of its future" by creating a "livable city" where one can "meet the most basic of human needs without having a car."[7]

The Coalition for Utah's Future performs a similar function in the fast-growing cities of northern Utah. With state support and funding, the group has held a series of Envision Utah meetings, asking residents to develop a vision for their region's future.[8] Yet the vision that comes out is always identical to smart growth. While the group claims to be merely an educational organization, it placed full-page advertisements in Salt Lake City newspapers endorsing rail transit just a few weeks before local elections on expanding the city's light-rail system.[9]

During the Envision Utah process, the group distributed a public opinion questionnaire that was heavily biased towards smart growth. One question asked whether people wanted lots, moderate, or little air pollution. The questionnaire included graphics showing a large, medium, or small sized clouds of pollution. Naturally, the smart-growth alternative was the one that supposedly produced the least pollution. Envision Utah's own predictions were that existing plans would produce only 0.4 percent more pollution than smart-growth—yet the cloud for existing plans was 40 percent larger than smart growth.[10] Clouds for other alternatives were even more disproportionate. Not surprisingly, most people favored the least amount of air pollution.

Do Oregonians and Utahns really want to live in high-density, mixed-use, transit-oriented developments? Are they willing to give up their cars and ride transit more often? When asked questions in this way, most people in both states say no. By asking biased questions and failing to present the real trade offs, Livable Oregon and Envision Utah manage to make it appear that local residents support density and traffic congestion over freedom of housing choice and mobility. Organizations with such strong agendas should not receive government funding.

Corporate Funding of Smart Growth

When smart-growth ideas such as rail transit projects are on the ballot, another set of funders appears. Most of the contributions to political committees favoring rail transit comes from companies likely to make money from the transit project. These include banks, electric companies (since much rail transit is electrically powered), engineering and consulting firms, and rail car manufacturers.

There is nothing wrong with these companies donating to the political campaigns of their choice. But it explains why rail projects are so popular. Buses can carry more people at higher speeds at a far lower cost than light rail. But buses don't require bond sales (which attracts campaign contributions from banks), electric power, engineering and technical consulting, or rail construction. Politicians sometimes say they favor rail over buses because it is easier to sell to voters; what they mean is that it is easier to raise campaign funds for rail construction.

Notes

1. Philanthropic Research, Inc., "1000 Friends of New Mexico Financial Data" and "Growth Management Institute Financial Data," www.guidestar.com.
2. Daniel T. Oliver, "Grantmakers Declare War on Suburbs: Fund Environmental, Urban Interests to Fight 'Sprawl,'" *Foundation Watch*, July, 1999, http://www.capitalresearch.org/fw/fw-0799.htm.
3. Energy Foundation, *Transportation Grants List*, http://www.ef.org/grantees/TransportationList.cfm.
4. Surdna Foundation, "1998–1999 Environmental Grants," http://www.surdna.org/envgrant.html.
5. Ibid, p. 9.
6. Livable Oregon, "Livable Oregon," http://www.livable.org/.
7. Jeff Hunter, "Development needs community's involvement," *Hood River News*, September 15, 1999, http://www.livable.org/Press/hoodriver.html.
8. Envision Utah, "What Is Envision Utah?" http://www.envisionutah.org/main.html.
9. Envision Utah, "Transportation Choices Newspaper Ad," August, 2000, http://www.envisionutah.org/ad.html.
10. Envision Utah, "Growth Questionnaire," http://www.envisionutah.org/survey_old.html.

Part Four

Dense Thinking

It's good-bye open space as Portland-area cities rush to rezone land to meet smart-growth population targets (pp. 79–82). Top: More than 11,000 acres of farms inside the urban-growth boundary are slated for development. This one is for sale to anyone who will build a high-density transit-oriented development. Bottom: The Top o' Scott Golf Course was zoned open space in 1980. In 1999, Clackamas County rezoned most of it for high-density residential and commercial development in order to meet Metro's population targets (p. 80).

15. Smart Growth Means Higher Densities

"**D**ense living is the geometry of humanity," claims auto-opponent Jane Holtz Kay[1] in her book, *Asphalt Nation*. The most important objective of smart growth is to increase the population density of U.S. urban areas. Smart-growth advocates say that higher urban densities will reduce congestion and air pollution, provide affordable housing and infrastructure, and protect open space. They claim that doubling densities reduces congestion by reducing per capita automobile use by up to 30 percent.[2] They sometimes add that high densities, combined with plans to limit highway construction, will save cities from becoming like Los Angeles.

Low-density development of the sort typically found in the suburbs is supposed to cause several problems. First, low densities combined with the separation of commercial from residential areas are said to force people to drive too much. This means that people who cannot drive are left stranded whereever they are. Too much driving also increases congestion, air pollution, and other problems associated with cars.

Second, low densities are supposed to be costly, not just for homeowners but for the government agencies that must provide water, sewer, schools, and other urban services to residents. Density advocates consider it painfully obvious higher densities mean shorter water and sewer pipes and therefore lower infrastructure costs. Low densities, meanwhile, are said to shift high infrastructure costs from the buyers of new developments to existing residents.

Third, low densities are alleged to consume too much land. Such land use is wasteful because, in the eyes of smart-growth advocates, no one really needs that much land for their own personal use. Large lot development forces the conversion of valuable farmland and other open space to pointlessly large backyards. All of these claims—that low densities significantly increase driving and infrastructure costs while wasting land—are myths that will be addressed later in this part of the book.

Density supporters use several techniques to increase neighborhood and urban

area densities, including:
- Infill;
- Redevelopment of low-density neighborhoods;
- Prescriptive zoning of vacant lands;
- Incentives to developers;
- Urban-growth boundaries; and
- Limits on rural development.

Infill

Infill, the development of vacant parcels in existing neighborhoods, is an innocuous-sounding method of increasing density. This idea is routinely endorsed by planners and city councils as well as many who might not normally support other parts of the smart-growth agenda. In actual practice, infill isn't as innocent as it sounds. For one thing, smart-growth infill is often at much higher densities than the surrounding neighborhood. When an existing neighborhood might have homes on lots of, say, 5,000-square-foot or more, smart-growth planners encourage infill of row houses on 2,500-square-foot lots. This added density increases local congestion and places new burdens on water, sewers, and schools and other infrastructure.

Smart-growth planners do not limit their infill dreams to vacant lots, but add what they call "underutilized" parcels as well. Sites now occupied by buildings in poor condition or by uses that planners deem incompatible with the area are often slated for infill development. This means that uses that local residents may value, but planners do not—such as auto repair shops or secondhand stores—may be replaced by high-density housing that imposes congestion and other costs on local residents.

Another step often endorsed in the same breath as infill is the rezoning of single-family neighborhoods to allow the addition of *accessory units*—also known as *granny flats*—to homes. An accessory unit is a complete apartment with kitchen and other living facilities and a separate entrance from the rest of the house. Planners often argue that baby boomers need these units to house their aging parents, but in fact their real goal is to increase densities.

Redevelopment of Low-Density Neighborhoods

Infill is just the beginning for neighborhoods that smart-growth planners target for redevelopment at higher densities. Often, planners want to replace existing low-density housing or commercial structures with mixed-use developments. A typical goal is to replace one- or two-story homes or shops with three- to five-story buildings containing retail shops and offices on the ground floor and apartments or condominiums on the upper floors. When planned along transit routes such projects are called *transit-oriented developments*.

To produce this kind of development, planners will rezone neighborhoods to much higher densities and wait for developers to buy existing homes, clear them, and build higher-density or mixed-use buildings. Traditionally, land zoned at higher densities is somewhat more valuable to developers than land with lower density zoning. But this does not mean that homeowners will see their property values rise when their neighborhood is rezoned. It is more likely that, during a transition period, their home values will fall as people who are not interested in living next to a high-density development sell out and move or convert their owner-occupied home to a rental. Planners hope that this decline in property values, combined with a growing market for recyclable materials from demolished houses, will encourage developers to buy homes and replace them with smart-growth projects.

Incentives for High-Density Development

Rezoning is usually not enough to promote smart-growth development, particularly the rapid redevelopment of existing low-density neighborhoods. Planners say that this is because developers are unfamiliar with the kind of developments smart-growth advocates envision. At least as important is the fact that the market for high-density housing in most urban areas is largely satisfied by existing inner-city neighborhoods, while the market for new, low-density housing remains strong. In any case, smart-growth programs often support high-density, mixed-use developments with property tax waivers, infrastructure subsidies, and direct grants. Incentives can also take the form of reduced red tape or density "bonuses" to developers who build to certain smart-growth standards.

One popular technique is to create an *urban-renewal district* and dedicate some of the property taxes collected in that district to redevelopment. This makes it appear that people in the district are paying for their local improvements, but this is a sham. Since the property taxes dedicated to redevelopment would otherwise have gone to schools, libraries, and other property-tax funded items, people in the city outside of the urban-renewal district must pay higher taxes, or lose services, in order to maintain services to the district. This method of financing is endorsed by the American Planning Association,[3] but MIT planning professor Bernard Frieden considers it an undemocratic way for planners to "shield their own ventures from budget reviews and voter approval."[4]

In scenes reminiscent of the urban-renewal programs of the 1960s, planners often justify such subsidies by describing inner-ring suburbs as "blighted" because they are occupied by low-income people. Sometimes planners dedicate public land, such as former schools, government offices, or even parks, to high-density development. In other cases, cities and regional governments have purchased private land, cleared it of existing structures, and resold it to developers—often at a discount from prevailing market rates—who promise to build high-density, mixed-use developments. As with urban renewal, most of the newly-built condominiums will sell for much higher prices than the displaced low-income people can afford.

Prescriptive Zoning on Vacant Lands

One of the goals of smart growth is to preserve farms, forests, and open space. But realistic planners know that some open spaces will be urbanized, particularly small farms or forests that have already been surrounded by other urban developments. Such areas give planners one of the greatest opportunities for imposing high-density zoning prescriptions because there usually aren't a lot of nearby residents to complain about the density.

Most zoning rules today specify maximum densities of, say, four or eight houses per acre, but allow developers to build at any lower density. Smart-growth zoning turns this around, prescribing minimum densities and encouraging developers to build to even higher densities. As a transition, planners may supplement existing zoning codes by requiring minimum densities of, say, 80 percent of the current maximum.

Some smart-growth zoning rules may allow someone who owns an acre that is zoned at, say, eight houses per acre to build one house—so long as that house is sited to allow future construction of the other seven homes. But other smart-growth zoning codes are stricter, forbidding any construction at all unless it is at the prescribed densities.

Urban-Growth Boundaries

Even when subsidized, it is hard to attract many people, particularly families with children, into high-density developments so long as low-density alternatives exist. To minimize such alternatives, smart-growth advocates support the use of urban-growth or urban-service boundary to limit new low-density developments at the urban fringe.

An urban-growth boundary is a legal limit outside of which urban development cannot take place. Many California cities have created what they call urban-growth boundaries, but the cities usually have no jurisdiction outside their own limits. So these boundaries have more often been used to produce the opposite of smart growth: They limit the density within the cities but do not control development outside of the cities. For smart-growth to work, rural areas must be zoned to limit or prohibit urbanization. Oregon overcame this problem through its 1973 state land-use law that forbade urbanization outside of urban-growth boundaries.

An urban-service boundary is a line beyond which local or regional governments will offer no sewer, water, or other services. Development can still take place outside that line provided there is well water and land suitable for septic tanks, which are often regulated by the state. But a large-scale suburban development, complete with shopping malls and highways to the urban area, are generally impossible without traditional urban services. The Twin Cities' regional government has imposed such an urban-services boundary, but counties outside the region's jurisdiction are not obliged to follow it, which allows some leapfrog development.

Restrictive Zoning of Rural Areas

To protect rural areas from urban encroachment, counties and states have passed increasingly restrictive rules on rural land use. Many states prohibit subdivision of farms and other rural lands into units smaller than five or ten acres. This can backfire when exurbanites who might have been happy living in a cluster development—say, fifty homes on ten acres surrounded by hundreds of acres of open space—are instead forced to cumulatively occupy hundreds of acres.

Although a few areas have allowed cluster developments, the more common response is simply to increase the minimum size lot required for new home construction. Some areas require forty acres, others 160 or more. Oregon found that even 160-acre lot sizes did not slow rural development enough to satisfy land-use activists, so—as described on page 150—it has imposed even stricter rules, including the requirement that owners of 160 acres or more must earn $80,000 per year farming land before they can build a home on it.

Notes

1. Jane Holtz Kay, *Asphalt Nation: How the Automobile Took over America and How We Can Take It Back* (New York, NY: Crown, 1997), p. 300.
2. Federal Transit Administration, *Transit and Urban Form* (Washington, DC: US DOT, 1996), volume 1, page 12.
3. American Planning Association, *Modernizing State Planning Statutes: The Growing Smart Working Papers* (Washington, DC: APA, 1996),
4. Bernard Frieden and Lynn Sagalyn, *Downtown, Inc.: How America Rebuilds Cities* (Cambridge, MA: MIT, 1989), p. 251.

Population Density Facts

All densities expressed in people per square mile and are based on the 1990 Census unless otherwise noted. Numbers are often rounded for sake of clarity.

Densities of Selected Nations

Asia

Singapore	12,000
Taiwan	1,725
South Korea	1,200
Japan	825
India	815
China	335

Australia	6

Europe

Netherlands	1,175
Belgium	850
United Kingdom	625
Germany	600
Italy	510
Switzerland	460
Denmark	320
France	275
Sweden	55
Norway	35

North America

Mexico	125
United States	75
Canada	8

Source: Census Bureau, Statistical Abstract of the United States 1995 (Washington, DC: Department of Commerce, 1996), table 1361, based on 1995 population estimates.

Urban Areas

Average U.S. urbanized area	2,600
Densest—Los Angeles	5,800
Least dense—Dothan, AL	630
Lowest density major urban area—Atlanta	1900
Highest density small urban area—Davis, CA	5,000

Cities

The densest major city in America: New York at 24,000.
   Density of Manhattan: 52,000
   Density of Staten Island: 6,500

Other dense central cities:
   San Francisco: 15,500
   Chicago: 12,250
   Boston: 11,800
   Philadelphia: 11,700
   Miami: 10,100

Other dense towns:
   Union City, NJ: 45,800
   Guttenberg, NJ: 43,000
   West New York, NJ: 37,500
   Hoboken, NJ: 26,250
   Maywood City, CA: 23,900

Americans living in cities or towns with more than 10,000 people per square mile: 18 million
Americans living in cities or towns with less than 1,000 people per square mile: 40 million
Average density of cities over 100,000: 3,100
Average density of all cities and towns in U.S.: 1,970

Rural Areas

Percent of U.S. that is rural (outside of all cities, towns, or villages): 96.4

Average density of rural areas	17
State with densest rural area—Connecticut	175
Number of states with rural densities over 100	4

(Rhode Island, Massachusetts, and New Jersey)
State with least dense rural area—Alaska   0.3
Number of states with rural densities under 10   14
(Kansas, Nebraska, the Dakotas, and every western state except California and
Washington)
Density of rural California   14
Source: 1990 Census

 ## Web Tools: Population Densities

Look up the 1990 density of your state, county, and city at http://
www.census.gov/population/www/censusdata/density.html. However,
do *not* use densities of *metropolitan areas* at this site, as they include all of the land
in the counties in which cities are located, not just the urbanized land. Densities
of *urbanized areas* are not available on the Census Bureau web site but can be
found at http://www.demographia.com/db-ua90.htm. Approximate 1998 densities of urbanized areas can be found at http://www.fhwa.dot.gov/ohim/hs98/
roads.htm, table HM-72. By the time you read this, 1999 data may be available at
http://www.fhwa.dot.gov/ohim/ohimstat.htm.

The Density-Is-Normal Myth

Myth: Today's low-density suburbs are abnormal; most people have always lived in high-density cities.

Reality: Most Americans, and most other people in the world, have always lived in low densities. The true historical exceptions were high-density cities of the late nineteenth century.

Dense living may be the geometry of Manhattan, but it is not now and never has been the lifestyle of most Americans or indeed most people on the planet. Although turn-of-the-century urban planners considered crowded cities to be one of the major social problems of the age, more than 60 percent of Americans in 1900 lived in rural areas. The 1920 census was the first to find half of all Americans in urban areas. But by that time, low-density suburbs were rapidly expanding, so a majority still lived in lower densities. In 1960, urban areas held 70 percent of Americans. But 40 percent of that 70 percent, or 28 percent of the total, lived in the suburbs. This means that only 42 percent lived in the central cities that tend to be higher in density.

Just how dense does Jane Holtz Kay mean when she says "dense living is the geometry of humanity"? How dense must cities be before smart-growth advocates are satisfied? Smart-growth proponents applaud Portland for planning to increase its urban density to 4,800 per square mile. But density advocates want to increase the density of San Francisco even though, at better than 15,500 people per square mile, it is already the second densest major city in the U.S.[1]

Table one shows average densities for major cities and their urbanized areas. These densities may mask wide variations. New York City, for example, has 52,000 people per square mile in Manhattan but only 6,500 per square mile on Staten Island. Some cities such as Indianapolis and Nashville have low average densities because they have incorporated much of their suburbs, but their inner areas are no doubt much denser. Nineteenth-century cities, such as San Francisco, New York, and Boston, tend to be more than twice as dense as their urban areas. Cities built mainly after the automobile (and air conditioning), such as Phoenix, San Jose, and Houston, tend to have densities about the same as their urban areas.

Table One: 1990 Densities of Major U.S. Cities & Urbanized Areas
(People Per Square Mile)

City	Central City	Urbanized Area
New York	23,700	5,400
San Francisco	15,500	4,200
Chicago	12,300	4,300
Boston	11,900	3,100
Philadelphia	11,700	3,600
Miami	10,100	5,400
Washington	9,900	3,600
Baltimore	9,100	3,200
Providence	8,700	2,800
Buffalo	8,100	3,300
Los Angeles	7,400	5,800
Detroit	7,400	3,300
Minneapolis	6,700	2,000
Cleveland	6,600	2,600
Pittsburgh	6,600	2,200
Milwaukee	6,500	2,400
St. Louis	6,400	2,700
Seattle	6,200	3,000
Cincinnati	4,700	2,400
San Jose	4,600	4,200
Honolulu	4,400	4,600
Louisville	4,300	2,700
Toledo	4,100	2,500
Sacramento	3,800	3,300
Fresno	3,600	3,400
Portland	3,500	3,000
San Diego	3,400	3,400
Omaha	3,300	2,800
Denver	3,100	3,300
Las Vegas	3,100	3,000
Houston	3,000	2,500
Atlanta	3,000	1,900
Albuquerque	2,900	2,200
Dallas	2,900	2,200
San Antonio	2,800	2,600
New Orleans	2,800	3,900
Tuscon	2,600	2,400
Memphis	2,400	2,400
Charlotte, NC	2,300	1,900
Phoenix	2,300	2,700
Indianapolis	2,000	2,000
Salt Lake City	1,500	3,100
Kansas City	1,400	1,700
Nashville	1,000	1,200
Oklahoma City	700	1,200

Source: Census Bureau. Densities are rounded to the nearest 100.

According to the 1990 census, only 7 percent of the U.S. lived in cities denser than 10,000 people per square mile, and only 17 percent lived in urbanized denser than 4,000 people per square mile. A quarter of the population lives in rural areas whose densities are well under 200 people per square mile. Another quarter lives in cities or metropolitan areas whose densities are under 2,000 per square mile. By any measure, the median density of the U.S. is less than 2,000 per square mile. Table two shows the number and percentage of Americans living in various densities.

Table Two: Number of Americans Living Above Various Densities

Density in Pop/Sq.Mi.	Millions Above That Density	Percent Above That Density
20,000	7.6	3.0
15,000	9.4	3.8
10,000	18.0	7.3
7,000	30.5	12.3
6,000	38.3	15.4
5,500	41.4	16.6
5,000	45.4	18.2
4,000	58.5	23.5
3,000	83.2	33.5
2,800	91.3	36.7
2,500	101.7	40.9
2,000	121.8	49.0
1,500	141.2	56.8
1,000	166.4	66.9
500	180.7	72.6
All places	187.0	75.2
Rural	61.7	100.0
All U.S.	248.7	100.0

Source: Census Bureau.

No matter how we count, it is clear that most Americans live in fairly low densities. Less than a half of all Americans live in urban areas with densities of 3,000 per square mile or more. Only a third live in cities or other places with densities of 3,000 per square mile or more and more than half live in rural areas or places with densities below 2,000 per square mile.

Notes

1. Tim Redmond, "If you build it, they will come: But does S.F. really need another 50,000 yuppies?" SF Bay Guardian, September 1, 1999.

The Myth That Government Made Us Do It

Myth: Low-density suburbs have grown because of government subsidies and other policies favoring the suburbs over higher-density cities.

Reality: Americans began moving to the suburbs long before any of the government programs that supposedly favor the suburbs. In the past fifty years, government subsidies to the high-density cities far exceed subsidies to low-density suburbs.

"For more than a generation," says Milwaukee Mayor John Norquist, "urban sprawl sprung up with federal assistance—excessive road building, Federal Housing Authority (FHA) subsidized suburbanization and other inducements—that interfered with the free market." These programs "undermined the natural advantages of cities" and caused sprawl.[1] Are low-density suburbs a result of subsidies, government regulation, or personal choice? Some smart-growth advocates say that government actions promote sprawl; others go so far as to argue that people would prefer living in high-density cities but moved to the suburbs only because they were forced to do so by government policies.

In 1998, members of Congress formed a bipartisan sustainable development caucus, consisting of senators and representatives who supported smart-growth ideas. They asked the General Accounting Office to document whether federal subsidies or other federal policies were promoting sprawl. The General Accounting Office is known for its unbiased work on projects that it initiates, but when a member of Congress asks for its opinion, it often finds a way to provide an answer that the member wants to hear.

So most people were surprised when the General Accounting Office could not find any clear evidence that federal policies were promoting sprawl. The report admitted that "anecdotal evidence exists to support" the notion that federal programs promote low-density suburbanization. However, the report added, "limited data are available to document and quantify the extent of federal influence."[2]

Those who believe that federal subsidies promote low-density suburbs point to three main programs: federal mortgage loan subsidies, the Interstate Highway System, and sewer, water, and other infrastructure subsidies. They also point to local zoning and other regulations. As the Housing-Subsidies Myth will show, they have a weak case with respect to the mortgage loan subsidies. As the next three myths will show, they have no case at all regarding the other claims.

Notes

1. John Norquist, "Free Market: Key to Public Choice," *Commonground*, 2 (1, Winter, 1999): p. 30.
2. General Accounting Office, *Community Development: Extent of Federal Influence on "Urban Sprawl" Is Unclear* (Washington, DC: GAO, 1999), GAO-RCED-99-87, 81 pp.

The Housing-Subsidy Myth

Myth: Federal housing subsidies and discrimination against the inner cities promoted suburbanization.

Reality: Suburbanization was taking place long before federal housing subsidies. Mortgage loan subsidies may have enabled some people to afford slightly lower density suburban housing, but they did not influence the rate of movement to the suburbs.

Federal mortgage loan programs began during the Depression, when cities were overcrowded, people were desperately poor, and home ownership was widely viewed as a way out of both urban slums and poverty. As described in Kenneth Jackson's 1985 history of American suburbs, *Crabgrass Frontier*, the Federal Housing Administration (FHA) promoted suburbanization in three ways. First, it created a bias against multifamily homes by giving better terms on loans for single-family homes. Second, it created a bias against repairing existing structures by giving better terms on loans for new houses.[1] It also required that houses be used only as homes, and could not have facilities for stores, offices, or rental units.[2]

Third and most important, says Jackson, the FHA required that loans be judged for risk according to racial and other criteria that discouraged mortgages on inner-city houses. At least until 1948, the FHA would make no loans to blacks nor would it make loans in neighborhoods that had blacks living in them. Jackson cites one "bizarre and capricious" example of a black neighborhood in Detroit that was entirely surrounded by white neighborhoods. The FHA would not approve loans in the white neighborhoods until "an enterprising white developer built a concrete wall between the white and black areas."[3] Even after the FHA ended overt racial discrimination, it continued to redline lower-class neighborhoods on the grounds that they were poor risks for loans.[4] This became a self-fulfilling prophecy because houses that could not be sold were often abandoned, thus contributing to more rapid neighborhood decline.

Racial discrimination was a tragic part of American history and may continue today in some areas, but it did not significantly contribute to suburbanization. As Jackson himself notes, "The dominant residential drift in American cities had been toward the periphery for at least a century before the New Deal, and there is no reason to assume that the suburban trend would not have continued in the absence of direct federal assistance."[5] Suburbanization exploded after World War II partly because of government financing, but also because of "mass production techniques. . . , high wages, and low interest rates," says Jackson.[6] Urban economist Edwin Mills agrees, saying that, "It is almost certain that social issues [such as race discrimination] affecting the central cities have had a greater effect on *who* lives and works in suburbs than on *how many* live and work there" (emphasis in original).[7]

Similar responses apply to Jackson's claims of FHA biases against multifamily homes and mixed-use developments. The mid-twentieth-century housing market was saturated with multifamily and mixed-use housing, and such housing was widely regarded as inferior to the dream of single-family housing. FHA rules merely reflected the market reality that the value of such housing was declining and so did not provide good collateral for loans.

Notes

1. Kenneth T. Jackson, *Crabgrass Frontier: The Suburbanization of the United States* (New York, NY: Oxford University Press, 1985), p. 206.
2. Ibid, p. 208.
3. Ibid, p. 209.
4. Ibid, p. 213.
5. Ibid, p. 217.
6. Ibid, p. 241.
7. Edwin S. Mills, "Truly Smart 'Smart Growth,'" *Illinois Real Estate Letter*, Summer, 1999, p. 3.

The Interstate-Highway Myth

Myth: Interstate highways destroyed inner cities by encouraging people and businesses to move to the suburbs.

Reality: Without the congestion-reducing benefits of the urban interstates, business flight to the suburbs would have been faster and inner cities would have declined even more.

"Since 1956, the federal government has spent hundreds of billions of dollars to gouge our urban centers with six- and eight-lane freeways, which separated people and markets," complains Milwaukee's Mayor Norquist. "The freeways dispersed the economy, destroyed thousands of homes and businesses, and sucked millions of middle-class residents and businesses out to the suburbs."[1]

Early plans for the Interstate Highway System called for freeways to go around cities, but not through them. Highway opponents love to tell of President Eisenhower being angered to find an interstate freeway under construction in Washington, DC. Supposedly, when he signed the bill creating the Interstate Highway System he hadn't noticed that it had been modified to allow urban freeways. What the storytellers don't say is that Eisenhower was not concerned about the impacts of freeways on cities, which were universally thought to be positive at the time. Instead, he was a fiscal conservative who believed the Constitution allowed the federal government to build roads for interstate transportation, but not for urban commuters. On the same grounds, he would have opposed every piece of federal transit legislation ever passed.

What Mayor Norquist doesn't say is that urban interstates weren't imposed on the cities by a federal bully. Instead, they were demanded by Norquist's predecessor and other big-city mayors who vowed to oppose interstate highway legislation unless it were modified to include roads in their cities. They could see that the Interstate Highway System would be one of the biggest sources of pork barrel for many years and they wanted their share.

Americans were moving to the suburbs in record numbers well before Congress approved interstate highway funding in 1956. In 1950, the suburbs were growing ten times faster than the central cities and downtowns were rapidly declining.[2] As Harvard transportation Professor Alan Altshuler notes, "the central theory was [the downtowns] had been strangled and congested. And one way to bring them back was to deal with the congestion problem."[3] Urban interstates, the mayors hoped, would reduce inner-city congestion and slow the movement to the suburbs.

"In retrospect," says Altshuler, who served a term as the Massachusetts secretary of transportation, "it is not even clear that in simple economic terms, the mayors were wrong about the consequences of building the circumferentials [i.e., the interstates going around the cities] without building the inner city portion. . . . If the circumferentials had been built, but no radials, the decentralizing consequences might well have been even greater than they were."[4] As Altshuler points out, downtown decline slowed after interstate construction began.

Interstates greatly relieved inner-city congestion. Not counting local streets, urban interstates make up less than 6 percent of urban road miles and just 10 percent of lane miles today. Yet they carry nearly 30 percent of urban traffic—and at much higher speeds than on the arterials and collectors. One lane mile of the average urban interstate carries 14,000 vehicle miles of traffic per day, compared with 5,600 vehicle miles for a major arterial, 2,600 vehicle miles for a minor arterial, and 2,300 vehicle miles for a collector.[5] Interstates are also safer per passenger mile than other urban roads.[6]

Norquist's claim is that the urban interstates allowed businesses to escape the cities. But any business that is sick of congestion can load up a moving van and move to the suburbs. The reality is that, by reducing inner-city congestion, the urban interstates allowed businesses to stay in the cities and greatly slowed the decline of downtown areas. Indeed, it is possible that the downtown revitalizations that America witnessed in the 1980s could never have happened without the Interstate Highway System.

Notes

1. Quoted in Stephen Goldsmith, *The Twenty-First Century City: Resurrecting Urban America* (Washington, DC: Regnery, 1997), p. 90.
2. Kenneth T. Jackson, *Crabgrass Frontier: The Suburbanization of the United States* (New York, NY: Oxford University Press, 1985), p. 238.
3. Darwin Stolzenbach, *Interview with Professor Alan Altshuler, Former Secretary of Transportation, Massachusetts* (Washington, DC: American Association of State Highway and Transportation Officials, 1981), p. 3.
4. Ibid, pp. 3–4.
5. Federal Highway Administration, *Highway Statistics 1998* (Washington, DC: FHwA, 1999), tables HM-71. These calculations assume the average interstate has six lanes, while other freeways and arterials have four lanes, and collectors have two lanes.
6. Wendell Cox & Jean Love, *40 Years of the US Interstate Highway System: An Analysis* (Washington, DC: American Highway Users Alliance, 1996).

The Infrastructure Myth

Myth: Federal subsidies to communities for water and sewage facilities promote sprawl.

Reality: Most federal urban subsidies are to high-density areas.

I n the 1970s and 1980s, the federal government provided billions of dollars of funding to communities to build clean water and sewage treatment facilities. Smart-growth advocates today claim that this funding permitted low-density suburbanization that might not otherwise have occurred. Ironically, this funding was provided by the Environmental Protection Agency, which today is leading the federal war on sprawl.

The argument that federal infrastructure funding promoted suburbanization can only be valid if it costs more to extend water and sewer lines to low-density areas than it does to retrofit existing urban facilities to meet the needs of higher populations. Without the subsidies, it is presumed, communities could not afford to extend low-density suburbs. As noted in the Costs-of-Sprawl Myth (p. 278), the opposite is true: It costs far more to rebuild an existing city to accommodate higher densities than it does to extend infrastructure into vacant land. With or without federal infrastructure subsidies, communities would have used their limited funds as effectively as they could, which means they would have encouraged low-density suburbanization.

For the most part, federal subsidies have promoted density, not suburbanization. Total federal spending in the inner cities has far outweighed federal spending in the suburbs. Through 1998, federal grants to the cities have included:

- $114 billion (in 1998 dollars) on mass transit since 1963, most of which went to the cities;
- $117 billion on community development block grants and urban development action grants since 1975, most of which went to the cities;
- $43 billion on urban renewal between 1953 and 1986, virtually all of which went to the cities;
- More than $250 billion on public housing projects and subsidies since 1941, nearly all of which went to the cities.[1]

This totals to nearly $525 billion over 60 years, and more than $30 billion in 1999 alone. The vast majority of this money was spent in the cities as opposed to the suburbs. Much of it was directly aimed at propping up high-density areas that were declining as people left them for lower-density suburbs. By comparison, the water and sewer subsidies that supposedly contributed to sprawl totaled less than $14 billion, and much of this money went to the cities as well. Thus, infrastructure subsidies to low-density suburbs are a drop in the bucket compared to federal grants to high-density cities.

This is not to say that all of this money was effectively spent. Much of the spending on public housing projects and urban renewal proved disastrous for the cities. Spending on mass transit has done little other than to prop up one of the least efficient industries in the nation. Many of the luxury hotels and housing developments supported by urban development action grants subsequently went bankrupt. Federal grants aimed at supporting high densities is self-defeating because most people don't really want to live in such densities. The real federal bias might be the extent to which it has *not* spent money—and therefore created few disasters—in the suburbs.

Notes

1. Government Printing Office, *Federal Budget History*, (Washington, DC: GPO, 1999), Table 12.3-Total Outlays for Grants to State and Local Governments by Function, Agency, and Program: 1940-2004, http://w3.access.gpo.gov/usbudget/fy2000/sheets/hist12z3.wk4

The Local-Regulation Myth

Myth: Local zoning promoted suburbanization by forcing people to build to lower densities than they would have preferred in a truly free market.
Reality: Local zoning reflected personal preferences for low-density housing.

Smart-growth advocates say that low-density housing and auto-dependent design has been forced on the suburbs by inflexible zoning standards. Most zoning has long required a separation of uses, so that housing cannot be mixed with offices or stores. This prevents the kind of mixed-use, transit-oriented developments that smart growth promotes.

In reality, zoning codes for vacant areas are actually very flexible. Some people look at zones in vacant areas and see that they are for very low densities, such as ten-acre lot sizes. But this is often a "holding zone" aimed at discouraging development until the municipality can determine the best use for the land. As zoning historians Richard Babcock and Fred Bosselman write, "This 'wait and see' zoning has confused many analysts who think they can look at a zoning map and discover what future development the community welcomes. Studies that announce that the zoning of such-and-such area would accommodate only x thousand more people should always be taken with a grain of salt."[1]

Zones requiring the separation of uses are generally demanded by urban and suburban residents. The original zoning codes passed in the late 1910s and 1920s were for cities, not suburbs, and the codes separated uses because that is what city residents wanted. As Babcock notes, "The insulation of the single-family detached dwelling was the primary objective of the early zoning ordinances, and this objective is predominant today."[2]

Sociologist Herbert Gans found that, with respect to zoning, Levittown "residents were primarily concerned with status protection and wanted to make sure that commercial establishments did not infiltrate residential areas."[3] Most of the suburbanites he met were people who had moved from the inner city and were trying to escape high-density, mixed-use areas. In 1995, I learned that similar concerns motivated the residents of Oak Grove and other Portland-area neighborhoods.

Blaming sprawl on zoning overlooks the fact that many parts of the country have never adopted zoning. Yet the same low-density suburbanization takes place in those areas as in areas with strong planning and zoning laws.

A corollary to the zoning myth is that developers have somehow forced people to buy homes that they do not like. This makes no sense either. "If anything, the economy's entire thrust over the past four decades has been to offer paralyzing levels of choice," say Joel Garreau in *Edge City*. "People with money can live in this country in just about any fashion imaginable—including, if they so choose, in yeasty, artsy, diverse, walkable, renovated neighborhoods in the center city."[4] The fact that the suburbs are still growing faster than the central cities demonstrates that people prefer lower densities.

Notes

1. Richard F. Babcock and Fred P. Bosselman, *Exclusionary Zoning: Land Use Regulation and Housing in the 1970s* (New York, NY: Praeger, 1973), p. 11.
2. Richard Babcock, *The Zoning Game: Municipal Practices and Policies* (Madison, WI: University of Wisconsin Press, 1966), p. 3.
3. Herbert J. Gans, *The Levittowners: Ways of Life and Politics in a New Suburban Community* (New York, NY: Pantheon, 1967), pp. 385–386.
4. Joel Garreau, *Edge City: Life on the New Frontier* (New York, NY: Doubleday, 1991), p. 234.

The People-Want-Density Myth

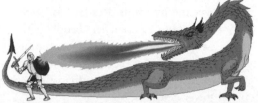

Myth: People would be glad to live in well-designed high-density neighborhoods if only developers would build such neighborhoods.

Reality: For most people, multifamily dwellings and other high-density neighborhoods are the last choice.

People would love to live in high-density, mixed-use areas where they can walk to the store and take a train to work, say smart-growth advocates, if only they had the opportunity. Of course, smart growth doesn't propose to give people a choice by loosening zoning laws; instead, it wants to rewrite zoning laws to require all future development to be at high densities.

In 1999 a public opinion firm called the Lazarus Group held focus groups in six different American cities to find out about attitudes towards growth. It learned that many people were upset about sprawl, traffic, and the loss of open space. But it did not find that those people would support higher density housing.

"People, especially those with children, are absolutely unwilling to move into higher density housing arrangements," concluded the group. "In the most constant and consistent response of the groups, people overwhelmingly indicated that there was no inducement that could be offered and no evidence which could be presented which would compel them to move to a more compact living arrangement." This finding held true "irrespective of income, race, gender, or previously stated attitudes about suburban overdevelopment." People perceive "a clear hierarchy of housing" from sharing an apartment through condominiums and row houses to detached single-family homes, and this perceived hierarchy is "unaffected by appeals from the critics of suburban development."[1]

People may accept more higher density housing in their city if they themselves don't have to live in or near it. Once they realize that smart growth means redeveloping many if not all existing neighborhoods, they will not give it much support.

Notes

1. The Lazarus Group, "Analysis of Research on Suburban Development Issues," July 1999, Richmond Virginia, p. 2.

16. Bucking the Trend

*A*ttempts to increase urban and suburban densities run counter to a world wide trend toward low densities and decentralization. In the United States this trend is at least 150 years old and is "deeply embedded in the urban growth process," says urban economist Edwin Mills notes.[1] The main factors influencing decentralization are technology and income. Railcars and later automobiles allowed people to live further and further away from their jobs. Distributed electrical power and telephone lines meant that people did not have to live in central cities to enjoy urban amenities. Increasing incomes made these technologies available to more and more people. As soon as they could afford it, a high percentage of families moved to the suburbs or other low-density areas.

The U.S. led the world in this trend, partly because incomes are higher here and partly because many American cities grew mainly after the automobile and other decentralizing technologies became available. But similar patterns can be found all over the world. Attempts to rebuilt cities to higher densities will be as successful as trying to make water flow uphill. Controls on low-density suburbanization will simply speed low-density *exurbanization*. If the suburbs are an attempt to combine the best of urban and rural areas, then the ultimate suburb is the *exurb*. Exurbs consist of small-town or rural housing occupied by people whose income has little or nothing to do with rural areas. This includes people who commute long distances to cities, telecommuters, small business owners who do not have to be located near a big city, and urban retirees.

Exurbanites can be distinguished from true ruralites by their sources of income and their values. Rural residents tend to earn their incomes from farming, forestry, mining, or other resource production, or by providing goods and services to those in such occupations. As such, they have a "wise use" view of the natural world, meaning they believe that conservation is worthwhile but ultimately resources exist to be used. Exurbanites tend to earn their income or have retired from income earned in urban occupations. They tend to be better educated and have higher than average incomes and they usually hold preservationist views of the natural world. Exurbanites may be hobby farmers, but not true farmers; they may grow trees, but don't feel comfortable cutting them; they may rely on all sorts of high-tech electronics, but are appalled by open-pit mining.

Exurbanization is not new; the term was first used in 1955.[2] But decreasing transportation costs and the increasing wealth and income of urban white collar workers and retirees has made exurbanization much more significant than in previous decades. In 1996, 176 million Americans lived in urbanized areas with populations of 50,000 people or more. Another 40 million lived in nonurbanized areas of metropolitan counties, meaning they lived in counties with urbanized areas but outside of the urbanized areas themselves. Many of these people are exurbanites. Finally, 53 million Americans lived in nonmetropolitan counties, and many of them are exurbanites as well. Only about 7.5 percent of all U.S. jobs are rural jobs. Yet the Census Bureau reports that 25 percent of Americans live in rural areas. Most of the 17.5 percent of rural residents who do not work in rural occupations are probably exurbanites. This is almost 48 million people.

Exurban researchers Arthur Nelson and Kenneth Dueker estimate that the U.S. exurban population has grown from about 40 million people in 1960 to 60 million in 1985. While their estimates of exurbanite numbers are rough, they may be correct in concluding that exurbia is growing faster than either the cities or suburbs.[3]

As in the suburbs, the jobs follow the people. Major manufacturing plans are opening in small towns that are long distances away from urban areas. In 1996, Motorola opened a one-million-square-foot cellular phone factory, employing close to 3,000 workers, in Harvard, Illinois, which is 40 miles from the edge of the Chicago metropolitan area and almost as far from the nearest interstate highway. Nearly half the workers commute from rural Wisconsin.[4] David Schultz, of Northwestern University, describes the movement of such factories to rural areas as "poison" for public transit. But automotive transportation makes it possible for both factories and workers to exist in very low density areas and both benefit from being far from congested cities.[5]

Smart growth rejects exurbia at least as emphatically as it rejects low-density suburbs. In 1995, a *Newsweek* article promoting smart growth noted that, in Holland, "a businessman seeking to live on a farm and drive into the city to work would have to request permission from the government—and he might not get it."[6] The magazine lamented the fact that the U.S. does not have similar rules.

Yet smart growth will have a difficult time trying to prevent people from moving to the exurbs. Oregon has restricted new subdivisions of farms and forests outside of urban-growth boundaries. But numerous parcels were subdivided before the new rules went into effect, and even Oregon can't keep its residents from moving to small towns. During the 1990s, the growth of Oregon's fastest growing county, Deschutes (which includes Bend), consisted almost entirely of exurbanites. Other fast-growing rural counties include Morrow, Crook, Jefferson, and Gilliam counties, all of which are even more remote from urban areas than Deschutes County.

Exurbanites "tend to locate where zoning is either nonexistent or is so lax as to be virtually nonexistent," observe Nelson and Dueker, possibly because they want to do things with their land that "cannot be accommodated in urban areas," or at least under urban zoning codes.[7] So one of their considerations in deciding how far from the city they will move is how far they have to be to find land-use rules that are compatible with their goals. Different people feel comfortable with different levels of regulation; those who like regulation less move to the less-regulated suburbs; those who oppose all regulation move to the minimally regulated exurbs.

Ultimately, exurbia is just as valid a lifestyle choice as central cities, suburbs, or rural areas. So long as people pay the full costs of their choices, no one should have a right to limit those choices. Efforts to restrict one choice or another will only be defeated by human ingenuity and unintended consequences. Smart growth restrictions on the suburbs, for example, will only accelerate the exurban trend. Even if only a small number act on this desire, the results will defeat smart-growth goals. For example, if smart growth can stop housing developments on half-acre lots, it may push two or three percent of the people who would have been happy in such a subdivision to build instead on a ten-acre lot instead. The result will be an even more rapid fragmentation of rural areas than before. If the goal is to protect rural open space from development, smart growth may produce exactly the opposite results.

Notes

1. Edwin S. Mills, "Truly Smart 'Smart Growth,'" *Illinois Real Estate Letter,* Summer, 1999, p. 2.
2. A.C. Spectorsky, *The Exurbanites* (Philadelphia, PA: Lippincott, 1955), 278 pp.
3. Arthur Nelson and Kenneth Dueker, "The Exurbanization of America and Its Planning Policy Implications," *Journal of Political Economy Research,* 9(2): p. 93.
4. Motorola, "Motorola Selects Harvard, Illinois as Site for Expansion of Its Cellular Telephone Business," http://www.motorola.com/GSS/CSG/Help/PR/pr940418.html.
5. David F. Schulz, "Reinventing Public Transportation," Remarks to the Region V Biennial Conference, Federal Transit Administration, May 24, 1994, http://www.iti.nwu.edu/pubs/schulz_5.html.
6. Jerry Adler, "Bye-Bye, Suburban Dream," *Newsweek,* May 15, 1995, p. 49.
7. Nelson and Dueker, "The Exurbanization of America," p. 96.

Urban Area Facts

This table lists the estimated 1998 population, land area, density, miles and lane miles of freeways, and daily miles driven on freeways (in thousands) for the nation's seventy-five largest urbanized areas. It also lists the 1990 split between auto (including motorcycles), transit (including taxis), and walking/bicycling commuters. Additional information about all 397 urbanized areas can be found at www.ti.org/urban.html.

Urban Area	Main State	Pop (1000s)	Area (sq mi)	Density (/sq mi)	Miles Fwy	Fwy Driving	Lane Miles	Commuters % Auto	Transit	W/B
New York	NY	16,407	3,962	4,141	1,142	96,808	6,604	65.5	26.5	8.0
Los Angeles	CA	12,600	2,231	5,648	643	121,554	5,244	90.3	4.7	5.0
Chicago	IL	8,070	2,730	2,956	477	48,426	2,653	81.1	13.7	5.2
Philadelphia	PA	4,546	1,350	3,367	352	23,555	1,734	83.2	10.3	6.5
San Francisco	CA	4,017	1,203	3,339	338	45,146	2,334	84.2	9.5	6.3
Detroit	MI	3,852	1,304	2,954	282	30,867	1,796	94.4	2.4	3.2
Dallas-Ft Worth	TX	3,722	1,712	2,174	583	46,737	3,229	94.7	2.3	3.0
Washington	DC	3,442	999	3,445	309	33,931	1,935	81.0	13.7	5.3
Boston	MA	2,904	1,138	2,552	215	22,254	1,307	82.4	10.7	6.9
Atlanta	GA	2,806	1,757	1,597	306	40,597	2,289	92.8	4.7	2.5
San Diego	CA	2,683	733	3,660	239	29,877	1,761	89.1	3.4	7.5
Phoenix	AZ	2,482	1,054	2,355	139	15,894	896	92.1	2.1	5.8
Houston	TX	2,396	1,537	1,559	400	39,567	2,429	92.5	3.7	3.8
Twin Cities	MN	2,322	1,192	1,948	311	25,503	1,542	90.3	5.4	4.3
Baltimore	MD	2,107	712	2,959	278	21,288	1,461	87.1	7.6	5.3
Miami	FL	2,066	545	3,791	120	12,546	754	91.6	4.3	4.1
St. Louis	MO	2,000	1,123	1,781	320	24,961	1,766	94.0	2.9	3.1
Seattle	WA	1,980	844	2,346	240	23,318	1,296	88.3	6.5	5.2
Tampa-St. Pete.	FL	1,863	1,294	1,440	125	8,149	648	94.2	1.4	4.4
Denver	CO	1,828	720	2,539	206	16,170	1,018	90.7	4.3	5.0
Pittsburgh	PA	1,768	1,112	1,590	284	10,911	1,190	86.0	8.0	6.0
Cleveland	OH	1,748	838	2,086	227	17,121	1,257	91.6	4.6	3.8
San Jose	CA	1,653	365	4,529	175	17,652	1,126	90.0	3.0	7.0
Portland	OR	1,471	468	3,143	137	12,021	698	89.4	5.6	5.0
Norfolk	VA	1,453	952	1,526	161	10,757	810	91.8	2.2	6.0
Fort Lauderdale	FL	1,441	489	2,947	109	11,228	718	91.6	4.3	4.1
Riverside-S. Bern.	CA	1,396	514	2,716	139	15,579	874	91.8	0.8	7.4
Kansas City	MO	1,375	1,034	1,330	374	18,222	1,715	95.0	2.1	2.9

Urban Area	Main State	Pop (1000s)	Area (sq mi)	Density (/sq mi)	Miles Fwy	Fwy Driving	Lane Miles	Commuters Auto	Transit	W/B
Sacramento	CA	1,353	383	3,533	105	11,142	679	91.8	2.4	5.8
Las Vegas	NV	1,283	270	4,752	77	5,880	396	91.5	1.9	6.6
Milwaukee	WI	1,243	512	2,428	114	8,859	609	90.1	4.9	5.0
San Antonio	TX	1,229	485	2,534	211	14,513	1,073	91.4	3.7	4.9
Cincinnati	OH	1,203	630	1,910	174	15,197	962	92.6	3.6	3.8
Orlando	FL	1,075	667	1,612	148	8,666	687	93.2	1.5	5.3
Buffalo	NY	1,072	564	1,901	139	5,796	633	90.0	4.5	5.5
New Orleans	LA	1,065	269	3,959	75	5,745	411	87.7	7.1	5.2
Oklahoma City	OK	1,030	711	1,449	147	8,731	729	96.0	0.6	3.4
West Palm Beach	FL	939	556	1,689	87	7,474	456	94.7	1.2	4.1
Memphis	TN	933	409	2,281	89	6,370	489	93.2	2.8	4.0
Indianapolis	IN	915	422	2,168	130	10,967	725	94.9	2.0	3.1
Columbus	OH	912	476	1,916	149	11,678	815	93.1	2.7	4.2
Providence	RI	900	515	1,748	117	7,904	630	92.6	2.6	4.8
Salt Lake City	UT	888	353	2,516	79	6,171	500	93.2	3.1	3.7
Jacksonville	FL	839	727	1,154	145	9,026	685	81.4	10.1	8.5
Louisville	KY	799	384	2,081	137	9,897	668	94.0	3.2	2.8
Tulsa	OK	760	394	1,929	112	5,846	530	95.8	0.9	3.3
Honolulu	HI	693	135	5,133	69	5,656	400	81.2	9.4	9.4
Tucson	AZ	662	312	2,122	33	1,913	172	89.8	3.2	7.0
Birmingham	AL	659	609	1,082	126	8,327	673	96.7	1.2	2.1
El Paso	TX	653	227	2,877	51	3,685	289	91.7	2.8	5.5
Rochester	NY	617	335	1,842	100	5,389	497	3.2	91.6	5.2
Nashville	TN	613	571	1,074	139	9,451	725	1.7	95.4	2.9
Richmond	VA	611	406	1,505	115	7,139	643	3.7	92.6	3.7
Augusta	GA	610	371	1,644	85	3,091	359	1.0	94.0	5.0
Springfield	MA	602	422	1,427	77	3,847	383	0.6	95.5	3.9
Hartford	CT	593	366	1,620	108	7,573	608	3.7	92.4	3.9
Dayton	OH	592	369	1,604	92	5,557	467	2.0	94.5	3.5
Tacoma	WA	586	341	1,718	55	5,099	296	3.0	91.8	5.2
Charlotte	NC	572	299	1,913	82	6,203	429	1.7	95.0	3.3
Austin	TX	554	314	1,764	100	7,837	541	3.3	92.0	4.7
Omaha	NE	544	221	2,462	60	2,951	292	2.0	94.3	3.7
Akron	OH	537	356	1,508	87	5,101	419	2.4	94.0	3.6
Fresno	CA	537	168	3,196	30	1,906	168	1.5	92.9	5.6
Oxnard	CA	531	190	2,795	58	5,844	345	1.4	95.0	3.6
Sarasota	FL	502	464	1,082	10	579	56	0.6	94.7	4.7
Grand Rapids	MI	495	318	1,557	68	3,413	290	1.2	95.2	3.6
Toledo	OH	494	255	1,937	71	3,591	319	1.8	93.9	4.3
Albany	NY	490	365	1,342	104	4,976	546	4.2	89.6	6.2
Wilmington	DE	490	254	1,929	56	4,385	320	4.2	91.0	4.8
Albuquerque	NM	486	192	2,531	43	3,728	229	1.8	93.1	5.1
Allentown	PA	457	187	2,444	65	2,916	283	1.3	92.8	5.9
New Haven	CT	455	230	1,978	77	4,892	380	3.3	90.5	6.2
Savannah	GA	452	420	1,076	78	2,640	316	3.7	90.9	5.4
Charleston	SC	427	251	1,701	51	2,475	221	1.9	92.2	5.9
Columbus	GA	420	319	1,317	82	2,243	383	1.3	90.1	8.6

Source: All data from Federal Highway Administration, Highway Statistics 1998, except commuting data which are from the 1990 Census.

The Density & Open Space Myth

Myth: Increasing urban densities will help protect open space.
Reality: Increasing urban densities threatens the urban open spaces that urbanites value with infill and other developments, while it equally threatens rural open spaces with exurbanites escaping urban congestion.

Protecting open space is enormously popular, so smart-growth advocates mention it as often as possible. Al Gore has made it the centerpiece of his public statements about livability, promising to provide billions of dollars in federal and local funds to "preserve open spaces for future generations."[1] But smart-growth proposals for open space are exactly the opposite of what most urban and suburban residents want.

Behind the density-and-open-space myth is another smart-growth myth that you won't hear voiced very often: Backyards don't count as open space. Andres Duany skirts this issue when he argues that letting people use their private backyards instead of "communal" open spaces reduces their sense of community.[2] Planners don't count backyards when inventorying the open space. In some cases, if they see those yards at all they consider them ripe for development.

In contrast, most urban and suburban residents consider private yards to be an important component of open space. Focus groups held by the Lazarus Group found that Americans are concerned about open space, but one of their solutions to declining open space is "expanding the lot sizes of houses." People "flat out rejected" the idea of increasing urban densities "to create more collective open spaces. In fact, the respondents came to precisely the reverse conclusion: the answer to the perceived shrinkage of open space was to create less dense housing situations and thereby enhance individual open space."[3]

Another smart-growth presumption is that vacant lands in urban areas don't count as open space unless they are publicly owned or zoned as open space. Everything from vacant lots to farms and woodlands that are intermingled with urban developments are considered ripe for development, preferably as high-density, mixed-use projects. Yet nearby residents often enjoy such "vacant" lands as open space.

Increasing residential densities will have a surprisingly small effect on land consumption. Purely residential areas make up less than half of most urban areas. Within residential areas, streets, sidewalks, parks, schools, and other public spaces contribute to the gross land area consumed but not to net density. So doubling net densities might reduce land consumption by less than a quarter.

Smart growth not only threatens the urban open spaces that people use and value, it threatens the rural open spaces it claims to want to protect. Increasing numbers of retirees, telecommuters, and self-employed people are discovering that they no longer need cities. Many can locate almost anywhere in the U.S., desiring only commercial air service within a reasonable distance. Such people will remain in cities only if the cities are made as attractive as possible. If smart growth succeeds in significantly increasing the density and congestion of American urban areas, then many people will become exurbanites, moving to small towns or rural areas. Even if only a fraction of people can afford to do so, a small number of exurbanites living on ten- to forty-acre lots will consume far more land than larger numbers of suburbanites on the quarter- to half-acre lots that are demonized by smart growth.

Open spaces, including private yards as well as public parks, are important parts of urban areas. Smart growth is harmful to the open places that urbanites value the most while it does little to insure protection for rural open spaces.

Notes

1. Al Gore, "Remarks Prepared for Livability Announcement," January 11, 1999.
2. Andres Duany, Elizabeth Plater-Zyberk, and Jeff Speck, *Suburban Nation: The Rise of Sprawl and the Decline of the American Dream* (New York, NY: North Point Press, 2000), p. 60.
3. The Lazarus Group, "Analysis of Research on Suburban Development Issues," July 1999, Richmond Virginia, p. 2.

 ## Web Tools: Open Space by State

How much of your state has been urbanized and how much is open space? For one answer, see pages 438–439 of this book. For another answer, go to http://www.census.gov/population/www/censusdata/density.html and obtain the total land area of your state from table one. Subtract the total land area of "places" in table three. The remainder may include a few rural roads, scattered homes, and farm buildings, but is mostly open space.

The Density & Congestion Myth

Myth: Smart growth can reduce congestion.
Reality: Smart growth's real goal is to increase congestion.

Sprawl is "a primary cause of congestion," says the Surface Transportation Policy Project.[1] "The consequences of sprawl [include] traffic congestion [and] longer commutes" says the Sierra Club.[2] Suburban "patterns of growth have created... congestion, pollution, and isolation" says Peter Calthorpe.[3] "Suburban areas [have] proved to be such a traffic nightmare," says Andres Duany, because "everyone is forced to drive."[4]

Smart growth will "ease traffic congestion," says Vice President Al Gore. One of the most important ways in which it claims to do so is by increasing urban densities. Higher densities will supposedly put people closer to work, to markets, and to other people who they might like to visit, thus making walking or cycling more feasible. Higher densities will also make mass transit more attractive since there is more likely to be a bus or train going from where you are to where you want to go. Those who do drive won't have to drive as far, thus supposedly reducing vehicle-miles traveled.

This myth can be broken into the following three myths:
1. The myth that sprawl causes congestion, discussed starting on page 252;
2. The myth that density reduces congestion, page 257; and
3. The myth that smart growth aims to reduce congestion, page 260.

Notes

1. Surface Transportation Policy Project, "Why Are the Roads So Congested?" (Washington, DC: STPP, 1999), 8 pp.
2. Sierra Club, *The Dark Side of the American Dream* (San Francisco, CA: Sierra Club, 1998), http://www.sierraclub.org/transportation/sprawl/sprawl_report/.
3. Peter Calthorpe, *The Next American Metropolis: Ecology, Community, and the American Dream* (New York, NY: Princeton Architectural Press, 1993), p. 9.
4. Andres Duany, Elizabeth Plater-Zyberk, and Jeff Speck, *Suburban Nation: The Rise of Sprawl and the Decline of the American Dream* (New York, NY: North Point Press, 2000), p. 22.

The Myth that Sprawl Causes Congestion

Myth: Low-density suburbs increase congestion because they force people to drive more.

Reality: Suburbanization is the solution to congestion.

Each year, the Texas Transportation Institute publishes a report on congestion in America. In 1999, the Surface Transportation Policy Project followed the Texas congestion report with a report of its own claiming that the Texas data proved that sprawl causes congestion.[1] "As growth sprawls outward, jobs, housing, and services grow farther apart," says the report. Such sprawl, claims the report, is "a primary cause of congestion." The report claimed to be based on a "rigorous analysis" of Texas Transportation Institute data—but it did not include this analysis with the report. Instead, the report's logic was:

- The amount of driving in cities is growing faster than the population growth;
- Therefore, most of the difference between the growth in driving and the growth in population must be due to sprawl.

Rather than use Texas Transportation Institute data, the Policy Project refers to a 1992 report by Alan Pisarski that estimates that increases in driving are due to the causes shown in table one. "As much as 69% of the growth in driving between 1983 and 1990 was caused by factors influenced by sprawl," says the Policy Project. "These factors include the same people driving farther, as well as a decrease in carpooling and a switch from bicycling, walking or transit to driving."[2]

In fact, all of the changes that the Policy Project blames on sprawl are really due to other factors. The *reduction in passengers per vehicle* (which the Policy Project calls carpooling even though most multi-passenger vehicles are on family business, not commuting) is due to a reduction in household sizes. Between 1983 and 1990, average household size fell from 2.80 to 2.63 people per household—a 5.8 percent drop.[3] In that same period, average vehicle occupancy fell from 1.75 to 1.64 people per vehicle—a 6.3 percent drop.[4] This suggests that more than 90 percent of the decrease in vehicle occupancy is due to shrinking family sizes. "Primarily," agrees Pisarski, reductions in occupancy "are a product of decreasing family size and increasing vehicle availability," which reflects increasing incomes.[5]

Table One: Factors Contributing to the Growth in Driving

Increase in population	13%
Increase in trips taken	18%
Increase in trip lengths	**35%**
Decrease in passenger per vehicle	**17%**
Switch from other modes to driving	**17%**
Total	100%

Source: Alan Pisarski, Travel Behavior Issues in the 90's *(Washington, DC: FHwA, 1992), p. 14.* **Bold face** *indicates factors that the Surface Transportation Policy Project says are "influenced by sprawl."*

The *switch from other modes to driving* is also due to rising incomes making cars available to more people. This switch is found in dense, transit-oriented cities such as New York and San Francisco as much as in the suburbs, indicating it is not a sprawl-related phenomenon. According to Pisarski, 56 percent of the decline in transit usage was in central cities, while only 41 percent was in the suburbs.[6] The largest declines in transit usage were in the transit-intensive Northeastern cities.[7]

The *increase in trip lengths* may be partly influenced by low-density suburbanization, but not in the way the Policy Project implies. Instead of being due to "jobs, housing, and services growing farther apart," it is a response to the lower congestion found in low-density areas. Lower congestion means that people can live in a desirable area further from work without taking more time to commute. Lower congestion means that, instead of shopping at an expensive grocery store a half mile away, people can drive five miles to a superwarehouse store and save far more than the dollar or so it costs them to drive the extra distance. Increasing trip lengths are more due to increases in income than to suburbanization. Pisarski observes that "both central city and suburban trip lengths have shifted toward longer trips."[8] A major component of increasing trip length is among women, whether urban or suburban. The growth in women's travel in the 1980s and 1990s have "clearly. . . affected the overall growth in passenger miles of travel" says Pisarski.

What about the Policy Project's "rigorous analysis" of Texas Transportation Institute data? The report invites readers to "contact STPP for detailed methodology" used in this analysis. When contacted, the Policy Project sent a three-paragraph "blurb" (their description) briefly describing the analysis but including no data and few results.[9] The analysis supposedly used Texas Transportation Institute data to compare congestion with changes in population densities between 1992 and 1997. But—for 1992 only—it used a different set of population densities from those calculated by the Texas Transportation Institute.

Replicating what the project says it did using Texas Transportation Institute data reveals that changes in density are totally unrelated to changes in driving. If sprawl increased driving, then decreased densities should correlate with increased per capita driving. Yet, as shown in figures one and two, there is no correlation whether comparing 1992 and 1997 data or the longer (and thus more valid) period between 1982 and 1997.[10] Other factors, such as income and family size, must influence driving far more than density. Why is this conclusion so different from the Policy Project's unpublished analysis? When asked, the Policy Project failed to respond, but the answer must be that the densities that the project substituted for 1992 returned misleading results.

Figure One: Changes in Density vs. Changes in Per Capita Driving

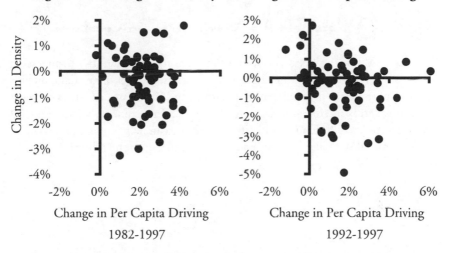

Whether comparing 1982 or 1992 data with 1997 data, the relationship between the change in urban area densities and changes in per capita driving is no better than random. Statistically, the r-squared for 1982–1997 data is 0.005, while for 1992–1997 data it is 0.017. Source: Texas Transportation Institute data for each urban area, available at http:// mobility.tamu.edu/study/usmap.stm.

"The traffic consequences of suburbanization are benign," say University of Southern California planning professors Peter Gordon and Harry Richardson. In fact, they add, "suburbanization has been the dominant and successful mechanism for coping with congestion."[11] Low-density suburbs are a major solution to, not a cause of, congestion.

Notes

1. Surface Transportation Policy Project, "Why Are the Roads So Congested?" (Washington, DC: STPP, 1999), 8 pp.
2. Ibid, p. 5.

3. Census Bureau, "Intercensal Estimates of Total Households by State," www.census.gov/
    population/estimates/housing/sthuhh7.txt.
4. Patricia Hu and Jennifer Young, *Draft Summary of Travel Trends: 1995 Nationwide
    Personal Transportation Survey* (Oak Ridge, TN: US DOE, 1999), table 15.
5. Alan Pisarski, *Travel Behavior Issues in the 90's* (Washington, DC: FHwA, 1992), p. 12.
6. Ibid, p. 19.
7. Ibid, p. 23.
8. Ibid, p. 61.
9. Reed Ewing, email to the author, March 8, 2000.
10. Texas Transportation Institute data for each urban area are available at http://
    mobility.tamu.edu/study/usmap.stm.
11. Peter Gordon and Harry Richardson, "Congestion Trends in Metropolitan Areas," *in*
    National Research Council, *Curbing Gridlock: Peak-Period Fees to Relieve Traffic Conges-
    tion* (Washington, DC: National Academy Press, 1994), volume 2:1–31.

Web Tools: Urban Congestion

While the Texas Transportation Institute's calculations of congestion
are not perfect, they have an excellent time series of raw data, including miles of roadway, miles driven, population, and urban area densities for most
major urban areas and for all years from 1982 to 1997 at http://mobility.tamu.edu/
study/usmap.stm. The Thoreau Institute's web site can help you use these data to
prepare a mobility report for your region at www.ti.org/mobrep.html.

The Myth That Density Reduces Congestion

Myth: Increasing urban densities will reduce congestion because more people will walk, bike, or ride transit.

Reality: Increasing density leads to slight reductions in auto usage and significant increases in congestion.

Doubling neighborhood densities, says the Federal Transit Administration, will reduce driving by 20 to 30 percent.[1] Higher densities are supposed to reduce congestion by letting people walk or ride transit instead of driving, and when they do drive they won't have to drive as far. If this reasoning were valid, Manhattan and Brooklyn would be the least congested parts of America while rural areas would be the most congested. In fact, the data show that urban density does not significantly influence the amount of driving people do.

Figure one shows a visible but weak relationship between density and driving in the nation's 391 major urban areas. While driving tends to fall as densities increase, it is very slight: Increasing the density of the average urban area by 10 percent reduces miles driven by just 0.2 percent. Meanwhile, at any given density there is a wide range of driving levels, which means that other factors influence driving more than density.

The urban areas with the highest miles-driven per person are not, as might be expected, large areas such as Los Angeles or New York. The five highest are Newburgh, NY; Petersburg, VA; Asheville, NC; Hickory, NC; and Myrtle Beach, SC. But the results are little different when the same calculations are made for only the 50 largest urban areas: Increasing the density of the average urban area by 10 percent reduces driving by just 0.3 percent. When only urban areas whose densities are greater than 2,000 people per square mile are counted, the results are no better than random (the slope is -0.001 and the r-squared is 0.03).

Similar results are found when comparing auto commuting with density. The 1990 census asked one out of six people how they commuted to work. Figure two compares the percentage of people who commuted by car with the density of each

Figures One & Two: Driving and Auto Commuting by Density

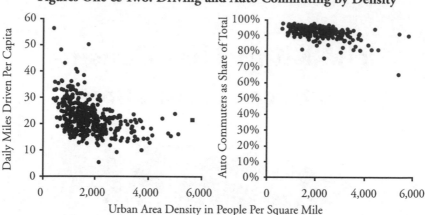

Urban Area Density in People Per Square Mile

The relationship between density and miles of driving (figure one) or density and share of people who commute by auto (figure two) is visible but weak. Statistically, the r-squared of the data in figure one is 0.03, which is no better than random, while the r-squared of the data in figure two is 0.28. Source: figure one—Census Bureau; figure two—Federal Highway Administration.

urban area. Calculations suggest that for every 1,000-person per square mile increase in density, the share of people driving to work drops by 2.4 percent.[2] To reduce auto usage to 50 percent, the density of an average urban area must increase to about 20,000 people per square mile.

More than 80 percent of commuters drive to work in every urban area but New York and the two college towns of Iowa City, Iowa, and State College, Pennsylvania. The other urban areas with low (but above 80 percent) rates of auto commuting are mainly nineteenth-century cities such as Boston, Philadelphia, Washington, Chicago, and San Francisco.

The results are not significantly different when looking at the 23,435 different cities, towns, and villages identified by the Census Bureau. At densities below 2,000 people per square mile, density has no significant effect on commuting behavior. Between 2,000 and 6,000 people per square mile, a 1,000-person per square mile increase in density reduces auto commuting by less than 1 percent. Above 6,000 per square mile, auto commuting declines more rapidly, but this is significantly influenced by a few nineteenth-century cities. Taking out New York, Chicago, San Francisco, Philadelphia, Washington, Boston, and Baltimore practically eliminates any effects of density on commuting. Each increase of 1,000 people per square mile reduces auto commuting by less than 1.6 percent.

All of these numbers point to the same results: Regardless of the existing density, a 1,000-person per square mile increase in density will reduce auto commuting by no more than 1 to 2 percent. Doubling the density of, say, the Seattle metropolitan area from its current 3,000-per-square mile to 6,000 will reduce the share of auto commuting by little more than 3.6 percent. Doubling the density of Honolulu, the nation's fourth-densest metropolitan area in 1990, will reduce commuting by little more than 5.4 percent.

So how can the Federal Transit Administration conclude that doubling densities reduces driving by 20 to 30 percent? This conclusion is based on Census Bureau statistics and survey data that show that people living in higher density neighborhoods tend to drive less. But comparing individual neighborhoods within an urban area introduces a sampling bias. People who live in high density neighborhoods don't drive less because of the density. Instead, people who can't drive or who want to drive less—mainly singles or couples with no children—choose to live in high density neighborhoods because these tend to be better served by transit or be more accessible on foot or bicycle. MIT planner Paul Schimek found that "greater neighborhood residential density is associated with lower household vehicle travel," but that this was mostly explained by "income and household size."[3] Forcing a family of four to live in a high-density neighborhood won't reduce their driving needs.

Even if the Federal Transit Administration were right, and doubling density reduced per capita driving by 30 percent, the result would be *more* congestion, not less. To reduce congestion after doubling density, per capita driving would have to fall by more than 50 percent. A 50-percent decline means that, with twice the number of people, there will be exactly as many autos on the road as before. Less than 50 percent means more cars on the road. A 30-percent per capita decline increases total driving by 40 percent, which would cause a huge increase in congestion unless 40 percent more roads were built—which smart-growth advocates would oppose.

Smart-growth, of course, includes other prescriptions aimed at reducing driving, including transit-oriented developments, pedestrian-friendly design, and balancing housing and jobs. The effects of these will be examined later in this book. But density alone will not significantly reduce driving.

Notes

1. Federal Transit Administration, *Transit and Urban Form* (Washington, DC: US DOT, 1996), volume 1, page 12.
2. Calculated using the least-squares method.
3. Paul Schimek, *Household Motor Vehicle Ownership and Use: How Much Does Residential Density Matter?* (Washington, DC: Transportation Research Board, 1996).

The Myth That Smart Growth Wants to Reduce Congestion

Myth: The goal of smart growth is to reduce congestion.
Reality: The real goal of smart growth is to increase congestion.

If density only increases congestion, then why do smart-growth supporters advocate density as a solution to congestion problems? The answer is that smart growth's real goal is to increase congestion, not reduce it. Of course, this is not a message that smart-growth advocates want known. Some smart-growth followers may actually believe that density reduces congestion. But many of the movement's leaders realize that the opposite is true. Privately—and sometimes publicly—they will admit that increased congestion is a good thing: If it does not convince many people to walk or take transit, at least it will punish those who continue to drive.

National Public Radio reporter Steve Inskeep reported on *All Things Considered* that "a few planners have stopped trying to ease traffic congestion. Instead, they're embracing congestion. They want to create more of it." Inskeep went on to say that these planners "want to replicate places like Hoboken, New Jersey. . . though it is a nightmare for commuters at rush hour."[1]

Who are these planners? Start with Portland's Metro, which says that "congestion signals positive urban development."[2] Portland's U.S. Representative and former City Councilor Earl Blumenauer waxes enthusiastic over congestion. He thinks some congestion "is exciting. It means business to the merchants. It means an exciting street life. It's the sort of hustle and bustle—and people don't mind going slow."[3]

Portland planners are not the only ones who favor congestion. The Twin Cities Metropolitan Council wants to build no new roads in that region for the next twenty years. "As traffic congestion builds," the council says, "alternative travel modes will become more attractive," including the buses that happen to also be run by the council and the light-rail line that the council wants to build.[4]

With crime on the wane, congestion has become the number one frustration for many urban residents. Smart-growth advocates don't dare admit that their real goal is to increase congestion. Instead, they rely on studies that optimistically suggest that density will reduce per capita driving to mislead people into believing that smart-growth plans will reduce congestion.

Notes

1. Steve Inskeep, "Commuting IV," *All Things Considered*, May 30, 1997. Available at http://iris.npr.org/plweb-cgi/fastweb?getdoc+npr+npr+21403+1+wAAA+congestion.
2. Metro, *Regional Transportation Plan Update* (Portland, OR: Metro, March 1996), p. 1-20.
3. Quoted by Inskeep, "Commuting IV."
4. Metropolitan Council, *Transportation Policy Plan* (St. Paul, MN: Metro Council, 1996), p. 54.

Smart Growth Doesn't Work Here Either

Myth: Sound land-use planning and heavy investments in transit have made European cities more livable and less auto-dependent than American cities.

Reality: Despite the fact that most European governments have imposed smart-growth-like policies for the past fifty years, European central cities are losing population, their suburbs are rapidly growing, transit ridership is stagnant, and auto ownership and driving are rapidly increasing.

"The models" for smart growth "already exist," says James Kunstler. "They're called London, Paris, Amsterdam, Prague, Munich, Oxford, Perugia, and Zurich."[1] Many advocates of smart growth wistfully wish that American cities could be as dense and auto-free as the ones in France, Germany, or Sweden. Europeans are less auto-dependent than Americans, they say, because their cities are denser, inhospitable to cars, and have excellent mass transit systems. As Joel Garreau says, many people "always rather hoped [the future] might look like Paris in the 1920s."[2]

Planner David Popenoe's favorite city is Stockholm. "In Stockholm," Popenoe writes, "only 7 percent of households have two cars, while 45 percent own no automobile at all." This is "not because Swedes cannot afford cars (although taxes make cars much more expensive than in the United States), it is because they do not need cars," claims Popenoe. "Sixty percent of all Stockholm journeys to work are made by public transportation, and another 20 percent on foot."[3]

Stockholm residents can get along without cars, says Popenoe, because Swedish planners took the time during World War II to "consider carefully the kind of urban housing that would be best." They "decided to continue Sweden's prewar urban tradition of apartment living."[4]

European environmentalists who visit the U.S. today are smug because Europeans drive less than Americans and therefore appear less auto dependent. Of course, most European countries are denser than the United States. Outside of Scandinavia, European nations are four to sixteen times denser than the U.S. But national density alone does not account for Europe's denser cities and lower rates of auto driving. After all, California and Florida are nearly as dense as France, while New Jersey and Rhode Island are nearly as dense as the densest European nations.

Many people ascribe differences between Europe and the U.S. to sound planning in Europe. For example, Karin Book and Lena Eskilsson, researchers in the Department of Social and Economic Geography at Lund University, Sweden, recently compared the auto-dependent American cities of Phoenix and Salt Lake with three European cities. The least auto-dependent city that they examined was Halle-Neustadt, which was built by the East Germans between 1964 and 1978. As of 1989, when the East German government fell, the city had the incredibly high density of around 70,000 people per square mile (Manhattan is only 50,000 per square mile).[5]

Book and Eskilsson describe Halle-Neustadt as a "good socialist city" because everyone lives in nearly identical apartments.[6] Most have two bedrooms because the government decreed "that the ideal family consisted of four family members and that the number of flat rooms should be one less than the number of family members."[7] The government discouraged car ownership by placing most of the parking on the outskirts of the city "at a relatively large distance from the residential houses."[8]

The Swedish researchers consider Halle-Neustadt a success, but in terms of reducing auto usage it was apparently a success only so long as the East German government kept its residents poor through inept economic planning. Book and Eskilsson chose "to focus on the socialist period" when the city met their ideal.[9] But they note that since 1990 the city's population density has declined while automobile ownership has "reached nearly the level of western Germany," meaning there are well over twice as many cars as planners anticipated. The "car traffic chaos" is the number one complaint of urban residents today:[10] "The cars are parked everywhere—on pavements, bike-ways, yards and lawns." As a result, the city is now talking about building new parking garages, which Book and Eskilsson worry will "undermine" the "planning concept of concentrating the parking places on the city's outskirts."[11]

To be fair to Book and Eskilsson, they don't necessarily approve of the authoritarian government needed to create a Halle-Neustadt. They note "that cities where public interests control physical development and cities where private interests are the most powerful are opposites": The former are compact, smart-growth-like cities, while the latter are low-density American-like cities. While the latter are auto dependent, the researchers admit that the former "tend to become monotonous and even boring." Of the cities they studied, their favorite, it appears, was Freiburg, Germany—a medieval city founded in 1120 and largely built centuries before there were either automobiles or urban planners.

The idea that Europe is better than the U.S. because it is less auto dependent has been promoted by Australian planners Jeffrey Kenworthy and Felix Laube (with the help of Peter Newman and others). Their massive 1999 book, *An International Sourcebook of Automobile Dependence in Cities*, presents data from more than forty-six cities around the world.[12] They conclude that European cities are less auto dependent, and therefore better, because they are denser, inhospitable to cars, and have excellent mass transit.

European countries, both east and west, can boast low auto usage as a result of severe government policies, including exorbitant taxes on cars and fuel and highly restrictive land-use laws. These policies "include every item that has been on this country's environmental wish list for the past 30 years," says economist Charles Lave of the University of California, Irvine. "The degree of governmental restriction upon personal freedom [that is found in Europe] would be unprecedented in this country."[13]

The personal preferences of European residents appears to have played very little role in setting these policies. Planning in Stockholm was done by "the elite and powerful," David Popenoe admits, and "the housing desires of individual residents was not a serious input. Indeed, a public opinion poll at the time in Stockholm showed that a majority of people wanted single-family homes. Needless to say, the people did not get them."[14] "Swedish housing densities are a planners' alternative," concludes Popenoe, an alternative that sounds very much like smart growth in the U.S. "In Amsterdam, in 1989," says Joel Garreau, "they were still holding symposia at which one of the key questions was: 'Should architects take consumer preference into consideration in the design of housing?' "[15]

Beyond questions of freedom and personal preference, there are two enormous holes in the European case for smart growth. First, government policies imposed huge unintended costs on their citizens. Second, they failed to do what smart-growth planners say they will do: discourage suburbs and auto usage.

The unintended costs of smart-growth-like policies in Britain are well documented by planning historian Peter Hall. In 1947, the British government passed the Town and Country Planning Act, which "effectively nationalized the right to develop land." Land outside of urban areas could not be developed. Land inside of urban areas was developed to high densities.[16]

In many parts of England, says Hall, people "found themselves uprooted into hurriedly constructed system-built flats lacking amenities, environment, community: lacking, in fact, almost anything except a roof and four walls."[17] High-density, low-rise apartments, the sort favored by smart-growth planners, "proved a failure." Like American housing projects, they were beset by crime and vandalism, making them " 'hard-to-let', i.e. lettable only to the poorest and most disorderly families."[18]

On a more general level, the artificial limit on the land available for housing led to an "inflation of land and property values, on a scale never previously witnessed."[19] The real problem, says Hall, was "a design solution laid down on people without regard to their preferences, ways of life, or plain idiosyncrasies; laid down,

further, by architects who—as the media delighted to discover—themselves invariably lived in charming Victorian villas."[20] Hall concludes that "The remarkable fact was how long it took for anyone to see that it was wrong."[21] Brookings
Institution researcher Pietro Nivola points out that "a recent report by McKinsey
and Company concluded that lagging productivity of the British economy derives in part from land-use controls that hinder entry and expansion of the most
productive firms."[22]

But for all their flaws (which, many planners would say, could be corrected
with better planning), didn't European policies at least prevent sprawl and auto-
dependency? Far from it. In fact, Europe is not ahead of the United States; it is
behind and catching up fast.

"An interesting phenomena has taken place in the past twenty years," says
Rutgers University political scientist James Dunn. "While many Americans were
wishing, vainly, that the United States could become more like Europe, Europe
became more like us! Auto ownership has been growing at a faster rate in Europe
than in the United States, and suburban development is proceeding apace."[23]

Kenworthy & Laube's book clearly documents this by presenting data from
1960, 1970, 1980, and 1990 for each of their forty-six cities. Amsterdam, often
cited as a good, non-auto dependent city, experienced a tripling of car ownership
between 1960 and 1990. The central city's population declined by 30 percent,
while suburban populations grew. As a result, its average population density fell
by nearly half.

The same story can be found in nearly every European city:

- *Inner city populations are falling.* Between 1960 and 1990, Copenhagen's population fell by 33 percent, Frankfurt's by 35 percent, London's by 28 percent,
  and Zurich's by 17 percent. Paris alone gained 2 percent but only because
  Kenworthy and Laube added 41 percent to its land area;
- *Suburban populations are growing.* Between 1960 and 1990, Copenhagen's
  suburban population grew by 35 percent, Frankfurt's by 41 percent, Paris' by
  88 percent, and Zurich's by 64 percent;
- *As a result, urban population densities are declining.* Between 1960 and 1990,
  Copenhagen's density fell by 30 percent, Frankfurt's by 47 percent, London's
  by 35 percent, Paris' by 33 percent, and Zurich's by 22 percent.[24]

Table one shows that, from 1960 to 1990, nearly all European urban areas, as
defined by Kenworthy & Laube, lost population but greatly expanded their land
area. Driving per capita has increased several times over while the transit's share of
motorized travel has fallen dramatically. The only urban areas whose densities are
increasing are in the United States. Only one city, Stockholm, shows an increase
in transit's share of travel.

Collectively, the European urban areas tracked by Kenworthy & Laube lost
2.2 million people between 1960 and 1990. Where did they all go? In most cases,
it appears that they moved to suburbs that are outside the urban areas defined by

Kenworthy & Laube. In other words, the real urban areas are much larger, and densities much lower, than they indicate. No doubt per capita driving is even greater and transit shares lower in those suburbs.

"The desire for the single-family home is international," says Herbert Gans, "and even exists in countries that cannot afford to satisfy it." Confirming Popenoe's comments, Gans found this desire "among Swedes who must live in apartment complexes," and he notes that others have reported it in England, Ghana, and elsewhere.[25] Because of this desire, Europeans, like Americans, are moving to the suburbs.

Table One: Percent Changes in Urban Form, 1960–1990

	Population	Land Area	Density	Miles Driven Per Capita	Transit Share
Amsterdam	-9.5	61.4	-43.9	475.0	-56.8
Boston	15.0	72.8	-33.4	240.6	-69.8
Brussels	-5.7	26.2	-25.3	171.3	-54.9
Chicago	14.0	65.1	-31.0	138.5	-60.6
Copenhagen	-12.8	24.6	-30.0	340.2	-45.0
Denver	88.9	175.4	-31.4	70.0	-43.5
Hamburg	-9.8	54.6	-41.7	224.5	-50.2
London	-16.4	29.1	-35.3	190.3	-16.7
Los Angeles	75.7	43.5	22.5	31.1	-3.7
New York	9.4	28.1	-14.7	104.6	-55.5
Paris	26.9	88.7	-32.7	174.6	-34.2
Phoenix	263.4	198.3	21.8	42.1	-13.0
San Francisco	96.7	53.8	-2.9	96.7	-23.1
Stockholm	-16.6	2.9	-18.9	157.1	51.4
Tokyo	104.9	147.2	-17.1	207.7	-18.9

Source: Jeffrey R. Kenworthy and Felix B. Laube, An International Sourcebook of Automobile Dependence in Cities 1960-1990 (Boulder, CO: University of Colorado, 1999), chapter 3.

This move is made possible by the automobile: European auto ownership is growing three times as fast as in the U.S.[26] Germans own as many autos per capita as Americans and France and Sweden are not far behind.[27] Europeans drive less than Americans, but they are catching up there too. In 1991, residents of Britain, France, Germany, and Sweden all drove 50 to 60 percent as many miles per capita as those in the U.S.[28] By 1997, they were up to 70 to 75 percent.[29] Between 1991 and 1997, auto driving in Paris grew by nearly 3 percent per year, while transit ridership was stagnant.[30]

Like those in the U.S., many European transit systems are experiencing declining shares of urban travel.[31] In 1960, 59 percent of commuters in Brussels used transit; by 1990 it was down to 35 percent. Similar declines are found in Frank-furt, Berlin, London, and many other cities. In some cities where transit's share was stable, auto usage grew but walking and cycling declined. In the European Union as a whole, 82 percent of all surface motorized travel is by car and only 18 percent is by rail, bus, or trolley—not that much different from the U.S.[32]

David Popenoe's Stockholm is no exception. In fact, though he was writing in the mid 1980s, Popenoe was able to give Stockholm an appearance of low auto ownership only by using 1970 data. Contrary to Popenoe's claim, the low auto ownership of 1970 must have been because the Swede's couldn't afford cars; as their incomes rose between 1970 and 1990, per capita auto ownership increased by 56 percent and transit's share of commuter traffic fell.

The *International Sourcebook on Auto Dependence* records a strange phenom-enon: Every European urban area in the book except Paris and Zurich lost popu-lation between 1970 and 1990. In most cases the losses were 10 percent or more, and the collective loss for ten cities was more than 2 million people. Where did all of these people go?

The book answers this question for Stockholm. Although the municipality of Stockholm lost 17 percent of its people (a loss of 134,000) after 1960, the *county* of Stockholm gained nearly 30 percent (a gain of 370,000). The book includes a map showing that more than 90 percent of the county is urbanized. But it does not list the urbanized land area, transit usage, or other data for the county except for population, motor vehicle numbers, and miles driven. Population densities in the county are low, while auto ownership has significantly increase and per capita driving more than doubled between 1960 and 1990.

Kenworthy and Laube simply refuse to see this. "Stockholm is unique in the sample of cities in this book in recording a marginal decline in the absolute level of car use experienced in the Municipality area between 1980 and 1990," they proclaim. "It is perhaps not coincidental that the Municipality of Stockholm is the only city in the sample to have experienced an increase in density between 1980 and 1990."[33] But auto driving in the *county* increased between 1980 and 1990, and the density of its urbanized areas probably declined—though we don't know for sure because the book does not list urbanized land areas for the county.

No doubt similar migrations to distant suburbs have taken place in other Eu-ropean urban areas, but are not recorded in the book. Wendell Cox, for example, points out that the urban areas of London, Frankfurt, and Munich all extend well beyond Kenworthy and Laube's boundaries. "This treatment tends to make data look more comparatively favorable for public transit," says Cox.[34]

The real differences between European and U.S. travel habits are not primarily due to differences in density or to planning. Instead, they are mainly due to differ-ences in personal income and in urban histories.

"The tough anti-auto policies in Western Europe have been overwhelmed by a far stronger force: the growth of personal income,"[35] says economist Charles Lave.

"In worldwide perspective, rapid growth of automobiles began in the United States because we were richer than other nations. But other nations soon headed down the same path as their incomes increased. . . . The desire for personal mobility seems to be unstoppable."[36]

Kenworthy & Laube's claim that their data show that Lave is wrong. "The cost of cars and the wealth of cities do not provide reliable or consistent evidence in explaining the degree of dependence on the automobile in different cities," they say. Instead, "urban form, especially higher urban density, is a key and consistently strong factor in helping to explain the level of car use in a city." But the data on which they base these claims is limited and ignores important historical factors.

They do not have data on per capita incomes over time, but for some cities they do list per capita gross regional products (GRP) and costs of driving for 1990. Gross regional product overestimates European personal incomes, relative to the U.S., because European tax rates are higher. Even so, their data show that European driving costs are 66 percent higher than in the U.S. while per capita gross regional products are just 18 percent higher. This suggests that European auto ownership and driving should be catching up to, but not even with, the U.S.—which is exactly the case. People in Australian and wealthy Asian cities also face higher driving costs and lower personal incomes than in the U.S., which explains why they tend to be further behind.

Kenworthy & Laube's other mistake is to compare individual city pairs without considering historical differences between those cities. For example, they say that "New York has 36 percent less car use per capita than Houston, but is actually 10 percent higher in GRP per capita." Based on such comparisons, they conclude that differences between cities "cannot be explained by simple economic factors alone." Of course, Lave never claimed that "simple economic factors alone" explained car usage. But he did claim that, as wealth increased, car usage would increase. Although Kenworthy & Laube do not include wealth data for any year but 1990, it is safe to say that, from 1960 to 1990, wealth increased in every city in their sample, and the book does show that auto usage also increased in every city.

In claiming that higher urban densities are "key" to "explaining" lower car usage, Kenworthy & Laube imply that increasing urban densities will reduce auto driving. Here they make the familiar smart-growth mistake of confusing cause and effect. Cities that can't afford autos will have higher densities. When people start to buy autos, densities decline. The densities are an effect of auto ownership, not the other way around. If density were enough to discourage auto usage, then no one in dense urban areas such as Amsterdam and Brussels, whose 1960 densities were greater than New York City, would have begun driving. But they did begin driving and the densities of those regions have since declined by 25 to 45 percent.

Differences in auto usage between cities can be explained by two major sets of factors: economic and historical. They can be summed up in the question: At what time in the city's growth did people's incomes become sufficient to own and drive autos—including enough to pay for any tax penalties that governments charge for auto driving? If a city is still new by the time income reaches that stage, then the city will be built to auto densities and transit will play little role. New York and most European cities fall in this category. If the city is largely or fully formed by the time income reaches that stage, then it will be far denser than is comfortable for auto usage. New developments on the urban fringe will aim to accommodate the auto, but inner city densities will decline only slowly. For a time, the city will appear more transit- and pedestrian-friendly, but that will fade as people express their mobility by leaving.

This historical difference explains why New Yorkers drive less than Houstonians, Europeans drive less than Americans, and most of the other differences between cities that the book's authors can't explain by "simple economic factors alone." Virtually all of the forty-six cities in the book fit one of these two patterns. Perhaps the most important bias in the book is the most subtle: the repeated use of the term "auto dependence," as if the automobile cripples us rather than enables us to be more productive and enjoy more things in life.

"When Europeans build new, they don't build more charming places reminiscent of old Paris, old Rome, old London," says Garreau. "Their modern stuff is frequently worse than our urban landscapes. Check out the mainland side of Venice. Many of the high-rise apartments ringing Paris and London have all the Stalinist charm of the Cross Bronx Expressway."[37] No wonder that Peter Hall found in Stockholm that "attempts to persuade everyone to live in apartments failed" and much of its suburban area today "is almost indistinguishable from its counterparts in California and Texas."[38] Smart-growth advocates may like the idea of apartments better than low-density suburbs, but given a choice most people will pay extra to live in their own private homes on their own plot of land.

Many European cities differ from American ones in one important respect: European air is significantly dirtier than in the United States. European countries tried to treat pollution by repressing auto driving. The U.S., of course, successfully reduced auto emissions through clean technology rather than by trying to change driving habits.

"Space is one of America's plentiful resources," says Pietro Nivola. He thinks it is absurd "to expect that space should be utilized as parsimoniously here as in countries with precious little of it."[39] It is similarly absurd to treat the incredible mobility that Americans enjoy as some sort of irrational "dependence," especially when Europeans are demonstrating that high densities do not reduce people's desire to travel by auto.

"Asthetes sometimes assume that erring in the direction of Europe or Japan would somehow enable American cities to emulate the showcases abroad," says

Nivola. "In reality, the face of the American metropolis, however stringently planned for higher densities, would resemble, at best, the rest of the industrial world's banal modernites—not Paris but Brussels, not Venice but Hamburg, not Kyoto but Osaka."[40]

The more people use Europe as a shining example of smart growth, the more they undermine the case for smart growth. Europe proves that most people want to live in low densities and they want to drive to their destinations no matter what barriers elite government planners try to put in their way. American cities that try to become as repressive as those in Europe will impose huge costs on their residents even as they fail to significantly reduce auto driving.

Notes

1. James Howard Kunstler, *Home from Nowhere: Remaking Our Everyday World for the 21st Century* (New York, NY: Simon & Schuster, 1996), p. 79.
2. Joel Garreau, *Edge City: Life on the New Frontier* (New York, NY: Doubleday, 1991), p. 8.
3. David Popenoe, *Private Pleasure, Public Plight: American Metropolitan Community Life in Comparative Perspective* (New Brunswick, NJ: Transaction, 1985), p. 43.
4. Ibid, p. 61.
5. Karin Book and Lena Eskilsson, *Transport, Built Environment and Development Control: A Comparative Urban Study* (Lund, Sweden: Dept. of Social and Economic Geography, 1998), pp. 107–109.
6. Karin Book and Lena Eskilsson, presentation at Transatlantic Research Conference on Social Change and Sustainable Transport, Berkeley, CA, 11 March 1999.
7. Book and Eskilsson, "Transport," pp. 109–110.
8. Ibid, p. 110.
9. Ibid, p. 104.
10. Ibid, p. 108.
11. Ibid, p. 111.
12. Jeffrey R. Kenworthy and Felix B. Laube, *An International Sourcebook of Automobile Dependence in Cities 1960-1990* (Boulder, CO: University of Colorado, 1999), 704 pp.
13. Charles Lave, "Cars and Demographics," *Access* 1 (Fall, 1992):4–11.
14. Ibid.
15. Joel Garreau, *Edge City*, p. 237.
16. Peter Geoffrey Hall, *Cities of Tomorrow: An Intellectual History of Urban Planning and Design in the Twentieth Century* (Cambridge, MA: Blackwell, 1988; updated to 1996), p. 304.
17. Ibid, p. 225.
18. Ibid, p. 226.
19. Ibid, p. 305.
20. Ibid, p. 226
21. Ibid, p. 225.
22. Pietro S. Nivola, *Laws of the Landscape: How Policies Shape Cities in Europe and America* (Washington, DC: Brookings, 1999), p. 52.
23. James A. Dunn, Jr., *Driving Forces: The Automobile, Its Enemies, and the Politics of Mobility* (Washington, DC: Brookings Institution, 1998), p. 185.
24. Kenworthy and Laube, *An International Sourcebook*, chapter 3.

25. Herbert J. Gans, *The Levittowners: Ways of Life and Politics in a New Suburban Community* (New York, NY: Pantheon, 1967), p. 417.

26. Lave, "Cars and Demographics," p. 4.

27. Federal Highway Administration, *Highway Statistics 1998* (Washington, DC: FHwA, 1999) table IN-3.

28. FHwA, *Highway Statistics 1993,* table IN-4.

29. FHwA, *Highway Statistics 1998,* table IN-4.

30. Christian Gerondeau, "Mass Transit—A Tale of Two Cities' Transportation," *Atlanta Journal*, November 1, 2000, http://www.accessatlanta.com/partners/ajc/epaper/editions/wednesday/opinion_93ff7cebe4aba15510f1.html.

31. Ibid.

32. Ibid.

33. Kenworthy & Laube, *International Sourcebook*, p. 341.

34. Wendell Cox, personal communication, August 5, 2000.

35. Lave, "Cars and Demographics," p. 4.

36. Ibid, p. 10.

37. Joel Garreau, *Edge City*, pp. 236–237.

38. Peter Hall, *Cities in Civilization* (New York, NY: Pantheon Books, 1998), pp. 877–878.

39. Pietro S. Nivola, *Laws of the Landscape: How Policies Shape Cities in Europe and America* (Washington, DC: Brookings, 1999), p. 5.

40. Ibid, p. 49.

Web Tools: European Cities

Additional data for the cities shown in table one and several more as well can be found at www.ti.org/europedata.html.

The Density & Air Pollution Myth

Myth: Increasing urban densities will reduce air pollution because more people will walk, bicycle, or ride transit.

Reality: Air quality problems are strongly associated with high densities because densities concentrate pollutants and often lead to pollution-causing traffic congestion.

One of the many ironies of smart growth is that the EPA and other smart-growth supporters use federal air quality goals to promote higher densities. But increasing densities is more likely to reduce air quality than increase it for two reasons.

- Urban air quality violations are usually the result of concentrations of pollutants, which can cause health problems for local residents. Higher densities are more likely to result in such concentrations.
- Density is more likely to result in congestion, and autos pollute more in congested, stop-and-go traffic.

Automotive air pollution is a complex matter. The amount of pollution cars produce depend on such things as:

- How well a car is maintained;
- The make and model of car;
- Whether the car is warm or cold, as catalytic converters don't work until they are warmed up;
- How much the car drives in stop-and-go traffic, where pollution is higher due to acceleration and the cooling of the catalytic converter;
- The concentration or density of traffic, particularly for carbon monoxide;
- How fast the car is going.

Speed is a particularly important factor. Nitrogen oxides are minimized at about 20 miles per hour but are not significantly greater until speeds exceed 50 miles per hour. Hydrocarbons and carbon monoxide are minimized at about 50 miles per hour. All emissions are much higher at speeds below 15 miles per hour than at speeds above 60 miles per hour: At 10 miles per hour, they can be twice as high as at 60.[1]

Despite this complexity, the Environmental Protection Agency oversimplifies pollution problems. While it deals with auto maintenance through inspection-and-maintenance programs, the EPA largely ignores the other factors when it evaluates urban transportation plans. Instead, the main factor the agency considers is how many miles are driven. Yet reducing miles driven will not necessarily reduce air pollution. Imagine a transportation plan that:

- Promotes stop-and-go traffic by increasing congestion;
- Uses traffic calming to slow cars on major streets to below 20 miles per hour;
- Builds light-rail lines that lead many people to take short drives in cold cars from home to the light-rail stations rather than longer drives in cars that get fully warmed up;
- Increases population densities resulting in more concentrated traffic.

Such a plan might reduce the total miles people drive (though probably not by much). But each of those miles will be far dirtier, on average, than the miles driven in a plan that adds road capacity to maintain traffic flows. For example, cars can produce three times as much pollution in stop-and-go traffic than in free-flowing traffic. In dense cities, says Brookings Institution fellow Pietro Nivola, "the concentration of population, and of foul air, exposes more inhabitants to a serious health hazard."[2]

Table One: Average Urban Area Density by EPA Air Pollution Rating

Extreme	5,600
Severe	3,362
Serious	2,378
Moderate	2,077
Marginal	1,744
None	1,505

Source: Density from 1990 U.S. Census of Population and Housing; 1990 smog ratings from EPA Office of Air Quality and Standards.

Table one shows that areas with cleaner air have, on average, lower densities than areas with more polluted air. The congestion and concentration of pollutants found in higher density areas overwhelm any slight reductions in auto driving that people may do in high-density areas.

Notes

1. David J. Brzezinski, Phil Enns, & Constance J. Hart, *Facility-Specific Speed Correction Factors (Draft)* (Washington, DC: EPA, 1999), figures 5a through 5d, http://www.epa.gov/oms/models/mobile6/m6spd002.pdf.
2. Pietro S. Nivola, *Laws of the Landscape: How Policies Shape Cities in Europe and America* (Washington, DC: Brookings, 1999), p. 42.

The Affordable-Housing Myth

Myth: Low-density housing is unaffordable because it consumes so much valuable land.

Reality: High densities are strongly correlated with significant increases in land and housing costs.

ow-income housing advocates and home builders use two slightly different terms when they discuss housing costs. To the former, *affordable housing* means housing that is affordable to low-income people, such as the 20-percent of people with the lowest income in a region or people whose income is half of the region's median. To builders, *housing affordability* means the share of houses for sale that are affordable to people with the *median* income in a region. Both measures are important, but if housing is not affordable to those of median income, it is certainly not affordable to low-income families.

Smart growth advocates often cite suburban housing costs as a reason for adopting smart-growth policies. But they rarely say how their policies will make housing affordable. There is a good reason for this: Smart growth's prescriptions for density and urban-growth boundaries make single-family housing unaffordable to people with both low and median incomes.

The National Association of Home Builders publishes a quarterly ranking of housing affordability in major urban areas. The ranking is based on the percentage of homes in the area affordable to families of median income. The list shows that, while density is not the only factor in housing affordability, higher densities tend to be associated with less affordable housing. Dividing the Home Builders' list into fourths, table one shows that the less affordable regions tend to have higher densities.

Higher densities are a response to higher land prices; if there is a scarcity of land, people will bunch up. If there is no scarcity, many people will choose to live in lower densities. The only way smart growth can increase densities is to create an artificial land shortage, driving land prices up. Such high land prices make housing less affordable.

Density is not the only factor affecting affordability. Local economic and geographic conditions all play a role. One important factor is the supply of land. Urban-growth boundaries create an artificial shortage of land, making land for housing less affordable. This process is plainly visible in Oregon, which established urban-growth boundaries around its cities in the late 1970s. Those boundaries included enough vacant land for an estimated twenty years worth of growth.

Table One: Density and Affordability
(Density in Population Per Square Mile)

Most Affordable Regions	1,426
Second Most Affordable Regions	1,886
Second Least Affordable Regions	2,079
Least Affordable Regions	2,520

Source: *National Association of Home Builders,* Housing Opportunity Index, Third Quarter 1999 *(http://www.nahb.com); densities from FHwA,* Highway Statistics 1998, *table HM-72. A few urban areas were not included in the comparison because the boundaries used by the home builders were different from the boundaries used by the Federal Highway Administration.*

In the 1980s, Oregon cities were among the most affordable housing markets in the nation. By 1996, they were among the least affordable. As of the last quarter of 1998, three Oregon cities—Portland, Eugene, and Medford—were among the nation's six least affordable housing markets. One more—Salem—was in the top fifteen.[1] Oregon cities have grown rapidly in the 1990s, but this growth alone does not account for Oregon's unaffordable housing. Many other cities have grown faster, including Albuquerque, Chattanooga, Denver, Las Vegas, Phoenix, and Raleigh, yet none of these are among the twenty least affordable cities.

While all four of Oregon's housing markets regularly make the home builders' list of unaffordable regions, most of the least-affordable cities are in California. California cities have implemented various forms of growth control since the 1970s. While these controls are not the same as smart growth, they have had the same effect as Oregon's urban-growth boundaries, which is to limit the amount of land available for new homes. California growth controls have included:

- Limits on the number of building permits allowed each year;
- Purchases of huge blocks of land as regional parks and open spaces, including more than 15 percent of the total land supply in the San Francisco Bay Area;[2]
- Local requirements that any increases in density or housing be approved by a vote of the people;
- Public involvement processes that make it so easy for people to halt or challenge development that, in one case, says zoning expert Bernard Frieden, "a lone boy scout doing an ecology project was able to bring construction to a halt on a 200-unit condominium project."[3]
- Even where public challenges don't stop developments, they often lead devel-

opers to change their plans "from moderate-priced to high-priced luxury units," says planner David Dowell.[4]

Promoters of smart growth and growth controls emphatically deny that these policies lead to higher housing prices. "The development industry is at work," says growth control advocate Eben Fodor, "trying to convince policymakers that growth controls will have negative effects on housing affordability, and therefore should be abandoned."[5] He claims that growth controls may "result in a better distribution of affordable housing than market-driven growth," but only because "cities acting to control growth may also be more proactive about housing policies."[6]

Yet the reality is that growth "controls inevitably make housing expensive," says economist Edwin Mills. Moreover, they "contribute to home prices that are not only high but unstable as well."[7] "The higher housing costs caused by growth controls reflect a net loss to society," says economist William Fischel. Even if the controls are designed to produce more compact development, as in Oregon, adds Fischel, they can "cause developers to go to other communities that are farther from the central city, thus contributing to metropolitan sprawl."[8]

"Advocates of growth and compactness controls may believe that the benefits of such controls outweigh the costs," says Mills. "I have no idea what such benefits might be (and am unable to find a coherent argument that substantial benefits exist). But advocates of controls should face the fact that an inevitable implication of the government actions they espouse is much more expensive and unstable metropolitan area housing."[9]

One difference between California's growth control's and Oregon's smart-growth policies is that the former drive up the costs of both single-family homes and apartments. Oregon's policies, so far, have not made apartments unaffordable to median income people. But most of the new apartments built in Portland are luxury buildings. Says *Oregonian* reporter Gordon Oliver, "There are few apartments, new or old, that are affordable to people earning less than 50 percent of the region's median income."[10]

In both Oregon and California, the rise in housing prices has hit poor people the hardest because housing prices in their neighborhoods have increased the fastest. Poor neighborhoods contain some of the most affordable housing left in Portland and other Oregon cities, so they are soon invaded by middle-class newcomers who can't afford new homes or housing in middle-class neighborhoods. This has caused housing costs to rise the fastest in low-income neighborhoods. Such gentrification is good for land values and property taxes, but not for poor people.

As Fodor suggests, Portland has responded to escalating home prices by being "proactive about housing policies." The Portland city council recently passed a requirement that all new developments of sixteen housing units or more must include a certain percentage of affordable housing. This will force developers to subsidize a few poor people by increasing the prices of other housing. Yet at the rate new housing is constructed, it will take hundreds of years for this policy to provide housing for all low-income Portlanders. Along with other Portland programs, such as its smart-growth design code, this policy will ultimately make housing even less affordable for most poor people.

Notes

1. National Association of Home Builders, *Housing Opportunity Index, Fourth Quarter 1998* (Washington, DC: NAHB, 1999).
2. David E. Dowall, *The Suburban Squeeze: Land Conservation and Regulation in the San Francisco Bay Area* (Berkeley, CA: UC Press, 1984), p. 15.
3. Bernard J. Frieden, *The Environmental Protection Hustle* (Cambridge, MA: MIT, 1979), p. 6.
4. David E. Dowall, *The Suburban Squeeze: Land Conservation and Regulation in the San Francisco Bay Area* (Berkeley, CA: UC Press, 1984), p. 141.
5. Eben Fodor, *Better Not Bigger: How to Take Control of Urban Growth and Improve Your Community* (Stony Creek, CT: New Society, 1999), p. 12.
6. Ibid, pp. 44–45.
7. Edwin S. Mills, "Truly Smart 'Smart Growth,'" *Illinois Real Estate Letter*, Summer, 1999, p. 7.
8. William Fischel, "What Do Economists Know about Growth Controls? A Research Review," *in* David Brower, David Godschalk, and Douglas Porter, eds., *Understanding Growth Management: Critical Issues and a Research Agenda* (Washington, DC: Urban Land Institute, 1989), pp. 59–86.
9. Mills, "Truly Smart 'Smart Growth,'" p. 7.
10. Gordon Oliver, "Apartment hunters move in on deals," *The Oregonian*, December 6, 1999.

Web Tools: Housing Affordability

How affordable is housing in your urban area? Find out at http://www.nahb.org/facts/default.htm. Point to "Housing opportunity index" and click on "HOI, major markets, listed alphabetically" or "listed by rank" for the latest information. The table shows the percentage of homes in each housing market that are affordable, using standard mortgage criteria, to families of median income. You can also use the data to calculate the ratio of median home sales price to the median income. In the most affordable cities, the ratio is about 1.5 to one, while in the least affordable cities it is about five to one.

The Costs-of-Sprawl Myth

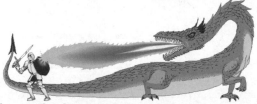

Myth: High-density development reduces infrastructure and other costs.

Reality: Studies of actual municipal expenses show that higher densities cost taxpayers more.

In 1973, the Council on Environmental Quality published a report titled *The Costs of Sprawl*.[1] The report concluded that high-density, planned communities were much less costly to build or live in than low-density sprawl and that sprawl produced more air pollution and other environmental impacts than planned developments. Based on detailed models of several different kinds of urban developments—including typical sprawl, high-density developments, and planned unit developments—*The Costs of Sprawl* contained a wealth of numbers indicating that costs of housing, utilities, public services, and roads were all significantly higher in low-density communities. The report was definitive, persuasive, and has been quoted countless times by planners and civic leaders.

The report was also totally wrong.

The authors of the report made the classic mistake of failing to verify their assumptions against reality. As a result, they left out major costs and made other cost assumptions that were simply wrong. For example, *The Costs of Sprawl* focused on capital costs rather than operating costs. Yet, in the long run, operating costs are greater than capital costs. The report also focused on on-site services while it underestimated the costs of schools and roads.

The report also unfairly compared high- and low-density housing costs. The housing units in the high-density areas that it modeled not only occupied less land than those in low density, they were smaller. Naturally, all else being equal, a smaller house or apartment will cost less than a big one. An important point missed by those who cite *The Costs of Sprawl* is that most of the variation in costs among the alternatives it studied was not infrastructure but costs to the home buyer. Obviously, a 2,000-square-foot single-family home is going to cost more than a 1,200-square-foot condominium. But home buyers know that and those who buy 2,000-square-foot homes are clearly willing to pay the price.

Moreover, *The Costs of Sprawl* didn't really evaluate the costs of high-density vs.

low-density cities. Instead, it assumed a fixed number of people per square mile in all of its models and simply left more unoccupied open space in the high-density models. True high-density cities, with higher populations per square mile, would have very different costs than those modeled by *The Costs of Sprawl.*

Helen Ladd, of Duke University's Institute of Policy Sciences, went to the real world to compare the costs of high- vs. low-density cities. Specifically, she gathered cost data from 247 counties that contain well over half the population of the U.S. Ladd found that, at population densities less than 250 per square mile—which is roughly one house every eight acres—higher densities indeed reduce public service costs. But above 250 people per square mile, costs increase with higher densities. At the highest densities Ladd studied—24,000 people per square mile or roughly 14 units per acre—per unit public service costs were nearly 50 percent higher than at the density of one house per eight acres.[2]

The Costs of Sprawl authors assumed that commuters in low-density sprawl would spend more than an hour a day in their cars, while commuters in high-density planned developments would spend under 38 minutes per day. In the real world, however, suburban commuters spend only about five more minutes per day commuting than those who live in central cities—and make up for that by spending less time traveling to shopping areas.[3] *The Costs of Sprawl* also claimed that water pollution and other environmental costs were lower in its high-density models. But it assumed that there were no environmental costs associated with the unoccupied open space that is saved by higher densities. In fact, farms tend to consume far more water and generate far more water pollution than urban areas.

The biggest mistake made by those who cite *The Costs of Sprawl* is to apply its conclusions to urban infill. Even if a new high-density development did have lower infrastructure costs per home than a new low-density development, those costs are very different than the cost of rebuilding a low-density neighborhood to higher densities. Yet the American Farmland Trust wrongly argues that, "While revitalizing urban centers may be costly, it is still usually less expensive than building new cities—infrastructure and all—at the urban edge."[4]

"The undistorted market price of land is normally lower, not higher, on the 'edge' than it is downtown," points out Pietro Nivola, of the Brookings Institution. He adds that, "Laying in new capital investment on suburban sites may generally cost less, not more, than replacing (or 'revitalizing') the downtown's depreciated buildings, streets, sewers, and other basic installations."[5] As a result, "there is little basis for a conclusion that moving people into cities rather than scattering them in suburbs would deliver basic services less wastefully."[6] Altshuler and Gómez-Ibáñez agree that "the cost of creating an additional unit of sewage or water carrying capacity may be much higher than the unit cost of existing capacity if the old sewage or water lines must be dug up and replaced with larger ones."[7]

After surveying numerous cost-of-sprawl studies and doing some himself, Rutgers University planning professor Richard Burchell concludes that urban infill will save 20 percent over the cost of low-density development at the suburban fringe.[8] But he assumes that no new roads, schools, sewer, water, or other infrastructure will be needed to serve the higher density redevelopment. This might be true for small increases in density, but it will not be true for the huge density increases needed to halt low-density suburbanization in growing urban areas.

Even if Burchell were correct and low-density suburbanization does cost more than infill, Anthony Downs points out that "Burchell's studies do not quantify any of the benefits that millions of Americans believe they receive from sprawl—and for which they may be willing to pay notable additional costs." Burchell's estimate of the total cost of sprawl to the nation is only about $10 billion per year. Downs notes that this is "only 0.12 percent of the gross domestic product" which was $8.5 trillion in 1998. Downs believes that "these are relatively small amounts that U.S. beneficiaries of sprawl might be quite willing to pay to continue enjoying its benefits."[9] In fact, they probably already are paying most of those costs.

University of Southern California urban planning professors Peter Gordon and Harry Richardson conclude that, "The economic and resource 'efficiency' of compact development has never been adequately demonstrated."[10] Nivola asks, "if low density is the mode desired by U.S. consumers, and they are willing to pay for it, in what sense, if any, is it inefficient?"[11] If there are cases in which low-density residents are not paying all of the costs of their lifestyles, the appropriate policy is to find ways for them to be self sufficient, not to try to force them to live in high densities.

Notes

1. Real Estate Research Corporation, *The Costs of Sprawl* (Washington, DC: CEQ, 1973).
2. Helen Ladd, "Population Growth, Density and the Costs of Providing Public Services," *Urban Studies* 29(2):273–295.
3. Alan Pisarski, *Commuting in America II* (Washington, DC: Eno Transportation Foundation, 1996), p. 91.
4. "Competition for Land," *American Farmland*, vol. 17, no. 3 (Fall, 1996), p. 15.
5. Pietro S. Nivola, *Laws of the Landscape: How Policies Shape Cities in Europe and America* (Washington, DC: Brookings, 1999), p. 36.
6. Ibid, p. 37.
7. Alan Altshuler and José Gómez-Ibáñez, *Regulation for Revenue: The Political Economy of Land Use Exactions* (Washington, DC: Brookings; Cambridge, MA: Lincoln Land Institute, 1993), p. 73.
8. Robert Burchell, "The Impacts of Continued Sprawl: Growing Another Way and Its National Cost Savings," speech delivered at the Colorado Forum, August 4, 1999.
9. Anthony Downs, "Some Realities about Sprawl and Urban Decline," *Housing Policy Debate* 10 (4): 964.
10. Peter Gordon and Harry Richardson, "Are Compact Cities a Desirable Planning Goal?" *Journal of the American Planning Association* 61(1), http://www.smartgrowth.org/library/apa_pointcounterpoint/apa_sprawl.html.
11. Pietro S. Nivola, *Laws of the Landscape*, p. 35.

Part Five

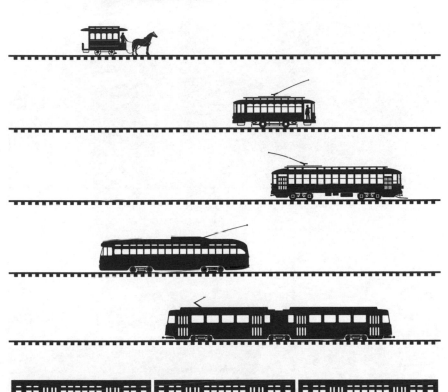

The Rail
Transit Fantasy

Portland's light rail averages only 20 miles per hour (top), *so even in stop-and-go traffic freeway drivers get to their destinations faster than on light rail.*
Feeder bus at Orenco light-rail station (bottom). *Feeder buses are lightly used because many light-rail riders drive to the station and most people don't ride the light rail anyway.*

17. The Transit Problem

As speedy and convenient as automobiles are, many people are too young, too old, or too disabled to drive, or too poor to own an auto. Unless they are chauffeured by friends or relatives or can afford to hire a driver, these people will not enjoy the mobility available to those who own and can drive autos. Such people deserve access to an efficient transit system that can take them where they need to go at a reasonable cost.

Smart growth will not provide that transit system. Smart growth's dual goals of increasing urban density and attracting motorists out of their cars lead to super-expensive rail projects that often force cash-strapped transit agencies to reduce transit services to those who really need it. Many transit officials strongly support smart growth because they want more transportation dollars diverted to their agencies and because rail transit represents an ego-boosting feather in their caps.

"Transit can and should play an important role" in America's cities, says David Luberoff of Harvard's Kennedy School of Government. "There's no reason, however, why that means relying on rail, which is basically a nineteenth-century technology, to meet the 21st century's demands."[1] What makes transportation analysts apoplectic about rail transit is not simply that it is obsolete technology, but that it is *expensive* obsolete technology. Money spent on rail construction and operation is money that cannot be used to do things that actually help both transit and auto users. Smart-growth advocates may consider this a virtue because money spent on rails might otherwise be spent on the highways they hate.

Rail transit is *high-capacity transit*, meaning that it can carry more people than conventional buses. While this is claimed to be a virtue, it is actually a drawback because America's typically low-density urban areas have little need for high-capacity transit. The few regions that have the densities to support rail transit— mainly New York—already have it. Of course, smart-growth's goal is to increase urban densities enough to support rail transit, but the increases needed for rail to truly make a difference in most urban areas are not likely to ever happen.

"The failure of U.S. transit policy has not been its inability to reverse the increase in automobile ownership and use nor to slow the suburbanization of population and employment," says UCLA planning professor Martin Wachs in *Science* magazine. "A far greater problem has been its failure to adapt transit service to the emergent conditions."[2] Since rail only makes sense in the densest areas, the "appropriate response" would have been buses, and smaller buses rather than larger ones. But buses are less politically attractive than rail because they create few local jobs and profits. Even transit systems that rely on buses have been encouraged by federal funds to buy needlessly high-capacity buses that are expensive to operate.

When urban streetcar systems were built around the turn of the twentieth century, most jobs, stores, and entertainments were downtown while housing radiated away from the downtowns along the streetcar lines. A hub-and-spoke transit system served this type of urban area very well. The automobile allowed jobs, stores, and entertainment to move to scores if not hundreds of different centers in today's urban areas. While downtown may be the largest of these centers, it is the destination for only a small share of urban trips. A hub-and-spoke transit system provides poor service to this type of urban area.

"With a pen and a local map, trace the trips you take in a typical week to work, shopping, school, to socialize or to see the doctor, for entertainment or some other recreation," suggests Gene Berthelson, a senior planner with the California Department of Transportation. Then do the same for your neighbors. "Imagine what your map would look like if you plotted all the trips for your entire neighborhood." No rail transit line will serve more than a tiny fraction of those trips.[3]

"I want to live in one place, work in a second place, and play in a third," says Joel Garreau. "If that's what you want, the very least you need technologically is a form of individual transportation that goes where you want to go when you to go. Trains just don't cut it. Trains require you to go where someone else wants you to go when someone else wants you to go."[4] Of course, to smart-growth supporters, that is rail's big advantage. But all the evidence points to the conclusion that rails won't even produce the results that smart growth promises.

Rather than redesign urban areas to serve obsolete transit systems, transit agencies should redesign their transit systems to serve modern urban areas. This means making more use of low-capacity transit, such as minibuses and vans, that may run on flexible routes rather than on fixed schedules. To be as effective as possible, transit agencies may have to give up their legal monopolies and encourage private operators to take over some or all transit services. These and other alternatives to rail transit are discussed in more detail in chapters 21 (p. 338) and 37 (p. 507).

Notes

1. David Luberoff, "What Can Transit Do?" *Governing*, November, 1999.
2. Martin Wachs, "U.S. transit subsidy policy: in need of reform," *Science*, June 30, 1989, p. 1547.
3. Gene Berthelson, "How Far Can the Trolley Take Us?" *Sacramento Bee*, March 6, 1994, p. F1.
4. Joel Garreau, Keynote Speech, *in* Metro, *Building a livable future: 1991 regional growth conference proceedings* (Portland OR: Metro, 1991).

Transit Facts

More than three hundred U.S. urban areas have transit service. But two out of three transit rides are taken in just seven regions: New York, Chicago, Los Angeles, San Francisco, Washington, Philadelphia, and Boston. Few Los Angeleans use transit, but Los Angeles makes it on the list simply because it has so many people. The other six join Honolulu and a few college towns as the only urban areas where transit has more than a 3 percent share of motorized transport. In only two other major urban areas—Seattle and New Orleans—does transit have more than a 2 percent share, and both are less than 2.5 percent.

Number of metropolitan areas tracked by the Census Bureau in 1998: 398
    Number with transit systems: 314
    Portion of all U.S. transit trips carried in the top seven transit markets: 66.5%
    Portion of transit passenger miles carried in the top seven transit markets: 69.6%

Share of urban area motorized passenger miles carried by transit in 1998:
    All U.S. urban areas: 1.8%
    New York: 9.6%
    Boston: 4.1%
    San Francisco: 4.0%
    Chicago: 3.6%
    Washington: 3.6%
    Philadelphia: 3.4%
    Los Angeles: 1.5%
    All other urban areas over 1 million people: 1.0%
    Urban areas of 200,000 to 1 million people: 0.6%
    Urban areas of 50,000 to 200,000 people: 0.4%

Per capita miles of transit use by urban area in 1998:
    All U.S. urban areas: 239
    New York: 978

Washington: 521
San Francisco: 513
Boston: 511
Chicago: 435
Philadelphia: 345
Los Angeles: 190
All other urban areas over 1 million people: 145
Urban areas of 200,000 to 1 million people: 78
Urban areas of 50,000 to 200,000 people: 57
Source: National Transit Database, table 27, for 1998 transit passenger miles; Highway Statistics 1998, table HM-72, for urban area vehicle miles (multiplied by 1.6 to get passenger miles).

Share of commuter trips carried by transit in 1990:
All U.S. urban areas: 6.8%
New York: 26.5%
Washington: 13.7%
Chicago: 13.7%
Boston: 10.7%
Philadelphia: 10.3%
San Francisco: 9.5%
Los Angeles: 4.7%
Honolulu: 9.4%
Pittsburgh: 8.0%
Iowa City: 7.9%
Baltimore: 7.6%
New Orleans: 7.1%
Seattle: 6.5%
Atlantic City: 5.6%
Portland: 5.6%
The Twin Cities: 5.4%
All other major U.S. metropolitan areas: Under 5%
All other urban areas over 1 million people: 4.2%
Source: 1990 Census

Web Tools: Transit

What is transit's share of passenger travel in your urban area? Get 1998 transit passenger miles from http://www.ntdprogram.com/ NTD/NTDData.nsf/1998+TOC/Table27/$File/T27_32.pdf. Get 1998 daily vehicle miles from http://www.fhwa.dot.gov/ohim/hs98/tables/hm72.pdf. Multiply the latter by 365 to get the annual total and by 1.6 to get passenger miles. Add transit passenger miles to auto passenger miles and divide the sum into transit passenger miles to get transit's share.

The High-Capacity-Transit Myth

Myth: One rail line can carry more people than an eight-lane freeway.

Reality: Very few rail transit lines carry as many people as even one lane of a typical urban freeway.

Rail transit is high-capacity transit. Rail advocates often say that rail lines can potentially carry as many people as an eight-lane freeway. While rail's capacity is high, New York is the only U.S. city with population densities high enough to support such a high capacity. As a result, New York City subways are the only rail transit lines in the nation that carry more people than a single lane of a typical urban freeway.

Table one shows that, among the three basic kinds of rail lines, only heavy rail comes close to achieving the productivities of a freeway lane—and then only in New York City. New York heavy and commuter rail lines are more than twice as productive as even the second highest cities. Not counting New York, the average heavy-rail line produced about 12,900 passenger miles of travel per mile, little more than half what a typical freeway lane produces.

Table One: Productivity of Freeways and Rail Transit

(Daily passenger miles per route mile of rail line or lane-mile of freeway)

	Light Rail	Commuter Rail	Heavy Rail	Freeway
Average[1]	4,620	3,766	22,043	23,724
Average[2]	4,300	2,222	12,890	23,769
Highest	8,664	6,770	38,296	37,091
Highest city	San Diego	New York	New York	Los Angeles
Second highest	7,728	3,948	15,960	30,946
Second city	St. Louis	Chicago	Washington	Chicago

1. Fifty largest urbanized areas.
2. Fifty largest areas minus the highest.

Source: Freeway data from FHwA, Highway Statistics 1998, *table HM-72; transit data from FTA,* National Transit Database 1998, *tables 19 and 27. Light-rail lines in Seattle, Memphis, and Galveston are excluded as they are mainly tourist lines.*

Light-rail productivities are a small fraction of either heavy rail or freeway lanes. The average freeway lane is nearly three times as productive as the most productive light-rail line and more than five times as productive as the average light-rail line. Commuter rail is even less productive than light rail. Outside of New York City, the average commuter rail mile produces less than a tenth as much travel as a lane-mile of urban freeway. The Detroit and Miami people movers, which are not listed in the table, average only 1,600 passenger miles per mile.

In the table, each mile of rail line is a *directional route mile*, meaning a mile of traffic in one direction. A rail line connecting two points ten miles apart provides twenty directional route miles. In general, then, cities should invest in:

- Heavy rail only if a directional route mile of heavy-rail line costs less than half as much as a mile of freeway lane;
- Light rail only if a mile of light-rail costs less than one-fifth as much as a mile of freeway lane; and
- Commuter rail only if a mile of commuter-rail costs less than one-eleventh as much as a mile of freeway lane.

In fact, most rail systems cost far more than these amounts. While building a single lane-mile of freeway costs around $5 million to $10 million (see the Expensive-Highway Myth, p. 368), the average light-rail line now being built or considered for construction in the U.S. is expected to cost around $40 to $50 million per route mile (see the Inexpensive-Rail-Transit Myth, p. 319), which is $20 to $25 million per directional route mile. Heavy rail is usually much more expensive, while commuter rail costs vary depending on the condition of the track. While freeways can sometimes cost much more in urban centers, where land costs are highest and mitigation is most needed, most urban growth is taking place in the suburbs where highway costs are lower.

Passenger miles are only one way to measure the productivity of transportation alternatives. Speed, safety, and comfort are other ways, but freeways tend to beat transit on these counts as well. This suggests that one dollar spent on freeway construction can produce as much benefit as $12 to $25 spent on light rail.

Web Tools: Rail Transit

If you live in a city with rail transit, how productive is your rail system? Table 19 from the 1998 *National Transit Database*, http://www.fta.dot.gov/ntl/database.html, has rail directional route miles. Table 27 has annual passenger miles of travel. Divide route miles into passenger miles. Divide by 365 to get daily passenger miles per route mile. Compare with the daily miles of vehicle travel per freeway lane mile in your urban area in http://www.fhwa.dot.gov/ohim/hs98/tables/hm72.wk4. Multiply vehicle miles by 1.6 to get passenger miles. You can find a summary of all these data at http://www.publicpurpose.com/ut-ot-rail&fwy98.htm.

18. Transit History

America's transit industry traces its roots to 1827, when the first urban stage coach line began in New York City.[1] The development of steam trains and horsecars in the 1830s reduced costs and made transit available to more people. By 1880, American cities had 10,000 miles of horse car lines that required over 100,000 horses that dumped a million pounds of manure on city streets each year.[2] In 1871, private entrepreneurs built the New York elevated, carrying masses of people on short trips for a nickel apiece. New York also saw the first cable car in 1868 and the first subway in 1870.

Outside of New York City, transit really boomed only after electric streetcars were fully developed around 1890. Streetcars had such tremendous cost advantages over other forms of urban transportation that, by 1910, almost every American city with more than 10,000 people had one or more streetcar lines, nearly all of which were built with private funds. Streetcars had a major effect on urban form. No longer did masses of workers need to live within walking distance of factories. Never again would a city be built like New York, with high densities of people in a central location. Instead, cities took on the shape of a seastar, with people living in the arms along the streetcar lines which all converged upon the downtown employment center. Canny real estate developers built hundreds of streetcar lines from their suburban developments to downtowns, effectively subsidizing the streetcar lines by the sale of homes. The streetcars were supplemented by interurban electric rail lines, faster and heavier than local streetcars, which connected nearby cities. Eventually, most cities saw the consolidation of all the independent streetcar and interurban lines into one or two companies.

The streetcar's dominance was short-lived. By the mid 1920s, more than half of all American households owned an automobile. U.S. transit ridership peaked at 17.3 billion trips per year in 1926, and then slowly but steadily declined until 1930. Well before the Depression, transit companies began to cut service on little-used lines, and many interurban lines simply shut down. When the Depression hit, the slow decline turned precipitous. By 1933, ridership had fallen to two-thirds of its 1926 peak.[3] While the transit industry was temporarily boosted by World War II's gasoline restrictions, after 1946 it resumed its decline.

Figure One: Auto and Transit Passenger Miles Per Year

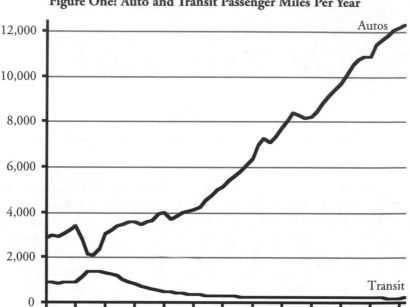

Source: APTA, Transit Fact Book, *and FHwA,* Highway Statistics. *The* Transit Fact Book *does not have passenger miles of travel for most years; this chart assumes 5 miles per unlinked trip.* Highway Statistics *also lacks passenger miles for urban areas; this chart assumes 1.6 passengers per vehicle mile. Only car and truck miles are counted, not buses.*

Figure one tells the story of twentieth-century transit by comparing auto and transit passenger miles since 1936 (the earliest year for which data are available for autos). In 1936, the average urbanite rode 900 miles by transit and went 2,800 miles by auto, giving transit a 24 percent market share of urban motorized travel. This declined to just 1.6 percent in 1997 as per-person transit travel declined to 200 miles while auto travel exceeded 12,000 miles.

The transit industry has two ways of counting riders. A transit user who rides one bus, then transfers to another bus, is counted as one *originating ride* or *linked trip*, but two *boarding rides* or *unlinked trips.* To the transit rider, a linked trip is a single trip, and the transfer from one bus to another is merely a nuisance. But the Federal Transit Administration requires transit agencies to report statistics in terms of unlinked trips, which tends to exaggerate the number of trips really taken by transit users. While the percentage varies by transit system, linked trips average about 80 percent of unlinked trips.[4] Because linked-trip data are not available, the ridership figures in this book are unlinked trips and are therefore roughly 25 percent higher than the true number of transit trips. This book also uses passenger miles, which are a better measure of transit productivity than unlinked trips.

Despite declining ridership, the U.S. transit industry was mainly privately owned and covered its own costs through 1964. But in that year, Congress passed the first federal urban transit legislation. The law encouraged cities to buy the privately owned transit systems and promised federal funding for capital improvements such as new buses. By 1970, nearly all urban transit was public—and nearly all of it was subsidized, both for capital and operating costs. Despite the new buses and subsidies, transit ridership continued to decline through the 1960s and early 1970s. In 1920, 54 million urban Americans took an average of 287 transit trips per year. By 1972, more than 150 million urban and suburban Americans rode transit an average of just 43 times a year. Total ridership had fallen from the 1926 peak of 17.6 billion trips to 6.6 billion trips per year.

The gasoline crisis reversed this trend: In 1973, ridership rose for the first time since 1946. It continued to rise, slowly, until it reached 8.9 billion annual rides in 1989, a 36-percent increase over 1972. But in terms of rides per capita, transit did little better than hold its own: The average U.S. urbanite took 48 transit rides in 1989, just 11 percent more than in 1972. By comparison, in the same time period per capita urban motor vehicle travel grew by 54 percent.

To support this meager transit ridership, federal, state, and local governments poured increasing subsidies into transit systems. Annual transit subsidies averaged $5.5 billion during the 1970s,[5] $13.6 billion in the 1980s. and $19.2 billion in the 1990s (all in 1999 dollars).[6] The Clinton-Gore administration wants to increase federal transit subsidies by at least another 10 percent in the 2000s.

Yet these subsidies have produced minimal results. In fact, transit ridership fell from 1989 to 1995. While it has increased since then, transit analyst Wendell Cox estimates that much of the increase is attributable to the New York City transit system's 1997 policy of allowing free transfers between subways and buses. Cox estimates this increased unlinked trips by 7 percent but linked trips by only 1.6 percent.[7] Even at the higher number, the numbers of rides per urban resident remained below the 1972 level.

The American Public Transportation Association claims that 1999 ridership was greater than any year since 1960.[8] Resurgence or not, public transit has become one the most inefficient industries in the nation, thanks in large part to its heavy subsidies. In terms of vehicle hours of service per dollar of input, transit productivity declined by 40 percent between 1964 and 1985. Yet privately owned bus companies increased their productivity by 8 percent in the same period.[9] In terms of passenger miles or riders per dollar, transit is even worse.

One problem is that the "subsidy money encouraged government meddling in transit operations, asking transit systems to undertake a variety of activities unrelated to their traditional goals," says University of California economist Charles Lave. "The subsidies sent the wrong signals to management and labor," adds Lave. "Management interpreted the message to mean: efficiency was no longer primary; rather, it was more important to expand passenger-demand and to provide social services. . . . Labor interpreted the message to mean: management now has a Sugar Daddy who can pay for improvements in wages and working conditions."[10]

One of the reasons for the high labor costs is an agreement made when Congress first began subsidizing transit that public transit agencies would hire only union labor. In most cities and states, labor unions and taxi drivers have successfully lobbied for legislation giving the transit agencies monopolies on mass transit. Any auto or van owner who agrees to give people rides in exchange for money risks violating these laws. Thus, the transit agencies have no competition and no reason to provide the most efficient transit.

One of the fastest rising costs in the early 1990s was the cost of providing transit for disabled passengers. The Americans with Disabilities Act required agencies to provide special buses for these riders. The cost per ride of these services is typically six-and-one-half times as great as the cost per ride for ordinary bus service.[11] This law, says Brookings Institution analyst Pietro Nivola, "added major financial obligations to our teetering transit systems."[12] Other federal mandates, including "buy America" requirements and drug testing, also boost transit costs. Paying for these mandates may have forced transit agencies to cut service or at least to not grow it as fast as they otherwise might.

While the above problems are important, transit also suffers from an ideological problem. It is not enough to provide transit to those who need it; transit agencies also feel a need to provide transit to those who don't need it, namely people who drive autos. The desire to get people out of their automobiles has led transit agencies to neglect their core riders, namely people who are too young or too old to drive or too poor to afford autos. As Lave says, "routes were extended into inherently unprofitable areas," such as auto-rich middle-class suburbs.[13] Between 1989 and 1993, transit agencies in central New York, Chicago, Los Angeles, and San Francisco all cut their transit services. But suburban transit agencies in the same urban areas all increased their transit services. The result was a decrease in urban riders and an increase in suburban ones. But the gains did not equal losses, and overall ridership in these urban areas declined.[14]

The neglect of core riders in an effort to reduce auto driving is most visible in the cities that built rail transit in the past twenty years. Rail transit is often promoted as the way for transit to gain middle-class riders. "There's a social stigma attached to buses," claims Paul Weyrich of the Free Congress Research and Education Foundation, and he urges cities to build rail transit to attract middle- and upper-middle class riders.[15] But the expense of building rail transit for the middle class often meant cutting bus transit for the poor who really depend on transit. Six of the ten cities that built rail transit since 1980 experienced an overall decline in ridership by 1995.[16] In Los Angeles, a bus-rider's union composed of minority groups and backed by the NAACP filed a racial discrimination lawsuit against the transit agency for cutting their bus services in order to build a rail line into white neighborhoods.[17]

The 1990 census revealed that, in most American cities, more people walk and bicycle to work than take transit. For non-commuter traffic, transit is even less important. Transit is important for those who need it, but it remains insignificant as a means of reducing congestion or other urban problems.

Notes

1. American Public Transportation Association, *Transit Fact Book 1999*, table 94, "Milestones in U.S. Transit History."
2. Mark Mills, "Transportation Fuels—Electricity," in *Encyclopedia of Energy Technology and the Environment* (New York, NY: John Wiley, 1995), p. 2698.
3. American Public Transit Association, *Transit Factbook* (Washington, DC: APTA, various years).
4. Wendell Cox, "US Urban Public Transport Ridership from 1900," http://www.publicpurpose.com/ut-us1900.htm.
5. Wendell Cox, "US Public Transport Subsidies from 1960," http://www.publicpurpose.com/ut-ussby.htm
6. APTA, *Transit Fact Book 1999*, tables 14, 18, and 25.
7. Wendell Cox, "US Urban Public Transport Annual Ridership (5 Modes) & Ridership per Capita: From 1970," http://www.publicpurpose.com/ut-95pc5.htm.
8. APTA, "Public Transportation Ridership Continues to Soar," http://www.apta.com/news/releases/rides1q2000.htm.
9. Charles Lave, "It Wasn't Supposed to Turn out Like This: Federal Subsidies and Declining Transit Productivity," *Access* 5 (Fall, 1994), p. 21.
10. Ibid, p. 25.
11. Brian Taylor and William McCullough, "Lost Riders," *Access* 13 (Fall, 1998), p. 27.
12. Pietro Nivola, *Fit for Fat City: A "Lite" Menu of European Policies to Improve Our Urban Form*, Brookings Institution Policy Brief #44, January 1999, http://www.brook.edu/comm/policybriefs/pb044/pb44.htm.
13. Lave, "It Wasn't Supposed to Turn out Like This," p. 25.
14. Stacy Davis, *Transportation Energy Data Book Edition 19* (Oak Ridge, TN: Department of Energy, 1999), table 2-12.
15. Paul Weyrich, presentation at the Minneapolis community forum on light rail, February 3, 2000.
16. Peter Gordon, "Does Transit Really Work? Thoughts on the Weyrich /Lind 'Conservative Reappraisal,'" Reason Public Policy Institute,
17. Consent decree in Labor/Community Strategy Center, et al. v. Los Angeles MTA, 10-26-96, available at http://www.ldfla.org/decree.html.

NEW YORK CASE STUDY

The Transit-Rider's Dream

T he United States has two kinds of urban areas: New York and everywhere else. In a nation where urban transit is practically inconsequential, New York is the transit king. Nearly a third of all U.S. transit rides and more than 60 percent of all rail transit rides take place in the New York urban area. More than a quarter of New York-area commuters reported in the 1990 census that they rode transit to work—almost twice the percentage of the next highest urban area.

Why does transit work in New York when it works practically nowhere else in the America? New York is the only U.S. urban area that has Manhattan, a 28-square-mile island jammed with 1.5 million people at a population density greater than 52,000 people per square mile. Though a few neighborhoods in Brooklyn and the Bronx have higher densities, nowhere in the U.S. as large as Manhattan has anywhere near that density. But it is the employment density, not the population density, that makes Manhattan really special, since the island has at least 20 percent more jobs than residents. This means that most of the workers must come from off the island, and transit is a good way for them to get there.

Table One: The New York Urbanized Area

	1950	1990	1998
Population (thousands)	12,342	16,044	16,407
Land area square miles	1,255	2,966	3,962
Density	9,830	5,400	4,140

Source: Census Bureau for 1950 and 1990, FHwA, Highway Statistics 1998 for 1998. FHwA land area data are not exactly comparable with Census Bureau data since they use slightly different criteria for determining urbanized area boundaries.

New York is also the only U.S. urban area with numerous suburbs that are denser than most city centers. Brooklyn, the Bronx, and Queens all have densities well over 10,000 people per square mile, as do Newark, Jersey City, Yonkers, and at least a half dozen other suburbs that each house more than 50,000 people. These high-density residential areas combined with the extremely high density

work center gave rail a 22.5 percent share of 1990 commuter traffic and nearly an
8 percent share of all motorized passenger miles.

Table Two: The City of New York

	1950	1990	1998
Population (thousands)	7,892	7,323	7,420
Land area square miles	315	309	309
Density	25,046	23,700	24,000

Source: Census Bureau. Land area and density for 1998 are estimated.

San Francisco, Boston, Philadelphia, Washington, and Chicago have high-density employment centers, but few high-density suburbs, so rail transit in these
cities carries no more than 10 percent of commuters and less than 3 percent of all
motorized travel. Los Angeles has several large high-density suburbs, including
East Los Angeles, Santa Ana, and Bellflower. But it has no center of concentrated
employment: Downtown Los Angeles contains less than 4 percent of the region's
jobs. As a result, rail transit in Los Angeles has proven practically useless. Most
other urban areas have neither high-density employment centers or high-density
suburbs, so rail transit in all other U.S. cities carries less than 2 percent of commuters and less than 0.5 percent of motorized travel.

Figure One: New York Area Densities
(people per square mile)

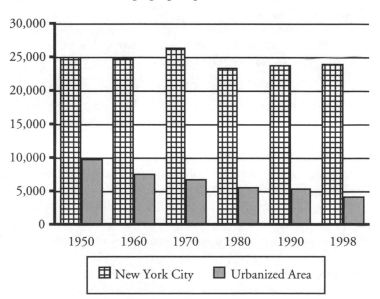

A city center with very high job densities surrounded by suburbs many of which are very dense themselves turns out to be an optimal environment for transit, especially rail transit: About three out of four New York-area transit trips are by rail. Similar conditions are found in many European cities. But they aren't found in other American cities, so it makes no sense to build new rail transit lines in this country.

The New York urban area is not all as dense as Brooklyn. The Census Bureau said that the region's average 1990 density was only 5,400 people per square mile. As figure one shows, the region's density has steadily declined for decades. The Federal Highway Administration, whose criteria is not exactly the same as the Census Bureau's, says that the region's density was only 4,100 per square mile in 1998. Manhattan's density declined steadily from its peak of 82,000 people per square mile in 1910 to 50,000 people per square mile in 1980.[1] It had increased slightly since then, but is not likely to ever again reach 80,000.

Table Three: New York-Area Transportation

Miles of freeway per million people	70
Annual miles driven per capita	5,731
Passenger miles per capita	9,170
Annual transit miles per capita	978
Annual transit trips per capita	173
Auto commuters	65.5%
Transit commuters	26.5%
Walk/cycle commuters	8.0%

Source: FHwA, Highway Statistics 1998, FTA, Transit Profiles 1998, 1990 Census. All data from 1998 except commuting data, which are from 1990. Passenger miles per capita are 1.6 times miles driven per capita.

The New York area mainly uses heavy rail and commuter rail, not light rail. But New Jersey Transit recently opened the first leg of a planned 20.5-mile light-rail line extending from the Hudson River waterfront, across from the World Trade Center, through Jersey City to Bayonne. New Jersey Transit hoped to save money by having a private company both build and operate the line. But the first 9.6-mile segment cost more than $103 million per mile, which is far greater than average. The total project will cost $2.1 billion, making it the most expensive public works project in New Jersey history.[2] The cost of every new transit ride is expected to be more than $22, suggesting that buses would have been far less expensive.

The line meets heavy-rail trains from Manhattan and serves the most densely populated region of New Jersey. So planners confidently predicted that New Jersey commuters would abandon their autos and make their line "the heaviest traveled light rail system in the nation."[3] Immediately after opening, they expected to attract 14,400 riders per day. As it turned out, after six weeks ridership was still under 4,200 riders per day.[4] Since the light-rail cars average just 18 miles per hour, it is not surprising that they have attracted few people out of their automobiles. Planners' projections of eventually attracting 100,000 riders per day are wildly optimistic. While it is clear to objective observers that light rail makes no sense even in the densest communities, New Jersey Transit naturally warns that it is "too early to pass judgment" on the line and are planning to build more miles of expensive light rail in both the northern and southern parts of the state.[5]

New York City, and especially Manhattan, is crammed full of the four- to five-story, mixed-use buildings that smart-growth planners love. Manhattan was the inspiration for Jane Jacobs' "lively neighborhoods" that planners now describe as "pedestrian friendly." So planners must be disappointed to find that walking and cycling play a fairly small role in New York life. According to the 1990 census, just 8.1 percent of New York-area commuters get to work on foot or bicycle. This is only a little higher than the national average of 5.1 percent. In New York City itself, the share is 11.3 percent, which is not particularly high. Though Boston's population density is less than half of New York's, 15 percent of Boston commuters say they walk or cycle to work. The cities with really high levels of walking and cycling tend to be college towns such as Cambridge and Berkeley.

New York is living proof that smart-growth policies will fail to significantly alter American travel habits. New York has the highest level of transit ridership in the nation, but only because New York has more than a million jobs concentrated in a small area. Smart-growth policies of maintaining a jobs-housing balance among towns and neighborhoods would prevent this from ever happening in other urban areas. New York also shows that mid-rise, pedestrian-friendly neighborhoods favored by smart-growth planners will not significantly increase walking and cycling.

Notes

1. Campbell Gibson, *Population of the 100 Largest Cities and Other Urban Places in the United States: 1790 to 1990* (Washington, DC: Census Bureau, 1998), http://www.census.gov/population/www/documentation/twps0027.html.
2. Federal Transit Administration, *Annual Report on New Starts—Proposed Allocation of Funds for Fiscal Year 2001* (Washington, DC: FTA, 2000), http://www.fta.dot.gov/library/policy/ns/ns2000/2000nsr.htm#_Toc477146663, http://www.fta.dot.gov/library/policy/ns/ns2000/2000nsr.htm#_Toc477146682.
3. Hudson Transportation Management Association, "Light Rail Background Information," http://www.hudsontma.org/lightrail.htm.
4. Amy Westfeldt, "Light rail ridership less than expected but growing slowly," *Bergen Record*, June 1, 2000, http://www.bergen.com/region/literail200006016.htm.
5. Tri-State Transportation Commission, "Hudson-Bergen Light Rail Reality Check?" *Mobilizing the Region*, #270, http://www.tstc.org/bulletin/20000522/mtr27005.htm.

The Roger-Rabbit Myth

Myth: A conspiracy of auto, oil, and tire companies demolished U.S. streetcar systems in order to force people to drive automobiles.

Reality: Buses' lower costs and greater flexibility led almost every streetcar system in the country to replace streetcars with buses.

An oft-repeated transit myth is that General Motors bought and scrapped supposedly efficient and popular streetcar lines around the country so that people would have to buy autos and drive. "The automakers have a history of mercenary acts, the most notorious of which was portrayed in the 1988 film, *Who Framed Roger Rabbit?*" says Andres Duany.[1] James Kunstler, who opens his book, *The Geography of Nowhere*, by quoting from *Roger Rabbit*, describes the General Motors history as "a systematic campaign to put streetcar lines out of business all over America."[2]

The reality is very different. In the 1930s and 1940s, streetcar companies all over the nation recognized that buses were less expensive to purchase and more flexible to operate than streetcars. Rather than build streetcar lines to new suburbs, they purchased buses. As bus operating costs declined, transit companies also began replacing worn-out streetcar lines with buses.

General Motors, Firestone Tire, and Chevron Oil saw a market opportunity, so they created the National City Lines, a company that took over streetcar companies that were buying buses to make sure that they purchased buses, tires, and fuel from GM, Firestone, and Chevron. This is called "vertical integration" and is not much different from the company that sells you telephone service also trying to sell you a telephone.

Vertical integration, however, can be a problem when it runs afoul of antitrust laws. General Motors had a near monopoly in the market for buses. The federal government brought an antitrust lawsuit against the company for trying to maintain this monopoly by not letting other manufacturers sell buses to National City Lines. While the courts concluded that it was legal for General Motors to own transit companies, the company was convicted and fined $5,000 for not letting those companies accept bids from other bus manufacturers. No one at the time accused GM of trying to destroy transit systems, only of trying to make money from the natural transition from streetcars to buses. As it turned out, all but four or five of the hundreds of transit lines that were *not* purchased by National City Lines also converted their streetcars to buses, a conversion motivated by buses' many advantages over streetcars.

One of the largest of the roughly one hundred transit lines that National City Lines bought was the Los Angeles Railway. National City did *not*, however, buy the Pacific Electric line, which ran the Los Angeles red cars featured in *Roger Rabbit*. Both Pacific Electric and Los Angeles Railway were pioneer bus operators, and they began converting rail to bus lines as early as 1923, two decades before National City purchased the Los Angeles Railway. The last streetcar lines in Los Angeles were not torn out by National City or Pacific Electric but by the Los Angeles Metropolitan Transit Authority, the public agency that bought Pacific Electric and the Los Angeles Railway in the 1950s. Thus, it was a public agency, not a General Motors conspiracy, that finally converted Los Angeles streetcars to buses.[3]

Years later a congressional staff member named Bradford Snell resurrected the General Motors antitrust case and claimed that General Motors' true goal was to drive transit companies out of business so that transit riders would be forced to buy automobiles. "The noisy, foul-smelling buses turned earlier patrons of the high-speed rail systems away from public transit, and, in effect, sold millions of private automobiles," claimed Snell.[4] Snell's charges have been endlessly repeated by automobile opponents ever since. "General Motors' ultimate goal was to replace public transportation with private transportation, meaning the car," says Kunstler.[5]

In fact, says Sy Adler, an associate professor of urban studies at Portland State University, "everything Bradford Snell wrote. . . about transit in Los Angeles was wrong."[6] "Buses were clearly a better way to go and would have taken over with or without GM,"[7] says University of Arizona transportation researcher Sandra Rosenbloom. *Who Framed Roger Rabbit?* was a wonderful movie, but it was, after all, largely a cartoon and should not be taken literally. Yet the movie has been credited with helping to convince Congress to pass the Intermodal Surface Transportation Efficiency Act in 1991, which increased federal spending on transit at the expense of highways.[8]

In a detailed analysis of Snell's claims, Hawaiian transportation expert Cliff Slater observes that, far from driving people away from transit, buses were welcomed by transit riders because buses were faster, safer, more comfortable, and could go places the rails didn't go. Where Snell claims that the 1936 replacement of many New York streetcars with buses by a GM affiliate was "the turning point in the electric railway industry," Slater notes that the buses led to a 62-percent increase in ridership. Nationwide streetcar ridership peaked in 1920, but bus-plus-streetcar ridership continued to grow until 1926. "Thus," says Slater, "it was the bus rather than the family automobile that caused the initial decline in street-car ridership." If anything, says Slater, the conversion of streetcars to buses was delayed by government regulators, who set fares based on a fair return on assets. Since streetcar systems required higher assets than buses, many companies retained streetcars longer than made financial sense in the hope that regulators would let them charge higher fares.[9]

Notes

1. Andres Duany, Elizabeth Plater-Zyberk, and Jeff Speck, *Suburban Nation: The Rise of Sprawl and the Decline of the American Dream* (New York, NY: North Point Press, 2000), p. 8n.
2. James Howard Kunstler, *The Geography of Nowhere: The Rise and Decline of America's Man-Made Landscape* (New York, NY: Simon & Schuster, 1993), p. 91.
3. Cliff Slater, "General Motors and the Demise of Streetcars," *Transportation Quarterly* 51(3, Summer 1997): 45–66, http://www.lava.net/cslater/TQ.HTM.
4. Bradford C. Snell, "American Ground Transport, A Proposal for Restructuring the Automobile, Truck, Bus, and Rail Industries," Part 4A, Appendix to Part 4, Hearings before the Subcommittee on Antitrust and Monopoly of the Committee on the Judiciary, United States Senate, A-1–A-103, 1974.
5. Kunstler, *The Geography of Nowhere*, p. 92.
6. Quoted in James A. Dunn, Jr., *Driving Forces: The Automobile, Its Enemies, and the Politics of Mobility* (Washington, DC: Brookings Institution, 1998), p. 10.
7. Quoted in "Divided Highways: The Interstates and the Transformation of American Life," Florentine Films, 1997, http://www.pbs.org/weta/dividedhighways/TRANSCRIPT.html.
8. Martha J. Bianco, *Kennedy, 60 Minutes, and Roger Rabbit: Understanding Conspiracy-Theory Explanations of the Decline of Urban Mass Transit*, Portland State University Center for Urban Studies Discussion Paper 98-11, November, 1998, http://www.upa.pdx.edu/CUS/PUBS/PDFs/DP98-11.pdf.
9. Cliff Slater, "General Motors and the Demise of Streetcars."

The Nostalgia Myth

Myth: Turn-of-the-century transit systems offered Americans greater mobility and livability than the transit-and-highway systems of today.

Reality: No transit system could possibly produce the mobility and other benefits provided by the automobile.

The Nostalgia Myth claims that Americans lived in an urban paradise, able to easily and cheaply go on streetcars to anywhere they wanted, before the automobile clogged up our streets. In fact, the average American in 1900 traveled less than 2,000 miles per year, nearly all of which was within 50 miles of home. Today, the average American travels close to 18,000 miles per year, nearly half of which is more than 50 miles from home.[1] More than 80 percent of both intercity and intracity travel today is by automobile and nearly half the remainder is by air. This means that our non-auto, non-air travel is little more than the 2,000 miles per year that the average American traveled in 1900.

Imagine that all of your travel today consists solely of the travel you do *not counting* travel by autos or air. That is about the amount of travel that Americans did in 1900. Clearly, autos have dramatically increased American mobility.

People nostalgic for pre-automotive American cities romanticize the dense residential areas, mixtures of residences and commercial uses, and convenience of streetcars and other early transit. These sentiments were not shared by residents of the time. Turn-of-the-century urban critics worried that high residential densities were unhealthy and provoked crime; that mixtures of commercial and industrial uses into residential areas reduced property values; and that early transit systems were inadequate, inconvenient, and too expensive for many people to use.

Urban mobility has given people much more freedom of choice, greater access to employers, retailers, and other businesses, and more opportunities to visit friends and participate in cultural and recreational activities. Employers, too, have access to a much larger labor pool, giving them the opportunity to improve their productivity, while retailers provide greater variety in response to a much larger consumer market.

Mobility has particularly transformed retailing. Americans take for granted the convenience of the supermarket, something that did not exist before autos were ubiquitous. Because supermarkets serve large numbers of people, they can offer customers more variety at lower prices than the corner grocery stores that preceded them. A typical American grocery store in 1912 sold just 300 different products.[2] Today's supermarkets typically sell 25,000 products, and some hypermarkets carry 100,000 to 200,000 or more products. Even if you personally do not drive, the supermarket you shop at is there only because most other people do drive.

More recent retail phenomena, such as club warehouses and category killers—stores such as Toys-R-Us and Circuit City—also depend on the automobile. Individual club warehouse stores typically serve regions with populations of 200,000 people or more. Automobility is essential for people to have the variety provided by the category killers and the price advantages provided by the club warehouses.

Life is more than working and shopping, of course, and automobiles are essential for many forms of recreation that Americans take for granted today. Many sports, hobbies, and entertainment activities owe their existence, or at least their variety and widespread availability, to the automobile. The automobile has enhanced almost everything we do—working, shopping, eating, recreating—and no transit system could possibly replace cars without seriously degrading our mobility and quality of life.

Notes

1. Bureau of Transportation Statistics, *National Transportation Statistics 1997* (Washington, DC: BTS, 1997), table 1-7.
2. William I. Walsh, *The Rise and Decline of the Great Atlantic & Pacific Tea Company* (Secaucus, NJ: Stuart, 1986), p. 29.

19. Smart Growth and Transit

Instead of reinventing transit to serve twenty-first century cities, the smart-growth solution is to pretend the twentieth century never happened and to rebuild American cities to fit nineteenth-century transit. This turns out to mean rebuilding urban areas to primarily serve the 5 to 10 percent of people who walk or ride transit instead of the 90 percent of people who use cars. Smart growth calls for:

- Building high-cost rail lines along major corridors radiating from central city downtowns;
- Promoting high-density redevelopment of neighborhoods along those rail corridors;
- Locating new jobs either downtown or in various urban centers on rail or other transit corridors; and
- Discouraging or forbidding new low-density development that conventional transit does not easily serve.

Smart-growth advocates say they support rail transit because it attracts riders who would not take a bus; it gives people more transportation choices; and it promotes high-density neighborhood redevelopment. In fact, the real reasons why rail is such an important part of smart growth are more insidious:

- Because rail is far more expensive than buses, it becomes an important source of federal pork barrel and thus attracts support from many who many not care about smart growth's other goals.
- Highways are also pork barrel. But highways are neither popular nor particularly needed in central cities; instead, they are both needed and often welcomed in the suburbs. Central city officials, who are typically the most powerful elected officials in a region, thus prefer rail pork over highway pork, because their cities, not the suburbs, will get most of it.
- Rail's expense also gains the support of the contractors who will design and build the rail lines, the banks who will finance it, and the electric companies whose electricity will power it. One study notes that Los Angeles rail transit projects led to more lobbying activity than the entire California state government. Rail transit's designers are also often the same consultants who make

"wildly improbable forecasts" to support rail construction.[1]

• Once the rail lines are built, they become an excuse to rezone existing neighborhoods to higher densities. Residents who object are told that the rezoning is needed to promote rail ridership.

• The high expense of rail construction diverts funds that might otherwise go to highway construction into mass transit. This discourages new roads and promotes congestion—which smart-growth advocates hope will encourage people to live in higher densities.

Rail transit turns out to be highly successful at diverting federal funds away from highways and into transit and away from the suburbs and into the central cities. Unless supported by further subsidies to developers, rail transit has not been notably successful at promoting neighborhood redevelopment. Meanwhile, rail transit has been remarkably unsuccessful at reducing congestion or attracting many people out of their automobiles.

Notes

1. Peter Gordon and Harry Richardson, "Are Compact Cities a Desirable Planning Goal?" *Journal of the American Planning Association* 61(1), http://www.smartgrowth.org/library/apa_pointcounterpoint/apa_sprawl.html.

Transit Finance Facts

Capital subsidies to transit in 1998: $7.1 billion
  Operating subsidies to transit: $11.2 billion
  Total transit trips: 8.7 billion
  Subsidy per trip: $2.10
  Total transit passenger miles: 44.6 billion
  Subsidy per passenger mile: 41¢
  Source: APTA, *Transit Factbook 2000*.

As a rule of thumb, $1 spent on buses or new highway capacity has as much effect on reducing congestion as $6 to $50 spent on rail transit.

 ## Web Tools: Transit Finance

How much does your urban area spend on rail or bus transit? How much of the cost is recovered by fares? You can answer such questions using the National Transit Database, http://www.fta.dot.gov/ntl/database.html. For 1998:

- Operating expenses by mode are in http://www.ntdprogram.com/NTD/NTDData.nsf/1998+TOC/Table11/$File/T11_32.pdf.
- Passenger fares are in http://www.ntdprogram.com/NTD/NTDData.nsf/1998+TOC/Table-1/$File/T01_32.pdf. Fares are not broken down by mode.
- Capital expenses in 1998 by mode are in http://www.ntdprogram.com/NTD/NTDData.nsf/1998+TOC/Table10/$File/T10_32.pdf.
- To calculate cost per trip or passenger mile, get trips and miles from http://www.ntdprogram.com/NTD/NTDData.nsf/1998+TOC/Table27/$File/T27_32.pdf. Keep in mind that these are *unlinked trips*, meaning that someone who transfers from one bus to another gets counted as two trips.

The Balanced Transportation Myth

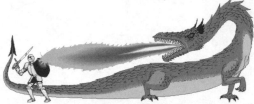

Myth: Transportation subsidies are unfairly biased towards autos and highways, so we must increase transit funding to provide balanced transportation.

Reality: Since at least 1975, transit subsidies have been tens to hundreds of times greater than highway subsidies, partly because highway user fees have been diverted to subsidize transit.

The Balanced-Transportation Myth may have been valid in 1962, when the U.S. transit industry was still earning a profit[1] while highway subsidies amounted to around $7 billion per year[2] (in 1998 dollars). But this imbalance was soon redressed by federal, state, and local subsidies to transit. In 1960, 95 percent of all transit systems were privately owned.[3] But during the 1960s, the federal government encouraged states and cities to purchase most local transit companies. By 1970, three out of four transit riders rode government-owned buses or railcars.[4] As government took over transit, it provided increasing levels of operating assistance and capital funding.

By 1975, taxpayers were paying half the costs of transit operations and capital improvements, or more than $4 billion per year.[5] While highway subsidies had increased to $14 billion per year,[6] subsidies per passenger mile were much greater for transit than highways. Highway subsidies were about two-thirds of a penny per passenger mile in 1962.[7] The total subsidy doubled by 1975, but passenger miles also doubled, so the subsidy remained about the same. Meanwhile, transit subsidies had increased from nearly zero in 1962 to more than 12 cents per passenger mile in 1975.[8] In fact, they were probably much greater than 12 cents per mile, but complete information on capital subsidies to transit is not available for years before 1984. At the very least, 1975 transit subsidies per passenger mile were sixteen times greater than highway subsidies.

Since 1975, the disparity has grown. Starting in the early 1980s, Congress was persuaded by the Balanced-Transportation Myth to begin diverting highway user fees to transit. These diversions balanced some of the local subsidies to highways so that overall highway subsidies declined.[9] Since 1987, total transit subsidies have been greater than total highway subsidies even though highways produce a hundred times more passenger miles than transit.[10] Highways also produce billions of ton miles of freight transport, so counting all highway costs against autos overestimates any subsidies.

In 1993, Congress began diverting more gas taxes to "deficit reduction." Although this stopped in 1999, during the mid-1990s transit subsidies per passenger mile were thousands of times greater than subsidies to highways. Highway user fees actually exceeded highway expenses in 1994 (figure one). Over the past thirty years, highway subsidies averaged less than a half cent per mile[11] while transit subsidies averaged more than thirty cents per mile (figure two).[12]

Far from being unfairly subsidized, highways are one of the most successful government programs ever. They provide trillions of passenger miles of transportation and billions of ton-miles of freight per year. Yet highways have cost taxpayers only about a half penny per passenger mile—falling to less than a tenth of a penny per mile in the past few years. At least since 1975, transit subsidies per passenger mile have been tens to hundreds of times greater than highway subsidies.

Figures One and Two: Transit and Highway Subsidies

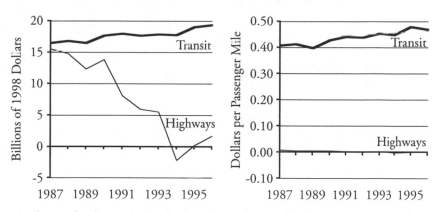

In the past decade, transit subsidies have increased to nearly $20 billion per year, while highway subsidies have fallen to near-zero—and were below zero in 1994—mainly because Congress diverted so many federal highway user fees to mass transit and other federal programs (figure one). The disparity in subsidy per passenger mile is even greater, with transit subsidies averaging 45¢ per mile while highway subsidies average a half cent per mile and are barely visible on the graph. Source: Highway data from FWhA, Highway Statistics 1996, 1997, 1998, and Highway Statistics Summary to 1995 (Washington, DC: FWhA, 1997). Transit data from APTA, Transit Fact Book 1998 (Washington, DC: APTA, 1998).

Notes

1. American Transit Association, *Transit Factbook 1966* (Washington, DC: APTA, 1966), table 1.
2. Federal Highway Administration, *Highway Statistics Summary to 1995* (Washington, DC: DOT, 1997), table HF-210.
3. American Public Transit Association, *Transit Factbook 1981* (Washington, DC: APTA, 1981), table 3.
4. Ibid.
5. Ibid, tables 5, 6, 19. All historic dollars converted to 1998 dollars using GNP price deflators published by the Department of Commerce.
6. FHwA *Highway Statistics Summary to 1995*, table HF-210.
7. Ibid, table VM-201. Vehicle miles converted to passenger miles by multiplying by 1.6.
8. APTA, *Transit Factbook 1981*, table 1.
9. Ibid, table HF-10 and U.S. DOT, *Highway Statistics Summary to 1995*, table HF-210.
10. FHwA, *Highway Statistics Summary to 1995*, table HF-210.
11. Federal Highway Administration, *Highway Statistics 1996* (Washington, DC: DOT, 1997), tables HF-10 and VM-2.
12. APTA, *Transit Factbook 1998*, tables 18, 21, 34.

The Funding Myth

Myth: More money for transit will boost ridership. We need to transfer highway dollars to transit and increase state and local taxes for transit agencies.

Reality: There has been no relation between transit funding and transit ridership. Despite huge increases in transit funding over the past two decades, ridership is stagnant.

A comparison of transit ridership with funding levels suggests that there is little relation between the two. Although transit received $180 billion in government funds in the past ten years—considerably more than in the previous decade—ridership declined from 1989 to 1995.[1] Between 1989 and 1995, transit funding increased by 15 percent but ridership fell by 13 percent.[2] Transit funding declined from 1995 to 1998, yet ridership increased.

This does not mean that less funding will increase ridership. But it does suggest that *how* transit agencies spend their dollars may be more important than *how many* dollars they spend. Much transit spending has been highly ineffective, including the billions of dollars spent on rail projects that carry few new riders.

In the 1970s, the transit agency for Portland, Oregon, attracted people out of their cars and onto transit at a cost of about $1 per new weekday ride.[3] The agency relied on inexpensive devices such as park-and-ride stations, increased bus frequencies, and free bus service in the downtown area. These inexpensive actions increased Portland transit's share of commuter traffic by 43 percent. Then, in the 1980s, Portland began building an expensive light-rail system. The agency estimates that attracting new riders to light rail will cost $9 to $22 per ride. To pay for these lines, the agency has reduced frequencies on some of its most popular bus routes in the urban core. Overall transit ridership declined during the 1980s.[4] While ridership has since recovered, transit's market share of commuter trips fell by 36 percent.

Like Portland, Sacramento relied on inexpensive service improvements to score a 58 percent increase in transit's share of commuter traffic in the 1970s. Then it built a light-rail line which opened in 1987. The result was a 33 percent decrease in market share in the 1980s.[5] In 1994, a California state transportation planner noted that,

> We have spent over $200 million on a light rail system and lost more than a
> million passengers a year. Reports on passenger mileage suggest that virtually
> all of the ridership on light rail has been drawn from the pre-existing bus
> system. There's no evidence that the trolleys have taken any vehicles off those
> highways.[6]

Similar stories can be told about rail projects in San Diego, Los Angeles, and
elsewhere. Even San Francisco's Bay Area Rapid Transit and Washington's Metro
systems had insignificant effects on transit's market share of commuters.

Figure One: Transit Subsidies and Ridership

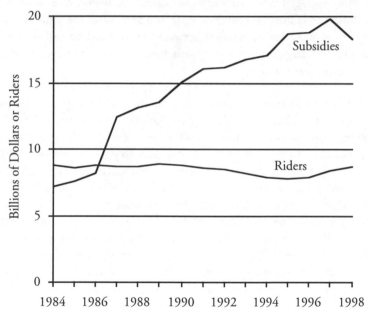

Source: American Public Transit Association, Transit Fact Book for 1998 *and* 1984 *(Washington, DC: APTA, 1984, 1998).*

Notes

1. American Public Transit Association, *Transit Factbook 1998* (Washington, DC: APTA, 1998), tables 18, 21, 32.
2. Ibid.
3. Don Pickrell, *Urban Rail Transit Projects: Forecast vs. Actual Ridership and Costs* (Cambridge, MA: US DOT, 1989), p. 60.
4. Tri-Met, "Ridership," internal memoranda on file at Tri-Met offices in Portland, Oregon.
5. Pickrell, *Urban Rail Transit Projects*, p. 58.
6. Gene Berthelson, "How Far Can the Trolley Take Us?" *Sacramento Bee*, March 6, 1994, p. F1.

The Morality Myth

Myth: Public transit is morally superior to private automobiles.

Reality: Most of transit's supposed advantages over the automobile are based on aesthetic judgments not shared by most Americans.

Since traditional, monopolistic transit cannot compete against the convenience and efficiency of the automobile, the Morality Myth turns to moral and emotional arguments to justify many transit policies. This moral argument is clear in the terms its advocates use to compare autos and modern cities with transit and New Urban areas:

- Automobiles are "isolating" and "depersonalizing," while those who build cars and roads are part of an "evil empire";[1]
- Transit promotes "community" and "public life";[2]
- Transit is cleaner and more energy efficient than autos;
- Driving causes congestion while transit relieves congestion;
- Autos have made cities and, especially, suburbs "monotonous," "placeless," and "scaleless."[3]
- Transit-oriented cities are "diverse," "civic," and "built at a human scale."

Some of these claims are flat out wrong. Others are essentially aesthetic judgments not shared by most of the people who find autos convenient and the suburbs pleasant. Yet we have been bombarded with the Morality Myth for so long that people who rarely use transit themselves readily agree to proposals giving transit unfair advantages over autos.

Many cities have changed or plan to change their traffic signals to give streetcars and buses priority over autos. Oregon has passed a law giving buses the right of way over cars when they pull from the curb into lanes of traffic. Other cities are converting traffic lanes that were open to all into bus-only lanes. Cities that are building rail transit lines typically spend two-thirds or more of their total transportation budgets on transit even though transit carries less than 2 percent of the motorized passenger miles in all but a few urban areas. Such programs end up delaying thousands of people to speed a few dozen transit riders.

These policies only make sense if transit has such an advantage over autos that it deserves special treatment. Does it consume less energy? No. Is it less expensive? Not by a long shot. Is it cleaner or safer? Not particularly. Is it faster? No, not even when traffic laws are biased in its favor.

The Morality Myth allows heavily subsidized transit riders to feel smugly superior to the auto users who pay for both the highways they drive on as well as most of the costs of the buses and rail lines used by transit patrons. The myth becomes dangerous when its believers try to turn that moral claim into government policy.

Notes

1. James Howard Kunstler, *The Geography of Nowhere: The Rise and Decline of America's Man-Made Landscape* (New York: NY: Simon & Schuster, 1993), p. 113.
2. Andres Duany and Elizabeth Plater-Zyberk, "The Second Coming of the American Small Town," *Wilson's Quarterly*, Winter 1992, pp. 19–48.
3. Jane Holtz Kay, *Asphalt Nation: How the Automobile Took over America and How We Can Take It Back* (New York, NY: Crown, 1997), p. 4, p. 20; Peter Calthorpe, *The Next American Metropolis: Ecology, Community, and the American Dream* (New York, NY: Princeton Architectural Press, 1993), p. 18.

20. Rail Transit Primer

Washington, DC, has spent some $10 billion federal dollars on a far-flung rail system that is very convenient for tourists and visitors. Yet fewer than 14 percent of all DC-area commuters use either bus or rail transit; more than 80 percent drive to work.[1] At best, the DC rail system has slowed the decline of transit, but it has not increased transit's share of urban travel. Subsidies amount to about $12 for each new rider.[2]

The San Francisco Bay Area spent almost as much money as Washington, DC, building the Bay Area Rapid Transit (BART) system. The many early problems with this system, including cost overruns, operational failures, and safety problems, were documented in Peter Hall's book, *Great Planning Disasters*.[3] Now, more than 20 years BART began service, total daily ridership remains less than eleven weeks worth of *growth* of Bay Area highway traffic.[4] Without BART, many riders would use other transit, so the BART system has an insignificant effect on traffic.

Los Angeles spent billions of dollars building three rail lines to middle-class suburbs. To pay for the lines, the transit operator has let bus service to poor and minority neighborhoods deteriorate. A bus riders union, backed by the NAACP, sued the transit agency for discrimination against minorities. In a 1996 out-of-court settlement, the agency agreed to boost its bus service and recently halted construction on one of the rail lines to pay for its bus operations. A transit operators' strike in 2000 highlighted the fact that Los Angeles' transit agency "is flush with billions of dollars to build more rail and bus projects, [but] it struggles to pay to operate what it already has."[5]

Twenty-five American urban areas have some form of rail transit. Most of these fall into one of four categories:

- *Heavy rail* consists of electric-powered vehicles that run in trains of two to ten cars on tracks that are in subways, elevated, or otherwise completely separated from pedestrian and auto traffic. Washington's Metrorail, San Francisco's BART, and New York subways are all heavy rail.
- *Light rail* consists of electric-powered vehicles that run singly or in trains of up to four cars on tracks that often share streets with pedestrians and auto traffic. Portland's MAX, the San Diego Trolley, and the Los Angeles green

and blue lines are all light rail, as are the San Francisco, Philadelphia, and New Orleans streetcar systems. The terms heavy and light rail refer to the weight of the vehicles, not the rails, which is about the same in each.

• *Commuter rail* consists of Diesel or electric locomotives pulling passenger trains usually on tracks shared with freight trains. Commuter rail lines such as the Long Island Railroad, Chicago's Metra trains, and California's CalTrains go longer distances and stop far less frequently than light or heavy rail.

• *People movers* consist of driverless low-capacity vehicles on rubber tires or magnetic levitation moving on fixed routes. Also known as "personal rapid transit" and "automated guideway transit," people movers can be found in Detroit and Miami.

There are, of course, other variations. The Chicago South Shore line is the nation's last *electric interurban*, which is midway between heavy rail and commuter rail. Other alternatives include the Seattle monorail, which is primarily a tourist attraction, and the Vancouver, BC, Skytrain, which is midway between a people mover and light rail. Most of the discussion in this book will be on the three major categories of light, heavy, and commuter rail since these are the modes being considered by most cities today.

Heavy rail and commuter rail can play a significant role in very high-density corridors such as those found in the New York metropolitan area, where well over half of all U.S. rail transit trips and passenger miles take place (figure one). It is doubtful whether such high-density corridors will ever be built in any U.S. urban area not already served by rail. Even in Chicago, San Francisco, and Washington, where rail transit carries two out of three transit passenger miles, rail transit has but a tiny share of the total transportation market.

Light rail makes no sense at all in any transportation market anywhere in the world. With capacities midway between buses and heavy or commuter rail, light rail might seem ideal for urban corridors that are not as heavily populated as those in New York but still fairly dense. But light rail is too slow and inflexible to effectively compete even with buses, much less autos. Buses can do anything better than light rail except divert huge gobs of federal tax dollars to central city pork barrel.

People movers attempt to combine the operational cost advantages of rail with the distributional advantages of low-capacity transit.[6] But for low-capacity transit to work, it must reach hundreds or thousands of destinations in an urban area. While streets preceded autos and are built incrementally as a region grows, people movers are ineffective until a huge network is built. The capital costs of such a system are so high that it is doubtful that any will ever be attempted. The people movers that have been built are extremely limited, often connecting only a handful of destinations. Low-capacity buses are far superior to people movers because they flexibly rely on the existing street network.

A major advantage of rails is supposed to be their exclusive right-of-way. Except for some segments of light rail, most rail riders do not have to contend with congested roads and streets. From a cost standpoint, however, this is a major draw-back as the costs of the rail line are attributable solely to the transit riders. Buses have an enormous cost advantage because they share the road with autos and trucks, whose drivers pay most of the costs. The solution to congestion is not to build an exclusive system for a tiny fraction of a region's residents but to reduce congestion for everyone.

Figure One: 1998 Share of Rail Passenger Miles by Urban Area

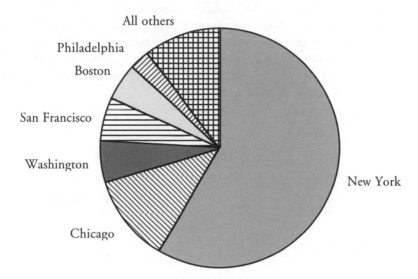

Source: Federal Transit Administration, 1998 National Transit Database *(Washington, DC: FTA, 2000), table 27.*

"Careful social benefit/cost studies conclude that most major highway invest-ments' benefits *exceed* their costs," says urban economist Edwin Mills. "Yet I have seen no careful study concluding that any metropolitan fixed rail investments in the last 35 years had benefits anywhere near as great as its costs."[7] Rail transit is advertised as producing all sorts of environmental and social benefits over buses or cars. But a close look at these benefits reveals that they are either negligible or, in some cases, not really benefits at all.

- *Speed*: Rail transit is capable of high speeds, but when frequent stops are accounted for actual speeds average around 20 to 30 miles per hour. Total trip speeds are far lower when counting the time taken to get to and from transit stations. Express buses with few stops can be far faster than rail transit.
- *Energy efficiency*: A full passenger train uses less energy per passenger than an auto. But rail transit cars are rarely full, so energy costs end up being about

the same or even higher than autos.

- *Cost*: Rail transit's operating costs can be—but often are not—lower than buses, but the construction costs are far higher. Both buses and rail transit cost far more per passenger mile than autos.
- *Ridership*: Few if any new rail lines produced significant transit ridership increases for their urban areas. In many cases ridership declines partly because bus services are cut to pay for the rail lines.
- *Safety*: Rail transit can be safe when the rail lines are competely separated from pedestrians and autos, as in heavy rail. But light-rail transit may be one of the most dangerous modes of transportation in America.
- *Neighborhood redevelopment*: Rail transit lines are often welcomed by urban officials eager to revitalize declining business and residential districts. But experience indicates that such redevelopment requires further subsidies. When offered without the rail transit, these subsidies alone are often enough to stimulate rail transit. So why build the rail line?

All of these issues are discussed in greater detail in the transit myths on the next few pages.

Notes

1. Census Bureau, http://venus.census.gov/cdrom/lookup.
2. Don Pickrell, *Urban Rail Transit Projects: Forecast Versus Actual Ridership and Costs* (Cambridge, MA: U.S. DOT, 1989), p. xv.
3. Peter Hall, *Great Planning Disasters* (Berkeley, CA: UC Press, 1981), pp. 109–137.
4. Myles Cunneen, personal communication, 1998.
5. Jeffrey Rabin, "MTA Strike Has Deep Roots in Agency's Past Mistakes," *Los Angeles Times*, September 19, 2000, http://www.latimes.com/news/state/20000919/ t000088492.html.
6. Taxi 2000, "Personal Rapid Transit: The Urban Transit Solution," http:// www.taxi2000.com.
7. Edwin S. Mills, "Truly Smart 'Smart Growth,'" *Illinois Real Estate Letter*, Summer, 1999, p. 4.

The Speedy-Rail-Transit Myth

Myth: Rail transit is fast.

Reality: Counting stops, the average heavy-rail line goes 30 miles per hour; the average light-rail line goes only 20 miles per hour. Add the time required to get to and from rail stations and rail is far slower than autos.

In 1996, transportation analyst Jonathan Richmond interviewed Los Angeles officials to find out why they favored spending billions of dollars on rail transit. A county supervisor said that "I believe that most businessmen would abandon the freeways and use the train because it would be so remarkably fast." If people "get on a light-rail car," one transit commissioner told Richmond, "I mean, they're—whoosh—gone." People generally associated trains "with images of speed," concluded Richmond.[1]

Most campaigns in support of rail transit proposals focus on rails' top speed— up to 80 miles per hour for heavy rail and commuter rail, around 55 miles per hour for light rail. Such speeds are deceptive since even the fastest trains must slow, stop, wait to unload and load passengers, and then slowly build up speed again at many stations along the route. When station stops are counted, the average speed of heavy-rail lines is about 30 miles per hour while commuter train speeds are variable but are generally under 40 miles per hour. The fastest light-rail line in the country averages 27 miles per hour, while the average light rail goes just 20 miles per hour.

Even these speeds are deceptive because they do not include the time taken to get to and from the rail stations. Most urban residents live no more than two or three blocks from a bus line, and suburban residents not much further than that. But rail networks are rarely as dense as bus networks, so people must first drive or take a bus to the rail station, then take a bus or walk from the station to their destination. Total trip time ends up being much longer that driving—which means rail transit will not attract many people out of their cars.

The 1990 census found that commuters who drove to work took an average of 21 minutes each way, while bus riders required 38 minutes. Light- or heavy-rail riders took 45 minutes and commuter rail took 58 minutes.[2] The longer transit times weren't due to greater distances: The distance auto drivers went tended to be longer than bus, light-, or heavy-rail commuters. The automobile's door-to-door convenience wipes out any gains due to the top speeds achieved by rail.

Notes

1. Jonathan E. D. Richmond, "The Mythical Conception of Rail Transit in Los Angeles," http://the-tech.mit.edu/~richmond/professional/myth.pdf.
2. Alan Pisarski, *Commuting in America II* (Washington, DC: Eno Transportation Foundation, 1996), p. 85.

The Inexpensive-Rail-Transit Myth

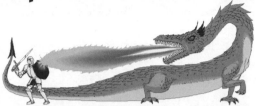

Myth: Rail transit costs less to build than freeways and less to operate than buses.

Reality: Rail transit costs far more to build than freeways and not significantly less to operate than buses.

R ail transit was originally proposed as a low-cost alternative to building more freeways and a way of saving money on transit operations. Neither of these promises turned out to be true. Although initial rail cost estimates are often low, costs tend to rapidly increase after cities decide to build. After they are built, they turn out to cost as much or more to operate as buses.

In 1973, the Oregon Railroad Commission estimated that the cost of installing four light-rail routes on recently abandoned or little-used Portland-area rail lines would cost less than $100 million.[1] Twenty-five years later, two lines were built and two more were on the drawing boards, and the actual or projected cost had reached $4 billion, more than forty times the 1973 original estimate.

This is the typical pattern for rail transit proposals. Public support is gained with low initial estimates. After public officials are sold on the idea, costs creep up as the project is shaped and new features added. After construction begins, estimates are revised upward so that when the project is done the transit agency can claim that it was completed under budget, hoping no one remembers that the initial estimate was much lower than the final budget.

A 1989 report by U.S. Department of Transportation researcher Don Pickrell found that nearly all recent rail projects cost far more than originally projected. As table one shows, the average rail project which he examined came in at 46 percent over budget and cost 78 percent more to operate than projected. As the next myth will show, the average project also carried less than half the projected ridership. A 1995 update by Robert Dunphy, of the Urban Land Institute, found that all but one system built after Pickrell's analysis followed the same pattern.[2]

"The systematic tendency to overestimate ridership and to underestimate capital and operating costs," concluded Pickrell, "introduces a distinct bias toward the selection of capital-intensive transit improvements such as rail lines."[3] One reason for this bias is that the federal government often pays a large share of rail construction and local officials regard federal dollars as "free money." Unlike buses, most rail money goes to local contractors, who therefore lobby for rail projects and give political support to officials who promote such projects.

Table One: Actual vs. Projected Rail Costs

City	Rail Type	Capital Cost	Operating Cost
Atlanta	Heavy Rail	58%	205%
Baltimore	Heavy Rail	60%	
Buffalo	Light Rail	61%	12%
Detroit	People Mover	50%	47%
Miami	People Mover	58%	84%
Miami	Heavy Rail	33%	42%
Pittsburgh	Light Rail	11%	
Portland	Light Rail	55%	45%
Sacramento	Light Rail	13%	-10%
Washington	Heavy Rail	83%	202%
Average		46%	78%

Source: Don Pickrell, Urban Rail Transit Projects: Forecast Versus Actual Ridership and Costs (Washington, DC: US Department of Transportation, Urban Mass Transportation Administration, 1989), table S-2. Blanks signify no available data.

"I have interviewed public officials, consultants and planners who have been involved in these transit planning cases," says business ethicist Martin Wachs, "and I am absolutely convinced that the cost overruns and patronage overestimates were not the result of technical errors, honest mistakes or inadequate methods. In case after case planners, engineers and economists have told me that they had to 'revise' their forecasts many times because they failed to satisfy their superiors. The forecasts had to be 'cooked' in order to produce numbers that were dramatic enough to gain federal support for the projects."[4]

Freeways sometimes cost more than their initial estimates as well. But are freeways more expensive than rails? A typical urban freeway costs $5 to $10 million per lane mile. The least expensive U.S. light-rail lines built in the last twenty years cost more than $10 million per mile; the average was more than $25 million.[5] Lines now on the drawing boards are projected to average $40 to $50 million per mile.[6] Heavy rail costs much more: Miami's heavy-rail line cost $88 million per mile, yet it was one of the least expensive of recent lines built.[7]

Such high costs would be worthwhile only if rail carries many more people than a freeway lane. But as shown in the Myth of High-Capacity Transit (p. 287), the New York City subway is the only rail line in the country that carries more people than a single lane of typical urban freeway.

Rail construction looks especially grim when compared with the costs of improving transit with new buses. A light-rail car may hold twice as many people and have double the life span of a bus. Yet the car alone will cost more than ten times as much as a bus—not counting the right of way, roadbed, tracks, or overhead wires that the car needs to operate. Rail makes sense only if it attracted many more riders than buses. As the Rail-Ridership Myth (p. 323) shows, it does not.

One way to significantly reduce costs might be to eliminate federal support for rail transit. Cities that built rail lines without federal funding spent as little as half as much as lines built with federal funding. Transit agencies probably use federal funds to gold plate their systems, not to build additional capacity or route miles.

Rail may be costly to build, but according to data published by the Federal Transit Administration it costs less to operate than buses. In 1997, the average urban bus service cost $2.04 per trip, while heavy rail cost only $1.43 and light rail $1.82.[8] But this comparison overlooks several factors that actually make rail more expensive than buses.

- Calculations of operating costs neglect the cost of reconstructing roadbeds and other rail facilities, which must be done every twenty years or so. Washington's Metro recently announced that it needs to find $150 million per year to replace cars, elevators, track, and other parts of its system that are wearing out after two decades of use.[9] The Federal Transit Administration counts such expenses as capital costs, but buses don't have to pay them.
- Most rail lines skim the cream of transit systems by replacing the most popular bus routes in the system. In 1997, the average bus picked up just three transit riders per vehicle mile of service. Heavy-rail cars average 4.5 riders per mile while light-rail cars average 6.5 riders per mile of service. If the buses they replaced carried more than 3.5 riders (for light rail) to 4.5 riders (for heavy rail) per mile of operation, then those bus routes cost far less to operate than the rail lines that replaced them.
- Most rail routes are supported by lightly patronized, and therefore expensive, feeder bus lines. This drags down average bus operating costs even though the feeder buses are really a cost of rail transit.

Commuter rail costs more per trip because the trips are much longer than ordinary transit. On a passenger mile basis, the seventeen major commuter rail systems in the U.S. cost about 30 cents per passenger mile to operate. Commuter bus services in New Jersey cost only 12 cents per passenger mile.[10]

To evaluate rail and other transit proposals, the Federal Transit Administration asks transit agencies to estimate how much each *new* transit rider will cost, including both operating costs and annualized capital costs. A new transit rider is someone who would not have used transit in the absence of the proposed project. For example, the Hiawatha light-rail line being planned from Minneapolis to Bloomington is projected to carry about 24,000 riders per weekday, but only about 9,300 of these are "new" riders—the rest would have taken the bus if the rail line were not built. The annual cost works out to $18.27 per new ride.[11]

The Federal Transit Administration also requires transit agencies to estimate the cost per new ride of improving bus service, the "transportation system management" alternative. This is invariably far less than the cost of rail. Metro Transit, the Twin Cities transit agency, projects that transportation system management in the planned light-rail corridor would attract new riders for just $7.75 per ride—well under half the cost of rail. If the money to be spent on light rail were spent on transportation system management throughout the Twin Cities, transit would gain 135 percent more riders than building light rail.

From this perspective, very few rail transit proposals make sense. But generous federal capital funding leads transit agencies to favor projects with high capital costs and low operating costs. In many urban areas, the capital cost of one rail transit line is enough to double the number of buses in the transit system. But doubling buses requires double the operating costs, which transit agencies can't afford. So agencies promote rail even though it will do little for transit passengers.

"Investment in rail transit has proven to be a terribly inefficient way to divert trips from automobiles," say University of California transportation experts Genevieve Giuliano and Kenneth Small. "The cost of providing bus service is lower than rail except in corridors with passenger volume much higher than those experienced in any North American metropolitan area not already served by rail transit."[12] This is also true of all rail transit systems built in the last thirty years.

Notes

1. Oregon Railroad Division, *Light Rail Transit: Portland Area Rail Corridor Study* (Salem, OR: PUC, 1973), 80 pp.
2. Robert Dunphy, "Review of Recent American Light Rail Experiences," *in* Transportation Research Board, *Seventh National Conference on Light Rail Transit* (Washington, DC: National Academy Press, 1995), pp. 106–107.
3. Don Pickrell, *Urban Rail Transit Projects: Forecast Versus Actual Ridership and Costs* (Washington, DC: US Department of Transportation, Urban Mass Transportation Administration, 1989), p. xi.
4. Martin Wachs, "Ethics and Advocacy in Forecasting for Public Policy," *Business and Professional Ethics Journal*, 9 (Spring, 1990), p. 141.
5. Robert Dunphy, "Review of Recent American Light Rail Experiences," p. 107.
6. Light Rail Central, "Lightrail Projects & Costs," http://www.lightrail.com/costs.htm. Costs not adjusted for inflation.
7. Don Pickrell, *Urban Rail Transit Projects: Forecast Versus Actual Ridership and Cost* (Washington, DC: US DOT, 1991), tables S-2 and 1-1.
8. Federal Transit Administration, *Transit Profiles: Agencies in Urbanized Areas Exceeding 200,000 Population, 1997 Report Year* (Washington, DC: FTA, 1998), pp. A-3–A-4.
9. Trigie Ealey, "Metro wants funds for major improvements," *Fairfax Journal*, November 3, 2000, p. A3, http://cold.jrnl.com/cfdocs/new/ffx/story.cfm?paper=ffx&section=st&snumber=01.
10. FTA, *Transit Profiles 1997*, p. 144.
11. Metro Transit, "New Starts Criteria Materials," September 1, 1999, p. 19.
12. Genevieve Giuliano & Kenneth A. Small, *Alternative Strategies for Coping with Traffic Congestion* (Berkeley, CA: UCTC No. 188, 1992), p. 4.

The Rail-Ridership Myth

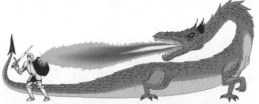

Myth: Rail transit can attract many more riders than buses.

Reality: Ridership on almost every rail line built in the last twenty-five years has been far lower than expected and in most cases is little more than previously rode the bus.

Conservative Paul Weyrich believes that middle-class people are more likely to ride "high-quality mass transit," meaning trains, than buses.[1] The public perception, a transit commissioner told researcher Jonathan Richmond, is that buses are "noise and dirty and slow," while rails are quiet, clean, and fast.[2] Based on these perceptions, rail advocates often presume that rail lines will attract more people out of their automobiles than simple improvements in bus service.

Consultants predicted that a Miami subway would carry more than 200,000 riders per day, yet it has never carried as many as 50,000 per day. As USC planning professors Peter Gordon and Harry Richardson point out, the consultants who made that prediction "had little trouble obtaining lucrative contracts in Los Angeles," where they predicted "more riders per mile than any U.S. subway, *including* New York's."[3] This prediction has also proven false.

U.S. Department of Transportation analyst Don Pickrell's report shows that most other rail proposals also vastly overestimated ridership (table one). Rail advocates claim that Pickrell's study was done too soon after the lines in Portland and other cities opened and therefore did not accurately show ridership. But in 1995, Robert Dunphy, of the Urban Land Institute, updated Pickrell's report and reached similar conclusions.[4] Dunphy found that the rail systems Pickrell had studied did not have "dramatic ridership growth to change the early assessment." Dunphy also looked at several newer systems, all but one of which was "following the pattern. . . of overestimating ridership and underestimating costs."

Of seven cities that built light-rail lines during the 1980s, four actually suffered significant losses in transit commuting between 1980 and 1990. Transit commuting in Baltimore fell by 9 percent, Denver by 17 percent, Portland by 20 percent, and Buffalo by 25 percent. Of the other three systems, Sacramento transit commuting grew by 2 percent, Los Angeles by 18 percent, and San Diego by

43 percent. Of light-rail lines that opened after Pickrell collected his data, "all were in cities with a net loss in transit commuting during the 1980s," says Dunphy. These included San Jose, St. Louis, and new lines in Baltimore and Denver. All of these except for St. Louis followed the pattern of costing more and carrying fewer riders than anticipated.

Table One: Actual vs. Projected Rail Ridership

City	Rail Type	Ridership
Atlanta	Heavy Rail	-63%
Baltimore	Heavy Rail	-59%
Buffalo	Light Rail	-68%
Detroit	People Mover	-83%
Miami	People Mover	-74%
Miami	Heavy Rail	-85%
Pittsburgh	Light Rail	-66%
Portland	Light Rail	-54%
Sacramento	Light Rail	-71%
Washington	Heavy Rail	-28%
Average		-59%

Source: Don Pickrell, Urban Rail Transit Projects: Forecast Versus Actual Ridership and Costs (Washington, DC: US Department of Transportation, Urban Mass Transportation Administration, 1989), table S-2.

St. Louis seems to have pioneered a new tactic: planners dramatically *underestimate* ridership so that, when the project is built, actual ridership will appear to be a great success. But light-rail ridership in St. Louis, per route mile, is not significantly greater than average and is less than in San Diego, Denver, and many other cities. Planners who follow this tactic apparently rely on pork-barrel rather than ridership to sell rail projects.

According to data gathered from numerous transit agencies by Portland transportation consultant Myles Cunneen, less than 30 percent of the riders of most recent light- and heavy-rail lines in the U.S. were previously auto drivers. The only exceptions were BART, at 35 percent, and the Philadelphia Lindenwold heavy-rail line, at 40 percent. If the goal is to get people out of their cars, Cunneen found, starting express bus service on high-occupancy vehicle lanes was much more successful. In most cases, half or more of the riders on such bus routes were former auto drivers.[5]

There are two major reasons why rail ridership is likely to be low.

- First, rail is slow. Though rail advocates often quote top speeds, average speeds for the typical light rail are only 20 miles per hour; the typical heavy rail averages just 30 miles per hour. Express buses, not to mention automobiles, can easily exceed these speeds.

• Second, as Garreau points out, rail doesn't go where people want to go. A rail line serves a very narrow corridor of land, and except in the New York urban area, densities are simply not high enough to support rail's theoretical capacities. This means most people who might use the rail line must first drive or take a bus to the rail station, which makes the journey take even longer. In contrast, a high-occupancy vehicle lane can serve express buses from many neighborhoods to downtown or other major centers.

"Research consistently shows that the comfort of a trip is not a prime determinant of the mode of travel to be chosen for making it," says Richmond. "The travel time, frequency of service and cost of a trip are more important." There is no reason why rails are necessarily any more luxurious than buses, but even if they are, people won't ride them if they don't go where the people want to go.

Notes

1. Paul M. Weyrich and William S. Lind, "Conservatives and Mass Transit: Is It Time for a New Look?" American Public Transportation Association, 1998.
2. Jonathan E. D. Richmond, "The Mythical Conception of Rail Transit in Los Angeles," http://the-tech.mit.edu/~richmond/professional/myth.pdf.
3. Gordon and Richardson, "Are Compact Cities a Desirable Planning Goal?" *Journal of the American Planning Association* 61(1), http://www.smartgrowth.org/library/apa_pointcounterpoint/apa_sprawl.html.
4. Robert Dunphy, "Review of Recent American Light Rail Experiences," *in* Transportation Research Board, *Seventh National Conference on Light Rail Transit* (Washington, DC: National Academy Press, 1995), pp. 106–107.
5. Myles Cunneen, "Passenger Former Mode: New Transit Projects," unpublished report.

The Myth That Transit Reduces Congestion

Myth: New rail lines will reduce congestion.
Reality: Rail transit's effect on congestion is insignificant in most American cities.

Rail transit advocates often claim that rail lines will attract a large percentage of people out of their autos, thus leaving the highways less congested. In fact, rail transit will have at best an insignificant effect on congestion. More likely, it will make congestion worse, particularly if it is light rail.

Recent plans for more than two dozen light-rail proposals typically projected less than a 0.3 percent reduction in auto traffic.[1]

- A proposed light-rail project in Minneapolis bluntly says: "Impacts of light rail on freeway traffic and congestion: None."[2]
- A St. Louis light-rail plan estimated that auto traffic in the proposed rail corridor would more than double in twenty years. "Comparing this level of demand with the reductions in peak auto travel due to new transit ridership indicates that the latter have little impact."[3]
- A San Diego light-rail plan says that "The traffic analysis did not reveal any substantial difference in LOS [levels of service; i.e., highway congestion] between the No Build, TSM [transportation system management], and Build Alternatives."[4]
- A Denver light-rail plan says that "Auto travel times will deteriorate significantly over today's levels by the year 2015 regardless of whether the no-build or LRT alternative is implemented."[5]

Many of the proposals nevertheless found a way to put insignificant effects in a positive light. The Denver plan, for example, said that, since light rail will remove 1,600 auto trips from the road in a region that generates well over 10 million trips per day, "the LRT alternative better addresses increased congestion levels" than not building the light rail.[6] Partly as a result of such distortions, the above cities all built or, in the case of Minneapolis, are planning to build light rail.

Salt Lake City's I-15 corridor plan, which called for both freeway expansion and light-rail construction, found that highway expansion would save drivers traffic delays at a cost of less than $5 per hour saved. Saving drivers' and transit riders' time with light rail would cost more than $35 per hour—over seven times as much per hour saved. "None of the [transit] improvements induce a large enough shift away from driving automobiles to significantly affect highway traffic volumes," concluded the plan—which didn't stop them from building the line.[7]

Transit has such a small share of travel in most cities that even doubling transit ridership will have a minimal effect. Outside of New York, transit carries an average of 1.5 percent of urban travel. While around 6 percent of commuters use transit, only about half of rush-hour traffic consists of commuters.[8] Thus, doubling transit commuting would only reduce rush hour traffic by about 3 percent. And no rail project will come anywhere close to doubling ridership. Transit agencies usually project a small increase in ridership in the rail corridor, which works out to a tiny increase for the urban area as a whole.

Outside of the top seven transit markets—New York, Boston, Chicago, San Francisco, Washington, and Philadelphia—the annual growth in auto driving exceeds the total amount of transit ridership in almost every U.S. urban area. This means that even if transit ridership could be doubled by attracting people out of their autos, the natural growth in driving would replace those autos in less than a year. Since most rail proposals result in far less than a doubling in transit ridership, any effects they have on congestion are nullified in a few days to a few weeks. For example, Salt Lake City's new light-rail line carries people about 80,000 passenger miles per day. Over the last six years, Salt Lake City auto traffic has been growing by more than 11,000 vehicle miles per week, so even if every light-rail rider was a former auto driver, traffic would have reached its pre-light-rail levels just seven weeks after the line opened.[9]

Outside of Washington, DC, and, possibly, San Francisco, if all of the rail transit systems built in the last thirty years were to disappear tomorrow, no one would notice a change in roadway congestion. Most rail transit riders would switch to buses, which is what they used before the rail lines were built. But even if they did not, there are too few rail riders to make a difference to the roads.

Instead of reducing congestion, rail transit is likely to increase it for two reasons. First is the cost of spending limited transportation funds on projects that are not likely to move great numbers of people. When a single freeway lane moves six times as many people as the average light-rail line, yet costs less than a fifth as much to build, it is foolish to expect that spending money on rail will improve mobility. Instead, it simply means that less money is available to do things that really can reduce congestion.

Rail lines, particularly light rail, also increase congestion by acting as an obstacle for auto and bus traffic. The construction of rail lines usually interferes with auto traffic. The operation of light-rail lines in city streets often obstructs autos and usually reduces roadway capacity. Typically, four-lane arterials are reduced to two automobile lanes and two light-rail lanes. Light-rail vehicles crossing streets every three to five minutes can significantly delay auto traffic.

This is one reason why streetcars were eliminated back in the 1930s through the 1950s. As Hawaiian transportation analyst Cliff Slater notes, "The great complaints about streetcars were always that they had to load and unload passengers without pulling into the curb." As a result, a 1933 Honolulu newspaper editorialized that "Honolulu is doing what all progressive mainland communities are nowadays doing: getting rid of street cars and replacing them with good size buses."[10]

Most light-rail proposals estimate the amount of time saved by transit riders who switch from bus to rail. Only a few have estimated the amount of time that light-rail interference with traffic will cost auto users. One that did so was the proposal for the Southwest Corridor light rail in Denver. The proposal estimated that light rail would save the average bus rider 19 minutes per ride, but that it would cost the average auto passenger 1 minute.[11] Since more than 95 percent of the passenger miles in the corridor are by auto, this means a net loss in travel time.

In short, rail transit in general will do little or nothing to relieve congestion. As Anthony Downs says, "communities that have built new public transit systems have not experienced much—if any—reduction in peak-hour automotive congestion."[12] Light-rail transit in particular is likely to make congestion worse.

Notes

1. Randal O'Toole, *ISTEA: A Poisonous Brew for American Cities* (Washington, DC: Cato Institute, 1998).
2. Minnesota Department of Transportation, *Central Corridor Draft Environmental Impact Statement* (St. Paul, MN: MN DOT, 1993).
3. Missouri Department of Transportation, *St. Clair County Corridor Draft Environmental Impact Statement* (St. Louis, MO: MO DOT, 1995), p. 4-15.
4. San Diego Metropolitan Transit Development Board, *San Diego East Urban Corridor Draft Environmental Impact Statement* (San Diego, CA: SDMTDB, 1985).
5. Denver RTD, *Southwest Corridor LRT Project Draft Environmental Impact Statement* (Denver, CO: RTD, 1995), p. ES-9.
6. Ibid.
7. Utah Department of Transportation, *I-15/State Street Corridor Draft Environmental Impact Statement* (Ogden, UT: UT DOT, 1990), p. 5-54, tables 5-9, 7-1, and 7-2.
8. Alan Pisarski, *Commuting in America II* (Washington, DC: Eno, 1996), pp. 3–4.
9. Ridership data from Utah Transit Authority; traffic data from Federal Highway Administration, *Highway Statistics 1992* and *1998* (Washington, DC: FHwA, 1992 and 1999), table HM-72.
10. Cliff Slater, "City rail plan is rubbish," *Honolulu Advertiser*, http://www.lava.net/cslater/trans2kc.htm.
11. Denver RTD, *Southwest Corridor LRT Project Draft Environmental Impact Statement* (Denver, CO: RTD, 1995), p. ES-9.
12. Anthony Downs, *Stuck in Traffic: Coping with Peak-Hour Traffic Congestion* (Washington, DC: Brookings, 1992), p. 30.

The Energy-Efficient Transit Myth

Myth: Transit saves energy.
Reality: Bus transit consumes far more energy per passenger mile than cars and rail transit consumes about the same amount as cars.

When the gasoline crises of the 1970s boosted transit ridership, people hoped that transit would play a major role in saving energy. But the real energy savings came from increased automobile fuel efficiency. In 1970, cars used twice as much energy per passenger mile as either rail or bus transit.[1] Drivers responded to high gasoline prices by buying cars that, by 1995, consumed almost 25 percent less energy per passenger mile.

Meanwhile, transit agencies tried to attract riders by adding energy-consuming amenities such as air conditioning and extending service to areas that made little use of transit.[2] Transit ridership was 22 percent higher in 1989 than 1970, yet bus transit consumed 50 percent more energy and rail transit 38 percent more energy per passenger mile than in 1970. When ridership fell after 1989, energy costs leaped again until by 1995 bus transit consumed 88 percent more energy and transit 56 percent more energy per passenger mile than in 1970. As a result, cars consumed far less energy per passenger mile than transit. Bus transit in 1995 used 26 percent and rail transit 3 percent more energy per passenger mile than cars. Light trucks—including minivans and sports utility vehicles—consumed more energy than rail transit but about the same as buses.

Increased ridership after 1995 helped reduce transit energy costs, particularly for rail transit. Rail's apparent advantage over cars, light trucks, and buses leads to arguments that building rail transit will help save energy. As usual, however, this overlooks some important considerations. First, building a new rail line consumes an enormous amount of energy. For example, Portland's Metro wants to build a light-rail line from downtown north to the Columbia River. The agency says that, after the line is built, it will save 63 million British Thermal Units (BTUs) of energy a day. But it also admits that building the line will cost 3.94 quadrillion BTUs—roughly 170 years' worth of the projected daily energy savings.[3] Since buses use roads whose energy-construction costs are shared with many other au-

Figure One: Energy Consumption by Mode, 1970 to 1997
(Btus per passenger mile)

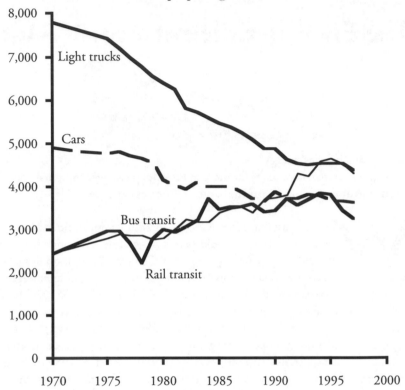

Source: Stacy Davis, Transportation Energy Data Book Edition 19 *(Oak Ridge, TN: Department of Energy, 1999), table 2-12. Assumes light trucks carry 1.6 passengers per mile.*

tos and trucks, the energy cost of adding buses instead of rails is negligible. The energy cost of building buses is much less than that of building rail cars, which weigh far more than buses. Second, rail and auto journeys are not really comparable. Rail transit usually requires some other form of transportation at one or both ends, while auto trips are generally from door to door, and often on a more direct route. Thus, from point to point autos may consume less energy than trips that include rail even if the rail itself costs less energy per passenger mile than cars.

Notes

1. Stacy Davis, *Transportation Energy Data Book Edition 19* (Oak Ridge, TN: Department of Energy, 1999), table 2-12.
2. Sharon Sarmiento, "Autos Save Energy," *Access* 8 (Spring, 1996): p. 41.
3. Metro, *North Corridor Interstate MAX Light Rail Project Final Environmental Impact Statement* (Portland, OR: Metro, 1999), p. 4-104.

The Clean-Transit Myth

Myth: Rail transit is pollution free.
Reality: Rail transit is only cleaner than other forms of transportation if it significantly alters travel habits, which it does not.

Rail transit will do very little to relieve air pollution problems for all of the same reasons that it will do little to relieve congestion: Too few people ride the rails; most of them were former bus riders; and any reduction in auto traffic is likely to be replaced with other autos due to latent demand. While it might be thought that replacing Diesel buses with electric transit is an improvement, the feeder buses needed to serve rail lines generally go as many if not more miles—and so pollute as much—as the buses the rail line replaced. Yet more people drive to rail stations, so the feeder buses typically run with very light loads.

To these are added some specific pollution problems with rail. Diesel-powered commuter rail generates quite a bit of pollution on its own. A lightly used commuter rail line could easily produce more pollution than the automobiles that might replace it.

Electric rail generates two sorts of pollution. First, most U.S. electricity is generated in coal-fired power plants. Substituting electric rail for autos or buses does not eliminate pollution, it just exports it to the location of the coal-fired power plant. Second, electric rail vehicles do not make continuous contact with the transmission lines or rail. The near-contacts result in sparks of electrical current arcing between the lines and the vehicle. Such electrical arcing can be a significant source of ozone, a major constituent of smog.

A final pollution problem has to do with the park-and-ride stations that are usually associated with rail transit. Significant numbers of transit riders use these park-and-ride lots. Analyses of the pollution effects of rail often presume that pollution is constant per vehicle mile of travel, so someone driving one mile to the park-and-ride lot is estimated to generate one-tenth as much pollution as if they drove ten miles to work. In fact, autos generate most of their pollution when their catalytic converts are cold, so driving to the park-and-ride station can cause nearly as much pollution as driving all the way to work.

The Transit-Safety Myth

Myth: Rail transit is much safer than automobiles.
Reality: Heavy-rail transit may be safer, but light-rail transit is more dangerous to pedestrians and autos.

Heavy-rail lines are generally kept completely separated from pedestrian and auto routes and so are relatively accident free. But light-rail lines often follow streets and come into frequent contact with pedestrians and autos. Light-rail vehicles also weigh significantly more than the heaviest trucks or buses. Getting hit by a modern streetcar is likely to produce fatal results. In the first thirteen months after Portland's west side light-rail line opened, streetcars struck and killed five pedestrians. Local residents blamed the quiet vehicles which offered little warning to people on foot. The transit agency blamed pedestrians for trespassing onto the tracks.[1]

In the first seven weeks of operation the Salt Lake City light-rail line suffered nine accidents. One accident demonstrated the incongruous results when putting 88,000- to 166,000-pound vehicles on the same streets as 2,000- to 4,000-pound vehicles (not to mention 100- to 200-pound pedestrians). A train of two light-rail vehicles moving at just 5 miles per hour struck an automobile on January 28, 2000. The two continued to move for one hundred feet before coming to a stop. The automobile, of course, was totaled. Fortunately the streetcar hit the car on the passenger side, which was unoccupied.[2] A few weeks later, the Salt Lake light rail hit and killed a pedestrian.[3]

In evaluating a light-rail plan for the Twin Cities, the Minnesota Department of Transportation compared the safety of light rail with buses and autos. Using data up to 1997 (and therefore not including Portland's recent experience), it found that:

- Light rail would produce more costly collisions per passenger mile than auto driving, but less costly than buses. The savings from moving bus riders to light rail would outweigh the costs from moving auto drivers to light rail.
- Light rail's savings over buses is due to its lower rate of personal injuries, as buses produce about twice as many injuries per passenger mile as light rail.

This is probably because rail vehicles take so long to stop that few occupants are hurt.

• Light rail has fewer collisions than buses but each collision does much more property damage for a net result that light rail collisions costs about 10 percent more per passenger mile.

• Light rail produces four times as many fatalities per vehicle mile and 60 percent more fatalities per passenger mile than buses.[4]

By assuming that a human life is worth $2.7 million, the department calculated that the savings produced by light rail having a lower injury rate than buses outweighed the cost of its greater fatalities and property damage. If a human life is worth much more than $2.7 million, however, then buses become less costly than light rail. In 1997, CSX Transportation was ordered by a Florida court to pay more than $50 million in a passenger's death.[5] As a result, CSX refused to provide a right-of-way for a proposed light-rail line in Orlando unless the line is elevated above the street. At a rate of $50 million per human life, Minnesota's light rail would not pay off.

People may question the morality of trying to put a price on a human life, though this is often necessary for benefit-cost analyses. The point here is that the Minnesota Department of Transportation (which supports building light rail) was willing to trade off increased fatalities in exchange for fewer personal injuries—a trade off that many would find questionable.

Notes

1. Nancy Keates, "Light-Rail Addition Comes to Portland At a Heavy Price: MAX Moves Lots of People—And Runs Some Down," *Wall Street Journal*, December 2, 1999, p. A1.
2. Amy Joi Bryson, "Crash derails TRAX for first time," *Deseret News*, January 28, 2000.
3. Jennifer Dobner and Zack Van Eyck, "Accident is 1st fatality for TRAX," *Deseret News*, March 29, 2000, p. A1.
4. Minnesota Department of Transportation, "Hiawatha Corridor LRT Benefit-Cost Analysis," November 4, 1999, tables 3 and 4.
5. Nancy Keates, "Light-Rail Addition Comes to Portland At a Heavy Price: MAX Moves Lots of People—And Runs Some Down," *Wall Street Journal*, December 2, 1999, p. A6.

The Neighborhood-Redevelopment Myth

Myth: New rail lines lead to neighborhood revitalization.
Reality: Unless supported by additional subsidies, neighborhood redevelopment near rail lines has generally been no faster than elsewhere.

Light rail "is not worth the cost if you're just looking at transit," admits John Fregonese. "It's a way to develop your community at higher densities."[1] Fregonese is currently helping Peter Calthorpe spread the gospel of smart growth to cities around the country, but at the time he said this he was the director of growth-management planning for Portland's Metro.

One of rail transit's biggest selling points is that it will lead to neighborhood redevelopment. Promoters of this idea openly call it the "field of dreams theory": Build it, and they will come. Unwary residents of poor inner-city neighborhoods hope that this means jobs and better (but still affordable) housing. Central-city officials dream of new investments revitalizing inner cities. To smart-growth advocates, redevelopment means increasing densities, preferably with mixed-use, transit-oriented developments.

A wide range of experiences and research studies suggest that all of these groups will be disappointed. Rail transit rarely leads to redevelopment unless that redevelopment is subsidized. On the other hand, redevelopment subsidies often lead to redevelopment even if no rail transit is present. Except for the fact that it provides an excuse to provide the redevelopment subsidies, the rail system is an unnecessary cost.

As described in the Field-of-Dreams Myth (p. 103), Portland's transit agency claims that light rail has stimulated $1.3 billion in developments. Yet most of the developments near Portland light rail are government buildings, government subsidized, or routine work that would have been done without the light rail. Ten years after the light-rail line opened, the line had not produced "any of the kind of development—of a mid-rise, higher-density, mixed-use, mixed-income type" that the city wanted.[2] As a result, the city and its suburbs began heavily subsidizing such developments with infrastructure subsidies, tax breaks, and in direct grants.

Portland is not the only urban area to have discovered that rail has failed to attract transit-oriented development. Six years after completing Los Angeles' blue light-rail line, say University of California researchers, "areas around stations remain unchanged—disinvested, forsaken, and decaying—denying planners' dreams of transit villages and depriving surrounding communities of their hopes for a better economic future." The state legislature passed a "Transit Village Act" and the city of Los Angeles adopted a "Transit-Oriented Districts" land-use policy. Yet so little development has taken place that "density at some stations increases as one moves away from transit stops."[3] Development did not take place because "there is no there there," say the researchers. "Most station areas lack any of the physical amenities intrinsic to neighborhood livability," such as parks, stores, and restaurants. "The New Urbanists' romantic image of a transformed inner city stands in stark contrast with the decay, unemployment, poverty, and crime that characterize these neighborhoods," the authors conclude.

As described in the San Francisco case study, BART failed to produce significant land-use benefits near most of its stations. Among other things, "housing growth in the San Francisco Bay Area has been much stronger outside BART corridors than near the stations."[4]

Residents of the Philips neighborhood in Minneapolis, where Minnesota Governor Jesse Ventura grew up, are hoping that the Hiawatha light-rail line now being planned will stimulate major improvements in their area. But Twin Cities planners have so little faith that rail will lead to revitalization that they have already budgeted millions of dollars to subsidize developments along the line.[5]

Given enough subsidies, developers will build anything. But rail does not seem to make much difference to developers' calculations even in cities such as San Francisco where rail's share of transportation is several times greater than most other urban areas. If neighborhood revitalization is the goal, then rail is not the appropriate tool.

Notes

1. Dee J. Hall, "The Choice: High Density or Urban Sprawl," *Wisconsin State Journal*, July 23, 1995.
2. Statement of Mike Saba, Portland City Planning Bureau, at the October 23, 1996, city council meeting, taken from a videotape of that meeting made by the city of Portland.
3. Anastasia Loukaitou-Sideris & Tridib Banerjee, "There's No There There; Or Why Neighborhoods Don't Readily Develop Near Light-Rail Transit Stations," *Access* 9:2–6.
4. Marlon G. Boarnet & Nicholas S. Compin, *Transit-Oriented Development in San Diego County: Incrementally Implementing a Comprehensive Idea* (Berkeley, CA: UC Transportation Center, 1996), UCTC No. 343.
5. Dan Wascoe, Jr., "Subsidies urged for rail-station areas," *Minneapolis Star-Tribune*, November 9, 1999, p. B7.

The Rail-Helps-the-Poor Myth

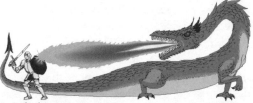

Myth: Rail transit helps poor people.
Reality: Most rail transit projects are aimed at middle-class, white neighborhoods.

Rail transit advocates sometimes argue that rail will give poor people greater access to jobs in other parts of urban areas. But, as built, rail transit lines often end up reducing transit service to the poor. This is because poor neighborhoods today are generally well served by bus routes. But rail projects are usually aimed at getting middle-class suburbanites onto transit, so they bypass the poor neighborhood. To make matters worse, transit agencies often cut back bus service in order to pay for rail construction and operations.

Because of this, the high cost of rail has provoked a backlash against rail construction in several cities. In New York, Los Angeles, and Philadelphia, bus riders successfully sued to halt spending on rail transit that forced cuts in bus service.[1] Los Angeles, for example, was spending billions of dollars on rail lines. Although Los Angeles voters agreed to pay for the lines with a sales tax, huge cost overruns led the agency to reduce bus service and increase fares to pay for the rail lines. Such policies drove ridership down from 1.6 million trips per day before rail construction began to 1.1 million trips per day by 1999.[2] This led blacks, Hispanics, and Koreans to charge that transit service to poor, minority neighborhoods was being cut to pay for rail service to middle-class, white neighborhoods.

Low-income and minority groups formed a bus riders' union and the NAACP sued on behalf of the union, charging the transit agency with discrimination. Bus riders were particularly incensed in July 1994, when the transit agency raised bus fares 23 percent but decided to spend another $123 million on a rail line to Pasadena.[3] In an out-of-court settlement, the agency agreed to restore bus service and to buy new buses.[4] In 1998, the agency decided to halt construction of at least one of the rail lines because it could not both build it and comply with the settlement. Yet by 2000, the agency faced a $44-million annual operating deficit. When the transit agency proposed to cover part of the deficit with another fare increase, transit riders threatened a fare strike. When the agency tried to save money by asking workers to accept fewer overtime hours, bus and train drivers went on a strike that lasted a month.[5]

A similar controversy can be found in San Francisco, where Muni spends a little over $225 million moving more than 200 million passengers per year. Meanwhile, BART spends $250 million moving just 80 million passengers per year, albeit on longer trips.[6] Muni is perpetually short of capital funds, while BART is spending around half a billion dollars extending its lines a few miles to San Francisco Airport.

"The growing dissonance between the quality of service provided to inner-city residents who depend on local buses and the level of public resources being spent to attract new transit riders is both economically inefficient and socially inequitable," say UC Berkeley planners Mark Garrett and Brian Taylor.[7] Rail transit is not a way of helping the urban poor. More often, it is a way of enriching construction companies.

Notes

1. David Luberoff, "What Can Transit Do?" *Governing Magazine*, November, 1999.
2. Findings of Fact and Conclusions of Law in Labor/Community Strategy Center, et al. v. Los Angeles MTA, http://www.thestrategycenter.org/Decree/findings.html.
3. Jeffrey L. Rabin, "Bus Riders Union Will Urge MTA Fare Strike," *Los Angeles Times*, July 9, 1999, p. B-3, http://www.busridersunion.org/body_7-9-99.html.
4. Consent decree in Labor/Community Strategy Center, et al. v. Los Angeles MTA, 10-26-96, http://www.ldfla.org/decree.html. Also see http://www.busridersunion.org/.
5. Jeffrey L. Rabin, "MTA Strike Has Deep Roots in Agency's Past Mistakes," *Los Angeles Times*, September 19, 2000, http://www.latimes.com/news/state/20000919/t000088492.html.
6. Federal Transit Administration, *Transit Profiles 1997* (Washington, DC: FTA, 1999), pp. 228–229.
6. Mark Garrett and Brian Taylor, "Reconsidering Social Equity in Public Transit," *Berkeley Planning Journal*, volume 13, pp. 6–27.

21. Alternatives to Rail Transit

S mart-growth plans to rebuild twenty-first century urban areas to nineteenth-century standards are unworkable, but transit remains a problem in
decentralized urban areas. Instead of moving from high-capacity buses to
higher-capacity rail cars, the solution is more likely to be found in lower capacity
transit systems that meet the needs of modern urban residents. Transit experts
have proposed numerous ideas to help transit agencies boost ridership and cope
with decentralization.

* *Dedicated busways* are often suggested as lower cost alternatives to light- or
  heavy-rail systems. However, these systems are still not very cost effective in
  moving people around.
* *Improved bus transit* on highways and streets shared with other vehicles, particularly designed around multiple hubs, is a better way of moving people
  around modern urban areas.
* *Jitneys* and *demand-responsive transit* provide the ultimate transit services to
  low-density areas.

These changes in transit services are described in more detail below. In addition, structural changes in transit agencies could allow competition with and between private operators who may be more efficient than government transit agencies. Such structural changes, including contracting out of transit operations and
ending transit agency monopolies, are discussed in detail in chapter 37 (p. 507).

Bus Rapid Transit and Busways

"Think rail, use buses," says the Federal Transit Administration of its *bus rapid
transit* program. As used by the agency, bus rapid transit includes "exclusive
transitways and HOV lanes" combined with "intelligent transportation systems
technology, priority for transit, cleaner and quieter vehicles, rapid and convenient
fare collection, and integration with land use policy."[1] Cleaner buses and improved
fare collection might be worthwhile, but exclusive busways are expensive and priority for transit and new land-use policies are both unnecessary and harmful to
urban traffic flows.

Busways are lanes of streets or highways that have been set aside exclusively for buses. A few cities, such as Pittsburgh and Ottawa, Ontario, have built highways exclusively for buses. When compared with light rail transit, the numbers are very favorable. Busways cost less than building rail lines, and because buses from many different places can get on and off the busway, the busway can end up moving far more people than a rail line.[2]

Yet the exclusivity of busways presents the same cost disadvantage as the exclusivity of rail lines. The cost of constructing an ordinary highway can be shared among all of the autos, trucks, and buses that use that highway. But the costs of building, maintaining, and operating an exclusive busway or rail transit line are solely attributable to transit riders. Busways are therefore rarely a good use of a region's limited transportation dollars.

High-occupancy vehicle (HOV) lanes are a step down in exclusivity from busways. These lanes, found today in many urban areas, are open to buses as well as cars with two or sometimes three or more occupants. The goal of such lanes is to encourage carpooling or transit by giving them a more speedy trip than single-occupancy vehicles. Yet HOV lanes have rarely boosted carpooling, with the result that the HOV lanes often appear nearly empty even when the other lanes are heavily congested. Since HOV lanes usually cost more to build than regular lanes, many analysts have concluded that the money can more effectively be spent building general-purpose lanes.[3]

If bus rapid transit means fast, efficient bus service without impeding other traffic flows, then it is a good idea. But if it means the same high costs and urban redevelopment as rail transit, then it is a waste of money and energy. As the next section will show, cities can have faster bus service at a low cost without creating more traffic jams.

Improved Bus Service

New rail transit lines can often increase transit ridership in the rail corridor—not because people like trains better than buses but because transit agencies usually offer significantly improved rail service over the previous bus service. These service improvements include greater frequencies, fewer stops and therefore faster trips, and easily identified destinations.

Conventional *local bus service* generally consists of buses every fifteen minutes to every hour that stop twelve or more times every mile. In the Twin Cities, routes 7 and 19, which operate every 11 to 30 minutes, take 50 to 61 minutes to go from the Mall of America in Bloomington to Nicollet Mall in downtown Minneapolis.[4]

Most cities supplement local bus routes with some *express bus service*. Express buses may run a short route of several stops at either end, and then travel long distances while making no stops, or perhaps only one or two stops. Express buses are much faster than local buses but often operate less frequently. Twin Cities express route 80, which runs roughly every half hour, takes 25 minutes to get from the Mall of America to Nicollet Mall with three stops. Express route 72M takes only 21 minutes with one stop, but runs only two or three times a day each way.

By comparison, light- or heavy-rail service typically runs every five to twenty minutes. This means that travelers can go the transit stations almost any time with confidence that a train will arrive soon. Rail transit typically stops more frequently than an express bus but far less frequently than a local bus route. For example, the Twin Cities' Hiawatha light rail is expected to run every 7.5 to 10 minutes from the Mall of America to downtown Minneapolis, with fifteen inter-mediate stops. Over most of the journey it will stop less than twice per mile, so travel time will be 31 minutes. This means that those who take express buses now will face longer journeys but those who take local buses will save time. New riders attracted to the light-rail line will be responding to its speed and frequency.

Rail has one other advantage over buses: ease or transparency of use. Except in New York and three or four other urban areas, most cities with rail transit have so few rail lines that it is easy to see where they go. In contrast, buses can go any-where and bus riders must be acutely aware of routes as well as schedules. As anyone who has taken a New York subway knows, this simplicity disappears as rail lines proliferate.

Cities sincerely interested in better transit could improve bus service in ways that replicate and improve on rail's apparent advantages without the expense of rail construction or the inconvenience of feeder buses. This means:
1. Running buses more frequently;
2. Adding semi-express routes that stop less frequently;
3. Hub-and-spoke design around multiple hubs; and
4. Clearly marking buses with colors that vary by destination, route, and fre-quency.

More Frequent Service: Transit riders are highly sensitive to frequencies. If a bus is scheduled every ten minutes from, say, 6:00 AM to 11:00 PM, then riders can dispense with schedules and simply show up at the bus stop any time. The simple step of increasing local bus frequencies from every 15 to 30 minutes to every 7 to 12 minutes can significantly increase ridership. This was one of the most success-ful tools used by Portland's transit agency during the 1970s.

Less Frequent Stops: Transit riders are also highly sensitive to speed. Express buses that make few or no stops between end points are popular, but only serve the people who need to go between those end points. Light rail is midway between an express bus and a local bus in that it stops one to two times per mile over most of its journey. *Limited bus service*—buses on light-rail schedules—could serve far more people than express buses yet be far faster than local buses and far less expensive than rail. Unlike rail, limited buses could serve several different routes between two end points, thus avoiding the need for feeder buses.

Multiple Hubs: Most urban bus systems still follow the streetcar hub-and-spoke pattern with just one downtown hub. Almost any trip from one place to another, neither of which are downtown, must go downtown and usually transfer to another bus. Partly due to downtown's political muscle, many freeway networks and most new rail systems follow this same pattern.

Modern urban areas have many employment, retail, and entertainment centers, some of which are equal in size and many of which are growing faster than downtown. The low-density suburbs around these centers are not well served by downtown-oriented transit. The solution is to connect every center with every other center using express or limited bus service. These bus routes would only go downtown if it happened to be on the most direct route between centers. Local feeder buses would radiate from each of the centers through residential areas.

The drawback of the multiple-hub system is that it requires many people to transfer more than once. Someone whose origin and destination are both outside of centers might have to transfer from a local bus to an express bus to another local bus. Though this drawback is shared with most rail systems, as a rule of thumb transit riders do not like to transfer more than once.[5] Transit riders who dislike transferring would probably drive to or be dropped off at park-and-ride stations at the centers just as they do for rail transit.

Clear Markings: The Washington Metro subway system has blue, red, green, yellow, and orange lines. All stations are clearly marked with the colors of the lines that go to those stations. This makes it easy to find the train that goes where you want to go. The difficulty with buses is that most cities have scores of bus routes yet there are only a few primary colors. The conventional solution is to identify buses by number. But when there are dozens of bus routes, this becomes too complicated for any but the most dedicated transit riders to understand.

The multiple hub-and-spoke system helps solve this problem since all express and limited buses and most local buses would be destined for one of just a few regional centers. The transit agency would identify each regional center with a characteristic color or logo: bright red or a rose for downtown Portland, brown or a beaver for Beaverton, and so forth. With appropriate creativity, different colors or symbols could be used for a score or more basic destinations. Buses would display a large flag or placard displaying this color or logo. A second logo would designate the kind of bus service offered: perhaps a checkered flag for express service, green for limited service, and yellow for local service. Bus stops would be correspondingly marked: large red markers where downtown-destined buses stop, checkered flags where express buses stop, and so forth.

This system remains a little more complicated than the five colors of the Washington subway. But residents would have a much easier time grasping the essentials and, freed by increased frequencies from worrying about schedules, could easily find their way around an urban area with little more than a map showing the colors or logos for each center.

Increased express and limited bus service serving multiple hubs sounds a little like a smart-growth dream. But I have no illusions that transit improvements will entice large numbers of auto drivers out of their cars. Instead, the goal of a speedy, decentralized, and transparent bus network is to provide better service at low cost for those who cannot or choose not to drive. At an overall cost that is probably less than the cost of a single rail line, this system would significantly improve transportation over an entire metropolitan area.

Jitneys and Demand-Responsive Transit

The basic problem with rail transit is that it is a high-capacity transit system that is unsuited for low-density, decentralized urban areas. The multiple-hub, express and limited bus services described above contemplate 30- to 72-seat buses, which are still relatively high in capacity. Yet conditions in many low-density areas call for truly low-capacity transit operations: vans or minivans providing people with door-to-door or nearly door-to-door service.

"The ideal transit system will take its passengers from door to door with no transfers, with little waiting—and it will fit the small number of persons having the same origin, the same destination, and the same schedule," says UC planning Professor Melvin Webber. "Only such a system can compete with the private car on its own grounds."[6] This is a perfect description of jitneys.

Jitneys are small—generally six- to twenty-four-passenger—vehicles that carry passengers over regular routes but allow flexible schedules.[7] They are generally privately operated and operators keep their own schedules. Naturally, they are more likely to operate during high demand periods and so meet the needs of transit users. While they may follow regular routes, drivers are often willing to diverge from those routes to meet the needs of passengers.

Atlantic City, New Jersey, relies on a non-subsidized jitney service that has operated since 1915. Nearly 200 jitneys operate on four different routes 24 hours a day, seven days a week.[8] New York has long had jitney services, though they usually have not been legal. But recently the city authorized a private van service in Brooklyn.[10] Several towns in New Jersey operate public jitneys that connect neighborhoods with New Jersey Transit train stations.[11] The city of Miami created a jitney service that now carries well over 40,000 people per day—three-quarters of whom were previously driving cars. Riders say they like it because it is fast, convenient, and inexpensive.

In some places in the U.S., jitney service has developed spontaneously. The

San Francisco Bay Bridge has toll-free lanes for vehicles with three or more people. University of California planning Professor Melvin Webber observes that "Solo drivers now stop at BART stations and bus stops to pick up two passengers—strangers who've been waiting in polite queues."[10] This saves the drivers $1 and a twenty-minute wait in line.

Jitneys are far more common in third world countries, where they are often the main components of local transit.[12] More than 40 percent of black commuters in South Africa ride some 105,000 unsubsidized minibuses to work in the nation's major metropolitan areas.[13] (By comparison, all U.S. urban transit agencies operate less than 44,000 buses.[14]) As described below, the main obstacle to jitney service in the U.S. is laws giving transit agencies legal monopolies over public mass transit.

Demand-responsive transit is another low-capacity transit service sometimes called *dial-a-ride* or *smart jitneys*. A cross between a jitney and a taxi, demand-responsive minibuses pick people up at their door and drop them off at their destinations with intervening stops to pick up and drop off other people. Transit riders call to order service, and a central operator routes the most appropriate bus to their door. Operators would use computer systems that keep track of the locations and destinations of minibuses in service, perhaps with the help of the geographic positioning satellite system. It may even be possible to completely automate calls for service using touch-tone phones.

Under the Americans with Disabilities Act, most U.S. urban transit agencies must provide demand-responsive transit to disabled people. Such services are very costly per passenger, partly because of the expense of handicapped-accessible buses but mainly because the costs of the service are spread among very few riders. A first step toward demand-responsive service could be to simply expand the number of people using the existing service. In many places, opening transit to private competition as described in the next section could lead private operators to spontaneously begin such service with low or no subsidies.

Because most cities in the U.S. rely solely on taxis and high-capacity buses or rail cars for public transportation, the idea of replacing some or all of the 44-seat buses now in service with 7-passenger minivans or 15-passenger vans seems strange and unrealistic. But "the ideal transit system will take its passengers from door to door with no transfers, with little waiting—and that it will fit the small number of persons having the same origin, the same destination, and the same schedule," notes Webber. "Only such a system can compete with the private car on its own grounds."

An even better transit system might combine the improved bus service previously described with jitneys and smart jitneys. Instead of the two-tiered public transport system we have today—transit and taxis—this would create a three-tiered system with three different price levels. People riding the express, limited, and local buses would continue paying about a dollar a ride; people taking taxis would continue paying by the mile, while people using the jitneys might pay $2 to $5 a ride. This would give people more choices and allow them to tailor their public transport usage to their needs and income.

Notes

1. Federal Transit Administration, "Bus Rapid Transit," http://brt.volpe.dot.gov/.
2. John F. Kain, "The Case for Bus Rapid Transit," *Nieman Reports*, Winter, 1997, pp. 39–43.
3. Joy Dahlgren, "Are HOV Lanes Really Better?" *Access* 6 (Spring, 1995): 25–29.
4. Metro Transit schedules, http://www.metrocouncil.org/transit/index.asp.
5. Joel Garreau, *Edge City: Life on the New Frontier* (New York, NY: Doubleday, 1991), p. 467.
6. Melvin Webber, "The Marriage of Autos and Transit: How to Make Transit Popular Again," *Access* 5 (Fall, 1994):26–31.
7. Daniel B. Klein, Adrian T. Moore, and Binyam Reja, "Free to Cruise: Creating Curb Space for Jitneys," *Access* 8 (Spring, 1996), p. 2.
8. Atlantic City Jitney Association, "Atlantic City Jitneys," http://www.virtualac.com/jitney.
9. Cascade Policy Institute, "Tri-Met, Jitneys & Curb Rights: Exploring Transit Alternatives," 1999, http://www.cascadepolicy.org/archive/moore.htm.
10. Kelly Heyboer, "Towns to split $3.5 million for rail shuttles," *Star-Ledger*, August 19, 1998, http://www.gsenet.org/library/21trn/jitneys-.txt.
11. Melvin Webber, "The Marriage of Autos and Transit: How to Make Transit Popular Again," *Access* 5:26–31.
12. Ibid.
13. Cascade Policy Institute, "Tri-Met, Jitneys & Curb Rights."
14. Federal Transit Administration, *Transit Profiles: Agencies in Urbanized Areas with Population Greater than 200,000, 1997* (Washington, DC: FTA, 1999), p. A-3, and *Transit Profiles: Agencies in Urbanized Areas with Population Less than 200,000, 1997*, p. A-3.

Part Six

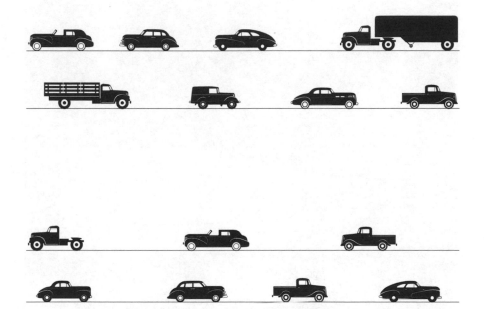

Highways and Mobility

Traffic calming barricades are designed to slow traffic and they also can remove some on-street parking (top, see p. 349).

Portland is imposing traffic calming on many major travel corridors by blocking right turn lanes and barricading parts of the left-turn lanes (bottom, see p. 113). In some cases, four-lane streets will be converted to two-lane streets, with the extra space used for bike lanes and/or wider sidewalks.

22. The Politics of Stasis

```
SIGNALS
TIMED
TO
REQUIRE
FREQUENT
STOPS
```

In 1993, Los Angeles opened the seventeen-mile, eight-lane Century Freeway. At over $100 million per mile, or about $15 million per lane mile, and a total cost of more than $2 billion, some called it the most expensive road in the world.[1] That title is being superseded, however, by Boston's Central Artery, dubbed the *Big Dig* by local residents and the *megaproject* by transportation analysts.[2] The state of Massachusetts calls the Central Artery "the largest, most complex, and technically challenging highway project ever attempted in American history."[3] Scheduled for completion in 2004, the Big Dig is currently projected to cost $12.2 billion for 161 lane miles of traffic, or a whopping $75 million per lane mile.

These two highways, as well as many other central city freeways built in the last thirty years, were constructed only after years of local debate. Although suburbanites make far fewer objections to freeways in their vicinity, the war on sprawl has made construction or expansion of any urban or suburban highways controversial.

Between the mid-1950s and the mid-1970s, U.S. urban freeway networks grew by about 5 percent each year.[4] Despite their detractors, these freeways produced enormous benefits: speeding traffic, reducing travel and shipping costs, relieving congestion on other roads, and increasing safety. During this time, urban travel grew by nearly 5 percent per year, with increasing amounts of it on the freeways. After the mid-1970s, however, rising costs due to inflation combined with increasing hostility to roads slowed freeway construction rates to less than 2 percent per year. Yet urban travel continued to grow by close to 4 percent per year, leading to huge increases in congestion. The Texas Transportation Institute estimates that, from 1982 to 1997, the average amount of time each auto driver in major urban areas was stuck in traffic nearly tripled.[5] "The politics of stasis," says interstate highway historian Mark Rose, "has displaced the politics of growth."[6]

Smart growth descended from this anti-auto political movement. Although smart-growth advocates frequently use people's worries about congestion as a way of gaining support for their cause, their real goal is to *increase* congestion. This can be seen by carefully reading smart-growth plans for various urban areas. Many of

these plans include policies that:
- Promote congestion;
- Limit new road capacity;
- Reduce existing road capacities; and
- Reduce mobility standards.

Promoting Congestion

"It is widely assumed," says Anthony Downs, "that high levels of peak-hour high-way congestion will stimulate public transit patronage."[7] Although Downs and most other objective analysts have concluded that this is not true, transit agencies and their supporters still promote the idea either because they believe it is true or to gain large federal grants. As commuting expert Alan Pisarski predicts, increasing congestion "will lead to searches for. . . transit 'magic bullets' to solve mobility problems [and] increasing calls for growth controls."[8] That, of course, is what smart-growth advocates are counting on.
- The Twin Cities' Metropolitan Council is minimizing new highway construction in the region for twenty years. "As traffic congestion builds," says the council, "alternative travel modes will become more attractive," including mass transit.[9]
- The Port of Portland, which is helping pay for a light-rail line to Portland's airport, says that one of the elements needed for "successful airport rail" is a "congested highway and roadway access system."[10]
- Metro projects that its plan for Portland will triple local traffic congestion. But far from being bad, says Metro, "Congestion signals positive urban development."[11]

Opposing New Road Capacity

While smart-growth advocates often say they desire a "balanced transportation system," in fact their real goal is to transfer as much road funding to transit or other purposes as possible and to spend what road funding remains on maintenance instead of new construction. A recent report by the Surface Transportation Policy Project criticizes the states for spending too many federal transportation dollars on road construction and not spending enough on transit or other alternatives. "Funding that had been going to repair roads and bridges and provide people transportation choices is now going to build new and wider highways," which the group describes as a "negative trend."[12]

In fact, during the 1990s, total federal spending on surface transportation increased by more than 50 percent, enabling increases in spending on transit, repair, and new highways. But the Policy Project is upset because the *percentage* of spending on transit hasn't increased during the decade. Increased spending on either transit or repair, of course, would force a decrease in spending on new road capacity. Even as the group opposes new highway construction, it also opposes increased spending on highway reconstruction, claiming that stories of crumbling roads and bridges is a "false crisis" perpetuated by the highway lobby.[13]

Each year, Friends of the Earth and the budget watchdog group Taxpayers for Common Sense publish *Road to Ruin*, a list of federal road projects that the two groups think should be stopped. Some of the roads on the list are pure pork and probably aren't needed. But others are proposed in congested areas and the groups oppose them because they will reduce congestion and allow more people to live in low-density suburbs.[14] The Sierra Club web site maintains a list of highway projects that it opposes, along with links to the club's chapters that are fighting local projects.[15]

Restricting Existing Road Capacity

Traffic engineers used to pride themselves on improving traffic flows. One technique was to time traffic lights to allow traffic to move at a steady speed. Signs were often posted that read, "SIGNALS SET FOR 30 MPH" or some such speed. Times have changed. Traffic planning is now run by regional planners, not traffic engineers. Today, a sign on the Mystic Parkway in the Boston suburb of Medford, Massachusetts reads "SIGNALS TIMED TO REQUIRE FREQUENT STOPS." Boston's Metropolitan District Commission, which manages parks and parkways, wants people to know that no one driving on a Boston-area parkway should expect to get where they are going in a reasonably short period of time.

"A few planners have stopped trying to ease traffic congestion," discovered *All Things Considered* reporter Steve Inskeep. "Instead, they're embracing congestion. They want to create more of it. Several cities are experimenting with making streets narrower, so traffic moves more slowly. It's called *traffic calming*." Inskeep added that, "Traffic calming experts want to replicate places like Hoboken, New Jersey, though it is a nightmare for commuters at rush hour." Portland's U.S. Representative Earl Blumenaeur told Inskeep that narrow, busy streets can improve a neighborhood by making it "too crowded. And that is congestion that is exciting. It means business to the merchants. It means an exciting street life. It's the sort of the hustle and bustle—and people don't mind going slow."[16]

Traffic calming consists of roadway barriers and other techniques designed to slow traffic and reduce roadway capacities. "Traffic calming can be defined as the restraining of automobile traffic through the use of measures which physically alter the operational characteristics of a roadway," says Kris Jacobson, a planner for the city of Stoney Creek, Ontario.[17] Originally designed as a safety measure to reduce speeding on neighborhood streets, traffic calming is now eagerly endorsed by anti-auto groups for use on major collectors and arterials. On these roads, the real purpose of traffic calming is to make it harder for people to drive. In such cases, traffic calming represents a major turnaround for transportation agencies, which have traditionally tried to reduce congestion.

Like so many phrases coined by smart-growth planners, traffic calming plays on public fears, in this case, the fear of road rage. Some reporters have been gulled into believing that traffic calming is a cure for road rage—as if people irritated by congestion will be relieved to drive even slower.[18] In fact, traffic calming has nothing to do with road rage, which itself is a very rare phenomena that has little to do with congestion.

The city of Portland spends about $2 million per year on traffic calming. Table one, from Portland's web site, indicates that a few traffic calming devices are aimed at pedestrian safety, but most are intended to reduce traffic speeds or volumes. Portland even evaluates the "effectiveness" of each device by how much it reduces speeds or volumes. For one device only, the city wryly notes that "some drivers consider it a disadvantage."

Many traffic calming devices also reduce the available parking on the street. Smart-growth planners consider this a side-benefit because less parking will force some people to drive less. Cul-de-sacs and diverters on neighborhood streets also reduce the "connectivity" of streets, which is ironic because Peter Calthorpe and other smart-growth architects criticize the suburbs for lacking connectivity and recommend that cul-de-sacs be forbidden.

Traffic calming is an especially serious problem when applied to the busy streets that link neighborhood streets with freeways and other major highways. "Boulevarding" is the application of numerous traffic calming devices, including curb extensions, pedestrian refuges, and median barriers, to major arterials. Boulevarding can turn arterials with four major lanes of traffic, plus a continuous left turn lane and auxiliary right turn lanes, into streets with just two to four lanes of traffic, an occasional left-turn lane, and no right-turn lanes. Boulevarding's median strips limit an auto driver's ability to reach businesses on the opposite side of a highway. The curb extensions eliminate right-turn lanes, so anyone who slows to turn right forces everyone behind them to slow down as well. Turning commercial arterials—derisively known as "strip malls"—into boulevards can devastate retailers and other local businesses.

"The engineering manuals demonstrate statistically that roads carry more traffic at 30 MPH than they do at higher speeds," says Andres Duany. "As cars breach 30 MPH, they begin to spread apart, and this increased vehicle spacing results in a drop in roadway capacity."[19] Duany is misreading his highway manuals: What he says is true when applied to a freeway, but when planners slow traffic on a major arterial by making lanes narrower, removing right-turn lanes, and adding speed bumps, they reduce the streets capacity as well as slow it down. Besides, telling people that throughput is greater at slower speeds doesn't make them feel better about driving 30 miles per hour on a 70-mile-per-hour highway. Traffic engineers

Table One: Traffic Calming Devices
Speed Reduction

Speed Bumps: Speed bumps are intended to reduce vehicle speeds. Fourteen-foot speed bumps are very effective at encouraging 25 MPH vehicle speeds. Twenty-two-foot speed bumps are very effective at encouraging 30 MPH vehicle speeds.

Traffic Circles: Traffic circles are raised islands placed in an intersection. . . . Traffic circles require drivers to slow to a speed that allows them to comfortably maneuver around them. The primary benefit of traffic circles is they reduce the number of angle and turning collisions. An additional benefit is they slow high-speed traffic. . . .

Chicanes: A chicane changes a street's path from straight to serpentine. A chicane may be constructed to give the illusion, from a distance, that a street no longer continues. A chicane is intended to reduce vehicle speeds with less impact on emergency vehicles.

Entrance Treatments: Entrance treatments consist of physical and textural changes to streets and are located at key entry ways into a neighborhood. . . . The intent is a reduction is speed. Entrance treatments have minimal influence on drivers' routine behavior.

Pedestrian Safety

Pedestrian Refuges/Slow Points: Pedestrian refuges narrow the roadway available to a driver, provide a visual cue to drivers that they are in a popular pedestrian area, and provide a refuge for pedestrians so they can cross a street one half at a time, if they prefer. Pedestrian refuges are effective pedestrian amenities but have minimal influence on a driver's behavior.

Curb Extensions: Curb extensions narrow the street by widening the sidewalk or the landscaped parking strip. . . . Curb extensions effectively improve pedestrian safety by reducing the street crossing distance and improving sight distance. They may also slightly influence driver behavior by changing the appearance of the street.

Raised Crosswalks: Raised cross walks are cross walks constructed 3-4 inches above the elevation of the street. . . . Raised cross walks are intended to reduce vehicle speeds specifically where pedestrians will be crossing a street. . . .

Reduce Traffic Volume

Diagonal Diverters: Diagonal diverters place a barrier diagonally across an intersection, disconnecting the legs of the intersection. Strategically located diagonal diverters reduce traffic volumes on a street. . . . Advantages: Effectively reduce traffic volumes. Can restrict vehicle access while retaining bicycle and pedestrian access. Disadvantages: Prohibit or limit access and movement. While this is the purpose of diversion devices, some drivers consider it a disadvantage. Restricts access for emergency and transit vehicles.

Semi-Diverters: Semi-diverters are curb extensions or islands that block one lane of the street. . . . Strategically located, semi-diverters can effectively reduce traffic volumes on a street. . . .

Median Barriers: A median barrier is a concrete curb or island that is located on the centerline of a street and continues through the street's intersection with a given cross street. Strategically located median barriers reduce traffic volumes on a street. Median barriers prevent left turns from the through street and left turns and through moves from the cross street. . . .

Cul-de-sacs: Cul-de-Sacs close one end of a street. Portland uses Cul-de-sacs according to the conditions and needs of a given street. . . . Cul-de-sacs are very effective at reducing cut-through and general traffic volume.

Vehicle Exclusion Lanes: Exclusion lanes are lanes for a particular class of vehicle, excluding all others. The most common examples are the bus-only, bicycle and car pool/diamond lanes. . . . The effectiveness of exclusion lanes varies with the location of their placement. . . .

Choke Points: Choke Points are curb extensions placed mid block to narrow the roadway to 14' or the equivalent of one travel lane. Choke Points are intended to reduce traffic volumes by making the roadway narrow so that only one car at a time can pass through it. . . .

Source: City of Portland, Traffic Calming Devices, http://www.trans.ci.portland.or.us/ Traffic_Management/trafficcalming/ DEVICES/DEVICES.HTM.

know this: That's why they grade high-speed traffic conditions with low through-put "A" while low-speed traffic with high throughput is graded "E."

Traffic calming has limited benefits for pedestrians and bicyclists, and those benefits can usually be achieved in ways that don't interfere with auto traffic. For example, bicyclists are attracted to quiet neighborhood streets parallel to major arterials that have been turned into clearly marked bike routes, especially if the number of stop signs on those streets is limited. They are less attracted to riding on busy arterials even if the traffic on those arterials has been slowed slightly by narrowing the lanes. At least one traffic calming practice—turning one-way streets into two-way streets—significantly reduces pedestrian safety. Studies show that changing two-way to one-way streets typically reduces accidents by 20 to 60 percent.[20]

One important side effect of traffic calming is increased air pollution. A study of traffic calming in Portland, Maine, found that traffic calming, by slowing traffic, increased hydrocarbon emissions by 46 percent. As a result, the Federal Highway Administration stopped spending federal air quality funds on traffic calming in the area.[21]

Fire districts and other emergency service providers often have serious objections to traffic calming devices that slow traffic. The Portland Fire Bureau studied speed bumps and traffic circles with video cameras and concluded that each bump or circle would delay fire trucks by up to 10 seconds—seconds that can be critical when people's lives are involved.[22] Political considerations muted the fire bureau's objections. But some analysts believe that traffic calming could end up costing far more lives than it could possibly save. "Traffic calming devices are a tradeoff of the perception of increased safety from speeding vehicles for the real risk to citizen survivability from delays to emergency response," says Boulder resident Kathleen Calongne.[23] According to calculations by physicist Ronald Bowman, the deaths from impediments to emergency services are likely to far exceed the lives saved by traffic calming.[24] An analysis by an assistant fire chief in Austin, TX, found that traffic calming "loses 37 lives" to heart attacks caused by a delay in emergency service vehicles "for every life saved" due to fewer auto-pedestrian collisions.[25]

Traffic calming is bad for commuters and bad for businesses. Cities that follow Portland's example will impose huge congestion costs on their residents with few benefits for anyone.

Reducing Mobility Standards

Most state and local highway departments use mobility standards, also known as performance or levels-of-service standards, to rank potential transportation investments. As described in the Portland case study, transportation engineers grade highway congestion or *levels of service* (LOS) from A to F, with A being free-flowing traffic and F being stop-and-go traffic. A typical mobility standard "uses

LOS C as a design standard and LOS D as the minimum tolerable operating standard."[26] In other words, roads are built to provide enough capacity to keep congestion at or above level of service C and capacity is supposed to be added if congestion gets worse than level of service D.

An important purpose of this concept was to insure that road funds are allocated based on where they are needed, not on pork barrel. If roads in one area consistently provide level of service A while roads in another area often provide only level of service D or E, then too much money has been spent in the former area and not enough in the latter. A quiet goal of smart-growth advocates today is to eliminate or relax these standards so dollars can be spent on rail transit, which does little to reduce congestion, or traffic calming, which increases congestion, even if highway congestion increases to E or F levels. As the Portland case study notes, Portland transportation planners have applied a mobility standard of level of service F to area freeways and streets that are paralleled by light-rail lines in the hope that congestion drives people to use light rail.

Notes

1. Joseph Dimento, Drusilla Van Hengel, and Sherry Ryan, "The Century Freeway: Design by Court Decree," *Access*, 9 (Fall, 1996): 7.
2. David Luberoff, Alan Altshuler, and Christie Baxter, *Mega-Project: A Political History of Boston's Multibillion Dollar Artery/Tunnel Project* (Cambridge, MA: Harvard University, 1994), 238 pp.
3. The Central Artery/Tunnel Project, "Central Artery/Tunnel Project," http://www.bigdig.com.
4. These numbers are approximate based on data in Federal Highway Administration, *Highway Statistics Summary to 1995* (Washington, DC: FHwA, 1996), table HM-220.
5. David Schrank and Tim Lomax, *1999 Annual Mobility Report: Information for Urban America* (College Station, TX: Texas A&M, 1999), table 4.
6. Mark Rose, *Interstate: Express Highway Politics, 1939–1989* (Knoxville, TN: University of Tennessee Press, 1990), p. xi.
7. Anthony Downs, *Stuck in Traffic: Coping with Peak-Hour Traffic Congestion* (Washington, DC: Brookings, 1992), p. 30.
8. Alan E. Pisarski, "Issues in Transportation and Growth Management," *in* David J. Brower, David R. Godschalk, and Douglas R. Porter (eds.), *Understanding Growth Management: Critical Issues and a Research Agenda* (Washington, DC: Urban Land Institute, 1989), p. 125.
9. Metropolitan Council, *Transportation Policy Plan* (St. Paul, MN: Metropolitan Council, 1996), p. 54.
10. Port of Portland, *PDX Light Rail Slide Show*, slide 2, "Successful Airport Rail," 1999.
11. Metro, *Regional Transportation Plan Update* (Portland, OR: Metro, March 1996), p. 1-20.
12. Barbara McCann, Roy Kienitz, and Bianca DeLille, *Changing Direction: Federal Transportation Spending in the 1990s* (Washington, DC: STPP, 2000), p. 5, http://www.transact.org/Reports/Cd/tea21color.pdf.
13. Hank Dittmar and Donald D. T. Chen, *Crying Wolf: The False "Crisis" of America's Crumbling Roads and Bridges* (Washington, DC: STPP, 1996), http://www.transact.org/

Reports/Wolf/wlfmn.htm.

14. Bryan Knowles and David Hirsch, *Road to Ruin: The 50 Worst Road Projects in America* (Washington, DC: Taxpayers for Common Sense, 1999), http://www.taxpayer.net/TCS/RoadRuin/R2R.pdf.

15. Sierra Club, "Projects in the Balance," http://www.sierraclub.org/sprawl/transportation/highways.asp.

16. Steve Inskeep, "Commuting IV," *All Things Considered*, May 30, 1997, http://www.npr.org/ramfiles/970539.atc.04.ram.

17. Kris Jacobson, *Traffic Calming*, http://www.netaccess.on.ca/~jacobson/calming.html

18. Sarah Glazer, "Putting the Brakes on Pushy Drivers," *The Oregonian*, July 23, 1997, p. A13.

19. Andres Duany, Elizabeth Plater-Zyberk, and Jeff Speck, *Suburban Nation: The Rise of Sprawl and the Decline of the American Dream* (New York, NY: North Point Press, 2000), p. 196n.

20. Oregon State Highway Department, *A Study of One-Way Street Routings on Urban Highways in Oregon* (Salem, OR: Oregon State Highway Commission, 1959), p. 15.

21. Letter from Steven Beningo, Federal Highway Administration, to John Melrose, Maine Department of Transportation, on Stevens Avenue Traffic Calming Report, August 13, 1998, http://www.speedhumps.com/archives/pollution.htm.

22. Crystal Atkins and Michael Coleman, "The Influence of Traffic Calming on Emergency Response Times," *Institute of Traffic Engineers Journal*, August 1997, p. 42.

23. Kathleen Calongne, "Problems Associated with Traffic Calming," October, 1999, http://www.users.uswest.net/~erinard/problems_associated_with_traffic.htm.

24. Ronald Bowman, "Deaths Expected from Delayed Emergency Response Due to Neighborhood Traffic Calming," April, 1997, http://members.aol.com/raybowman/risk97/eval1.html.

25. Leslie W. Bunte, Jr., "Traffic Calming Programs & Emergency Response: A Competition of Two Public Goods," professional report prepared in partial fulfillment of the requirements for the degree of Master of Public Affairs, University of Texas at Austin, 2000.

26. D&M Group, *Highway Level of Service Technical Memorandum: I-15 North Corridor* (Salt Lake City, UT: UT DOT, 1998), p. 1.

Web Tools: Urban Mobility

How mobile are people in your urban area? Compare miles of roads by type (interstates, other freeways, other arterials, collectors, and local streets) with miles of travel for each type in http://www.fhwa.dot.gov/ohim/hs98/tables/hm71.wks (Lotus format) or http://www.fhwa.dot.gov/ohim/hs98/tables/hm71.pdf (Acrobat format) for nearly 400 urban areas.

Highway Finance Facts

Federal highway user fees paid in excess of federal highway expenses:
  1921 to 1998: $47.5 billion
  1998: $3.7 billion

State highway user fees paid in excess of state highway expenses:
  1921 to 1998: $124.5 billion
  1998: $6.6 billion

Local highway expenses in excess of local highway user fees paid:
  1921 to 1998: $783.1 billion
  1998: $17.9 billion

Total highway expenses in excess of total highway user fees paid:
  1921 to 1998: $611.1 billion
  1936 to 1998: $451.1 billion
  1998: $7.6 billion

Total vehicle miles driven:
  1936 to 1998: 71.2 trillion
  1998: 2.6 trillion

Subsidy per vehicle mile driven:
  1936 to 1998: 0.6¢
  1998: 0.3¢

Sources: FHwA, Highway Statistics Summary to 1995, tables HF-210 and VM-201; FHwA, Highway Statistics 1996, 1997, and 1998, tables HF-10 and VM-1. All dollars are adjusted for inflation to 1998.

The Air Pollution Myth

Myth: Automotive air pollution is getting worse every year.
Reality: Air pollution controls have significantly cleaned up urban air, while attempts to discourage auto driving have had little or no effect.

Air pollution is the chief social cost of driving, though autos also pollute storm sewer runoff. The best and most successful way of treating these costs is to treat them directly by regulating emissions, as has so successfully been done for auto air pollution, or by charging auto drivers pollution fees if they drive dirty cars. Attempts to reduce auto driving are indirect approaches that will do little about pollution or other social costs.

Automotive air pollution was a serious problem when Congress passed the Clean Air Act in 1970. Thanks to that law, urban air has been getting cleaner ever since. Although urban auto travel has nearly doubled, most automotive air pollutants, including hydrocarbons (also known as volatile organic compounds or VOCs) and carbon monoxide, have declined by 40 percent or more.

For example, in 1997 urban Americans drove passenger cars nearly 92 percent more miles than in 1970, yet various pollutants declined by 31 to nearly 100 percent (table one). Total driving, including light and heavy trucks, increased by 174 percent in that time period, yet most pollutants declined by 40 to nearly 100 percent. The major exception was nitrogen oxides, which declined by only 5 percent, because federal pollution standards for cars don't apply to light trucks or Diesels. A minor exception is sulphur dioxide: Autos are not a major source of that pollutant so they haven't been targeted with tight pollution standards.

Nearly all of this decline is due to the requirement that new cars be built with catalytic converters and other pollution reduction equipment. By comparison, the nation has spent billions of dollars on mass transit, but today's urban transit systems consume more energy, and probably pollute as much, per passenger mile as autos.[1] The EPA rates the New York metropolitan area, whose multiple high-density centers come closest to smart growth's preferred pattern of development, as having "extreme" air pollution problems. Transit and smart growth do not reduce pollution.

Table One: Urban Driving and Pollution, 1970 and 1997

	1970	1997	% Change
Passenger Cars			
Billion Miles Driven	496	951	92
Million Tons CO	63.8	26.8	−58
Million Tons NOx	4.2	2.9	−31
Million Tons VOCs	9.1	2.7	−70
Million Tons SO2	132	128	−3
Million Tons PM-10	224	56	−75
Tons Lead	142,918	12	−100
All Motor Vehicles			
Billion Miles Driven	570	1,560	174
Million Tons CO	88.0	50.3	−43
Million Tons NOx	7.4	7.0	−5
Million Tons VOCs	13.0	5.2	−60
Million Tons SO2	411	320	−22
Million Tons PM-10	443	268	−40
Tons Lead	171,961	19	−100

Source: Pollution: EPA, http://www.epa.gov/ttn/chief/trends97/appndA.pdf. Miles driven: FHwA, Highway Statistics Summary to 1995, table VM-201; FHwA, Highway Statistics 1998, table VM-2.

University of California economists Kenneth Small and Camilla Kazimi estimated that in 1992 the cost to human health of Los Angeles air pollution was 3 cents per vehicle mile. They predicted that this would fall "to half that amount in the year 2000" due to cleaner cars.[2] The costs would be considerably lower, they added, outside of Los Angeles, the nation's most polluted city. Based on these estimates, they concluded that policies that reduce emissions from autos are worthwhile, but that "our findings do not provide much support for policies to reduce motor vehicle use overall."[3]

New cars produce only a fraction of the pollution emitted by the average car on the road. A pollution fee that made motorists pay for the pollutants they emit would encourage people to drive cleaner cars, but would not greatly reduce auto travel. That may be why many smart-growth advocates and other auto-hostile interests are not enthusiastic about proposals for a pollution emissions fee. Their goal is to reduce auto driving, not clean the air. Air pollution may be just an excuse they use for their heavy-handed regulation.

The Environmental Protection Agency first tried to regulate driving after Congress passed the 1970 Clean Air Act. But members of Congress and other elected officials strongly protested, so the agency concentrated on the pollution-reduction technologies that ultimately did so much to clean the air.[4] But in the 1990s, the EPA returned once again to the idea of using congestion and regulation to try to reduce the amount people drive. For example, Congress appropriates $1 billion per year for a congestion mitigation/air quality (CMAQ) fund. But the EPA doesn't want to spend CMAQ dollars on projects that reduce congestion because less congestion might simply encourage more people to drive.[5] Similarly, the EPA's Transportation Partners program (see chapter 12) focused exclusively on reducing driving, not cleaning the air.[6]

All the available research shows that policies aimed at discouraging driving won't work. In 1993, the EPA and U.S. Department of Transportation prepared a joint review of the effectiveness of transportation control strategies. "Based on preliminary indications," the report found, transportation control measures such as huge investments in transit, employee commute options, and strict land-use regulation "have not yet been shown to significantly reduce emissions." In 1995, a group of experts gathered by the Transportation Research Board—a branch of the U.S. Department of Transportation—concluded that "curbing growth in motor vehicle travel by limiting highway capacity is at best an indirect approach for achieving emissions reductions from the transportation sector that is likely to have relatively small effects" on air pollution.[7]

Future improvements in air quality are not going to come from forcing people to live in dense cities, forcing employers to convince their employees not to drive, or forcing taxpayers to pay for expensive rail transit. Instead, the air will get cleaner the way it has gotten cleaner in the past: by building cleaner cars. One reason this is true is that people seem to drive more regardless of the costs or restrictions that the EPA or others try to impose upon them.

Given that Americans will continue to drive more, there are several ways to further clean up the cars they drive. One is to solve the cold starts problem. Catalytic converters work poorly until they are warmed up, so most pollution from new cars comes from the first few minutes of cold operation. Building preheaters into the catalytic converters can eliminate this problem. A second solution is to reduce stop-and-go traffic by treating congestion at selected locations. The most congested routes in most cities are not the freeways but are arterials and collectors whose speeds are often below 45 miles per hour. Better signals, roundabouts, and other improvements to smooth traffic flows can reduce pollution.

Other improvements in technology are on the horizon. So-called zero-emission vehicles (electric cars) appear both imaginary (all vehicles pollute, though the pollution may come from a coal-fired power plant that generates the electricity) and expensive. But ultra-low-emission cars, such as gas-electric hybrids, will do far more to clean the air than any transportation control measures. Such ultra-clean cars pollute less at speed than pre-1970 autos polluted standing still with their engines turned off. Mainly by keeping the catalytic converters at their most effective temperature, the Toyota Prius and Honda Insight emit less than 10 percent of the pollution produced by typical new cars and less than 1 percent of the pollution from pre-1970 cars.[8] An independent test of the Insight could not detect any nitrogen oxides.[9] Unlike all-electric cars, their cost is little or no more than current gas-powered cars. Certainly, they will cost less than a radical redevelopment of all of America's urban areas.

Notes

1. Sharon Sarmiento, "Autos Save Energy," *Access* 8 (Spring, 1996):41.
2. Kenneth A. Small & Camilla Kazimi, "On the Costs of Air Pollution from Motor Vehicles," *Journal of Transport Economics and Policy* 29(1): p. 28.
3. Ibid, p. 29.
4. Arnold M. Howitt, Joshua P. Anderson, and Alan A. Altshuler, *The New Politics of Clean Air and Transportation* (Washington, DC: US DOT, 1997), p. 37.
5. Ibid, p. 25.
6. Environmental Protection Agency, *Transportation Partners 1997 Annual Report* (Washington, DC: EPA, 1998), Executive Summary, p. 1.
7. Transportation Research Board, *Expanding Metropolitan Highways: Implications for Air Quality and Energy Use* (WADC: TRB, 1995), p. 8.
8. Hideshi Itazaki, *The Prius That Shook the World: How Toyota Developed the World's First Mass-Production Hybrid Vehicle* (Tokyo, Japan: Nikkan Kogyo Shimbun, reprinted in English by Toyota, 1999), pp. 176–178.
9. InsightCentral.net, "Insight Emission Levels," http://www.InsightCentral.net/emissions.html.

23. Other Anti-Road Policies

In addition to the policies described in chapter 22, smart-growth activists use a number of other techniques to annoy auto drivers. While it is doubtful that any of these policies will significantly reduce the amount of driving Americans do, they will greatly increase the aggravation urbanites face on a day-to-day basis. These policies and tactics include:

- Diverting highway funds away from highways;
- Suppressing auto traffic;
- Giving traffic preferences to transit;
- Emphasizing so-called pedestrian-friendly design that may actually be more dangerous for pedestrians and cyclists; and
- Linking highway funding to air pollution targets

Diverting Highway Funds Away from Highways

Gasoline taxes, weight-mile truck taxes, and other highway fees were originally conceived of as user fees. These fees aimed to provide road funding in proportion to the amount of driving people did. The people who thought up such fees never imagined heavily congested ten-lane freeways or fuel-efficient cars eating into the revenues. In contrast, highway opponents describe any highway user fees spent on highways as a "subsidy." They view highway user fees as funds that they can capture to spend on transit.

Until 1973, Congress and most state legislatures dedicated all highway user fees to highways, roads, and streets. But in 1973, the state of Massachusetts convinced Congress to allow cities to cancel interstate highway projects and use the funds for mass transit instead. Massachusetts argued that this was a states-rights issue, that "Montana shouldn't tell Massachusetts how to spend its money."[1] Portland and Boston were among the cities that took advantage of the law to use highway funds to build rail transit.

This law prevailed until 1983. By then, inflation had led to shortfalls in road funding and highway interests wanted an increase in federal gas taxes. Transit interests opposed the increase unless they got a share, so Congress increased taxes by 5¢ per gallon and dedicated one of those cents to transit. From then on, transit received a 20 percent share of any increases in gas taxes that Congress used for transportation.[2] Numerous state legislatures also diverted gas taxes to transit. By the mid-1990s, New York, Massachusetts, New Jersey, Connecticut, and Maryland were each spending hundreds of millions of dollars of highway user fees on transit. Florida, Michigan, Wisconsin, and Virginia also spent tens of millions of gas taxes on transit.

In 1990, Congress increased gas taxes by 5 cents a gallon and dedicated half the increase to "deficit reduction"—meaning non-transportation activities. This further diluted the idea that highway taxes were a user fee. In 1993 the amount of gas taxes going to deficit reduction was increased to 4.1 cents.

Highway opponents scored a significant victory with Congressional passage of the Intermodal Surface Transportation Efficiency Act (ISTEA) of 1991. In addition to dedicating funds to transit, the law made a large share of funds "flexible," meaning that they could be spent on either transit or roads. Other highway funds were made available for planning, historic preservation, and all sorts of other activities.

Congress reauthorizes federal transportation funding about every six years. In 1998, flush with the budget surplus, Congress decided to end the diversion of gas tax revenues to deficit reduction. But the Transportation Efficiency Act for the Twenty-First Century (TEA-21) still left open the possibility of a large share of funds going for transit and other non-highway purposes. The Clinton Administration has proposed significant increases in funding for non-highway purposes. The next several years will see battles over the use of these funds.

Suppressing Driving

Attempts to suppress driving are known as *transportation demand management* (TDM). TDM practices range from efforts to promote carpooling to regulations requiring employers to somehow convince their employees to reduce automobile commuting.

"Mild" or optional TDMs include such things as:
- High-occupancy vehicle lanes to promote carpooling;
- Discounts or free passage for carpools on toll roads;
- Transit improvements;
- Construction of bike ways;
- Efforts to promote telecommuting.

Except for some of the more expensive transit improvements, most of these programs do not cost very much, but neither were they very effective.[3] More restrictive TDMs include:
- Restrictions on parking;
- Land-use regulations aimed at discouraging driving;

- The misnamed *employee commute options* (ECO) program, which required employers to convince their employees to reduce driving.

Portland's smart-growth plan is using all of these techniques, but elsewhere few have been tried other than the ECO program. All evidence has found that ECO has a high cost but does little to reduce congestion or air pollution. Yet many major cities require it for the simple reason that Congress mandated it in the Clean Air Act Amendments of 1990 for regions with severe air pollution.[4]

In a typical ECO program, businesses with more than 50 employees are given a choice between simply reducing their employees' commuting by 10 percent or writing and implementing a detailed plan for reducing commuting. If they choose the first option, they are required to track their employee's driving habits and can be severely fined if they do not meet their targets. Most employers choose the second option, which allows employers to do such things as buy free transit passes for all of their employees. If none of their employees use the passes, the employer is not fined so long as it carried out its plan.

Transportation demand management differs from *transportation system management* which consists of low-cost measures, such as synchronizing traffic signals, designed to use the existing transportation system more efficiently.[5] Together, TDM and TSM are called *transportation control measures*. Smart growth advocates oppose transportation system measures, which they describe as "measures that lessen auto pollution without changing automobile dependence."[6] Instead of using our transportation system more efficiently, it appears, their goal is to use it as inefficiently as possible.

Giving Preference to Transit

Although less than five percent of the trips taken in most American cities are by transit, smart-growth calls for giving transit preference over automobiles on city streets. This preference is expressed by changing rules governing the right of way and by giving transit vehicles priority recognition at signaled intersections.

Bus-only or high-occupancy vehicle lanes are common in many cities. These lanes often increase congestion because they dedicate a large share of roadway surface to vehicles that carry relatively few passenger miles. Despite the installation of high-occupancy vehicle lanes in many cities, average vehicle occupancies continue to decline. Bus-only lanes tend to be in downtowns or other congested areas, or precisely where congestion relief is needed. By dedicating entire lanes of traffic to a few transit vehicles, this policy effectively increases congestion unless those transit vehicles are very numerous or very full. Cities should carefully examine bus-only or high-occupancy vehicle lanes to insure that they are truly reducing, not increasing, congestion.

Other transit preferences are less obvious than bus-only lanes. Oregon recently passed a state law giving buses the right of way when they pull away from the curb into a lane of traffic.[7] Ordinarily, parked vehicles turning into a traffic lane must yield right of way to moving traffic in the lane. But the Oregon law reverses this for buses, so that moving traffic must slow or stop every time a bus pulls away from a curb. A typical bus may pull into traffic about fifty times per hour. Giving such buses the right of way imposes far more delays on automobile passengers than the time it saves for transit riders simply because the latter are far fewer in number.

Another transit preference is to give transit vehicles priority at traffic signals. This has been implemented for several light-rail lines and has been proposed for buses. The traffic signals sense when a light-rail vehicle is in the area and turns red for automobile cross traffic, giving the light rail the green. Again, this delays far more auto passengers than it saves time for transit riders.

An implicit judgment behind such transit preferences is that transit is somehow more morally sound that autos and so deserves advantages. This is the same rationale for the argument that rail transit is needed because rail cars, unlike buses, won't get stuck in traffic with the automobiles. Other than this questionable moral judgment, transit preferences make no sense at all unless they can be proven to effectively reduce congestion at a reasonable cost.

Bicycling and Walking

Smart growth calls for building bikeways and pedestrian-friendly environments. Traffic calming and boulevards are designed to discourage driving and emphasize walking and cycling. Implicit behind these programs are two erroneous assumptions:

1. Autos and walking/cycling are mutually exclusive: The only way to make neighborhoods and business districts attractive to pedestrians and cyclists is to make them unattractive to motorists.
2. Bike lanes, barriers in roads, and other traffic calming or boulevarding practices will increase bicyclist and pedestrian safety.

In fact, it is easily possible to conceive of ways to make areas more bicycle and pedestrian friendly without reducing automobility. Moreover, it turns out that traffic calming, bike lanes, and other so-called pedestrian-friendly designs make streets more dangerous for pedestrian and cyclists, not less.

John Forester is a cyclist who has studied bicycle safety and street design for more than two decades. He has done something that few smart-growth advocates have ever done: studied bicycle accident statistics and personally observed thousands of bicyclists in hundreds of different traffic conditions. He has concluded that the safest cyclists are the ones who "act and are treated as drivers of vehicles."[8]

On the other hand, Forester has found that some of the most dangerous riding conditions are created when bicycles and pedestrians are merged together on bike paths. "Bike paths are the most dangerous type of facility we know," he says, "two-

and-one-half times more dangerous than roads."[9] Bike lanes, too, are somewhat more dangerous than simply riding as a vehicle in traffic because they "increase the number of errors by both cyclists and motorists."[10]

Traffic calming, says Forester, is "simply anti-car" and makes roads more dangerous for bicycles. Traffic circles force motor vehicles into the shoulders where bicyclists may be and curb extensions force bicycles into the flow of motor vehicle traffic. Moreover, speed bumps and other things that slow traffic are "counterproductive because the prime way to make cycling more useful is to encourage faster cycling."[11] Smart growth suggests that we "redesign our cities to significantly shorten travel distances" in order to make cycling more attractive. But, as Forester notes, "that will take decades, if it occurs at all. . . . In the meantime, cyclists still have to ride the present distances," which means that anything that slows bicyclists down will discourage cycling.[12]

The most effective way of improving bike safety is to train cyclists the same way we train drivers, and Forester's book, *Effective Cycling*, has helped more than 100,000 cyclists ride on ordinary city streets.[13] Unfortunately, says Forester, too many transportation planners treat bicycles as toys and assume that "the cyclist doesn't understand the traffic system, has poor judgment of traffic, and doesn't care to obey the laws."[14] By comparison, says Forester, "British cyclists take their place in traffic and ride properly, and most think nothing about it."

Beyond education, "there are many improvements that make cycling easier," says Forester. These include "shoulders or wide curb lanes (these are the same as far as cyclists are concerned), traffic signals that respond to bicycles, right-turn-only lanes to separate straight-through cyclists from right-turning traffic, protected left turn signal phases and lanes, drain grates that don't catch wheels, more space at diagonal railroad crossings so cyclists can turn perpendicular to the tracks, better bicycle parking facilities, and more."[15]

Along with most active cyclists, Forester is particularly annoyed that traffic signal detectors often cannot detect bicycles. "It is foolish to expect cyclists to obey the law and have respect for your profession," he told the Institute of Transportation Engineers, "when the equipment that you install won't allow them to obey the law and may kill them as well."[16]

Unfortunately, few transportation planners have studied Forester's work or done their own studies of bicycle safety. As a result, Forester regretfully observes that 86 percent of federal bikeway dollars since 1991 have gone for "off-road paths and trails," which Forester considers the most dangerous; "13 percent for bike lanes, and 1 percent for bicycle parking or bicycle connections to public transit."[17]

Many traffic calming practices may actually be more dangerous for pedestrians as well. One practice used in Portland is to convert one-way streets back to two-way streets. When these streets were first made one-way streets, generally in the 1950s, the change resulted in a huge reduction in accidents, and in particular in reduced pedestrian accidents. Typically, pedestrian accidents declined by half to two thirds.[18] The reason is simple: On a one-way street, pedestrians need only worry about traffic coming from one direction and are less likely to step in front of cars. Moreover, with synchronized traffic signals, one-way streets offer plenty of lengthy gaps between groups of cars, so pedestrians have many safe opportunities to cross.

Linking Highway Funding to Air Pollution Targets

ISTEA significantly changed federal transportation policy by linking transportation funding to the Clean Air Act Amendments (CAAA) of 1990. The law required every state and metropolitan planning organization to prepare transportation plans. Metropolitan areas that did not meet Environmental Protection Agency air quality standards were required to focus their plans on cleaning up the air.

"CAAA and ISTEA effectively proclaim air quality as the primary goal—or dominant constraint on—U.S. transportation policy," say a team of Harvard transportation analysts.[19] In other words, air quality trumps all other urban concerns, including congestion, transportation costs, and the preferences of local residents. While clean air is a worthwhile goal, the law and its subsequent implementation were based on simplistic and sometimes incorrect assumptions about the relationship between autos and air quality.

Although cars pollute more in congestion than in free-flowing traffic, the law limited spending on highway capacity increases in polluted regions, thus helping to insure that they would stay polluted. Under the law, urban regions with serious air pollution problems can have their federal highway funding completely withheld until they adopt an approved transportation plan that promises to clean the air. The EPA originally allowed regions to continue building highways that had already been funded, but in 1998 it told Atlanta that it would approve no new highway projects until the region wrote an approved air quality plan.[20] In 1999, a lawsuit by the Sierra Club successfully halted many existing road projects in Atlanta as well.[21]

ISTEA created a billion-dollar-per-year *congestion mitigation air quality* (CMAQ) fund which was supposed to help communities reduce congestion and improve air quality. However, the EPA tries to discourage regions from using the fund to reduce congestion and instead promotes such things as rail transit.[22] Many cities have used CMAQ funds to improve traffic signalization, which should both reduce congestion and improve air quality. But other cities have used CMAQ funds to support light-rail projects and subsidize transit-oriented development, both of which are more likely to increase congestion than improve air quality.[23] As noted in "Suppressing Driving" (p. 362), the law also required areas with severe air pollution to adopt *employee commute option* (ECO) plans, even though research has shown that such plans would "produce relatively little in the way of emission reductions, at significant cost."[24]

Another requirement in regions with poor air quality is an annual or biannual inspection-and-maintenance program for motor vehicles built since 1970. This program is supposed to insure that the air pollution control equipment on such vehicles is working properly. But, as University of California economist Charles Lave says, all they really do is insure that autos are "clean for a day." California's biannual inspection program, says Lave, "worked harder and harder at making that one day cleaner and cleaner, while ignoring the car's performance on the other 729 days." Lave compared the inspection system "to a program that 'controls' drunk driving by scheduling drivers for a breathalyzer test every two years." Although California has proven that the program works poorly, the EPA is requiring cities to use a new testing program that is more expensive, more time-consuming, and no more likely to improve air quality. The agency rejected an alternative, developed by University of Denver chemist Donald Stedman, of distributing inexpensive infrared sensors along roadways which could constantly monitor air emissions and identify polluting vehicles. The owners of such offending vehicles would receive a notice in the mail to bring their car in for inspection and, if needed, repair. This would be less expensive for the government, less time consuming for auto drivers, and do more to clean the air than the EPA's program.[25]

ISTEA's emphasis on planning resulted in a cumbersome, bureaucratic process that was easily captured by anti-auto groups. In fact, the Federal Transit Administration criticized some cities for not going out of their way to involve cyclists and transit riders in their transportation planning.[26] Even though auto trips greatly outnumber other trips in every urban area, the Department of Transportation never urged cities to go out of their way to involve auto drivers in planning.

In reviewing the implementation of ISTEA planning, the Harvard analysts note that "the environmentalists have been most aggressive" in metro-area plans. "They asked for voluminous information about existing planning processes and made clear their intent to review, critique, and, if necessary, litigate to assure that planning under CAAA and ISTEA was done property."[27]

The analysts also worried that some planners might engage in "a considerable 'stretching' (and perhaps significant 'cooking') of the planning results to minimize the need for painful policy choices to reduce pollution."[28] But in regional planning agencies enchanted by the smart-growth ideology, the danger is just the opposite: that planners will cook their books to make any policy except smart growth appear to be bad for air quality. The analysts note that "some advocates, not at all analytically inclined, stay attached to favored policy positions—for example, transit enhancements or transportation control measures—whether or not they are supported by the 'numbers.'"[29]

Notes

1. Darwin Stolzenbach, *Interview with Professor Alan Altshuler, Former Secretary of Transportation, Massachusetts*, AASHTO Interstate Highway Research Project, June 8, 1981, p.

36.

2. George Smerk, *The Federal Role in Urban Mass Transportation* (Bloomington, IN: Indiana University Press, 1991), 391 pp.

3. Arnold M. Howitt, Joshua P. Anderson, and Alan A. Altshuler, *The New Politics of Clean Air and Transportation* (Washington, DC: US DOT, 1997), p. 20.

4. Ibid, pp. 20–21.

5. Ibid, p. 20.

6. Barbara McCann, Roy Kienitz, and Bianca DeLille, *Changing Direction: Federal Transportation Spending in the 1990s* (Washington, DC: STPP, 2000), p. 7, http://www.transact.org/Reports/Cd/tea21color.pdf.

7. Tri-Met, "Yield to Buses!" http://www.tri-met.org/yield.htm.

8. John Forester, "Review of Bicycle-Safety-Related Research Synthesis," http://www.johnforester.com/Articles/Facilities/bsrrs.html.

9. John Forester, "Objective and Psychological Explanations for Differences in the Bicycling Programs of Different Nations," paper presented at the VeloCity Conference, Montreal, 1992, http://www.johnforester.com/Articles/Social/psychnat.html.

10. John Forester, "The Government's Use of Pseudo-Scientific Propaganda," http://www.johnforester.com/Articles/Social/law01.html.

11. John Forester, "The National Bicycling and Walking Studies," 1994, http://www.johnforester.com/Articles/Facilities/nbwsrev.html.

12. John Forester, "Review of Bicycle-Safety-Related Research."

13. John Forester, *Effective Cycling* (Cambridge, MA: MIT Press, 1983).

14. John Forester, "Improving Bicyclists' Traffic Behavior by Changing National Attitudes," paper presented at the 1988 annual convention of the Institute of Transportation Engineers, http://www.johnforester.com/Articles/Social/natattit.html.

15. John Forester, "Review of Bicycle-Safety-Related Research."

16. John Forester, "Improving Bicyclists' Traffic Behavior."

17. John Forester, "Review of *Bicycling Renaissance in North America?*" *Transportation Research*, September-November, 1999, http://www.johnforester.com/Articles/Social/Bicycle%20Renaissance.html.

18. Oregon State Highway Department, *A Study of One-Way Street Routings on Urban Highways in Oregon* (Salem, OR: Oregon State Highway Commission, 1959), p. 15.

19. Arnold M. Howitt, Joshua P. Anderson, and Alan A. Altshuler, *The New Politics of Clean Air and Transportation* (Washington, DC: US DOT, 1997), p. 12.

20. David Goldberg, "3 advocacy groups sue over highway projects," *The Atlanta Constitution*, January 21, 1999, p. B4

21. Associated Press, "Road work restricted in Atlanta," *The Augusta Chronicle*, June 22, 1999, p. C7.

22. Howitt, et al., *The New Politics of Clean Air*, p. 22.

23. See, for example, Federal Highway Administration, *CMAQ Annual Reports (FY 1997)* (Washington, DC: FHwA, 1998), http://www.fhwa.dot.gov/environment/cmaq97rp.pdf.

24. Howitt, et al., *The New Politics of Clean Air*, p. 21.

25. Charles Lave, "Clean for a Day: California versus the EPA's Smog Check Mandates." *Access* 3 (Fall, 1993):3–7.

26. Federal Transit Administration, *Review of the Transportation Planning Process in the Minneapolis-St. Paul Metropolitan Area* (Washington, DC: FTA, 1993), p. 30.

27. Howitt, et al., *The New Politics of Clean Air, p. 34.*

28. Ibid, p. 32.

29. Ibid.

The Expensive-Highway Myth

Myth: Highways are expensive and produce little benefit.
Reality: Highways cost far less per passenger mile than rail transit and are essentially self funding.

The high costs of such roads as the Century Freeway or the Boston Central Artery get quoted so often that many people think they are typical. In fact, average costs are much lower. In Portland, the cost of building arterials—roads with grade-level crossings of other roads and streets—or adding new lanes onto existing arterials is about $2.5 million per lane mile. Limited-access freeway costs are about double, at $5 million per lane mile, mainly due to cost of overpasses and on- and off-ramps.[1] Stretches of freeway with no overpasses or exits cost about the same as arterials.

This means that a four-lane expressway will cost roughly $10 million per mile, while a four-lane freeway will cost around $20 million per mile. Costs will be significantly higher only if most of the highway is elevated or depressed. In Portland, one new stretch of elevated freeway with numerous elevated on- and off-ramps connecting with other freeways and arterials is expected to cost about $50 million per lane mile. The Boston Central Artery reached $75 million per lane mile because most of it is in a tunnel. Elevating or depressing freeways is usually proposed to minimize effects on inner city neighborhoods. In most suburban areas, $2.5 to $5 million per lane mile is a reasonable cost for arterials and freeways.

A mile of freeway lane in major urban areas typically carries around 16,000 to 18,000 vehicles per day. In Los Angeles, the number rises to 23,000 per day. Daily freeway flows in less-congested urban areas average around 8,000 vehicles per lane mile. Arterial lane miles carry about 6,000 to 8,000 vehicles per day. Since arterial costs and flows are each about half that of freeways, the cost per passenger mile is about the same. But since freeways are both faster and safer than arterials, they provide better service and therefore more value per dollar.

The average freeway lane mile in the nation's fifty largest metropolitan areas provided about 5.8 million miles of vehicle travel in 1998. At the national average of 1.6 people per vehicle, this equals nearly 9.3 million passenger miles. When counting all 391 urbanized areas, the numbers are slightly lower: about 8.0 million passenger miles per lane mile in 1998.[2] Each lane mile of Los Angeles freeway produced an incredible 8.5 million vehicle miles, or 13.5 million passenger miles, of travel in 1998. As shown in the High-Capacity Transit Myth (p. 287), highways produce about six to fifteen times as many passenger miles of travel, per dollar of construction cost, as light-rail transit.

Notes

1. Metro, *Interim Federal Regional Transportation Plan* (Portland, OR: Metro, 1995), chapter 5.
2. Federal Highway Administration, *Highway Statistics 1997* (Washington, DC: FHwA, 1998), table HM-72.

 ## Web Tools: Highway Subsidies

Get all the data you need to calculate highway subsidies in your state from http://www.fhwa.dot.gov/ohim/ohimstat.htm. For any given year, you will need to download tables HDF, SF-1, LGF-1, LGF-2, and VM-2. From table HDF, add together the following for your state:
• The amount of federal highway user fees that are diverted to mass transit;
• The amount of federal highway user fees diverted to (from) other states or for general purposes.
These are the *diversions*. Ignore state diversions because they are accounted for in table SF-1. Then add together the following:
• Appropriations from state general funds from table SF-1;
• Other imposts from table SF-1;
• Miscellaneous from table SF-1;
• Federal funds from other agencies from table SF-1; and
• Total dispersements by local governments from table LGF-2.
From this sum, subtract the following from table LGF-1:
• Motor fuel and vehicle tax revenues;
• Tolls;
• State highway user imposts; and
• Federal FHwA funds.
What is left are the *supplementary funds*. Subtract the diversions from the supplementary funds. If the result is negative, there is no subsidy: Road users are subsidizing something else. If the result is positive, there is a subsidy. To calculate the subsidy per vehicle mile, divide the subsidy by the total number of vehicle miles driven in your state shown in table VM-2. To get the subsidy per passenger mile, divide again by 1.6.

The Dangerous-Highway Myth

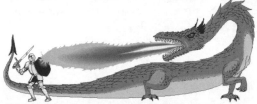

Myth: Automobile driving, especially on freeways, is far more dangerous than transit or other forms of transportation.

Reality: Driving in urban areas, especially on freeways or other major roads, is as safe or safer than mass transit.

Everyone knows that driving on urban freeways is one of the most dangerous forms of transportation possible. Auto-hostile people can hardly mention automotive safety without talking about the "carnage" on our highways. As is so often the case, what "everyone knows" is wrong. Nearly 42,000 people died on American highways in 1998, and that is certainly a tragedy. But it is less well known that:

- Urban roads are safer than rural roads;
- Freeways are the safest of all roads in urban or rural areas;
- Urban driving is safer than urban transit;
- Other than motorcycles, the most dangerous form of urban motorized travel may be light-rail transit.

Table one compares fatality and injury rates for various methods of travel. The table indicates that cars, trucks, and urban transit have roughly the same safety records. Data for trucks and intercity buses apply only to occupants, so are not strictly comparable to the others. Although passenger car fatalities are slightly higher than transit fatalities, a closer look at the data reveals that urban auto travel is much safer than transit.

Although Americans do more than 60 percent of their driving in urban areas, urban areas account for just 40 percent of roadway fatalities. Moreover, as shown in table two, the most dangerous roads are not the freeways or arterials but local neighborhood streets where urban transit rarely ventures. In general, *the faster the design speed of a highway, the safer it is.* Although table two includes all forms of highway travel, passenger cars and light truck numbers overwhelm all others so the safety rates in the table can largely be attributed to those vehicles. Since urban fatalities are just two-thirds of the average and urban serious injuries are 94 percent of average, the fatality and injury rates for cars in table one can be reduced

Table One: Safety by Transportation Mode
(Fatalities or Injuries Per Billion Passenger Miles, average of 1990–1996)
Fatalities

Passenger car	9.4
Urban transit	7.3
Trucks	7.6
Intercity Bus	0.2
Motorcycle	228.6
Air carrier	0.6
General aviation	67.7

Injuries

Passenger car	990.6
Urban transit	1,364.7
Trucks	4,002.8
Intercity Bus	161.1
Motorcycle	5,948.1
Air carrier	0.2
General aviation	36.4

Source: Bureau of Transportation Statistics, National Transportation Statistics 1998, tables 1-10, 3-1, 3-2. Trucks includes both light and heavy trucks. Numbers for trucks and intercity buses not truly comparable with others because they only include occupants.

accordingly. Urban passenger car fatalities would be 6.2 per billion passenger miles, which is 15 percent less than urban transit fatalities.

Table three shows that, in terms of fatalities, light rail is the most dangerous form of urban transit, causing 80 percent more fatalities per passenger mile than autos and nearly three times the fatality rate of urban interstates. This is because light-rail vehicles weigh many times more than buses or cars and thus are unable to quickly stop after hitting a pedestrian or another vehicle. Commuter rail has high fatality rates for the same reason, while heavy rail is safer because it is completely separated from pedestrians and other vehicles. Light-rail vehicles are very safe to ride in because they rarely stop suddenly enough to do more than shake up passengers. But it is dangerous to be a pedestrian in a city with light rail. The rates in table three do not include 1999, when Portland's westside light-rail line alone killed five pedestrians, a rate of about 100 per billion passenger miles.

Table Two: Safety by Highway Type
(Rate per billion passenger miles, 1998)

	Total Fatalities	Total Injuries	Serious Injuries	Pedest. Fatalities	Pedest. Injuries
Rural					
Interstate	7.9	256.9	39.9	0.5	3.8
Other Principal Arterial	14.7	549.1	79.3	0.9	6.5
Minor Arterial	17.1	739.0	100.0	1.1	7.8
Major Collector	17.8	845.8	118.4	0.9	9.9
Minor Collector	22.0	997.3	117.7	1.0	12.8
Local	24.3	1,392.6	125.9	2.0	26.9
Total Rural	15.6	689.7	88.4	1.0	9.4
Urban					
Interstate	3.9	453.0	32.8	0.6	7.4
Other Freeways	5.1	670.0	46.8	0.9	16.7
Other Principal Arterial	8.8	1,244.1	91.1	2.2	33.9
Minor Arterial	7.3	1,237.2	101.6	1.6	42.0
Collector	6.7	994.9	89.4	1.2	46.4
Local	8.9	1,848.4	99.1	2.3	104.9
Total Urban	6.8	1,065.5	76.0	1.5	38.7
Total U.S.	10.2	918.7	80.9	1.3	27.2

Source: FHwA, Highway Statistics 1997, table FI-1. Table FI-1 shows rates per vehicle mile. To be comparable with table one, these rates were divided by 1.6 to get rates per passenger mile. Pedestrian fatalities and injuries are included in totals in addition to being shown separately.

Table Three: Transit Safety by Type
(Fatality and injury rates per billion passenger miles, 1991–1996)

	Fatalities	Injuries
Bus	4.4	1,058.5
Light Rail	11.2	573.3
Heavy Rail	3.6	28.3
Commuter Rail	8.1	31.7

Source: Bureau of Transportation Statistics, National Transportation Statistics 1998, table 3-30. Rates include collisions with pedestrians and other vehicles but not suicides.

24. Highway History

Despite several decades of campaigning by anti-auto writers and activists, Americans today own more autos than ever before. But automobiles are not much use without good roads to drive on. Before automobiles, the United States already had extensive city street and rural road networks, a fact which is usually forgotten by auto opponents who claim that a huge percentage of land has been "dedicated" to the automobile. But the roads, especially rural roads, were generally of poor quality, suitable for horses but not rubber-tired vehicles.

According to the Federal Highway Administration, in 1921—the first year for which data are available—Americans owned only 10 million motor vehicles yet the U.S. already had 3.1 million miles of public roads.[1] More than seventy-five years later, Americans own twenty times as many autos yet road mileage has increased by just 25 percent to 3.9 million.[2] More than 90 percent of the increase in road mileage has been city streets, which grew from 304,000 miles in 1941 to 820,000 miles today.[3] This mirrors the 150 percent increase in urban population during that time period.

Few of the early roads were good enough for automobiles. In 1941, the first year for which such data are available, just 18 percent of the nation's roads were paved, compared with 61 percent today.[4] In addition to being paved, roads today are wider than they were in 1921. But even here the data are surprising: Only about 200,000 miles of roads, or just 5 percent, have more than two lanes.[5] The vast majority of the 3.9 million miles of roads are rural two-lane roads or quiet neighborhood streets. Yet Americans do more than half of all their driving on the 5 percent of roads with more than two lanes.[6]

Through much of the nineteenth century, many intercity roads in the U.S. had actually been built as toll roads by private entrepreneurs.[7] But before motorcars, animal-drawn wagons were too slow and inefficient to compete against railroads, so intercity roads were few. As first bicycles and then automobiles became popular, the demand for better roads grew. But who should build them?

Americans have traditionally been suspicious of letting politicians make such decisions as where and how roads should be built. The nineteenth-century spoils system and pork barrel were not likely to produce roads where they were really needed. At the same time, controversies over the railroads led people to worry that private roads would lead to monopolies and price gouging.

The Progressive Movement, led by President Theodore Roosevelt, offered an alternative: scientific management by experts. Transportation engineers would use objective criteria, not political power, to decide where roads should go. In 1905, Congress created the Office of Public Roads and specified that the person in charge must be a scientist. Roosevelt appointed Logan Page, a geologist who specialized in testing road materials. Page, says a Federal Highway Administration historian, "believed that scientific experts could best address the nation's road problems by applying apolitical judgment, based on irrefutable data, free of political taint and corrupt influence."[8]

The Progressive ideal was endorsed by the Good Roads movement, led by bicyclists and automobilists. The movement gained support from farmers who wanted all-weather, farm-to-market roads; from the Post Office, which wanted to deliver mail in rural areas; and even from the railroads, which saw roads as a way for farmers to get their products to the rail lines. The first state highway legislation came in 1889, when a New Jersey law allowed counties to sell property-tax-backed bonds for roads and to assess adjacent landowners up to one-third of the cost of the roads.[9] In 1916, Congress authorized $75 million over five years to be given to states with highway departments for rural road construction.[10]

Funding roads out of property or income taxes did not produce very rapid results. So automobilists conceived the idea of paying for the roads with a tax on gasoline. This would insure that those who used the roads paid the cost. The oil industry supported the tax because it would increase the demand for its products. In 1919, Oregon was the first state to levy a tax on gasoline and dedicate the revenues to roads.[11] The federal government started collecting gasoline taxes in 1932.[12] Local governments continued to use property and other taxes to pay for city streets and some county roads, but after 1940 state and federal governments paid their shares of road costs almost exclusively out of highway user fees.

While Progressives expected that agencies such as highway bureaus would be run solely by the experts, the expenditure of hundreds of millions and later billions of dollars naturally led to political interference.

- Oregon passed the first gas tax in 1919 only after legislators spent an entire day drawing and redrawing the proposed highway map until most legislators' homes were served.[13]
- During the Depression, funds were diverted from projects that served transportation needs to projects that could provide work for the unemployed.[14]
- Rural legislators hold power disproportionate to rural residents' numbers in many states, with the result that rural areas probably get more transportation dollars than can be justified based on the amount of rural travel.
- Similarly, low-density states such as Montana and Alaska hold power in the U.S. Senate disproportionate to their populations, with the result that many

of these states get more federal highway funds than their auto drivers put into the fund, while dense states such as California and Georgia get less.

In addition, some planners wanted to use highway money to achieve social goals, rather than just transportation goals. Urban planners, for example, hoped to use highway funds to reshape American cities and the people living in them.[15]

Despite these pressures, transportation engineers were able to convince most state and city transportation agencies to follow objective criteria in locating and building roads. Traffic engineers classify congestion as *levels of service* (see p. 385). A road offering service level A has no congestion. Grade B has light congestion, all the way down to grade F, which is bumper-to-bumper, stop-and-go traffic. The engineers convinced most cities and states to adopt standards that all roads and streets should provide a certain level of service—generally a minimum of C or D—and that transportation dollars should be allocated primarily to maintain this service level. Level of service goals were reinforced by state funding of roads out of gas taxes and other highway user fees. If congestion led people to cut back on driving, it would also reduce highway revenues. This gave the engineers an incentive to spend the money where it was most needed.

Federal funding of highways created more problems for the engineers' goal of meeting traffic needs. In the 1930s, many people wanted to use federal funds to build interstate highways similar to Germany's autobahns. But Thomas MacDonald, who directed the Bureau of Public Roads from 1919 through 1953, believed that the primary need for freeways was in the congested cities, not the rural countryside.[16] When Congress first considered President Eisenhower's proposed Interstate Highway System in 1955, the original plans called for highways skirting around cities, not going through them. This proposal failed. The bill passed in 1956 with support from the cities after it was amended to include highways that went through the cities, as MacDonald wanted, not just around them.

Other political decisions in the 1956 bill would have a major effect on America's highways. Early proposals for the Interstate Highway System conceived of a flexible design: two lanes and at-grade railroad and highway crossings where there was little traffic, more lanes and limited access highways where traffic was greater.[17] The later decision to build all interstates to a four-lane, limited-access minimum standard would mean that funds spent building little-used roads in thinly populated states would not be available to relieve congestion in more crowded areas.

Another early proposal was to fund interstates at least partly from tolls. But truckers objected to tolls because of delays at tollbooths. They convinced Congress to specify that no tolls could be charged on any road built with the help of federal funds. Existing tollroads, located mainly in the Northeast, were grandfathered in, but this decision contributed to a belief on the part of many that toll-free roads were some sort of constitutional right.

Urban planners played a modest role in highway debates. They supported inner-city freeways in the hope that such freeways would play a role in their urban-renewal programs. Planners were less concerned with congestion relief than with saving the cities. They wanted roads built in a way that would shape their ideal city. If the traffic wanted to go one way and the planners wanted it to go another, then the traffic was wrong and should be ignored.

In the 1920s, planners hoped that roads would get people out of the crowded cities, which they did.[18] According to historian Mark Foster, "the majority of planners enthusiastically endorsed both automobility and the suburban movement."[19] In the 1950s, planners tried to accelerate suburbanization by building roads through "blighted" neighborhoods, which outraged many residents. They also wanted, but did not get, the authority to use highway dollars to clear the neighborhoods around the highways, forcing people to move out, and rebuilding them the way they saw fit.[20] While some highways played a role in urban renewal, the engineers remained dominant and planners did not really begin to get their way until the 1990s. They are now using their influence to reverse the trends their predecessors supported in the 1920s through the 1960s.

In 1950, University of Michigan transportation economist Shorey Peterson argued that transportation funding decisions should be made strictly on the basis of meeting traffic needs. Attempting to use highway dollars to achieve some greater social good, warned Peterson, would simply lead to decisions made primarily on the basis of pork barrel, not the public interest.[21] This is exactly what happened when federal gasoline taxes were diverted to mass transit instead of highways.

On a micro-level, the judgments of transportation engineers about highway location and design held sway for many years, but not without plenty of political interference at a macro-level. For example, although Congress claims it supports the idea that state highway departments should decide how to spend federal transportation dollars, it puts hundreds of "demonstration projects" in the home districts of powerful senators and representatives into each transportation bill.

The 1956 highway legislation also contained some perverse incentives for states. The law allocated funds based on the states' initial estimates of how much interstate highways in their states would cost. This initially led states to pad their estimates so as to get a healthy share of the funds. But the Federal Highway Administration strictly monitored estimates to prevent this. So states developed an alternative tactic of underestimating costs so that they could get extra highways in the system. Once in, they could be funded later at more realistic costs.[22] Another quirk in administration led to a bonanza for engineering consulting firms: When state agencies did design work themselves, they had to keep elaborate records of employee time. But they could avoid this by contracting work to outside engineering firms, which soon became a powerful interest group.[23]

By the early 1970s, engineering judgments about new roads came under increasing criticism, especially with respect to urban freeways. Some of that criticism was valid. For example, by focusing solely on traffic, engineers ignored the effects of freeways on neighborhoods. Freeways increased the value of adjacent vacant land, and the land near such freeways was generally used for commercial or industrial development. But noise, congestion, and other freeway effects could greatly reduce the value of adjacent residential land. Freeways could also split neighborhoods, leaving one half of the neighborhood less accessible to urban centers and urban services than the other. This could lead to a decline in property values throughout the cutoff neighborhood, and not just near the freeway.

Other criticisms were not so valid. For example, *Power Broker*, Robert Caro's biography of Robert Moses, who oversaw construction of many of the highways in New York City, accused Moses of discriminating against poor people by building parkways with clearances too low to allow buses. This meant, claimed Caro, that only those wealthy enough to afford an automobile could visit parks and recreation areas. This misrepresents Moses' goal, which was to provide safer highways by separating autos from trucks.

In the 1970s, highway engineers met an even more significant obstacle to their goal of minimizing congestion: a funding shortfall. Inflation, rising urban land values, and increasing demands for mitigation of highway impacts dramatically raised construction costs. In at least one case, highway funds were used to build housing for people displaced by the freeway.[24] But even without such costs, highway revenues could not keep up with inflation because gas taxes were on a per gallon basis, rather than on a per dollar basis like ordinary sales taxes. The fuel-efficient cars of the late 1970s and 1980s only made the problem worse because people could drive more while paying less gasoline taxes.

Due to such problems, new highways started falling behind traffic growth long before the highway controversies of the 1970s. In 1975, California Governor Jerry Brown announced that the state would shift priorities away from building new freeways. But in fact, "freeway development in California began a precipitous decline in 1967," says University of North Carolina planning Professor Brian Taylor. "In other words, California had stopped building freeways years before the state announced its intent to stop building freeways."[25]

Nationwide, Taylor calculates, highway construction dollars (adjusted for inflation) per vehicle mile of travel actually peaked in 1959. Since 1980, construction expenditures per mile of travel "have remained fairly stable at. . . about one-third of the 1959 peak."[26] Taylor concludes that the increasing urban congestion of the last few decades is not primarily due to highway opponents. "Even if the Brown Administration had announced in 1975 that the state remained committed to implementing the 1959 freeway plan, it is unlikely that any additional miles of freeway would have been built" without "an extraordinarily new financial commitment to freeways."[27]

Nevertheless, after 1970 politics played an increasing role in highway location decisions or in vetoing roads despite congestion problems. In Massachusetts, for example, the official state policy starting in the early 1970s was that no new lanes would be built on highways inside Boston's Route 128 beltway "because those

lanes would, by inducing more traffic, bring pressure to bear for still more highway construction and undermine the state's strategy of relying on transit to meet
urban mobility needs."[28] In 1973, Massachusetts convinced Congress to allow
states to cancel proposed urban interstate freeways and use the funds for mass
transit instead. This law expired in 1983, after which a share of gas taxes and other
highway user fees was dedicated to mass transit. After 1991, *flexible funds*—federal highway revenues that states could spend on either highways or transit—took
another bite out of highway dollars.

The diversion of highway money to mass transit increasingly politicized transportation decisions. Although some states complain that they do not get their fair
share of federal highway funds, only fifteen states have received less than 100
percent of what their drivers paid into the fund, and none got less than 84 percent.[29] But most of the mass transit money went to a few large cities. Between
1991 and 1996:

- DC's expensive Metro system got $15 for every dollar DC highway users put
  into the fund;
- New York transit agencies got more than $5 for every dollar New York high-
  way users put into the fund;
- Oregon and New Jersey transit agencies got nearly $4 for every dollar their
  highway users put into the fund;
- At the other end of the scale, thirty-eight states got less than their highway
  users put into the fund;
- Half the states got less than 60 cents per dollar; and
- A dozen states got less than 25 cents per dollar.[30]

DC's high ratio is partly explained by the fact that most of the gasoline in the
Washington metro area is purchased in Maryland or Virginia, not DC. New York
and its New Jersey suburbs are the one urban area where heavy investments in
mass transit may make sense. But why is Oregon near the top of the list? Simple:
Oregon's senator, Mark Hatfield, was ranking Republican member of the Senate
Appropriations committee.

In general, the winner or *recipient states* turned out to be mostly ones, such as
New York, Oregon, Illinois, and California, with expensive rail transit projects.
The loser or *donor states* were either states with no big cities or states with big
cities that did not build expensive rail projects. This explains why light rail became so popular in the 1990s: Arizona, Colorado, Florida, Minnesota, Tennessee,
and Washington are among the many donor states whose urban leaders felt pressured to get their share of mass transit funds by proposing big rail projects when
Congress reauthorized transportation funding in 1998.

Notes

1. Federal Highway Administration, *Highway Statistics Summary to 1995*, table HM-210.
2. Federal Highway Administration, *Highway Statistics 1998*, table HM-12.

3. Ibid.
4 FHwA, *Highway Statistics Summary to 1995*, table HM-212.
5. FHwA, *Highway Statistics 1998*, table HM-20. This counts interstates, other freeways, and major arterials. Table HM-35 says that just 160,000 miles of the Federal Aid Highway System have more than two lanes; the remaining 40,000 are local arterials.
6. FHwA, *Highway Statistics 1998*, table VM-2.
7. Daniel B. Klein & Chi Yin, *The Private Provision of Frontier Infrastructure: Toll Roads in California, 1950–1902* UCTC No. 238
8. Richard F. Weingroff, "Federal Aid Road Act of 1916: Building the Foundation," *Public Roads*, Summer, 1996, http://www.tfhrc.gov/pubrds/summer96/p96su2.htm.
9. Spencer Miller, Jr., "History of the Modern Highway in the United States," in Jean Labatut and Wheaton J. Land (eds.), *Highways in Our National Life: A Symposium* (Princeton, NJ: Princeton University Press, 1950), p. 90
10. Ibid, p. 91.
11. Robert Bradley, *Oil, Gas, and Government: The U.S. Experience (volume 2)* (Lanham, MD: Rowman & Littlefield, 1996), p. 1370.
12. FHwA, *Highway Statistics Summary to 1995*, table FE-101A.
13. Robert Bradley, *Oil, Gas, and Government*, pp. 1375–1376.
14. Richard F. Weingroff, "The Federal-State Partnership at Work," *Public Roads*, Summer, 1996, http://www.tfhrc.gov/pubrds/summer96/p96su7.htm.
15. Mark Rose, *Interstate: Express Highway Politics, 1939–1989* (Knoxville, TN: University of Tennessee Press, 1990), p. 55–57.
16. Ibid, p. 20.
17. Richard F. Weingroff, "Federal-Aid Highway Act of 1956: Creating the Interstate System," *Public Roads*, Summer, 1996, http://www.tfhrc.gov/pubrds/summer96/p96su10.htm.
18. Mark S. Foster, *From Streetcar to Superhighway: American City Planners and Urban Transportation, 1900–1940* (Philadelphia, PA: Temple Univ. Press, 1981), p. 92.
19. Ibid, p. 177.
20. Mark Rose, *Interstate*, pp. 56–57.
21. Shorey Peterson, "The Highway from the Point of View of the Economist," in Jean Labatut and Wheaton J. Land (eds.), *Highways in Our National Life: A Symposium* (Princeton, NJ: Princeton University Press, 1950), pp. 190–200.
22. David Luberoff, Alan Altshuler, and Christie Baxter, *Mega-Project: A Political History of Boston's Multibillion Dollar Artery/Tunnel Project* (Cambridge, MA: Harvard University, 1994), p. 30.
23. Ibid, p. 133.
24. Joseph Dimento, Drusilla Van Hengel, and Sherry Ryan, "The Century Freeway: Design by Court Decree," *Access* 9 (Fall, 1996): 10.
25. Brian D. Taylor, "Why California Stopped Building Freeways," *Access* 3 (Fall, 1993):31.
26. Ibid, p. 32.
27. Ibid, p. 31.
28. David Luberoff, Alan Altshuler, and Christie Baxter, *Mega-Project*, p. 62.
29. FHwA, *Highway Statistics 1998*, table FE-221.
30. Federal Transit Administration, "Comparison of Projected Federal Highway Trust Fund Receipts for the Mass Transit Account to Federal Apportionments and Allocations for Transit, FY 1992 - 1997" (Washington, DC: FTA, 1997), 1 p.

The Subsidized-Highway Myth

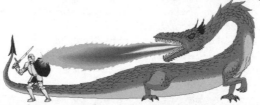

Myth: Americans drive so much only because highways are heavily subsidized.
Reality: Most costs that are claimed to be "subsidies" are actually paid for by automobile users.

Claims that highways are subsidized are greatly exaggerated by shoddy analyses. Highway opponents often claim that all federal and state highway expenditures are a subsidy even though they are paid almost exclusively out of highway user fees such as gas taxes. A *subsidy* is a cost paid by someone other than the user; costs paid by the user cannot be a subsidy. Yet auto opponents have claimed many other "subsidies" that are actually paid by highway users, including auto insurance, road tolls, and time wasted due to congestion.[1]

Other so-called subsidies include:[2]

- *The lost taxes from free parking*—If employers and shopping malls charged employees and customers to park, they would have to pay taxes on the income. The fact that they don't is considered a subsidy. Should employers also charge workers for their offices and desks?
- *Property taxes lost from land cleared for freeways*—This is more than made up for by the huge increase in property taxes from the increased values of land next to the freeways.
- *The military cost of defending Middle Eastern oil*—If the U.S. spent money only to defend oil, it would not spend money in the Balkans, Somalia, or other parts of the world. As Brookings Institution economist Pietro Nivola says, "U.S. armed forces would need to defend the Gulf regardless of how much or little Americans drive their cars."[3]
- *Trade deficits due to people buying foreign autos*—"Deficits" are not a subsidy, and foreign automakers provide many benefits through innovation and lower costs.
- *Low gasoline taxes*—Since gas taxes are higher in Europe, low U.S. taxes are supposed to be a subsidy. But the failure to charge more taxes is not a subsidy to autos any more than the IRS's failure to tax one hundred percent of your income is a subsidy to your family.

- *Cellular phones*—Jane Holtz Kay counts as subsidies "such pricy corollaries as cellular phones to save time spent behind the wheel."[4] I recently used my cell phone when riding BART. Was I subsidizing transit?
- *Loss of transportation options*—Public transit has supposedly shrunk because people have chosen the auto as being more economical and convenient. In fact, transit service today is probably far better (and certainly more subsidized) than it was a hundred years ago.[5]

After reviewing the literature on auto subsidies, University of California researchers James Murphy and Mark Delucchi concluded that most calculations are "of limited use" because they "rely on outdated, superficial, nongeneralizable, or otherwise inappropriate studies."[6] Delucchi estimates that total subsidies to the auto to be less than 7 cents per mile—although he includes congestion and highway accidents, which are paid for mainly by highway users.[7]

Table One: Highway Subsidies in 1996

Disposition of Highway User Fees (billions)

	Federal	State	Local	Total
Highway user fees	$30.3	$53.6	$2.8	$86.6
Diverted to mass transit	3.1	2.5	.8	6.4
Diverted to non-transportation	5.6	7.6	.1	13.4
Collection expenses		2.9		2.9
Spent on highways	$21.5	$40.6	$1.9	63.8
Spending on Highways (billions)				
Highway user fees	21.5	40.6	1.9	$63.8
Property taxes			5.0	5.0
General funds	1.0	1.9	10.0	12.9
Other taxes and fees	.2	1.9	1.4	3.5
Total taxes spent on highways	22.7	44.4	18.3	85.2
Highway Subsidies (billions)				
Taxes spent on highways	$1.2	$3.7	$16.4	$21.3
Diverted user fees	8.7	10.1	.9	19.7
Net subsidies to highways	–$7.6	–$6.3	$15.5	$1.7

Source: Federal Highway Administration, Highway Statistics 1996, table HF-10. Data may not add due to rounding. This table and related text presumes that a small amount of federal highway money given to territories is spent on highways in those territories.

An accurate analysis of highway and auto subsidies must first recognize that gasoline taxes paid by auto drivers were designed to be a user fee. Spending non-road-related taxes or government funds on roads may represent a subsidy. But that subsidy may be partially offset by highway user fees that are diverted to mass transit or other purposes. The true measure of road subsidies is total government spending on roads minus total receipts from highway users. Table one shows that, in 1996, $19.8 billion of highway user fees were diverted to transit or non-transportation purposes, while $21.4 billion of non-highway taxes were spent on roads. This leaves a net 1996 subsidy of $1.7 billion. Note that all of the subsidies are local: The federal and state governments collected more from highway users than they spent on highways.

Historically, this has typically been the case. State subsidies to roads pretty much ended around 1930. In almost every year since then, the states collected more highway user fees than they spent on roads. Despite efforts by highway interests to dedicate state gasoline and other user fees exclusively to roads, only eight states do so today: Forty-two states divert some highway user fees to transit and forty states spend some highway user fees on non-transportation projects. Since 1921, highway users have paid states $124 billion (in 1998 dollars) more than the states spent on highways.[8]

Between 1941 and 1956 and since 1989, the federal government also collected more highway fees than it spent on roads. In 1998 dollars, these surpluses outweighed deficits in other years since 1921 by a total of $48 billion.[9] Congress imposed a tax on gasoline in 1932 but felt no obligation to spend it all on roads until 1957, when it created the so-called Highway Trust Fund. If it were a true trust fund, the trustees would be legally obligated to spend it on the fund's beneficiaries, meaning the auto drivers who pay into it. But in 1983 Congress diverted one cent of federal gas taxes, which were then nine cents, to mass transit. In 1990, the tax was increased by another nickel, with another penny going for mass transit. In 1993, another 4.3 cents per gallon was added, all of which went for non-transportation purposes. In the decade ending in 1998, a total of $62 billion was siphoned from highway user fees to transit and general purposes.

Local governments have subsidized roads and streets to the tune of $783 billion, an average of $10 billion per year, since 1921. In the past decade, local subsidies have averaged $15 billion per year. More than half of these subsidies in 1996 came from just seven states—New York, Texas, California, Minnesota, Georgia, Wisconsin, and New Jersey—even though those same states account for only 31 percent of total U.S. highway expenses.[10] This suggests that subsidies could be reduced if some of these states changed their tax structure.

Many of these local subsidies may be subsidizing something other than the automobile. American cities had streets and rural areas had roads before they had cars and they would still need those streets and roads if cars disappeared tomorrow. Many pre-auto streets and roads were paid for with local funds such as the funds now being used. If your property taxes pay to maintain the street in front of your house, are you subsidizing the automobile or just paying for the benefits of having access to the rest of the city?

For the sake of argument, though, let's charge all of these subsidies against the automobile to see how much people who drive and ride in autos are subsidized per passenger mile. Since 1936, the earliest year data are available, road subsidies have averaged less than a half penny per passenger mile (in 1998 pennies). They reached as high as 3.6 cents per passenger mile in the 1930s, mainly due to the job-creation efforts of the New Deal. Since 1941, they have never exceeded three-fourths of a penny per mile and in the last decade they have averaged less than two-tenths of a penny per mile. As noted in the Balanced-Transportation Myth, transit subsidies are hundreds of times greater, averaging 45 cents per passenger mile in recent years.

Actually, it is not fair to compare transit and highway subsidies per passenger mile because highways do more than just carry people. In recent years, American highways have carried almost a billion ton-miles of freight per year. The city streets that receive the preponderance of local highway subsidies are an especially critical component of this movement; even if all intercity freight were shipped by rail, urban roads would still be needed for the final delivery of most goods. Unlike roads, urban transit serves no such dual function.

This is not to excuse the highway subsidies. Auto drivers should pay their own way and local road departments should not have to rely on other taxes. The main point, however, is this: Adding 45 cents per passenger mile to transit fares would severely depress transit ridership, but adding two-tenths of a cent per passenger mile to the cost of driving is not going to have much effect on people's behavior. As Peter Muller observes, the "permanently higher fuel prices" of the 1970s were accompanied by "the revival of growth in nonmetropolitan areas for the first time in nearly a century as the city spilled into exurbia and beyond."[11]

Notes

1. For example, see Stephen B. Goddard, *Getting There: The Epic Struggle between Road and Rail in the American Century* (New York, NY: Basic Books, 1994), p. 255.
2. Most of these are from studies cited by the Sierra Club, "America's Autos on Welfare: A Summary of Subsidies," 1999, www.sierraclub.org.
3. Pietro S. Nivola, *Laws of the Landscape: How Policies Shape Cities in Europe and America* (Washington, DC: Brookings, 1999), p. 17.
4. Jane Holtz Kay, *Asphalt Nation: How the Automobile Took over America and How We Can Take It Back* (New York, NY: Crown, 1997), p. 121.
5. Alan Pisarski, *Commuting in America II* (Washington, DC: Eno, 1996), p. 85.
6. James J. Murphy and Mark A Delucchi, "A Review of the Literature on the Social Cost of Motor Vehicle Use in the United States," *Journal of Transportation and Statistics* 1(1):15–42 (January, 1998).
7. Mark Delucchi, "Should We Try to Get the Prices Right?" *Access* 16 (Spring 2000), p. 17.
8. Federal Highway Administration, *Highway Statistics Summary to 1995* (Washington, DC: FHwA, 1996), table HF-210; FHwA, *Highway Statistics 1996, 1997,* and *1998,* table HF-10.
9. Ibid.
10. FHwA, *Highway Statistics 1996,* table LGF-21.
11. Peter O. Muller, "Transportation and Urban Form: Stages in the Spatial Evolution of the American Metropolis," *in* Susan Hanson (ed.), *The Geography of Urban Transportation* (New York, NY: Guilford Press, 1986), p. 46.

25. Understanding Congestion

Surveys consistently show that urban Americans consider congestion to be one of the biggest problems in their cities. For example, a poll commissioned by the Pew Center for Civic Journalism found that more than one out of three Americans considered congestion to be a "big problem" where they live and nearly one out of three considered it to be a "small problem."[1]

Yet congestion is hardly a recent phenomenon. "Traffic congestion was already a serious problem in the 1920s," says geographer Cliff Ellis.[2] In fact, congestion in major cities preceded the automobile. In 1900, traffic jams "were so bad that police often had to break them up using billy clubs."[3] A New York City traffic jam in 1867 led a young boy named William Eno to a lifelong pursuit of finding ways to reduce congestion. He eventually founded the Eno Transportation Foundation and today is known as the "father of traffic regulation."[4]

As noted in the Portland case study (p. 111), traffic engineers use a concept called *levels of service* to describe traffic conditions (table one). Level of service A means no congestion and free-flowing traffic, while level of service F is near gridlock. Notice that C produces more than twice as much traffic volume as A with little deterioration in speed. Going to level of service D results in a small increase in volume at the cost of a significant reduction in speed and safety. The road's capacity is reached at level of service E, but speeds are lower still and driver stress is high. Level F is stop-and-go traffic, which means both speeds and volumes are low and irregular. The volume numbers in table one are estimates; transportation engineers do not have a precise measure of road capacities. In fact, highway capacities may have increased in recent years simply because drivers are willing to drive closer to one another at a given speed.[5]

Volumes increase even though speeds decline at service levels D and E because at lower speeds drivers are willing to drive closer to the cars in front of them. But as speeds fall, there is a limit to the increase in volume that is possible by driving closer together. Obviously, two cars cannot be closer than touching one another. Level of service E is considered "unstable" because a slight disruption can cause cars to slow down so much that traffic throughput falls. This bumps the level down to F, that is, to stop-and-go traffic.

Table One: Levels of Service
(volume of cars per lane per hour)

LOS	Traffic Conditions	Volume
A	Free flow, low volumes and densities, high speeds, drivers unaffected by other vehicles	700
B	Reasonably free flow, speeds restricted somewhat by traffic, reasonable freedom to select speeds	1,120
C	Speeds remain near free flow, freedom to maneuver noticeably restricted	1,645
D	Speeds decline, freedom to maneuver further reduced, traffic speed has little space to absorb disruptions	2,015
E	Unstable flow, at or near capacity, freedom to maneuver extremely limited and level of comfort for driver is poor	2,200
F	Breakdown in flow, speeds and volumes can drop to zero	

Source: Wolfgang Homburger, et al., Fundamentals of Traffic Engineering *(Berkeley, CA: UC, 1996), pp. 8-2–8-2. Volumes are for limited access freeways; volumes for multi-lane highways are similar though at slower speeds.*

Suppose a freeway has service level C, so the traffic is somewhat heavy but speeds are free flowing. If someone suddenly slows down, then the car behind has to slow down, and the car behind that. This sends a *shock wave* down the highway so that many cars end up slowing down a little. At level of service C, the spaces between the cars are sufficient for traffic to quickly get back up to speed.[6] But at service level D, it may take many minutes for traffic to get back up to speed. At service level E, traffic flows are likely to breakdown and remain down until the number of people entering the highway falls well below the highway's capacity.

Slowdowns leading to shockwaves or breakdowns in traffic flows can be unpredictable, such as when a traffic accident occurs. Such unpredictable slowdowns are called *incident-related congestion*. But slowdowns during *peak-period congestion* generally happen at predictable locations such as:
- On- and off-ramps;
- The junction of two highways; or
- Places where two highway lanes merge into one.

These predictable locations, or *bottlenecks*, are often the result of poorly designed roads or roads built when traffic levels were much lower than today. For example, many older freeways have on-ramps that quickly turn into off-ramps. Traffic getting on must move one lane to the left while traffic that wants to get off must move right to get on the off-ramp. Such *weaving* is not a problem at low traffic levels but can cause considerable slowdowns, shockwaves, and flow breakdowns at high traffic levels. Most freeway designers today would avoid situations requiring such weaving, but the cost of retrofitting older freeways can be very high. One simple technique that many states are using is ramp metering, which reduces the likelihood that shockwaves at on ramps will reduce the level of service to F.

Congestion on arterials and collectors differs from freeways and is usually associated with stop lights and stop signs. The sequence of stop lights on a grid of busy streets can be arranged to allow a smooth flow of traffic at a preset speed *if* the streets are all one-way streets. On two-way streets, however, light sequences cannot be arranged to allow vehicles to go more than one or two blocks without stopping. For this reason, traffic engineers favor one-way streets in busy downtown grids. One-way streets are also significantly safer for pedestrians. Businesses in such areas face a trade off: One-way streets mean that only half the traffic will pass buy each store front; but two-way streets mean an increase in congestion that may lead people to avoid the business area entirely.

Busy, two-way arterials can maintain reasonable traffic flows if stop lights are placed no closer than about a half-mile apart and are programmed to provide sequential flow in the dominant direction of traffic. In other words, inbound traffic will have smooth flows in the morning while outbound traffic will have to stop more frequently. In the afternoon this sequence is reversed. Many cities are using federal funds to invest in improved traffic signalization in order to reduce congestion and the air pollution that results from stop-and-go traffic.[7]

Serious congestion can result when stop lights must be placed closer than a half-mile together on major arterials. Peak-period traffic is often delayed because cars cannot pass through a light even when it is green because the lanes ahead are filled with autos waiting for the next light to turn green.

One solution is to use rotaries, also known as roundabouts. Given the same land area as ordinary signalized street intersections, rotaries have lower flow capacities than traffic signals, but are less likely to result in breakdowns in flows. Rotary flow capacities can be increased by using more land. Rotaries are popular in many other nations but are rarely used in the U.S., partly because the U.S. developed traffic signals instead. Today traffic engineers are hesitant to build rotaries because they fear that Americans would not understand how to use them.

Highway planning would be a lot simpler if travel were equally distributed through all hours of the day. Instead, a huge percentage of travel takes place during morning and afternoon rush hours. This is partly because businesses find it convenient to be open during similar hours so they can interact with one another.[8] Even if businesses were willing to stagger work hours, families with multiple workers would find it inconvenient for them to have different schedules.

Business hours are not the only cause of rush-hour congestion. Nearly 40 percent of morning rush-hour traffic and 60 percent of afternoon rush-hour traffic is not commuter traffic.[9] Obviously, there are many reasons why people find it particularly beneficial to travel during those hours. While certainly not welcome, congestion is voluntary to the extent that people consider the value of driving during peak periods exceeds the cost of delay and aggravation. As Downs says,

"Many commuters are willing to travel long distances or to tolerate the time wasted in heavy traffic so they can work and live where they choose."[10]

When faced with peak-hour congestion, potential travelers have several choices:

1. Drive anyway and accept that speeds will be slower than in free-flowing traffic;
2. Plan to leave earlier or later to avoid peak hours;
3. Find an alternate route that is less congested;
4. Use an alternate mode such as transit, walking, or cycling;
5. Don't go—telecommute, combine or *chain* several activities into one trip, or otherwise take fewer trips; or
6. Change the origin, destination, or both, perhaps by moving home or workplace to less congested areas.

University of California researchers surveyed hundreds of San Diego city employees to find out how they responded to congestion. The most common response was to shift travel times by leaving from home earlier or work later or adopting a flextime work schedule. Nearly as many people continued to drive in peak-period traffic while reducing the stress or cost of such driving by improving their car stereo system or buying and using a cell phone while driving. Even though most of those surveyed worked in a downtown area, very few changed to a different mode of travel such as transit.[11]

The city employees interviewed by UC researchers did not have the option of moving their work place. Yet most new job growth is taking place in the suburbs. "When a company moves," Joel Garreau observes, "the commute of the chief executive officer must always become shorter."[12]

The available evidence indicates that most of those who choose not to drive during peak periods prefer some strategies over others:

• Huge numbers of people time shift, which is why the number of congested hours per day tends to increase;
• Businesses and residents are rapidly moving to less congested areas, which of course is called sprawl;
• While some people may skip trips, telecommuting remains small and trip chaining is mainly done by women, suggesting that it is a response to family responsibilities more than a response to congestion;
• While there is some movement to alternate routes, most routes tend to quickly become equally congested at all times;
• Very few appear to shift to other modes. Despite increasing congestion, per capita transit ridership has remained constant for about a decade.

In short, time shifting is the most important short-run alternative to peak-period congestion, and location shifting is the most important long-run alternative. Trip reduction and route shifting are probably less important alternatives and mode shifting is insignificant.

The Texas Transportation Institute collects data on miles of driving and highway lane miles for sixty-eight urban areas. The most recent data cover every year from 1982 through 1997. Based on these data, the institute calculates levels of congestion, the amount of delay experienced by auto drivers, and the costs of such congestion in terms of wasted fuel, drivers' time, and so forth.[13]

To make these calculations, the institute relies on generalized assumptions about the capacity of freeways and other major highways to carry traffic flows. For example, the institute might assume that all freeways can carry 2,000 cars per lane-mile each hour, while arterials can carry 1,600 cars per lane-mile each hour. In fact, there are significant variations among highways. Cities with older highway networks, such as New York, Philadelphia, and Boston, are more likely to have lower capacities per lane-mile and more bottlenecks than cities with newer highways, such as Dallas, Phoenix, and Atlanta. Peter Gordon and Harry Richardson found that the correlation (r-squared) between the institute's results and average rush hour speeds reported in the Nationwide Personal Transportation Survey was "just 0.09, not significantly different from zero."[14]

This means that the institute's estimates of congestion, delay per driver, and similar measures are not comparable between cities. However, estimates of *changes* in congestion over time are more likely to reflect reality because large urban areas cannot rebuild enough highways in just fifteen years to significantly change average lane-mile capacities. Thus, Texas Transportation Institute data cannot reliably say that congestion in, say, Phoenix is worse than in Philadelphia. But it can suggest whether the *change* in Phoenix congestion over the past ten to fifteen years is more or less than the change in Philadelphia congestion.

The institute also calculates such things as the number of hours of delay imposed on drivers and the number of gallons of fuel spent idling in stop-and-go traffic. Again, these calculations are merely first approximations. While they are useful, they should not be considered exact, especially when comparing one urban area with another.

The institute carefully does not take a stand on how congestion should be relieved. Its reports note that it could be reduced by adding road capacity, reducing driving (perhaps by increasing vehicle occupancy), shifting the hours of driving (perhaps through congestion pricing), and improving the efficiency of existing roads (by, for example, changing the timing of traffic lights)—although such efficiency improvements would not show up in the institute's calculated results.

The institute's data have been used by groups on all sides of the debate. For example, the Surface Transportation Policy Project claims that institute data show that sprawl causes congestion (although it has not released its analysis; see The Myth that Sprawl Causes Congestion, p. 253). Meanwhile, the Buckeye Institute, an Ohio think tank, uses institute data to show that congestion has increased more in cities that built new rail transit lines than in other urban areas.[15] But the difference between the two—a 29-percent increase in congestion for areas with new rail transit compared to a 22-percent increase for other urban areas—is too small to be very meaningful.

What the Texas Transportation Institute data clearly show is that motor vehicle traffic is increasing faster than roadway capacities in almost every major U.S. city. In rural areas, where there is plenty of surplus capacity, this would not be a problem. But in congested urban areas, increases in driving lead to more congestion, more delay, more air pollution, and more wasted fuel. While the exact numbers may be debatable, the general results are not. The question is what to do about it.

Notes

1. Princeton Survey Research Associates, "Straight Talk from Americans – 2000," Pew Center for Civic Journalism, http://www.pewcenter.org/doingcj/research/r_ST2000nat1.html#sprawl.
2. Cliff Ellis, "Professional Conflict over Urban Form: The Case of Urban Freeways, 1930 to 1970," in Mary Corbin Sies and Christopher Silver (eds.), Planning the Twentieth-Century American City (Baltimore, MD: Johns Hopkins, 1996), pp. 262–279.
3. Mark Mills, "Transportation Fuels—Electricity," in Encyclopedia of Energy Technology and the Environment (New York, NY: John Wiley, 1995), p. 2698.
4. John A. Montgomery, Eno: The Man and the Foundation (Washington, DC: Eno Transportation Foundation, 1988), p. 1.
5. Federal Highway Administration, Highway Capacity Manual, Third Edition (Washington, DC: FHwA, 1994).
6. Shock wave animations can be viewed at http://www.cs.berkeley.edu/~zephyr/shock/index.html.
7. See, for example, Federal Highway Administration, The Congestion Mitigation and Air Quality Improvement Program FY 1997, (Washington, DC: FHwA, 1999), http://www.fhwa.dot.gov/environment/cmaq97st.pdf.
8. Anthony Downs, Stuck in Traffic: Coping with Peak-Hour Traffic Congestion (Washington, DC: Brookings, 1992), p. 15.
9. Alan Pisarski, Commuting in America II (Washington, DC: Eno, 1996), pp. 3–4.
10. Anthony Downs, Stuck in Traffic, p. 16.
11. Patricia Mokhtarian, Elizabeth Raney, & Ilan Salomon, "Behavioral Response to Congestion: Identifying Patterns and Socioeconomic Differences in Adoption," in Sandra Rosenbloom, ed., Women's Travel Issues: Proceedings from the Second National Conference (Washington, DC: US DOT, 1997), p. 719, http://www.fhwa.dot.gov/ohim/womens/chap38.pdf.
12. Joel Garreau, Edge City: Life on the New Frontier (New York, NY: Doubleday, 1991), p. 468.
13. David Schrank and Tim Lomax, 1999 Annual Mobility Report: Information for Urban America (College Station, TX: Texas A&M, 1999), http://mobility.tmu.edu.
14. Peter Gordon and Harry Richardson, "Congestion Trends in Metropolitan Areas," in National Research Council, Curbing Gridlock: Peak-Period Fees to Relieve Traffic Congestion (Washington, DC: National Academy Press, 1994), volume 2:1–31.
15. Buckeye Institute, "Rail Transit Fails to Reduce Congestion," Policy Note, February 1999, http://www.buckeyeinstitute.org/policy/1999_2.htm.

Congestion Facts

Each year the Texas Transportation Institute publishes its latest estimates of urban congestion. These are widely reported because they quantify something urban drivers know: that highway congestion is getting worse. As described in chapter 25, comparisons between urban areas for a specific year are unreliable. Costs and speed estimates are also very approximate. However, the Texas data can be used to compare changes in congestion over time.

Texas Transportation Institute Congestion Data

| | Annual Per Driver | | | Freeway | | Travel Rate Index | | |
Urban Area	Delay	Fuel	Cost	Speed	1997	1992	1987	1982
Albany, NY	8	13	$140	59	107	107	104	103
Albuquerque, NM	39	57	650	46	123	116	110	105
Atlanta, GA	68	106	1,125	43	136	120	121	116
Austin, TX	53	82	880	46	129	121	118	116
Bakersfield, CA	8	12	155	55	110	107	104	103
Baltimore, MD	47	72	780	46	128	124	120	115
Beaumont, TX	12	18	225	56	107	105	103	102
Boston, MA	66	98	1,095	45	134	128	118	114
Boulder, CO	6	0	110	59	109	106	104	103
Brownsville, TX	3	0	50	57	108	107	104	102
Buffalo, NY	7	11	115	55	109	108	106	104
Charlotte, NC	41	61	680	47	129	124	113	108
Chicago, IL	44	65	720	41	139	134	132	123
Cincinnati, OH	31	50	525	47	126	125	115	110
Cleveland, OH	20	33	345	48	123	112	108	105
Colorado Springs, CO	16	23	275	51	120	114	106	103
Columbus, OH	30	47	515	48	125	120	112	109
Corpus Christi, TX	8	13	110	56	107	107	108	107
Dallas, TX	58	92	975	45	130	122	120	117
Denver, CO	45	70	760	44	134	126	117	114
Detroit, MI	62	92	1,010	43	135	129	122	119
El Paso, TX	12	20	205	51	114	113	109	105
Eugene, OR	8	12	120	58	110	107	105	104
Fort Worth, TX	38	60	640	47	124	117	114	110
Fresno, CA	19	26	315	53	119	117	110	108

Urban Area	Annual Per Driver Delay	Fuel	Cost	Freeway Speed	1997	Travel Rate Index 1992	1987	1982
Ft. Lauderdale, FL	31	47	$515	46	128	123	117	112
Hartford, CT	23	38	390	53	113	115	111	106
Honolulu, HI	29	45	510	49	126	126	121	121
Houston, TX	58	90	960	42	136	129	132	130
Indianapolis, IN	52	79	865	47	127	116	109	106
Jacksonville, FL	35	53	580	50	120	119	112	109
Kansas City, MO	28	44	475	52	118	110	108	105
Laredo, TX	6	0	90	59	112	107	107	106
Las Vegas, NM	34	50	575	43	137	128	119	114
Los Angeles, CA	82	122	1,370	36	151	150	141	131
Louisville, KY	40	63	680	49	124	119	111	107
Memphis, TN	29	44	480	48	124	114	110	107
Miami, FL	57	83	930	40	136	134	126	121
Milwaukee, WI	25	39	425	44	127	123	115	110
Minneapolis, MN	34	53	570	45	130	119	114	108
Nashville, TN	46	71	765	51	118	111	110	108
New Orleans, LA	25	37	400	47	125	128	131	121
New York, NY	38	58	640	46	135	131	126	122
Norfolk, VA	34	52	570	48	125	119	118	113
Oklahoma City, OK	18	29	305	52	115	109	105	103
Omaha, NE	31	45	510	53	120	118	113	109
Orlando, FL	41	60	670	44	130	130	122	117
Philadelphia, PA	27	40	445	48	127	123	121	118
Phoenix, AZ	35	51	580	41	132	126	124	117
Pittsburgh, PA	15	22	245	54	118	117	115	110
Portland, OR	52	80	885	44	133	125	121	114
Providence, RI	21	32	360	50	121	117	112	107
Sacramento, CA	38	59	645	47	127	123	117	111
Salem, OR	15	21	215	52	114	109	104	102
Salt Lake City, UT	23	36	400	47	128	118	109	107
San Antonio, TX	26	42	435	49	121	117	118	111
San Bernardino, CA	47	74	815	41	132	129	123	112
San Diego, CA	36	59	635	42	136	134	127	112
San Francisco, CA	58	91	995	40	144	144	146	137
San Jose, CA	45	69	765	44	134	134	132	119
Seattle, WA	69	106	1,165	39	146	146	127	116
Spokane, WA	11	16	200	54	112	108	105	103
St. Louis, MO	52	79	845	48	130	119	115	113
Tacoma, WA	29	47	500	43	129	126	117	108
Tampa, FL	41	48	650	51	123	123	124	121
Tucson, AZ	28	38	450	51	126	118	115	113
Washington, DC	76	116	1,260	41	142	139	132	127

Annual per-driver estimates of delay are in hours, fuel wasted in gallons, and cost in dollars. Freeway speed is at the peak hour. The Travel Rate Index is roughly the delay encountered at the peak hour: An index of 150 means a 50-percent longer journey than at off-peak hours; 100 means no delay. Source: Texas Transportation Institute, 1999 Annual Mobility Report: Information for Urban America *(College Station, TX: Texas A&M, 1999).*

Smart Growth's Poster Child

Myth: Los Angeles is the epitome of sprawl, a low-density area covered with freeways.

Reality: The Los Angeles metropolitan area is the epitome of smart growth, as it has the highest density and the fewest miles of freeway per capita of any U.S. urbanized area.

To most people, Los Angeles is the epitome of an unlivable city. The Texas Transportation Institute says it is the most congested city in America.[1] The Environmental Protection Agency says that it suffers from the most extreme air pollution.[2] The Sierra Club describes Los Angeles as "the granddaddy of sprawl" and says it is "standard for the worst that sprawl has to offer: over-dependence on the automobile, gut-wrenching traffic congestion, unhealthy air pollution, and paved-over open space."[3]

Most people who live outside the Los Angeles metropolitan area—which includes Anaheim, Burbank, Long Beach, Pasadena, Pomona, and Santa Ana, among other nearby cities—agree that they don't want their city to become another Los Angeles. The question is: What policies should a city follow to avoid becoming as congested and polluted as LA? The conventional wisdom is that Los Angeles is a sprawling, low-density area covered with freeways. If this is true, the best way to save other cities from becoming like Los Angeles is to stop building roads and start building and rebuilding neighborhoods to higher densities.

Table One: The Los Angeles Urbanized Area

	1950	1990	1998
Population (thousands)	4,001	11,403	12,600
Land area square miles	869	1,966	2,231
Density	4,600	5,800	5,650

Source: Census Bureau for 1950 and 1990, FHwA, Highway Statistics 1998 for 1998. FHwA land area data are not exactly comparable with Census Bureau data since they use slightly different criteria for determining urbanized area boundaries.

As is so often true in the smart-growth world, the conventional wisdom is wrong. In this case, it is spectacularly wrong. Los Angeles is not only not the epitome of sprawl, it is the epitome of smart growth.

- At more than 5,600 people per square mile, the Los Angeles urbanized area has the highest density of any metropolitan area in the nation.[4]
- Los Angeles is significantly denser than the New York metropolitan area (4,100 per square mile, including northeastern New Jersey).
- Los Angeles is also one of the few major urban areas to get denser in the past half century. Where New York's urban density has fallen by half, Los Angeles' has increased by nearly a quarter.[5]
- Los Angeles has the jobs-housing balance called for by smart growth, with more than one hundred major employment centers, none of which have more than 4 percent of the region's jobs.

Table Two: The City of Los Angeles

	1950	1990	1998
Population (thousands)	1,970	3,485	3,598
Land area square miles	451	469	469
Density	4,370	7,425	7,670

Source: Census Bureau. Land area and density for 1998 are estimated.

Figure One: Los Angeles Area Densities

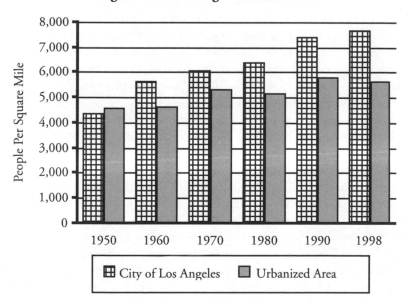

Not only is Los Angeles the nation's densest urbanized area, it is one of the few whose density has increased since 1950. Source: Census Bureau, Federal Highway Administration.

Smart growth also calls for less road construction, demanding instead rail transit lines surrounded by transit-oriented developments.

- At 51 miles per million people, Los Angeles has the fewest number of miles of freeway per capita of any U.S. city.[6] This is less than half the average of U.S. urban areas, which is 112 miles per million.
- Los Angeles has been spending billions of dollars building a rail system that is turning out to be a colossal failure.
- Los Angeles is planning transit-oriented developments near at least eight rail stations and has zoned for such developments near many more stations.[7]

Table Three: Los Angeles-Area Transportation

Miles of freeway per million people	51
Annual miles driven per capita	7,921
Passenger miles per capita	12,674
Annual transit miles per capita	190
Annual transit trips per capita	45
Auto commuters	90.3%
Transit commuters	4.7%
Walk/cycle commuters	5.0%

Source: FHwA, Highway Statistics 1998, FTA, Transit Profiles 1998, 1990 Census. All data from 1998 except commuting data, which are from 1990. Per capita passenger miles are 1.6 times miles driven.

To promote these transit-oriented developments, planning authorities have used "incentive zoning," which rewards developers of high-density areas by reducing fees or regulatory requirements. Los Angeles and Long Beach redevelopment agencies have also provided tens of millions of dollars in public funds to support such developments.[8] Yet only a few developments have taken place and they have done little or nothing to change regional travel habits.[9]

Los Angeles' reputation for terrible congestion results not from low-density sprawl, but from the region's combination of the nation's highest metropolitan densities with the fewest number of freeway miles per capita. The high population produces by far the most vehicle miles traveled per square mile of any major U.S. city—twice the average of the fifty largest urban areas and 22 percent more than its nearest competitor, San Jose.[10] With so few miles of freeways per capita, those cars get jammed in daily congestion.

In 1994, smart-growth planners in Portland, Oregon, compared the nation's major urban areas with their goals for Portland. They concluded that, "In public discussions we gather the general impression that Los Angeles represents a future to be avoided." Yet "with respect to density and road per capita mileage it displays an investment pattern we desire to replicate" in Portland.[11]

- Portland's plan calls for increasing population densities from under 3,000 people per square mile to nearly 5,000 people per square mile.[12] Only Los

Angeles, Honolulu, and Bangor, Maine, are higher.
- The plan also calls for reducing per capita freeway mileage from more than 100 miles per million residents to under 70 miles per million.[13] Of major urban areas today, only Los Angeles, Miami, and Philadelphia are lower.
- Portland's plan calls for several expensive rail lines similar to those recently built in Los Angeles.

If Los Angeles is "the standard for the worst" American cities, then why do smart-growth planners want to replicate Los Angeles in Portland and other cities? The answer is that smart-growth advocates care less about how people live today than about how they want people to live. They want people to live in the same neighborhood as most of their friends and relatives, so that they won't have to drive to visit them. They want people to shop at a corner grocery store, where prices are high and selection is low, instead of driving to a supermarket. They want people to both live and work on a rail transit line so they won't have to drive to work.

That's not how people live today. They may get to know their neighbors, but their real friends—the people with whom they share hobbies and interests—are scattered all over town. They shop for price and value and don't want to be limited to one grocery store. And their workplaces are as widely distributed around the city as their friends, so few people would benefit from a rail line that doesn't go where they need to go.

To understand why this won't happen, consider Los Angeles. Less than 5 percent of all jobs in the metro area are in downtown L.A. Only one other place in the area, Long Beach, has a comparable number of jobs. Instead, employment is distributed in over 100 centers all around the area. The distance from one end of the Los Angeles area to the other can be over 60 miles. Even in a smaller urban area such as Portland, the distance from one edge of the metro area to the other is over 30 miles. Few people will walk or bicycle the distances that they need to visit friends, go to work, recreate, or shop.

This lack of a concentrated center is what bothers people about Los Angeles. Los Angeles "finds its order in chaos, and its structure is that is has no structure," says writer David Olin. H. L. Mencken once disdainfully called the city "nineteen suburbs in search of a metropolis." Yet historian Kevin Starr calls it "a true world city," noting that it is "the second-largest Korean city" and "the third-largest Mexican city on the planet." According to urban analyst Michael Dear, Los Angeles' lack of a center is "prototypical of the way cities are going to go in the future."[14] But, as Joel Garreau says, that is actually the way cities have been growing since around 1920.[15]

With the possible exception of New York, American cities are all heavily decentralized. Jobs, recreation, friends, retailers are all well distributed throughout metropolitan areas. The U.S. could spend trillions of dollars on rail transit and not provide enough lines to get people from where they are to where they want to go. Smart growth doesn't even aim to do the one thing that would make cities more like New York, which is to concentrate hundreds of thousands of jobs in one small central area.

In short, smart growth doesn't save cities from becoming like Los Angeles. It turns them into Los Angeles. To avoid turning into Los Angeles, cities should allow low-density residential and commercial development and build cost-effective transportation systems that will easily move people around the area.

Notes

1. Texas Transportation Institute, *Urban Roadway Congestion Annual Report 1998* (College Station, TX: Texas A&M, 1998), table 1.
2. Environmental Protection Agency, *National Air Quality and Emissions Report, 1994* (Washington, DC: EPA, 1995).
3. Sierra Club, *The Dark Side of the American Dream* (San Francisco, CA: Sierra Club, 1998), p. 4. Available at http://www.sierraclub.org/transportation/sprawl/sprawl_report/.
4. Federal Highway Administration, *Highway Statistics 1998* (Washington, DC: US DOT, 1996), table HM-72.
5. Census Bureau, *1950 Population Census: Volume II—Characteristics of the Population, Part 1* (Washington, DC: Census Bureau, 1953), table 17.
6. FHwA, *Highway Statistics 1998*, table HM-71.
7. City of Seattle Strategic Planning Office, "Los Angeles Transit-Oriented Development Case Studies," http://www.ci.seattle.wa.us/planning/todstudy/CS04.htm.
8. Ibid, table 4-4.
9. Marlon Boarnet & Randall Crane, *L.A. Story: A Reality Check for Transit-Based Housing* UCTC No. 250.
10. FHwA, *Highway Statistics 1998*, table HM-72.
11. Metro, *Metro Measured* (Portland, OR: Metro, May 1994), p. 7.
12. Metro, *Region 2040 Recommended Alternative Technical Appendix* (Portland, OR: Metro, 9-15-94).
13. Ibid.
14. Olin, Mencken, Starr, and Dear quotes from Carl Nolte, "Los Angeles — It's Our Destiny," *San Francisco Chronicle*, August 31, 1999.
15. Joel Garreau, *Edge City: Life on the New Frontier* (New York, NY: Doubleday, 1991), p. 25.

The Myth That New Roads Increase Congestion

Myth: We can't build our way out of congestion because new roads simply become congested as soon as they are built.

Reality: Adding road capacity pin congested areas provides enormous benefits in terms of shorter trips, safer travel, and more valuable travel.

"For decades traffic experts have observed the capacity of more highways to simply breed more traffic," claims Jane Holtz Kay.[1] It is a mark of the success of the anti-auto movement that this absurd proposition has become fully accepted and frequently repeated by mayors, governors, vice presidents, and other intelligent people. Of course, with urban travel growing twice as fast as urban road capacities for two decades, congestion is severe and new capacity is quickly saturated by the existing demand. But to use this as an argument against building roads makes as much sense as arguing that Ford should make Edsels instead of Mustangs because the Mustangs are sold as fast as they are built.

There is no doubt that urban congestion is increasing. In 1975, 41 percent of urban freeway miles were congested during rush hours. By 1993, this had increased to 69 percent. The increase isn't due to more freeways. It is due to more driving without a similar increase in freeways. In the past two decades, the number of cars in the U.S. has increased by half, while the number of miles those cars travel has increased by three-quarters. Yet the number of road miles has increased by less than 3 percent.

The notion that new roads only increase congestion implies two equally absurd assumptions:

- *The demand for automobile travel is infinite and can never be sated.* Anyone who has driven interstate highways in such states as South Dakota or Wyoming knows that it is easily possible to build excess capacity that remains only partially used for decades.
- *Urban auto travel produces no benefits and is merely a deadweight loss on society.* Auto travel produces benefits for travelers as well as nearly everyone else.

Building new capacity in a congested route, perhaps by adding new lanes on a freeway, produces several important benefits.
- People who were driving that route during peak periods save time;
- People who were time shifting to avoid congestion can drive at a time that is more valuable to them;
- Businesses that had moved to avoid congestion may be replaced by other businesses that benefit from the added road capacity;
- Those who reduced travel to avoid congestion can go back to traveling again;
- People who had moved to alternate routes switch back to the route with new capacity, thus reducing congestion on those alternate routes;
- Some who used other modes save time or money by switching to autos.

Referring to time shifters, route shifters, and mode shifters, Anthony Downs says that new capacity leads to a "triple convergence" of travel to the new route.[2] Downs' attitude towards this convergence is almost defeatist: "Expanding roadway capacity does not fully eliminate peak-hour traffic congestion, or even reduce the intensity of traffic jams during the most crowded periods—although these periods will be shorter."[3] Yet such a triple convergence represents huge benefits in terms of more convenient travel, shorter trip times, and lower costs.

"In 1996, the amount Americans drive every day grew at the relatively modest rate of 3%," says Barbara McCann of the Surface Transportation Policy Project. "If road space were to keep pace with that increase in driving, we would have had to build 245,335 additional miles of roadway in just one year (that's 184,664 lane miles more than were actually built), consuming about 560 square miles of land. The cost for these roads would exceed $171 billion."[4] McCann hugely inflates the amount and cost of new roads that are needed by assuming that the entire U.S. network must be expanded by 3 percent. In reality, only a tiny percentage of U.S. roads are congested, and therefore a relatively small expansion is needed to keep up with demand.

Auto opponents insist that new construction leads to *induced travel*, as if road builders are putting guns to Americans' heads and making them drive more.[5] In fact, travel that is "induced" by added capacity is actually travel that had been repressed or shifted by capacity shortages.

After collecting urban congestion data for more than a decade, the Texas Transportation Institute says that "additional roadway reduces the growth in travel delay experienced by motorists."[6] Tim Lomax, the coauthor of the institute's congestion reports, notes that cities such as Phoenix and Houston have reduced their congestion by adding new highway capacity.[7] Among the data published by the Texas Transportation Institute are the number of freeway lane miles, the miles driven, and the population of 68 urban areas in 1982 and 1997. If new roads lead to an increase in driving, then urban areas with the greatest increase in new lane miles between 1982 and 1997 would also see the greatest increase in per capita driving. But the correlation between these two numbers is no better than random.

Imagine if AT&T or MCI discovered that people using their services were frequently discouraged by "all circuits are busy" messages. Furthermore, the company found that building more long-distance transmission facilities reduced the congestion, leading people to make more long-distance phone calls. Would the company decide to stop building new facilities and let people's attempts to make calls be frustrated by busy signals? Of course not—though it would make sure that people paid enough to cover the costs of the service.

An important difference between long-distance phone competitors and highways is that the latter are a government-run monopoly. The progressives who endorsed such government monopolies believed they would be more efficient and that they would not attempt to earn excess profits by deliberately creating shortages. Yet such deliberate shortages are exactly what smart-growth advocates recommend for urban road systems.

States and cities can do three things to reduce congestion:

- Identify and relieve bottlenecks such as inadequate on- and off-ramps and poorly designed junctions between freeways.
- Relieve rush hour congestion by charging peak-period tolls. Peak-period tolls will shift some non-commuter traffic, which makes up half of rush hour congestion, to other times. As Downs says, with peak-period tolls, "triple convergence would be replaced by triple divergence."
- Add capacity where it is needed, funded when possible by peak-period tolls.

Americans want to move. Congestion is not caused by too many roads, but by not enough roads, poorly designed roads, and poorly priced roads. The solution to congestion is not to immobilize people but to fix the road network so that it serves public demand and insures that people pay the cost of the service they use. New roads are not the only solution to congestion, and often not the most effective solution. But the idea that new roads increases congestion is completely wrong.

Notes

1. Jane Holtz Kay, *Asphalt Nation: How the Automobile Took over America and How We Can Take It Back* (New York, NY: Crown, 1997), p. 15.
2. Anthony Downs, *Stuck in Traffic: Coping with Peak-Hour Traffic Congestion* (Washington, DC: Brookings, 1992), p. 27.
3. Ibid, p. 29.
4. Barbara McCann, "New Roads Aren't the Only Answer to Congestion Woes," Surface Transportation Policy Project, 1999, http://www.transact.org/Toolmonth/tools.htm.
5. Sierra Club, "New Study Says New Highways Cause, Not Relieve, Up to 43% of Tri-State Traffic Jams," http://www.sierraclub.org/sprawl/transportation/cincy.asp.
6. David Schrank and Tim Lomax, *1999 Annual Mobility Report: Information for Urban America* (College Station, TX: Texas A&M, 1999), p. IV-11.
7. Texas Transportation Institute, *Urban Roadway Congestion Annual Report 1998* (College Station, TX: Texas A&M, 1998), table 3; Elizabeth Farnsworth, "Hurry Up and Wait," interview with Tim Lomax of the Texas Transportation Institute on *All Things Considered*, 10 November 1996.

26. The Real Problem
with Highways

As the Subsidized-Highway Myth describes (p. 380), one of the great myths about American highways is that they are heavily subsidized. In fact, federal and state governments have, for the most part, collected more money in gas taxes and other highway user fees than they have spent on roads. While local governments have tended to spend more on roads than they collect from road users, these local subsidies have been at least partially offset by the diversion of federal and state gas taxes to mass transit and other uses.

The fact that highway subsidies are small doesn't mean that highway finances always make sense. When you buy a gallon of milk at the grocery store, the store learns that you like milk and orders new stocks of milk. Supermarket pricing therefore acts as a signal from you the consumer to the store managers, letting the managers know what you like. Prices also act as signals from food producers to you, letting you know that, for example, Ben & Jerry's ice cream costs more than the store-brand of ice milk.

Highway funding fails to provide these signals. When you pay the tax on a gallon of gasoline, highway officials don't know whether you drive mainly on urban freeways or rural roads. This ambiguity leaves plenty of room for political interference in transportation funding, and some highways have clearly been built mainly because they were in the districts of powerful members of Congress, not because they were truly needed. Gas taxes also fail to give you signals about the relative cost of roads: When you enter an urban freeway at rush hour, you are not particularly aware that it costs far more to provide peak capacities than to build the street connecting your neighborhood with that freeway.

The dominant method of funding highways out of gas taxes for autos, weight-mile taxes for trucks, registration fees, and other assorted road taxes may have made sense when those taxes were first devised. In the early part of the twentieth century all roads were one- or two-lane roads and except in city centers most were lightly used. Transportation issues are far more complex today.

The free market can coordinate the production and distribution hundreds of thousands of different goods and services because each one is separately priced. Prices help consumers decide how much to buy and producers decide how much to make. Despite being self funded, highways are not comparably priced.

- Whether a driver uses a freeway, an arterial, or a local street, the cost in gas tax is about the same.
- Someone driving a 50-mile-per-gallon compact car consumes nearly as much road space as someone driving a 15-mile-per-gallon sports-utility vehicle, yet the former pays far less in highway user fees.
- Someone driving during rush hour places far greater stress on the transportation network than someone driving a similar vehicle at midnight, yet both pay about the same user fee.

Improved pricing will produce several benefits. first, it would reduce congestion if driving during congested periods cost more. Second, in reducing congestion it would also reduce the total cost of building roads since road capacities would not need to be as great. Third, it would make transportation agencies more responsive to users because their revenues would depend on providing excellent services. The first steps towards such a pricing system are described in chapter 36.

The other major problem with highway finance is centralized control at the federal level. Federal policies have severely distorted local transportation facilities. First, federal financing of 90 percent of interstate highway costs may have led state highway departments to overbuild interstate highways in some places. By funding construction but not maintenance, Congress expected the states to build no more than they could afford to maintain. Instead, many states built far more than they can maintain. Federal funding also led states to spend more on interstates than they spent on freeways that they paid for themselves. This is partly because federal laws include numerous costly requirements, such as "buy America" provisions. But it is also because state agencies using "free" federal money tend to spend more lavishly on rights of way, landscaping, and other amenities.[1]

A second problem is that the federal government insisted on a consistent design standard for all interstates. As late as 1945, the federal government contemplated that interstate highways would use a flexible design: two lanes and at-grade railroad and highway crossings where there was little traffic, more lanes and limited access highways where traffic was greater.[2] But this flexibility disappeared when the act was passed, and all interstates were required to have at least four lanes and limited access.

This made interstates more expensive in rural areas such as Wyoming or South Dakota. But it also made them more expensive in urban areas. In the 1940s and early 1950s, transportation planners in Los Angeles had planned an extensive network of arterials throughout the region. These would not be limited access roads but would carry traffic at 45 or 50 miles per hour. But with passage of the interstate highway legislation, the federal government would only help pay for 70-mile-per-hour, limited-access roads. These ended up costing much more per mile than the arterials that were originally planned and so Los Angeles' freeway network is much smaller than the planned network of arterials.[3] It is difficult to imagine how Los Angeles would be different today if the original, lower-speed network had been built.

Another string that Congress attached to federal highway funds was that no highway built with federal funds could charge tolls. This curtailed the expansion of highly successful toll roads such as the Pennsylvania Turnpike. This turnpike, which federal officials predicted would collect tolls from only a few hundred cars each day, almost immediately attracted tens of thousands of motorists every day. Congress' elimination of this restriction in 1991 has led to some long overdue experimentation with electronic tolls, congestion tolls, and other practices that will both reduce congestion and help highway officials plan future investments.

The huge influx of federal funds provided for the Interstate Highway System probably blinded many transportation engineers to the potential damage freeways could do to inner-city freeways. Certainly, federal funding for rail transit and the current federal push for smart growth is blinding many urban planners to the desire of local residents to protect their neighborhoods from density and mixed-use developments. At the same time, freeways have greatly increased personal mobility, improved the movement of freight within urban areas, and produced many other social benefits, while the benefits of rail transit are barely measurable.

While no system is perfect, the nation's highways come close to Wendell Cox's description of the Interstate Highway System as "the best investment a nation ever made"[4]—or at least the best investment a government ever made. No one can predict how different America's highways would be if they were built with private, local, or state funds instead of with the support of federal funds, but it is clear that the highways that have been built have produced enormous gains in mobility, shipment of goods, and the wide distribution of a variety of foods and other consumer items to hundreds of millions of Americans. Still, the highway finance system is far from perfect. Changing the ways highways are funded will do more to congestion and other highway problems than diverting highway funds to other uses.

Notes

1. Robert W. Poole, Jr., *Defederalizing Transportation Funding* (Los Angeles, CA: Reason Foundation, 1996), pp. 4–5.
2. Richard F. Weingroff, "Federal-Aid Highway Act of 1956: Creating the Interstate System," *Public Roads*, Summer, 1996, http://www.tfhrc.gov/pubrds/summer96/p96su10.htm.
3 Darwin Stolzenbach, *Interview with Professor Alan Altshuler, Former Secretary of Transportation, Massachusetts*, AASHTO Interstate Highway Research Project, June 8, 1981.
4. Wendell Cox & Jean Love, *40 Years of the US Interstate Highway System: An Analysis* (Washington, DC: American Highway Users Alliance, 1996), http://www.publicpurpose.com.

The Myth of the Long Commute

Myth: Every year, people spend more and more of their time sitting in their cars going to and from work.

Reality: Average commutation times have remained at about 22 minutes each way for years. Times in the suburbs are about the same as times in the cities.

"Instead of spending two more hours a day with our families and friends," say Andres Duany and Elizabeth Plater-Zyberk, "we have chosen to spend them competing with our fellow citizens for that scarce commodity called asphalt."[1] Duany and Plater-Zyberg reflect the popular belief that urbanites spend more and more time commuting each year. In fact, data collected by the Census Bureau and Federal Highway Administration show that average commuting times have remained remarkably constant for years at about 22 or 23 minutes each direction.

The 1980 census found average travel times of 21.7 minutes, while the 1990 census found that this had increased to 22.4 minutes. In 1990, about one out of eight commuters spent 45 minutes or more commuting each way, but one out of six took under 10 minutes.[2] The slight increase in travel time probably does not reflect congestion. According to the Federal Highway Administration, commute distances have increased faster than travel times, indicating that average commute speeds are rising.[3] Moreover, commuting times are roughly the same across all cities and across different types of commutes: suburbs to suburbs, suburbs to central city, and central city to suburbs. "The travel times from each origin to all destinations are almost identical," says Alan Pisarski, author of *Commuting in America*. "This suggests that people's selection of homes and job sites take into account some sense of what is a reasonable amount of time for work travel."[4]

Gordon and Richardson reach the same conclusion. "Rational commuters will, sooner or later, seek to escape congestion by changing the location of their homes and/or their jobs." As a result, commuting times remain about the same even in cities such as Houston and Los Angeles that cover thousands of square miles. In fact, they say, "This type of adjustment is easier to make in large dispersed metropolitan areas with alternate employment subcenters and a wide variety of residential neighborhoods."[5]

In other words, if average commuter times are about the same everywhere, it is because people want to live about twenty or so minutes from work (see chapter 28). A close look at the data reveals that average commuting times in big cities such as Houston and Los Angeles are a bit longer than in smaller cities such as Portland or Albuquerque. But this is due to the way the data were collected. Census Bureau figures average commuting times within each urban area. So commuters from Salem to Portland (which are two different urban areas) or from Santa Fe to Albuquerque (likewise) don't get counted in, while commuters traveling similar distances in Los Angeles or Houston do get counted.

One factor that does significantly affect average commuting times is the method of travel. Auto commuters who drive alone take about 21 minutes, while bus and light-rail commuters average closer to 40.[6] This isn't because mass transit commuters go further; on average they don't go as far. Instead, it is because mass transit is slower: an average of 13 miles per hour compared with more than 30 miles per hour by car. The modes taking the least time, by the way, are walking and cycling, but they are also the shortest distances: 0.2 and 2 miles respectively.

If commuting times are remaining constant, then why do people think they are getting worse? The answer is that congestion is getting worse, but people adapt to it by relocating their homes or work. This is one of the reasons why so many companies are moving their offices and factories from the central cities to edge cities: to be closer to their workers. As Gordon and Richardson say, "Suburbanization has become the dominant and successful congestion reduction mechanism."[7]

In other words, our urban areas are evolving in response to population and congestion. And they aren't doing it in the ways planners would like, by becoming denser and more compact. Instead, they are moving the other way. Efforts to make cities more compact will impede the most important congestion reduction technique available: that of moving homes and offices to less congested areas.

Notes

1. Andres Duany and Elizabeth Plater-Zyberk, "The Second Coming of the American Small Town," *Wilson's Quarterly*, Winter 1992, pp. 19–48.
2. Census Bureau, *1990 Census Lookup*, http://venus.census.gov/cdrom/lookup.
3. Patricia Hu and Jennifer Young, *Draft Summary of Travel Trends: 1995 Nationwide Personal Transportation Survey* (Oak Ridge, TN: US DOE, 1999), table 25, http://www-cta.ornl.gov/npts/1995/Doc/trends_reportl8.pdf.
4. Alan Pisarski, *Commuting in America* (Washington, DC: Eno, 1989), p. 58.
5. Peter Gordon and Harry Richardson, "Are Compact Cities a Desirable Planning Goal?" *Journal of the American Planning Association* 61(1), http://www.smartgrowth.org/library/apa_pointcounterpoint/apa_sprawl.html.
6 Alan Pisarski, *Commuting in America II* (Washington, DC: Eno, 1996), p. 85.
7. Peter Gordon and Harry Richardson, "Are Compact Cities a Desirable Planning Goal?"

Part Seven

The Land-Use

Transportation

Connection

Sunshine Dairy, a Portland transit-oriented development *with housing upstairs and shops on the ground floor (top). Such developments may be attractive to many people, but Portland officials have found that the market for such housing is so low that they now offer twenty-years of property tax waivers to developers who build them.*

A neotraditional mixed-use development in Orenco *(bottom). Though near light rail, a huge parking lot in back (visible on the right side of the photo) attests to the fact that most residents and customers still drive (see p. 62).*

27. Changing How We Work and Live

Parts four, five, and six covered density, transit, and highways separately. But modern urban planners strongly believe that transportation and land use cannot be planned separately. Instead, the two are intimately related. Streetcars and automobiles led to a profound transformation in urban land uses. The key claim of smart-growth planners is that, by regulating land uses, they can turn this around and significantly influence people's transportation choices. If this claim is wrong, then smart growth is futile.

"The alternative to sprawl is simple and timely," says architect Peter Calthorpe. "Neighborhoods of housing, parks and schools placed within walking distance of shops, civic services, jobs and transit—a modern version of the traditional town."[1] Some of the ideas planners have for producing this vision include:

- *Transit-oriented developments*, meaning high-density mixed-use centers located on transit lines or next to rail transit stations. People living in the developments will be able to walk to shops and ride transit to other parts of the city. To further discourage driving, some transit-oriented developments are built with fewer parking spaces than residences.
- *Pedestrian-friendly design*, including sidewalks, bike paths, and other pedestrian facilities. In retail areas, pedestrian friendliness means that stores front on the street, with no setback for parking. Parking, if the stores provide it at all, should be in back. In residential areas, design codes may require large porches and garages recessed behind the front of the house.
- *Main streets*, meaning travel corridors with mixtures of retail shops and offices at the ground level and apartments and condominium above.
- *New Urban single-family residential patterns* that emphasize gridded streets rather than cul-de-sacs; narrow streets to discourage driving and minimize parking; small lots so more homes will be within walking distance of commercial areas; and more row houses instead of detached homes.

The utopian smart-growth vision of living within walking distance to a grocery store and taking light rail to work is attractive to many people. But it doesn't take much thought to realize that planners have confused cause and effect. Historically, the land use-transportation connection is clear: improved transportation led to changes in urban land uses. Smart growth claims to reverse this: Regulating land uses will lead people to use different forms of transportation. But if land use determines travel choices, then why did people who lived in high-density, mixed-use nineteenth-century cities take so readily to automobiles in the first place?

The traditional answer is that congestion did not immediately appear when the auto was invented; instead, it grew slowly as more people purchased autos. This ignores the fact that downtown streets in major cities were congested with streetcars, wagons, carriages, horses, and pedestrians long before the automobile was popular. The auto was attractive because it allowed people to get away from the congestion, initially for their homes and later for their businesses.

For decades, transportation planners focused on meeting travel demand. When new areas grew, they built roads to those areas. When older areas became congested, they added lanes or safety features to increase speeds. The idea of manipulating land-use patterns in order to influence travel behavior did not become popular until the mid 1980s.[2] Even today it is more accepted by transportation planners than by transportation engineers.

Planners are asking urban residents to give up their freedom to choose how they use their own land and, to some extent, how they travel around the urban area in order to achieve some greater social goods. The greater social goods that planners promise include clean air, open space, reduced congestion, affordable housing, and easier access to work, shopping, and recreation areas. "The basic difficulty of urban growth all over the world," says a Brookings Institution scholar, "is that decisions about the use of urban land are being made by a host of private parties without the guidance of comprehensive plans or community goals."[3]

For some people, personal freedom of choice is more important than whatever benefits can be gained with "guidance" from centrally written comprehensive plans.[4] But what if smart growth is just plain wrong? What if land-use and transportation planning are more likely to dirty the air, speed the development of open space, increase congestion and housing prices, and make travel more stressful and consumer goods more expensive? Then the debate about personal freedom vs. social goods, as important as it may be in other contexts, is irrelevant.

Notes

1. Peter Calthorpe, *The Next American Metropolis: Ecology, Community, and the American Dream* (New York, NY: Princeton Architectural Press, 1993), p. 16.
2. Marlon G. Boarnet & Nicholas S. Compin, *Transit-Oriented Development in San Diego County: Incrementally Implementing a Comprehensive Idea* (Berkeley, CA: UC Transportation Center, 1996), p. 1.
3. W. Owen, *The Accessible City* (Washington, DC: Brookings, 1972).
4. See, for example, Thomas Sowell, "Urban Sprawl, Liberal Gall," *Joplin Globe*, June 30, 1999, http://www.joplinglobe.com/archives/1999/990630/oped/story3.html.

Land Use Facts

The Natural Resources Conservation Service inventories U.S. farm lands every five years. Using a statistical sampling procedure, the inventory also estimates the amount of developed and urbanized land. The 1997 inventory claimed to find a dramatic increase in the rate of urbanization, which Vice President Gore used to raise alarms about urban sprawl. However, numbers in the inventory did not agree with the Department of Agriculture's Census of Agriculture. Several months after releasing the data, the Natural Resources Conservation Service withdrew it, saying it had found errors. A few of the 1997 numbers are listed below with the warning that urbanized percent may be too high.

Percentage of U.S. including Alaska that is farm, forest, or open space 96.4
    Percentage not counting Alaska   92.9

Percentage of U.S. not counting Alaska that is:

Range land	27.0
Forest land	26.8
Crop land	25.2
Pasture land	8.0
Conservation reserve	2.2
Other rural	3.8
Rural roads & railroads	2.9
Urbanized	4.2

Source: 1997 Natural Resources Inventory.

The Smart-Growth Myth

Myth: Smart-growth planning can design communities that allow people to walk to many of their destinations and significantly reduce driving.

Reality: The population densities required to significantly reduce driving are staggeringly high.

According to smart-growth advocates, the "ideal community" is one in which people can "walk to the store, the library, the post office, or the bank."[1] So for smart growth to work, then population densities must be high enough for businesses to have enough customers within walking distance to keep them going. Smart growth won't work if businesses in pedestrian-friendly neighborhoods must attract hordes of auto drivers from other areas in order to survive.

A modern large supermarket needs to draw patrons from a community of about 40,000 people.[2] This is known as the *trade population* of this type of store. Grocery stores with smaller trade populations will either fill in a niche market that draws people from a larger area or have very limited selections. For example, a convenience store, which sells only about a quarter as many different products as a conventional supermarket, can survive with a trade population of just 6,000 people.

Joel Garreau says that, as a rule of thumb, "the farthest distance an American will willingly walk before getting into a car" is 600 feet. However, "if you do everything you can to make casual use of the automobile inconvenient at the same time that you make walking pleasant and attractive, you maybe, just maybe, can up the distance an American will willingly walk to fifteen-hundred feet." He adds that "this at the substantial risk of everybody saying forget it and choosing not to patronize your highly contrived environment at all."[3]

The population density required to place 40,000 people within 1,500 feet of a grocery store is almost 124,000 people per square mile. That's about two-and-one-half times the density of Manhattan. Even if everyone were willing to shop at a limited-selection convenience store, the density required to place 6,000 people within 1,500 feet of that store is 18,600 people per square mile—more than the density of the city of San Francisco. While lots of people walk in Manhattan and San Francisco, there is also plenty of auto traffic in both.

Portland's smart-growth plan calls for raising the region's population density from just under 3,000 people per square mile to 4,800 per square mile. No other urban area in the country has considered even this large an increase in density. This density is far too low to have a significant effect on people's transportation habits.

Notes

1. Oregon Department of Transportation, "Smart Development Primer," http://www.lcd.state.or.us/issues/tgmweb/smart/primer.htm.
2. Michael Rothschild, *Bionomics: Economy as Ecosystem* (New York, NY: Holt, 1990), p. 372.
3 Joel Garreau, *Edge City: Life on the New Frontier* (New York, NY: Doubleday, 1991), p. 464.

28. Smart-Growth Commuting

        Surveys show that commuting makes up a little more than a third of all urban travel.[1] Morning and evening rush hour travel places the greatest stress on urban transportation systems. Since commuting for most people is fairly consistent—the same origin and destination every day—it seems to be a problem most easily solved using transit and smart-growth planning. Indeed, transit has around four times the market share of commuter travel than other travel, but that means just 6 percent for commuting compared with less than 1.5 percent for everything else.

To analyze commuting and land use, planners and economists build models of urban areas. Like a model airplane, a model of an urban area does not need to perfectly mimic reality; it only needs to reasonably approximate it. Standard model-building techniques start with simplifying assumptions. The results of simple models are tested against reality. When the model fails to agree with reality, some of the simplifying assumptions are replaced with better data or relationships. Eventually, the model's predictions are close enough to reality that they can be used to predict the effects of changes in various policies, technologies, or prices.

Imagine that all of the jobs, stores, schools, and urban entertainment in your city were located downtown. How far away would people live from the city center? This is the question posed by the *monocentric model* of an urban area. The model assumes that everyone wants to live as close to their work as they can afford. Naturally, land for housing nearest the city center would be the most expensive, both because potential home builders would have to compete for the land with offices, stores, and other uses, but also because people who lived there would enjoy the lowest transportation costs. Land is less expensive further away from downtown, but there is a trade off: the further you live from downtown, the greater your transportation costs.

The model predicts that, for a typical urban area, people will live an average of one mile from their work. The economists and planners who put together the model then looked at the real world and found that, on the average, urbanites live about seven miles from work. The model underestimates "actual average commutes by a factor of seven!" exclaim several University of California economists.[2]

It is interesting to see how the economists and planners responded to this difference between theory and fact. The economists said, "If the model differs from reality, there must be something wrong with the model." They tried to make the model more complex by allowing jobs to locate in many centers distributed throughout the city, rather than just one downtown center. But even a *polycentric model* of an urban area came up with average commute distances of a little over two miles—less than a third of reality.

"Naturally we don't expect the real world to fit the monocentric model perfectly," say the economists, "but being off by a factor of seven or even three is hard to swallow."[3] So the economists went further and asked if some of their other assumptions might be wrong, such as the assumption that everyone wants to live as close to work as possible. Maybe people have other priorities when choosing where to live, such as the quality of schools, the nature of the neighborhoods, proximity to recreation areas, or the fact that two people in the household work and their jobs are located some distance apart. Adding "idiosyncratic tastes" into the model turned out to produce results that were closer to reality.[4]

Planners came to a completely different conclusion. If the model differs from reality, they said, there must be something wrong with reality. The cities are inefficiently designed, leading people to waste their time commuting. Numerous articles in the planning literature deal with "excess" or "wasteful" commuting and how cities must be redesigned to eliminate it.[5] "In urban planning," says James Scott in his book, *Seeing Like a State*, "it is a short step from parsimonious assumptions to the practice of shaping the environment so that it satisfies the simplifications required by the formula."[6]

Some planners were only slightly appeased by the polycentric model; to them, polycentric is another word for sprawl. But smart growth has come to accept the polycentric city and now sees it as the solution to rush-hour congestion. The goal, say smart-growth planners, is to achieve a *jobs-housing balance* in all neighborhoods and communities so that no one has to travel very far to get to work.[7] As described in the Myth of Balanced Jobs and Housing (p. 416), this turns out to be exactly the wrong prescription for reducing driving.

Smart growth also calls for increasing urban densities. As noted in the Myth That Density Reduces Congestion (p. 257), even at the highest densities, a 1000-person-per-square-mile increase in density reduces auto commuting by just 1.6 percent. The urban areas with the lowest rates of auto commuting are low not because they are dense overall but because they have dense, nineteenth-century downtown employment centers. This can be shown by comparing census data with data from the Federal Transit Administration[8] and Federal Highway Administration.[9] Miles driven, transit ridership, and other data can be compared for each of nearly 300 urban areas using a standard statistical test known as r-squared. An r-squared close to 1 indicates close correlation while close to zero indicates no correlation. R-squared does not reveal whether one factor causes the other, only whether they are correlated; sometimes, two factors may be correlated because both are influenced by some other cause.

The data show a strong correlation between population and miles of driving (r-squared = 0.93), but not between density and driving (0.18). In other words, as cities get bigger, no matter how dense they are, total miles driven tend to increase proportional to population. Density has a low correlation with any other data, including transit trips per capita (0.23), the share of auto (0.18) or transit commuters (0.19), per capita driving (0.12), or per capita transit riding (0.19). Thus, density is not a good way to influence driving or transit ridership. Instead of being correlated with population density, transit riding is strongly correlated with the level of transit service, as measured by the revenue miles of transit service per square mile of land. The correlation between service level and transit trips per capita is 0.74; transit passenger miles per capita is 0.78; and the percent of transit commuters is 0.62.

Transit ridership is only moderately correlated with the share of transit service that is rail transit. For the thirty-two largest urban areas, twenty-two of which have rail transit, the correlation between transit trips per capita and percent rail transit is 0.43. But these results are dominated by the nineteenth-century cities of Boston, Chicago, New York, Philadelphia, Pittsburgh, and San Francisco. When only twentieth-century cities with recently-built rail lines are considered, such as Los Angeles, Miami, and Dallas, the correlation between transit rides per capita and percent rail transit is just 0.18, suggesting that rail service does not significantly boost transit ridership.

Transportation consultant Wendell Cox reached similar conclusions after reviewing rail transit in five cities that he considered "rail success stories": Tokyo, New York, London, Paris, and Hong Kong. To be successful, he found, rail must serve cities whose core-area population densities that are "many times that of more automobile-oriented urbanized areas in the United States." In addition, the cities must have central business districts that have huge numbers of jobs: 750,000 or more, while most in the U.S. range between 50,000 to 200,000. Given these prerequisites, Cox says, only heavy rail or commuter rail will work: light rail is simply too slow to compete with autos.[10]

In sum, the most important factors in minimizing auto commuting and maximizing of transit commuting are having a large concentration of people and jobs in one location and having a high density of transit service to that location. Population density has almost no effect on commuting. Rail transit has very little effect. No matter how much they increase their densities and how many miles of rail transit they build, twentieth-century cities will not increase transit commuting above about 17 percent of the total, or reduce auto commuting below about 75 percent, unless they also force most jobs into their downtown areas.

Some planners hope that telecommuting will reduce the need for automobiles and encourage people to live in smart growth's pedestrian-friendly neighborhoods.

Helen Couclelis, of the University of California at Santa Barbara, has studied telecommuters and found just the opposite: "At the same time as we have been increasing the substitution of telecoms for travel, we have been increasing travel." The reason, she found, is that "activity is disintegrating." "Activities that used to be associated with a single location (e.g., my 'workplace') are now increasingly scattered among geographically distant locations (e.g., my office, home, associate's home, hotel room, car, train, or plane)."[11] Thus, telecommuting may simply be one more factor leading to an increase in the demand for mobility.

Notes

1. Mary Jane Vincent, Mary Ann Keyes, and Marshall Reed, *Nationwide Personal Transportation Survey 1990: Urban Travel Patterns* (Washington, DC: FHwA, 1994), table 2-1.
2. Alex Anas, Richard Arnott, & Kenneth A. Small, "Urban Spatial Structure," *Journal of Economic Literature* 34:1426–1464.
3. Ibid, p. 1444.
4. Alex Anas, "Taste Heterogeneity and Urban Spatial Structure: The Logit Model and Monocentric Theory Reconciled," *Journal of Urban Economics*, 28(3): 318–335.
5. See, for example, John Phcher, "Urban Travel Behavior As The Outcome Of Public Policy," *Journal of the American Planning Association*, 54(4): 509–520; and B. Hamilton, "Wasteful Commuting Again," *Journal of Political Economy*, 97 (1989): 1498–1504.
6. James C. Scott, *Seeing Like a State: How Certain Schemes to Improve the Human Condition Have Failed* (New Haven, CT: Yale University Press, 1998), p. 141.
7. Robert Cervero, "Jobs-Housing Balance Revisited," *Journal of the American Planning Association*, 62(4): 492.
8. Federal Transit Administration, *National Transit Database 1997* (Washington, DC: US DOT, 1999), http://www.ntdprogram.com.
9. Federal Highway Administration, *Highway Statistics 1997*, tables HM-71 and HM-72.
10. Wendell Cox, "Urban Rail Success Stories," March, 2000, http://www.publicpurpose.com/ut-railsuccess.htm.
11. Helen Couclelis, "From Sustainable Transportation to Sustainable Accessibility: Can We Avoid a New 'Tragedy of the Commons?'" Presentation at the *Transatlantic Research Conference on Social Change and Sustainable Transport*, Berkeley, CA, 11 March 1999.

The Myth of Balanced Jobs and Housing

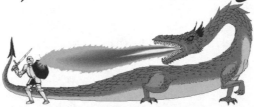

Myth: Planners can reduce driving by balancing jobs and housing.

Reality: The urban areas with the lowest rates of auto commuting have the most unbalanced jobs and housing.

Smart-growth planners today seek to "balance" jobs and housing, meaning they want to locate more offices and other job centers in residential areas and put more residences in or near places that are primarily employment centers. The theory is that people will tend to live near where they work and so will be able to walk to work—or at least won't have to drive as far.

A scrutiny of modern urban areas reveals that this theory is 100 percent wrong. The major urban area with the best jobs-housing balance is Los Angeles. Most jobs in the Los Angeles region are spread among more than one hundred different job centers. Out of 4.6 million jobs in the region, only 200,000 are located in downtown Los Angeles.[1] No job center has more than 4 percent of all the jobs in the region. If planners are correct, people in Los Angeles should be able to live fairly close to their jobs and thus not have to commute as much by auto. By comparison, the major urban area with the worst jobs-housing balance is New York. Out of 10.5 million jobs in the region, over 2.3 million, or more than 22 percent, are located in Manhattan.[2] No other U.S. urban area comes close to this amount of job concentration.

Based on these figures, the balanced jobs-and-housing theory would predict that Los Angeleans drive less and are more likely to use walking or transit to commute to work than New Yorkers. Of course, exactly the opposite is true. Residents of the New York urban area are twice as likely to walk to work and five times as likely to take transit to work as Los Angeleans. Meanwhile, residents of the Los Angeles area put 42 percent more miles on the odometer each year than those in New York.[3]

Rather than distributing employment across the urban area, concentrating it is more likely to reduce driving. But planners who attempt to locate all new offices, factories, stores, and other employers downtown will soon find major employers leaving or refusing to enter the region. While few people outside of southern California think of Los Angeles when they imagine a livable urban area, even fewer outside of New York think of New York.

The problem with balancing jobs and housing is that people don't choose their homes based solely, or even primarily, to be near work. In fact, as described in the Accessibility Myth (p. 109), most people don't even like to live near their work and prefer to locate more than 15 minutes away. Since cars are faster than transit or walking, people who drive have greater flexibility in where they live since they can live farther away and still be within the desired 15-to-20 minute zone. Further complicating commuting is the growth of two-income households. Even if one member of the household can live near their job, the other probably cannot. They often choose to live midway between the jobs, requiring both to drive, instead of locating so that one can walk.

As the Myth of the Long Commute (p. 403) notes, commuting times have stayed remarkably constant, at around 22 minutes, for many years. USC planners Gordon and Richardson say this has happened despite apparent increasing congestion because jobs are moving to the suburbs, where most urban residents live.[4] Indeed, the U.S. Department of Transportation surveys show that, although commuting times have remained about the same, commuting distances have increased, meaning speeds are getting faster.[5] Between 1983 and 1995, average automobile commute speeds increased from 30 to 35 miles per hour. Again, this is probably because more jobs are in the suburbs where congestion is lower. All of these things suggest that jobs-housing imbalances are self-correcting.

Yet planners are not satisfied with a natural tendency towards a jobs-housing balance. In a study of San Francisco Bay area jobs and housing, Robert Cervero finds that some suburban towns "are nearly perfectly balanced, yet fewer than a third of their workers reside locally, and even smaller shares of residents work locally." As a result, "even if jobs-housing balance is attained," says Cervero, "it does not guarantee self-containment or reduced external commuting." "Jobs followed labor markets," he concludes, but housing "did not follow jobs."[6] As Harvard University transportation analysts Alan Altshuler and José Gómez-Ibáñez say, "the jobs-housing imbalance research suggested that severe imbalances were a self-correcting phenomenon and that limits existed to the willingness or abilities of households and businesses to locate close to one another."[7]

In other words, a company may open an office in a town with a "surplus" of workers. But the people living in the town already have jobs elsewhere, while the housing in the town is already occupied so workers in the new office must come from elsewhere. Cervero's solution is building more high-density housing for the new workers, an action he says is prevented by "NIMBY resistance." It doesn't seem to have occurred to Cervero that perhaps people don't want to work and live in the same neighborhoods or that they might prefer living in low-density residential areas rather than having a shorter commute. As Anthony Downs observes, "People's willingness to commute long distances has repeatedly undermined attempts to shorten commuting times by building housing near workplaces and encouraging workers to occupy that housing."[8]

Since the highest rates of transit commuting and lowest auto commuting are found in urban areas with highly concentrated employment centers, mandating a jobs-housing balance forces a dispersal of jobs that reduces transit's ability to attract riders. This means that the smart-growth goal of creating a jobs-housing balance in various parts of each urban area will have exactly the opposite of the intended effect. Instead of reducing driving, it will greatly limit transit's ability to serve commuters. As Cervero's data show, people doggedly refuse to live near where they work, so improving the job-housing balance will also do little to promote walking and cycling by commuters. This doesn't mean it is a good idea to try to force all jobs downtown; only that smart-growth's prescription will fail.

Planners' efforts to balance jobs and housing often involve enormous distortions of the economy. If an area has more jobs than workers, they will subsidize more housing. Meanwhile they subsidize jobs in other areas that have more workers than jobs. Taxpayers must pay for both subsidies, yet the result is that neither the employers nor the residents are located where they really want to be.

It is likely that the goal of balancing jobs and housing is politically driven. As described in the Subsidized-Development Myth (p. 517), commercial developments produce tax revenues that are important to many cities. Distributing jobs is politically popular among urban and suburban officials because it means that those revenues are more fairly shared among the municipalities in a region. But anyone who thinks that balancing jobs and housing will reduce driving is deluding themselves.

Notes

1. Jeffrey R. Kenworthy and Felix B. Laube, *An International Sourcebook of Automobile Dependence in Cities 1960-1990* (Boulder, CO: University of Colorado, 1999), p. 209.
2. Ibid, p. 249.
3. FHwA, *Highway Statistics 1997*, table HM-72.
4. Peter Gordon, Harry Richardson, and Myung-Jin Jun, "The Commuting Paradox: Evidence from the Top Twenty," *Journal of the American Planning Association*, 57(4): 416–420.
5. Patricia Hu and Jennifer Young, *Draft Summary of Travel Trends: 1995 Nationwide Personal Transportation Survey* (Oak Ridge, TN: US DOE, 1999), table 25.
6. Robert Cervero, "Jobs-Housing Balance Revisited," *Journal of the American Planning Association*, 62(4): 492.
7. Alan Altshuler and José Gómez-Ibáñez, *Regulation for Revenue: The Political Economy of Land Use Exactions* (Washington, DC: Brookings; Cambridge, MA: Lincoln Land Institute, 1993), pp. 74–75.
8. Anthony Downs, *Stuck in Traffic: Coping with Peak-Hour Traffic Congestion* (Washington, DC: Brookings, 1992), pp. 16–17.

Growth Control in the Bay Area

T he San Francisco-Oakland-San Jose urbanized area has a combined population of more than 5.7 million people, making it the fourth largest metropolitan area in the country after New York, Los Angeles, and Chicago. San Francisco itself is the second densest major city in the country, but its population of 750,000 people is actually exceeded by San Jose's 860,000, who live at only about a quarter the density of San Franciscans.

Table One: The San Francisco-Oakland Urbanized Area

	1950	1990	1998
Population (thousands)	2,017	3,629	4,017
Land area square miles	287	874	1,203
Density	7,040	4,150	3,340

Source: Census Bureau for 1950 and 1990, FHwA, Highway Statistics 1998 for 1998. FHwA land area data are not exactly comparable with Census Bureau data since they use slightly different criteria for determining urbanized area boundaries.

The Bay Area was one of the first U.S. urban areas to build a modern rail transit system. As described in Peter Hall's *Great Planning Disasters*, the Bay Area Rapid Transit (BART) system cost far more than expected and carries far fewer riders than anticipated.[1] In 1997, BART carried 80 million riders almost 1 billion passenger miles.[2] That sounds like a lot, but 1997's growth of automobile travel in the San Francisco-Oakland area (not counting San Jose) was nearly 4.8 billion passenger miles per year, or almost five times as much as BART's total use.[3] Without BART, many rail riders would probably use other forms of transit, so it does not appear that BART is doing much to relieve Bay Area congestion.

Robert Cervero, one of the nation's strongest proponents of transit-oriented developments, has studied San Francisco's BART line in depth. He admits that BART's effects on metropolitan development have been "fairly modest" and confined mainly to downtown San Francisco and two or three suburban station areas.[4] BART "has not triggered hoped-for levels of reinvestment in downtown Berkeley, Oakland, or Richmond." In fact, "Population has grown faster away from BART than near it," he says.[5] He concludes that "our findings confirm that the land use benefits of investments in rail are not automatic."[6]

Table Two: The City of San Francisco

	1950	1990	1998
Population (thousands)	775	724	746
Land area square miles	45	47	47
Density	17,386	15,500	15,875

Source: Census Bureau. Land area and density for 1998 are estimated.

One of the few communities which Cervero says has been extensively redeveloped since the construction of BART is Walnut Creek. Walnut Creek has plenty of high-density housing, a lively little downtown area, and a startling number of high-rise office buildings. In fact, as noted in Joel Garreau's book, it is a classic edge city.[7] "Edge cities are most frequently located where beltway-like bypasses around an old downtown are crossed at right angles by freeways that lead out from the old center," says Garreau.[8] Walnut Creek achieved its status not because of BART but by being at the junction of a radial freeway, California 24, and a ring freeway, Interstate 680.

Figure One: San Francisco Area Densities

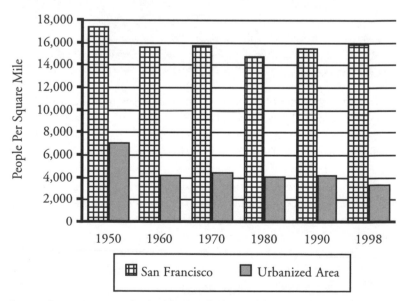

Source: Cemsus Bureau, Federal Highway Administration.

Table Three: San Francisco-Oakland-Area Transportation

Miles of freeway per million people	84
Annual miles driven per capita	7,738
Passenger miles per capita	12,381
Annual transit miles per capita	513
Annual transit trips per capita	102
Auto commuters	84.2%
Transit commuters	9.5%
Walk/cycle commuters	6.3%

Source: *FHwA*, Highway Statistics 1998, *FTA*, Transit Profiles 1998, *1990 Census. All data from 1998 except commuting data, which are from 1990. Passenger miles per capita are 1.6 times miles driven per capita.*

Walnut Creek has a lively, upscale downtown, with many fancy stores such as a Williams-Sonoma kitchen shop and numerous restaurants. Its streets are jammed with cars much of the day and evening, but nothing is far from one of the three freeway exits serving Walnut Creek. People who work downtown drive there and park in the municipal parking garage for just $2 per day. Notably, the BART station was a good fifteen-minute walk from the liveliest areas of Walnut Creek, while the area close to the station mainly consists of a few sterile office buildings and a variety store with a huge parking lot. The 1990 census reports that 84 percent of Walnut Creek commuters drive to work while 13 percent use transit and less than 3 percent walk or bicycle. This rate of transit usage is higher than for the San Francisco Bay Area as a whole, but at the expense of walking and cycling: Auto usage is almost exactly the same as for the metropolitan area.

The other areas whose redevelopment Cervero credits to BART are downtown San Francisco, Pleasant Hill, and Fremont. However, John Landis and David Lotzenheiser, Cervero's colleagues at the UC Berkeley City Planning Department, could not find any evidence that office buildings located near BART stations commanded any rent premiums over ones further away. This was true in Walnut Creek, Fremont, and Berkeley as well as San Francisco. With no rent premium, it is unlikely that BART by itself stimulated much development.

Downtown San Francisco has enjoyed a building boom like many other downtowns, and like those other downtowns the boom is partly due to various tax subsidies offered by the city aimed at maintaining the city's preeminence over the region. BART may be one of those subsidies, but it is not very effective. Landis and Lotzenheiser noted that, in San Francisco, "a coordinated combination of transit investments, land clearance and site assembly, zoning policy, and development restrictions have located almost all office development in the downtown area." Their analysis led them to conclude that "transit investments by themselves are unlikely to attract (or concentrate) new office development."[9]

Cervero himself reached similar conclusions regarding residential development.

Some apartments around BART stations had lower vacancy rates than apartments further away. But "when we looked more closely we found that the higher occupancy levels associated with BART reflected improved building quality, not access to BART."[10] Cervero says "Fremont has a mix of transit-oriented developments." Pleasant Hill has rezoned the area near its BART station for multifamily housing, but the area lacks a significant retail section. "Around most other stations," says Cervero, "few significant land-use changes have occurred."[11]

The Bay Area may also be the nation's leader in the use of growth controls to manage growth. The terms *growth control* and *growth management* are sometimes used interchangeably, but this book uses them in two very different ways. Growth control includes policies that limit the costs of growth by limiting growth itself, such as through a city ordinance limiting the number of building permits that may be granted each year. Growth management includes policies that limit the costs of growth by directing where growth should take place such as through an urban-growth boundary. It does not limit growth, and so it is more acceptable to home builders and other developer interests. But growth management does dictate which lands may or may not be developed.

A city by itself cannot implement growth management because it cannot control the land outside its borders. Growth management will only work when cities work in cooperation with county, regional, or state governments that have the authority to control development over a large area. But such cooperation is difficult because individual cities and towns have conflicting incentives. When California voters passed proposition 13, in 1978, they severely limited the revenue cities could collect in property taxes and made them dependent instead on sales tax revenues. This gave cities incentives to compete with one another for commercial developments, which collect sales taxes, while they tried to push residential developments elsewhere.

Because the San Francisco Bay region does not have a powerful regional government, growth controls rather than growth management became the favored techniques. Some cities limited the number of building permits granted each year; others limited the percentage growth that would be allowed; others zoned much of their land to very low densities to minimize their school costs. "Nowhere else in the nation do communities so aggressively restrict developers," wrote David Dowell in 1984.[12]

Bay Area environmentalists fervently embraced growth control ideas in the hope of reducing pollution and protecting open space. For example, they convinced city and county governments to place more than 15 percent of the region's land in regional parks.[13] Local governments went along with this because park lands would not contribute to their school liabilities.

Cities were also persuaded to create elaborate developmental review processes which make it easy to delay or stop new home-building projects. When challenged, developers often responded by reducing the density of their proposed developments—with a corresponding increase in the price of individual homes. For example, David Dowell describes a proposal to build 2,200 homes on 685 acres in the Caballo Hills above Oakland. After eight years of objections from nearby property owners, the developer ended up getting permission to build just 150 homes. The price of homes that were built ended up being six times greater than the homes that were originally planned.[14] In another case, reported planner Bernard Frieden, "a lone boy scout doing an ecology project was able to bring construction to a halt on a 200-unit condominium project."[15]

Transportation expert Alan Pisarski observes that "the most vocal supporters of growth controls" are "people who moved to suburbs to gain certain amenities" and then sought to maintain those amenities by keeping other people out.[16] In short, they wanted to keep densities low. While this may be a reasonable goal, a major effect of the way growth controls have been implemented is that the Bay Area has long been the nation's least affordable housing market.[17] Long before Bay Area housing prices reached today's levels, when a tiny, two-bedroom tract home on a small lot can sell for $400,000 in Walnut Creek and $700,000 in Palo Alto, Dowell wrote that "astronomical housing costs are shattering what can best be described as the American dream."[18]

Growth controls have extended well outside the borders of the San Francisco-Oakland-San Jose urbanized areas. Due to growth controls, housing prices in Santa Cruz, which is south of San Jose, "are at least 10 percent higher than they would have been in the absence of controls," says researcher Paul Niebanck. "The result is that many households that could have afforded to buy into the Santa Cruz County market no longer have that option, and many more will be excluded over time."[19]

As wrong as it is, smart growth is based on a clear vision of what an urban area should look like. Bay Area growth opponents had no such clear vision. Instead, says Frieden, they used whatever argument they could find to object to just about any development. The Sierra Club opposed "suburban housing on the grounds that it would generate unnecessary long-distance commuting" but opposed "new housing near the central cities on the grounds that it would use up scarce open space there." Another group opposed housing in the valleys "because the valley soil is better suited to farming" even as it opposed housing on hillsides "because it claims hill developments will increase the chances of landslides."[20]

Although the Sierra Club has endorsed smart growth, the San Francisco chapter of the club strongly promoted ballot measures in several Bay Area towns that would require a vote of the people for any zoning change, and density increase, or any time as few as ten homes were constructed within a quarter of a mile of one another.[21] In the face of an intense campaign waged by local home builders, the measures failed, but they demonstrated that the even many Sierra Club members support density and compact development only if it is somewhere else.

Similar sentiments were expressed by residents of Berkeley when the local planning bureau proposed a smart-growth plan that called for increasing densities to house 13,000 new residents. Planners said that new housing was needed to maintain a walkable community and to "encourage sufficient new construction to meet Berkeley's fair share of regional housing needs."[22] The plan proposed to increase height limits to allow construction of mid-rise apartment buildings in many parts of the city. "People would be mystified to wake up and walk down College Avenue"—a busy, narrow thoroughfare surrounded by one- and two-story structures—"and find four-story buildings," commented Nancy Carleton, the chair of Berkeley's zoning board.

Local residents mobilized to oppose the plan, which they said would "destroy" Berkeley "by bulldozing neighborhoods and overbuilding in the name of progress." One opponent, Becky O'Malley, blamed developers for the plan. "Speculators hiding behind the smart-growth banner have started drawing their bull's-eyes on attractive viable cities like San Francisco and Berkeley," she said. While O'Malley found smart-growth goals "laudable," she said that "In Berkeley we've done our 'fair share' decades ago. We're the third densest city in the Bay Area, right behind San Francisco and Emeryville."[23]

Berkeley residents have a long history of opposing further density increases. In the 1970s, the city council passed the Neighborhood Preservation Ordinance, which prevented developers from building multifamily housing in single-family neighborhoods. Although four BART stations have been located in Berkeley for decades, UC city planning professor Robert Cervero notes that these BART stations have seen little transit-oriented development. This is mainly, Cervero laments, due to "NIMBY [not in my backyard] resistance."[24]

The pressure to increase densities comes from the booming Silicon Valley combined with numerous growth controls elsewhere in the Bay Area. These restrictions have slowed suburbanization, so new residents are willing to accept higher densities. But existing residents don't like it. Based on objections raised at a September, 1999, hearing, the Berkeley Planning Commission ordered planners to start over. The plan showed, however, that smart growth can help create a sense of community—by bringing people together to oppose it. The only positive thing said about the plan at the hearing was that it "was a fabulous organizing tool."

Even residents of politically correct San Francisco object to more density in their city. Writers in the left-wing *San Francisco Bay Guardian* wage a continuous editorial campaign against the conversion of warehouses and other old buildings into "lofts." They are even more outraged by proposals for high-rise developments. "Does San Francisco really need another 50,000 yuppies?" asks *San Francisco Bay Guardian* writer Tim Redmond. Noting that "San Francisco in 1999 is becoming a bedroom community for Silicon Valley," Redmond says that most new residents today are "white, college-educated people" who make "the city less interesting and less diverse." "The place to increase density is the spread-out, suburban areas of the peninsula," he concludes.[25]

Notes

1. Peter Hall, *Great Planning Disasters* (Berkeley, CA: UC Press, 1981), pp. 109–137.
2. Federal Transit Administration, *Transit Profiles, Agencies in Urbanized Areas Exceeding 200,000 Population: 1997 Report Year* (Washington, DC: FTA, 1998), p. 229.
3. Federal Highway Administration, *Highway Statistics 1997* and *1998* (Washington, DC: FHwA, 1998 and 1999), table HM-72.
4. Robert Cervero, Carlos Castellanos, Wicaksono Sarosa, & Kenneth Rich, *BART @ 20: Land Use and Development Impacts* UCTC No. 308.
5. John Landis and Robert Cervero, "BART and Urban Development," *Access* 14 (Spring, 1999): p. 4.
6. Ibid, p. 15.
7. Joel Garreau, *Edge City: Life on the New Frontier* (New York, NY: Doubleday, 1991), p. 436.
8. Ibid, p. 37.
9. John Landis and David Lotzenheiser, *BART Access and Office Building Performance* (Berkeley, CA: UCTC, 1995), p. 24.
10. John Landis and Robert Cervero, "BART and Urban Development," p. 13.
11. Robert Cervero, Carlos Castellanos, Wicaksono Sarosa, & Kenneth Rich, *BART @ 20: Land Use and Development Impacts* (Berkeley, CA: UCTC No. 308, 1995).
12. Ibid, p. 14.
13. David E. Dowall, *The Suburban Squeeze: Land Conservation and Regulation in the San Francisco Bay Area* (Berkeley, CA: UC Press, 1984), p. 15.
14. Ibid, pp. 141–142.
15. Bernard J. Frieden, *The Environmental Protection Hustle* (Cambridge, MA: MIT, 1979), p. 6.
16. Alan E. Pisarski, "Issues in Transportation and Growth Management," *in* David J. Brower, David R. Godschalk, and Douglas R. Porter (eds.), *Understanding Growth Management: Critical Issues and a Research Agenda* (Washington, DC: Urban Land Institute, 1989), pp. 123–133.
17. National Association of Home Builders, *Housing Opportunity Index, First Quarter 1999*, http://www.nahb.com/mandl.html.
18. David Dowall, *The Suburban Squeeze*, p. 9.
19. Paul Niebanck, "Growth Controls and the Production of Inequality," *in* David J. Brower, David R. Godschalk, and Douglas R. Porter (eds.), *Understanding Growth Management: Critical Issues and a Research Agenda* (Washington, DC: Urban Land Institute, 1989), 193 pp., p. 115.
20. Frieden, *The Environmental Protection Hustle*, p. 9.
21. *Contra Costa Times*, "CAPP Initiatives," http://www.hotcoco.com/election99/capp.htm.
22. Berkeley Planning Department, *General Plan Update Berkeley 2000-2020: A Framework for Public Decision-Making* (Berkeley, CA: City of Berkeley, 1999), http://www.ci.berkeley.ca.us/planning/advplan/genplan/draftgp3.html.
23. Berkeley Free Press, "Berkeley General Plan," *Berkeley Free Press*, September 15, 1999, p. 1.
24. Robert Cervero and John Landix, "The Transportation-Land Use Connection Still Matters," *Access* 7 (Fall, 1995): p. 8.
25. Tim Redmond, "If you build it, they will come: But does S.F. really need another 50,000 yuppies?" *San Francisco Bay Guardian*, September 1, 1999.

29. Smart-Growth Shopping

Smart-growth planners are especially hopeful that transit-oriented development and pedestrian-friendly design can change peoples' shopping behavior. Locating housing directly above the shops will provide stores with a ready market. Fronting stores on the street will keep pedestrians from being intimidated by a sea of parking between the sidewalks and the front door. Limits on parking will discourage people who live further away from driving to the stores.

Yet shopping has already undergone several revolutions since the development of the automobile, each of which rely on peoples' increasing mobility. Ninety years ago, most grocery shopping was in public markets. Meat, tea and coffee, dairy, baked goods, produce, and other goods were displayed in independently owned stalls. Shoppers would order their items at each stall, and a clerk would serve them or go to a stock room and pick them up.[1] In many cases, the stores then delivered the goods to people's homes. This labor-intensive method reflected the low labor costs at the time.

Many historians credit the 1916 opening of Piggly Wiggly in Memphis with being the first true self serve.[2] That store gave customers wire baskets and arranged the aisles so that customers would have to pass every item in the store before reaching the checkout stand. Later self-serve stores gave customers more freedom, but all greatly reduced labor costs and allowed the grocers to slash prices. By 1940, public markets were rapidly disappearing.

"The invention that made [self-service] work was the car," says a history of Fred Meyer Stores, the first self-service operation in Portland. "Previously, people had to take the trolley to the shopping area, so carrying packages back home was difficult. With a car, people could take their purchases with them."[3]

The first true supermarket opened in 1930 and the first freestanding store with its own parking area in 1932. Transportation experts called these stores "park and shops," indicating their dependence on the automobile.[4] Where a public market or corner grocery might have carried a few hundred different products, the supermarkets sold 12,000 products or more. They could do so only by having a larger customer base: Pedestrian-based stores had a trade area of 5,000 people, while supermarkets had a trade area of around 40,000 people. Perhaps a quarter of the people within a store's trade area actually shopped at each store.

Without automobiles, the 40,000 customers needed to insure supermarket variety cannot reach the stores. Without such a large customer base, the store cannot provide as wide a selection of products. So the automobile and truck have made a much wider selection of goods available to people at much lower prices.

The connection between autos and shopping was understood by auto manufacturers long ago. In the 1920s, advertisements for Chevrolet bragged that a car was "proving a wonderful help to many housekeepers, more than paying its low cost of upkeep through the economics of time and money saved in cash and carry shopping." Another ad reminded urbanites that cars would allow them "to buy eggs, vegetables, poultry, and small fruits directly from the farmer, fresh and cheap."[5]

Since World War II, supermarkets have grown in size and variety. The largest supermarkets sell 25,000 or more products and serve trade populations of over 100,000 people. Grocery store evolution did not stop with the supermarket. In 1988, grocery store ecologists counted seven different species of grocery stores (table one). This doesn't include, among others, club warehouse stores or hypermarts such as Fred Meyer's all-in-one grocery, drug, variety, and home-improvement stores which stock as many as 225,000 different products.

Table One: Grocery Store Species

	Number of Products	Size in Square Feet	Trade Population	Trade Area Radius (mi.)
Convenience store	3,500	2,600	6,000	0.5
Limited assortment	900	10,000	65,000	4.0
Conventional supermarket	12,000	24,500	40,000	2.0
Superstore	17,500	39,000	55,000	2.5
Food/drug combo	25,000	48,000	65,000	2.5
Warehouse	10,500	32,000	75,000	5-10
Super-warehouse	16,000	60,000	125,000	5-10

Source: Michael Rothschild, Bionomics: Economy as Ecosystem (New York, NY: Holt, 1990), pp. 372–373.

Aside from greater selection, customers benefit from auto-based shopping in another way: Intense competition keeps prices lower. Store owners know that, if their prices are too high, shoppers will simply get in their cars and drive to the next store a mile or so away. Competition also makes stores more receptive to customer demands for new products and responsive to customer complaints about poor-quality products.

Do we really need supermarkets that carry 25,000 or more different products? My kitchen shelves and refrigerator hold only about two hundred different foods. Larger families might have more, but few are likely to have as many as a thousand. Yet everyone has different tastes. The two hundred foods on my shelves may only include a handful of the two hundred or so foods on your shelves. A store that serves only 5,000 to 10,000 people won't be able to stock enough items, especially fresh goods, to satisfy our modern diverse tastes.

The last decade has seen the growth of another new species of grocery: the public market. Like the public markets of a century ago, these often consist of independent stalls each selling different types of foods. They are generally in high-density central cities and serve single professionals or double-income-no-children households. They emphasize high-quality (and high-priced) ready-to-serve or heat-and-serve foods for busy workers who have no time to make elaborate dinners. While intriguing in many ways, they serve a narrow market and few of them rely mainly on pedestrian traffic. Instead, the streets around them are usually jammed with sport-utility vehicles looking for parking.

Smart growth's ideas for retailing seem to have been thought up by people who do most of their grocery shopping at such public markets. The idea is that if enough such markets are built surrounded by enough high-density housing, then people will walk to the grocery store instead of driving their cars. That may work for one- or two-person households earning professional salaries, but it won't work for working-class families of four or five that watch every grocery dollar and stock up on staples when they are on sale. Ask the families with full shopping carts in the checkout lines at Costco or Cub Foods if they would be happier buying high-priced foods from an inner-city public market.

In support of walkable retail areas, planners often cite many inner-city neighborhoods with "transit villages" or "main street" shopping areas. To see whether these traditional shopping areas really do reduce auto driving, Ruth Steiner, of the University of California at Berkeley city planning department, studied six shopping districts in the Bay Area. Four were within a half mile of a BART station. One was an old suburban shopping center, but the other five had "continuous sidewalks fronting clusters of retail shops." All were within walking distance of a moderately high-density neighborhood.

Steiner found "that significant numbers of customers in each of these shopping districts did indeed walk there. Excluding the old suburban shopping center, to which only about 10 percent of customers walked, 25 to 50 percent of customers reached the other five shopping districts on foot." Yet Steiner found that "despite this high frequency of walking, the promise of less automobile traffic is not realized." First, "a significant percentage of each neighborhood's residents drove" and very few came by transit. Second, because the shops were unable to survive solely on local business, they offered specialty products to "induce high levels of traffic" from outside the local neighborhood, and nearly all of these customers drove. Her "counts and surveys taken during average (not major) shopping days reveal levels of traffic and parking demand in excess of comparable standards for peak demand." Steiner concludes that anyone building a pedestrian village "must provide plenty of parking."[6]

Smart growth, of course, doesn't confine itself to groceries. Home Depots, WalMarts, and other big-box retailers are equally targets of smart growth because they all benefit from people's freedom to drive to their stores. Jane Holtz Kay approvingly quotes a planner who calls such stores an "attack on Main Street."[7] But the real attack comes not from the stores but from the consumers who appreciate the wider selection and lower prices that can be offered by larger stores.

This doesn't mean that there is no future for small shops on main streets. Streets of such shops are often very successful because they have identified niche markets: antiques, designer boutiques, upscale food and clothing, specialty books, or other unusual merchandise. But they can only support such niche markets by attracting customers from large areas, customers who must drive to get there. Thus, the main streets that city officials point to with pride are the ones most clogged with autos.

Smart-growth planners have a different idea for achieving the quantity of business needed to support pedestrian-oriented markets: Increase densities by building "mid-rise, mixed-use developments."[8] This means four- to five-story buildings with stores and offices on the ground floor and housing above. This turns out to be unrealistic as well.

Among the rules of thumb formulated by developers and repeated by Joel Garreau is the "one-story-climb law," which says that most Americans will only climb one flight of stairs. This means that any multifamily housing taller than three stories must have an elevator. But an elevator raises the cost of construction so much that it cannot be justified for a housing complex unless the building is at least six stories tall.[9]

In other words, developers have learned, through hard experience, that four- to five-story residential buildings make no economic sense. So of course such buildings are the goal of smart-growth planners. In Portland, Oregon; Berkeley, California; and elsewhere, planners have proposed to rezone streets of one- and two-story homes and businesses into ones allowing—or even requiring—four- and five-story buildings. This represents a huge increase in local densities and will turn streets that are now open to the sun much of the day into narrow canyons reminiscent of much of Manhattan. Of course, developers will build them only if they are subsidized or if other smart-growth policies have so driven up housing prices that people are willing to pay a premium to live even in a high-density mid-rise.

Will such developments do any better at reducing auto driving? Many planners point to studies showing that people living in high densities own fewer cars and drive less. For example, the 1995 *Nationwide Personal Transportation Survey* found that 31 percent of households in neighborhoods with densities greater than 10,000 people per square mile have no autos, whereas the nationwide average is 8 percent. But once again it is important not to confuse cause with effect. Do people live without cars because they live in high-density neighborhoods? Or do they live in high-density neighborhoods because they can or must live without cars?

Robert Cervero's studies of high-density housing near BART and other rail stations found that most residents were "young households without children" or "professional workers making relatively good salaries," again mostly without children. Cervero is encouraged by the fact that people in these developments have fewer cars per household than average. However, this is because the households are small: 80 to 90 percent of the households in his study have only one or two people. On a *per person* basis, residents own 17 percent *more* cars than average.[10] Taking families with children out of the suburbs and putting them in transit-oriented developments will not necessarily reduce their driving needs. As UC transportation experts Marlon Boarnet and Nicholas Compin note, "it is unclear how much of the benefit of transit-based housing is more convenient residences for current transit users, as opposed to encouraging automobile commuters to use transit."[11]

Even if transit-oriented developments did influence transportation choices, redeveloping existing neighborhoods using such patterns will take decades or more. As University of Southern California planning Professor Genevieve Giuliano points out, transportation systems and housing in U.S. cities are already highly developed, they have very long lives so that most of it will still be around twenty or even fifty years from now. She adds that, due to such factors as telecommuting, "transportation is of declining importance in the locational decisions of households and firms." Thus, "transportation policy efforts would have to be truly extreme to have a significant impact on urban form."[12]

After studying transit-oriented development plans for San Diego, Boarnet and Compin concluded that such plans are "most likely to be implemented slowly and incrementally." Barriers such as neighborhood resistance, desires by local governments to obtain uses that produce high tax revenues, and desires by developers to build projects that make money means that "the revolutionary prospect that land use can boost rail transit ridership faces a long, incremental implementation process."[13]

Another study in Los Angeles assumed that 75 percent of all new jobs and 65 percent of all new residents could be located in transit-oriented developments near rail stations. Yet the study projected that only 7 to 10 percent of commuters would end up using transit. The study concluded that "even if anticipated land use changes were to occur, travel patterns would not change very much, because the overall regional pattern of land use would not change very much."[14]

The idea that 65 to 75 percent of urban growth could be concentrated around new rail stations is pretty unlikely in any case. Brookings economist Anthony Downs calculated that, to accommodate normal growth in transit-oriented development, every U.S. city with more than a million residents would have to build new rail lines longer than the 200-mile-long Washington Metro system each decade. "Realistically, it may not be feasible to accommodate all or even most urban growth in. . . transit-oriented developments. The feasibility of applying them on a large scale is weakened by the high cost of building the rapid-transit links among them."[15] Even if new growth were all compact, it wouldn't matter much, adds Downs. "Around 85 percent of urban development that will exist in 2020 is already here," says Downs, "So even if future growth occurs in very dense forms. . . . transportation will still be greatly dominated by private automotive vehicles."[16]

Other smart-growth ideas, such as gridded streets instead of cul-de-sacs, narrow streets, and small lots are supposed to reduce driving in neighborhoods of single-family homes. Robert Cervero surveyed residents of Rockridge, a traditional grid-pattern community near the University of California, and Lafayette, a low-density suburb. The two towns are just two BART station stops apart, but are completely different in character. He found that residents of both were equally inclined to ride BART, but that Rockridge residents were sixteen times more likely to walk, bicycle, or take the bus while Lafayette residents were 36 percent more likely to drive.[17] Cervero attributes this to differences in neighborhood design. It is more likely due to the fact that a high percentage of Rockridge residents are students or childless professionals while a high percentage of Lafayette residents are families with children.

Marlon Boarnet and UC Irvine colleague Sharon Sarmiento did a much more detailed study of travel data which controlled for personal data such as education, income, and number of children under 16, as well as for land-use data such as population density, proximity to stores and employment, and whether they lived on gridded streets. They found that the personal data strongly influenced travel behavior but that "the influence of the land use variables is quite weak." In other words, "the concern that persons choose residential locations based in part on their desired travel behavior appears to be quite valid."[18]

In some cases, Boarnet and Sarmiento found "land use policies designed to promote less travel can actually induce more travel." For example, "people who live in areas with more of a gridded street pattern accumulate more miles of non-work automobile travel."[19] Boarnet's UC Irvine colleague Randall Crane explains why this might be so: "An open circulation pattern that makes for short trip distances can also stimulate trip taking: shorter trips take less time and therefore cost less."[20] Gridded, open-circulation street plans are a goal of smart growth.

Crane's own study of detailed travel data for over 2,000 San Diegans "found *no evidence that the neighborhood street pattern affects either car-trip generation or mode choice*" (emphasis in the original).[21] Crane thinks that such smart-growth concepts such as gridded streets and mixed-use neighborhoods "offer a generally thoughtful and attractive alternative to what many consider ugly or banal about conventional suburban development." But, he goes on, "there is no convincing evidence that these designs influence travel behavior."

Smart growth's "transportation benefits have been advertised as facts rather than hypotheses,"[22] says Crane, adding that "planning research addressing these issues has for the most part failed to separate hype from hypothesis,"[23] Crane concludes that smart growth ideas "remain a wobbly foundation indeed for current transportation policy."[24]

Changes in transportation technology, from the horse car to the streetcar to the automobile, have had tremendous effects on urban land-use patterns. Each of these technological improvements has given increasing numbers of people a choice between the high-density cities mandated by previous technologies and low-density suburbs. Most have chosen to live in lower density areas.

"Land use changes are unlikely to produce major changes in metropolitan form or, more pertinently, transportation demands," says transportation expert Alan Pisarski. "Although the relationship between land use and transportation is undeniable, it is also rather remote."[25] As architects Maurice Culot and Leon Krier put it, "A street is a street, and one lives there in a certain way not because architects have imagined streets in certain ways."[26]

Notes

1. Michael Rothschild, *Bionomics: Economy as Ecosystem* (New York, NY: Holt, 1990), p. 130.
2. Progressive Grocer, "Preface to a revolution: 1900-1922," http://www.progressivegrocer.com/1922.htm.
3. Fred Meyer Stores, "The Birth of One-Stop Shopping," http://www.fredmeyer.com/fms/fmshist/histbirth.shtml.
4. Joseph Barnett, "The Highway in Urban and Suburban Areas," *in* Jean Labatut and Wheaton J. Land (ed.), *Highways in Our National Life: A Symposium* (Princeton, NJ: Princeton University Press, 1950), p. 150.
5. Martin Wachs, "The Automobile and Gender: An Historical Perspective," *in* Sandra Rosenbloom, ed., *Women's Travel Issues: Proceedings from the Second National Conference* (Washington, DC: US DOT, 1997), p. 104, http://www.fhwa.dot.gov/ohim/womens/chap6.pdf.
6. Ruth Steiner, "Traditional Shopping Centers," *Access* 12 (Spring, 1998): 8–10.
7. Jane Holtz Kay, *Asphalt Nation: How the Automobile Took over America and How We Can Take It Back* (New York, NY: Crown, 1997), p. 275.
8. Mike Saba, Portland Planning Bureau, quote from the October 23, 1996, city council meeting taken from a videotape of that meeting made by the city of Portland.
9. Joel Garreau, *Edge City: Life on the New Frontier* (New York, NY: Doubleday, 1991), pp. 465–466.
10. Robert Cervero & Val Menotti, *Market Profiles of Rail-Based Housing Projects in California* (Berkeley, CA: UCTC No. 242, 1994).
11. Marlon G. Boarnet & Nicholas S. Compin, *Transit-Oriented Development in San Diego County: Incrementally Implementing a Comprehensive Idea* (Berkeley, CA: UC Transportation Center, 1996), p. 3.
12. Genevieve Giuliano, "The Weakening Transportation-Land Use Connection," *Access* 6: (Spring, 1995): pp. 8–9.
13. Ibid, p. 20. See also Marlon Boarnet & Randall Crane, *Public Finance and Transit-Oriented Planning: New Evidence from Southern California* (Berkeley, CA: UC Transportation Center, 1995), pp. 23–24.
14. Genevieve Giuliano, "The Weakening Transportation-Land Use Connection," p. 7.

15. Anthony Downs, *New Visions for Metropolitan America* (Washington, DC: Brookings Institution, 1994), p. 227.
16. Anthony Downs, "Some Realities about Sprawl and Urban Decline," *Housing Policy Debate* 10 (4):969.
17. Robert Cervero & Carolyn Radisch, *Travel Choices in Pedestrian Versus Automobile Oriented Neighborhoods* (Berkeley, CA: UC Transportation Center, 1995).
18. Ibid, p. 23.
19. Marlon G. Boarnet & Sharon Sarmiento, *Can Land Use Policy Really Affect Travel Behavior? A Study of the Link between Non-Work Travel and Land Use Characteristics* ((Berkeley, CA: UCTC No. 342, 1996), p. 25.
20. Randall Crane, "Travel by Design?" *Access* 12 (Spring, 1998): p. 6.
24. Ibid, p. 7.
22. Randall Crane & Richard Crepeau, *Does Neighborhood Design Influence Travel?: A Behavioral Analysis of Travel Diary and GIS Data* (Berkeley, CA: UC Transportation Center, 1998).
23. Randall Crane, *On Form Versus Function: Will the "New Urbanism" Reduce Traffic or Increase It?* (Berkeley, CA: UC Transportation Center, 1995).
24. Ibid.
25. Alan E. Pisarski, "Issues in Transportation and Growth Management," *in* David J. Brower, David R. Godschalk, and Douglas R. Porter (eds.), *Understanding Growth Management: Critical Issues and a Research Agenda* (Washington, DC: Urban Land Institute, 1989), p. 128.
26. Maurice Culot & Leon Krier, "The Only Path for Architecture," *Oppositions* 14 (1978): 38–53.

The Excessive-Driving Myth

Myth: Sprawl forces people to drive too much.
Reality: A major part of the increase in driving comes from more women and low-income people getting jobs and taking care of their families.

Driving in the United States is increasing two-and-one-half times faster than the rate of population growth. There are several reasons why auto driving continues to increase even after experts predict that the demand for auto travel is "saturated." First, increases in income, especially during America's recent economic boom, also lead to increases in driving. This is both because more low-income people are buying cars and because everyone is driving more as the cost of driving decreases relative to their incomes.

Second, America's work force is growing faster than its population. In particular, a higher percentage of women enter the work force each year. For other reasons, women's driving is growing especially fast. Women under 65 take more trips each day than men[1] and they are more likely to do *trip chaining*, meaning they have several destinations on each trip, than men.[2] While they still drive fewer miles than men, the growth of women's driving is about twice as fast as that for men.[3]

Because much of recent increases in driving are among women and low-income people, efforts to restrict driving may fall especially hard on these groups. Transportation researchers Sandra Rosenbloom and Elizabeth Burns say that driving restrictions would cause women to suffer several major problems, including:

- They would have to pay more child care expenses because alternative travel modes are slower;
- Trip chaining, such as combining shopping or chauffeuring or children with work-related trips, would be more difficult if not impossible;
- They would find it more difficult to respond to home or school emergencies;
- They would be more concerned than men to the dangers of walking or riding transit.[4]

Smart-growth advocates claim that rail transit helps women and low-income people by giving them more "choices."[5] But choices are meaningless if they are not usable and worse than meaningless if their expense closes out other, more usable, options. Rosenbloom points out that, in low-income households, women are more likely to drive a car to work than men—probably because they use the car for trip chaining—and so restrictions on travel would especially hurt low-income women.[6]

Other researchers have found that low-income people "are pouring dollars into car ownership at a surprisingly high rate," even when transit is readily accessible. This indicates that they themselves believe that car ownership is superior to transit. "Transit-based solutions to the mobility problems" of people on welfare "may neither be optimal nor true long-term solutions to the mobility issues that welfare recipients face."[7] Another study found that the best way to help part-time workers is "to make automobiles more accessible" to such people.[8] Smart growth is the wrong solution for reducing urban poverty.

Notes

1. Patricia Hu and Jennifer Young, *Draft Summary of Travel Trends: 1995 Nationwide Personal Transportation Survey* (Oak Ridge, TN: US DOE, 1999), p. 22, http://www-cta.ornl.gov/npts/1995/Doc/trends_reportl8.pdf.
2. Nancy McGuckin, *Examining Trip-Chaining Behavior: A Comparison of Travel by Men and Women* (Washington, DC: US DOT, http://www-cta.ornl.gov/npts/1995/Doc/Chain2.pdf.
3. Patricia Hu and Jennifer Young, *Draft Summary of Travel Trends: 1995 Nationwide Personal Transportation Survey* (Oak Ridge, TN: US DOE, 1999), p. 38, http://www-cta.ornl.gov/npts/1995/Doc/trends_reportl8.pdf.
4. Sandra Rosenbloom & Elizabeth Burns, *Why Working Women Drive Alone: The Implications for Travel Reduction Programs* (Berkeley, CA: UCTC #274, 1994).
5. Hank Dittmar, "From Wooing Soccer Moms to Demonizing Welfare Mothers: A Legislative and Policy Context for Women's Travel," *in* Sandra Rosenbloom, ed., *Women's Travel Issues: Proceedings from the Second National Conference* (Washington, DC: US DOT, 1997), p. 668, http://www.fhwa.dot.gov/ohim/womens/chap35.pdf.
6. Sandra Rosenbloom, "Trends in Women's Travel Patterns," *in* Sandra Rosenbloom, ed., *Women's Travel Issues: Proceedings from the Second National Conference* (Washington, DC: US DOT, 1997), p. 24, http://www.fhwa.dot.gov/ohim/womens/chap2.pdf.
7. Alissa Gardenhire and William Sermons, "Understanding Automobile Ownership Behavior of Low-Income Households: How Behavioral Differences May Influence Transportation Policy," *in* Transportation Research Board, *Conference on Personal Travel: The Long and the Short of It* (Washington, DC: US DOT, 1999), pp. 14–15, http://www.fhwa.dot.gov/ohim/travelconf/garden.pdf.
8. Joint Center for Political and Economic Studies, *Equitable Transportation Access in the Journey to Work for Part-Time Workers* (Washington, DC: FHwA, 1999), p. 5-4, http://www.fhwa.dot.gov/ohim/equit/Chap5.pdf.

30. Greenbelts

The part of Vice President Al Gore's plan to curb urban sprawl that received the most publicity was a proposal for a huge federal fund that cities could use to purchase open space and greenbelts. No doubt Gore pushed this the hardest because voters are particularly receptive to protecting open space. Open spaces and parks are certainly important for urban livability, but Gore's proposal was questionable for two reasons.

First, open space purchases are politically popular because voters see them as a tool for minimizing population densities. But Gore's greenbelts have exactly the opposite goal: increasing urban densities by limiting development at the urban fringe. As long ago as 1928, regional planning advocate Benton MacKaye urged the use of continuous greenbelts around urban areas as "dams and levees for controlling the metropolitan flood."[1] As described by Andres Duany, these greenbelts would be combined with transportation and urban service policies to prevent leapfrog development outside the belts. Duany likes greenbelts better than urban-growth boundaries because he thinks it will be more difficult for people who want to live in low densities to leap a broad greenbelt than to simply cross a growth boundary. He also fantasizes that their location will be based on "objective environmental criteria" rather than on political considerations.[2]

Second, as planned by Gore, federal funding would come with many strings attached. Cities could get open-space funds only if they adopted auto-hostile policies and forced higher densities on their residents. Such policies would do more harm to urban livability than the open spaces federal funds might buy.

Contra Costa County, just east of San Francisco Bay, has spent tens of millions of dollars purchasing huge regional parks and greenbelts. Most of these parks are in the highlands, which make poor wildlife habitat. The parks have a few trails used by a few hardy hikers. But generally they receive very little public use. It is likely that most county residents have never set foot in one. Though paid for by county taxpayers as a whole, the main beneficiaries have been the few people who own homes next to the parks. So much Bay-area land has been included in parks and open spaces that it has significantly contributed to making the area the least affordable housing market in the nation.[3]

Portland voters passed a "green spaces and parks" bond measure that authorized $135 million to purchase open spaces. To date, more than 80 percent of the acres purchased have been greenbelt lands outside the urban area. The regional government that is buying the land has no plans to develop most of the greenbelt for public use. Instead, most of it will be left as "wildlife habitat" that is inaccessible to most members of the public. As open space inside the urban-growth boundary is rapidly being developed, many voters feel cheated because they expected that the funds would be used for recreational parks inside the urban area.

This is the standard smart-growth prescription. As Duany says, greenbelts should consist of "wetlands, habitat for endangered species and communities of species, forests and large woodlots, steep slopes, cultural resources, scenic areas, view-sheds for highways, agricultural land, and current and future parks." The "current and future parks" is almost an afterthought, suggesting that, except for those who live next to such greenbelts, few people will get to use most of them.

Voters who think that greenbelts will reduce densities, provide neighborhood playgrounds for their children, and recreation areas for their families will be sorely disappointed by smart growth. Rather than buying lands that are far from and inaccessible to most urban residents, cities should concentrate on providing neighborhood parks and open spaces that residents can use on a regular basis.

Notes

1. Benton MacKaye, *The New Exploration: A Philosophy of Regional Planning* (New York, NY: Harcourt, Brace, 1928), p. 178.
2. Andres Duany, Elizabeth Plater-Zyberk, and Jeff Speck, *Suburban Nation: The Rise of Sprawl and the Decline of the American Dream* (New York, NY: North Point Press, 2000), pp. 143–144.
3. David E. Dowall, *The Suburban Squeeze: Land Conservation and Regulation in the San Francisco Bay Area* (Berkeley, CA: UC Press, 1984), p. 15.

Open Space Facts

The Open Space Myth (p. 155) discussed problems with the 1997 Natural Resources Inventory, which apparently overestimated the area of urbanized land in many states. Still, even these data show that a remarkably small percentage of the United States has been developed (including urban areas and rural roads and railroads) or urbanized (including just urban areas). The inventory did not cover Alaska, but Alaska urbanized data can be taken from the 1990 Census. This exaggerates urbanized area since the census counted all land within city limits as urbanized even though Alaska city limits include mostly undeveloped land. Note that areas include only land, not water.

Developed and Urbanized Areas by State
(thousands of acres)

State	Land Area	Developed Area	Urban Area	Percent Developed	Percent Urban
Alabama	33,424	2,410	1,823	7.2	5.5
Alaska	365,482		103	0.0	0.0
Arizona	72,964	1,675	1,246	2.3	1.7
Arkansas	34,037	1,501	996	4.4	2.9
California	101,510	5,687	4,952	5.6	4.9
Colorado	66,625	1,706	1,182	2.6	1.8
Connecticut	3,195	897	823	28.1	25.8
Delaware	1,534	238	213	15.5	13.9
DC	39	39	39	100.0	100.0
Florida	37,534	5,449	4,867	14.5	13.0
Georgia	37,741	4,238	3,534	11.2	9.4
Hawaii	4,163	186	159	4.5	3.8
Idaho	53,488	811	445	1.5	0.8
Illinois	36,059	3,262	2,544	9.0	7.1
Indiana	23,158	2,356	1,846	10.2	8.0
Iowa	36,017	1,803	839	5.0	2.3
Kansas	52,661	2,882	1,070	5.5	2.0

State	Land Area	Developed Area	Urban Area	Percent Developed	Percent Urban
Kentucky	25,863	1,955	1,418	7.6	5.5
Louisiana	31,377	1,693	1,339	5.4	4.3
Maine	20,966	747	582	3.6	2.8
Maryland	7,870	1,291	1,189	16.4	15.1
Massachusetts	5,339	1,549	1,463	29.0	27.4
Michigan	37,349	3,764	3,360	10.1	9.0
Minnestoa	54,010	2,361	1,535	4.4	2.8
Mississippi	30,527	1,656	1,094	5.4	3.6
Missouri	44,614	2,653	1,743	5.9	3.9
Montana	94,110	881	409	0.9	0.4
Nebraska	49,510	1,268	557	2.6	1.1
Nevada	70,763	416	325	0.6	0.5
New Hampshire	5,941	642	549	10.8	9.2
New Jersey	5,216	1,849	1,803	35.4	34.6
New Mexico	77,823	1,325	793	1.7	1.0
New York	31,361	3,373	2,919	10.8	9.3
North Carolina	33,709	4,181	3,556	12.4	10.5
North Dakota	45,251	1,152	271	2.5	0.6
Ohio	26,445	3,797	3,431	14.4	13.0
Oklahoma	44,738	1,997	1,290	4.5	2.9
Oregon	62,161	1,296	886	2.1	1.4
Pennsylvania	28,995	4,336	3,901	15.0	13.5
Rhode Island	813	205	187	25.2	23.0
South Carolina	19,939	2,325	1,880	11.7	9.4
South Dakota	49,358	1,035	366	2.1	0.7
Tennessee	26,974	2,618	2,182	9.7	8.1
Texas	171,052	8,984	7,126	5.3	4.2
Utah	54,339	760	505	1.4	0.9
Vermont	6,154	346	241	5.6	3.9
Virginia	27,087	2,805	2,302	10.4	8.5
Washington	44,035	2,214	1,686	5.0	3.8
West Virginia	15,508	986	745	6.4	4.8
Wisconsin	35,920	2,543	1,844	7.1	5.1
Wyoming	62,603	716	261	1.1	0.4
Total	2,307,351	104,859	80,419	4.5	3.5

Sources: 1997 Natural Resources Inventory except AK and DC, which are from Statistical Abstract of the U.S. *Alaska urban acres are from Census Bureau, 1990 Census of Population and Housing (1990 CPH-2-1) (Washington, DC: Commerce, 1993), table 51. Total developed area is slightly underestimated because it does not include Alaska.*

The Small-Town Myth

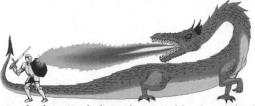

Myth: Smart-growth planning helps urban neighborhoods look like small towns.
Reality: Smart-growth's density and mixture of uses looks more like Brooklyn
than small towns.

Fairview Village, a moderately high-density, neotraditional subdivision near
Portland, "recaptures the look, feel of small-town America" headlines the
Oregonian, Portland's leading newspaper. "Welcome to the good old days,"
says the article. Such features as wide front porches, alleys, and garages facing the
rear make the development "a scene out of small-town America." "There's a real
sense of community," says one resident.[1]

Almost any article lauding neotraditional, new urban, or smart-growth planning eventually promises to make your gargantuan urban area feel like a small
town. It's true that many older homes in small towns have broad front porches
and garages in the back. But older homes in cities and prewar suburbs did too;
that's the way houses were built before almost everyone owned their own car. But
Fairview Village also has row houses, which you will rarely find in small towns.
Nor will you find house lots barely big enough to hold the house, four- and five-
story apartment buildings, heavily mixed uses, inadequate parking, traffic calming, gold-plated light-rail lines, or (in most cases) proposals to plan everything for
the next twenty years.

Since leaving Oak Grove, I've moved into a small Oregon town of about 2,900
people. At 1,100 people per square mile, Bandon's density is about a third that of
Portland. Except for an occasional odd house, no building is taller than two stories. Some of the older homes have garages in back; some of the newer ones have
garages in front; most are nice looking either way. Front porches are almost nonexistent because the climate does not encourage them. People walk around a lot
because there is so much open space for them to walk in. There is no public mass
transit, but the 1990 census found that nearly 15 percent of the employed residents walked or bicycled to work (not counting those who work at home)—well
ahead of the cities of New York or San Francisco.

In 1936, a fire wiped out more than 90 percent of the town. Inspired by the

New Deal, urban planning was all the rage then, so the state hired a Portland planner to write a new plan for Bandon. He found that the town's density was far too low and so he proposed to shove all housing into a smaller area. Instead of being on the highway through town, he put all businesses in a location within walking distance of most of the homes. At a town meeting in March 1937, the planner reported, residents unanimously approved the plan.[2] Yet they then ignored it, rebuilding their town to the same low density as before and leaving the businesses where they were. It is probably a good thing, for the town depends on out-of-town travelers for much of its retailing, and many businesses probably would not have survived being off the highway.

Today I cannot detect any more or any less of a sense of community than I felt in Oak Grove. When the state of Oregon proposed to densify a part of the town, people rose up in protest just as they had done in Oak Grove. People go to high school football games, join the Friends of the Library, and enjoy Fourth of July fireworks sponsored by the local fire department just as they did in Oak Grove. But they don't have to deal with traffic, unaffordable housing, or developers trying to turn golf courses into housing because no other land remains available to development.

Like Portland and many of its suburbs, Bandon has some tax-increment finance districts that allow the city council to spend property taxes on pet projects and special interests without getting voter approval. Bandon residents overwhelming voted for property tax reform when it was on the statewide ballot several years ago, but a loophole in the law left tax-increment financing alive. If Bandon truly had a stronger sense of community than Portland, residents would probably have banded together to get rid of these undemocratic taxes long ago.

In promising a small-town atmosphere, smart-growth advocates are appealing to a nostalgia that most Americans have for a distant (and, on close examination, usually not so rosy) past. But in almost every important respect—density, traffic congestion, mass transit, mixed uses, and government regulation—smart growth is exactly the opposite of small town life.

Notes

1. Connie Potter, "Fairview Village: New east Multnomah County subdivision recaptures look, feel of small-town America," *The Oregonian*, 2 May 1999, p. H-1.
2. Harry Freeman, *Plan for Bandon, Oregon*, Oregon State Planning Board, March, 1937.

Overwhelmed by Smart Growth

Because the term *smart growth* is so new, even many planners don't realize that smart-growth ideas have already been tried, and failed, in the U.S. In 1979, San Diego's regional planning agency, the San Diego Association of Governments (SANDAG), implemented a plan very much like smart growth. Its plan called for four zones in and around the city:

- In *urbanized* areas, where infrastructure was already in place, developers were encouraged to "infill" vacant sites, developments were fast tracked, and development fees were minimized.
- A *planned urbanized* area outside the urbanized zone would allow developers to pay impact fees on a "pay as you go" basis for all public facilities including schools, libraries, even freeway interchanges.
- An *urban reserve* would be limited to 10-acre home sites for at least 20 years.
- An *environmental* zone would have no development.

According to Nico Calavita, a planning professor at San Diego State University, this plan led to "frantic overbuilding. . . in the urbanized tier. One after another, single-family neighborhoods were invaded by multifamily dwellings, many of them insensitively designed."[1]

As a result of this "on-slaught of newcomers," community facilities were "overwhelmed." "Freeway congestion and sewer breakdowns became commonplace." In 1990, the city estimated that "it would cost over $1 billion to make up the infrastructure shortfall." These overdevelopments were probably a response to the high development fees in the "planned urbanized" area.

Table One: The San Diego Urbanized Area

	1950	1990	1998
Population (thousands)	433	2,348	2,683
Land area square miles	134	690	733
Density	3,240	3,400	3,660

Source: Census Bureau for 1950 and 1990, FHwA, Highway Statistics 1998 for 1998. FHwA land area data are not exactly comparable with Census Bureau data since they use slightly different criteria for determining urbanized area boundaries.

Table Two: The City of San Diego

	1950	1990	1998
Population (thousands)	334	1,111	1,221
Land area square miles	99	324	342
Density	3,726	3,425	3,570

Source: Census Bureau. Land area and density for 1998 are from http://www.sannet.gov/general-plan/facts/statistics.shtml.

Meanwhile, "development interests used the political process to eviscerate plans" in the urban reserve. In 1984, for example, the city approved a 5,000-acre project in this zone. This led to a 1985 initiative requiring voter approval for future developments in the "future urbanized" area. While this seemed to give environmental interests the upper hand, it proved short lived.

California's recession in the early 1990s led the city to cut development fees in the "planned urbanized" area in half. Lot sizes in the "future urbanized" were reduced from 10 acres to 4 acres. Meanwhile, little effort was made to minimize development in the "environmental" zone.

"It is likely that most of the urban reserve will eventually become an exurban enclave for the rich and the super-rich," says Calavita. "In addition to their four-acre lots, they will have access to tens of thousands of acres of open space, while in the urbanized communities—where most middle and lower income families live—open space and parkland are lacking."

Figure One: San Diego Area Densities

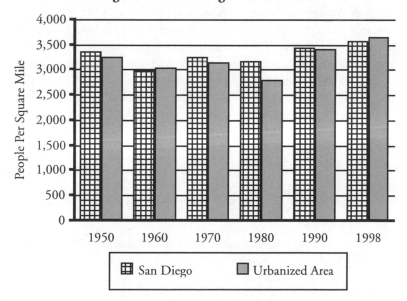

Souce: Census Bureau and Federal Highway Administration.

Table Three: San Diego-Area Transportation

Miles of freeway per million people	89
Annual miles driven per capita	7,848
Passenger miles per capita	12,557
Annual transit miles per capita	188
Annual transit trips per capita	35
Auto commuters	89.1%
Transit commuters	3.4%
Walk/cycle commuters	7.5%

Source: FHwA, Highway Statistics 1998, FTA, Transit Profiles 1998, 1990 Census. All data from 1998 except commuting data, which are from 1990. Passenger miles per capita are 1.6 times miles driven per capita.

Nor does it appear that San Diego's 1979 plan has changed local travel habits. Although the region boasts both light-rail and commuter rail services, transit accounts for less than 1.5 percent of motorized travel. San Diego's excellent weather allows for more than the average share of walking and cycling, but efforts to promote transit-oriented developments have been hampered by neighborhood resistance and lack of a market for such housing.[2]

Despite the failure of the 1979 plan, the San Diego Association of Governments is now promoting a modernized smart-growth plan based on high-density centers at light-rail transit stations and minimum density standards for all future developments. Higher densities are needed, says SANDAG, because "anything less than 5 or 6 units per acre is a wasteful use of urban land." The association estimates that 408,000 housing units are needed in the next twenty years to accommodate growth. It wants to increase the average density of new homes from 3.7 units per acre to 4.8 units per acre, which it claims will save 400,000 acres.[3] Yet the difference between 3.7 and 4.8 units per acre times 408,000 units is 25,000 acres, not 400,000. Still, the SANDAG plan appears to be on its way toward implementation by the area.

Notes

1. Nico Calavita, "Vale of Tiers: San Diego's much-lauded growth management system may not be as good as it looks," *Planning* magazine, March 1997, pp. 18-21.
2. Marlon Boarnet & Randall Crane, *Public Finance and Transit-Oriented Planning: New Evidence from Southern California* (Berkeley, CA: UC Transportation Center, 1995), pp. 23–24.
3. SANDAG, "2020 Cities/County Forecast Land Use Alternatives," SANDAG Board of Directors Report #99-2-7, February 26, 1999.

Part Eight

Smart-Growth Government

To prove its commitment to recycling, Portland's Metro rebuilt an old Sears store into offices for its planners at a cost of $30 million when a new building would have cost only $15 million (top, p. 189). Several years later officials learned that toilets in the building weren't hooked up to the city sewer lines and instead were pouring raw sewage into the Willamette River—a problem that would not have happened if they had simply built a new building. **Property owners and merchants in downtown Portland** (bottom) are the biggest beneficiaries of Metro's plan (p 182).

31. Regional Government

7n 1973, a right-wing publisher called the Independent American Newspaper issued a little book titled *Beware Metro and Regional Government!* Subtitled "an exposé of those who seek to destroy local self-government," the book is full of factual errors and paranoid delusions tying metropolitan and regional governments to the Rockefellers, the Council on Foreign Relations, and other favorites of conspiracy theorists.[1] At the same time, the book contains a glimmer of truth: Regional urban governments tend to restrict freedom and local self determination. In fact, according to many advocates of regional governments, the ability to impose such restrictions on local property owners and municipalities is one of their primary advantages.

USC planning professors Harry Richardson and Peter Gordon call it an "astounding paradox" that as the governments of Eastern Europe, Russia, and so many other parts of the world have given up central planning, the United States is embracing it. "Ironically the collapse of central planning in Eastern Europe was the direct result of pressures for democracy and freedom," they say, while the growth of planning in the United States "was essentially anti-democratic."[2]

Smart growth is profoundly anti-democratic. While it gives lip service to public involvement, its real goal is to overcome personal preferences and the democratic processes used in local governments. Smart-growth advocates say that the social or collective good outweighs individual freedom. But ultimately, all decisions are made by individuals, not by some amorphous "collective." Who gets to decide what is the social good or what is in the collective interest of a community? No matter what the answer, the final decision will not be made by a collective but by individuals who are subject to their own personal preferences and ideologies.

Smart-growth government is designed to insure that individuals with certain ideologies make decisions for everyone—decisions that most people would probably not make for themselves. The tools used to insure this outcome include regional governments, planning, pseudo-public involvement processes, and increasingly restrictive zoning and other regulations.

Regional governments are not an international conspiracy. But they are a result, in part, of federal edicts. In 1962, Congress required that transportation

447

projects in urbanized areas of 50,000 or more in population be based on a con-
tinuing, comprehensive, urban transportation planning process undertaken co-
operatively by the state and local governments. In 1965, the Bureau of Public
Roads (predecessor to the Federal Highway Administration) required the creation
of a planning agency for each urbanized area. These planning agencies came to be
known as *metropolitan planning organizations* (MPOs).

Also in 1965 Congress required that urban areas seeking grants from the Department of Housing and Urban Development create regional planning organizations controlled by boards of elected officials representing most or all of the
residents in the regions. A typical board might consist of the mayors or city coun-
cillors from the major and some of the minor cities in the region and county
commissioners to represent people in the unincorporated areas.

Between 1965 and 1980, the departments of Transportation and Housing and
Urban Development wrote increasingly stringent planning rules for the regional
councils and MPOs. The Urban Mass Transit Administration (later the Federal
Transit Administration) joined with the Federal Highway Administration in writing joint transportation planning rules. While the law only required long-term
transportation planning, the new rules required short-term capital improvement
and operational plans as well. While the original focus was on congestion reduction, the new rules placed greater emphasis on energy and environmental concerns. The rules also allowed the Department of Transportation to send plans that
it did not like back to the drawing board, although that rarely happened.

The Reagan administration attempted to decentralize the planning process by
eliminating most of the planning rules that were not specifically required by law.
Under the new rules, plans were certified by the states, taking away the Department of Transportation's veto power. Planners, naturally, were unhappy with the
deemphasis on planning and refer to the 1980s as a period of "deterioration."[3]

Such decentralization was reversed in 1991 when Congress passed the
Intermodal Surface Transportation Efficiency Act (ISTEA), which contained numerous planning requirements for states and urban areas. The law required every
urban area to write a detailed transportation plan and tied that planning to federal
air quality targets. Regions with serious air pollution problems were required to
undertake certain activities, such as ordering employers to reduce the amount of
commuting their employees do by auto, and federal transportation funds could
be denied to polluted urban areas that did not have transportation plans that
satisfied the Environmental Protection Agency.

Initially, the EPA allowed polluted regions to go ahead with highway projects
that had already been approved. But then a Sierra Club lawsuit against Georgia
highway authorities halted construction of roads in the Atlanta metropolitan area
because that region did not yet have an approved plan. The Georgia legislature
responded by creating the Georgia Regional Transportation Authority, whose governor-appointed commission would be one of the most powerful regional govern-

ments in the nation.

ISTEA required public involvement in transportation planning, but this did not assure that planning would be democratic. Spurred by grants from liberal foundations and the Environmental Protection Agency, transit and bicycle groups stacked the planning processes in many cities, while auto groups that might have represented the people taking 80 to 90 percent of urban trips remained asleep at the wheel. The Federal Transit Administration sometimes criticized MPOs that failed to get enough transit and pedestrian groups involved in their planning, even though transit and walking played little role in the transport of those regions.[4]

Other interests also took advantage of MPOs and regional planning:

- Central city officials saw MPOs as a way of extending their reach over the suburbs.
- Urban planners viewed MPOs as tool for imposing order on the chaos that they called urban sprawl.
- Developers, environmentalists, and other special interests hoped they could use MPOs to bend local governments to their preferences.

Today, more than 300 MPOs are scattered across the country.[5] Some are little more than post office boxes; others are much more powerful. The Department of Housing and Urban Development endorses the creation of "a super agency" to "promote more rational development" in urban areas. Such agencies should have "the authority to stop construction of highways or shopping malls that don't promote smart growth."[6]

The Environmental Protection Agency also promotes regional government. In an article titled "Becoming Regional" on the smartgrowth.org web site, Harriet Tregonning, the director of EPA's Urban Policy Division, says that "many federal agencies" are supporting regional governments that can address "poorly planned development" because "local solutions are often too narrow." Local governments, for example, "try to solve congestion with more freeways," but regional governments would "make our communities less reliant on cars."[7]

The advantage regional governments have over local governments, says Anthony Downs, is that regional governments "can take controversial stands without making its individual members commit themselves to those stands. Each member can claim that 'the organization' did it or blame all the other members."[8] In other words, the regional government can subvert the democratic process by doing things for "the greater social good" that local voters would ordinarily oppose.

Downs appears to view regional governments as altruistic organizations that will automatically seek to maximize net social benefits. Like any bureaucracy, however, a regional government tends to grow. Once established, it takes on more and more authority until it has the power to become exceptionally intrusive on the lives of urban-area residents. Given that power, interest groups will pressure it to use its power to obtain special benefits for those groups—which they usually claim are in the "greater social good."

"We 'good people' were breakfasting at the Graduates Club," recounts New Haven resident Paul Bass. "We talked about the unenlightened people in the suburbs. How can we make them care more about the poor, unfortunate people in the city? The question became: How do we shove regional government down their throats?"[9]

Most central city officials have long been frustrated by the reluctance of their suburbs to be annexed into the main city. On average, central cities make up only a third of the residents of metropolitan areas. Yet they are the largest political entity in their regions and so have a disproportionate share of power. They welcome MPOs as a way of gaining power over the suburbs that insisted on independence for so long.

Planners, too, saw MPOs as a way of gaining power over the suburbs, many of which had no zoning codes or significant planning staffs. Douglas Porter, of the Urban Land Institute, notes that there is a "gap between the daily mode of living desired by most Americans and the mode that most city planners and traffic engineers believe is most appropriate." The "gap" is that "Americans generally want a house on a large lot and three cars in every garage, or rather on the highways," yet planners object to the "low-density sprawl and dependence on roads and highways."[10] Moreover, worries Porter, most local governments are likely to give people what they want rather than what planners think they should have. Porter recommends closing this gap by giving regional governments "powers to require local plans to conform to regional or state goals." He laments that "relatively few regional agencies can coerce local governments to respect regional plans."[11]

Porter admits that "this straightforward model of intergovernmental behavior breaks down in practice" because the regional governments end up getting captured by some powerful interest group. He cites specific examples of regional planners in Denver favoring the central city over the suburbs in their plans. Even though suburban populations were growing and Denver's was shrinking, the planners forecast growth for Denver and, based on that forecast, denied resources to the suburbs that they needed to cope with their growth. "These accommodations to fit forecasts to local policies appear to be quite common," says Porter, yet this doesn't suggest to him that perhaps regional governments won't produce the benefits he seeks.

Without regional governments, say many planners, local governments will not only fail to solve regional problems, they will actually make them worse because they will be more responsive to their local constituents than to the greater social good. The proliferation of local governments—school districts, water districts, sewer districts, fire districts, and other service districts on top of cities and counties—is often cited as duplicative and inefficient, with the implicit or explicit claim that a single region-wide government would be more efficient. "We have

238 communities each with their own zoning and funding system," complains a Philadelphia transit official to a sympathetic Jane Holtz Kay.[12]

So far, only a handful of regional government have the kind of authority smart-growth advocates seek. Portland's Metro is one; Atlanta's new Georgia Regional Transportation Authority is another. The Twin Cities Metropolitan Council does not have as much power as either the Portland or Atlanta governments, but still more than most other metropolitan planning organizations. A few cities have acquired power over their suburbs through annexation (Indianapolis, San Antonio) or city-county mergers (Nashville). In most other urban areas, smart-growth planners must still rely on persuasion rather than coercion.

Notes

1. Phoebe Courtney, *Beware metro and Regional Government!* (Littleton, CO: Independent American Newspaper, 1973), 149 p.
2. Harry W. Richardson and Peter Gordon, "Market Planning: Oxymoron or Common Sense?" *Journal of the American Planning Association* 59(3) [Summer, 1993]: pp. 347–352.
3. National Association of Regional Councils, "About MPOs," http://narc.org/ampo/def.html.
4. For example, see Federal Transit Administration, *Review of the Transportation Planning Process in the Minneapolis-St. Paul Metropolitan Area* (Washington, DC: FTA, 1993), p. 30.
5. For a complete list, see the Federal Highway Administration's directory of MPOs at http://www.bts.gov/tmip/MPOlist/mpoindex.htm.
6. Department of Housing and Urban Development, *State of the Cities 1999* (Washington, DC: HUD, 1999), p. 21.
7. Harriet Tregoning, "Becoming Regional: A Federal Role," http://www.smartgrowth.org/library/tregoning_ground.html.
8. Anthony Downs, *Stuck in Traffic: Coping with Peak-Hour Traffic Congestion* (Washington, DC: Brookings, 1992), p. 133.
9. Paul Bass, "A Bad 'Good' Idea," *New Haven Advocate*, April 16, 1998, p. 6.
10. Douglas Porter, "Regional Governance of Metropolitan Form: The Missing Link in Relating Land Use and Transportation," *in* Transportation Research Board, *Transportation, Urban Form, and the Environment* (Washington, DC: TRB, 1991), p. 65.
11. Ibid, p. 68.
12. Jane Holtz Kay, *Asphalt Nation: How the Automobile Took over America and How We Can Take It Back* (New York, NY: Crown, 1997), p. 301.

Web Tools: MPOs

Identify and locate your metropolitan planning organization at http://www.bts.gov/tmip/MPOlist/mpoindex.htm. This web site provides MPO addresses but not their web sites. Many metropolitan planning organization web sites are listed at http://www.narc.org/links/member.html.

The Regional-Issues Myth

Myth: Only regional governments can handle the problems of modern metropolitan areas.

Reality: Regional governments are undemocratic and tend to be controlled by special interest groups.

Jane Jacobs defines a region as "an area safely larger than the last one to whose problems we found no solution."[1] Yet proponents of regional government argue that problems that local governments handle poorly can be solved at a regional level. According to Anthony Downs, such issues include "traffic congestion, air pollution, large-scale adsorption of open space, extensive use of energy for movement, inability to provide adequate infrastructures to accommodate growth because of high costs, inability to locate certain region-serving facilities like new airports that have negative local spillover effects, and suburban labor shortages because of inadequate low-income housing near new jobs."[2] "Regional growth patterns require regional governance," concludes Downs.[3]

Downs's argument carries a strong assumption that he never acknowledges: that a regional government will actually solve his list of problems and not make them worse. He necessarily assumes that regional governments will be as rational as he is, that they will not become tools of special interest groups or enamored with the latest inane urban planning fad, and that they will have access to and use all of the information they need to make wise decisions at a regional scale.

"All bureaucracies make mistakes, but megacity bureaucracies tend to make big, big mistakes," said Jane Jacobs when opposing metropolitan government for the Toronto area. "What is worse, they tend thereafter to be paralyzed with respect to correcting their mistakes or learning from them."[4] As a long time observer of urban planning, Jacobs knows that planning at any scale requires simplifying assumptions. These simplifying assumptions go into a "model" of the thing being planned, which may be a sophisticated computer model or simply an idea in the planner's head. If the simplifying assumptions turn out to be wrong, then the plan will also be wrong. Larger scale plans require greater simplification and magnify both the chances for and the scale of any error.

Jacobs further argued that regional government would be "less responsive than what we have now, more prone to costly error because less on top of detailed realities, more inert and very likely more vulnerable to favoritism and hidden agendas at the expense of taxpayers." Of course, Downs believed that the ability of regional government to impose hidden agendas was a virtue, but also believed that they would impose *his* agenda and not someone else's.

Portland shows that Downs' prediction that regional councils can "take controversial stands without making its individual members commit themselves to those stands" is valid, largely because few people were watching. People who are quick to protest when a proposal is made to develop a nearby property remain complacent about regional planning because it is so nebulous and vague. As Jacobs predicted, this gives special interests the opportunity to work the process to their advantage. Gerald Ford notes that "a government powerful enough to give you everything you want is powerful enough to take from you everything you have."

The claim that some issues are regional in nature overlooks the fact that the United States has a long history of state and local government cooperation without a coercive overseer. Highways reaching the borders of states and cities met roads in adjacent states and jurisdictions long before the federal government required comprehensive transportation planning. Similar cooperation can deal with traffic congestion, open space protection, and other supposedly regional issues.

There are some situations where local governments do not have an incentive to cooperate. Most state tax systems reward cities for commercial land uses and penalize them for residential areas. Thus, cities end up in competition for commercial developments while they try to burden their neighbors with the residential developments. This has become a particular problem in California, where cities get much of their funding from sales taxes instead of property taxes. Regional government can supposedly overcome these types of problems.

But if regional government creates more problems than it solves, then alternate solutions must be found to apparently regional problems. For example, some states require local cities to share the tax revenues from commercial developments, thus taking away the incentive to attract commercial uses and drive away residential developments. State legislation might also be used to give local cities and towns incentives to protect open space and solve other supposedly regional problems without actually creating regional governments.

Notes

1. Jane Jacobs, *The Death and Life of Great American Cities* (New York, NY: Random House, 1961), p. 410.
2. Anthony Downs, "How America's Cities Are Growing: The Big Picture," *Brookings Review*, Fall, 1998, pp. 8–9, 11
3. Quoted by Andres Duany, http://www.periferia.org/publications/Quotes.html.
4. Jane Jacobs, "Deputation given to the Standing Committee on General Government conducting hearings on The City of Toronto Act - Bill 103," February 3, 1997.

The Bigger-Is-Better Myth

Myth: One regional government will be more efficient than scores or hundreds of local governments.

Reality: Local governments are more responsive to local taxpayers and thus often end up wasting less money subsidizing special interest groups.

Regional advocates argue that the proliferation of hundreds of local governments and special districts is inefficient. "American cities have been especially susceptible to the notion that 'bigger is better,'" says Kenneth Jackson in his history of the suburbs, *Crabgrass Frontier*. "In many cases, the cry for efficiency was a mask for the desire to exploit and to control; it might be termed the local or downtown brand of urban imperialism. Often the large merchants and businessmen of the central business districts sought to eliminate neighborhood governments that in their view inhibited progress."[1]

Regional government, says Herbert Gans, represents "the downgrading of local democracy." The Levittown which he studied was inhabited by mostly lower-middle-class citizens, while its critics were mostly "cosmopolitan upper-middle-classes." The residents were satisfied with their community and with being able "to determine their own destiny and to do so by majority rule." The elites considered "such satisfaction irrelevant" and wanted to build "utopias" which reflected their "philosophies and styles of life."[2] Advocates of regional governments "see only the advantages for the larger area, but ignore the very real disadvantages for local communities."[3] "If the community is genuinely democratic, I would begin with the value judgment that local democracy is of high priority, and that its costs must be accepted along with its benefits," says Gans. "If democracy is important, one cannot set up another, nonpolitical criterion for decision-making every time the decision goes the wrong way."[4]

Portland's Metro claims to have overcome Gans' concerns with democracy by having a democratically elected council. Yet a local government is almost always more democratic than a regional one because local residents have more of an incentive and are more likely to get involved in the local government. Moreover, they are more likely to share similar concerns and preferences and thus less likely to try to impose some minority view on the majority.

Gans was not impressed by arguments that the greater social good outweighed local preferences. "Issues in the holistic public interest are also rare," he said. "Although intervenors often claimed their own demands were so important that they justified the rejection of individual interests, I cannot think of a single issue in this category in Levittown's short history."[5]

Howard Husack, a researcher at Harvard's Kennedy School of Government, believes that urban problems should be dealt with by making governments smaller, not bigger. Different people want different things from their local governments, he says. Smaller jurisdictions make it possible for local governments to cater to the needs of their residents, resulting in both better services and lower costs. Studies of school districts have found that, "even after controlling for race and income," he says, "students from metro areas with many separate school districts had higher math and reading scores than students from areas with large 'unified' districts."

Former Albuquerque Mayor David Rusk argues that regional governments can allocate resources to poor neighborhoods that need them more. In fact, says Husack, what usually happens is that resources are spend in the parts of the city "with the most political influence." This may mean, for example, taking property taxes that would ordinarily pay for schools and spending them on light rail, urban renewal, or subsidies to downtowns.

Husack points out that, in Dade County, Florida, and Los Angeles, California, "local activists not only are rejecting efforts to create bigger jurisdictions, they also are trying to create smaller governments by advocating secession from existing counties and cities." The leaders of these movements, he says, are seeking more control of their own affairs. "They sense that as government jurisdictions get larger, control gradually melts away from voters." He concludes that, "rather than seeking to expand cities, perhaps we should break them up into an array of neighborhood-based governments that would set their own property tax rates, elect their own officials, and give city residents the same control that their suburban counterparts take for granted."[6]

The democratic aspects of regional versus local governments may be responsible for a paradox about density and urban-service costs. Numerous cost-of-sprawl studies—based mostly on hypothetical numbers—claim that higher density development requires lower urban-service costs than low-density development. Harvard researchers Alan Altshuler and José Gómez-Ibáñez say that "sprawl and low density appear to increase the burden new development imposes on infrastructure, but only slightly."[7] Yet a comparison of actual public service costs with densities by Helen Ladd, of Duke University, found that costs increase with density.

Why would urban service costs be higher in higher density cities? Ladd says that part of the problem is that the cost-of-sprawl studies consider mainly capital costs, yet operating costs are higher in high-density areas.[8] But another consideration is that high-density cities tend to be bigger cities. In larger cities, voters tend to have less control over their municipal governments, which are more likely to be captured by special interest groups. The higher urban-service costs in high-density areas may partly reflect subsidies to such special interests rather than actual higher costs associated with density. This becomes one more argument against regional government: It costs too much.

Notes

1. Kenneth T. Jackson, *Crabgrass Frontier: The Suburbanization of the United States* (New York, NY: Oxford University Press, 1985), pp. 144–145.
2. Herbert J. Gans, *The Levittowners: Ways of Life and Politics in a New Suburban Community* (New York, NY: Pantheon, 1967), p. 397.
3. Ibid, p. 42
4. Ibid, pp. 396–397
5. Ibid, p. 398.
6. Howard Husack, "The Case for Breaking Up the Cities," Taubman Center, Kennedy School of Government, http://www.ksg.harvard.edu/taubmancenter/ARTICLES/cities.htm.
7. Alan Altshuler and José Gómez-Ibáñez, *Regulation for Revenue: The Political Economy of Land Use Exactions* (Washington, DC: Brookings; Cambridge, MA: Lincoln Land Institute, 1993), p. 74.
8. Helen Ladd, "Population Growth, Density and the Costs of Providing Public Services," *Urban Studies* 29(2):273–295.

32. Planning

uring World War II, Kenneth Arrow, who later won the Nobel prize in economics, worked as a weather forecaster for the Air Force. Part of his team's job was to forecast the weather a month in advance. But their long-range forecasts were no better than random, so they asked to be relieved of the task. They were told that, "the Commanding General is well aware that the forecasts are no good. However, he needs them for planning purposes." This seems to be the attitude of many city officials: Urban planning doesn't work, but they need it for planning purposes.

As a profession, urban planning has been around for nearly a century. Most towns and rural counties employ at least one planner and most cities and urban counties have entire planning bureaus. This seems amazing since most urban planning's track record is hardly stellar. Cities rarely gave planners lots of power, but two instances in which they did were urban renewal and public housing. Both ended in disaster.

Urban renewal programs of the 1950s and 1960s are case studies of planning disasters. In the 1950s, downtown residents were mostly poor, often single men, living in one-room apartments and tenements. During the next two decades, planners and other progressives encouraged the federal government to take two actions that would profoundly affect downtown areas for a generation.

First, concerned about the plight of the mentally ill confined to state hospitals that were little better than prisons, the federal government gave states incentives for releasing harmless patients. Federal agencies promised to monitor these people to insure they took the medicines they needed and could otherwise take care of themselves. Most of these people ended up in one-room apartments and hotels in downtown areas. Second, concerned about downtown slums, the federal government granted cities huge sums for urban renewal. This money was usually spent condemning and knocking down slums, tenements, and one-room apartments and replacing them with civic buildings, high-class theaters and art centers, luxury housing, and concrete-and-brick plazas.

Due to the actions of one arm of the federal government, hundreds of thousands of people released from mental hospitals by another arm of the federal gov-

457

ernment suddenly had nowhere to live. The agencies that promised to monitor those people found that there was little political or budgetary reward from helping people who didn't vote, and ended up counseling the middle class "worried well" instead. Many of the permanently homeless people in our cities today are victims of these benevolent federal programs.[1]

Failing to foresee this effect, urban planners rejoiced in urban renewal. But the mentally ill were not the only victims of urban renewal. Jane Jacobs's 1963 book, *The Death and Life of Great American Cities*, showed that urban renewal usually transformed living, vital neighborhoods into lifeless concrete monuments or dangerous low-income housing projects. Jacobs tells many stories of neighborhoods where, despite heated protests from the residents, planners evicted people, tore down buildings, and built new housing that soon became far worse than anything that had preceded renewal. Sometimes, after tearing down the older housing, cities ran out of money and the blocks remained vacant, like some bombed-out European city after the war.

Jacobs's book came out just as increasing sums of federal money were becoming available for urban renewal. Naturally, planners hated and reviled the book for many years. Today it is considered a classic and is often cited by planners who claim to have changed their ways. In fact, planners say that one goal of smart growth is to turn dreary suburban neighborhoods into Jacobs's urban villages. Some planners even dream of repeating urban renewal in the suburbs: condemning and buying several blocks of "blighted" low-density suburbs, tearing down the buildings, and replacing them with transit-oriented developments. They obviously failed to carefully read Jacobs's book.

"I hope no reader will try to transfer my observations into guides as to what goes on in towns, or little cities, or in suburbs which still are suburban," she admonished. "We are in enough trouble already from trying to understand big cities in terms of the behavior, and imagined behavior, of towns. To try to understand towns in terms of big cities will only compound confusion."[2] As sociologist Herbert Gans pointed out in his review of Jacobs' book, not everyone wants to live in an urban village.[3]

Although planners today frequently refer to Jacobs in their work,[4] Jacobs has no love for urban planners. In a book on a completely different subject, she refers to one person as a "know-it-all (who also possessed a supposed knowledge of the future) who wades into a piece of the world and its population with visions of how to transform the whole shebang and proceeds to try to do it. The people who founded and shaped the Soviet Union were such types. So were many imperialists who lorded it over colonies in Africa and Asia. So were American slum-clearers, public-housers, and city planners. The World Bank today is full of such types. The visions differ; the hubris and impulse do not."[5]

Architecture critic and one-time planning enthusiast Peter Blake notes that Jacobs showed "that virtually all modern dogma regarding the planning and design of cities was seriously flawed; that chaos was often preferable to order, that variety was preferable to neat uniformity, that small was better than big, and that the ways in which communities developed and grew, naturally, was much more in keeping with the way a free and egalitarian society wanted to function than the sort of predetermined orderliness suggested by such heroes of mine and of my generation as Le Corbusier."[6] Smart growth planners who cite her work to back up their schemes have completely missed her point.

One of the problems with urban renewal is that it removed large numbers of low-income housing units and replaced them mainly with luxury housing. To compensate, planners convinced the government to build low-income housing projects. These turned into their own disasters. One of the most famous, Pruitt-Igoe in St. Louis, was designed by a distinguished architect and received numerous awards. It contained 2,800 apartments in thirty-three identical buildings. Although the government spent nearly as much building Pruitt-Igoe as top-grade luxury apartments, the complex was a complete disaster. The architect's highly praised design left much of the complex extremely vulnerable to criminals, and by 1970 only about a third of the units were occupied. In 1972, as famously recorded on film, the government blew up the complex after just seventeen years.[7]

"Of the past half-century's urban policy blunders in the United States," says Brookings Institution urban expert Pietro Nivola, "few have left a more distinctive, and deadly, mark than the decision to condense a critical mass of impoverished residents into isolated inner-city housing complexes. Many (though not all) of these became pits of blight, crime, and social decay that have abetted the exurban flight of the American middle class. The postwar crime wave in Washington, D.C., for example, can be traced in no small part to the relocation of thousands of poor families from old neighborhoods surrounding the Capitol into new housing projects."[8]

All over the world, planners have produced similar disasters. In Hong Kong, planners tried to build satellite cities that would have both housing and jobs. Nine such satellites were built housing hundreds of thousands of residents—but the jobs never materialized. Planners didn't expect China to initiate economic reforms that attracted the blue-collar factories that they had hoped would move into the satellite cities. So the satellites are now bedroom communities with serious congestion problems and three-hour commutes to jobs in Hong Kong. Other examples are described in the case study on European cities.

As described in the Planning Myth (p. 142), planning disasters are not exceptional, they are inevitable. Despite their scientific pretensions, planners can't predict the future any better than anyone else, nor can they know what millions of people want or need. Lacking this knowledge, they rely on outdated models and fall back on fads such as urban renewal or smart growth. Even if the models have a logical foundation, government planning is inherently political, so the fads become warped to benefit powerful interests such as downtown businesses or construction companies.

Planners claim that their services are needed to help cities prepare for the future. But, to paraphrase Stewart Brand, "All plans are predictions, and all predictions are wrong." No one thirty years ago could predict the personal computer, the internet, or the growth of the dot-com industry. These things have profoundly changed American travel, shopping, and work habits. Writing a plan for today without knowing about such new technologies would lock you in to an obsolete city.

Although we can't predict the future, we know what life is like today. And our cities today are very different than they were a hundred years ago. For example, as *Edge City* author Joel Garreau points out, "We have not built an old downtown from raw ground in seventy-five years." Yet, he goes on, many planners "have a mental image of the gritty centers of the Industrial Age—Chicago, Cleveland, Pittsburgh, New York—as the standard form of American city."[9]

For most people today, downtowns are either irrelevant or, at best, one of many interesting destinations in our cities. Yet planners have spent an inordinate amount of time—and uncountable billions of tax dollars—attempting to "save" downtowns. For example, you would think that Los Angeles planners would have learned from their mistake of building so many freeways into downtown LA. After all, LA's downtown produces less than 5 percent of all the economic activity in the Los Angeles urban area. Yet planners focused a multi-billion dollar rail system on downtown—and wonder why so few people ride it. Of course, the attention planners pay to downtowns is a reflection of downtown's political power. The fetish for rail transit is similarly due to its huge cost, which creates all sorts of constituencies for its construction.

Melvin Webber, professor emeritus at the University of California (Berkeley) Department of City Planning, writes that planners are "heir to the postulates of the Enlightenment with its faith in perfectibility."[10] As Joel Garreau explains, "planners seemed to think that human behavior was malleable, and that nobody was better equipped by dint of intelligence and education than they to do the malleting."[11] The planning literature is permeated with the idea that properly designed cities and streets can transform human behavior: reduce crime, put people to work, get people to drive less, or fix whatever happens to be the social problem of the day.

Planners, Webber notes, love a quote attributed to Winston Churchill: "We shape our cities and then our cities shape us." If true, then whoever has the power to shape cities has power over human behavior. Many planners never questioned whether it was ethical to exercise that power or whether doing so would produce all sorts of unintended consequences. The only question was how. "Many came to believe that something akin to social engineering would soon be possible," says Webber of the planning profession in the 1960s. "If only we could accumulate sufficient scientifically derived knowledge of urban systems and if only we could apply that knowledge to social maladies, we could surely ameliorate troubling social problems."[12]

What results from this, says urban activist Robert Goodman, "is an insistent pattern of arrogant and repressive programs by many prominent, and not so prominent, planners, politicians and corporate leaders, usually in the cause of solving what has been called the 'urban crisis.'"[13] As Peter Blake writes of his own education as a modern architect in the 1930s, "the thought that 'planning' was, just possibly, antithetical to life in a free enterprise society, and antithetical to the kind of colorful chaos that seemed to characterize cities in an egalitarian democracy—well, that thought never crossed our minds. In fact, the few people who occasionally questioned our absolute certitudes were thought to be hopelessly reactionary."[14]

Planners are only a part of an age-old struggle between personal freedom and the social good. "The modern state, through its officials, attempts with varying success to create a terrain and a population with precisely those standardized characteristics that will be easiest to monitor, count, assess, and manage," says Yale political scientists James Scott in *Seeing Like a State*. "The utopian, immanent, and continually frustrated goal of the modern state is to reduce the chaotic, disorderly, constantly changing social reality beneath it to something more closely resembling the administrative grid of its observations."[15]

Scott observes that foresters try to plant forest lands "with same-aged, single-species, uniform trees growing in straight lines in a rectangular flat space cleared of all underbrush."[16] The same principles apply "in urban planning as in forestry," he says. Take, for example, zoning for retails stores. "Once planners applied the formula for a certain number of square feet of commercial space, parceled out among such categories as food and clothing, they realized that they would then have to make these shopping centers monopolistic within their areas, lest nearby competition draw away their clientele. The whole point was to legislate the formula, thereby guaranteeing the shopping center a monopoly of its catchment area. Rigid, single-use zoning is, then, not just an aesthetic measure. It is an indispensable aid to scientific planning, and it can also be used to transform formulas posing as observations into self-fulfilling prophesies."[17]

"The great weakness in the case made by planners," says transportation expert Alan Pisarski, "is its inability to demonstrate that planners' goals parallel or support public preferences. The dialogue thus takes on the character of a diatribe, in which those who 'know better' prescribe how the 'masses' should live."[18]

Unfortunately for planners, Americans are notably resistant to restrictions on their personal freedom. Michael McCormick, the author of smart-growth legislation passed by the Washington state legislature, lamented this fact in a speech he gave at a 1997 planning conference held in Vancouver, BC. "I like British Columbians because of their willingness to be governed," he stated. "They accept regulation and I just think, wouldn't it be great if we could have that south of the border?"[19] Fortunately for Americans, we don't.

Notes

1. E. Fuller Torrey, MD, *Nowhere to Go: The Tragic Odyssey of the Homeless Mentally Ill* (New York, NY: Harper & Row, 1988), 256 pp.
2. Jane Jacobs, *The Death and Live of Great American Cities* (New York, NY: Vintage, 1963), p. 16.
3. Herbert J. Gans, "City Planning and Urban Realities: A Review of The Death and Life of Great American Cities," *Books in Review* 1961:170–173.
4. For example, see Roger Montgomery, "Is There Still Life in *The Death and Life?*" *Journal of the American Planning Association*, Summer, 1998, pp. 269–274.
5. Jane Jacobs (ed.), *A Schoolteacher in Old Alaska: The Story of Hannah Breece* (New York, NY: Random House, 1995), p. 215.
6. Peter Blake, *No Place Like Utopia: Modern Architecture and the Company We Kept* (New York, NY: Alfred Knopf, 1993), p. 290.
7. Peter Geoffrey Hall, *Cities of Tomorrow: An Intellectual History of Urban Planning and Design in the Twentieth Century* (Cambridge, MA: Blackwell, 1988; updated to 1996), pp. 235–238.
8. Pietro Nivola, *Fit for Fat City: A "Lite" Menu of European Policies to Improve Our Urban Form*, (Washington, DC: Brookings Institution Policy Brief #44, 1999), http://www.brook.edu/comm/policybriefs/pb044/pb44.htm.
9. Ibid, pp. 104–105.
10. Melvin M. Webber and Frederick C. Collignon, "Ideas that Drove DCRP," *Berkeley Planning Journal* Volume 12, pp. 1–19.
11. Joel Garreau, *Edge City: Life on the New Frontier* (New York, NY: Doubleday, 1991), p. 222.
12. Webber and Collignon, "Ideas that Drove DCRP."
13. Robert Goodman, *After the Planners* (New York, NY: Simon & Schuster, 1971), p. 11.
14. Peter Blake, *No Place Like Utopia: Modern Architecture and the Company We Kept* (New York, NY: Alfred Knopf, 1993), p. 35.
15. James C. Scott, *Seeing Like a State: How Certain Schemes to Improve the Human Condition Have Failed* (New Haven, CT: Yale University Press, 1998), pp. 81–82.
16. Ibid, p. 82.
17. Ibid, p. 141.
18. Alan E. Pisarski, "Issues in Transportation and Growth Management," *in* David J. Brower, David R. Godschalk, and Douglas R. Porter (eds.), *Understanding Growth Management: Critical Issues and a Research Agenda* (Washington, DC: Urban Land Institute, 1989), pp. 126–127.
19. Michael McCormick, speech before the joint convention of the Washington Chapter of the American Planning Association and the Planning Institute of British Columbia, Vancouver, BC, April 23, 1997.

Ted's Aggressive Agenda

I n November, 1998, Minnesota voters elected former professional wrestler Jesse Ventura as governor in a tight, three-way race. Ventura promised to revolutionize state politics, and his campaign brought many people to the polls who had never voted before. Among other things, Ventura said he would abolish the Metropolitan Council, the Twin Cities' agency that many planners regarded as the second most powerful regional government in the nation after Portland's Metro. While "relatively few regional agencies can coerce local governments to respect regional plans," says the Urban Land Institute's Douglas Porter, "the Portland and Twin City regional agencies possess substantial powers to influence local decision making on land use issues."[1] Many Twin Cities' suburbs resented the agency's control of things that they thought should be local, such as where to build sewer and water facilities.

Ventura also widely distributed his statement of "beliefs and budget principles," including: "Spend the people's money on things that are needed, not things that are nice." This led many people to think that he would oppose a light-rail proposal then being considered by the Metropolitan Council.

Table One: The Twin Cities Urbanized Area

	1950	1990	1998
Population (thousands)	986	2,080	2,322
Land area square miles	232	1,064	1,192
Density	4,254	1,956	1,948

Source: Census Bureau for 1950 and 1990, FHwA, Highway Statistics 1998 for 1998. FHwA land area data are not exactly comparable with Census Bureau data since they use slightly different criteria for determining urbanized area boundaries.

The Met Council (as Minnesotans call it for short) had published a "regional blueprint" and a "transportation policy plan" in 1996 that proposed various smart-growth ideas, including:

- Concentrating development inside the beltline freeways that circle the area;[2]
- Limiting development outside of an "urban reserve boundary" by refusing to extend sewer and water services;[3]
- Giving local jurisdictions "housing density benchmarks to make the 2040 Urban Reserve last at least 40+ years";[4]
- Outside the urban reserve, limiting development to one house every 40 acres in agricultural areas and to one house every 10 acres in other rural areas;[5]
- Limiting the expansion of urban roadways for twenty-five years;
- Emphasizing transit and transit-oriented development.

Table Two: The City of Minneapolis

	1950	1990	1998
Population (thousands)	522	368	352
Land area square miles	54	55	55
Density	9,697	6,700	6,400

Source: Census Bureau. Land area and density for 1998 are estimated.

The council admitted that the region's roads "are approaching or exceeding capacity," but said that "the social and environmental constraints are too great to continue with large highway expansion programs to escape congestion."[6] So that council decided that "expansion of roadways will be very limited in the next 25

Figure One: Twin Cities Area Densities

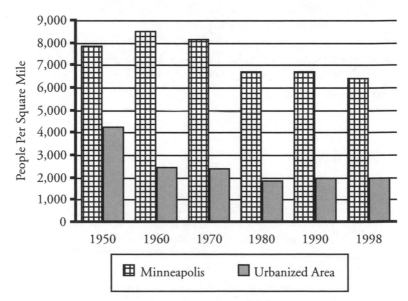

Source: Census Bureau and Federal Highway Administration.

years."[7] The only highway expansions that would be seriously considered, said the plan, were the addition of high-occupancy vehicle lanes to three freeways.[8]

Table Three: Twin Cities Transportation

Miles of freeway per million people	134
Annual miles driven per capita	8,833
Passenger miles per capita	14,133
Annual transit miles per capita	108
Annual transit trips per capita	28
Auto commuters	90.3%
Transit commuters	5.4%
Walk/cycle commuters	4.3%

Source: FHwA, Highway Statistics 1998, FTA, Transit Profiles 1998, 1990 Census. All data are 1998 except commuting data, which are from 1990. Passenger miles per capita are 1.6 times miles driven per capita.

"As traffic congestion builds," said the plan hopefully, "alternative travel modes will become more attractive."[9] The Met Council also operates the regional bus system, known as Metro Transit. Although the council has the authority to plan how all transportation funds in the region will be spent, the only funds that the council itself spends are for transit—highway funds are spent by other agencies. A plan that emphasized transit over highways therefore enhances the council's budget and power.

The Twin Cities transit system needed some good news, because Metro Transit saw ridership decline from about 100 million trips per year in 1970 to 62 million trips per year in 1997. Minnesotans like to say that they don't mind the weather, but they don't like standing at a bus stop in the cold of a Minnesota winter, or the heat of a Minnesota summer, any more than anyone else. Yet far from being a problem, transit's decline is symbolic of a booming economy that has made auto ownership affordable to almost everyone who is physically able to drive. The Twin Cities today enjoys one of the lowest rates of unemployment and highest average incomes of major midwestern cities.

The Twin Cities is also one of the most mobile regions in the country. The region has well above the average number of freeway miles per capita—about 135 miles per million people as compared to the U.S. urban area average of about 114. Its non-freeway arterials are broad and often paralleled by frontage roads so that local traffic doesn't interfere with through movement of cars and trucks. This means that the region has far less congestion than the average urban area. Although it has a population of more than 2.3 million people who collectively drive more than 56 million miles per day,[10] it is the largest metropolitan area rated by the Environmental Protection Agency as having no air pollution problems.

Minneapolis, St. Paul, and their suburbs are built around dozens of lakes, yet even when counting only land the region has a low population density of about 1,900 people per square mile.[11] Broad streets and thoroughfares provide plenty of room for bicyclists, but cycling is strictly a seasonal form of transportation as few are willing to brave the winter's cold and ice on a two-wheeled vehicle. The low congestion and low population density may be important reasons why the region's economy is thriving despite being so far from the nation's Sun Belt.

Rather than see these things as positive features of a healthy, livable region, the Metropolitan Council worried about poverty and the decline of certain neighborhoods and suburbs.[12] While these are problems worth worrying about, it is not clear how increased densities and reduced mobility can solve them. Instead, these policies would probably aggravate the problems and certainly irritated many suburban officials. So Ventura's talk of abolishing the Metropolitan Council was welcomed by many people. Since the governor appointed the members of the council, his voice would carry a lot of authority over its future.

Instead of abolishing the council, however, Ventura replaced all of the members of the council who might resist smart growth with smart-growth advocates. As chair of the council, he appointed Ted Mondale, a state senator and son of the former vice-president. Mondale was known for having "an aggressive agenda" in favor of light rail and containing urban sprawl.[13]

Mondale soon made it clear that his agenda was much more extreme than that of the previous Metropolitan Council. Although transit carries only 5 percent of the region's commuters and less than 2 percent of other trips, the Met Council had been spending half the region's federal transportation dollars on transit. This wasn't enough for Mondale, who proposed to increase transit's share to 70 percent.[14] He also announced that the council would be tougher on suburbs whose plans didn't call for high-density housing and mass transit. "Where are your transit plans?" Mondale said he was asking suburbs. "Where's your density?"

"If we're giving money to communities that are thumbing their noses" at the council's priorities, asked Mondale, "then what's it all about? It's a charade!"[15] Under pressure from the Met Council, the town of Rosemont agreed to rezone an area for much higher densities despite "spirited community opposition."

Naturally, the council's policies were controversial, especially as land prices began to rise in response to the limits the council placed on the urban boundary. In response, Mondale said he would be willing to expand the urban boundary slightly if the suburbs promised to fill in the areas with high-density, transit-oriented developments. "What we're getting now is not what we want," he said.[16]

Light rail was even more controversial. With support from Governor Ventura, the legislature had agreed to put up $100 million in funding for a light-rail line that was expected to cost $446 million. The rail funding legislation was a part of a larger, last-minute package, and rail opponents complained that the legislature was not allowed to vote on rail by itself. Ventura's support for light rail may have been influenced by the fact that the first line was going to go through Minneapolis's

Phillips neighborhood, where he grew up. This inner-city neighborhood was a combination of housing, commercial, and industrial facilities, and many considered it to be "in decline." Architectural renderings gratuitously renamed the neighborhood "Ventura Community" and promised lots of green trees and colorful gardens if light rail was built. Beneath the natural colors, their plans called for infilling every private vacant lot with high-density housing or offices.

Planners predicted that light rail would inspire businesses to locate thousands of new jobs in the neighborhood. Local businesses made it clear that their main interest was getting a new freeway on-ramp to connect them with Interstate 35W. "Lack of [freeway] access has had an adverse impact on businesses, institutions, and residences," they said.[17] But they supported light rail if it was part of a package. Neighborhood residents were excited about redevelopment that planners said the light rail would inspire. But to make sure that such redevelopment took place, planners set aside $9 million to subsidize such activities.[18]

Legislative opponents of the rail project managed to include a provision in the law requiring the Minnesota Department of Transportation do a benefit-cost analysis demonstrating whether rail was the most cost efficient solution to the region's transportation problems. The department analysis counted a wide variety of social benefits, including air pollution reductions, time savings for transit riders, and the reduction in accident losses. The analysis did not include any social costs, such as the amount of time auto drivers would lose due to the increased congestion caused by light-rail vehicles running in city streets. The department found 42 cents worth of benefits for every dollar in costs.[19] Naturally, they considered this to be cost effective and the governor endorsed the plan.

Mondale warns that if the region relied on roads it would have to spend $15 to $20 billion to keep up with congestion over the next twenty years.[20] But using light rail to relieve congestion will cost far more. The Metropolitan Council estimates that the line will reduce regional auto traffic by 9,000 trips per day. Twin Cities auto traffic grows by that many trips each week, so the region would have to build a new light-rail line every week just to maintain congestion at current levels. Over the next twenty years, this would cost about $1 trillion.

The plan ran into trouble on grounds other than cost, however. The state had hired Parsons Brinkerhof to oversee construction, including selecting which company would get to build the line. Two major construction firms with rail experience bid on the project: Bechtel and Raytheon. No one seemed to mind that Parsons Brinkerhof was a partner with Bechtel on several other projects, including construction of Boston's $12 billion central artery. But then the engineer—a former Bechtel employee—that Parsons Brinkerhoff placed in charge of the project rejected Raytheon's bid on the grounds that Raytheon was not financially capable of building such a major project. Since Raytheon was building light-rail lines elsewhere, this reason made no sense.

A local judge ruled that the engineer had acted inappropriately. The Federal

Transit Administration told the state that this apparent conflict of interest could jeopardize federal funding for the project, so the state asked a different company, O'Brien Kreitzberg of San Francisco, to manage the project. In the meantime, cost estimates have risen to about $625 million.[21]

Ventura's goal is to get the rail line operating before the end of his first term of office. While legislative opponents were unable to withdraw state funding, federal funding is not yet assured. But supporters are so confident that the line will be completed that the state has already ordered light-rail vehicles.

Notes

1. Douglas Porter [Urban Land Institute], "Regional Governance of Metropolitan Form: The Missing Link in Relating Land Use and Transportation," *in* Transportation Research Board, *Transportation, Urban Form, and the Environment* (Washington, DC: TRB, 1991), p. 68, p. 74.
2. Metropolitan Council, *Regional Blueprint* (St. Paul, MN: Metropolitan Council, 1996), p. 49.
3. Ibid, pp. 47–48.
4. Ibid, p. 49.
5. Ibid, pp. 52–53.
6. Metropolitan Council, *Transportation Policy Plan* (St. Paul, MN: Metropolitan Council, 1996), p. 17.
7. Ibid, p. 54.
8. Ibid, pp. 72, 76.
9. Ibid, p. 54.
10. Federal Highway Administration, *Highway Statistics 1998* (Washington, DC: FHwA, 1999), table HM-72.
11. Ibid.
12. Metropolitan Council, *Regional Blueprint*, p. 11.
13. Patricia Lopez Baden, "Ventura's choice of Ted Mondale for Met Council sends signals" *Star Tribune*, January 27, 1999.
14. David Peterson and Laurie Blake, "More money on mass transit, less on highways," *Star Tribune*, October 1, 1999.
15. David Peterson, "Mondale says Met Council has big plans," *Star Tribune*, October 11, 1999.
16. David Peterson, "Met Council will formally give cities more room to grow," *Star Tribune*, March 23, 2000.
17. Phillips Partnership, *I-35W Access Project: The Phillips Partnership Transportation Initiative* (Minneapolis, MN: Phillips Partnership, 1999), 1 p.
18. Dan Wascoe, Jr., "Subsidies urged for rail-station areas," *Star-Tribune*, November 9, 1999, p. B7.
19. Minnesota Department of Transportation, "Hiawatha Corridor LRT Benefit-Cost Analysis," November 4, 1999, p. 9.
20. Ted Mondale, presentation at the Regional Growth Seminar for Realtors, St. Paul, MN, December 8, 1999.
21. Doug Grow, "Wink, wink: This is really for our own good," *Star-Tribune*, October 1, 2000, http://webserv3.startribune.com:80/stOnLine/cgi-bin/article?thisSlug=GROW01&date=01-Oct-2000&word=krinkie.

The Public-Involvement Myth

Myth: Public involvement helps people democratically produce the cities and
neighborhoods they want.
Reality: The public involvement processes used by urban planners are neither
democratic nor do they accurately measure regional opinion.

Planners say they want to help people have and maintain the kind of neighborhoods they want. Most planning efforts include a public involvement
process: slick publications, open houses, invitations to comment, public hearings. Yet comprehensive land use planning was originally considered a job for
experts—architects, scientists, people who had received training in technical planning concepts. "Comprehensive land-use planning, at least as it has been proposed in the United States, is incompatible with democratic processes," says economist Robert Nelson. "In fact, planning was very explicitly intended by its early
proponents to take the place of political decision making for many areas of government activity. . . by removing key decisions from this process and putting
them in the hands of technical experts, i.e., planners."[1]

Planners lost their credibility as experts during the 1950s and 1960s when they
imposed their controversial and destructive urban-renewal programs on many
inner-city neighborhoods. While the 1926 Supreme Court was impressed by planners' expertise, by 1966 zoning attorney Richard Babcock could "sense a growing
skepticism on the part of the courts toward the usefulness of the planner. . . .
There is an increasing judicial suspicion that planners. . . drift where the wind
blows strongest."[2]

Planners responded to their lost credibility by promoting public involvement
in planning. A plan written with the help of the residents of a city or neighborhood was much more likely to withstand political and judicial scrutiny than a
plan imposed on people without their agreement. Yet planners remain ambivalent
about public involvement. In 1988, surveys by University of Maryland planning
theorist Howard Baum found that:

- Four out of five planners believe in public involvement during the first stage
  of planning, when problems are identified.

- But less than half believe that the public has the skills needed to help identify goals.
- Fewer than two out of five planners believe that citizens can understand alternative goals well enough to choose among them.

Baum says planners chafe at any political "constraint on their effectiveness," but few recognize that such constraints stem partly from "public concerns about limiting the role of experts in democratic decision making." Most planners "insist on reasserting a traditional planning role without, or in spite of, acknowledgment that public expectations of planning have changed." In fact, says Baum, nearly half the planners surveyed believed that "planners should have more power [and] should receive more support [and] larger budgets for their efforts."[3]

In the 1960s, Herbert Gans noted that Levittown's town planner "often appealed for popular support of planning through 'citizen participation,' but he gave people no opportunity to participate, and his actions indicated that he only wanted them to assent to his proposals," observed Gans. "Levittowners who wanted to talk to him found it difficult to see him, and when they succeeded, he was insensitive to their concerns."[4] The planner's master plan required that "future houses be sited in 'cluster subdivisions,' a series of cul-de-sacs surrounded by public open space." The planner claimed that houses on a conventional grid "create urban sprawl," which Gans called "ludicrous." Today's planners say exactly the opposite, but, Gans noted, the cluster subdivision was "a current fad in site planning."[5] The planner's "policies were irrational," concluded Gans, "and they asked attitude as well as behavioral changes from people, requiring their conversion to his vision of the community without taking their demands or needs into account."[6]

After talking with dozens of planners and architects, Joel Garreau concluded that planning was more about visionary idealism than technical expertise. In addition to thinking "that human behavior was malleable," planners "believed that the physical environment they wanted to shape could and would shape society. The places they would like to plan would lead, they believed, to fundamental, welcome, and long-overdue changes in human mores and human attitudes."[7]

The idea that good design will improve human morals and attitudes goes back at least to the nineteenth century utopian movements. It was fundamental to the thinking of many architects, including both Le Corbusier and Frank Lloyd Wright. Someone who believes this is not going to give much consideration to the wants and desires expressed by people living in today's cities. After all, those people are victims of poor design, and thus their preferences are suspect. We know what's best for them, and if they disagree now they will find out how right we were once we've imposed it on them.

This may sound paranoid. But this attitude isn't much different from that of the planner interviewed by Garreau who wants to "limit people's movement" by "enormously" raising the cost of driving in order to force Americans to live closer together. As Baum found in his surveys, "only a minority [of planners] accept. . .

that citizens can provide a sense of what is acceptable and what is not acceptable to the community."

As a democratic tool, planning leaves much to be desired. While planners may be wrong in thinking that citizens lack the technical expertise to get involved, they would be right in thinking that citizens lack the incentive to get involved. The process of preparing a comprehensive plan is long and tedious, and few people will get or stay involved unless a plan clearly threatens something they value. This gives planners and their supporters opportunities to manipulate public sentiments during the planning process. One important technique is to rewrite the language so that soothing, positive terms are substituted for planners' real intentions:

- Obstructing roads and creating congestion is called *traffic calming*;
- Roads built with highway user fees are *subsidized*;
- Transit funded by highway user fees is *balanced transportation*;
- Spending money on rail transit that few people will use is called *creating choices*;
- Auto-hostile design is *pedestrian-friendly* design;
- Requiring developers to build a few units of low-income housing at the expense of all other home buyers is called *creating affordable housing*;
- The mobility provided by automobiles is called *auto dependency*;
- House lots larger than 5,000 square feet are *wasteful*;
- Most deceptively, policies that increase congestion, making housing unaffordable, and raise taxes are called *smart growth*.

Visioning processes used by planners in Oregon, Utah, and elsewhere supposedly help people to choose their own futures. In fact, no matter what people say they want, the processes always end up with the same proposals: density, rail transit, and pedestrian-friendly design. The very idea of visioning—the notion that we can decide on what the future should be like and impose that idea on people in the future—is incompatible with human freedom and technological change.

"It is in that very ability of a social organization to promote a repressive ideology while masking its effects in the mannerisms and rhetoric of 'freedom,' 'democracy,' and 'opportunity' that we find one of the unique forms of repression in both this country and the Soviet Union," says Robert Goodman, who describes himself as an "advocacy planner" defending "the disenfranchised" against the planners. "The planners' own form of ostensible 'value free,' 'scientific' methods have contributed to this repression."[8]

Growth control advocate Eben Fodor urges people to "use democracy to control the growth machine." He quotes H. L. Mencken as saying, "The cure for the [ills] of democracy is more democracy."[9] Only Fodor knows why he substituted the word "ills" for Mencken's original word, but it is clear why he quoted Mencken out of context: "Childish credulity is visible in the doctrine that the cure for the evils of democracy is more democracy. This is like saying that the cure for crime is more crime."[10] Smart-growth advocates probably don't appreciate some of

Mencken's other famous statements either, such as: "There is always a well-known solution to every human problem—neat, plausible, and wrong."[11]

The various 1000 friends and other smart-growth groups might not agree with Fodor's slow-growth philosophy. But like him, they will use "democracy" when it is to their advantage, while they oppose democracy when it is not. Their idea of democracy is a public involvement process accessible only to the professional interest group lobbyists, one that makes the real decisions before members of the public find out what is going on. As Peter Gordon and Harry Richardson say, "the growth in local enforcement and regulation in the United States was essentially anti-democratic."[12]

Notes

1. Robert Nelson, *Zoning and Property Rights: An Analysis of the American System of Land-Use Regulation* (Cambridge, MA: MIT, 1977), p. 192.
2. Richard Babcock, *The Zoning Game: Municipal Practices and Policies* (Madison, WI: University of Wisconsin Press, 1966), p. 83.
3. Howell Baum, "Problems of Governance and the Professions of Planners: The Planning Profession in the 1980s," *in* Daniel Schaffer (ed.), *Two Centuries of American Planning* (Baltimore, MD: Johns Hopkins, 1988), pp. 279–302
4. Herbert J. Gans, *The Levittowners: Ways of Life and Politics in a New Suburban Community* (New York, NY: Pantheon, 1967), p. 393.
5. Ibid, p. 391.
6. Ibid, p. 395.
7. Joel Garreau, *Edge City: Life on the New Frontier* (New York, NY: Doubleday, 1991), p. 222.
8. Robert Goodman, *After the Planners* (New York, NY: Simon & Schuster, 1971), p. 12.
9. Eben Fodor, *Better Not Bigger: How to Take Control of Urban Growth and Improve Your Community* (Stony Creek, CT: New Society, 1999), p. 35.
10. H. L. Mencken, *Minority Report: H. L. Mencken's Notebooks* (New York, NY: Knopf, 1956), p. 29.
11. H. L. Mencken, *Prejudices: Second Series*, (New York, NY: Knopf, 1920), p. 158.
12. Harry W. Richardson and Peter Gordon, "Market Planning: Oxymoron or Common Sense?" *Journal of the American Planning Association* 59(3) [Summer, 1993]: pp. 347–352.

33. Zoning

Nineteenth-century architects and urban visionaries laid out many plans for redesigning cities. But those plans were frustrated because they had no way of influencing private property owners short of actually buying their land. That changed in 1916 when New York City passed the first comprehensive zoning ordinance. Though initially conceived by retailers who wanted protection from the growing garment district, the idea quickly expanded to protect areas of single-family homes from invasions of apartment dwellings.

Early zoning laws were designed "to protect residential neighborhoods from commerce, industry, and undesirable immigrants," says Stewart Brand.

Soon, legal barriers clattered into place all over the cities—residential here and here, commercial center in there, industrial out yonder. No more unsanitary high-density living areas (there had been a health problem). No more mixed living and working (there had been nightmarish sweatshops). And no melting pot; these cities would be stratified strictly by economic class, creed, and race. It would all be efficient and just, because experts were in charge.[1]

The people who developed zoning were not architects or planners but lawyers—almost a necessity since most people at that time believed that government had little or no right to interfere with private property owners. To bolster their legal position, the lawyers turned to architects and professional planners as "experts" who could scientifically show that cities benefited from zoning.

They lost the first great zoning case in district court. Interestingly, the judge ruled against them not because zoning violated the rights of property owners but because it violated another constitutional right, the right of people to travel and live wherever they wanted. Zoning was unconstitutional, he said, because its purpose was "to classify the population and segregate them according to their income or situation in life." His decision, however, was overturned by the Supreme Court, which was impressed by the weight of "experts" the lawyers rallied to their cause. "The matter of zoning has received much attention at the hands of commissions and experts," wrote the court, "and the [favorable] results of their investigations have been set forth in comprehensive reports."[2]

In its 1926 decision, the court supported zoning as a legitimate device for controlling nuisances. Under traditional nuisance law, people could prevent the opening of, say, a dump in their neighborhood as something that would reduce the value of their property by much more than it would add to the value of the property on which it was located. The Supreme Court concluded that an apartment house, when located in a neighborhood of single-family homes, was just such a nuisance. "Under these circumstances, apartment houses, which in a different environment would be not only entirely unobjectionable but highly desirable, come very near to being nuisances."[3]

Before World War II, most zoning ordinances were *cumulative*: An area zoned for single-family homes could only have single-family homes, but an area zoned for multifamily homes could also have single-family homes. An area zoned commercial could also have homes, while an area zoned industrial could also have commercial or residential developments. Since a single-family home could hardly be considered a nuisance to an apartment, retailer, or factory, the lawyers believed that any other type of zoning would be unconstitutional.

By the end of World War II, however, the lawyers had mostly been replaced by planners. Confident of their ability to determine the "right" use for any piece of land, planners made zoning more completely *exclusive*: Areas zoned industrial could not have retail stores; areas zoned commercial could not have housing. "If the industrial pigs were to be kept out of the residential parlor," comments zoning attorney Richard Babcock, "then those who enjoyed the parlor should most certainly stay out of the pen."[4] Since planners could not possibly guess the appropriate ratio of single-family, multifamily, commercial, and industrial land their cities would need in the distant future, this less-flexible zoning concept is responsible for many of the land "shortages" cities suffer today.

Zoning is also often a victim of political compromise. Babcock points out that interest groups often use zoning to limit competition. For example, have you ever wondered why downtown areas have so few gasoline stations? It is because the zoning in many downtowns forbids new gas stations—but grandfathers in the old ones. Naturally, the existing gasoline dealers strongly supported this zoning.

"There is no doubt that zoning is often regarded as a convenient and intentional device to limit competition," says Babcock. "A few years ago the Detroit retail gasoline dealers petitioned the Detroit Common Council to revise the municipal zoning ordinance to prohibit any more gas stations. In 1957 the Chicago Independent Grocers' Association, whose members sell package beer, endorsed an amendment to the Chicago zoning ordinance which allowed nonconforming grocery stores to remain in residential areas but provided that taverns in the same districts would be eliminated in seven years."[5]

Smart-growth zoning codes go beyond exclusive to *prescriptive*. A traditional zoning code might set *minimum* lot sizes of 10,000 square feet, but would allow homes on larger lots (an acre is 43,560 square feet). But smart-growth zoning codes set both minimum and maximum lot sizes. The 5,000-square-foot lot that is the minimum in a suburb might be the maximum a smart-growth code would allow, and 2,500-square-foot lots—50-feet by 50-feet—might be preferred. Row houses and low-rise apartments with as many as thirty-five units per acre are more preferable. Mid-rise mixed-use buildings with fifty housing units plus offices and retail are even better. Smart-growth codes may also mandate design features such as porches or window placements.

Andres Duany says that plans should be "drawn with such precision that only the architectural detail is left to future designers."[6] Such rigid zoning is "not just an aesthetic measure," says planning critic James Scott. "It is an indispensable aid to scientific planning, and it can also be used to transform formulas posing as observations into self-fulfilling prophesies."[7]

Today, most cities in the U.S. have zoning. The largest exception is Houston. Planners often point to Houston as an example of what happens when you don't have planning and zoning. In fact, Houston's sprawl is little different from the sprawl around Atlanta or St. Louis. Moreover, the people living in most of Houston's neighborhoods feel just as protected from nuisances as people living in a zoned city. As described in the Houston case study (p. 501), its neighborhoods rely on protective covenants to achieve the same end as zoning.

Robert Nelson notes that either covenants or zoning divide land ownership into two "bundles" of property rights. One bundle, the rights to own, use, and sell the land for its current use, is kept in the hands of individual owners. The other bundle, the right to change to a different land use, is held collectively. As practiced in Houston, covenants have an important advantage over zoning: Groups of landowners can together decide to change the land use of their neighborhood. Under zoning, only the government can change it. But "the process of transition under zoning," says Nelson, "produces many misunderstandings and great ill will between neighborhood residents and developers. . . . Developer strong-arm tactics and even corruption of public officials have been required to bring about transfers of the zoning rights needed to allow development of new land uses."[8]

The difficulties of changing zoning can inspire corruption and bribery. One developer told a *Harpers* writer investigating corruption in zoning, "We know where we stand now—$25,000 for zoning for a trailer park in this county. Why upset things by talking about it?"[9] Commenting on such corruption, law professor Bernard Siegan asks, "Can one justify an institution where consumer demand can frequently only be satisfied by resorting to illegal or morally and socially questionable tactics?"[10] When corruption is revealed, people tend to blame the people involved, not the system that provoked the corruption. But it is unreasonable to expect that zoning adopted today will make sense ten or twenty years from now. If there is no orderly way to change, then changes will be disorderly. As Joel Garreau quotes a successful Maryland developer, "There is no zoning, only deals."[11]

This leads to the second advantage of covenants over zoning: Covenants actually give landowners better protection than zoning. Since government can change zoning on a whim, anyone with the right connections can make their property much more valuable by using those connections. Most neighborhood residents can tell stories of some piece of land near their neighborhood that they thought was zoned for one use and instead was suddenly developed for some other use.

In fast-growing urban areas such as Portland, corruption is less of a threat to many neighborhoods than idealism. People who want to protect the character of their neighborhoods are told it is their duty to accept "their share" of the newcomers. "Or would you rather have sprawl?" The neighborhoods most threatened by idealism are those by a light rail line, since planners want to boost ridership by getting as many people as possible within a quarter mile of light-rail station.

Though many planners blame urban blight on the automobile, Andres Duany and many planners blame zoning as much or more. Says Randall Arendt, a planning professor at the University of Massachusetts, zoning "is why America looks the way it does. The law is the major problem with the development pattern."

In fact, there is plenty of evidence that America would look pretty much the way it does even without zoning. Houston and many suburban towns lack zoning yet are not significantly different from areas with zoning. But having blamed sprawl on zoning, planners say they are going to fix the problems caused by their predecessors using more—and more prescriptive—zoning. Instead of forbidding mixed uses, they will mandate them. Instead of forbidding apartments from single-family neighborhoods, they will require them. Can planners fix the problems they themselves have created? "Better zoning is no more the answer to no zoning," says Siegan (echoing H. L. Mencken), "than better censorship is to no censorship."[12]

Notes

1. Stewart Brand, *How Buildings Learn: What Happens After They're Built* (New York, NY: Viking, 1994), p. 78.
2. Robert Nelson, *Zoning and Property Rights: An Analysis of the American System of Land-Use Regulation* (Cambridge, MA: MIT, 1977), p. 64.
3. Richard Babcock, *The Zoning Game: Municipal Practices and Policies* (Madison, WI: University of Wisconsin Press, 1966), p. 4.
4. Ibid, pp. 127–128.
5. Ibid, p. 74.
6. Andres Duany, Elizabeth Plater-Zyberk, and Jeff Speck, *Suburban Nation: The Rise of Sprawl and the Decline of the American Dream* (New York, NY: North Point Press, 2000), p. 228.
7. James C. Scott, *Seeing Like a State: How Certain Schemes to Improve the Human Condition Have Failed* (New Haven, CT: Yale University Press, 1998), p. 141.
8. Ibid, pp. 88–89.
9. Alfred Balk, "Invitation to Bribery," *Harper's Magazine*, October, 1966, p. 18.
10. Bernard Siegan, *Land Use Without Zoning* (Lexington, MA: Lexington Books, 1972), p. 196.
11. Joel Garreau, *Edge City: Life on the New Frontier* (New York, NY: Doubleday, 1991), p. 223.
12. Siegan, *Land Use Without Zoning*, p. 144.

The Market-Failure Myth

Myth: Market failure leads to urban sprawl, pollution, and other environmental problems that can only be cured by planning.

Reality: Most environmental problems are the result of government failure, not market failure, and markets often are the key to solving those problems.

There may be no paradox between the worldwide dismantling of authoritarian regimes and the U.S.'s leanings to command-and-control urban policies. People want security and stability. Central planning failed to provide that security and stability; it couldn't even provide basic necessities—in the late 1980s, the average Soviet grocery store had less than a dozen different products for sale. So people demanded change. But people will also want change if they feel insecure in a market economy. When New York City adopted the nation's first comprehensive zoning ordinance in 1916, its advocates justified it by saying:

> New York City has certainly reached a point beyond which continued unplanned growth cannot take place without inviting social and economic disaster. It is too big a city, the social and economic interests involved are too great to permit the continuance of laissez faire methods of earlier days.[1]

Today, the same arguments are heard in cities throughout the nation as justifications for even more planning and regulation. To most economists in the U.S., the main justification for government intervention in private affairs is the failure of the marketplace: monopolies, externalities such as pollution, and public goods such as scenery. Gordon and Richardson address these points in a proposal for "market planning." They point out that:

- Far from being monopolies, "most markets are reasonably competitive."
- Externalities are due to "unenforced private property rights" and the "appropriate action is not regulation by planners" but, where needed, establishment and enforcement of those property rights.
- True public goods are rare. Most of "what passes for public goods can be provided by the private sector almost as easily as by the public sector."[2]

Some say that markets are efficient but inequitable, and that planners must intervene to insure equity. But when government planners and regulators are captured by wealthy special interests, their plans usually make the inequities worse. "The evidence suggests that market approaches are more likely to result in efficiency with equity," say Gordon and Richardson, "while planning efforts often result in inefficiency with inequity." For example, planning has often discriminated against the poor by destroying low-income housing.

Gordon and Richardson argue that regulatory approaches have failed, and that more successful approaches would instead rely on incentives and the power of the market. For example, they point to "a market success story surpassing the wildest dreams of energy planners": In 1988, people drove their cars 286 billion miles more than in 1978, but they used 10 billion gallons less fuel. This increase in efficiency was due almost entirely to market-driven gasoline prices giving people incentives to buy more fuel-efficient cars.

Garreau observes that planners and architects have fallen into an "intellectual ambush" that leads them "to dismiss the value of the marketplace." They assume that they know how people should live, and since Americans aren't living that way, they conclude either that markets aren't working or that they are evil. "It can't be that they like it. It must be that capitalism enslaves them, and the developers give them no choice."[3]

"There is a temptation to say that economics is not enough; there should be some additional limitations, perhaps just enough to insure that the strips along roads and highways will be more aesthetically pleasing," says Bernard Siegan. "One might then ask: aesthetically pleasing to whom? But the bigger problem comes from entrusting this power to some person or some groups who necessarily have their own values and beliefs."[4] We don't give that power to others in the areas of speech, press, and religion, Siegan points out. Why should we do it for land use?

Markets are powerful forces, far more so than the regulatory tools used by planners. As Jack Linville, a designer now in the private sector who once worked for the American Planning Association, told Garreau, "planners and architects [are] trying to fight against a surge that is just overwhelming."[5] The inevitable results when government tries to regulate the market are unintended consequences that often cause more harm than the problems regulation were supposed to solve.

Notes

1. Robert Nelson, *Zoning and Property Rights: An Analysis of the American System of Land-Use Regulation* (Cambridge, MA: MIT, 1977), p. 190.
2. Harry W. Richardson and Peter Gordon, "Market Planning: Oxymoron or Common Sense?" *Journal of the American Planning Association* 59(3, Summer, 1993): pp. 347–352.
3. Joel Garreau, *Edge City: Life on the New Frontier* (New York, NY: Doubleday, 1991), p. 234.
4. Bernard Siegan, *Land Use Without Zoning* (Lexington, MA: Lexington Books, 1972), p. 144.
5. Garreau, *Edge City*, p. 232.

Part Nine

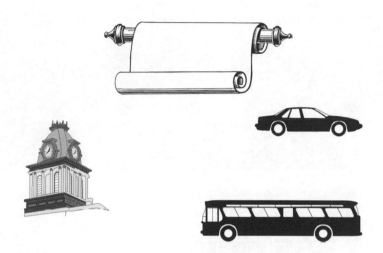

The American
Dream Alternative

Smart growth jeopardizes the American dream of home ownership and mobility. Portland's smart-growth plan has made the region one of the least affordable housing markets in the nation. Portland planners project that the region's emphasis on transit even though most people will continue to drive will triple congestion and quintuple the time wasted in traffic. These plans hit poor people the hardest. Fortunately, the American dream alternative shows that home ownership and mobility are compatible with a clean environment, protection of accessible open space, low taxes, and other measures of urban livability. Bottom photo by Myles Cunneen.

34. Basic Principles

The American Dream alternative

This book has scrutinized smart growth and its many flaws. Inevitably, someone will ask, "What is the alternative?" Fortunately, since we have looked much closer at how cities work than most smart-growth adherents, we can develop an alternative that solves many urban problems without smart growth's costs. I call it the *American dream alternative* because this name conveys the near-universal desire for freedom of choice in housing, mobility, and a quality environment.

The American dream alternative will work for any large, urban area. I encourage readers to alter and improve the alternative to fit the specifics of their region. The main goal of presenting the alternative here is to show that urban problems can be solved without coercion and expensive-but-useless public-works projects; that in fact central planning, coercion, and subsidies won't work as well as self determination, incentives, and user fees.

The American dream alternative has practically the same goals claimed by smart-growth advocates: to protect the livability of urban areas by minimizing congestion and pollution and protecting open space. But the alternative also places a high priority on individual freedom and efficiency—two goals that smart-growth advocates sometimes pay lip service to but, by their actions, apparently do not particularly value. Where the American dream alternative particularly differs from smart growth is in the *means*—the tools used to achieve the goals.

- Where smart growth is based on a vision of how people ought to behave in the future, the American dream alternative gives people freedom to choose what they want.
- Where smart growth would compel people to follow its vision, the American dream alternative allows people to pursue their own visions but uses incentives and feedback relationships to insure that people pay the full cost of their choices.
- Where smart growth has targets for population densities and jobs, the American dream alternative proposes user fees to deal with such problems as congestion and pollution.
- Where smart growth relies on the wisdom of planners, the American dream

481

alternative relies on individual actions prompted by appropriate incentives.
- Where smart growth treats problems indirectly, the American dream alternative treats the source of the problems.
- Where smart growth relies on centralization, the American dream alternative decentralizes as much as possible.

The American dream alternative is based on six fundamental principles:

1. *Solve today's problems*—Don't try to dictate to the future.
2. *Insure freedom and responsibility*—Give people freedom of choice but make sure they pay the actual cost of their choices;
3. *Decentralization*—Decisions made at the most decentralized level possible are most likely to be efficient and equitable;
4. *Protect and create property rights*—Property rights and markets are the most effective and democratic tools available for allocating scarce resources;
5. *Design transportation facilities for mobility*—Don't use transportation as a social engineering or land-use tool;
6. *Base policies on facts, not perceptions*—Policies and decisions based on unverified perceptions are likely to become expensive mistakes.

1. Solve Today's Problems

The American dream alternative focuses on solving today's problems, not trying to create a future utopia. This means, for example, removing major traffic bottlenecks, spending public money as effectively as possible, and reforming transit to make it responsive to the needs of transit riders, not to the objectives of planners.

USC planners Harry Richardson and Peter Gordon might consider the American dream alternative to be an example of *market planning*. But the planning profession, with its authoritarian impulses, its emphasis on aesthetics, and its belief in human malleability, is unsuited to the task of solving urban problems. Cities could go a long way towards solving their problems by simply firing all of their planners. If nothing else, this would save money. In the American dream alternative, most of the activities now being done by urban planners—planning, zoning, design—would be turned over to individuals or neighborhood councils.

One of the common tactics of urban planners today is to ask members of the public to "envision" the future of their city—say twenty to fifty years in the future. Once a future is envisioned, the natural next step is to try to legislate it into existence through zoning codes, taxes, subsidies, and so forth. The problem is that no one really knows what the future will be like or what future urban residents will want. One thing is certain: The forces that have promoted decentralization—telecommunications, mobility, distributed electrical power—are stronger than ever. So attempts by urban governments to recentralize their populace are doomed to fail. Instead of attempting to create utopias in fifty years, cities should treat livability problems such as congestion and pollution today.

2. Freedom of Choice and Responsibility

People should be free to choose how and where they want to live, work, shop, and recreate, and how they get from one place to another. But people should be responsible for their choices, meaning that they should pay the full cost. Rather than try to social engineer people's choices by, for example, charging high fees for low-density housing and subsidizing high density, governments should provide a level playing field, making sure that any user fees cover costs but otherwise not favoring any density or intensity of use.

"Truly smart growth would require governments to 'get the prices right' for the services they provide," says urban economist Edwin Mills. "It would also require them to permit people maximum freedom as to where and how they live and create jobs."[1] This is the basis of the American dream alternative's principle of freedom and responsibility.

3. Decentralization

Important decisions about housing, transportation, and other urban issues should be made at the most decentralized level possible.
- Housing decisions now being made by cities and counties should be made by families and individuals.
- Land-use and zoning decisions now being made by state and regional governments should be made by neighborhood associations.
- Transportation decisions now made by federal and state governments should be made by cities or private entrepreneurs.

Decentralization will make these decisions more responsive to public needs and desires and less beholden to special interests. The decisions made by individuals, neighborhood associations, and local governments are also likely to save money and come closer to solving real problems than decisions made by higher levels of government. Movements to consolidate governments or service districts or create regional governments should be discouraged because bigger governments tend to be more expensive and less responsive to public needs and desires.

4. Protect and Create Property Rights

Property rights are not an artificial structure created by wealthy people to oppress the poor. They are the result of a centuries-long evolutionary process seeking an efficient and just means of allocating scarce resources. Property rights encourage trade, which allows people to express their personal preferences through the market. The market, in turn, is arguably the most democratic institution ever devised:
- Far more Americans participate in the market than vote in an election year;

- Markets allow people to "vote" as often as they want and on as many issues as they want instead of just for a few officials and ballot measures;
- Markets protect minority rights: People who "vote no" in a market do not have to pay for things that other people buy, while people who "vote yes" usually win even if they are in the minority.

People fear that markets and property rights give undue power to the wealthy. But the wealthy have much more control over government than they do markets. Bill Gates cannot force me to use Windows; Bill Clinton can force me to pay for bombs and light-rail lines that I think do more harm than good. Markets cater not to the rich but to anyone willing to pay the cost, which is why the vast majority of American families own their own homes, autos, and other things that are only available to the wealthy in less market-oriented nations. Recent trends toward mass customization—tailoring goods and services to individual needs—are giving people even more power over their daily lives.[2]

Environmental problems are not caused by markets but by the lack of a market for air, water, wildlife, and other resources. Instead of cumbersome regulation that is often warped to benefit the wealthy and powerful, government can solve many of these problems by creating property rights and markets for such resources. Three urban issues where markets can be especially useful replacements for current government regulation are air pollution, transit, and traffic congestion.

5. Transportation for Mobility

Transportation facilities should be designed to help people go where they want to go, not to socially engineer their lifestyles and destinations. While turning transportation over to the private sector may be too radical for many people to contemplate, government spending on transportation should be based on user fees as far as possible and should focus on promoting mobility, not trying to control land uses.

While some transit subsidies may be needed for low-income, disabled, and other people who have no access to autos, such subsidies can be minimized by reinventing transit agencies and promoting private transit services. Mobility goals should rule out the possibility of spending most of a region's transportation dollars on construction of transit facilities that only a tiny percentage of the region will use. Traffic calming on collectors or arterials would also be ruled out; traffic calming would be allowed in neighborhoods only if the neighborhoods actually want them and they are compatible with service vehicles.

6. Base Policies on Facts, Not Perceptions

Government policies are bound to go wrong when Congress bases spending decisions on movies such as *Roger Rabbit* and opinion-makers such as *The Economist* cite *The Simpsons* to justify their derision of the suburbs. Many of the concerns raised by the war on sprawl are based on demonstrably false perceptions, such as the perception that an evil conspiracy destroyed public transit or that the suburbs are sterile. Government officials who make decisions based on perceptions without verifying whether they are correct are likely to impose huge costs on urban residents and the nation as a whole.

Chapter 35 will show how these principles apply to housing, open space, and other land-use issues. Chapter 36 will focus on highways and congestion while chapter 37 will discuss transit. Chapter 38 will suggest some ways to reduce air pollution while chapter 39 will describe institutional changes needed to apply these principles to urban areas.

Notes

1. Edwin S. Mills, "Truly Smart 'Smart Growth,'" *Illinois Real Estate Letter*, Summer, 1999, p. 7.
2. W. Michael Cox and Richard Alm, *The Right Stuff: America's Move to Mass Customization* (Dallas, TX: Federal Reserve Bank of Dallas, 1999), http://www.dallasfed.org/htm/pubs/anreport/arpt98.pdf.

 ～Web ⊤ools: ᗩmerican ᗪream

See www.ti.org/dreamalt.html to find out how you can customize the American dream alternative for your region.

35. Land Use

Many cities without zoning have developed other institutional arrangements aimed at protecting local property values. One common such arrangement is a neighborhood association combined with protective covenants on the land in the neighborhood. These covenants can be changed by a vote of the residents of the neighborhood. This allows residents to have a say in how their immediate neighbors use their property but little say in how more distant lands are used.

Covenants and neighborhood associations are often initiated by property developers. Developers know that a $200,000 home on a quarter-acre lot will sell faster, and may even sell at a premium price, if the buyers are secure that the land around them will not be turned into junkyards, factories, or other uses incompatible with their home. Some neighborhoods have been created exclusively for retirees, others for families with children. People who want to live in an area with no zoning can often choose between a variety of neighborhoods with varying degrees of protective covenants.

Such neighborhood associations have several advantages over zoning:

- The people making decisions about the neighborhood are intimately familiar with it and are the ones who care most about its future.
- Because neighborhoods are small, planning problems are far less complicated than those for an entire city.
- Since major decisions about changing covenants would probably require a majority vote, there is less opportunity for corruption than there is in zoning.
- Different neighborhoods are likely to come up with a wide variety of rules, from none at all to very strict, giving home buyers a wider range of choices than are found in cities with a few zoning categories.

Such neighborhood associations are the essence of land-use planning in Houston[1] and many new suburbs that are protected by covenants instead of zoning codes.[2] In 1999, some 42 million Americans lived in neighborhoods covered by 205,000 community associations—including condominiums and cooperatives.[3] Surveys show that most residents are very satisfied with their neighborhoods and the associations that help manage them.

To extend the advantages of covenants and neighborhood associations to areas that are now zoned, University of Maryland public policy Professor Robert Nelson proposes that state legislatures enact a process allowing urban neighborhoods to create associations:

1. A group of property owners representing 60 percent of the neighborhood (by property value) would petition to form a neighborhood association. The petition would describe the boundaries and a "constitution" showing how the association would be governed.
2. The state would certify that the neighborhood met certain standards such as that it is contiguous and has reasonable boundaries.
3. The neighborhood would then negotiate a service transfer agreement with the local municipality. Some neighborhoods might just take over zoning, but others might take care of streets, garbage collection, snow removal, and even police protection.
4. During a one-year waiting period, all local property owners and residents would be informed and would get a chance to discuss the proposal.
5. A state supervised election would be held. Nelson suggests that the proposal would be passed only if both the owners of at least 90 percent of all property (by value) and 75 percent of individual unit owners voted yes.[4]

The last requirement seems unduly strict. People who care about freedom and property rights abhor the idea of coercion, but such a huge supermajority could prevent any neighborhood association from ever forming. Reducing the percentages to no more than 60 percent should make it possible for cities to explore the benefits of neighborhood associations without risking any more coercion than is found in existing zoning codes. A few other features should also be considered:

- Existing zoning codes should form the initial protective covenants for the neighborhood. This would give residents and property owners assurance that changes would be incremental, not revolutionary.
- Any property owner on the border of a neighborhood association should be allowed to opt out of that association. If the property borders land that is zoned, opting out would mean the property would stay with municipal zoning. If the property borders another neighborhood association, the owner would have a choice of which neighborhood association to join.
- Neighborhood associations could receive funds from property taxes or other local sources that they can use for neighborhood improvements. Such improvements might include the purchase of land for parks, the purchase and obliteration of preexisting eyesores, or the installation of sidewalks or other pedestrian-friendly facilities.

The association would be free to write any and all rules for neighborhood use and development. The rules might be as simple as zoning with a minimum of 5,000-square-foot lots, or they might be much more specific, such as requiring people to tend their lawns and not to leaving motor vehicles in their front yards.

Preexisting uses would be grandfathered in so no one would be required to change an existing use without compensation. In most associations that exist today, changes in community rules must win the votes of two-thirds to three-quarters of association members.[5]

Zoning, says Nelson, is static and does not recognize changes in tastes or economic conditions. Thus, some areas get stuck in obsolete land-use patterns. Some cities "sell" zoning changes to developers by requiring developers to pay high impact fees or turn over some of their land to the city. But many people consider this unethical and a betrayal of existing neighborhoods. Nelson also notes that recent Supreme Court decisions, including the Tigard, Oregon Dolan decision, make such "sales" of zoning changes legally questionable.

Neighborhood associations can overcome all of these problems. Suppose a city has a surplus of areas with single-family homes and a shortage of apartments. Developers could approach neighborhood associations and offer to pay money or provide services in exchange for building apartments in the neighborhoods. No doubt the developers would also provide assurance that the apartments did not reduce property values. Some associations would accept, others would not. In this way, a city could evolve in response to changing conditions on a more voluntary basis than used by current planning and zoning.

How big would a neighborhood association be? Today's average neighborhood association with protective covenants serves around 200 people. This includes condominiums and cooperatives; neighborhood associations of mainly single-family homes may be larger. A typical neighborhood bounded by major commercial streets may have 300 to 800 homes. But the final determinations of the boundaries would be decided by the neighborhoods themselves and there is no reason why commercial streets would necessarily form the boundaries.

Alternatives that are worth considering include performance zoning and systems of tradable development rights. Performance zoning is based on outcomes, not prescriptions. Instead of dictating densities and land uses, a performance zoning code specifies that landowners cannot cause certain effects, such as noise, traffic, or pollution. So long as they can meet these goals, landowners can do whatever they want. Performance zoning was most successfully applied in Ft. Collins, Colorado.[6] However, the city recently overlaid a more conventional zoning system on the area because residents did not feel that performance zoning provided them with enough security. Neighborhood associations do not have that problem.

Under a system of tradable development rights, every property owner is given a tradable development credit, based perhaps on existing zoning. Anyone who wants to develop their property beyond existing zoning would have to purchase development credits from someone else. Under this system, certain areas could be protected from further development by downzoning them, yet leaving the tradable credits in the hands of property owners. While the owners could not develop their land, they could sell their credits to others who have the right to develop other lands. The problem with tradable credits is that it still requires a central planning authority to monitor credits, determine zoning, and decide which areas need further protection. The neighborhood association program is much more decentralized and more responsive to local desires to protect livability.

Neighborhood associations would completely replace zoning. They would protect neighborhoods not only from unwanted new developments on private property but from government imposition of developments that the neighborhood does not want. Yet they would allow orderly neighborhood transitions without people feeling that their land had been devalued without compensation.

Although neighborhood associations would have no land-use planning authority over land outside of their neighborhood, they could play a significant role in protecting open space. Some or all of the open space funds available to a region should be divided among the neighborhood associations which would have a free hand in how to spend them. Some might buy vacant land in their neighborhoods for parks. Others might improve existing parks. Still others might buy lands for open spaces outside of their individual neighborhoods, perhaps by pooling their money with other associations or donating it to regional park districts or organizations such as the Nature Conservancy.

The problem with open space is that those who get the benefits are usually not the same as those who pay the costs. Those who live near the open space, especially those who can view it from their homes, receive the greatest benefits. The costs are paid by those who actually own the open space. If they are private landowners who are prevented by zoning rules from developing their property, then they are effectively forced to subsidize their neighbor's views. If parks districts or other public entities own the open space, then taxpayers in general are paying for benefits that largely accrue to a few landowners. Since a homesite next to a large park tends to be more valuable than an ordinary homesite, the beneficiaries of public open space tend to be wealthier than average.

The solution is to create a fund that can be used purchase land or scenic easements from the owners of open space. Land can be used for parks. Easements will insure that their land remains open forever though it can still be used by the owner for agriculture, timber, or other preexisting uses. Where should open-space funds come from? A variety of sources is possible. Since real estate values are greatly enhanced by the presence of nearby open space, a real estate transfer tax or a property would come close to insuring that those who get the benefits of the open space are also those who pay the costs. If a majority or supermajority of property owners agree to it, neighborhood associations might be authorized to collect such a tax to be spent on neighborhood improvements and open space.

Whatever the source of funds, they should be given to the neighborhood association of the neighborhood in which the property was located. Federal or state funds granted to the region for open space protection could also be distributed to neighborhood associations. This would give neighborhood residents an incentive to maintain an active neighborhood association as well as give them control over the future of their neighborhoods. The neighborhood associations could spend their share of the funds buying land or easements for parks in their neighborhoods, but they might also be allowed to spend them on other neighborhood improvements such as pedestrian facilities or removal of blighted properties.

To provide for scenic protection on a regional scale, neighborhoods could donate a share of their funds—perhaps a third to a half—to an organization that purchases land or easements at the regional level. The organization could be a regional park district, but it could also be a nonprofit group such as the Nature Conservancy. Giving neighborhoods a choice will insure that the regional spending is responsive to local demands rather than to special interest groups.

The American dream alternative will protect more open space inside of urban areas than smart growth, thus allowing urbanites to have more frequent contact with parks, golf courses, urban farms, and other open spaces. Protecting the quality of existing neighborhoods might also slow the rate of exurbanization, which may do more in the long run for protecting rural open spaces than urban-growth boundaries or greenbelts.

Notes

1. Bernard Siegan, *Land Use Without Zoning* (Lexington, MA: Lexington Books, 1972), 271 pp.
2. Joel Garreau, *Edge City: Life on the New Frontier* (New York, NY: Doubleday, 1991), chapter 6.
3. Community Associations Institute, "Facts about Community Associations," http://www.caionline.org/about/facts.cfm.
4. Robert Nelson, "Privatizing the Neighborhood: A Proposal to Replace Zoning with Private Collective Property Rights to Existing Neighborhoods," *George Mason Law Review*, vol. 7(4): 827-880.
5. Community Associations Institute, "Inside Look at Community Association Homeownership" http://www.caionline.org/about/inside.cfm.
6. William D. Eggers, *Land Use Reform Through Performance Zoning.* (Los Angeles, CA: Reason Foundation, 1990), RPPI policy paper number 120.

The Selfish-Neighborhoods Myth

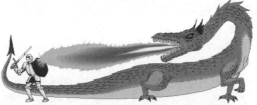

Myth: Neighborhoods that are allowed to decide their own futures will make selfish decisions that ignore the needs of other people.

Reality: Self-determination will give everyone more power over the livability of their neighborhoods.

Suburban critics claim that the suburbs are "exclusive," meaning that they are havens for the upper class or at best strictly segregate classes. One goal of smart growth is to create neighborhoods of mixed incomes. Giving neighborhood residents power over their own destinies will supposedly reinforce class segregation since residents will try to exclude lower-class people from living in their areas.

Today, the epitome of this class segregation is supposed to be the gated community. "When public services and even local government are privatized," worry urban planners Edward Blakely and Mary Gail Snyder in *Fortress America*, "what happens to the function and the very idea of a social and political democracy?"[1] Although gated communities reduce crime, worries over their effects on society have led many planners to call for bans on new gated developments.

Part of the problem is that critics of the suburbs have a romanticized view of the past in which the rich and poor lived next door to one another in high-density cities and therefore understood each other better than people do today. "Nobody objects to the walled towns of Europe and Asia, because they were home to a full cross section of society rather than a privileged elite," says Andres Duany. "The unity of society is threatened not by the use of gates but by the uniformity and exclusivity of the people within them."[2] Yet no one can argue that there is more racial or class discrimination today than one hundred years ago. Just the fact that the rich and poor were crammed more closely together in nineteenth-century cities doesn't mean that they understood one another or even encountered each other more than they do today. Although Theodore Roosevelt, Jr.'s father did much charitable work, Roosevelt did not believe that living conditions for New York's urban poor were as bad as claimed by labor lobbyists until Samuel Gompers personally guided the future president on a tour of Manhattan tenements. Roosevelt was so appalled that he became a leading champion of Gompers's reforms.[3]

Duany and the authors of *Fortress America* worry that people living in the insulated suburbs aren't willing to do their "civic duty" by paying taxes to subsidize the cities. "The people in the gated pods are the ones consistently voting down necessary taxes," frets Duany. "Not one penny more to support the inner city."[4] Yet many suburbanites know the devastating impact of urban renewal and public housing projects and have witnessed billions of dollars wasted on light-rail boondoggles. Perhaps they are simply less confident than Duany that spending more of their tax dollars on the inner city will actually do any good.

Critics of the suburbs "may have matters almost entirely backwards," suggests one public policy analyst. "The real inequality may not be the social divisions resulting from economically and socially segregated patterns of living in the suburbs," says University of Maryland Professor Robert Nelson. "Rather, the greatest inequality may be the denial of a similar private opportunity to people in the inner city." Instead of seeking "to undermine suburban powers of exclusion," central city supporters should try "to bring suburban powers of exclusion into the inner city." After all, crime is a greater problem for the inner-city poor than it is for suburbanites. "Few things would do more to improve the overall quality of inner city life than a significant reduction in crime."

Nelson suggests letting inner city neighborhoods form neighborhood associations with real power over land use and selected urban services would help them improve their neighborhoods. Nelson points out that St. Louis allows such neighborhood associations to "take over ownership of their streets," in effect creating inner-city gated communities. Many neighborhoods have done this to reduce crime and improve property values.[5]

A successful democracy does not depend on everyone living cheek-to-jowl with one another. But it does depend on giving everyone the opportunity to use successful institutions that can improve the quality of their lives. If homeowners' associations and gated communities can work in the suburbs, they may also work in the cities. All that is necessary is that planners and city officials not stand in their way and instead make such possibilities available to urban residents.

Notes

1. Edward J. Blakely and Mary Gail Snyder, *Fortress America: Gated Communities in the United States* (Washington, DC: Brookings Institution, 1997), p. 3.
2. Andres Duany, Elizabeth Plater-Zyberk, and Jeff Speck, *Suburban Nation: The Rise of Sprawl and the Decline of the American Dream* (New York, NY: North Point Press, 2000), p. 45.
3. Nathan Miller, *Theodore Roosevelt: A Life* (New York, NY: Morrow, 1992), pp. 143–144.
4. Duany, et al., *Suburban Nation*, pp. 44–45.
5. Robert Nelson, "Privatizing the Neighborhood: A Proposal to Replace Zoning with Private Collective Property Rights to Existing Neighborhoods," *George Mason Law Review*, 7(4): 827–880.

36. Highways

*T*raffic congestion is the most commonly cited urban complaint, and smart growth is guaranteed to make it worse. The solution to congestion is not to simply stop building roads any more than it is to build millions of miles of new urban freeways. Congestion must be treated with a combination of construction, improved designs, and new financial arrangements that insure that people pay their fair share for highways. As commuting expert Alan Pisarski says, "Recent transportation problems are partly a one-time bubble and partly the result of long-term trends. Many problems would be resolved by a one-time reorganizing and reorientation of available road capacity along with construction of some new capacity."[1]

Paying a Fair Share

Gasoline taxes and other user fees have failed to provide enough revenue to keep up with highway maintenance needs and demands for new road capacities. Between 1980 and 1998, the number of miles of urban freeways in the U.S. grew by 40 percent, but the number of miles people drove on those freeways grew by 124 percent. One important problem is that fuel-efficient cars contribute less to the highway system even as they drive more miles. As 50- to 80-mile-per-gallon hybrid-electric cars are introduced to the market, this problem will only get worse.

Another problem is that meeting peak demand for highways is far more expensive than meeting average demand. When highways are built to meet peak demand, people alter their driving habits to use those highways. As a result, most highways are heavily congested during morning and evening rush hours. Gasoline taxes and other fees do not account for peak demand. Buying a gallon of milk at a supermarket gives the grocer a signal to stock another gallon of milk. But buying a gallon of gas does not tell highway departments when and where the buyer will be driving. The gas tax is the same whether people travel during rush hour or midnight and whether they drive on crowded urban freeways or little-used country roads. Raising gas taxes may discourage some auto trips but will do little for congestion because most of the trips that people can cut are non-peak-hour trips.

"Most U.S. roads," says economist Gabriel Roth, "are still in the 'command economy,' the kind that failed so spectacularly in the Soviet Union." As such, "roads suffer from the typical command economy characteristics: poor maintenance, congestion, and insensitivity to consumer needs."[2] The solution, says Roth, is to charge a fee to use highways that varies depending on the time of day. The fee would be highest during the peak of rush hour, while it would be very low or zero at night. Such fees are commonly called *congestion pricing*. Taking a lesson from smart-growth rhetoric, congestion pricing advocates are increasingly using the term *value pricing* because prices are proportional to value.

Value pricing is very common in businesses that experience predictable fluctuations in traffic:

- Long-distance telephone companies charge more for calls made during weekdays than evenings and weekends (although this is disappearing as fiber-optics increase capacities);
- Airlines and hotels charge more during peak vacation periods than during other times of the year;
- Electric utilities in the north often charge more in the winter, while utilities in the south charge more in the summer, and some charge more during the day than late at night;
- Some museums charge more on weekends than on weekdays;
- Prices of clothing and other goods are often lower after Christmas than in November and December.

"The existence of congestion implies inadequate supply and/or pricing of travel facilities," says urban economist Edwin Mills. The appropriate response, he adds, is to make sure that "the price of using a facility [is] set equal to the cost."[3] Since it costs more to build enough roads to meet peak demand than to meet average demand, people who drive during peak periods should pay more than those who do not.

Whenever the demand for a good or service exceeds the supply, some sort of rationing is needed. As Peter Gordon and Harry Richardson note, on our highways "congestion has become the dominant rationing mechanism."[4] Value pricing works better than congestion because time wasted in congestion is a deadweight loss for society, whereas money spent on rush-hour tolls can be used to maintain and expand road capacities.

Distributing radio transponders to auto and truck drivers makes value pricing possible without traffic-delaying toll booths. When drivers pass through a toll area, the fee at the time they are driving can be either charged to their credit card or deducted from a prepaid amount that is recorded in the transponder. The prepay option would resolve privacy questions because no one would ever know who was using a prepaid transponder. Toll stations might be set up at *choke points* distributed around an urban area. Such choke points would include bridges, canyons, and other places where drivers would have little ability or incentive to get off the highway for a short distance to avoid paying the fee. Or they might be applied to new highways or to new lanes built onto existing highways.

Value pricing is successfully being used by a private road company in Orange County, California. The company invested $130 million in a four-lane highway paralleling a crowded freeway. Tolls range from 75 cents at night to $3.75 during rush hour and cars with three or more people, disabled plates, or zero-emission power receive substantial discounts. The company has sold 124,000 transponders and collects about $20 million in revenue each year. Users of the highway claim they can save 10 to 20 minutes—and sometimes much more—in each direction. Another value-priced road is in San Diego County.

As more cities implement value pricing, it will eventually be possible for someone to travel coast to coast using a single transponder to pay any tolls. Transponders could also be incorporated into other devices: In Finland, people use cell phones to pay for items purchased from vending machines. There is no reason why cell phones could not double as the transponder for value-priced roads. Whatever is used as a transponder could also be used to pay for gasoline or other items. Recently, several McDonalds restaurants in Orange County installed equipment to let people use their highway transponders to pay for food purchased in the drive-through.[5]

Residents of the Northeast and a few other states are used to toll roads, and introducing value pricing should not be a problem there. People in other states who drive exclusively on non-tollroads often react in horror to the idea of value pricing. Yet there are several ways of making value pricing politically palatable.

- Value pricing can be introduced on newly-built lanes or on lanes now dedicated to high-occupancy vehicles. This gives people a choice between spending more time in traffic on the free lanes or saving time by spending a little more money on the toll lanes.
- To give people confidence that they are getting what they pay for and not simply paying another tax, all fees collected should be dedicated to expansion and maintenance of the highways used by those who pay the fees.
- Where value-priced tolls are used to pay for highway expansions, the fees collected could be offset by a reduction in gasoline taxes equal to the amount that would have been spent on those highway expansions.

The main reason why value pricing is not widely used for highways is that, for thirty-five years prior to 1991, Congress prohibited states from charging tolls for roads built with federal money. The 1991 transportation bill rescinded this and actually provided pilot funds for several cities to experiment with value pricing. Portland, Oregon, was one of those cities, but Metro, the regional planning agency, is clearly lukewarm to the idea, and its planning documents rarely mention it. In what is probably an echo of Metro's attitude, the *Oregonian* says that "At best congestion pricing is a solution that might supplement light rail."[6] Apparently, planners find it easier to create highway congestion and major shortages of single-family housing than to ask people to pay a highway toll.

Planners usually underestimate how people will respond to changes in pricing. During the 1970s energy shortages, planners predicted that fuel consumption would continue to increase at exponential rates. In fact, with higher prices, people bought fuel-economy cars, and the energy "crisis" of the 1980s was one of low oil prices due to a drop in demand.

Only 60 percent of urban traffic during the morning rush hour and 40 percent of the afternoon rush hour is commuter traffic. Much of the remainder is traffic that could easily reschedule to another time of day. Just as high daytime long-distance fees encourage people to make personal calls in the evenings, congestion fees would give the noncommuter traffic an incentive to travel during non-rush hour periods. The fees might also convince some businesses to save their employees money by scheduling different work hours.

In fast-growing cities, value pricing would not end the need for new urban roads—nothing will do that, particularly not rail transit. But value pricing would provide a new source of funding as well as give highway planners more accurate information about where such roads should be built. More important, value pricing should reduce the peak-hour demand for any particular road by at least 20 percent.

An alternative to value pricing would be the complete privatization of urban road networks. This would effectively produce the same end result, since many private road owners would use value pricing. While privatization may be too big a change to be politically realistic, cities and states can offer private companies the opportunity to build major new roads that are needed in urban areas. These companies could pay for the roads by collecting tolls. Such private roads are rare because they were once forbidden by federal law. But Congress repealed this law in 1991 and some places, including Virginia and California have begun to experiment with the idea. Private interests will only invest in such roads, however, if they can be assured that the government will not build roads that will compete with them.

In sum, value pricing treats the source of congestion problems by creating incentives to minimize peak-hour congestion and giving both decentralized highway users and highway providers feedback about when and where to travel and build roads.

Transportation Design

Improved transportation designs cannot solve all congestion problems but can provide some relief. Some of these improvements aim to smooth the flow of traffic. Others aim to eliminate or reduce bottlenecks. Such improvements include:
- Synchronizing traffic signals so that drivers do not have to stop at every light;
- Replacing some signals with roundabouts, particularly where several signals

are located close to one another leading to traffic stack ups because no more than one or two cars can get through one of the signals at a time;

- Installing ramp meters on freeways so that traffic joining the freeway minimally interferes with traffic already on the freeway;
- Rebuilding exit ramps on older freeways to allow higher speed exits;
- Rebuilding on- and off-ramps where the traffic must weave across lanes in short distances;
- Rebuilding the junctions between major highways to reflect current traffic flows.

New Construction

Though freeways make up less than 3 percent of urban roads and streets, their capacities are so much greater than other highways that they carry well over a third of all urban traffic. Even if freeway expansion or a new freeway does not eliminate congestion, it produces significant benefits by allowing people to travel at more convenient times, giving people access to more jobs and other urban resources, and relieving congestion on other routes.

In general, the judicious use of value pricing should greatly reduce the need for new urban freeways. At the same time, some new roads will be needed, and value pricing will help provide the revenues to pay for such roads. As a general rule, highway expansions aimed at relieving congestion should be paid for exclusively with value-priced tolls. Completely new roads designed to provide new connections between areas could be paid for with a combination of tolls and the existing highway user fees.

Highway opponents often point to the lack of space for new roads in built-up areas and the cost of removing existing buildings and disrupting neighborhoods. Tollway expert Peter Samuel points out several ways in which road capacities can be increased without significantly increasing the amount of land dedicated to roads.

- Movable barriers: On roads where morning peak traffic is mainly in one direction and afternoon is in the other, movable barriers make it possible to create reversible express or toll lanes at a minimal cost in extra space.[7]
- Tunnels: Recent advances in technology have greatly reduced the cost of tunneling. Samuel reports that Norway builds tunnels for as low as $6.5 million per lane mile, which is not significantly more than a lane mile of ordinary freeway in the U.S.[8]
- Auto-truck separation: Since autos are smaller, lanes dedicated to autos can be narrower and thus more lanes can be built in a fixed amount of space.
- Double-decking: If lower decks were dedicated to autos, they would need a mere seven feet of clearance, reducing the visual impact of the upper decks. "Given that ingenuity can create new kinds of space for roads," says Samuel,

"glib statements that we are 'running out' of space for new roads are. . . misleading." He adds, however, that "state highway authorities have generally been very slow to use" some of these techniques.[9] This may be one argument for more private freeways whose owners could be willing to try innovative ideas. While most freeways have traditionally been built by government agencies, recent experiments in private roads have proven successful so long as the government does not build competing roads.

Notes

1. Alan E. Pisarski, "Issues in Transportation and Growth Management," IN David J. Brower, David R. Godschalk, and Douglas R. Porter (eds.), *Understanding Growth Management: Critical Issues and a Research Agenda* (Wsahington, DC: Urban Land Institute, 1989), 193 pp., p. 125.
2. Gabriel Roth, "How to Solve Our Highway Problems," *Consumers' Research*, June, 1997, p. 11.
3. Edwin Mills, "Truly Smart 'Smart Growth,'" *Illinois Real Estate Letter*, Summer, 1999, p. 4.
4. Peter Gordon and Harry Richardson, "Congestion Trends in Metropolitan Areas," *in* National Research Council, *Curbing Gridlock: Peak-Period Fees to Relieve Traffic Congestion* (Washington, DC: National Academy Press, 1994), volume 2:1–31.
5. Peter Samuel, "Toll dat Big Mac, Pal," *Tollroads Newsletter*, 45 (January, 2000), p. 4.
6. Editorial, "If not light rail, what?" *The Oregonian*, July 28, 1995, p. C8.
7. Peter Samuel, *How to "Build Our Way out of Congestion"* (Los Angeles, CA: Reason Foundation, 1999), p. 24.
8. Ibid, p. 22.
9. Ibid, p. 24.

The Lexus-Lane Myth

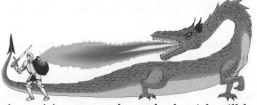

Myth: Congestion pricing means that only the rich will be able to drive on uncongested roads.

Reality: Value pricing will help relieve congestion for everyone.

American highways are one of the most egalitarian institutions in the world. Almost every American family has access to an automobile, and everyone who has an auto has equal access to highways. At first glance, value pricing seems to reduce this equality. In fact, value pricing increases equity in two important ways.

First, value pricing insures that those who get the benefits of peak-period transportation are the ones who pay the cost. Value pricing of roads is no less egalitarian than a supermarket. Almost every American shops at or eats foods purchased from a supermarket. Sometimes people (if they are meat eaters) buy hamburger, other times they buy steak. If the government ordered that hamburger and steak be sold at the same price, there would be long lines for the steak and lots of hamburger would go to waste. The difference in price helps insure that food is efficiently used and gives everyone a choice. Though some people eat steak more often than others, nearly everyone who eats meat will enjoy it once in a while.

Ordinary tollroads insure that the people who use a particular road are the ones who are paying for it. The builders of the nation's first major throughways such as the Pennsylvania Turnpike and the New Jersey Turnpike found that people readily paid a fee on top of gas taxes to hasten their journey over the time it would take to go on conventional two-lane roads. But such tolling could actually make congestion worse: If the time advantage of driving on a limited-access highway is greater in congested periods, then people will be more willing to pay the toll during rush hour than other hours of the day.

Value pricing solves this problem by sending people signals about the cost of relieving congestion. A non-value-priced urban highway that contains enough lanes to satisfy peak-period demand would be largely unutilized during much of the rest of the day. Value pricing encourages people to shift their driving time to other times, thus reducing the need for such an expensive highway system. While

congestion itself also encourages time shifting, the time and fuel wasted in congestion are deadweight losses. Value pricing produces revenue that can be used to
relieve congestion while it saves people time.

A second way that value pricing increases equity is by making alternatives to
congestion accessible to everyone. The wealthy and powerful always have alternatives to congestion. They can hire chauffeurs so they can work or play while someone else drives. They can afford to shift their travel to non-peak times. In a few
cases, they can have motorcades clear the streets for them or take a helicopter or
some other uncongested mode of transportation.

Value pricing won't give everyone a chauffeur-driven limousine. But it does
give everyone who needs or wants to bypass congestion the ability to do so at a
relatively low price. Obviously, the price has to be high enough to turn some
people away or it would not reduce congestion. But the people turned away will
not all be poor while the people who pay the toll will not all be wealthy. Like
hamburgers and steak, value pricing gives people a choice and few will make the
same choice all the time. Instead, each person will decide each time they get on a
highway with a value-price option: How bad is the congestion? How much time
will I save if I pay the toll? And most important, how much of a hurry am I in
right now?

Civic Clubs and Tollways

Not many people, perhaps, regard Houston as their favorite city. A monument to the oil industry, the nation's fourth largest city is much closer to the epitome of sprawl than Los Angeles. According to the 1990 census, the city of Los Angeles is two-and-one-half times as dense as Houston and the Los Angeles urbanized area is more than twice as dense as Houston's urbanized area.

This makes sense. Much of Los Angeles was developed after the turn of the century, when streetcars were still the dominant form of transportation. As a result, LA is really the streetcar city that Andres Duany claims he loves so well. Houston, meanwhile, had to wait for air conditioning before it could really grow. By that time, the streetcars had been almost completely replaced by cars. In fact, Houston's first freeway was built on the route of a former streetcar line.[1]

Houston's freeways are one reason why Houston is worth examining, since the region's aggressive road construction program has made it one of the few urban areas in the country that has kept congestion under control—at least according to the Texas Transportation Institute. Houston is special for two other reasons as well. First, it is beginning to experiment with value-priced toll roads, which is helping to pay for those new highways. Second, it has no zoning, instead relying on neighborhood associations and deed restrictions. These things make Houston the urban area that comes closest to the American dream alternative.

Table One: The Houston Urbanized Area

	1950	1990	1998
Population (thousands)	701	2,901	3,434
Land area square miles	270	1,177	1,537
Density	2,600	3,021	2,234

Source: Census Bureau for 1950 and 1990, FHwA, Highway Statistics 1998 *for 1998. The 1998* Highway Statistics *has the wrong population for Houston; the population here is estimated based on Census Bureau data. FHwA land area data are not exactly comparable with Census Bureau data since they use slightly different criteria for determining urbanized area boundaries.*

"Houston is the hair shirt of the city planners," says zoning expert Richard Babcock. When frustrated planners meet in a bar, "some poor soul is bound to suggest that zoning must stink because Los Angeles has had zoning for forty years, Houston never, and what the hell is the difference!"

Table Two: The City of Houston

	1950	1990	1998
Population (thousands)	596	1,631	1,787
Land area square miles	160	540	600
Density	3,726	3,021	3,000

Source: Census Bureau. Land area and density for 1998 are estimated.

"For generations," Babcock continues, Houston land use has depended on restrictive covenants placed in the deeds by developers. "Almost every acre of land in the city is subjected to private restrictions over use, size, or cost of house, yard requirements, height of building, and all the other baggage customarily found in our zoning ordinances."[2] These restrictions are not always enforced, and neighborhoods that make no effort to enforcement eventually lose the legal right to them.

Thus, many neighborhoods have self-appointed watch dogs who monitor land use and make sure that local deed restrictions are enforced. In 1998, Weldon

Figure One: Houston Area Densities

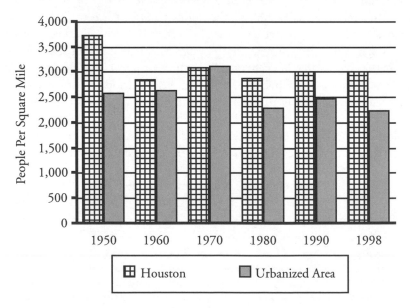

Source: Census Bureau, Federal Highway Administration.

Tiedt was named Neighbor of the Year by his Ridge Crest neighbors for keeping an eye on the area, notifying people who are violating the covenants, and sending thank you notes to those who fix the problems. By being diplomatic, he almost never has to resort to legal measures, and his neighbors take pride in their community.[3]

Houston has a planning department, and a large part of its work is in helping people like Mr. Tiedt and the neighborhood associations or civic clubs that they belong to protect their neighborhoods. Such protection ranges from removing junk vehicles from yards to cleaning up derelict buildings and making sure that new construction complies with local requirements.

Residents of neighborhoods that have no deed restrictions can petition to create such restrictions by getting signatures from half the local property owners. If restrictions already exist, they can petition to change them, but must get signatures from all local property owners. Either way requires the help of a lawyer, and the city has arranged for Houston attorneys to offer pro bono services to low-income residents seeking to create or change local deed restrictions.[4] The city also offers small grants to low-income neighborhoods to cover the costs of petitioning and filing fees.

In some neighborhoods, the deed restrictions written by the original developers sunset after so many years, and the neighborhood associations must vote to retain or change the restrictions at that time.[5] In all these ways, the system is flexible and capable of evolving to meet local needs.

The city planning department offers many more services to neighborhood associations, including an annual Neighborhood Connections Conference, a seven-week Leadership Institute for local leaders, a Technical Assistance Resource Center, and matching grants for landscape beautification and other local improvements.[6]

Houston residents have voted against creating a zoning system more than once. Wealthy neighborhoods felt adequately protected by their restrictive covenants and so were not particularly in favor of zoning. Many poor neighborhoods had lost their deed restrictions by lack of enforcement, so zoning advocates thought that they would support the idea. Instead, the strongest opposition came from these neighborhoods. Many of the residents of these neighborhoods had opened small shops or businesses in their homes and feared that zoning would force them to shut down.[7]

Babcock observes that, contrary to the planners, there *is* a difference between Los Angeles and Houston neighborhoods: Los Angeles was better at maintaining "residential purity" while Houston neighborhoods were more likely to have developed a mixture of uses.[8] This is just the sort of evolution that smart-growth planners endorse today, though of course Houston's mixed uses are not usually at the high densities called for by smart growth.

One measurable result of Houston's lack of zoning is that it saves taxpayers' money. Houston has three-and-one-half times as many people as Portland, and more than four times the land area. Its planning department, including the office of neighborhood assistance, has a budget of $9.5 million in 2000.[9] The 2000 budget for Portland's Bureau of Planning is more than $10.6 million, plus the separate Office of Neighborhood Involvement will spend another $4.1 million to help neighborhood associations who have far less authority over their areas than those in Houston.[10] Thus, Portland spends nearly $30 per resident on planning functions that cost Houstonians just $8 apiece. Of course, this doesn't count the planning budget for Metro, Portland's regional government, which is probably similarly larger than Houston's metropolitan planning organization.

Another result is that Houston's housing market is considerably more affordable than Portland's. A median-priced home in the Houston area costs a little more than twice as much as the region's median income, whereas in Portland it costs more than three times as much.[11]

Houstonians take more transit trips and ride more transit miles per year than San Diegans. But they also drive more. In fact, Houston-area residents drive nearly 10,000 miles per year, while residents of most other major urban areas drive around 7,000 to 8,000 miles per year. This isn't just because Houston is a large, low-density area that requires people to drive a lot to get anywhere. After all, people in such urban areas as Newburgh, New York; Asheville, North Carolina; and Myrtle Beach, South Carolina all drive far more than those in Houston. One reason why Houstonians drive more may be that they can: Houston has more than 700 lane miles of freeway per million people, compared to an average of just over 500 for the twenty-five largest urban areas. Smart-growth advocates would say this proves that building roads is self-defeating, but a better interpretation is that giving people the opportunity to go where they want to go creates urban vitality.

Table Three: Houston-Area Transportation

Miles of freeway per million people	116
Annual miles driven per capita	9,771
Passenger miles per capita	15,634
Annual transit miles per capita	223
Annual transit trips per capita	40
Auto commuters	92.5%
Transit commuters	3.7%
Walk/cycle commuters	3.8%

Source: FHwA, Highway Statistics 1998, FTA, Transit Profiles 1998, 1990 Census. All data from 1998 except commuting data, which are from 1990. Passenger miles per capita are 1.6 times miles driven per capita.

Between 1982 and 1997, Houston opened more than one thousand lane miles of new freeway, a 75-percent increase. This was faster than the population growth of just 30 percent over the same time period. Miles of driving grew by 62 percent over this period, so the faster growth of freeways allowed for much congestion relief. Since miles of driving grew faster than the population, it is obvious that per capita driving grew as well. But this wasn't because of the new roads: Per capita driving in Atlanta grew twice as fast as in Houston, yet Atlanta's freeway capacity barely kept up with population growth. As noted in the Myth That New Roads Increase Congestion, the correlation between per capita driving and road construction is no better than random.

Of course, Houston already had an extensive freeway system in 1982, but as in most places gas taxes were proving inadequate to keep up with congestion. So, in 1983, the region's voters agreed to build new roads with toll financing. The region's first tollway opened in 1988. By 1997, the region had nearly 60 miles of tollways, representing more than a third of the increase in lane-miles.

In 1992, Houston's was one of the first toll systems in the country to offer electronic tolling. In 1999 the system collected more electronic tolls than any other tollroad system outside of New York City.[12] Currently most tolls are the same regardless of time of day, but the tollroad authority estimates that switching to value pricing would increase traffic by 15 to 25 percent because the tolls would better match the relative time-savings offered by using the roads.[13] Future toll roads in the region are likely to use value pricing, but the authority has not yet decided to shift the existing tollways.

Houston is also experimenting with high-occupancy/toll (HOT) lanes. High-occupancy vehicle lanes built on the Katy Freeway presented a problem: hardly anyone used them when they were limited to cars with three or more people but they were too congested when cars with two people were allowed. So Houston's Metropolitan Transportation Board decided to allow cars with two people to use the lane if they paid a toll during rush hour. This increased usage of the lane while still giving it a considerable speed advantage over general purpose lanes on the freeway. The board would like to let cars with just one person pay a toll to use the lane, but so far has not received permission to do so from the federal government, which helped pay for the lane.[14]

Houston's reputation as a sprawling urban area is as much due to its huge population as to its low density. After all, Cincinnati, Columbus, Kansas City, Norfolk, Oklahoma City, and the Twin Cities urban areas all have significantly lower population densities than Houston, but people rarely accuse those areas of being the epitome of sprawl.

Houston isn't perfect. The air is dirty, but that's due to oil refineries rather than to local auto driving. There is a strong push for a light-rail line, which will do nothing about congestion but which the region's transit agency says will "enhance the national and international image of the Houston region."[15] This only proves that the desire for expensive civic monuments is universal. But Houston's problems would be found in any metropolitan area of three to four million people.

What makes Houston interesting is its willingness to find different ways to solve those problems.

Notes

1. Dan Feldstein, "A rare quiet interlude for area's first freeway," *Houston Chronicle*, June 27, 1999, http://www.chron.com/cs/CDA/printstory.hts/traffic/freeways/284969.
2. Richard Babcock, *The Zoning Game: Municipal Practices and Policies* (Madison, WI: University of Wisconsin Press, 1966), p. 25.
3. Houston Planning and Development Department, *Connections: A Resource for Neighborhoods* (Houston, TX: City of Houston, 1999), p. 10.
4. Ibid, p. 19.
5. Bernard Siegan, *Land Use Without Zoning* (Lexington, MA: Lexington Books, 1972), p. 34.
6. Houston Planning and Development Department, "Neighborhood Programs," www.ci.houston.tx.us/departme/planning/program_serv.htm.
7. Babcock, *The Zoning Game*, pp. 27–28.
8. Ibid, p. 28.
9. City of Houston, *Fiscal Year 2000 Budget* (Houston, TX: City of Houston, 2000), p. IV-12, www.ci.houston.tx.us/citygovt/mayor/budget/00bud/V1IV_PLN.pdf.
10. City of Portland, *F.Y. 2000 Budget volume 1*, (Portland, OR: City of Portland, 2000), p. 71, www.ci.portland.or.us/finance/ADOPTED/FinancialSummaries1.pdf
11. National Association of Homebuilders, "Housing Opportunity Index," www.nahb.org.
12. Peter Samuel, "Electronic Tolls in North America," *Tollroads Newsletter*, 35 (January, 1999), p. 6.
13. Peter Samuel, "Houston's HCTRA Building Westpark," *Tollroads Newsletter*, 44 (November-December 1999), p. 15.
14. Peter Samuel, "Houston's Katy Pricing to Continue," *Tollroads Newsletter*, 33 (November, 1998), p. 13.
15. Metro, *20 Most Frequently Asked Questions about Light Rail* (Houston, TX: Metro, 1999), p. 20.

37. Transit

hapter 21 presented a number of efficient alternatives to rail transit, including express buses, limited buses, jitneys, and demand-responsive transit. But the real problem with urban transit is less the size of the transit vehicles than it is the institutional design of the transit agencies themselves. As heavily subsidized legal monopolies, many transit agencies appear more interested in building empires than in providing better transit service.

Transit subsidies have made the user cost of transit—but not its convenience or speed—competitive with autos. The subsidies have also made the agencies so top heavy with bureaucracy that they are inflexible and slow to respond to changing transportation patterns and new technologies. Transit fares pay for less than 40 percent of operating costs and less than 28 percent of operating and capital costs together. Local and state taxes pay for most of the operating expenses while federal taxes—mostly highway user fees—pay for most of the capital costs.

On top of that, many states grant transit agencies legal monopolies on public transportation. Except for licensed taxis and, sometimes, nonprofit organizations, no one is allowed to run transit services competitive with the public agencies. "When a single company can capture 60 percent of its revenues through taxation, and is protected from any direct competition, there is no incentive to provide services that people really want," says the Cascade Policy Institute's John Charles. "The services are totally politicized; we get whatever the pork market will bear."

The solution is to deregulate mass transit so that private operators can compete against the local public transit agency. This could result in several different innovations, including contracting out transit operations; granting or selling curb rights to private companies; and jitney services.

One moderate reform of transit agencies is known as *competitive tendering* or *contracting out* transit service. The agency defines a standard of service and invites competitive bids from private operators able to provide that service. A few routes may be so popular that they can actually pay for themselves, in which case the operator might actually pay the transit agency for the right to offer the service. In most cases the service would still be subsidized, but the buses and drivers would be privately owned and employed.

A number of American cities contract out some or all of their bus services. Las Vegas contracts out 100 percent of its bus system and has the lowest operating cost of the fifty largest transit agencies in the country.[1] In 1989, the Colorado legislature directed Denver to contract out 25 percent of its system. This saved the agency an average of 40 percent per route and a cumulative total of $100 million over ten years. The legislature recently directed the agency to increase competitive tendering to 35 percent.[2] Other cities that contract out some transit services include Indianapolis, San Diego, Los Angeles and Houston. Outside of the U.S., London, Stockholm, Copenhagen, and Auckland all contract out 50 to 100 percent of their transit systems. The experience in these cities has been that contracting out saves enough money for the cities to boost service on other lines.[3]

Critics charge that contracting out allows private operators to "skim the cream" of transit operations, that is, to run the most profitable lines while the agency is left with the least profitable ones.[4] In fact, such operations can potentially "skim the deficit" by reducing agency costs and freeing up agency resources for improvements on other transit lines. It doesn't matter to the operator whether the line is profitable or not, since bids are adjusted accordingly. What matters is that private operators can often provide service at a lower cost than public agencies.

Contracting out is not always the best solution. A University of California study of 141 transit agencies that contracted anywhere from 0 to 100 percent of services, found that contracting out could save money but "is certainly not a panacea," meaning it is not guaranteed to radically reduce costs.[5] Still, it is a viable option in many cities whose transit agencies are plagued by high overheads and declining productivity.

Vouchers are an alternative system of creating competition for transit service. When counting both capital and operating costs, the typical American transit rider gets a $2 to $3 subsidy every time they get on a bus, and generally much more when they get on a rail car. John Charles has suggested that, instead of giving the subsidy to the transit agencies, states or cities should give it directly to the transit riders in the form of vouchers. They can use the vouchers to take a bus, train, taxi, or other private or public transportation service. The operator might charge them $1 on top of the voucher, or $5, or nothing at all depending on the service. The operator then turns the vouchers into the state or local government for reimbursement.

One problem with this system is that it could encourage operators to steal each others riders by duplicating service on popular routes. To prevent this, several transportation experts at the University of California have proposed that cities sell exclusive and transferable curb rights—the right to pick up riders at various potential stops. "A carefully planned transit system based on property rights would rid the transit market of inefficient government production and overregulation" while it avoids the problems of "cutthroat competition" among rival operators.[6]

Whether vouchers, curb rights, or some other system is involved, private operation of transit in decentralized urban areas is likely to promote truly low-capacity transit operations such as the jitneys and smart jitneys described in the previous section. But the real benefit of competition is that the transit system that arises may be completely different from whatever we can predict today because competitive systems rapidly evolve and tailor themselves to local conditions. Thus, the streetcar-based single-hub transit systems that, due to administrative inertia, nearly all U.S. urban areas still have would be replaced with whatever happens to best meet the needs of each individual city.

An alternative is to have the transit agencies themselves run demand jitneys. Most transit agencies already provide a demand-responsive service, but only for disabled passengers. While the agencies could expand this service, they probably could not do it as efficiently as private operators. Since jitneys are potentially profitable, they could be operated privately at no cost to the public.

A major advantage private operators have over public agencies, other than lower overheads, is that they can hire nonunion employees. Virtually all public transit agencies have union contracts that pay significantly higher wages than private industry—sometimes higher even when the private industry is unionized. Thus, unions can be expected to oppose public transit deregulation.

However, Indianapolis Mayor Stephen Goldsmith found that the problem is often not union pay scales but bureaucracy and obsolete work rules. When he proposed privatizing urban services, he allowed public employees to bid on the contracts. They were often the successful low bidders and found ways to significantly streamline operations without reducing either wages or services.[7]

In sum, public transit deregulation will do far more to provide transportation to those who cannot drive than building an expensive, inflexible light-rail system. By providing better service at lower cost, deregulated transit systems will also carry far more people—and in turn do more to reduce auto traffic—than current transit systems.

Notes

1. Wendell Cox, "Competition, Monopoly, and Public Policy," paper presented to the 5th International Conference on Competition and Ownership in Passenger Transport, May, 1997. http://www.publicpurpose.com.
2. Wendell Cox, "Legislature Mandates Increase in Mandatory Competitive Tendering to 35 Percent in Denver," May, 1999, http://www.publicpurpose.com.
3. Cox, "Competition, Monopoly, and Public Policy."
4. Jane Holtz Kay, *Asphalt Nation: How the Automobile Took over America and How We Can Take It Back* (New York, NY: Crown, 1997), p. 313.
5. William McCullough, Brian Taylor, and Martin Wachs, "Does Contracting Transit Service Save Money?" *Access* 11 (Fall, 1997): 22–26.
6. Daniel B. Klein, Adrian T. Moore, and Binyam Reja, *Curb Rights: A Foundation for Free Enterprise in Urban Transit* (Washington, DC: Brookings, 1997), 148 pp.
7. Stephen Goldsmith, *The Twenty-First Century City: Resurrecting Urban America* (Washington, DC: Regnery, 1997), pp. 20–22.

38. Air Quality Incentives

Urban air pollution has declined significantly in the past three decades because of federal laws requiring pollution control devices on new automobiles. Thanks to those devices, many cities with once-dirty air haven't violated federal air quality standards in years even though Americans today drive two-and-one-half times as many miles as in 1970.

Significant progress can still be made in reducing automotive air pollution with some fairly simple steps. One possibility is to increase pollution standards for light trucks to the level allowed for passenger cars. In 1970, when light trucks were mainly pick ups, they were so few in number that setting a looser standard for them did not seem to be a problem. Today, the vast majority of new cars on the road are minivans, sport-utility vehicles, or other light trucks.

A second possibility is to encourage people to use preheaters for their catalytic converters. New cars produce many times more pollutants when they first start up than after they (and their catalytic converters) have warmed up. In some cities, cold-start pollution may exceed all other automotive air pollution even if a only small fraction of total driving is done when engines are cold.

A third solution is to encourage people to drive more fuel efficient autos. While pollution is not exactly proportional to fuel consumption, in general more fuel efficient cars produce less pollution. The new petroleum-electric hybrid vehicles, which get 60 to 80 miles per gallon, are expected to produce very little pollution.

Given that such simple steps can be taken to reduce air pollution still further, the question remains of how to do them. The traditional answer is to impose them by law or regulation. With a stroke of a pen, the standards applying to passenger cars can be broadened to include light trucks. The state of California has already required that 10 percent of autos sold in that state produce zero emissions by 2003.[1]

An alternative to laws and regulations is to give people incentives to reduce their pollution by charging them for the pollution they generate. It may not be possible for anyone to own the air, but it is possible to charge people fees for the rights to use that air. A pollution fee would be based on the amount of pollution each car produces per mile times the number of miles the car is driven each year.

The fee could be paid on a monthly basis or at the time owners update their registration. The advantage of a fee is that it gives people a choice of which technology they want to use to reduce pollution and may even promote the development of innovative techniques that no one today is considering.

A University of California study estimated that the cost to human health of auto air pollution for "the average car on the road in Los Angeles in 1992 is $0.03 [per vehicle mile], falling to half that amount in the year 2000."[1] Diesels and cars made before federal air pollution laws cost much more while brand-new gasoline vehicles cost less. Costs are probably lower, the study added, in "areas lacking the mountain barriers to trap pollutants in the Los Angeles air basin." Thus, pollution fees might range from 0.5 cents to 10 cents per mile depending on the type of vehicle. At these rates, someone who drives 10,000 miles a year would have to pay $50 to $1,000 per year in fees, with the average being about $150. Such fees might lead people to reduce their driving slightly, but more important they would give people powerful incentives to replace polluting cars with cleaner autos.

There are several ways to monitor pollution and collect fees. The simplest, but least effective, is to simply charge a flat fee per mile for each model of motor vehicle depending on the amount of pollution the average vehicle of that model produces. The problem with this is that individual cars of the same model can produce widely varying levels of pollution depending on how well they are maintained or how they are driven. This method also does not account for cold starts: Someone driving 50 miles in a single trip each day would pay the same amount as someone taking the same model on ten 5-mile trips per day, each starting from a cold engine. Yet the latter car would generate far more pollution. Still, this method will encourage people to drive cars that are known to produce the least pollution.

A more effective method is to use remote sensors to measure the actual amount of pollution produced by each vehicle. This would mean distributing hundreds or thousands of remote sensors around each urban area. The sensors would measure the pollution from each car and photograph the license plate of that car. Over the course of a month or a year, each car would be measured several times and the owner could be billed based on the average reading times the number of miles they drive. This would cost less than testing every single car each year or two.

An even more effective method would be to install sensors in each motor vehicle. Such sensors would continuously measure the pollution emitted by the auto and so would accurately account for cold starts, stop-and-go driving, and other variations. The sensors could be combined with an electronic transponder for toll roads. This alternative could be combined with remote sensors by asking people to voluntarily have sensors installed and giving them discounts on the pollution fees if they do. People who fail to install the sensors might pay a flat fee depending on their model of vehicle.

Income from the pollution fees could be used for many things. First, since congestion causes cars to emit far more pollution, a portion of the revenues could be used for congestion-reduction programs. These might include building more highways, mass transit, or building bicycle and pedestrian facilities. Second, a share of the revenues could be used to purchase and destroy particularly polluting engines. This might include autos built before current air pollution standards. It could also include some two-cycle engines, since these typically pollute far more than new cars. For example, some urban areas have given purchasers of electric lawnmowers a rebate for junking a functioning gasoline mower. This could significantly reduce the pollution from two-cycle engines.

Who would get to decide how to spend the funds? A regional air pollution authority could too easily be captured by special interest groups. An alternative would be to let individual neighborhood groups decide how to spend the funds generated in their areas. They could spend them directly on pollution-reducing activities or donate them to regional nonprofit groups dedicated to reducing pollution. This would create a competitive environment for cleaning up the air and give groups incentives to find better and more efficient ways to do it.

A variation would improve the incentives still further but be administratively more difficult. This would substitute tradable pollution permits rather than pollution fees. All car owners would be given a permit to pollute as much as their car is legally allowed to pollute. Make those permits tradable so that anyone who buys a new car will be required to buy a permit for the amount of pollution that car would be expected to produce. Owners of a pre-1970 cars can junk their cars and sell their permits to a couple of dozen purchasers of brand new cars.

Tradable permits might be politically palatable because they don't require fees paid to the state. They also have the advantage that the government can systematically reduce overall pollution by buying permits and not using them. But as described here, tradable permits may be unfair because older cars aren't driven as many miles as newer ones. While older cars pollute more on a per mile basis, they tend to produce less pollution each year than newer cars because they go fewer miles. This alternative might be worth considering if the administrative and social problems of incorporating mileage into the permit can be resolved.

In short, there are many ways pollution emissions fees can give people incentives to drive cleaner automobiles and generate funds that can be used to reduce pollution and pollution-causing activities such as congestion. State and local governments should experiment with the various alternatives described here to see which works best.

Notes

1. California Environmental Protection Agency Air Resources Board, *California Exhaust Emission Standards and Test Procedures for 2003 and Subsequent Model Zero-Emission Vehicles* (Sacramento, CA: CA EPA, 1999), section C-2.
2. Kenneth A. Small & Camilla Kazimi, "On the Costs of Air Pollution from Motor Vehicles," *Journal of Transport Economics and Policy* 29(1):28.

The Pay-to-Pollute Myth

Myth: Charging pollution fees allows people to pay to pollute.
Reality: Pollution fees give people incentives not to pollute and to find the most efficient way of reducing pollution.

Many people believe that pollution is bad and that it is wrong to be able to pay to do something bad. Pollution fees, they say, would allow wealthy people to pollute air that other people have to breathe. But pollution is not evil, it is simply a form of consumption. When we pollute the air or water, we are consuming clean air or clean water. Paying to consume clean air or clean water is not necessarily different from paying to consume food, clothing, or housing.

Federal laws and regulations have clearly helped clean America's air and water. Lead, carbon monoxide, and hydrocarbon emissions are well below the amounts they were thirty years ago. To a large degree, however, regulations have dealt with simple issues: Lead is bad, cars can run without lead, so ban lead in gasoline. New cars today pollute less than 5 percent as much as cars built thirty years ago. The next step is more difficult: how to reduce pollution to 1 percent or a half percent or even a smaller percentage of thirty years ago?

The great advantage of paying for something is that the payment creates an incentive to produce more and consume less of that thing. If people have to pay for their auto's air pollution, the auto industry will find ways to build new cars that pollute less and even to modify existing cars so they pollute less. No one today can accurately guess the most effective way of reducing pollution tomorrow, so a regulatory solution, such as requiring manufacturers to make a few electric cars, may not find the best way.

Under our current system, wealthy people can pollute more by driving bigger cars. With pollution fees, they would have to pay fees equal to the cost of their pollution. Those fees would be used to clean up the air in various ways. Thus, pollution fees give everyone an incentive to pollute less even as they make everyone who continues to pollute pay to clean up the air or water. The result will be much less pollution than the regulatory system that exists today.

39. Institutions

At its heart, smart growth is a struggle between the *centralizers*, who want to push decisions up to the regional, state, and national level; and the *decentralizers*, who want to push decisions down to the state, local, and individual level. Centralizers argue that local decisions are inefficient because they allow people and cities to impose costs on others. While such inefficiencies exist, decentralizers argue that decisions made by regional or national governments tend to be even more wasteful because they are more responsive to pork barrel politics and more likely to try to impose some moral ideal on other people.

While a case can be made for both side, most of the problems with decentralized government can be corrected by using such tools as value pricing and pollution emissions fees to insure that people pay the full costs of their actions. If that is the case, the argument for regional or other centralized government falls apart.

In short, with appropriate institutional design, regional problems can be adequately handled by local agencies and individuals. While revolutionary in some ways, the following ideas are a natural extension of American desires for decentralized government and the success of the free enterprise system:

- The best thing Congress can do for America's urban areas is to stop funding them: Eliminate the federal gas tax, federal housing programs, and other urban programs and let state and local governments decide their own futures.
- Local streets are built by developers and maintained by neighborhood associations with funding out of local gas taxes, property taxes, or whatever funds the local government thinks are appropriate.
- Urban freeways are built and maintained by local public or private toll authorities. Value pricing would be used to moderate congestion and provide income for both new capacity and maintenance of existing roads.
- Other arterials and collectors would be built and maintained by toll or non-toll authorities depending on tolling technologies and local desires. Where congestion is modest, funding of such roads out of gasoline taxes may make sense. Severely congested roads should be considered for value pricing.
- Different kinds of transit can be provided by a variety of local agencies and private transit companies. Government funding for transit should be in the

form of vouchers to transit users, not grants to transit providers, thus giving the users a choice of services in a competitive environment.

- Land-use decisions would be made by neighborhood associations, which presumably would offer a range of lifestyles from neighborhoods with very strict rules to ones with no rules at all. Neighborhood associations might also have the option of taking over street maintenance, schools, and other local services.

- Regional open space and scenery would be protected by various public parks districts and private organizations competing for various funds, some of which are provided by the neighborhood associations.

- Neighborhood associations could also decide how to spend pollution emission fees generated by residents of their neighborhoods. They could spend them on local pollution reduction projects or donate them to regional organizations that would compete for funds and spend them on such activities as buying and scrapping high-emission vehicles; transit vouchers for people in polluted areas; or subsidizing the installation of pollution-reduction technologies.

Smart growth promises severe increases in congestion throughout urban areas, which may lead to increased air pollution. It also promotes the loss of urban open space to infill, the destruction of many existing neighborhoods, and unaffordable housing. These negative effects result from the smart-growth strategy of treating problems indirectly through regulation and manipulation of government spending rather than treating individual problems directly. In contrast, the American dream alternative aims to solve congestion and pollution problems and resolve conflicts over land use and open space by giving people the tools to treat these problems directly in their local areas.

Congestion would be relieved by a combination of congestion tolls and new facilities and transit funded by those tolls. Toll roads would also create incentives for private road companies to build and operate highways on private rights of way. The regionally elected transportation board would keep the combination of congestion and fees as pain free as possible.

Pollution would be relieved by emissions fees that give auto users incentives to minimize pollution. Moreover, the fees would provide funds that could be used to reduce pollution by eliminating the most polluting motors and by funding transit or other pollution-reducing activities.

Neighborhoods would be protected through a process of self determination. This will also assure a diversity of neighborhoods instead of all neighborhoods being expected to fit the "new urbanist" or some other mold.

Scenery and open space would be protected by a system of parks and scenic easements. The cost of scenic easements would be paid by the beneficiaries: the people who buy land in the region, and most particularly those whose properties have the best views.

Overall, the American dream alternative should significantly lower congestion and pollution and make more livable neighborhoods. The major drawback, some will say, is that the lack of an urban-growth boundary does not guarantee the protection of farms, forests, and open space. In fact, this proposal will probably protect more open space than smart growth. Some of the protected open space will be inside of current urban areas. Some areas outside of current urbanized zones will be developed. But this proposal greatly reduces the incentives to leap-frog development beyond existing areas. The net result should be more open space at any particular time.

These proposals are designed to minimize the hidden costs of growth to urban residents. But one cost remains: the subsidies that states and localities often give to corporations to build factories, offices, or other developments in those areas. Growth subsidies are a vicious circle. People move into a city, so the city subsidizes factories to provide jobs for them. In response, more people move in. Some politicians worry that average incomes in their regions are lower than in some other regions and want to subsidize jobs to increase local income levels. But as University of Montana economist Thomas Power has shown, people are willing to earn less to live in places with a high quality of life. Trying to match incomes with places whose quality of life is lower will merely attract people until the local quality of life is no better than elsewhere.[2]

The apparent solution is to stop giving tax breaks and other subsidies to agents of growth. The problem is that it is not always easy to distinguish between a subsidy and an appropriate public investment. As noted in the Subsidized-Development Myth, most local tax structures effectively overtax commercial areas to pay for the schools needed by residential areas. A town that is all residential with no commercial uses thus must either charge significantly higher taxes or run short of educational funds. In such a situation, it may be reasonable for the town to offer an infrastructure subsidy to a commercial developer whose developments will help pay for schools for decades into the future.

Rather than argue over whether this is a subsidy or not, the best solution is to decentralize government spending to as local a level as possible so that local taxpayers will best be able to monitor spending on infrastructure and other public services. In most cases this means the city or town; some public services could be taken over by neighborhood associations. Decentralization will force cities and towns to compete with one another but will also give local residents the greatest say in local spending.

Notes

1. Quoted by Andres Duany, http://www.periferia.org/publications/Quotes.html.
2. Thomas M. Power, *The Economic Value of the Quality of Life* (Boulder, CO: Westview, 1980), 144 pp.

The Subsidized-Development Myth

Myth: New development cannot pay for itself and must be subsidized by existing residents.

Reality: In most states, all residential areas consume more services than they pay in taxes and are subsidized by commercial and other uses.

In fast-growing regions, smart-growth and no-growth advocates each play on residents' fears that their taxes are subsidizing the often expensive homes built for newcomers. Studies often compare the tax revenues that government can expect to collect from a new residential development with the costs of government services to that development. Invariably, the revenues are less than costs. The natural conclusion is that existing residents must be subsidizing the new ones.

This conclusion is wrong. In fact, if you compare tax revenues from existing residential areas with the costs of services to those areas, you would find that existing areas also lose money. If both existing and new residential areas cost more than they pay in taxes, then who makes up the difference? The answer is commercial and other nonresidential uses. This is because tax rates on commercial and residential areas tend to be about the same, yet the commercial areas do not add to local school services, which normally makes up the largest share of the local tax bill. The commercial areas therefore effectively subsidize residential areas.

"For every $1.00 of tax revenue that comes in from a residential subdivision, as much as $1.22 goes out to provide services, especially schools," says Joel Garreau. "By contrast, for every $1.00 of tax revenue that comes in from commercial development, at most thirty-two cents is required in expenditures, usually for roads." This explains, says Garreau, "why elected officials feel they must encourage commercial development or die."[1] While the numbers vary from place to place, a study of tax revenues and municipal costs in seven states comes to the same conclusion.[2] Attempts to make new subdivisions "pay for themselves" through developer fees can impose an unfair burden on new home buyers unless the fees are adjusted to account for the surplus from new commercial areas that will serve those subdivisions. Such *developer impact fees* often really mask an effort to slow or halt growth.

Of course, commercial areas aren't really subsidizing residential areas because businesses benefit from schools in many ways. But when fiscal impact studies attribute all school costs to new residential areas they will inevitably, and erroneously, conclude that those residential areas are being subsidized. The real problem with existing tax structures is that they sometimes encourage communities to attract commercial development while dumping residential development onto adjacent towns. Density will not solve this problem.

Notes

1. Joel Garreau, *Edge City: Life on the New Frontier* (New York, NY: Doubleday, 1991), p. 465.
2. American Farmland Trust Farmland Information Center. *Cost of Community Services Studies Fact Sheet*, 1998. http://farm.fic.niu.edu/fic-ta/tafs-cocs.html.

40. Conclusions

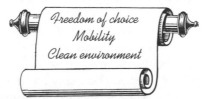

Freedom of choice
Mobility
Clean environment

The American dream alternative was originally designed for my hometown of Portland, Oregon. Just as Portland's smart-growth planning has become a model for smart growth in other cities, the American dream alternative provides a model for alternatives to smart growth in other cities. Starting with the American dream alternative, you can create a proposal that will help you create and preserve the livable, congestion-free cities that you want for your future.

The American dream alternative is a sharp contrast to smart growth, which begins by sacrificing personal freedom and mobility in order to protect urban livability and ends up sacrificing livability in a futile attempt to control people's lives and lifestyles. The American dream alternative shows that personal freedom and mobility are compatible with and even essential for urban livability.

When debates over public policy get emotional, people often confuse *means* with *ends*. If you are not for smart growth, they say, then you must be for paving over the countryside. Yet smart growth uses the wrong means *and* the wrong ends.

- Why should people in one of the least populated parts of the world be so panicked about running out of land that they support costly boondoggles and unpopular restrictions on personal freedom?
- Why should regions spend most of their transportation budgets on rail-transit systems that will never carry more than 1 or 2 percent of regional travel?
- Why should we build light-rail lines to reduce congestion and then densify neighborhoods along the lines to boost ridership, which—since most people still won't use transit—makes congestion worse than ever?
- Why should we redesign cities for the 10 to 20 percent of people who walk, bicycle, or use transit while making them hostile to the 80 to 90 percent of people who use autos—when we could improve conditions for both?
- How can people think congestion will be reduced by significantly increasing population densities without similarly increasing highway capacities?
- Why should we destroy urban open spaces that people value in the name of protecting rural open spaces, 95 percent of which aren't in danger anyway?
- Why should a nation with a low average population density model its cities after those in nations whose densities are many times more?

Smart growth has become popular because the growth spurred by our decentralized society can appear just as threatening and unstable as the stagnation produced by central planning. Congestion, pollution, poverty, and loss of urban open spaces are real problems. Yet smart growth's vision of nicely designed yet incredibly congested cities, stupendously expensive transit systems, and increasingly restrictive rules and regulations aimed at curbing people's freedom of choice is unacceptable in America. Even if it were acceptable, a vision based on myths and folklore will make cities less livable, not more so.

The American dream of letting people choose how they want to live, while insuring they pay the full costs of their choices, can solve all of the problems that smart growth claims to address, with none of its disadvantages.

- Neighborhoods can be controlled not by distant planners but by the residents and landowners in those neighborhoods.
- Congestion and pollution can be managed with incentives and user fees.
- Open space and scenery can be protected by insuring that those who most benefit from scenic views will pay most of the cost.
- Poverty can be reduced by giving poor people the same advantages available to the wealthy: better schools, safer streets, and greater mobility.

Freedom of choice, incentives, and neighborhood self-determination will create far more livable urban areas than regulation, subsidies, and regional control. Our brightest future will come from fact-based policies that solve today's problems by combining freedom with responsibility and by decentralizing decisions as far as possible. With such policies, Americans will have every reason to be proud of our cities, our suburbs, our wide open spaces, our transportation systems, and the wondrous opportunities they provide to all our residents.

Appendices

Resources
& Glossary

Row houses add density to a neighborhood that once consisted solely of single-family detached homes (top). Portland planners now regret permitting so many row houses because they aren't dense enough—they would have preferred that developers build high-density transit-oriented developments.

An advertisement at the construction site of Beaverton Round (bottom) doesn't hint that the transit-oriented development has gone bankrupt despite nearly $10 million in subsidies (see photo on title page).

Appendix 1. Resources

A. Key Resources

This book cites hundreds of books, reports, articles, and web sites. This appendix lists some of the most outstanding sources of information on all sides of the issue. At the very least, everyone interested in urban issues should do the following four things.

First, get on the internet if you are not already on it. The World Wide Web can be a great way for you to get information and email can be the best way for you to stay in touch with other people.

Second, subscribe to:
- *Access* magazine, a free publication of the University of California Transportation Center. Twice a year, *Access* includes summaries of recent research on urban transportation and planning. All of the back issues except #2 are still in print; ask for your free copies. To subscribe and order back issues, email access@uclink4.berkeley.edu.
- The Thoreau Institute's free urban email newsletter, which provides updates and information on urban issues. To subscribe, send an email to urban@ti.org.
  Third, read:
- James Dunn's book, *Driving Forces*, the best pro-mobility book published in recent years;
- Joel Garreau's *Edge City*, the best book about what is happening to our cities and suburbs today.
  Fourth, visit the following web sites:
- The Competitive Enterprise Institute's sprawl links (http://www.cei.org/pubs/1999/simmons%20%26%20wyatt.html) give access to many useful reports, including some cited below.
- The Public Purpose (http://www.publicpurpose.com) is a wealth of data about transit, transportation, and urban development. From the web site you can also subscribe to a useful transport policy discussion group.
- The Reason Public Policy Institute (http://www.rppi.org) has many reports on transportation and sprawl on line.

- The Thoreau Institute (http://www.ti.org/urban.html) has reports, fact sheets, op-eds, and articles about smart growth, sprawl, and mobility.

B. Books

Pro-planning and pro-smart growth book writers have been far more prolific than those with alternative views. Here is a selection of some of the most influential and interesting books on all sides.

Pro-Mobility

James A. Dunn, Jr., *Driving Forces: The Automobile, Its Enemies, and the Politics of Mobility* **(Washington, DC: Brookings Institution, 1998), 230 pp.**
    Dunn updates John Rae's *The Road and the Car* by making a strong case that the "automobile system has been nothing if not sustainable for about a century now."
John Rae, *The Road and the Car in American Life* **(Cambridge, MA: MIT Press, 1971), 390 pp.**
    Rae attempts to answer the many anti-auto books written in the late 1960s. While Rae is a respected scholar, the fact that this book was funded by auto manufacturers may have tainted it. It is also somewhat dated.

Anti-Auto, Anti-Sprawl

Peter Calthorpe, *The Next American Metropolis: Ecology, Community, and the American Dream* **(New York, NY: Princeton Architectural Press, 1993), 175 pp.**
    Written before new urbanism became as coercive as it is today, Calthorpe reasonably argues that people should be given a choice between low-density suburbs and transit-oriented developments. That's fine as long as no coercion or subsidies are required to build the transit-oriented developments.
George Dantzig and Thomas Saaty, *Compact City: A Plan for a Livable Urban Environment* **(San Francisco, CA: Freeman, 1973), 244 pp.**
    One of the earliest formal arguments for controlling and densifying low-density suburbs.
Andres Duany, Elizabeth Plater-Zyberk, and Jeff Speck, *Suburban Nation: The Rise of Sprawl and the Decline of the American Dream* **(New York, NY: North Point Press, 2000), 290 pp.**
    The latest anti-suburbs book written by some of the leading gurus of smart growth.
Peter Katz. *The New Urbanism: Toward an Architecture of Community* **(New York, NY: McGraw-Hill, 1994), 245 pp.**
    A coffee table book featuring pretty photos of the few new urban communities that have been built and architects' drawings of the many that have not.
Jane Holtz Kay, *Asphalt Nation: How the Automobile Took over America and How We Can Take It Back* **(New York, NY: Crown, 1997), 418 pp.**
    The latest and perhaps the most popular in a long history of anti-auto books,

Asphalt Nation is an emotional diatribe with little evidence to support its many claims.

James Howard Kunstler, *The Geography of Nowhere: The Rise and Decline of America's Man-Made Landscapes* (New York, NY: Simon & Schuster, 1993), 303 pp.

Kunstler's ravings against the suburbs have proven popular if not rational. His sequel, *Home from Nowhere*, is an influential argument for new urbanism.

Philip Langdon, *A Better Place to Live: Reshaping the American Suburb* (New York, NY: Harper Perennial, 1994), 270 pp.

Langdon is a dedicated inner-city dweller who thinks everyone would be happier if they lived the way he does.

Alternative Views of Planning

Stewart Brand, *How Buildings Learn: What Happens After They're Built* (New York, NY: Viking, 1994), 243 pp.

Brand's scathing critique of architects makes you wonder: If architects can't design decent buildings, what makes them think they can design decent cities?

Joel Garreau, *Edge City: Life on the New Frontier* (New York, NY: Doubleday, 1991), 546 pp.

A magnificent and objective view of current urban trends. Garreau started out believing in planning and ended up very skeptical.

Peter Geoffrey Hall, *Cities of Tomorrow: An Intellectual History of Urban Planning and Design in the Twentieth Century* (Cambridge, MA: Blackwell, 1988; updated to 1996), 502 pp.

An excellent history documenting urban planning's many failures and few successes.

Jane Jacobs, *The Death and Life of Great American Cities* (New York, NY: Vintage, 1963), 458 pp.

The classic critique of urban planning when planners were doing urban renewal. Now planners want to do suburban renewal and often cite Jacobs as their inspiration. But she dislikes planners far more than she dislikes the suburbs.

James C. Scott, *Seeing Like a State: How Certain Schemes to Improve the Human Condition Have Failed* (New Haven, CT: Yale University Press, 1998), 445 pp.

Blasts urban planners for being tools of an authoritarian state.

Zoning

Robert Nelson, *Zoning and Property Rights: An Analysis of the American System of Land-Use Regulation* (Cambridge, MA: MIT, 1977), 259 pp.

Suggests a process for cities to eliminate zoning and create neighborhood associations with the power to enforce and change protective covenants.

Bernard Siegan, *Land Use Without Zoning* (Lexington, MA: Lexington Books, 1972), 271 pp.

An analysis of Houston, which relies on protective covenants and homeowner associations rather than zoning to protect neighborhoods.

Urban Transportation

Anthony Downs, *Stuck in Traffic: Coping with Peak-Hour Traffic Congestion* (Washington, DC: Brookings, 1992), 210 pp.

Downs' analytical skills are highly respected, yet he seems to fall short when he applies them to urban issues. Here he mixes incisive data analyses with many unsupported conclusions and endorses regional governments on the strange theory that such governments will do good if they are given unlimited power.

George M. Smerk, *The Federal Role in Urban Mass Transportation* (Bloomington, IN: Indiana University Press, 1991), 391 pp.

An objective analysis of federal transit programs through 1990, Smerk shows that federal funding has benefited transit bureaucracies but played little or no role in reducing urban congestion or air pollution.

C. Reports

Pro-Mobility

Peter Samuel, *How to "Build Our Way out of Congestion"* (Los Angeles, CA: Reason Foundation, 1999), RPPI report #250, http://www.rppi.org/wecanbuild.html.

Contrary to anti-auto rhetoric, "out-of-the-box" thinking can conquer urban roadway congestion.

Samuel Staley, *The Sprawling of America: In Defense of the Dynamic City* (Los Angeles, CA: Reason Foundation, 1999), RPPI report #251, http://www.rppi.org/sprawl.html.

Provides a market-based perspective of suburban growth and challenges many underlying principles of the anti-sprawl movement.

Pro-Smart Growth

Sierra Club, *The Dark Side of the American Dream: The Costs and Consequences of Suburban Sprawl* (College Park, MD: Sierra Club, 1998), 28 pp., http://www.sierraclub.org/transportation/sprawl/sprawl_report/index.html.

Influential, thought provoking, and wrong on just about every count, the Sierra Club's report is an easy introduction to smart-growth arguments.

Urban Transportation

Donald Camph, *Dollars and Sense: The Economic Case for Public Transportation in America* (Washington, DC: Citizen Action, 1997), 95 pp.

Claims that the benefits of investments in transit "far outweigh the costs." For an alternative view, see John Semmens' report below.

James V. DeLong, *Myths of Light Rail Transit* (Los Angeles, CA: Reason Foundation, 1998), RPPI report #244, http://www.rppi.org/ps244.html.

Light rail transit fails to relieve congestion, help the poor, or do many of the other things claimed for it.

Robert T. Dunphy, "Review of Recent American Light Rail Experiences," in Transportation Research Board, *Seventh National Conference on Light Rail Transit* (Washington, DC: National Academy Press, 1995), pp. 104–113.

Updates Don Pickrell's study (below) and concludes that "Light rail is expensive [and] will not reduce traffic congestion."

Federal Highway Administration, *Transportation Air Quality: Selected Facts and Figures* (Washington, DC: US DOT, 1996), 35 pp.

Useful source of air pollution data and references to further information.

General Accounting Office, *Community Development: Extent of Federal Influence on "Urban Sprawl" Is Unclear* (Washington, DC: GAO, 1999), 81 pp. GAO/RCED-99-87, http://www.gao.gov/new.items/rc99087.pdf.

The GAO found no evidence that federal subsidies caused or accelerated sprawl.

Arnold M. Howitt, Joshua P. Anderson, and Alan A. Altshuler, *The New Politics of Clean Air and Transportation* (Washington, DC: US DOT, 1997), 43 pp.

A candid summary of interviews with dozens of state and local planners.

Randal O'Toole, *Urban Transit Myths* (Los Angeles, CA: Reason Foundation, 1998), RPPI report # 245, , http://www.rppi.org/ps245.html.

Transit plays an important role in moving people who cannot drive, but efforts to use transit to get significant numbers of people out of their cars have failed.

Don Pickrell, *Urban Rail Transit Projects: Forecast Versus Actual Ridership and Costs* (Cambridge, MA: US DOT, 1989), 144 pp.

US DOT researcher Pickrell found that most rail transit lines built in the last two decades cost far more but carried far fewer people than planners predicted when cities decided to build the lines.

Alan Pisarski, *Commuting in America II* (Washington, DC: Eno Transportation Foundation, 1996),

This sequel to the 1987 book of the same name is packed with data about commuting. The report provides little support for smart-growth arguments that densification and rail lines can reduce auto driving.

Robert W. Poole, Jr., and Michael Griffin, *Shuttle Vans: The Overlooked Transit Alternative* (Los Angeles, CA: Reason Foundation, 1997), RPPI report #176, http://www.rppi.org/es176.html.

Door-to-door van transit offers a low-cost, feasible, and proven alternative to reduce emission and traffic congestion in greater Los Angeles.

John Semmens, *Rethinking Transit "Dollars & Sense": Unearthing the True Cost of Public Transit* (Los Angeles, CA: Reason Foundation, 1998), RPPI report #243, http://www.rppi.org/ps243central.html.

Discusses how the highly-touted report *Dollars & Sense* is plagued with inflated numbers, omissions, and outright falsehoods to make the case that public transit offers a "handsome" return on investment.

U.S. Department of Transportation, *A Guide to Metropolitan Transportation Planning Under ISTEA: How the Pieces Fit Together* (Washington, DC: US DOT, 1995), 42 pp.

Slightly outdated by passage of TEA-21, this publication still is the best introduction to federally mandated transportation planning available.

U.S. **Department of Transportation,** *Transportation Conformity: A Basic Guide for State & Local Officials* (Washington, DC: US DOT, 1997), 22 pp.
Introduction to the relationship between transportation and clean air laws.

D. Magazines, Journals, and Articles

Magazines and Journals

Access, **published twice a year by the University of California Transportation Center, 108 Naval Architecture Building, University of California, Berkeley, CA 94720-1720, 510-643-5454, 510-643-5456 fax, access@uclink4.berkeley.edu.**
An excellent source of recent research on mobility and urban planning—and it's free!

Innovation Briefs, **published bimonthly by the Urban Mobility Corporation, 1050 Seventeenth Street NW #600, Washington, DC 20036-5503, 202-775-0311, 202-775-4867 fax, korski@erols.com.**
Short articles about transportation and urban planning.

Tollroads, **published at 301 East Third Street, Frederick, MD 21701-5316, 301-631-1148, 301-631-1248 fax, tollroads@aol.com.**
Monthly newsletter on toll roads and road price issues. Naturally, charges a toll.

Articles

"Bye-Bye, Suburban Dream," by Jerry Adler, *Newsweek,* May 15, 1995 pp. 40–53.
This fourteen-page article enthused about smart growth when it was still called new urbanism and contained only one paragraph suggesting that anyone thought that it might not work.

Peter Gordon and Harry Richardson, "Are Compact Cities a Desirable Planning Goal?" *Journal of the American Planning Association* 61(1), http://www.smartgrowth.org/library/apa_pointcounterpoint/apa_sprawl.html
Demolishes the smart-growth claims that low-density suburbs cause congestion and that higher densities are better.

Helen Ladd, "Population Growth, Density and the Costs of Providing Public Services," *Urban Studies* 29(2):273–295
Ladd, a researcher at Duke University, shows that, contrary to the "cost of sprawl" claim, urban infrastructure costs increase with density.

E. World Wide Web Sites

Pro-Smart Growth

American Public Transportation Association: http://www.apta.com/

American Planning Association: http://www.planning.org
Congress on the New Urbanism: http://www.cnu.org
Surface Transportation Policy Project: http://www.transact.org
EPA-developed smart-growth web site: http://www.smartgrowth.org
Sierra Club anti-sprawl: http://www.sierraclub.org/transportation

Alternative Views

Americans Against Traffic Calming: http://www.io.com/~bumper/ada.htm
Cascade Policy Institute: http://www.CascadePolicy.org
Competitive Enterprise Institute urban sprawl links: http://www.cei.org/pubs/1999/
    simmons%20%26%20wyatt.html
LibertySearch.com: http://www.libertysearch.com/Environment/Urban_Sprawl/
National Motorists Association: http://www.motorists.org/
Oregon Transportation Institute: http://www.hevanet.com/oti
Pacific Research Institute: http://www.pacificresearch.org/action/action17.html
Reason Public Policy Institute: http://www.rppi.org
Thoreau Institute: http://www.ti.org/urban.html
University of California Transportation Center: http://socrates.berkeley.edu/~uctc/

Data Sources

Census data: http://venus.census.gov/cdrom/lookup 1990 lookup
Congestion: http://mobility.tamu.edu/
Highway Statistics: http://www.fhwa.dot.gov/ohim/ohimstat.htm
Natural Resources Inventory: http://www.nhq.nrcs.usda.gov/CCS/NRIrlse.html
National Transit Database: http://www.bts.gov/ntda/ntdb/, http://
    www.ntdprogram.com/NTD/ntdhome.nsf/Docs/Publications?OpenDocument
National Transportation Statistics: http://www.bts.gov/ntda/nts/
TEA-21: http://www.fhwa.dot.gov/tea21/index.htm (contains the complete text of
    the act as well as summaries of the important parts of the law)
Transit Fact Book: http://www.apta.com/stats/index.htm
Transportation Energy Data Book: http://www-cta.ornl.gov/data/tedb19/

Government Agencies

Census Bureau: http://www.census.gov/
U.S. Department of Transportation: http://www.dot.gov
U.S. Environmental Protection Agency: http://www.epa.gov
U.S. EPA grants database: http://www.epa.gov/envirofw/html/gics/gics_query.html
U.S. General Accounting Office: http://www.gao.gov

Appendix 2. Glossary

A. Geographic Terms

central city includes the area within the legal boundary of the major city in an urban area, such as Chicago, Denver, or St. Louis. A few urban areas, such as the Twin Cities and San Francisco-Oakland, may have multiple central cities.

city includes only areas within the legal limits of an incorporated city.

exurb refers to a rural area or small town that has a growing population of former urban residents who have moved on retirement or because their work no longer requires them to remain in an urban area.

metropolitan statistical area is a Census Bureau term that includes all of the land in the county or counties that include the urbanized area in and around a central city. The Census Bureau also defines **partial** metropolitan statistical areas, particularly for urban areas that cross state lines, and **combined** metropolitan statistical areas that include all partial areas in a single urban area. Metropolitan statistical areas provide useful data for things like jobs and population but not for densities because large portions of some of the counties in many metropolitan statistical areas are rural. For densities, use *urbanized area* data.

nineteenth-century cities is a term used in this book to refer to cities largely built up before the development of the automobile. They have dense centers with a high percentage of jobs located in the center. The classic example is New York: Manhattan is ten times denser than the New York urban area as a whole. While nineteenth-century cities are distinguished by densely populated urban cores, even more important are their dense employment centers. This allows for relatively high transit usage by commuters because so many commuters work in a central location.

place includes a city, village, borough, or "census-defined place," i.e., any concentration of people.

suburb generally includes all urbanized land outside of the legal limits of a central city.

twentieth-century cities is a term used in this book to refer to cities largely built up after the auto. They may have downtowns but do not have high concentrations of people and jobs in one central location. San Jose, whose central city is just 8 percent denser than the urban area as a whole, is a prime example. Jobs in twentieth-century cities tend to be spread throughout the area. Other than San Francisco, urban areas outside of the Northeast and Midwest tend to be twentieth-century cities.

urbanized area includes all developed land in and around the central city. As used by the Census Bureau, it includes all the land in a central city of 50,000 or more people plus all adjacent land with a population density greater than 1,000 people per square mile (roughly one house every two acres).

B. Planning Terms

Ahwahnee principles are a set of ideas written by a group of architects and planners at the Ahwahnee Lodge in Yosemite National Park. The ideas reconcile the differences between new urbanism and neotraditionalism, generally leaning towards designing communities to reduce auto dependency.

growth control generally includes policies designed to limit the rate of growth of a city or metropolitan area.

growth management generally includes policies designed to determine *where* and *how* growth takes place without limiting the *rate* of growth.

metropolitan planning organization (MPO) is a government agency or body made up of representatives of most or all residents in an urban area. Initially mandated by the Federal Housing Authority in the 1960s solely to determine how federal housing (and later transportation) funds would be allocated within each urban area, later laws gave MPOs the responsibility to write regional transportation plans. Some MPOs have also gained various amounts of land-use planning authority.

neotraditional refers to a style of neighborhood design first advocated by Andres Duany and Elizabeth Plater-Zyberk. It includes homes with large front porches, deemphasized garages, alleys, mixes of commercial and residential, and other features of so-called "traditional" neighborhoods, that is, neighborhoods built around the turn of the century.

new urbanism refers to a style of neighborhood design first advocated by California architect Peter Calthorpe. Where neotraditionalism is more concerned with individual home design, new urbanism is more concerned with reducing auto usage through densities, street layouts, and transit-oriented and pedestrian-friendly design. Originally proposed as an idea for developers to voluntarily try, new urbanism soon turned into a movement demanding that zoning codes mandate certain densities and development patterns.

smart growth is a term first popularized by Maryland Governor Parris Glendening to refer to his proposal that the state mandate urban-growth boundaries, transit-oriented design, and other new-urban ideas. The term has now become broadly accepted by the Environmental Protection Agency and others to embrace government-enforced, new-urban policies.

urban-growth boundary is a politically drawn line outside of which development is limited or forbidden.

urban-service boundary, a variation on an urban-growth boundary, is a line outside of which a city or county plans to provide no urban services such as sewer or water lines.

C. Transportation Terms

arterials are major through streets, usually with four or more lanes. Technically, freeways are arterials, but as used in this book *arterials* means non-freeway arterials.

collectors are minor through streets, usually with just two lanes.

commuter rail refers to transit that operates on existing rail lines that often also carry freight. Trains of rail cars are pulled by Diesel or electric locomotives. Top speeds are typically 60 MPH. Commuter rail lines go longer distances and make fewer stops than light or heavy rail. Major commuter rail systems can be found in New York, Boston, and Chicago.

congestion tolls are tolls that vary by time of day: higher during rush hour, lower or free during non-peak periods.

employee commute options (ECO) is a program requiring employers to adopt plans to reduce the amount of commuting their employees do in single-occupancy vehicles. Proven to be ineffective but mandated by federal law in heavily polluted (extreme or severe) urban airsheds.

freeways include all limited-access roads; the "free" in freeway means free of stop lights and stop signs, not free of tolls.

heavy rail is a form of transit that uses electric-powered vehicles that may form long trains that run on an exclusive right of way. Top speeds may be 80 MPH and average speeds as much as 40 MPH. Washington, DC's Metro is an example of heavy rail.

high-occupancy toll lane (HOT lane) is a highway lane dedicated to single-occupancy vehicles that pay a toll or high-occupancy vehicles that go toll-free.

high-occupancy vehicle (HOV) includes buses and cars with three or more (or sometimes two or more) people. A *high-occupancy vehicle lane* is a highway lane dedicated at least some hours of the day to high-occupancy vehicles.

inspection and maintenance (I&M) programs require regular (usually at time of reregistration) inspection and maintenance of motor vehicles to insure that they comply with air pollution standards. Effectiveness is highly debated, but mandated by federal law in fairly polluted (extreme, severe, or serious) urban airsheds.

Interstates are freeways that are part of the Interstate Highway System.

levels of service are measures of highway traffic flow conditions.

light rail is a form of transit that uses lightweight, electric-powered vehicles that are usually run singly or in pairs. They may run on an exclusive right of way but often run in streets. Top speeds are typically around 50 MPH while average speeds are only around 20 MPH. The term refers to the weight of the vehicles, not the weight of the rails. San Diego's trolley is a form of light rail.

local streets are neighborhood streets that provide very little through traffic.

new transit rider is a transit rider attracted by an improvement such as rail or better bus service who previously used cars or another mode of travel.

nonattainment area is an urban area that experiences violations of federal air quality standards. The Environmental Protection Agency rates nonattainment as *extreme, severe, serious, moderate*, and *marginal*. Various federal requirements and funding restrictions are imposed on nonattainment areas depending on the rating.

single-occupancy vehicle (SOV) includes cars with a driver and no passengers.

transportation control management or **measures** cover a wide range of transportation strategies including transportation demand management and transportation system management.

transportation demand management or **measures** include actions designed to change travel behavior, and in particular to reduce single-occupancy vehicle travel. TDMs range from mild measures such as government-promoted voluntary carpooling, high-occupancy vehicle lanes, transit improvements, and bike paths, to highly restrictive measures such as parking limits, mandatory carpooling, and land-use regulations.

transportation system management or **measures** include policies and projects aimed at making a more efficient use of existing transportation networks. This may include improved traffic signals, on-ramp metering, telecommuting, congestion warning systems, and programs that encourage alternative work hours, carpooling, transit, and cycling or walking.

vehicle-miles traveled is an estimate of the number of miles all motorized road vehicles travel in a particular area.

D. Zoning Terms

downzoning indicates new zoning or rezoning to a lower density or less intensive development. For example, farm land that is unzoned or zoned to allow low-density residential might be downzoned to limit development to one house every 40 or more acres.

exclusive zoning limits development within each zone to the type of development allowed by that zone. For example, new residences may not be built in commercial or industrial zones. Developments may be at significantly lower densities than allowed by a zone; for example, an "R-5 zone" allows housing on lots as small as 5,000 square feet, but lots may be any size larger than that. This is the sort of zoning many communities adopted from the 1960s to the 1980s.

hierarchical zoning creates zoning levels, traditionally (from higher to lower levels) industrial, commercial, multifamily residential, and single-family residential. An area in any level of zoning may be used for any purpose in *or below* that level. For example, an area zoned commercial may be used for residential but not industrial. This is the sort of zoning communities adopted from the late 1910s to the early 1950s.

performance zoning is based on outcomes, not prescriptions. The zoning code specifies the desired outcomes or limits, such as noise, traffic, or pollution. So long as landowners can meet these limits, they are free to do what they want with their land.

prescriptive zoning tightly specifies the type of development that is allowed in each zone and leaves little option to developers. Prescriptive zoning typically sets density floors as well as ceilings and may prescribe such things as the size of the front porch, the location of the garage, and so forth. A number of communities are adopting prescriptive zoning in the 1990s.

takings refers to the fifth amendment of the U.S. Constitution which states that government may not take private property for public purpose without compensation. Courts have ruled that zoning is not a taking that requires compensation so long as the property being zoned still has a significant economic value—regardless of what the property owners want.

upzoning indicates a rezoning to a higher density or more intensive development. For example, a neighborhood of single-family homes may be upzoned to multifamily residential or a mixed-use (commercial plus residential) zone. Some prescriptive upzonings from single-family to multifamily have required that a single-family home that burns down must be replaced with a multifamily home.

Index

535

About the Author

Randal O'Toole is senior economist with the Thoreau Institute, a non-profit group that seeks solutions to environmental problems using incentives rather than government regulation. During the 1980s, O'Toole became one of the nation's leading experts on national forest planning, which led to his first book, *Reforming the Forest Service*, published by Island Press in 1988.

In the 1990s, he did in-depth studies of other conservation agencies and issues including national parks, endangered species, and state lands and resources. Many of his reports and articles on these subjects are available at www.ti.org. As a native Oregonian who grew up in Portland, O'Toole became involved in Portland-area smart-growth planning in 1995, when he lived in the Portland suburb of Oak Grove. His research and articles on light-rail transit helped convince Portland and Oregon voters to reject new light-rail proposals in 1996 and 1998.

The Oregon Environmental Council gave O'Toole its prestigious Richard L. Neuberger Award in 1978. In 1981, the Oregon Natural Resources Council gave O'Toole its David Simons Award for Vision. The Yale University School of Forestry and Environmental Studies named O'Toole its McCluskey Conservation Fellow in 1998. In 1999 he was a visiting scholar at the University of California College of Natural Resources. In 2000 O'Toole was the Milton R. Merrill Visiting Professor of Political Science at Utah State University. He currently lives in Bandon, Oregon.